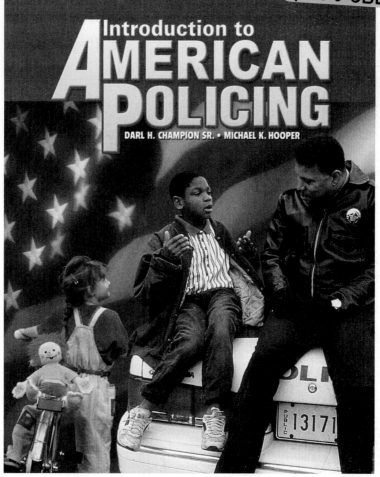

Introduction to AMERICAN POLICING

DARL H. CHAMPION SR. • MICHAEL K. HOOPER

Darl H. Champion, Sr., Ed.D.

Chairman of the Department of Sociology, Social Work, and Criminal Justice
Methodist College
Fayetteville, North Carolina

Michael K. Hooper, Ph.D.

Senior Law Enforcement Consultant
California Commission on Peace Officer Standards and Training (POST)

New York, New York   Columbus, Ohio   Chicago, Illinois   Peoria, Illinois   Woodland Hills, California

The McGraw-Hill Companies

 **Higher Education**

INTRODUCTION TO AMERICAN POLICING

Published by McGraw-Hill, a business unit of The McGraw-Hill Companies, Inc.,
1221 Avenue of the Americas, New York, NY, 10020. Copyright © 2003 by The
McGraw-Hill Companies, Inc. All rights reserved. No part of this publication may be
reproduced or distributed in any form or by any means, or stored in a database or
retrieval system, without the prior written consent of The McGraw-Hill Companies,
Inc., including, but not limited to, in any network or other electronic storage or transmission, or broadcast for distance learning.

Some ancillaries, including electronic and print components, may not be available
to customers outside the United States.

This book is printed on acid-free paper.

     7 8 9 0 WDQ/WDQ 0

ISBN 978-0-02-800915-5

MHID 0-02-800915-0

www.mhhe.com

Expanded Contents

PART 2 POLICE ROLE AND ORGANIZATION   117

PART 3 THE MAKING OF A POLICE OFFICER 203

PART 4   BEHAVIOR, INTEGRITY, AND THE LAW   287

PART 5   THE DELIVERY OF EFFECTIVE POLICE SERVICES
415

INTRODUCTION TO AMERICAN POLICING

LEARNING SYSTEM

This book is designed to help you learn. It contains 15 chapters, organized into six parts. You will be able to study more efficiently if you use the guidelines of the integrated learning system detailed below.

1. **Concept Preview** The chapter opener introduces the key concepts.
2. **Concept Development** The chapter text explains concepts in a structured, visual format.
3. **Concept Reinforcement** In-Text examples, graphics, and special features enhance and strengthen learning.
4. **Concept Review and Application** End-of-Chapter exercises and activities encourage you to review and apply what you have learned.

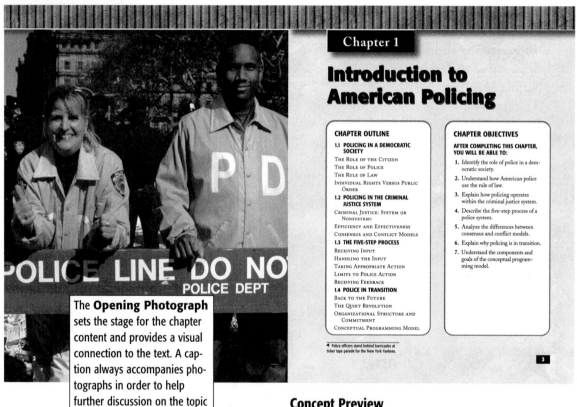

The **Opening Photograph** sets the stage for the chapter content and provides a visual connection to the text. A caption always accompanies photographs in order to help further discussion on the topic illustrated.

Chapter 1

Introduction to American Policing

CHAPTER OUTLINE

1.1 POLICING IN A DEMOCRATIC SOCIETY
THE ROLE OF THE CITIZEN
THE ROLE OF POLICE
THE RULE OF LAW
INDIVIDUAL RIGHTS VERSUS PUBLIC ORDER

1.2 POLICING IN THE CRIMINAL JUSTICE SYSTEM
CRIMINAL JUSTICE: SYSTEM OR NONSYSTEM?
EFFICIENCY AND EFFECTIVENESS
CONSENSUS AND CONFLICT MODELS

1.3 THE FIVE-STEP PROCESS
RECEIVING INPUT
HANDLING THE INPUT
TAKING APPROPRIATE ACTION
LIMITS TO POLICE ACTION
RECEIVING FEEDBACK

1.4 POLICE IN TRANSITION
BACK TO THE FUTURE
THE QUIET REVOLUTION
ORGANIZATIONAL STRUCTURE AND COMMITMENT
CONCEPTUAL PROGRAMMING MODEL

CHAPTER OBJECTIVES

AFTER COMPLETING THIS CHAPTER, YOU WILL BE ABLE TO:

1. Identify the role of police in a democratic society.
2. Understand how American police use the rule of law.
3. Explain how policing operates within the criminal justice system.
4. Describe the five-step process of a police system.
5. Analyze the differences between consensus and conflict models.
6. Explain why policing is in transition.
7. Understand the components and goals of the conceptual programming model.

◀ Police officers stand behind barricades at ticker tape parade for the New York Yankees.

Concept Preview

Chapter Outline introduces the topics that will be discussed in a chapter. Scan the outline to familiarize yourself with the subject matter.

Chapter Objectives alert you to the major concepts to learn. Turn the objectives into questions and, as you read the chapter, look for the answers to the questions.

Concept Development

The Heading Structure shows the relationship among the topics covered within a chapter and breaks the material into easy-to-understand segments. Scan the headings to locate the information that will help you answer the questions you derived from the chapter objectives.

Key Terms are defined when introduced and are printed in boldface type so that they are easy to locate. Terms and definitions are also repeated in the margin and in the glossary.

Important Concepts and Data are depicted in visual format to make them easier to understand and to study.

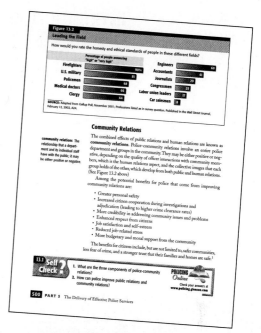

Concept Reinforcement

Computer On Patrol provides updates on the most recent technology developments.

CopTalk zeroes in on communication and interpersonal skills.

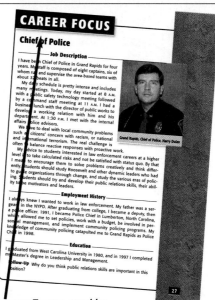

Ethics Issues opens up the debate on key ethics and integrity issues.

Police Procedure focuses on issues relevant to day-to-day police operations.

Career Focus provides first-person accounts with law enforcement professionals.

Concept Review and Application

Summary By Learning Objectives sums up each chapter's major themes. The summary is organized by chapter objectives and provides you with general answers to the questions you posed when you began the chapter.

Key Terms consolidate the policing and criminal justice vocabulary that is introduced in the chapter. If you cannot remember what a term means, the page reference allows you to locate it quickly within the chapter.

Questions for Review re-examine key points from the chapter content. These questions can help you review for exams.

Experiential Activities allow you to expand your knowledge by putting yourself in a specific law enforcement situation and apply the chapter's concepts.

Critical Thinking Exercises develop your critical thinking skills and provide you with law enforcement practice scenarios.

Web Patrol Exercises complete the experiential exercise section. They invite you to use the Internet to do further research on chapter-specific questions.

Part Review Questions conclude each part. These 15 questions are a good way to check quickly whether you remember key facts and concepts.

Patrol: The Backbone of Policing

Summary By Learning Objectives

1. Identify the basics of traditional patrol.
Police patrol is a multifaceted concept that involves a visible police presence for the purpose of deterring crime, observing conditions that might lead to crime occurrence, and apprehending people who have committed crimes or who might be about to commit crimes. In the course of their exposure to crimes, intelligent patrol officers draw on their experience to develop strong observational skills. In addition to maintaining a deterrent presence, officers perform a wide variety of noncriminal service functions.

3. Explain police methods for prioritizing service delivery.
To better manage the workload of patrol officers, calls for service are prioritized, and differential response is used so that responses to

problem at hand. This team of officers does not respond to routine citizen calls for service; the remaining members of the patrol handle all the calls for service. In a directed-patrol scheme, no officers are assigned shift-long responsibility for a special crime problem. Instead, officers are requested to spend any available time in the special crime problem area.

4. Learn about the value of foot patrol.
Foot patrol has enjoyed a resurgence in the era of community policing because it has been shown to be highly effective for reducing fear levels among neighborhood residents. It is also an ideal vehicle for stimulating the police-citizen interaction essential for mobilizing the community. Also, the nature of foot patrol enables police officers to treat conditions of disorder that have been shown to foster crime occurrence. While there are many advantages to foot patrol, it does need to be recognized as a support service for motorized patrol.

5. Describe the problem-solving approach to policing.
The problem-solving concept has had a pronounced influence on policing. More than any other factor, it has stimulated proactivity in policing. In addition to getting at the root causes of problems, this approach can result in a reduction of repeated calls for service at the former problem location. The reduction permits officers to spend more time on newly emerging problems. A problem-solving strategy, referred to as

strategy. Closely associated with the problem-driven approach to policing is the broken windows theory. This concept is an analogy to describe the relationship between disorder and crime. The originators of the broken windows concept believed strongly that serious crime flourishes in areas in which conditions of disorder have been unaddressed. Broken windows has proven to be a viable concept in the quest to restore order along urban streets through the problem-solving approach.

6. Learn the principles of community policing.
Community policing is an organizational philosophy based on a set of values emphasizing problem-solving partnerships between community members and the police. Both the community and the police work together to identify, prioritize, and solve crime problems to attain improved quality of life in their community. The community-police partnership is the essence of the concept of community policing. For a community to unite and actively support a program of community policing, the major

---

Key Terms

patrol (p. 418)
preventive patrol (p. 419)
omnipresence (p. 419)
team policing (p. 422)
split-force patrol (p. 423)
directed patrol (p. 424)
differential response (p. 425)

beat profiling (p. 429)
problem-oriented policing (POP) (p. 431)
SARA (p. 432)
broken windows theory (p. 434)
community policing (p. 437)
Big Six (p. 437)
empowerment (p. 440)

Questions for Review

1. Why is patrol referred to as the backbone of policing?
2. What is the twofold purpose of preventive patrol?
3. Discuss the relative importance of the preliminary investigation conducted by patrol officers in the context of the total criminal investigation.
4. What is a key factor distinguishing the split-force concept from directed patrol?
5. What is differential response, and how does it operate?

6. What are the unique benefits of foot patrol?
7. Briefly describe each stage of the SARA problem-solving technique.
8. How does the broken windows theory contribute to the problem-solving approach?
9. Identify the key elements that constitute community policing.
10. Which groups comprise the Big Six?

Experiential Activities

11. Using SARA
Your city has seen convenience store robberies increase over the past five years. Since the problem began, 45 of 47 San Luis convenience stores have been robbed at least once. Nearly half were robbed five or more times. Convenience stores account for only 18 percent of small service businesses, but they account for 50 percent of the robberies. The police have also learned that 75 percent of the convenience store robberies have taken place between the hours of 7:00 P.M.

and 5:00 A.M. One clerk was present in 92 percent of the crimes. In addition, 24-hour convenience stores were robbed 77 percent more than ones that closed by 11 P.M. Perform a SARA-method analysis of the situation.
  a. What will be your first steps in solving this problem?
  b. At what point will you consider this crime problem resolved?
  c. How would you determine whether this is a specific crime trend?

Critical Thinking Exercises

18. Underaged Drinking in the Park
You are a police officer assigned to a patrol unit. Your patrol beat includes a popular park, which is open daily from 6:00 A.M. until 10:00 P.M. After closing, particularly on weekend evenings, the quiet park is used extensively by local teenagers who drink and use drugs in the parking lot.
  When the problem involved only local juveniles, your department chose to ignore it because they were not making noise or committing other crimes. Recently, juveniles from other communities have been joining the locals. The average number of cars has increased from 3 to nearly 20. The juveniles are loud and unruly, and leave a large amount of broken bottles behind. Homeowners who reside near the park have delivered a petition to your chief, demanding immediate action.
  a. As a night watch officer, whose shift begins at 4:00 P.M. and ends just after midnight, how would you handle the problem on the night shift?
  b. What can you do to communicate to the homeowners that the problem is not being resolved?

19. Mobilizing the Big Six
If you had been assigned a specific beat as a community-policing officer, how would you sustain the interest and active involvement of the Big Six, especially other municipal departments, in the community-policing concept?

Experiential Activities continued

12. Involving the Community
Using the scenario in exercise 11. Consider what convenience stores could do, or what a city ordinance could require in order to make conditions safer between 7:00 P.M. and 5:00 A.M.
  a. Can changes in working conditions of convenience store employees help reduce crime?
  b. How can the employees help you in preventing further crime and in arresting suspects?
  c. What do you think you could learn from community group discussions?

13. Causes of Crime
Your police department has been unable to stem your city's increasing drug-dealing problem. The narcotics division is convinced that if more resources were allocated to fighting the drug problem, other crime problems such as robberies would be resolved. Your chief cannot do so without reducing the patrol division. This would make residents feel less safe.
  a. Do you agree with the narcotics division's belief?
  b. Devise a way in which the narcotics division can get more resources depleting the foot patrol.
  c. How would you present your decision to citizens?

14. A Virtual Visit
Tune in to PoliceScanner.com (click on at **www.policing.glencoe.com**). Listen to least three police departments' communication centers and jot down the first ten calls monitored for each agency.

  a. Which call suits a problem-solving approach?
  b. Which call requires a split-force approach?
  c. What difficulties did you encounter during decision making?

Web Patrol

15. Crime Prevention
Visit an officer's crime prevention page for the Cook College Community Policing Unit (of Rutgers University, NJ) by clicking on the link at **www.policing.glencoe.com**. *How do sites like this help serve the community and improve the quality of life?*

16. Community-Oriented Policing
Visit the U.S. Department of Justice's page for Community-Oriented Policing Services by clicking on the link at **www.policing.glencoe.com**. Read about the grant funding and training services.

Questions for Review

1. Define professionalism and explain how the concept applies to policing.
2. What is integrity?
3. Why does scientific management apply to policing?
4. Who was August Vollmer and what did he contribute to the field of law enforcement?
5. Which parts of the body does stress affect?
6. How can police corruption be prevented?
7. Write out the basic text of the Miranda Warning.
8. Name the three stages of the body's reaction to stressor.
9. What is discretion?
10. Should police officers be familiar with the exclusionary rule? Why or why not?
11. What is probable cause?
12. What is eustress?
13. Explain the importance of the Code of Ethics.
14. Name three types of pretrial identification procedures.
15. Why is the reading of the Miranda Warning required before an interrogation?

ADDITIONAL STUDY AND TUTORIAL RESOURCES

To assist you in learning and applying the policing and criminal justice concepts introduced within this volume, Glencoe/McGraw-Hill provides several supplementary resources.

Report-Writing Guidelines

Appendix A in this text outlines the basic steps of effective report writing, a key, and often challenging, ingredient of police work.

Essential Spanish for the Law Enforcement Officer

For quick reference, this text's Appendix B lists words and phrases that are indispensable for basic communication in Spanish.

PageOut Distance Learning Course

Technology and the Web enable instructors to teach beyond the walls of the classroom. With **PageOut**, a versatile and easy-to-use program, this entire course is available in an Internet format.

Instructor Resource Manual

A valuable teaching tool, the IRM includes answers to the text's activities and questions, as well as some targeted extra practice and advanced research activities. This manual also contains a CD-Rom with PowerPoint® presentations and an electronic testbank.

www.policing.glencoe.com

This site was developed specifically as a supplement to this text. It provides you with extra practice and self-tests as well as reinforcement tools for report writing, information about professional organizations, and all the links you will need to complete the textbook activities.

www.glencoe.com/ps/cjustice/

This Glencoe Web site is dedicated to the field of criminal justice and is updated monthly. There, you will find relevant career profiles and tips, articles on the newest technological developments and background information about criminal justice issues currently in the news.

Student Success in Law Enforcement Operations

With the purchase of this volume, you have taken a major step toward achieving your career goals in your study of American law enforcement. To ensure your success, you must take full advantage of the many informational features, learning aids, and pedagogical structures that are provided. You will gain a broad, comprehensive, and holistic understanding of law enforcement and its application in the criminal justice system. That knowledge will serve you well as a strong foundation for other more specialized courses in criminal justice and the social sciences.

This book is divided into 15 chapters that are organized in six parts to provide a logical approach to understanding the evolution of American policing and its contemporary form and functions.

The first three chapters (Part 1) examine the context and history of policing within the criminal justice system. Special features are introduced and consistently reappear thereafter. **Career Focus** provides profiles of law enforcement professionals based on live interviews that focused on their backgrounds, daily work routines, challenges specific to positions, and career advice for students. **CopTalk** zeroes in on communication skills. **Computer on Patrol** offers updates on technological developments. **Police Procedure** provides vignettes for critical thinking exercises. **Ethics Issues** opens up debate on key ethics and integrity issues. **Self Checks** measure retention of facts and concepts. **Myth and Fact** debunks common misconceptions about policing. **FYI** presents little-known facts that complement the text. Each chapter concludes on a **Review and Applications** section that provides ample opportunity to practice and deepen understanding of key concepts. **Web Patrol** identifies Web sites where additional insight and knowledge can be acquired on various police topics. Finally, each part ends on a series of 15 review questions.

Part 2 (Chapters 4 and 5) discusses the police role and organization. You will learn about the functional roles of police in a democratic society, emerging roles of the police, and the structure and nature of law enforcement at the municipal, state, and federal levels. The nature of private security and its relationship with public protective services is also examined.

Part 3 (Chapters 6 and 7) details the making of a police officer. The processes of recruitment, selection, and training are explored. Protocols for development of essential skills involving communications, critical thinking, and problem solving are studied.

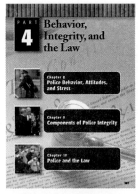

Part 4 (Chapters 8, 9, and 10) analyzes police behavior, integrity, and the conformance to the rule of law. Stress and its effect on the individual and the organization is assessed. The components of integrity, i.e., professionalism, discretion, and ethics, are emphasized. Powers of arrest, search, and seizure are reviewed against the backdrop of the U.S. Constitution.

Part 5 (Chapters 11, 12, and 13) looks at the delivery of police services. Here, all aspects of the "backbone of policing," i.e., police patrol, are studied. Other line functions involving detective, juvenile, traffic, and undercover operations are examined in the context of their respective missions and operational environments. The police-community relations discussion entails explanation of attitude formation, methods for improving relations between the police and community, understanding diversity, and responding to citizen complaints.

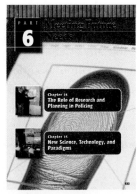

Part 6 (Chapters 14 and 15) addresses vital topics that are often overlooked in policing texts: research/planning, application of new technologies, and the future of policing.

Why Study Law Enforcement?

Law enforcement is the principal initiator of the criminal justice system and the most visible representative of government. Law enforcement wields an enormous range of power and discretion, ranging from issuance of a traffic citation to the taking of a human life. Law enforcement is unique among the criminal justice system components in the period of deliberation allotted for decision-making. The decisions made by law enforcement are often life changing, but the time within which they may be made may amount to only seconds.

Law enforcement personnel are also the preservers of our democracy. The police exist for the purpose of ensuring freedom from disorder and from those criminal acts that interfere with the freedom to pursue personally and socially fulfilling objectives. Their actions in this context range from ensuring the rights of individuals to assemble for peaceful demonstrations to battling violent rioters.

The police are also one of only two public safety entities relied upon 24 hours daily to perform a host of public service functions that involve neither violations of criminal law nor preservation of democracy. Whether it involves a missing sewer cover along a busy boulevard or a disoriented senior citizen, the police must initiate action to reduce the potential for harm.

Thus, the police are an extremely important force within not only the criminal justice system but also society at large. The importance of learning about the functioning of this particular governmental entity cannot be overstated. Understanding its intricacies is as important as understanding the underpinnings of freedom itself—if not central to its preservation.

How to Study Law Enforcement

As stated, here is a detailed and, we believe, foolproof strategy for succeeding in your law enforcement course. (The strategy can also be applied successfully in other courses.) Before beginning, however, it is important to emphasize three qualities that are important in the learning process and that we cannot teach you: *desire*, *commitment*, and *perseverance*. Unless you are willing to apply those three qualities to your study of policing, we cannot guarantee success. ***Introduction to American Policing***, like any other course, builds in stages. Information presented in later chapters often assumes knowledge of information introduced in earlier chapters. You cannot afford to fall behind and then expect to catch up in one massive cramming session. To get off to a good start, prepare yourself before the course begins by setting learning goals, organizing your time, studying your syllabus, and examining your own learning style.

Set Learning Goals for Yourself

The purpose of setting goals is to understand exactly what you plan to accomplish. Ask yourself what you want out of this course. Is it a specific grade? Perhaps you need an A or a B to keep up your grade average. Perhaps you need a certain body of knowledge from this course to get into a higher-level course. Perhaps you need a specific set of skills. You may be taking this course to meet a requirement for your job, to attain a personal career goal, or simply to satisfy your curiosity about the subject. Be forewarned, however—if you set your goals too low, you are likely to achieve only those low goals. For example, if you are not interested in the course but are taking it only because it is required of all majors, you should not be disappointed if you earn less than an A or a B.

Organize Your Time

Now that you have set your goals, you need to organize your time to accomplish them. Time management allows you to meet your goals, and still have time for activities. It helps you work smarter, not just harder. As a rule of thumb, for every class hour, allow two study hours. If an exam is coming up, allow more study time. Plan to study when you are most alert. You will retain information longer if you study on a regular basis, rather than during one or two cramming sessions. Either before or after a study session, have some fun! Timely breaks from studying enhance the learning process.

Study Your Syllabus

Usually the course syllabus is available on the first day of class, but sometimes it is available sooner. If you can get a copy early, you will be that much ahead. The syllabus is your map for navigating the course. It should define the goals or objectives of the course, specify the textbook and supporting materials to be used, and explain course requirements, including the method or formula for determining final grades. The syllabus will also include a course schedule indicating when particular topics will be covered, what material needs to be read for each class, and when tests will be given. Other useful information on a course syllabus may include the instructor's name, office location, phone number, and office hours, and perhaps, the types of extra credit or special projects you may complete. Keep the syllabus in your notebook or organizer at all times. Review it at the beginning of each class and study session so you will know what course material will be covered and what you will be expected to know. Write down important due dates and test dates on your calendar.

Eight-Step Study Plan to Maximize Your Learning

This plan is based on research that shows people learn and remember best when they have repeated exposure to the same material. This technique not only helps you learn better but can also reduce anxiety by allowing you to become familiar with material step by step. You will go over material at least six times before you take an exam.

Step 1: Use a Reading Strategy

In most cases, you will be asked to read material before each class. The SQ3R (Survey, Question, Read, Recite, and Review) method can help you get the most out of the material in every chapter of your book. Reading the material before class will acquaint you with the subject matter, arouse your interest in the subject, and help you know what questions to ask in class.

Survey By surveying an assignment, you are preparing yourself for a more thorough reading of the material.

Read the Chapter Title, the Chapter Objectives, and the Chapter Outline What topics does the chapter cover? What are the learning objectives? Do you already know something about the subject?

Read the Summary by Chapter Objectives This will give you an overview of what is covered in the chapter.

Look for Key Terms Key terms are the names for words associated with the important concepts covered in the chapter. Key terms are printed in bold-face type in the text. Definitions of the key terms appear in the margins near the text in which they are introduced.

Question Turn the chapter objectives into questions. For example, if the objective is, "State a basic definition of law," turn it into a question by asking yourself, "What is a basic definition of law?" Look for the answers to your questions as you read the chapter. By beginning the study of a chapter with questions, you will be more motivated to read the chapter to find the answers. To make sure your answers are correct, consult the summary at the end of the chapter.

You can also write a question mark in pencil in the margin next to any material you don't understand as you read the chapter. Your goal is to answer all your questions and erase the question marks before you take an exam.

Read Before you begin a thorough reading of the material, make sure that you are rested and alert and that your reading area is well lit and ventilated. This will not only make your reading time more efficient, but help you understand what you read.

Skim the Material Generally, you will need to read material more than once before you really understand it. Start by skimming or reading straight through the material. Do not expect to understand everything at once. You are getting the big picture and becoming familiar with the material.

Read, Highlight, Outline The second time, read more slowly. Take time to study explanations and examples. Highlight key terms, important concepts, numbered lists, or other items that will help you understand the material. Most students use colored highlighting markers for this step. Put question marks in pencil in the margin beside any points or concepts you don't understand.

Outline the Chapter in Your Notebook By writing the concepts and definitions into your notebook, you are using your tactile sense to reinforce your learning and to remember better what you read. Be sure you state concepts and definitions accurately. You can use brief phrases to take more extensive notes for your outline, depending on the material.

Apply What You Read In policing, as in any other course, you must be able to apply what you read. The experiential activities and critical thinking exercises at the end of each chapter allow you to do this. Complete those activities and exercises when you have finished studying the chapter.

Recite In this step, you do a self-check of what you have learned in reading the chapter. Go back to the questions you formed from the chapter objectives and see if you can answer them. Also, see if you can answer the Questions for Review at the end of each chapter. Try explaining the material to a friend so that he or she understands it. These exercises will reveal your strengths and weaknesses.

Review Now go back and review the entire chapter. Erase any question marks that you have answered. If you still don't understand something, tab that spot or mark it in your text. These items are the questions you can ask in class.

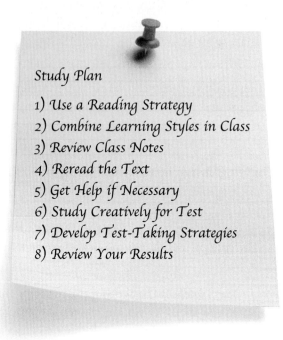

Study Plan

1) Use a Reading Strategy
2) Combine Learning Styles in Class
3) Review Class Notes
4) Reread the Text
5) Get Help if Necessary
6) Study Creatively for Test
7) Develop Test-Taking Strategies
8) Review Your Results

Step 2: Combine Learning Styles in Class

Think of the time you spend in class as your opportunity to learn by listening and participating. You are combining visual, aural, and tactile learning styles in one experience.

- **Attendance:** More Than Just Showing Up. Your attitude is a critical element. Attend class ready to learn. That means being prepared by having read and reread the assignment, having your questions ready, and having your note-taking materials organized. Because law enforcement, like other courses, builds in stages, it is important for you to attend every class. You cannot ask questions if you are not there, and you may miss handouts, explanations, or key points that often are included on a test. One final note: If you cannot attend a class, call the instructor or a classmate to find out what you have missed. You do not want to show up the next day and find out the instructor is giving a test!

- **Attention: Active Listening and Learning** During most classes, you spend more time listening than you do reading, writing, or speaking. Learning by listening, however, calls for you to become an active listener and participate in the class. This means you come to class prepared, you focus on the subject, you concentrate on what the instructor or other students are saying, and you ask questions. Block out distractions such as street noises or people walking by the classroom.

- **Participation** In reading the material before class, you will have made a list of questions. If those questions are not answered in class, then ask your instructor to answer them. If the instructor makes a point you do not understand, jot it down and ask him or her to explain it as soon as you can.

- **Note Taking** Why take notes? We forget nearly 60 percent of what we hear within one hour after we hear it. Memory is highly unreliable. This is why taking notes during class is so important. Note taking involves both listening and writing at the same time. You must learn not to concentrate too much on one and forget the other. Follow these tips for taking good notes:

Listen for and Record Main Ideas You do not need to write down everything your instructor or other students say. By reading your assignment before class, you will know what the main topics are. Listen for those topics when your instructor goes over the material in class, then take notes on what he or she says about them. If the instructor emphasizes the importance of a topic for a test, be sure to make a note of this information as well (for example, "This section really important for exam"). If you think you have missed a point, either ask your instructor to repeat or rephrase it right away, or mark the point with a question mark and ask your instructor about it later.

Use Outline Style and Abbreviations Set up your notes in outline style, and use phrases instead of complete sentences. Use abbreviations of symbols whenever possible (& for and, w for with, and so on). This technique will help you write faster to keep up with the instructor.

Step 3: Review Class Notes

Listening and taking notes are critical steps in learning, but reviewing your notes is equally important. Remember, repetition reinforces learning. The more times you go over material, the better you learn it.

Fill in the Blanks As soon as possible after a class, review your notes to fill in any missing information. Make sure you do it the same day. Sometimes you may be able to recall the missing information. If you can't, check your textbook or ask to see another student's notes to obtain what you need. Spell out important abbreviations that you may not recognize later.

Highlight Important Information Marking different types of information helps organize your notes. You want to find what you need when you need it. Try these suggestions for highlighting your notes:

1. Use different colored highlighting pens to mark key terms, important Supreme Court decisions, and other kinds of information. Then, you will know that green, for example, always indicates key terms; blue indicates Supreme Court decisions; and so on. This method will help you find specific information quickly and easily.

2. Write a heading such as "community policing" at the beginning of each key topic. These headings can either correspond to those in the chapter, or you may make up your own headings to help you remember key information.

Step 4: Reread the Text

After reviewing your notes, you are ready to reread the chapter to fix the concepts in your mind.

Read for Details

- Go over the key points and main ideas carefully. Make sure you understand them thoroughly and can explain them to someone in your own words.

- Review the Chapter Objectives (that you have turned into questions) and the Questions for Review. Make sure you can answer all the questions and that you understand your answers.

Mark Your Text

- Highlight any important terms or concepts you may have missed in your previous reading.

- Highlight any special feature boxes, e.g., "Myth/Fact" boxes, "FYIs," or figures you feel are important to remember.

- Erase any question marks in the margin that represent questions you have answered.

- Use stick-on notes to mark anything of which you are still unsure. Ask questions about those points in the next class, talk them over with other students, or make an appointment to meet with your instructor to discuss your questions.

Step 5: Get Help if Necessary

What if you have read the material, taken notes, and asked questions, and you still do not understand the material? You can get further help. As soon as it becomes apparent that you need some help, ask for it. If you wait until the semester is nearly over, it may be too late. Here are several sources of help.

Your Instructors Most instructors are willing to spend extra time with students who need help. Find out what your instructor's office hours are and schedule an appointment to go over the material in more detail. You may need several sessions. Remember to take notes during those sessions.

Study Groups Join a study group in your class, or start your own. What one person does not understand, another does. Study groups take advantage of each member's expertise. You can often learn best by listening and talking to others in such groups. Chances are that together, you will be able to master the material better than any one of you could alone. This is an example of power in numbers.

Learning Labs Many schools have learning labs that offer individual instruction or tutoring for students who are having trouble with course material. Ask your instructor or classmates for information about the learning labs in your college or university.

Private Tutors You might consider getting help from a private tutor if you can afford the fee. Although this route will cost you more, it may take only a few sessions to help you understand the material and keep up with the class. Check with your instructor about the availability of private tutors.

Step 6: Study Creatively for Tests

If you have read your assignments, attended class, taken notes and reviewed them, answered the Questions for Review, and completed the Experiential Activities and Critical Thinking Exercises, then you have been studying for tests all along. This kind of preparation means less stress when test time comes around.

Review: Bring It All Together You should enter all exam dates on your calendar so that you know well in advance when to prepare for a test. If you plan extra time for study during the week, you will not have to cram the night before the test.

During that week, bring together all your textbook notes, all your handouts, and other study materials. Reread them, paying particular attention to anything you marked that the instructor emphasized or that you had trouble understanding.

In addition to studying the Summary by Chapter Objectives, Key Terms, and Questions for Review at the end of each chapter, it is a good idea to make a summary sheet of your own that lists all the major points and other information that will be covered on the test. If you have quizzes or tests you have already taken, review them as well. Focus on the material you either missed or did not do well on before.

Do not hesitate to ask the instructor for information about the test, in particular:

- The types of test items he or she will use (multiple-choice, true-false, matching, fill-in-the-blanks, short answer, essay)

- What material, if any, will be emphasized, and what material, if any, will not be included

- How much time you will have to take the test

Step 7: Test-Taking Strategies

No matter how well you prepare for a test, you will feel some anxiety just before and even during the exam. This is natural—*everybody* feels this way. The guidelines in this section will help you manage your anxiety so that you can do your best.

Before the Test: Get Ready Use this checklist to help you prepare the night before or a few hours before an exam.

- Gather supplies: unless instructed otherwise, at least two sharpened pencils with good erasers, a watch for timing yourself, and other items if you need them (such as a blue book for essay exams).

- If the test is in your first class, get up at least an hour before the exam to make sure you will be fully awake.

- Eat well before the test, but avoid having a heavy meal, which can make you sleepy.

- Arrive early to review your notes and study materials.

Remember: Luck favors the prepared!

During the Test: Go for It! Memorize these strategies to help you during the exam.

- Follow the directions. Listen carefully to the instructor's directions and read the printed directions carefully. Ask questions if the directions are unclear.

- Preview the test. Take a few minutes to look over the entire test. This will give you an idea of how much time to allot to each of the components.

- Do the easier sections first. If you get stumped on a question, skip it for now. You can come back to it later. Finish with the harder sections.

- Go back over the test. If you finish ahead of time, double-check your work and look for careless errors. Make sure your writing is legible if you are taking an essay exam or an exam that requires short answers. Make sure that your name and other information the instructor requires are on the test papers.

Step 8: Reviewing Your Results

Never throw away any of your quizzes or tests. Tests give you direct feedback on your progress in the courses. Whether the test is a weekly quiz or a mid-term, do not just look at the grade and put the paper in your file or notebook. Use the results of each quiz or test to help you achieve your goals.

Learn From Your Successes First review the test for those questions you answered correctly. Ask yourself the following questions:

- What are my strongest areas? You will know which topics to spend less time studying for the next exam.

- What types of items did I find easiest to answer (multiple-choice, true-false, etc.)? You might want to start with these types of items on the next exam, giving you more time to work on the harder items.

Learn From Your Mistakes Look over your errors, and ask yourself these questions:

- What types of items did I miss? Is there a pattern (for instance, true-false items, Supreme Court decisions)?

- Did I misunderstand any items? Was it clear to me what each item was asking for?

- Were my mistakes the result of carelessness? Did I read the items incorrectly or miss details? Did I lose track of time? Was I so engrossed in a test section that I forgot to allow myself enough time to get through the entire test at least once?

Look back through the textbook, your notes, class handouts, and other study materials to help you understand how and why you made the mistakes you did. Ask your instructor or classmates to go over your test with you until you know exactly why you missed the items. Evaluating your errors can show you where you need help and what to watch out for in the next test.

Refine Your Action Plan: The Learning Spiral You can think of the eight-step action plan as an upward spiral. Each time you travel a full cycle of the plan, you accumulate more knowledge and experience. You go one turn higher on the spiral.

Use your test feedback and classroom work to help you refine your plan. Perhaps you need to spend more time reading the textbook or reviewing key terms. Perhaps you did not allow enough time for study during the week. Or you might need extra help from your instructor, your classmates, or tutors. Make adjustments in your plan as you tackle the next part of the course.

Acknowledgments

This book, like any other book, is the product of a collaborative effort. For their insightful reviews, criticism, suggestions, information, and inspiration, we would like to thank:

Laurie Anderson
Torrance Police Department

Cindy Bevan
South Bay Regional Public Safety Training Consortium

Robert Bohm
University of Central Florida

Jacquelyn Bush
Grand Rapids Police Department

David Scott Canevit
University of Wisconsin at Milwaukee

Jon Cella
Central Texas College

Jan Chauncey
North Carolina Justice Academy

Mark Conta
Los Angeles Police Department

Kenneth Digby
Fayetteville Technical Community College

Chief Harry Dolan
Grand Rapids Police Department

Vicky Dorworth
Montgomery College, Maryland

Will Ferel
West Palm Beach Police Department

Karen Finkenbinder
Carlisle Police Department

Bruce Gay
Campbell University

Robert J. Golden
Former FBI Agent

Victor Gonzalez
Humble, Texas Police Department

Robin Greene
Methodist College

Patrick Hauser
East Los Angeles College

A.H. Hill
North Carolina Highway Patrol

Mark Kroeker
Portland Department

Gregory I. Mack
New York Police Department

Larry Marshall
Marion Technical College

James McAuliffe
Seminole Community College

Greg Meyer
Los Angeles Police Department

Carl Milazzo
Americans for Effective Law Enforcement

Bernadette Muscat
York College

James Ness
Mesa Community College

Ni He
University of Texas at San Antonio

David Paul
South Bay Regional Public Safety Training Consortium

David Perez
South Bay Regional Public Safety Training Consortium

Josh Phillips
Fayetteville North Carolina Police Department

Anna Pilette
Las Vegas Metropolitan Police Department

Jim Pleszewski
Rowan Cabarrus Community College

Amanda Ritz
Methodist College

Jason Romlein
Penn State University

Margy Schaufelberger
San Diego Police Department

Darrel Schenck
Portland Police Department

Judy Schmidt
Penn State University

Don Stacy
North Carolina Justice Department

Tom Weber
Penn State University

Susan Wernicke
Kansas City Police Department

Kevin Williams
Los Angeles Police Department

Christie Wilson
Penn State University

Mike Wilson
Kansas City Police Department

Kathryn Zybeck
Methodist College

Finally, we would like to express our appreciation to our families and friends for their understanding and patience throughout the period we have worked on this project.

About the Authors

Darl H. Champion, Sr., Ed.D is the Chairman of the Department of Sociology, Social Work, and Criminal Justice Studies, Methodist College, Fayetteville, North Carolina. Prior to joining the faculty at Methodist College, Dr. Champion was employed by Fayetteville Technical Community College in Fayetteville, North Carolina for 18 years. During this time he served as a criminal justice instructor and departmental chairman for 11 years. In addition, Dr. Champion has taught for 23 years in the Security Management Graduate Program for Webster University. At both Methodist College and Webster University, he has been very involved in developing and teaching online courses. From 1985–1995 Dr. Champion served as a member of the North Carolina Criminal Justice Education and Training Standards Commission. Within the Commission he served on the Education and Training Committee and was Chairman of the Program Evaluation Sub-Committee, which administered the certification program for post-secondary criminal justice programs in North Carolina. Presently, Dr. Champion serves on the Governing Board of the Carolinas Institute for Community Policing. Also, Dr. Champion has served as a military police officer in the 82d Airborne Division and Special Agent with the United States Army Criminal Investigation Division. As a Special Agent with USACID, Lieutenant Champion acquired the reputation as a dedicated and meticulous investigator with a knack for intuitive thinking.

Lieutenant Champion acquired extensive experience in conducting major felony investigations, protective service missions, and risk analysis surveys.

Dr. Champion received his doctorate in adult education from North Carolina State University. He has authored articles and papers on subjects such as community policing; juvenile assessment centers; vision, paradigms, and paradigm pioneering in criminal justice; and police officers as critical thinkers. He has received awards for teaching excellence to include the 1986 Margaret Lange Willis Outstanding Criminal Justice Educator in North Carolina Award and the 1988 Teaching Excellence Award at Fayetteville Technical Community College. In 1988 he was a finalist for the North Carolina Outstanding Community College Educator Award.

Michael K. Hooper, Ph.D is a Senior Law Enforcement Consultant with the California Commission on Peace Officer Standards and Training (POST). Prior to joining the consultant corps at POST, he was a member of the Criminal Justice Program faculty at Penn State Harrisburg. He also served more than 23 years as a sworn member of the Los Angeles Police Department (LAPD). At LAPD, Lieutenant Hooper cultivated a niche as a tactical planner. He was involved in the creation and implementation of special tactical plans, including the Los Angeles Airport Anti-Terrorism Plan, the Venue/Vital Point Security Template for the Los Angeles Olympic Games, and the Los Angeles Aerial Damage Assessment Plan. He was also a first responder to the 1992 Los Angeles riots, the 1994 Northridge earthquake, and the 1996 Atlanta Olympics bombing, among myriad unusual occurrences.

Dr. Hooper received his doctorate in criminal justice from Claremont Graduate University. He has authored or co-authored several journal articles, book chapters, and books on community policing, police administration, emergency management, workplace violence, and riot prevention and control.

Dedication

To our esteemed and prolific colleague, Frank Schmalleger,
without whose support and encouragement this book would not
have been possible.

—Darl H. Champion, Sr. and Michael K. Hooper

PART 1

Introduction to American Policing: Roles and History

Chapter 1
Introduction to American Policing

Chapter 2
Policing in Ancient and English Times

Chapter 3
Policing and the American Experience

1

Introduction to American Policing

CHAPTER OBJECTIVES

AFTER COMPLETING THIS CHAPTER, YOU WILL BE ABLE TO:

1. Identify the role of police in a democratic society.

2. Understand how American police use the rule of law.

3. Explain how policing operates within the criminal justice system.

4. Describe the five-step process of a police system.

5. Analyze the differences between consensus and conflict models.

6. Explain why policing is in transition.

7. Understand the components and goals of the conceptual programming model.

◄ Police officers stand behind barricades at ticker tape parade for the New York Yankees.

1.1 Policing in a Democratic Society

The United States was created with the vision of a land of economic opportunity, freedom, and liberty for all. To the many immigrants who came as a result of political and religious oppression in Europe, the nation was like a beacon in a storm. In the early years of the republic, safety was the responsibility of local citizens who organized watches that patrolled the nighttime streets. It was not until the 1840s that uniform police forces appeared with regularity in American cities.

To understand the role of policing in a democratic society, one must first understand the role of citizens. Americans have certain rights and protections, which shape police procedure. These rights limit the actions that police can take against citizens. For example, police cannot interrogate suspects without informing them of their constitutional protection against self-incrimination. Police cannot arrest a suspect without being able to establish probable cause that the suspect committed a crime.

When police and citizens have a clear understanding of their respective roles, everyone benefits from the relationship between them. When one or both groups do not understand these roles, relations can become weak or hostile.

The Role of the Citizen

Dr. Mortimer Adler, the pre-eminent philosopher and educator of our time, has stated that Americans do not understand the role of their elected officials. He states very bluntly that "most Americans think of themselves as the subjects of government and regard the administrators in public office as their rulers, instead of thinking of themselves as the ruling class and public officials as their servants—the instrumentalities for carrying out their will."[1]

For example, most citizens willingly consent to searches even when police have no need or right to search them or when they are carrying illegal items such as drugs and guns. This is not because they want to get caught, but because they believe that they should not say no to the police.

Many Americans, it seems, are ignorant of the power that they hold. Over two hundred years ago, the American people formed a republic under a constitutional government. The main political office was citizenship. The citizens are the principal and permanent rulers. All other offices established by the Constitution are secondary and all, not some, elected officials answer to the people. The American people are the stewards of their government. When they fail to vote, remain ignorant of social and political issues, or fail to speak out, they give up their power to those they elect. For example, many

FYI

The Origins of *Police*

The word *police* appears for the first time in the Statute of Winchester. There appear to be two words that influenced its creation: 1. The Greek word *polis*, which means city-state, and 2. Another Greek word, *polites*, which means citizen.

SOURCE: A. C. German, F. D. Day, and R. R. J. Gallati, *Introduction to Law Enforcement and Criminal Justice* (Springfield, IL: Charles C. Thomas, 1978).

Americans complain about taxes or corporate subsidies they do not agree with, but they do not call their congressional representatives to demand change. In essence, they assume a secondary role in the democratic process.

The Role of Police

What does this have to do with policing in a democratic society? The answer is: everything. As the founder of modern policing Robert Peel stated, "The police are the public and the public are the police." This means that police are paid to give full-time attention to those duties that are actually the responsibility of every citizen—to police themselves.[2]

Police must provide effective strategies to maintain order while preserving the values of democracy.[3] As one community policing expert James Fisk said, "The police exist for the purpose of producing a value—the value of freedom—freedom from disorder and those criminal acts that interfere with the freedom to pursue personally and socially fulfilling objectives."[4] Two concepts that help define the role of police are the law of agency and perpetual loan:

- The **law of agency** is the concept that the police possess only the authority that is granted to them by society. Just as elected officials must answer to the people, the police also answer to the legitimate needs and expectations of the public.[5] American citizens choose to have police enforce the laws and make arrests, rather than take matters into their own hands, as families did in many ancient societies. Although citizens give up individual power by doing this, they do so in order to gain security and avoid being harmed by more powerful individuals.

  law of agency The belief that the police, who are the public's agent for providing law enforcement, possess only the authority that is granted to them by society.

- The concept of the **perpetual loan** is related to the law of agency. In this light, the authority of the police can be seen as a perpetual loan of the community's own power to the agents of law enforcement.[6] Citizens invest their individual power to influence a public agency like their police department. The fruits of this investment include increased security and safety.

  perpetual loan The belief that the authority of the police is loaned to them by the community.

The Rule of Law

Another concept that is essential to understanding crime and policing in a democratic society is the **rule of law**. Law, not the emotions or whims of human beings, is the guideline for what is acceptable and unacceptable human behavior. The rule of law, sometimes referred to as legality, provides a uniform way of making, interpreting, and enforcing the law. Law offers stability and direction to citizens who are free to move about society on a daily

rule of law Society's guideline for what is acceptable and unacceptable human behavior; sometimes referred to as legality.

RE-ELECT

Experience IS the difference.

Michelle B. Mitchell
Richmond City Sheriff

▶ **Law of Agency** Law enforcement officials can be elected to their positions, as this campaign poster shows.
In what other ways do citizens empower the police?

basis without giving much thought and consideration to the matter.[7] If a democracy uses the rule of law, law of agency, and perpetual loan consistently, the impact on the quality of life is enormous.

For example, imagine that a city has an outdated ordinance that requires tenants to pay a parking tax for parking on the street. This tax discriminates against tenants because homeowners are not required to pay it. When an apartment tenant gets a threatening letter from the city for not paying her parking tax, she protests the law to the mayor and says that the law is discriminatory. By doing this, she is saying that the law does not serve the needs of the people. The mayor refuses to do anything, and the tenant threatens to sue the city because the mayor is trying to ignore her power as a citizen. Knowing that he will lose such a lawsuit, the mayor relents and agrees to have the law removed from the books.

Police who follow the rule of law develop a relationship with the community that is focused on collaboration, not confrontation. They enforce the law in a fair and consistent manner that helps to maintain a democratic government. Suppose that Sgt. Leonard is assigned to begin a community policing program in a working-class neighborhood. In the past, this neighborhood has had poor relations with the police for two reasons:

1. Its high crime rate, which makes the citizens feel helpless and the police frustrated
2. Three police brutality incidents over the last five years. Although the officers who committed these acts were dismissed, citizens are still mistrustful

Sgt. Leonard makes a consistent effort to treat people fairly and communicate with the law-abiding members of the community. By doing this, he is obeying the rule of law, encouraging others to do the same, and building trust that he is protecting democratic values. Although he does not solve the entire crime problem, his efforts gradually raise the neighborhood's quality of life and reduce its crime rate—two primary goals of policing. This is the essence of good community relations.

The police are the most visible branch of government. How they treat the public will affect the public's impression of the government as a whole. For example, during the World Trade Center attack of September 2001, people saw police committing acts of bravery and their faith in American government rose. However, when people see police acting brutally, as they did during the civil rights protests of the 1950s and 1960s, faith in their government generally falls. To complicate matters, the actions of one officer can affect the public's perception of his or her entire department. They can even affect the public's view of all police. Therefore, police are continually in the spotlight, which can add stress to an already stressful job.

Individual Rights Versus Public Order

Lawmakers have always struggled to protect Americans' individual rights while maintaining public order. This conflict has resulted in two different criminal justice philosophies:

MYTH	FACT
Police work generally involves handling violent crimes like murder, rape, robbery, and aggravated assault.	Police work sometimes involves these crimes, but they are a small fraction of the total crime rate. Police more frequently deal with ordinance violations such as loud parties and other nuisances, property crimes such as burglary and auto theft, and various types of family violence such as spouse abuse and child abuse.

ETHICS ISSUES

Excessive Force

Gary and his partner Austin are on foot patrol. As they are walking down the main street, they see a man run from a hardware store followed by a woman, who is wearing a clerk's smock and nametag. Gary and Austin apprehend him. During the arrest, he struggles to get free, and Austin pushes him on the chest. The man yells in pain, and soon blood appears. It appears that he concealed in his jacket several sharp implements. Austin inadvertently pushed a paring knife nearly an inch into his chest.

The man is threatening to sue the police for alleged excessive use of force.
Explain whether you believe that excessive force was used.

- **Individual rights advocates** focus on protecting the constitutional rights of those who come in contact with, or are processed through, the criminal justice system. They believe that suspects should be read their rights and treated as innocent until proven guilty. They believe in protecting suspects as well as victims and witnesses.
- **Public order advocates** believe that when criminals threaten public safety, the interests of society take priority over the criminals' individual rights.

The challenge is to balance the two philosophies so that both the public and its rights are safe. Are these two issues mutually exclusive? Can Americans keep their freedom and maintain a high level of public safety and order?

Consider the heated debate over the Second Amendment, which guarantees citizens the right to bear arms but also calls for a "well regulated militia." Public order advocates say that guns threaten public safety and social order by allowing people to take away the most basic right of all—the right of life. Individual rights advocates disagree because they feel that the constitutional right to bear arms should be protected more than social order.

This debate has shaped laws regarding firearm possession. Citizens can still own guns, but there are legal restrictions in place to reduce the social harm caused by guns. The negative side to this constitutional right is that thousands of Americans die in gun-related incidents every year.

Another point of contention between individual rights and public order advocates is the First Amendment right to peaceful assembly, which allows citizens to gather and assemble in support of, or against, an issue. This right can be complicated because people can gather for any reason, whether their message is considered acceptable, radical, or offensive. For example, Ku Klux Klan members are allowed to assemble even though many people are offended by their organization.

Peaceful assembly becomes an issue when it is used to prevent others from exercising their rights. When police are working in a protest situation, they must be able to distinguish the fine line between peaceful and aggressive protesting. The police must protect the right to assemble, but at the same time protect citizens from violence. Protestors who block traffic, barricade buildings, or make death threats are disrupting the social order and infringing upon the rights of others. Therefore, the police serve to protect rights, but also to prevent the abuse of those same rights. By doing this in a balanced way, both individual rights and public order are maintained.

 **1.1 Self Check**

1. Compare the role of the citizen with the role of the police.
2. Why is the rule of law so important to safeguarding people's rights?

POLICING *Online*
Check your answers at
www.policing.glencoe.com

Policing is part of a complex system known as the **criminal justice system**. The criminal justice system is the government's use of police, courts, and corrections to prevent, control, and reduce crime and delinquency. Police officers, probation and parole officers, public defenders, prosecutors, and judges are all components of different parts of this system. A **crime** is a voluntary and intentional act that a person commits, or allows to occur by neglecting a lawful duty. It is prohibited by law and punishable in the name of the state. **Delinquency** is the same behavior when it is committed by juveniles. **Justice**, the goal of the criminal justice system, can be defined as the ideal of fairness, applied in an objective and consistent manner.

Criminal Justice: System or Nonsystem?

The word *system* can be defined as a group of components that are interdependent, interrelated, and interacting toward a common goal. When a system fails to demonstrate those qualities, it can be said to function as a **nonsystem**. Issues such as jurisdictional and operational problems, differences in roles and goals, people problems in the form of different attitudes and values, and issues such as incompetent judges, poorly managed courts, absence of standards, and poorly trained officers can have such consequences on the criminal justice system that it becomes a nonsystem.

For example, the criminal justice system is sometimes called a nonsystem because of the following issues, to name a few:

- The complexity of the criminal justice system
- Difficulties in planning, coordination, and cooperation
- Staff incompetence in police, courts, or corrections
- Opposing opinions between members of different components of the systems, such as between police and prosecutors, judges and legislators, and police and correctional authorities
- Behavior by one component that undoes the work of another, such as when police and prosecutors compile a strong case against a defendant to ensure his or her conviction, but he or she is released almost immediately by an overcrowded prison system
- Staff corruption or brutality
- Poor or inconsistent relations between members of the criminal justice system and the public

The components of the criminal justice system are referred to as subsystems. These include police, courts, and corrections. Just as the primary goal of the criminal justice system is the prevention, control, and reduction

criminal justice system The government's use of police, courts, and corrections to prevent, control, and reduce crime and delinquency.

crime A voluntary and intentional act that a person commits, or allows to occur by neglecting a lawful duty; prohibited by law and punishable in the name of the state.

delinquency The same behavior as a crime, but committed by juveniles instead of adults.

justice The ideal of fairness, applied in an objective and consistent manner; the goal of the criminal justice system.

nonsystem A nonfunctioning system in which components fail to recognize their relationships, depend upon each other, and work together in a way that promotes its goal.

of crime and delinquency, each of the components has a separate subgoal. For police, it is preventing and controlling crime and maintaining order. The courts judge offenders to determine innocence or guilt. For corrections, the goal is incarceration and/or monitoring offenders on probation or parole with a focus on rehabilitation.

These subsystems are interdependent, interrelated, and interacting toward a common goal. Each component is dependent on one another for its existence. Courts need the police to generate cases for prosecution. Corrections need the courts to provide convicted offenders for the correctional programs. The sequence involved in processing an offender highlights the interrelatedness of these components. For example, an arrest by police must occur before a trial can be conducted. (See Figure 1.1 on page 11 for an illustration of this process.) Finally, the components interact with each other. Any police investigation or enforcement campaign is often coordinated with the district attorney's office to ensure efficient use of resources.

Many argue that the criminal justice system is a functioning system because its three components—police, courts, and corrections—are actually

Computer On Patrol

Violent Crime Information Center

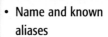

Multimedia and Megan's Law

Megan's Law requires state and the federal governments to register individuals who have been convicted of sex crimes against children. However, few people know exactly how law enforcement uses technology to inform communities about registered sex offenders.

In California, for example, all law enforcement agencies in jurisdictions with a population of 200,000 or more are required to make the CD-ROM available for public viewing. The CD-ROM, which may be viewed at the law enforcement agency where it is housed, contains the following information:

- Name and known aliases
- Age and sex
- Physical description, including scars, marks, and tattoos
- Photograph, if available
- Crimes resulting in registration
- County of residence
- Zip code (based on last registration)

Think About It What are your state's reporting requirements under Megan's Law? Visit the links provided at **www.policing.glencoe.com** and click on your state for more information.

SOURCE: "Registered Sex Offenders (Megan's Law)." State of California Department of Justice, Office of the Attorney General: http://caag.state.ca.us/megan/.

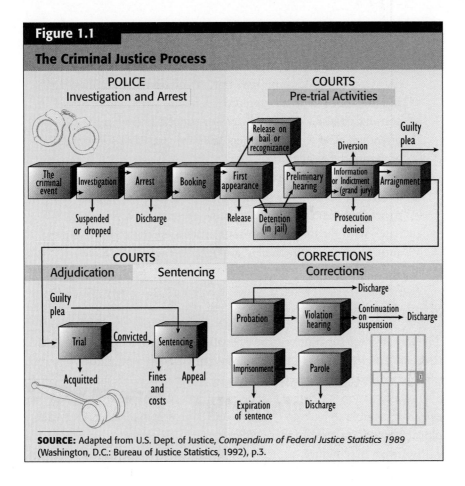

Figure 1.1

The Criminal Justice Process

SOURCE: Adapted from U.S. Dept. of Justice, *Compendium of Federal Justice Statistics 1989* (Washington, D.C.: Bureau of Justice Statistics, 1992), p.3.

related to each other, depend upon each other, and work together as components. There are four reasons why these components make up a functioning system

1. **All of these subsystems have related goals** Corrections, police, and the courts work to reduce crime, enforce the law, and maintain order. The police help achieve these goals by investigating violations and arresting offenders. Courts prosecute these offenders while following due process. Prisons and jails provide a deterrent to potential criminals and prevent convicts from committing more crimes.

2. **The components depend upon each other to function and survive** Courts need the police to generate criminal cases for prosecution and corrections to punish criminals effectively. Corrections need the police to arrest criminals who deserve punishment, and they need the courts to provide convicted criminals for the correctional programs. Police need the court and correctional system to prosecute criminals and keep them off the streets.

3. **The subsystems need each other to maintain a sequence** This means that the criminal justice system needs to process suspects and defendants in a particular order so that **due process**, which is the system of procedural laws that safeguard constitutional rights, is protected. The three-step process begins when police arrest criminal offenders. Next, the courts process and sentence the offenders. And third, offenders are incarcerated or supervised on probation by corrections.

4. **The components work together for the common cause of enforcing the law and punishing criminals** For example, many police investigations and law enforcement campaigns are coordinated with the district attorney's office to share information and ensure a timely and efficient and effective use of resources.

Efficiency and Effectiveness

The way a system functions can be evaluated in terms of efficiency and effectiveness. Efficiency is producing a desired effect with a minimum of effort, expense, or waste while effectiveness is producing a desired result or outcome. The ideal situation is a system that demonstrates both of these qualities; however, it is possible to have an effective system that is inefficient. One example can be found in many modern police agencies. Saturating a dangerous area with officers may reduce crime, but it is not an efficient use of resources. Balancing the expense of services with small department budgets makes the effective use of resources a constant struggle for police management.

Consensus and Conflict Models

Another way to look at the criminal justice system, or at different types of policing, is as a consensus model or a conflict model. Both models provide insight into the American criminal justice system.

consensus model A system model in which subsystems work together in agreement to reach a similar goal, promote harmony, and maximize efficiency; in criminal justice, the shared goal is justice.

Consensus Model In a **consensus model**, components work together in harmony to reach a similar goal. In criminal justice, this shared goal is justice. The criminal justice system often displays the ability to move to consensus. In the consensus model there is sometimes short-term conflict, but in the end the system adjusts itself to maintain the balance.

One illustration of the consensus model can be seen in the period after the terrorist attacks of September 11, 2001. Americans voiced concerns about public safety and security regarding public transportation, large cities, and biological warfare. The police wanted to provide an effective response but felt hindered because of legal procedures that protected individual rights and slowed down the crime-fighting process. For example, police wanted to be able to wiretap suspects' phones or electronically eavesdrop on their computers, but privacy laws prevented them from doing so.

The criminal justice system responded by weighing the need for national security against the concerns of individual rights. As a result, Congress passed new laws that gave the police greater freedom in investigations of terrorism. These included looser requirements for obtaining a court order for a wiretap and longer detention periods for suspected terrorists.

Conflict Model In the **conflict model**, components work best when they are in conflict or disagreement. The conflict model should not be confused with a nonsystem. It is more like a system of checks and balances. This model is evident in the adversarial process of criminal trials; the prosecution and defense oppose each other for the best possible outcome. Another example is the safeguards that protect a person's due process rights. Although these safeguards can create conflict between police and the courts, especially in the areas of interrogation and evidence collection, they also serve justice by demanding high standards.

Still, this conflict can create tension. Suppose that citizens complain about local prostitutes loitering in their neighborhood. The police chief decides to arrest all of them. The additional arrests double the workload of the overworked and understaffed district attorney's office. If all of these prostitutes are convicted, the women's section of the local jail will be extremely overcrowded and jail officials will probably give most of them an early release.

Since the district attorney cannot prosecute every case, she suspends the sentences of the first-time offenders. This causes friction and conflict with the police chief, who feels that the D.A. is not supporting him, and the public, who sees the district attorney as being weak on crime. In the consensus model the police chief would have first talked with the district attorney and perhaps jail officials before taking any action. The chief would then know how much the D.A. and jail could support his plan. Because the emphasis would be on collaboration and cooperation, all sides could reach consensus and move to address the problem.

Although the conflict model has some benefits, especially the system of checks and balances, the goal of American criminal justice should be the consensus model. To allow the system to operate in constant conflict only distracts from the goal of justice.

conflict model A system model in which subsystems are believed to work best when they are in conflict, because they strive for the best possible outcome for themselves.

1.2 Self Check ?

1. What are the three main components of the criminal justice system?
2. What are the differences between the consensus model and the conflict model?

POLICING *Online*
Check your answers at
www.policing.glencoe.com

1.3 The Five-Step Process

Each of the three criminal justice subsystems operates by following a minimum of five steps.

1. Receiving input
2. Handling the input
3. Taking appropriate action
4. Limits to police action
5. Receiving feedback

Each one of these is equally important. When a police administrator is trouble-shooting or problem solving, he or she must consider all system elements together.

Receiving Input

Before a system can produce output, there must be some input. In policing, these inputs help indicate what kind of problems need to be solved, how they can be solved, and what citizens expect from their officers. Inputs can be broad, affecting a department's policies, or they can be specific, concerning only one particular crime. Some common police-related inputs are:

▶ **New York's top private investigator, Joe Mullen** Detectives and investigators must use the information they gather at a crime scene to solve the case.
In what other ways do detectives use the five-step process?

- Public fear of crime
- Annual police budgets
- 911 calls
- Judicial review of police practices
- Quality of entry-level personnel
- Physical evidence
- Local and state government traditions
- Federal, state, and local statutes
- Preservice social and political views of personnel
- Political environment of the community and region
- Community and subcommunity expectations of police
- Administrative and command styles of leadership
- Entry-level personnel requirements
- Preservice socialization of recruits
- Organizational structure of the department
- Styles of policing
- Prevailing economic conditions
- Police-press relations[8]

Online

Remember, one of
your best resources is
www.policing.glencoe.com

Handling the Input

Clearly, police systems face input from many different sources. How they handle information such as calls for help or physical evidence is crucial to their success at all of the later stages of the criminal justice process. If a murder weapon is mishandled, for example, it may not be allowed as evidence in a trial.

On a broader scale, input affects the guiding principles of law enforcement agencies. The most obvious illustration is public demand. If citizens express concern about the growing number of thefts in a certain part of town, the local police will handle that input by considering ways to combat the problem.

Taking Appropriate Action

After a police department has processed information, it will take appropriate action to address the problem. To address the problem of theft in specific parts of town, for example, officers could urge residents to install burglar alarms and to report suspicious activity.

Deciding what is an appropriate action in policing can depend on a number of factors. Indeed, the number of various appropriate actions is as varied as the types of input to police. For example, a summary of one department's actions might include:

- 2,081 felony arrests
- 163 lives saved
- 17 positive newspaper editorials during the past 12 months
- 461 public letters of commendations
- 167 resignations from the department last year
- 23 false arrest suits during the past year
- Average patrol response time of 8.5 minutes
- Physical evidence samples collected in 1.6 percent of felony cases
- 4,567 arrestees processed
- 31 percent felony conviction rate during the past 12 months
- 4.7 percent personnel turnover rate last year
- 264 police recruits trained
- 12 percent Hispanic applicants for recruit training class
- 15 disciplinary actions taken last year
- 105 recoveries of stolen automobiles during the past 12 months
- 982 family disturbances handled
- 3,542 warnings issued to motorists[9]

Limits to Police Action

The controls that influence the operation of a police organization can be internal or external. Internal controls can include everything from policy and regulations, annual budget, internal standards, administrative attitudes, style of leadership, number of personnel assigned to internal affairs, and characteristics and capacity of communication systems. External controls focus on outside influences such as procedural laws governing the use of search, seizure, and arrest, or administrative laws that affect operation of the police organization and appellate court decisions.

Receiving Feedback

Every police agency has some method for monitoring and evaluating the actions taken by its employees. Some departments use community satisfaction surveys to determine how local residents feel about police services. They evaluate the responses to determine the community's most important concerns. In community policing, when officers receive feedback about their work, they seek information and then attempt to correct the problem.

This five-step process can also be seen in research, in which policing experts attempt to solve persistent problems with crime and police efficiency.

One famous example of this was the Kansas City Preventive Patrol Experiment in the early 1970s. In the past all police departments used random routine preventive patrol, which occurs when police patrol a neighborhood to announce their presence but do not focus on any specific section of that neighborhood. Random patrol was assumed to lower crime rates. Therefore, if police departments faced an increase in crime, they often increased the size of their patrol forces. Not until the Kansas City Preventive Patrol Experiment in the early 1970s did anyone ask (or answer) the fundamental question: "Does random routine preventive patrol reduce or prevent crime?"

Police researchers received input about the effectiveness of random patrol through the data they collected. Then they handled the input by comparing what they found in areas that used different numbers of patrol officers. This experiment, considered one of the most important pieces of police research ever conducted, found the surprising news that:

1. Increasing the number of officers conducting random patrol did not reduce crime or change the public's awareness of the police presence.
2. Reducing the size of the patrol did not bring about an increase in crime or an increased public fear of crime.[10]

This meant that increasing patrol forces to combat rising crime did not work, and reducing patrol units did not harm the community. As a result of this research, police experts took the appropriate action of finding a better approach: directed patrol, also known as targeted patrol. With directed patrol, patrol units limit and focus their police actions on high crime areas and hotspots. To determine which areas should be targeted they use crime mapping and their knowledge of their jurisdictions.

The feedback that they have received from police management, the public, and their follow-up research has shown this approach to be more successful. If police organizations hope to meet the policing challenges of tomorrow, they must continue to question assumptions and research better ways of providing services.

1.3 Self Check

1. What are the five elements of a system?
2. What did the Kansas City Preventive Patrol Experiment show?

POLICING *Online*

Check your answers at
www.policing.glencoe.com

1.4 Police in Transition

New technologies, training methods, and crimes keep policing in a perpetual state of transition. For example, drastic changes were suggested for the police selection process in the 1960s and 1970s. These suggestions included requiring applicants to pass a background check, successfully finish academy training and state certification, and complete at least some college education. Looking back, these improvements paved the way for community policing, in which officers are expected to be exceptionally ethical, friendly, and intelligent.

However, not all police departments adopted all of these suggestions. For example, few agencies today require college credits or a degree for incoming officers. Also, agencies did not adopt these suggestions in a uniform way. Some require eight weeks of academy training and some require six months of it. Therefore, community policing is being implemented with different degrees of success due to the different ways that police selection reform, and many other policing factors have changed in the past.

Back to the Future

In recent years, many departments have realized the value of returning to Sir Robert Peel's principles of policing. These nine guidelines for ideal police conduct, discussed in greater detail in Chapter 2, are:

1. Prevention of crime is the basic mission of the police.
2. Police must have the full respect of the citizenry.
3. A citizen's respect for law develops his respect for the police.
4. Cooperation of the public decreases as the use of force increases.
5. Police must render impartial enforcement of the law.
6. Physical force is used only as the last resort.
7. The police are the public and the public are the police.
8. Police represent the law.
9. The absence of crime and disorder is the test of police efficiency.[11]

These principles are regaining popularity because of their common sense and their positive attitude toward building relationships between the police and the community. In the wake of brutality scandals in New York and Los Angeles, departments are eager to strengthen those relationships.

The Quiet Revolution

Theories from the 1970s and 1980s shifted policing from a reactive approach to a more proactive one. Previously, officers waited until receiving a report or witnessing suspicious activity before acting to enforce the law. Although this worked well for certain common crimes, such as robberies, murders, drug dealing, and prostitution, it did not affect many other types of offenses. Less visible crimes like family violence and rape were more difficult to detect and, therefore, were often neglected.

Now, however, police are seeking out crime where they believe it is occurring and educating the public on how to prevent it. For example, law enforcement is using the Internet to find criminals who commit fraud, obscenity, and child abuse. Policing expert George Kelling calls this shift from reactivity to proactivity a **quiet revolution**.[12] He cites three reasons for its occurrence.

quiet revolution
The growth of community policing.

1. **Citizen disenchantment with police services:** Across the country, people have realized that traditional policing methods are not solving community problems. Members of minority communities especially feel police show little respect or understanding of their norms and values.[13]

2. **Research that questions the value of traditional police functions:** One famous example was the Kansas City Preventive Patrol Experiment of the 1970s. Researchers Skolnick and Bayley found a number of serious issues about traditional police methods and strategies, including:

   • Raising the number of police officers does not necessarily lower crime rates or increase the percentage of crimes solved.
   • Random routine preventive patrol neither reduces crime nor improves the chances of catching suspects.
   • Two-person patrol cars are no more effective than one-person cars in reducing crime or catching criminals.
   • Saturation patrolling, or heavy targeted patrol in a specific area, does not reduce crime. It only appears to do so temporarily, largely by displacing it to other areas.
   • The violent crimes that terrify Americans most, such as mugging, rape, robbery, burglary, and homicide, are rarely encountered by police on patrol.
   • Improving response time to emergency calls does not increase the likelihood of arresting criminals or even of satisfying involved citizens.
   • Crimes are not usually solved through criminal investigations conducted by police.[14]

3. **Officer and public frustration with the limits of the traditional policing role:**[15] Just as citizens are frustrated when officers do not exercise strong critical thinking and problem-solving skills, officers

are frustrated when their training or management does not encourage them to develop such skills. They often complain that they do not have any control over the causes of the crimes that they must deal with while on patrol. Over time, they become cynical at the inability of the criminal justice system to solve the problem. They may finally burn out and leave policing. Detective work is often considered the glamorous side of policing, and patrol work is often seen as only a stepping-stone to becoming a detective. At the same time, patrol officers handle the most complex and pressing problems in their communities. They are expected to do so in a timely manner without even the minimal rewards of recognition, salary raises, and status. Because of the lack of recognition or status, patrol work becomes less desirable, and sometimes incompetent and problem officers are assigned to patrol work because nobody else wants to do it.[16] To send these types of officers into the field to deal with the public can have disastrous results.

The New Policing Paradigm The result of this quiet revolution is **community policing**. To meet the challenges and demands of policing in the future, police must learn the new skills of community policing. They must be open-minded, unbiased, and sensitive to the concerns and problems of others.

community policing An interactive form of policing that requires officers to be friendly, openminded, unbiased, and sensitive to the concerns and problems of others; the new policing paradigm.

▶ **The New Paradigm of Community Policing** Building relationships with citizens is one of the goals of community policing.
How can officers achieve this goal?

Even if officers do not agree with a complainant's viewpoint, they should try to listen and understand the problem. Police should display empathy and compassion with sincerity, not in a rehearsed way. Police must also develop skill in:

- Planning
- Problem solving
- Organizing
- Interpersonal communications
- (Most importantly) Critical thinking

Online

Remember, one of your best resources is **www.policing.glencoe.com**

At the heart of the police transition to community policing is the question: "How do police identify and deliver high-quality services to the community?" In the past, the delivery of police services was accomplished in a reactive and unscientific manner, with little attention given to proactive policing. Today, the efficient delivery of police services requires a systematic process to 1) assess the needs of the public and 2) translate those needs into police services and programs that can be efficiently and effectively delivered to the community. In this way, police are becoming more sensitive to the needs of the community. They also have a better understanding of how their work affects the social environment.

Organizational Structure and Commitment

Two important factors in understanding the structure of an organization are:

- Role definitions
- Linking the police organization to the public

Role Definitions Within policing, role definitions are extremely important in order to achieve efficiency and have smooth transitions. For departments to operate effectively, they must be organized. Both management and officers must know the roles they are supposed to play to accomplish the goals and objectives of their department.

Department members who understand their roles clearly will know about, and be skilled in, the following processes of the organization:

- **Strategic planning** This is critical to the accomplishment of a department's mission because it allows the police department to prepare for the future.
- **Total quality management** Police departments, like private companies, will be productive only if they offer high-quality services.
- **Supervision** The supervision and leadership styles should promote the decentralized decision making that can be found in today's

community-oriented police departments. The department must attract and select candidates who have the requisite talents and ability to succeed within this new style of policing.

- **Staff development** Departments must provide training that develops the skills necessary for effective policing. Staff members must make lifelong learning a goal in all their development efforts.
- **Evaluation and accountability** Finally, departments must evaluate the performance of their officers. Valid evaluation is key to establishing accountability to the public.

Links to the Public The next factor is linking the police organization to its public. The public that the police serve can be classified into numerous subgroups characterized by:

- Ethnicity
- Religion
- Gender
- Economics
- Education
- Groups such as businesses, media, churches, civic groups, and educational institutions

Officers must study, analyze, and map the community, its people, and how crime affects each of them. Information collected can include any of the following:

- Basic demographics regarding age, gender, and ethnicity
- Information on economic status
- Employment rates
- Educational levels
- Availability and use of health services
- Availability and use of domestic violence programs
- Housing

Possible sources for this information include the U.S. Census, housing departments, social service agencies, colleges and universities, school boards, hospitals, courts, private physicians, and police departments. In-depth information on crime can also be obtained within police departments.[17] New technologies, such as Geographical Information Systems (GIS), allow departments to map city demographics, characteristics, and crime. Mapping may reveal a high concentration of Hispanic migrant workers in a community, and another community may have a number of elderly retirees.

Police departments should identify community leaders to discuss community issues and identify, assess, and analyze the needs specific to the targeted public. In community policing, many communities have established business associations and neighborhood groups who meet periodically with police to identify needs in their areas. Organizational structure and commitment will be stronger if police can follow the guidelines of a clear model.

Conceptual Programming Model

The 1973, the National Advisory Commission's *Report on the Police* recommended that:

> Every police chief executive should immediately develop written policy, based on policies of the governing body that provides formal authority for the police function, and should set forth the objectives and priorities that will guide the agency's delivery of police services. Agency policy should articulate the role of the agency in the protection of constitutional guarantees; the enforcement of the law; and the provision of services necessary to reduce crime, to maintain public order, and to respond to the needs of the community.[18]

The Commission was calling for a more structured approach to planning and delivering police services, as shown in Figure 1.2 on page 24. This **conceptual programming model** for the planning, design, and delivery of police services places a priority on needs assessment, design, implementation, and evaluation of police services. It focuses on the same philosophy, principles, and concepts as community policing does. Furthermore, it stresses

conceptual programming model A model for planning, design, and delivery of police services that focuses on needs assessment, design, implementation, and evaluation; and stresses quality and accountability.

Police Procedure

Fingerprinting and Photographing Suspects

Part of the standard booking process is the fingerprinting and photographing of adult suspects. Traditionally, juveniles were neither fingerprinted nor photographed to protect their privacy and to protect them from the stigma of a criminal record. Today, some jurisdictions are easing these restrictions so that juvenile records can be more complete.

Police may fingerprint arrested persons as long as they possess purpose and intent. In other words, if they have probable cause to believe that someone has committed a crime, they have the appropriate purpose and intent to fingerprint and photograph them to detect and prevent crime. In addition, police may fingerprint dead or injured persons who are in need of identification.

In addition to fingerprinting all of the foregoing, police themselves must be fingerprinted as a condition of employment. This also applies to private security officers.

Critical Thinking Is there anyone else who is (or should be) subject to mandatory fingerprinting in your jurisdiction?

Figure 1.2

Conceptual Programming Model for the Delivery of Police Services

→ Planning of Police Services ⎯→ Design and Implementation ⎯→ Evaluation and Accountability⎯
of Police Services   of Police Services

Feedback ←

I. Planning of Police Services

The Police Organization and Its Renewal Processes

Understanding of the commitment to the functions of the organization
◆ Philosophy
◆ Vision Statement
◆ Value Statement
◆ Mission Statement
◆ Goals and objectives

Understanding of the commitment to the structure of the organization.
◆ Role definitions
◆ Division of responsibility
◆ Internal and external relationships

Knowledge about and skilled in the processes of the organization.
◆ Strategic planning
◆ Total quality management
◆ Supervision and leadership
◆ Recruitment and selection of personnel
◆ Staff training and development
◆ Evaluation and accountability

Linking the Police Organization to Its Publics

Study, analysis, and mapping of the community, publics, and crime. Identify and interface with leaders of target publics.

Collaborative identification, assessment, and analysis of needs specific to target publics.
◆ Community surveys
◆ Public forums

II. Design and Implementation of Police Services

Designing Police Services

Translating analyzed needs into macro needs

Translating macro needs into service goals

Specify action/activities/roles and responsibilities

Identify operational constraints and potential obstacles

Establish timeframes

Resource Acquisition

Develop plans to market police services to both the police and the target publics

General plans for evaluating and assessing the effectiveness of police services

Implementing Police Services

Implementing strategies to market policing services to the police and the public

Delivery of police services/programs within established time frames

III. Evaluation and Accountability of Police Services

Evaluation and Accountability of Police Services

Determining quantitative and qualitative measures of successful policing
◆ Effectiveness
◆ Efficiency
◆ Equity

Assessing inputs and outputs Measure accomplishment of goals and objectives

Using evaluation findings for revisions, organizational renewal, and for accounting to police, public, and the profession

SOURCE: Adapted from Edgar J. Boone's Conceptual Programming Model.

quality and accountability. The conceptual programming model consists of three major stages:

1. Planning of police services
2. Design and implementation of police services
3. Evaluation and accountability of police services

The five key elements to effective service planning will be discussed first. In this stage there are two substages: 1) using the renewal process of the police organization and 2) linking the police organization to its public. In the first substage, the police organization must have an understanding and full commitment to its vision statement, values statement, and mission statement.

Vision Statement A **vision statement** illustrates the ideal beliefs and actions of an organization. For example, the vision statement of the Grand Rapids (MI) Police Department reads:

> The Grand Rapids Police Department shall lead in developing collaborative working partnerships with all our community and service providers, so that each and every citizen may enjoy the highest quality of life. Personalized community service shall be provided directly through Neighborhood Police Service Centers. Through our leadership, courage, and relentless pursuit of service excellence, the City of Grand Rapids will lead American cities into the 21st century.[19]

vision statement A statement that illustrates the ideal beliefs and actions of an organization.

CopTalk

Techniques for Talking

Police are well known for interviewing and interrogating witnesses and suspects. There are specialized techniques that should be developed for different types of interviews, such as dealing with:

- Scared or uncooperative witnesses
- Lying or uncooperative suspects
- Suspects who want to give information on other criminals in exchange for leniency
- Child victims or witnesses
- Dealing with several witnesses at a crime scene

In addition to interviews and interrogations, police use their communication skills in several other ways daily. This is especially true with community policing, in which police constantly meet and get to know residents and business owners of their community. It is also true for situations in which police regularly give warnings rather than make arrests. One common example of this is when someone violates a city ordinance by throwing a loud party.

What Do You Think? What are some ways in which police can develop their interviewing skills?

values statement A statement that declares an organization's values and beliefs in clear terms.

mission statement A statement that clearly and concisely describes what actions a department will take to achieve its vision and values.

Police and Gun Control

The Boston Gun Project is aimed at taking on a serious, large-scale crime problem: homicide victimization among youths in Boston. Between the late 1980s and early 1990s, Boston experienced an epidemic of youth homicide. Juvenile homicide increased by 230 percent from 1987 to 1990. The Gun Project was associated with a 63 percent decrease in youth homicides per month, a 32 percent decrease in shots-fired calls for service per month, a 25 percent decrease in gun assaults per month, and a 44 percent decrease in the number of youth gun assaults per month in the highest risk district (Roxbury).

SOURCE:
http://www.ncjrs.org/pdffiles1/nij/188741.pdf

Values Statement The vision statement provides the foundation for an agency's value statement. A **values statement** states an organization's values and beliefs, often in clear terms such as, "We believe that...." Another example from the Grand Rapids PD illustrates how this works:

- We believe the protection of life and property is our highest priority.
- We believe our Oath of Office and our Manual of Conduct define our highest standard of behavior.
- We value honesty, integrity, civility, and respect for ourselves and others.
- We value a trusting relationship with the community we serve.
- We believe our employees are our greatest asset and should be developed to their fullest potential.
- We value collaboration and the opportunity to work with other city agencies as partners in community-oriented government.
- We believe in open communication among all stakeholders.[20]

Mission Statement A **mission statement**, which follows a values statement, clearly and concisely describes what actions a department will take to achieve its vision and values. In Grand Rapids, for example, the department's mission statement is "to identify and solve problems in neighborhoods, by empowering police employees and holding them accountable to work in partnership with citizens, city services, schools, and other stakeholders."[21]

Goals and Objectives Finally, the department must identify its goals and objectives. In Grand Rapids (For a complete list, see Figure 1.3 on page 28) the goals are to:

- Encourage all members to be leaders
- Move its resources and decision making into the community
- Give citizens the ultimate responsibility for the safety and well being of their neighborhoods
- Recognize that neighborhood-based problem solving is a collaborative effort that focuses on the dynamics and root causes of crime and neighborhood decay
- Create an environment that encourages innovation in all aspects of our approach to policing[22]

In turn, each goal has objectives that must be achieved if the goal is to be accomplished. Goals are accomplished within a longer time frame that is normally greater than one year, and the objectives needed to reach these goals are set within a shorter time frame of less than one year.

Before moving to the design phase, police must assess criminal justice resources and strategies. This assessment is essential to determine which

CAREER FOCUS

Chief of Police

Job Description

I have been Chief of Police in Grand Rapids for four years. My staff is composed of eight captains, six of whom run and supervise the area-based teams with about 32 beats in all.

Grand Rapids, Chief of Police, Harry Dolan

My daily schedule is pretty intense and includes many meetings. Today, my day started at 8 A.M. with a public safety technology meeting followed by a command staff meeting at 11 A.M. I had a business lunch with the director of public works to develop a working relation with him and his department. At 1:30 P.M. I met with the internal affairs police advisors.

We have to deal with local community problems such as citizens' concern with racism, or national and international terrorism. The real challenge is often to balance reactive responses with proactive work.

My advice to students interested in law enforcement careers at a higher level is to take calculated risks and not be satisfied with status quo. By that I mean to encourage them to solve problems creatively and think differently. Students should study Roosevelt and other dynamic leaders who had to guide organizations through change, and study the various eras of policing. Students should try and develop their public relations skills, their ability to be motivators and leaders.

Employment History

I always knew I wanted to work in law enforcement. My father was a sergeant in the NYPD. After graduating from college, I became a deputy, then a police officer. 1991, I became Police Chief in Lumberton, North Carolina, which allowed me to set policies, work with a budget, be involved in personnel management, and implement community policing programs. My knowledge of community policing catapulted me to Grand Rapids as Police Chief in 1998.

Education

I graduated from West Carolina University in 1980, and in 1997 I completed my Master's degree in Leadership and Management.

Follow-Up Why do you think public relations skills are important in this position?

Figure 1.3

Goals and Objectives for Grand Rapids Police Department

Goal 1: Leadership and Empowerment
- Management must be willing to take risks and trust others.
- Managers must model behavior that others should follow and take responsibility for their own decisions.
- Develop comprehensive training to support the organizational mission.
- Encourage leadership and accountability at the line level and in the community.

Goal 2: Decentralization
- The department will establish six Neighborhood Police Service Centers (NPSCs) within the next two to three years (one of which will also include the downtown headquarters). Each NPSC will have its own management team, headed by a captain, with staff to fulfill neighborhood needs.
- The Grand Rapids Police Department will use restructuring, civilianization, despecialization, and other creative strategies to maximize sworn officer deployment.

Goal 3: Citizen Responsibility
- The department will promote and support initiatives that require everyone, especially parents and youth, to fulfill their responsibilities for enhancing the quality of life in the community.
- Develop strategies for holding property owners, landlords, and tenants responsible for maintaining their homes and yards and for businesses to do the same.

Goal 4: Problem Solving and Collaboration
- Prevent crime through proactive problem solving to deal with long-term and chronic problems and to improve the overall quality of life.
- Establish permanent partnerships with other service providers and citizens to enhance neighborhood safety and security.

Goal 5: Innovation
- Foster an atmosphere that promotes new ideas, creative thinking, and risk-taking.
- Research, develop, and use technology to enhance the department's ability to correct community problems.

SOURCE: Grand Rapids Police Department, *Back to the Future: How to Implement Community Policing as Part of Community-Oriented Police,* 1999, pp. 15-34

criminal justice resources are available and which are not. Areas examined might include:

- Policing strategies
- Training needs and capabilities
- Relationships with state and federal law enforcement agencies
- Prosecutorial priorities and workload

Service Design and Implementation The next stage of the conceptual programming model is service design and implementation. This includes the substages of designing police services and the implementation of police services. The design substage is more important because it strongly affects the delivery of police services. It begins with the police department and community leaders identifying a community's needs and finding the roots of the problems. Police also identify which resources are necessary, such as personnel, materials, time, money, and facilities.[23] When these resources are identified, police can work with the community to acquire them.

Service Evaluation and Accountability The final stage of the conceptual programming model is service evaluation and accountability. Along with goals, objectives, and action plans, police must also evaluate the effectiveness of their strategies. Evaluation is the bridge to accountability for effectiveness, efficiency, and equity in police services. Effectiveness is determining if the service or action plan achieved its goals and objectives, and efficiency is the best utilization of resources. Equity, or fairness, focuses on whether the department provided equal access to police services, equal treatment under the Constitution, and equal distribution of services and resources to all within the community.[24]

The three-step conceptual programming provides the basic steps that should be taken by all police departments when planning, designing, delivering, and evaluating police services. Although it does not provide answers for specific crime issues, it helps departments maintain guidelines and accountability to the public. Using this model promotes better police-community relations, which are based upon consensus rather than conflict. Unfortunately, many departments fail to follow this model and prefer to be reactive in their approach to crime and community problems. Many other departments, however, are realizing that consensus-based strategies are a better approach for the future.

1.4 Self Check

1. Explain the quiet revolution and the three reasons behind it.
2. What is the conceptual programming model?

POLICING *Online*

Check your answers at
www.policing.glencoe.com

Chapter 1

Introduction to American Policing

Summary By Learning Objectives

1. Identify the role of police in a democratic society.

Citizens empower the government and the police through their vote. Using the law of agency, society gives police authority to maintain order. Since this power is still owned by society, it can be seen as a perpetual loan of a community's power.

Police are the living expression of the law. They reflect the values, meanings, and potentialities of democracy. It is the police who ensure that citizens can exercise their freedoms. In a democratic society, it is a constant effort to balance individual rights with the need for public order.

2. Understand how American police use the rule of law.

The rule of law is essential to police functioning. It is society's guideline for what is acceptable and unacceptable human behavior. It provides a uniform way of making, interpreting, and enforcing the law in order to avoid emotional responses to crime and punishment.

Police who follow the rule of law develop a relationship with the community focused on collaboration, not confrontation. They enforce the law in a fair and consistent manner that helps to maintain a democratic government.

3. Explain how policing operates within the criminal justice system.

Police function within the criminal justice system, a complex system with three components that are interdependent, interrelated, and interacting toward a common goal. These three components are the police, courts, and corrections. The primary goal of the criminal justice system is the prevention, control, and reduction of crime and delinquency.

Just as the criminal justice system has subsystems, each component has a separate subgoal. For police, these are the prevention and control of crime and maintaining order. The courts have the goals of judging and sentencing offenders. Finally, the goal for corrections is incarceration and/or monitoring the offender on probation or parole with a focus on rehabilitation.

4. Describe the five-step process of a police system.

All systems have five steps:
1. Police receive input such as 911 calls.
2. They decide how to handle the input.
3. They take appropriate action.
4. They limit their actions based on procedural laws and public expectations.
5. They receive feedback from their management and the public.

All steps are equally important. When a police administrator is trouble-shooting or problem solving within a police system, he or she must consider every step together.

5. Analyze the differences between consensus and conflict models.

In a consensus model, subsystems work together in agreement to reach a similar goal and to promote harmony and efficiency among each other. In criminal justice, this shared goal is justice. The criminal justice system often displays the ability to move to consensus. In the consensus model there is sometimes short-term conflict, but in the end the system adjusts itself to maintain the balance.

In a conflict model, subsystems are believed to work best when they are in conflict or disagreement. It is important to understand that a conflict model is not a nonsystem. It is functioning, but works best by a system of checks and balances. Still, this conflict can create tension because the system can become fragmented.

6. Explain why policing is in transition.

Policing is always in transition because police must be prepared to meet the challenges of the future. In recent years, policing has returned to the principles of Robert Peel, who promoted police and community collaboration, as well as shared responsibility for crime-fighting among both groups. The nine guidelines Peel gave for ideal police conduct are:

1. Prevention of crime is the basic mission of police.
2. Police must have the respect of the citizenry.
3. A citizen's respect for law develops his respect for the police.
4. Cooperation of the public decreases as the use of force increases.
5. Police must render impartial enforcement of the law.
6. Physical force is used only as the last resort.
7. The police are the public and the public are the police.
8. Police represent the law.
9. The absence of crime and disorder is the test of police's efficiency.

A quiet revolution is occurring in the evolving policing philosophy of community policing. This revolution has been caused by the public's disenchantment with police services, research challenging old police assumptions, and a frustration with the traditional role of the police officer.

7. Understand the components and goals of the conceptual programming model.

In 1973, the National Advisory Commission's Report on the police recommended that police chief executives develop written policies and a structured approach to the planning and the delivery of police services. This model emphasizes needs assessment and planning, design, implementation, and evaluation of police services. In the planning stage the police organization must have a good understanding of its vision, values, and mission. In the next stage, the design, the police and the community identify needs, problems, and resources. Finally, the effectiveness evaluation determines whether the service or police action achieved its goals. This last step is the basis for accountability.

Key Terms

law of agency (p. 5)
perpetual loan (p. 5)
rule of law (p. 5)
individual rights advocates (p. 8)
public order advocates (p. 8)
criminal justice system (p. 9)
crime (p. 9)
delinquency (p. 9)
justice (p. 9)
nonsystem (p. 9)

due process (p. 12)
consensus model (p. 12)
conflict model (p. 13)
quiet revolution (p. 19)
community policing (p. 20)
conceptual programming model (p. 23)
vision statement (p. 25)
values statement (p. 25)
mission statement (p. 26)

Questions for Review

1. Explain how U.S. citizens can be considered the ruling class.

2. What is the role of police in a democratic society?

3. How does one find a balance between individual rights and public order?

4. What are the separate but related goals of police, courts, and corrections?

5. Compare and contrast the consensus and conflict models.

6. What are the three steps in the conceptual programming model?

7. What is meant by a proactive approach to policing?

8. How can departments evaluate the delivery of police services?

Experiential Activities

9. Ride-Along

Contact your local police department and ask to join an officer in a patrol car ride-along.

    a. What did you learn from the ride-along about the realities of policing?

    b. How did this experience make you more or less interested in policing as a career?

    c. What types of inputs does the officer receive while on patrol?

10. Meet the Dispatcher

One of the busiest, yet most invisible, employees of a police department is the dispatcher. Contact your local police department and ask if you can set up an interview with the dispatcher. Since dispatchers are very busy, you can offer to do it in person, by phone, or even by e-mail if he or she prefers.

Experiential Activities continued

a. How is the dispatcher's communication skill important to police officers?

b. How could the dispatcher's job be made easier?

c. How has your perception of a dispatcher's job changed because of this interview?

11. Informational Interviews

Contact a law enforcement agency in your area to set up an interview. Ask about what they look for in recruits, what their hiring needs usually are, and what qualities a person needs to succeed in their department.

a. What did you learn about the operations of a law enforcement agency?

b. How would you develop your interviewing skills for a law enforcement job?

c. What skills do you possess that would make you well suited for this agency?

12. Meet a Detective

Arrange an informal interview with a detective at your local police department. Prepare your questions so they revolve around differences between uniformed police and detectives.

a. List the differences between the two jobs.

b. What are the similarities?

c. What is the most challenging aspect of a detective's work?

Web Patrol

13. Officer Online

You can find a link to Officer.com at **www.policing.glencoe.com**. This site is often very opinionated, but offers insights on issues relevant to law enforcement. Read two of the news articles listed on the right-hand side of the page.

Based on the material you found on this site, what issues are important to today's officers?

14. Cops Who Care

Visit Cops Who Care through the link provided at **www.policing.glencoe.com**. Read the first page, then the Events section to learn about this multi-agency charitable organization.

Other than law enforcement, what can police do to help their communities and improve the quality of life?

15. Cybersnitch

Learn about Cybersnitch, an Internet-based crime reporting system that you can access through the link provided at **www.policing.glencoe.com**.

How does Cybersnitch help law enforcement fight high-tech crimes?

Critical Thinking Exercises

16. Choosing a Policing Career

You want a career in law enforcement. The counselor at your community college explains that a solid education would help you in any job, including policing. Your plans were to quit college, attend the academy, and enter police work with nine credits under your belt. Now you are not so sure.

   a. Do you feel that a college education would help you in a policing career?
   b. What further questions can you ask a police officer regarding how college could help in a policing career?

17. Academy Training

It is your first week of academy training, and you are completely disoriented. The drill instructors are yelling at you constantly, making you run until you are exhausted, and making fun of the way you put on your uniform. You expected this because you know that the drill instructors want to toughen the recruits. You have learned to stay calm when they are yelling and giving orders, but you begin to question if policing is right for you. You wonder what you can do to make it through your training.

   a. What are some ways that you can reduce your stress level? What about your physical exhaustion?
   b. Who can you talk to for moral support during this rough time?

18. Job Choices

About halfway through academy training, the sheriff's office calls you and asks you to come in for an interview for a position at the county jail. You do well at the interview and are offered a job as an officer at the jail. Before you accept the position, you talk to an officer at the local police department and a correctional officer at the jail. They give you two very different opinions. The local police officer thinks it is excellent experience because it puts you in an environment full of offenders, in which you have to learn to solve problems without relying on a gun. He feels that many rookies are nervous, which can make them too quick to use force, and he believes that correctional experience can help them and can benefit police officers in general.

The correctional officer thinks the opposite. He has been working as line staff for nearly 18 years, and he feels that once a person enters corrections, it is very difficult to find work elsewhere in the justice system. He tells you that his supervisor would give him bad performance ratings so he would not be able to find work elsewhere. Now you are concerned about becoming trapped in correctional work.

   a. Who seems to be correct, and why?
   b. What are the pros and cons of beginning a police career in corrections-related work?

Endnotes

1. M. J. Adler, (1987). *We hold these truths: Understanding the ideas and ideals of the Constitution.* New York: Macmillan Publishing Company.
2. E. Davis, (1981). Professional police principles. In *Critical issues in law enforcement* (pp. 14–15). Cincinnati, OH.
3. J. Lohman, (1981). Human relations and the law. In T. Johnson, G. Misner, and L. Brown, *The police and society: An environment for collaboration and confrontation* (p. 31). Englewood Cliffs, NJ: Prentice-Hall, Inc.
4. J. Fisk, (1974). Some dimensions of police discretion. In J. Goldsmith, & S. Goldsmith (Eds.), *The police community* (pp. 77–78). Pacific Palisades, CA: Palisades Press.
5. T. Johnson, Misner, G., & Brown, L. (1981). *The police and society: An environment for collaboration and confrontation.* Englewood Cliffs, NJ: Prentice-Hall.
6. J. Reiman, (1974). Police autonomy v. police authority: A philosophical perspective. In J. Goldsmith & S. Goldsmith (Eds.), *The police community* (pp. 228–229). Pacific Palisades, CA: Palisades Press.
7. Johnson, et al., op. cit., p. 32.
8. Ibid., 10.
9. Ibid., 11.
10. George Kelling et al., *The Kansas City preventive patrol experiment,* Washington, DC: The Police Foundation, 1974.
11. H. More, Ed. *Critical issues in law enforcement.* Cincinnati, OH: Anderson, 1981.
12. G.L. Kelling, Police and communities: The quiet revolution. *Perspectives on Policing,* U.S. Department of Justice, National Institute of Justice, Washington, DC, U.S. Government Printing Office, (1988), p. 1.
13. Kelling, loc. cit., p. 4.
14. J. Skolnick, & D. Bayley, *The new blue line.* New York: The Free Press, 1986.
15. Ibid., 4.
16. Kelling, op. cit., 4.
17. Bureau of Justice Assistance. *Neighborhood-oriented policing in rural communities: A program planning guide.* Washington, DC: U.S. Government Printing Office, (1994).
18. National Advisory Commission on Criminal Justice Standards and Goals. *Report on the police.* Washington, DC: U.S. Government Printing Office, (1973).
19. Grand Rapids Police Department. *Back to the Future: How to Implement Community Policing as part of Community-Oriented Community,* Grand Rapids, MI: Grand Rapids Police Department, 1999.
20. Ibid., 13.
21. Ibid., 14.
22. Ibid., 15–32.
23. Ibid., 53.
24. Ibid., 25. OR Ibid., pp. 64–70.

Chapter 2

Policing in Ancient and English Times

CHAPTER OUTLINE

CHAPTER OBJECTIVES

AFTER COMPLETING THIS CHAPTER, YOU WILL BE ABLE TO:

1. Understand the influence of the Code of Hammurabi.

2. Explain how early societies approached their law enforcement problems.

3. Describe early English law enforcement officials and their modern equivalents.

4. Explain how the English watch system evolved and why it was replaced.

5. Understand why the law enforcement strategies used throughout English history either succeeded or failed.

6. Discuss the importance of Peel's principles of policing.

◀ An English bobby escorts poor children in Plymouth.

The study of history offers an understanding of the bridges from the past to the present and to the future. The study of patterns of behavior in the past can help us understand the trends of today. If we are able to identify and project trends, we can prepare for the future. Why is modern policing the way that it is? To understand this, you must first understand police history and learn the origins of modern policing thought and practice. Many policing concepts were developed hundreds (or even thousands) of years ago to address problems that still exist today. Even crime problems that seem modern, such as gangs, have existed for centuries. This is why many modern policing strategies have been resurrected from the past.

As you read this chapter, you will see how the goal of policing—to fight and eliminate crime—has never differed. On the other hand, *how* the police have fought crime has changed and evolved over the centuries. You will learn what has succeeded, what has failed, and how police agencies have learned from this to create higher standards of policing today. As you read further chapters, you will also see that many policing issues, such as crime prevention and police-community relations, are still unresolved.

The Impact of History on Policing

Any study of police history can best be arranged in three broad periods: ancient policing (5000 B.C.–1066 A.D.), English policing (1066 A.D.–1850 A.D.), and American policing (1600 A.D.–present). Each of these periods has influenced the development of modern law enforcement. Many problems that affected ancient police have remained constant challenges through the ages. As such, they provide recruitment and personnel retention challenges, and the struggle to find the just punishment for a given crime has remained constant through the ages. Students and practitioners in criminal justice need to scrutinize history in order to understand the personalities and decision-making processes that have shaped American policing.

Figure 2.1 on pages 48 and 49 shows a timeline of ancient and English historical events. They can be summarized as follows:

- The present-day concept of criminal and civil law started with the Code of Hammurabi.
- The American concepts of democracy, rule of law, and justice are rooted in Greek civilization.

MYTH	FACT
American policing developed with very little outside influence.	**American policing is in fact descended from thousands of years of policing systems and practices. The policing of ancient Sumeria and Egypt, and later of Greece, Rome, and England, all contributed to the form of policing that Americans know today.**

- Greek law influenced Roman law, which in turn influenced English common law, which is the foundation of American law.
- The concepts of presidential security, urban policing, and public safety officers are seen in the Roman concepts of the praetorian guard, urban cohort, and vigiles, respectively.
- The tithing system in feudal England is the predecessor of the American neighborhood watch system and also shares similarities with today's community policing.
- The Magna Carta gave the United States the concept of due process and the right to a trial by jury.
- Sir Robert Peel created policing principles that are now the foundation of modern American policing.

All of these contributions have enriched the nature and quality of the American criminal justice system. By examining the ways in which people administered justice throughout history, we can see how and why our system works the way it does.

2.1 Self Check

1. What are some ways police history affects modern policing?
2. How far back can you trace the origin of the present-day concepts of criminal law and civil law?

POLICING *Online*
Check your answers at
www.policing.glencoe.com

2.2 Policing in Ancient Times

A formal and sophisticated criminal justice system did not exist in ancient times. To early man, the primary social unit was the tribe. There were no written laws; rather, customs and norms were the guides to individual conduct. If there was enforcement, it was the people who enforced the customs and norms. Crimes committed against a member of a tribe or clan were resolved by the injured party. In the case of crimes committed against the whole tribe or clan, the responsibility for addressing the wrong rested with the group.

Out of this practice arose the concept of **kin police**, in which family, tribe, or clan members assumed some responsibility for dispensing justice.[1] This was the first step in creating a police system for an established community. Kin police were used when needed, much like the posses of medieval England and the American West.

As tribes and clans formed larger groups and even nations, a need arose for uniform, written laws. These would provide a fair and just means to control personal behavior and commerce. As written laws developed, people also needed a legal system to administer justice. The human race was becoming civilized.

kin police An early policing system in which family, tribe, or clan members assumed responsibility for dispensing justice.

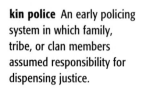

Remember, one of your best resources is **www.policing.glencoe.com**

The Sumerians and the Code of Hammurabi

By 5000 B.C., the civilizations of Egypt and Sumeria were evolving in the Middle East. In approximately 2400 B.C., Sumerians (who lived in what is now Iraq) started to develop their own laws and legal regulations. Under the ruler Ur-Nammu in 2050 B.C., they established a written legal code. Although the king had the primary responsibility for law and justice, in actual practice it was the Sumerian local officials, or *ensis*, who administered the law. This is similar to the way that government leaders today delegate police administration to chiefs and agency directors.[2]

Early Uses of Restitution An interesting feature of the Sumerian code was the use of fines as a punishment. This is a clear early example of restitution, the process of forcing criminals to take financial responsibility for their crimes. Unlike the present-day use of fines, in many ancient cultures offenders reimbursed victims and their families for serious crimes such as murder, rape, and aggravated assault. For example, under the Sumerian code, if a man cut off the foot of another man, he was required to pay the victim ten shekels of silver. Today, the most common use of fines is for minor offenses such as parking and traffic violations.

The Code of Hammurabi In 1901, French archaeologists working in Iraq uncovered artifacts containing the **Code of Hammurabi**, a collection of laws and edicts that were written during the rule of the Babylonian king Hammurabi. The code consisted of 28 paragraphs and provided guidance for legal procedure that addressed a variety of issues from civil matters to criminal acts. It was based on the concept of *lex talionis*, which means equal retaliation or "an eye for an eye."

The code provided legal protection to all classes of citizens, even for injustices committed by the rich and powerful against the poor. Although the law provided fewer rights and legal protections to women, children, and slaves than to free men, the code was still very humane for its time. It was also very complete: For example, it not only specified crimes but also penalties for non-compliance, unjust accusations, false testimony, and injustices committed by judges.

To make this code effective, an agent of the government was put in place to oversee the enforcement of these laws.[3] The code covers this by stating that messengers were responsible for enforcing the law.[4] These officials were an early form of police, and this is one of the first references to the role of policing in society.

Code of Hammurabi A collection of laws and edicts that provided guidance for a variety of issues, from civil matters to criminal acts; based on the concept of *lex talionis*.

lex talionis An ancient philosophy of justice, which means equal retaliation or "an eye for an eye."

Policing in Ancient Egypt

Policing in Egypt can be traced back to around 2900 B.C., when officials called Judges Commandment of the Police were responsible for the security of Egypt and its provinces. Eventually, specific individuals were assigned the responsibility of enforcing Egyptian laws and customs. Egyptian police were given a broad role that included not only law enforcement powers but also judicial authority. They were responsible for trying cases, passing judgment, and executing sentences[5] for any crimes under Egyptian law, such as stealing, cheating on taxes, grave robbing, or adultery.

The Police Draft To enforce the laws at the local level, Nubians from the southern part of the Egyptian empire were drafted into duty. This means that, as in today's military drafts, they were required to serve for a set amount of time as police officers. The fact that they had to be drafted may indicate that they had no personal desire to be police officers, which is very different from the types of people who become officers today.[6]

Role of the Vizier During Egypt's Eighteenth Dynasty (1575–1320 B.C.), pharaohs were involved in numerous military ventures and had to delegate the supervision of domestic responsibilities to subordinates. The most

vizier A high-ranking ancient Egyptian official who was the only person other than the pharaoh who could act on all civil matters.

important of these subordinates was the **vizier**, an official who had numerous titles and was the only person other than the pharaoh who could act on all civil matters. His responsibilities included:

- Overseeing the highest court of justice, which made him the equivalent of today's Chief Justice of the U.S. Supreme Court
- Collecting taxes across the kingdom, much like today's IRS
- Supervising Egypt's wars in a similar capacity as today's Secretary of Defense
- Acting as chief of police for the kingdom, which has no modern American equivalent but can be compared to an office in which one person supervises all police agencies simultaneously

As the official representative of the pharaoh, the vizier represented divine authority, perception, and justice. He wielded considerable power that he could use to further his own goals. However, the vizier was expected to be fair and equitable in his dealings with the people.[7]

New Police Units Ancient Egypt was a wealthy culture with a large amount of international commerce. Smuggling, especially along the coasts and delta of the Nile River, was a persistent crime problem. To put a stop to this problem, around 1400 B.C., King Amenhotep established customhouses and a marine patrol to guard the coast and delta areas. This was one of the

▶ **Ramses III** Ramses III strengthened the Egyptian police forces to protect tombs and graves more effectively. *Why was this function important in Egyptian sociaty?*

earliest forms of customs police.[8] In approximately 1340 B.C., Egypt went further and organized the River Security Unit to patrol the Nile. Their responsibilities included:

- Fighting piracy
- Searching ships for suspected smugglers
- Protecting business and commercial activity on the river

Another serious crime problem was grave robbing. In ancient Egypt, royal families were buried in tombs with valuables such as jewelry, sculptures, and expensively decorated coffins. Although most tombs were hidden underground, grave robbers were skilled at finding them. From 1198 to 1166 B.C., King Ramses III moved to increase the power and authority of police to prevent these types of crimes. Police units were assigned to 24-hour security duty at the tombs. Because the royal tombs were considered sacred, these police units were considered the most important police in Egypt. One of their innovations was using dogs to help guard property. Today dogs are used to protect property and also to help find criminal evidence.

FYI

Trials by Battle

In a trial by battle, a combatant could hire another person to stand in his place in battle. This stand-in individual came to be known as a *champion*. Today, to champion someone else's cause means to support it wholeheartedly.

SOURCE: H. A. Johnson and N. T. Wolfe, *History of Criminal Justice*, 2nd ed. (Cincinnati, OH: Anderson, 1996).

The Influence of Ancient Greece

The contributions of ancient Greek civilization to Western civilization are numerous. They include the Greek alphabet, the Olympic games, scientific reasoning, architectural design, sculpture, theater, epic poetry, and democracy. Any philosophical discussion on the topics of government, justice, virtue, or ethics brings forth the images of the great philosophers: Socrates, Plato, and Aristotle. The Greeks took great pride in the manner in which they administered justice. In many ways, they laid the foundation for the development and promotion of the rule of law in Western civilization.

The accomplishments of the Greeks were significant in creating a system of justice that was relatively fair for its period. Neighboring countries had great respect for the Greeks, and Grecian principles of law and justice still influence justice systems throughout the Western world.

Early Greek Justice Greek civilization began in about 2000 B.C. The Greeks' earliest system for administering justice was rooted in the philosophy of *lex talionis*, with the victim or his or her family dispensing retribution. Eventually, the king replaced the family as an arbitrator, or judge, between the victim and the accused. A victim of a crime could file a complaint against the accused, then the king would hear the case and decide on the defendant's guilt and punishment. This was similar to today's bench trials, in which criminal cases are heard without a jury, except there were no lawyers in that era. It was the first time that the state got involved in criminal trials and punishment and that criminals had to answer to the state instead of to other people.[9]

Early Greek police were kin police, but as Greece evolved, policing took on a more community-oriented approach. It was based on the organizing principle of the city-state, or polis. Each polis consisted of a city, which was usually walled and surrounded by farmland and other territory. It was an independent political unit with its own personality, laws, and customs.

Evolving Written Laws Athens was perhaps the first polis to have a regular process of law. One of the first sets of written laws was developed by the Athenian ruler Draco in 621 B.C. This **Draconian code** was very harsh. It called for the death sentence for many crimes, even property crimes. It also allowed an individual who was in debt to be sold into slavery to pay off the debt. These harsh laws made Athenians unhappy and set the stage for a crisis.

The resolution of this crisis came about 25 years later, when the revolutionary statesman Solon became the chief magistrate of Athens in 594 B.C. Solon saw the abuses of the law under the Code of Draco and set out to reform the Athenian law. His laws were considered very lenient for his era: For example, he outlawed selling debtors into slavery and limited the imposition of the death penalty to only the crime of murder. Solon tried to establish social and political equality, which was opposed by the aristocrats who ran large sharecropping systems in Athens. Solon's reforms were implemented by his successors even though some did not embrace the concept of democracy.[10]

Consider the case of one of the early rulers of Athens, Pisistratus (560–527 B.C.). Pisistratus staged an attack on himself in order to convince Athenians of the need for a security force to protect him. Citizens obligingly authorized the creation of a 50-member force. Pisistratus used this force, armed with wooden clubs, to maintain a tyrannical rule over Athens.[11] This was clearly one of the early instances of the abuse of publicly authorized police power. Athens became a democracy in 507 B.C., when another Athenian statesman, Cleisthenes, proposed a constitution that gave all citizens a chance to serve in the government. His reforms were implemented by his successors, and Athens finally became a democracy in 507 B.C.[12]

The Eleven During the rule of Pericles in 450–429 B.C., Athens maintained a police force that was supervised by a group of criminal commissioners known as The Eleven. The Eleven apprehended and punished criminals, processed arrests, and performed executions. For the murderer who rendered a confession on the scene, execution was immediate, and other serious cases were brought to court. The Eleven also oversaw the state prisons and dealt with less serious offenses.

Draconian code A very harsh ancient Greek code that made many crimes, even property crimes, into capital offenses; also allowed debtors to be sold into slavery.

◀ **Pericles's Eleven** Pericles
maintained the Athenian force
known as The Eleven that had
the power to arrest, try, and
execute criminals.
*Why do different people perform
these tasks in modern society?*

Innovations of Ancient Rome

The Roman Empire built upon the work of the Greeks and made several
important contributions to policing and the administration of justice. Some
of the most important developments were:

1. The Law of the Twelve Tablets
2. New police units created by Caesar Augustus
3. The creation of the *praetor*, a judge who changed the laws as needed

Law of the Twelve Tablets As early as 450 B.C. in ancient Rome, the lower
classes felt that the oral law needed to be written down in order to avoid
exploitation by the ruling classes. This first set of written laws, referred to
as the **Law of the Twelve Tablets**, appears to have been influenced by the
Greek laws developed by Solon. The Law of the Twelve Tablets grouped civil
and criminal law, legal procedures, and some social regulations. It was simply and logically organized and provided the lower classes with a presentation of the law that most people could understand. This simplicity better
armed the lower classes to protect themselves against tyranny.

Law of the Twelve Tablets
The first set of written law in
ancient Rome; grouped civil
and criminal law, legal procedures, and some social
regulations.

Policing under Emperor Augustus During the reign of the Emperor
Augustus (27 B.C.–14 A.D.), three types of police organizations developed in
Rome in response to different problems:

praetorian guard A Roman police force that existed mainly to protect the life of the emperor and his property, specifically his palace.

1. First, Augustus organized the **praetorian guard**, which existed mainly to protect the life of the emperor and his property, specifically his palace. The guard is an early example of presidential protection, as you can see today with the White House's Secret Service. The guard consisted of nine cohorts of 100 soldiers each. Personnel were recruited exclusively from Rome because Romans were believed to be the most loyal to their empire. Since the guard enjoyed shorter terms of service and higher pay than other members of the army, it attracted the best applicants and was considered the most prestigious unit.

urban cohort A Roman police force that dealt with problems of street crimes and mob violence by patrolling the streets and maintaining public order.

2. Augustus also created the **urban cohort**, which dealt with problems of street crimes and mob violence in Rome. The city prefect, the equivalent of a chief of police, commanded the force. Under his direction, three groups of 1,500 soldiers each would patrol the streets and maintain public order. The modern-day equivalent is the municipal foot patrol, although the urban cohort, at 4,500 soldiers, was much larger than most American police departments.

vigiles A special Roman corps of 7,000 men who served as both as fireman and night police.

3. In response to a need to improve fire protection, Augustus also organized the *vigiles*, a special corps of 7,000 men who served as both firemen and night police. The *vigiles* were organized into seven cohorts of 1,000 each, with each cohort being assigned to two of Rome's 14 regions.[13]

The Praetor By the third century B.C., the Roman system of justice was changing. As Rome expanded its empire by colonizing foreign lands, each new colony brought different sets of laws and legal systems. This made Rome a larger and more complex empire than before. The earlier principles of the Law of the Twelve Tablets were inadequate because they had become institutionalized and inflexible. Rome needed a body of law that was applicable to both Roman citizens and subjects in foreign colonies.

praetor A Roman judge who changed the law and created new laws as necessary.

To solve this problem, new laws developed from the annual edicts of the **praetor**, a judge who changed the law as necessary. In this respect, the praetor was like modern American judges who use case law, which is the use of case decisions to change the laws on far-reaching criminal issues such as the death penalty or a suspect's rights.

The praetor had jurisdiction in criminal matters and also possessed police powers. He often personally handled cases in which upper-class defendants denied their guilt. If defendants were from lower classes, he would assign a subordinate called a *quaesitor* to investigate and prosecute the case.[14] This combination of powers made the praetors and *quaesitors* a combination of today's detectives and prosecutors. Today, such roles are separated in order to maintain checks and balances within the criminal justice system.

Beneath the praetors and *quaesitors* were lower-ranking magistrates who policed the city, supervised the state prison, and executed criminals. Like The Eleven of ancient Greece, they had the authority to immediately execute anyone who confessed to a serious crime such as murder or was caught in the act of committing it.

By 450 A.D., the Roman Empire was declining rapidly and the system of justice was falling apart. The Roman legal code had become complicated and confusing because the Romans never repealed old laws as they created new ones. In 528 A.D., the Emperor Justinian ordered the old code to be revised to reflect current imperial laws; all older ones were repealed. Justinian's Code then became the foundation for teaching law during this period[15] and later had a tremendous influence on the development of legal systems in Europe and the Americas.

2.2 Self Check

1. Explain the concept of *lex talionis*.
2. What are four great contributions of ancient cultures to the development of policing?

POLICING *Online*
Check your answers at
www.policing.glencoe.com

2.3 Early English Policing

The American criminal justice system descends directly from the English system of justice. When English colonists first moved to the United States in the early seventeenth century, they brought their ideas for police, courts, and corrections. Although American criminal justice is now very different in some ways, it is still important to understand the English heritage and see its strong influence on American policing.

English Influences Before 1066 A.D.

The Romans invaded England in about 43 A.D. and maintained garrisons there until 436 A.D. While occupying England, they heavily influenced native government and law. The origins of English common law, which formed the foundation of American law, can be traced back to Roman legal codes discussed in the previous section. After 436 A.D., England's tribes formed small communities called *tuns* (the origin of the word *town*). It was here that policing evolved in England.[16] Tuns developed self-governing systems for local defense and the administration of justice that were the predecessors of today's local governments.

Punishment was administered according to the nature of the crime. Restitution was often used, and a system of fines was developed to match

Figure 2.1

The Development of Policing: A Timeline of Events

Year	Historical Event
To 5000 B.C.	Kin policing in tribes and clans.
2900 B.C.	Judges Commandment of the Police in Egypt responsible for security of Egyptian provinces.
2400 B.C.	Early Sumerian law written by Ur-Nammu.
2100 B.C.	Code of Hammurabi written and carried out by messengers, an early form of police. ▶
2000 B.C.	Greek civilization begins to develop.
1575-1320 B.C.	Egyptian vizier acts as a police chief to the pharaoh.
1400 B.C.	Egyptian King Amenhotep implements customs houses and marine patrol.
1198-1166 B.C.	Egyptians use dog patrols to guard royal tombs.
776 B.C.	Greek city-state, or polis, appears.
621 B.C.	Draconian code becomes the law of Athens.
560-527 B.C.	Pisistratus, ruler of Athens, uses armed force to maintain tyrannical rule of Athens.
450-429 B.C.	Pericles, ruler of Athens, maintains police force under the control of a group of magistrates called The Eleven.
450 B.C.	Law of the Twelve Tablets becomes the written law of Rome.
27 B.C.	Caesar Augustus, emperor of Rome, creates the praetorian guard (to guard the palace), urban cohort (to keep the peace in the cities), and the vigiles (combined police and firefighters).
43 A.D.	Romans invade England, influence the development of early English common law.
528 A.D.	Justinian Code becomes law of Rome.
600-800 A.D.	Tithing system, an early ▶ form of self-policing, appears in England; the shire reeve is the predecessor of the modern-day sheriff and performs law enforcement and judicial duties; the constable maintains the weapons and equipment of the hundred.

Figure 2.1

The Development of Policing: A Timeline of Events *(continued)*

Year	Historical Event
1066 A.D.	William the Conqueror invades England, reduces the power of the shire reeve.
1194 A.D.	King Richard creates the position of coroner, has knights travel the countryside swearing all young men (over age 15) to a loyalty oath to the king.
1215 A.D.	Magna Carta signed by King John, establishes the right to due process and trial by jury to the English people.
1252 A.D.	King Henry III creates the position of high constable to keep the peace; London organizes a watch system of unpaid citizens rotating off a roster.
1285 A.D.	Statute of Winchester issued by King Edward I to develop a systematic police system of watches and wards; the word *police* appears for the first time.
1361 A.D.	Justice of the peace, who had police and judicial powers, created by King Edward III.
1600-1800 A.D.	Industrial revolution begins; crime becomes a problem in England; English merchants, frustrated with increasing crime, hire their own private police force called merchant police.
1655-1657 A.D.	Oliver Cromwell creates the provost marshal, a military law enforcement official.
1737 A.D.	King George II authorizes the levying of a tax to pay the night watch.
1748 A.D.	Bow Street Runners, a plainclothes detective force, put in place by Henry Fielding.
1819-1820 A.D.	Two events reshape the thinking about a uniformed police force: (1) (1819) Peterloo Massacre results in mounted cavalry killing a number of protestors and (2) (1820) Cato Street Conspiracy involves the Bow Street Runners in a very successful undercover operation to stop a conspiracy to murder a number of high officials in the British government.
1829 A.D.	Robert Peel proposes to the British Parliament the creation of a uniform police force based on his principles of policing; Parliament agrees and the London Metropolitan Police Department is born.
1833 A.D.	Successful deployment of the new English police at Cold Bath Fields.
1835 A.D.	The Municipal Corporations Act requires all urban areas in England to establish a police force.
1839 A.D.	County Police Act establishes regular police forces for all counties in England.
1856 A.D.	Obligatory Act provides a model for standardization of police nationwide.

the seriousness of the crime. If a person was convicted of a crime but could not pay the fine, he or she was sentenced to serve the victim, the victim's family, or the *tun* for an appropriate period. This was similar to today's community service sentences. If the convict escaped to another village, the members of that community were expected to return him or her back. In cases where the offender could not be found, the accused's family or the community would have to pay the restitution.[17]

Tithing and the Frankpledge System Between 600 and 800 A.D., English towns and villages developed a new approach to community responsibility and crime prevention. The frankpledge or mutual pledge system, which originated in France around 600 A.D., required citizens to maintain the peace and assist in the protection of the community. At the heart of the mutual pledge system was the **tithing**, which was a group of ten families who were responsible for each other's behavior. The head of a tithing was called a tithingman. He was responsible for raising the hue and cry, a general alarm that was similar to an all-points bulletin, when a crime had been committed. Once the criminal was caught, the tithingman sentenced the offender.

Ten tithings were organized into a hundred, and the head of a hundred was an official called a reeve. Each month the reeve would meet with townspeople to discuss public safety. Within the hundred there was also the **constable**, who was responsible for supervising the weapons and equipment of the hundred. In later years, the role of the constable would evolve into a strictly policing role, and today in England and Canada officers are still called constables. Several hundreds were organized into a shire, which was equivalent to an American county. The head of the shire was a traveling official called a **shire reeve**, who had both law enforcement and judicial responsibilities. He could perform arrests and trials as well as pass sentences. He also had the power of *posse comitatus*, which allowed him to call able-bodied men of the shire together when he needed assistance. In more recent times, sheriffs of the American West revived this tradition by forming posses when they needed help hunting criminals.

Divine Intervention One way that early English law differed from Greek and Roman law was in its use of divine intervention. For about a thousand years after the Roman withdrawal, the English used the religious concept of divine intervention to determine a defendant's innocence or guilt. The problem with this method was that it did not rely on evidence but on the superstitious belief that God would intervene on behalf of defendants who were falsely accused.

If a case could not be resolved, the judge could require a trial by ordeal, in which the accused would be asked to place an arm in boiling water or carry a red-hot iron a certain distance before dropping it. If the accused was truly innocent, people believed that God would intervene and heal the scars. Needless to say, trials by ordeal led to the deaths of many innocent people.

---

tithing The heart of the English mutual pledge system, in which groups of ten families were held responsible for each other's behavior.

constable An early English officer who supervised the weapons and equipment of the hundred, which was ten tithings.

shire reeve A traveling official that was the head of the shire and had both law enforcement and judicial responsibilities.

posse comitatus A power of the *shire reeve* that allowed him to call able-bodied men of the shire together when he needed assistance.

The Middle Ages (1066–1500 A.D.)

During England's medieval period of 1066–1500, English policing changed drastically. Although the old frankpledge system remained, it became less prominent as kings and landowners built up more intricate and reliable systems of policing.

The Norman Conquest In 1066 William, the Duke of Normandy, invaded and defeated English troops at the Battle of Hastings. Immediately afterward, William the Conqueror set out to consolidate his hold on England. One way that he accomplished this was by breaking the power of the English tithing system. Although tithing still existed after the Norman conquest, it was less influential because tithingmen, reeves, and shire reeves held less power than the new law enforcement officers that William created.

William's changes focused on centralized control of the English government. To do this, he first divided England into 55 military areas with an officer of his choice in command. This took away the local law enforcement power of the old tithings and especially the shire reeves. Next, he took away the judicial powers of the sheriff and created a new judicial officer called the *vice comites*, a traveling judge who was the forerunner to today's federal circuit judge.[18]

vice comites A traveling judge who was the forerunner to today's federal circuit judge.

During his reign, William also introduced a new form of trial by ordeal called trial by battle. In trial by battle, the accused faced his accuser, often armed with sword and shield. They fought until one of them died, and the winner was considered guiltless for the same reason as in other trials by ordeal: because God protected those who were innocent. Therefore, these trials still did not rely on evidence or any other objective measure of guilt but on the physical strength of the victim.

The *Leges Henrici* With the governmental changes of William the Conqueror firmly in place, England now had a structure to support a more uniform application of justice. In 1166, the next king, Henry I, established a new legal code called the ***Leges Henrici*.** These new laws divided England into 30 judicial districts. They also made serious crimes—such as murder, robbery, arson, and counterfeiting—into breaches of the peace against the king.

> *Leges Henrici* A legal code that divided England into 30 judicial districts and made serious crimes into breaches of the peace against the king.

For the first time in English history, crimes were no longer acts committed against individuals, tuns, or shires but against the rulers.[19] This gave royal law enforcement and courts considerably more power against citizens and made citizens answer to a stronger system than before. This legacy continues today, although citizens now have many more rights and protections, which can be seen in how American defendants are charged. For example, if a person commits an ordinance violation in the city of Chicago, the charges read *City of Chicago v. Defendant.*

> **coroner** A person assigned to each shire who maintained death records, investigated sudden and unnatural deaths, handled forfeitures to the king, and performed other duties.

Seriousness of Crimes During this period, English courts began to make a distinction between serious and minor crimes. The same serious crimes that were already considered breaches of peace against the king, such as murder and robbery, were labeled felonious acts. *Felonious* means that they were committed by felons, who were individuals of the lowest degree. Today, these serious offenses are simply called felonies. Minor offenses were called misdemeanors, which means "acts of bad behavior."

The Creation of Coroners Richard I established the office of the **coroner** in 1194, and each shire was assigned a coroner. By 1275, Edward I had specified a long list of duties for the coroner:

- Maintaining death records
- Investigating sudden and unnatural deaths
- Handling forfeitures to the king (in certain cases, such as when a person was executed for a crime against the crown such as treason, all of the criminal's property was inherited by the king instead of by his or her family.)
- Managing lost or abandoned property
- Managing wandering animals
- Handling salvage of materials

Conservators of the Peace

In 1195, King Richard I selected certain knights to travel the countryside and swear all young males older than age 15 to a loyalty oath to the king. Eventually, these knights came to be known as peace wardens or conservators of the peace, and years later they would assume judicial powers.

Poaching Laws Many medieval laws failed to protect all citizens, and some specifically targeted commoners, who were people without lands or titles. One of the best-known examples is the discriminatory laws against poaching, the illegal hunting of animals. Under the Norman system, commoners could usually pick fruits and nuts and even chop down a limited number of trees. They could not, however, hunt animals in the forests because the forests were considered the property of landowners or the king.

To enforce anti-poaching laws, the English government created special laws, law enforcement units, and courts. For example, one law passed in 1360 held that a commoner owning a hawk, which was used to hunt other birds, could be sentenced to two years in prison.[20] Some of the new law enforcement positions were:

- Agisters who protected the grazing areas for deer
- Regarders who registered and declawed dogs, which were frequently used in hunting in the Middle Ages
- Foresters and rangers who enforced the laws protecting the game and forests

Commoners resented these laws because they did not apply to the higher social classes. Since commoners were overworked and mistreated, and in the eyes of the law were seen as owning "nothing but their bellies," they felt it was fair to poach. Poachers netted birds and snared rabbits, and some were brave enough to hunt deer and wild boars with crossbows. They also fished at night. In short, despite the harsh laws, "poaching nevertheless seems to have been practiced continuously on the most widespread scale."[21]

The Magna Carta The poaching laws were only one example of the many abuses of royal power, and they continued to increase during the reign of King John. Finally, in 1215, King John was forced to sign the **Magna Carta,** or Great Charter. The Magna Carta extended a number of rights to commoners and nobles, many of which are predecessors of rights found in the U.S. Constitution. For example:

- In Article 13, the people were permitted to practice all ancient liberties and customs. This can be seen as a predecessor of the First Amendment's rights to freedom of religion, speech, and assembly.
- In Article 39, people were given the right to a jury of one's peers. This right can be found today in the Sixth Amendment.
- In Article 39, due process was specified as another right of the people.[22] This extremely important right, which guarantees that all defendants will be tried and sentenced according to objective criminal procedures, can be found in the Fourteenth Amendment.

The Magna Carta forever changed the relationship of the English people to their government and later influenced the foundation of American freedom.

Magna Carta An English document that extended a number of rights to commoners and nobles, many of which are predecessors of rights found in the U.S. Constitution.

Police Procedure

Criminal Procedure—Then and Now

Many people take for granted the detailed procedural steps that American police are required to follow. These procedures have enormous implications for law enforcement and for citizens' rights. Compare the following differences between then and now:

- People could be jailed for lengthy periods of time based on mere suspicion that they committed a crime. Today, the detention of individuals for anything less than probable cause is forbidden, and the time limit is ordinarily 48 hours.
- Defendants could receive the death penalty based on witness accusations alone. In the case of witchcraft trials, some of this testimony may sound ridiculous to modern ears. Today in the United States, no defendant can be convicted of a capital crime based on witness testimony alone.
- Suspects were not informed of their rights, and commoners could be tortured into confessing crimes they did not commit. In fact, reading a suspect's rights is a procedure that did not begin until the 1960s.

Critical Thinking Name some other ways in which criminal procedure has changed over the years. What do you think were the driving forces behind these changes?

The Statute of Winchester By 1250, the tithing system was disappearing and English towns and villages needed better security. In an effort to restore security in towns and villages, King Henry III ordered all Englishmen to enroll in the national militia. In London, the militia was used to create a watch, with each member of the community rotating off a roster. Because this watch was unpaid, residents were permitted to find substitutes. This often resulted in local misfits and offenders serving on the watch,[23] which made some residents feel less safe than before.

To address this, in 1285, King Edward I issued the **Statute of Winchester**, which was a serious attempt to develop a police system of watches and wards, or guard forces, across England. The Statute of Winchester accomplished the following:

- It brought back the earlier concept of the hundred, where all members were responsible for the crimes committed within its boundaries. Once again, when a crime was committed within the hundred, the hue and cry would be raised throughout the entire shire.
- It required towns to watch the city gates from sundown to sunrise to ensure that each gate was closed during this time.
- It gave special consideration to protecting towns and villages during the harvest season, when farmers were in their fields and unable to protect their homes. The statute required that from May 26 to September 29, every city would provide six guards at each gate and a watch of 12 persons in every borough.

Statute of Winchester A law that attempted to develop a police system of watches and wards, or guard forces, across England.

- It provided that the watch and ward would be performed by community residents, who served on rotating shifts. Failure to serve often meant time in the pillory, a punishment device that consisted of a wooden frame with holes for the head and hands in which a person was placed and subjected to public ridicule. A similar device called the *stocks* consisted of a wooden frame with holes for the feet, in which a person sat. Both devices were used in England and colonial America to punish several minor offenses, including failure to serve watch, breaking the Sabbath, disobedience to one's parents or master, or begging without a license.
- It influenced the London law that required closing the city's gates at nighttime and established watches and wards. One of these watches was a special marching watch called a patrol, which was an early version of today's foot patrol. One difference from today's patrol officers is that the watches were not authorized to make arrests. Instead, all arrests were made by a civic official called an alderman.
- It granted authority for the creation of the office of **bailiff** in every town. The bailiff was responsible for checking on and observing all residents and lodgers during the nighttime. Every 15 days, he was also required to check up on strangers in town. To accomplish these tasks, the bailiff was assisted by sergeants. Today in the United States, bailiffs are officers, often employed by the sheriff's department, who can make arrests and are usually found in courtrooms to help keep order.

bailiff An officer, found in each English town, who was responsible for checking on all residents and visitors to that town.

Other Specialized Units and Positions Over the next 200 years, other specialized units and positions were developed:

- Around the year 1300, the English government created the *police des moeurs*, a special unit that regulated prostitution by registering prostitutes and ensuring they remained in certain parts of the city— the origin of today's red light districts.
- In 1361, Edward III resurrected the concept of peace wardens by creating the position of **justice of the peace**. Justices of the peace had both law enforcement and judicial powers and had to be knowledgeable about the law. They were gentlemen, which in that era meant that they were wealthy enough to not have to work for a living. They had the authority to pursue, arrest, sentence, and imprison offenders. With the creation of the justice of the peace came the development of bail, as offenders were granted pretrial release on certain conditions. Today in the United States, the justice of the peace is an officer of local governments who may hear minor criminal and civil cases, as well as perform marriages.

justice of the peace An official with law enforcement and judicial powers who had the authority to pursue, arrest, sentence, and imprison offenders.

Despite these improvements in law enforcement, the relationship between the king and his subjects became more strained. Part of the reason for this was that the English people felt that they were subject to more laws but without being given more rights. In 1434, Henry VI felt so threatened by rebellious subjects that he created the position of state informer. Citizens who uncovered treason against the king were rewarded and would be considered for the position.

As the medieval period came to an end, England had a much more sophisticated criminal justice system than it had 500 years earlier. When it began to colonize and influence other cultures, its system spread. Today the legal systems of the United States, Canada, Australia, New Zealand, and India are still influenced by the English system.

2.3 Self Check

1. What was the tithing system?
2. Explain the importance of the Statute of Winchester.

POLICING Online

Check your answers at
www.policing.glencoe.com

2.4 English Policing to Modern Times

By the end of the sixteenth century, England was becoming a world trader. As it colonized other countries, it became heavily involved in importing and exporting. The primary English export was wool. To meet the growing demand for wool, English sheep farmers needed larger grazing areas. They forced many smaller farmers to leave their land, and local officials did nothing to stop them. This resulted in a large migration of poor, dispossessed, and resentful people to English cities such as London.[24] As cities became overcrowded, crime started to spiral out of control and a policing crisis developed.

Seventeenth-Century Innovations

As crime increased in English cities, merchants were not satisfied with the quality of protection provided by the night watches. The English middle class, who were merchants or belonged to professions such as medicine or law, also resented having to serve on the watch and paid others to perform their watch duties. This made the quality of the watch even worse.

Merchant and Parochial Police In response to this situation, merchants decided to hire merchant police, an early form of paid private security, to protect their businesses.[25] Local governments also moved to create their own police, which they called parochial police.[26] Throughout England, cities were divided into neighborhoods called parishes. Initially, all citizens of the parish were required to serve on the parochial police, but later they paid parochial constables instead. The parochial police were an early form of municipal police, and the parishes were treated the same way as today's precincts or divisions are.

The Provost Marshal Between 1645 and 1660, England was not ruled by a king or queen because of a civil war. Between 1653 and 1658, it was led by High Protector Oliver Cromwell. During Cromwell's brief rule, he divided the country into 12 military districts with a **provost marshal** assigned to each district.[27] The provost marshal, a military official, led approximately 6,000 troops and maintained a strict control over English citizens. He acted as both police chief and judge. Today in the United States, the provost marshal still exists as a military police officer. In the army, the provost marshal maintains order and provides police functions within a command. In the navy, this officer supervises prisoners who are facing court-martial, much as civilian sheriffs supervise county jails.

Bellmen and Thief Takers In 1663, King Charles II created a system in London called the bellmen,[28] who were professional night watchmen who provided security from dusk to dawn. They were first welcomed by Londoners as an alternative to the rotating night watch but turned out to be so ineffective that they were nicknamed the "shiver and shake watch."

By 1692, England had a very high crime rate, and the English government started to offer monetary rewards to encourage citizens to become involved in the apprehension of thieves. These **thief takers** brought many criminals to justice, but not without a price. Many were not concerned with crime prevention at all but were criminals and informants themselves. They used their power to blackmail innocent people, such as by threatening to bring false charges against people unless they paid them not to. (Remember that there were no photographs or fingerprinting then, so it was easier to lie about a person's guilt.) They also often duped foolish individuals into committing crimes, then arrested them.

Today bounty hunters play a similar role in the United States by hunting and arresting outlaws for a reward. Their controversial and often violent tactics have helped them catch many criminals, but they have also led to unnecessary deaths, sometimes of innocent people. They have, therefore, drawn as much criticism as the thief takers did.

After decades of unhelpful tactics such as these, the English government finally realized that the night watch had to become a permanent paid occupation. In 1737, King George II authorized the first taxes to pay for the night watch.[29] Even though it was still ineffective, it seemed to be the only choice they had.

provost marshal Military official in charge of one of England's 12 military districts under the rule of Oliver Cromwell; acted as both police chief and judge.

thief takers Bounty hunters, often corrupt, who were given monetary rewards for apprehending and turning in criminals.

FYI

A Corrupt Thief Taker

Perhaps the most notorious thief taker was Jonathan Wild, the self-titled Thief-Taker General for Great Britain and Northern Ireland. It is said he was responsible for bringing some 75 felons to justice. His real success, however, came as a receiver of stolen property, which he often returned to the owners at a price. Between 1714 and 1725, Wild operated an organized and highly successful criminal enterprise. In the end, he was sent to the gallows for his crimes.

SOURCE: P. J. Stead, *The Police of Britain* (New York: Macmillan, 1985).

The Bow Street Runners

In 1748, the city of London hired Henry Fielding, a magistrate and author who was serious about curbing London's crime problem. Fielding's ideas were important to the evolution of policing thought and practice. In his 1751 publication, *An Enquiry into the Cause of the Late Increase in Robberies*, Fielding suggested that

1. Policing was a municipal function
2. London needed well-paid police officers
3. Some form of mobile patrol was needed to protect the highways
4. Separate runners were needed to move swiftly to the scene of a crime
5. A separate police court should be instituted

Several years later, Fielding and his brother John organized the Bow Street Station, which consisted of three sections:

1. A foot patrol to patrol inner-city areas
2. A mounted horse patrol in red uniforms to patrol the streets and highways up to 15 miles out from London
3. The **Bow Street Runners**, a plainclothes detective force whose responsibility was to move quickly to crime scenes and begin investigations. The Bow Street Runners were the first modern detective unit.[30]

Bow Street Runners
A plainclothes detective force whose responsibility was to move quickly to crime scenes and begin investigations; the first modern detective unit.

▶ **The Bow Street Runners**
Although the Bow Street runners failed to rid London of crime, they did win public support. *Why do you think this organization failed to stop London's crime?*

Computer On Patrol

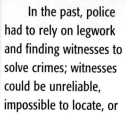

Technology and Investigation

In the early days of law enforcement, crime scene investigation was severely limited by the lack of technology. Although people knew that each individual had different fingerprints, it was not until the early twentieth century that police started to use fingerprints in criminal investigations. DNA profiling, which is also called genetic fingerprinting, was completely unknown.

In the past, police had to rely on legwork and finding witnesses to solve crimes; witnesses could be unreliable, impossible to locate, or nonexistent. Today, crime scenes can be reconstructed on computer to determine important information without the help of witnesses.

Think About It Name some aspects of criminal investigation that have stayed the same despite technology, and explain why.

The Bow Street Runners did not solve London's crime problems, but they won public confidence for their speedy and efficient responses to crime. This showed the English government that the public would support police units that were well organized and service oriented.

The London Metropolitan Police

During the nineteenth century, England faced a number of social problems related to the Industrial Age. Machines replaced individual manpower in many industries, and factory owners reaped tremendous profits at the expense of the physical and mental welfare of English men, women, and children. Industrialists used child labor extensively in factories, textile mills, and coal mines. Children began working as early as the age of five and often worked 16-hour days for low wages. As city populations grew and wages and working conditions declined, slum areas developed in the cities. These conditions led to a sharp increase in crimes such as:

- Bank robbery
- Counterfeiting
- Burglary
- Fencing, which is receiving and reselling stolen property
- Prostitution: About 25,000 prostitutes, many between the ages of 15 and 22, operated in the London area

Thousands of homeless children, many of them abandoned, roamed the streets. They were sometimes exploited as prostitutes, sent to prison-like conditions in government workhouses, or recruited by gangs and trained as thieves. Charles Dickens' classic novel *Oliver Twist* offers a candid view of social conditions and juvenile delinquency during this period.

In an effort to curb the uncontrollable crime rate, numerous strategies were tried:

- Rewards for evidence
- Harsher sentences (Courts offered longer prison terms, and in the early 1800s more than 160 crimes were punishable by death. Many of these capital offenses were minor crimes such as perjury.)
- Banishment, also called transportation, to the penal colony of Australia (People could be transported for seven years to life for crimes as minor as stealing a pound of butter or two yards of cloth.)
- Vigilante groups

The crime rate still did not decrease. Nothing appeared to work. This is an example that police agencies can bring up today when the public wants a "get-tough" approach to crime without first examining the causes of crime. Skilled police now know that preventing crime requires a more proactive, rather than reactive, approach.

The Need for a Police Force Because of the crime problems, by the 1820s there was an intense debate about creating a uniformed police force in London. This police force would wear distinctive uniforms and be under governmental control. There was much resistance to this idea since the English people were very suspicious of the government, and two events in 1819 and 1820 divided people's opinions even more:

- In 1819, the use of excessive force by a mounted cavalry unit against a gathering of protesters in Manchester resulted in 15 dead and hundreds injured. The Peterloo Massacre demonstrated what can happen when military forces, untrained in handling civil disturbances, are used to quell civil disorders. This led to public resistance against giving the police too much power.
- One year later, the Bow Street Runners infiltrated the Cato Street Conspiracy, a group of conspirators who planned to assassinate a number of government officials. Working undercover, the Runners collected evidence that ultimately resulted in the execution of all the conspirators. By doing this, the Bow Street Runners demonstrated that a disciplined and well-trained police force can be an effective alternative to military action.

The Cato Street Conspiracy swayed public opinion in support of a uniformed police force, but not entirely. It was not until 1829 that someone proposed an acceptable solution.

Sir Robert Peel Sir Robert Peel, England's Home Secretary, realized that the answer to the increasing crime problem in England was to select a group of well-trained officers who would prevent crime. In Peel's mind, there was no question that poor policing contributed to England's social disorder.[31]

In 1829, Peel proposed to Parliament "An Act for Improving the Police In and Near the Metropolis." At the heart of this proposal were **Peel's principles of policing**, which are still used today. These nine concepts are:

Peel's principles of policing A set of nine concepts created by Robert Peel as the foundation of the London Metropolitan Police; still in use today.

1. **Prevention of crime is the basic mission of the police.** The basic mission for which the police exist is to prevent crime and disorder as an alternative to the repression of crime and disorder by military force and to severe of legal punishment.
2. **Police must have the full respect of the citizenry.** The ability of the police to perform their duties is dependent on public approval of police existence, actions, and behavior and on the ability of the police to secure and maintain public respect.
3. **A citizen's respect for the law develops his respect for the police.** The police must secure the willing cooperation of the public in voluntary observance of the law to be able to secure and maintain the respect and approval of the public.
4. **Cooperation of the public decreases as the use of force increases.** The more officers use force, the less willing citizens will be to cooperate with the police.
5. **Police must render impartial enforcement of the law.** The police seek and preserve public favor not by catering to public opinion but by constantly demonstrating absolutely impartial service to the law, in complete independence of policy, and without regard to the justice or injustice of the substance of individual laws; by ready offering of individual service and friendship to all members of society without regard to their race or social standing; by ready exercise of courtesy and friendly good humor; and by ready offering of individual sacrifice in protecting and preserving life.
6. **Physical force is used only as the last resort.** The police should use physical force to the extent necessary to secure observance of the law or to restore order only when the exercise of persuasion, advice, and warning is found to be insufficient to achieve police objectives; police should use only the minimum degree of physical force that is necessary on any particular occasion for achieving a police objective.

Online

Remember, one of your best resources is **www.policing.glencoe.com**

7. **The police are the public and the public are the police.** The police at all times should maintain a relationship with the public that gives reality to the historic tradition that the police are the public and that the public are the police; the police are the only members of the public who are paid to give full-time attention to duties that are incumbent on every citizen in the interest of community welfare.

8. **Police represent the law.** The police should always direct their actions strictly toward their functions and never appear to usurp the powers of the judiciary by avenging individuals or the state or by authoritatively judging guilt or punishing the guilty.

9. **The absence of crime and disorder is the test of police efficiency.** The test of police efficiency is the absence of crime and disorder, not the visible evidence of police action in dealing with them.[32]

Peel realized that this new police force would never be effective if the laws still provided for severe punishments. The public would never help the police if they knew someone would be executed or sent to Australia for minor offenses. Peel knew that the law must be simple, fair, and just if the public

---

CopTalk

Skills That Never Change

One thing that has never changed about policing is the importance of good communication skills. Then as now, police must talk to others in order to understand their community, learn about crime problems, gather evidence, and obtain confessions. Therefore, police must develop a strong sense of whether someone is truthful and reliable.

Police everywhere rely on the same essential skills when talking to a suspect, witness, victim, or anyone else who is providing information. This includes understanding the importance of the following issues:

- The person's overall credibility
- The consistency of the story

- Whether the story sounds truthful or exaggerated
- Whether the person's verbal communication and nonverbal signals are consistent
- Whether a person's nonverbal signals (such as shifty eye contact) suggest that he or she is hiding something
- The person's previous relationship with others involved in an incident

What Do You Think? Do you think that good communication skills rely more on knowledge or on intuition? Explain.

CAREER FOCUS

Sheriff's Deputy

Job Description

I patrol the Del Rey (Florida) District. I have the basic beat of a patrolman: I work the road, report burglaries, theft, accidents, and accidents with injury. Days are never the same. Things can be dead silent and then, on a routine traffic stop, I can have someone who has a warrant out on them, who has narcotics, or who bails out of the car.

Will Ferel, West Palm Beach PD, Florida

During the day shift, there aren't so many hot calls as at night when we get domestic violence calls. Wednesday is often our busiest day, maybe because it's the half way point in the week and people are stressed. During football season, we have a lot of alcohol-related incidents.

The hardest part of the job is dealing with death of any kind. It's very hard when you have to notify family members, especially with child abuse cases or if a child is killed in a car accident. Our Sergeant always tells us to be prepared to face things we fear and put our "game face on." You may be forced to draw your weapon and shoot to defend somebody or to defend yourself. You have to be mentally ready to face danger.

My advice to students would be to do as many ride-alongs as you can and make sure that law enforcement is what you really want to do. If you do choose this job, then be enthusiastic.

Education and Employment History

I graduated from high school and did a degree in criminal justice. I went through the police academy in 1997. I also lived in Central America and became bilingual which is a big help in my job. I grew up in a small town. I knew a cop as I was growing up, and he was my ultimate idol. I went on my first ride-along when I was six.

Follow-Up How do you think this deputy's experience reflects a truly modern and American image of law enforcement?

were to respect the police. With this in mind, Peel also reformed the law and the punishments associated with it. In short, he revolutionized English criminal law.[33]

Sir Robert Peel knew exactly what type of candidate he wanted for his new police. He wanted young, respectable working-class men that were at least 5 feet 9 inches tall, under the age of 35, physically fit, literate, and possessing a perfect command of temper.[34] Today, all of these qualifications still apply. The only exceptions are the height and age restrictions, which American courts have found to be discriminatory.

The first commissioners of the metropolitan police, Colonel Charles Rowan and Richard Mayne, soon realized that recruiting and selecting a high-quality police force would not be an easy task. In policing, finding the right people for the job has always been a top priority but also a difficult challenge.

The uniform of the new police was a blue swallow-tailed coat, which was worn with a belt and a reinforced top hat. The coat and top hat were chosen to ensure that the uniform didn't take on a military appearance, which might intimidate the public. On the collar of the coat, a letter and number were attached to identify the officer and his division without giving any personal information. This approach is currently used in some American cities, such as New York, although many use nametags instead. Officers were given a rattle to signal other officers. In 1846, the rattle was replaced by a whistle, and in 1864 the top hat was replaced by a helmet.[35]

Personnel Retention Problems Initially the police department received more than 12,000 applicants, of whom 1,000 were selected and placed on immediate duty. In the first three years, 5,000 officers were dismissed and 6,000 were asked to quit.[36] Many of the dismissals and required resignations were for disciplinary actions related to drinking. In 1834, Commissioners Rowan and Mayne reported to a parliamentary select committee that four out of five dismissals were for drunkenness on duty.[37] A high turnover rate would remain a problem with the London Metropolitan Police Department for years to come, just as problems of substance abuse and high turnover still plague police agencies today.

Early Organization of the Police Department In late 1830, a major reorganization divided London into 17 divisions, with each division serving a population of 80,000. A superintendent was assigned to oversee each division, which consisted of eight patrol sections that were divided into eight beats. The total personnel for the metropolitan police consisted of 17 superintendents, 68 inspectors, 323 sergeants, and 2,906 constables.[38] As you can see, the role of constable had by now evolved into that of police officer.

The Beginnings of Training These early English police officers received only two weeks of training, which mainly focused on drill and sword exercises. Recruits received two afternoon lectures by a superintendent and were required to memorize a considerable amount of legal material. After training, each new constable was assigned to an experienced officer for about a week—then was on his own. Each constable was also required to serve through a probationary period.[39] This approach is an early version of today's academy training, field training, and probationary periods, although today these are much longer and more detailed.

At first, London citizens did not accept the new police. They referred to them as "raw lobsters" (which are dark blue) and "blue devils." Many felt that Peel had created the police to further his own ambitions and power by tightening the government's grip on the people.

Cold Bath Fields Incidents In May 1833, police moved to disperse a group of demonstrators at Cold Bath Fields who opposed the police. In the resulting melee, one officer was killed and several others were injured. The police's behavior at Cold Bath Fields was exemplary, and they were eventually cleared of any wrongdoing. Within months, public support for the new police improved dramatically,[40] and after ten years the English came to respect these new policeman, whom they now called *bobbies* after Sir Robert himself.

Over the next few years, police forces grew throughout England due to three more important parliamentary acts:

- The Municipal Corporations Act of 1835 required all urban areas in England to establish a police force.
- The County Police Act of 1839 established regular police forces for all 56 counties of England.
- The Obligatory Act of 1856 provided a model for the standardization of police nationwide. It was this model that shaped the English policing of today.[41]

The next chapter will look at the history of policing in America from the early colonial period, when American policing adopted English law and policing techniques, to the present. Special attention will be given to the key events that have shaped modern policing.

2.4 Self Check

1. Explain the thief takers program and tell whether it succeeded.
2. Who were the Bow Street Runners?

POLICING *Online*

Check your answers at
www.policing.glencoe.com

Chapter 2

Policing in Ancient and English Times

Summary By Learning Objectives

1. Understand the influence of the Code of Hammurabi.

The Code of Hammurabi, a collection of laws and edicts, provided guidance for legal procedure that addressed a variety of issues from civil matters to criminal acts. It was based on the concept of *lex talionis*, which means equal retaliation or "an eye for an eye." It was unique and influential because it provided legal protection to all classes of citizens, even for injustices committed by the rich and powerful against the poor. Also, it was the first known written law to require enforcement of the law by officers, who are referred to as messengers. Messengers were an early form of police, and this is one of the first references to the role of policing in society.

2. Explain how early societies approached their law enforcement problems.

Different early approaches were the following:
- Tribal cultures used kin police.
- Under the Code of Hammurabi, written law was created that required enforcement by messengers.
- The Egyptians created patrols to deal with the problems of smuggling and grave robbing and were also the first to use dogs to guard property.

- The Greeks developed the rule of law and policing within their city-states.
- The Romans created early security forces known as the praetorian guard, urban cohort, and *vigiles* and formulated the Justinian Code.

3. Describe early English law enforcement officials and their modern equivalents.

Some examples that you learned about in this chapter are the following:
- *Bailiff:* Bailiffs were responsible for checking on a town's residents and visitors. Today they usually work in courtrooms to maintain order.
- *Constable:* Early constables were responsible for supervising the weapons and equipment of the hundred. Today in England and Canada, they are police officers.
- *Coroners:* Then as now, coroners maintained death records and investigated sudden and unnatural deaths. In the past, they also handled other duties.
- *Justice of the peace:* Officials who had the authority to pursue, arrest, sentence, and imprison offenders. Today they may hear minor cases and perform marriages.

- *Patrol:* Patrol officers were originally a special marching watch in London; today, patrol officers are employed by every police department.
- *Provost marshal:* A military official that acted as both police chief and judge; today, the provost marshal is a military officer in charge of either maintaining order or supervising prisoners.
- *Ranger or forester:* Then as now, they enforced hunting and forest protection laws.
- *Sheriff:* The concept of the American sheriff originated from the early English shire reeve, a traveling law enforcement officer and judge.
- *Vice comites:* This was a traveling judge who was the forerunner to today's federal circuit judge.

4. Explain how the English watch system evolved and why it was replaced.

The earliest watch system started with the tithing system, in which every citizen was responsible for the security of his or her neighbors. By 1250, the tithing system was replaced by a watch and ward system, where local citizens were required to guard the city gates and streets during hours of darkness. In 1285, the Statute of Winchester attempted to develop a systematic police system of watches and wards across England. The watch and ward system was eventually replaced because it had many problems. Because it was unpaid work, many individuals paid others to pull their shifts. In some cases, this included misfits and offenders. Because it was inefficient, it was eventually replaced by a uniformed police force.

5. Understand why the law enforcement strategies used throughout English history either succeeded or failed.

Those that succeeded—such as the uniformed police force and the Bow Street Runners—were well organized and showed a service-oriented approach. They had clear and consistent standards and relied on dedicated professionals.

Those that failed—such as the watch and ward system and the thief takers scheme—were short-term remedies to more serious social problems. Also, their standards were inconsistent or nonexistent, and they relied on civilians rather than trained professionals. Because of this, some people who performed the night watch and some thief takers were offenders.

6. Discuss the importance of Peel's principles of policing.

Robert Peel formulated nine concepts that would evolve into the basic principles of policing. One of these concepts was that "the police are the public and the public are the police." This is perhaps the most important because it shows that the police are paid to do what is incumbent upon every person to do: police themselves. Public support and cooperation are essential to the effectiveness of any policing effort. This tenet may be considered as the very beginning of community policing. Today, Peel's principles of policing are the foundation of policing in America because of their consistent emphasis on high standards and accountability.

Key Terms

kin police (40)
Code of Hammurabi (p. 41)
lex talionis (p. 41)
vizier (p. 42)
Draconian code (p. 44)
Law of the Twelve Tablets (45)
praetorian guard (p. 46)
urban cohort (p. 46)
vigiles (p. 46)
praetor (p. 46)
tithing (p. 50)
constable (p. 50)
shire reeve (p. 50)

posse comitatus (p. 50)
vice comites (p. 51)
Leges Henrici (p. 52)
coroner (p. 52)
Magna Carta (p. 53)
Statute of Winchester (p. 54)
bailiff (p. 55)
justice of the peace (p. 55)
provost marshal (p. 57)
thief takers (p. 57)
Bow Street Runners (p. 58)
Peel's principles of policing (p. 61)

Questions for Review

1. What was the significance of the early written laws?

2. What influence did the early Greeks and Romans have on the early English?

3. What is the origin of the word *town* and how does it relate to policing?

4. What was the purpose of the tithing system?

5. What was the Magna Carta, and how has it influenced American law?

6. How did the Statute of Winchester change policing?

7. What social problems created high crime in England? Name the various efforts that were made to remedy the crime rate.

8. What was the most effective solution to England's crime problems, and which solutions were not effective?

9. Which of Peel's principles of policing do you feel are most important, and why?

10. Why are these principles considered the foundation of modern-day policing?

Experiential Activities

11. The Athenian Constitution
Visit your local library or go online to find Aristotle's Athenian Constitution. A good source is available at **www.policing.glencoe.com**. Read Section 1.

a. According to Aristotle, which ruler or statesman was most just?

b. What are the themes of the poems by Solon that are listed here?

c. How does this text relate to policing today?

Experiential Activities continued

12. Self-Defense in Ancient Times

Read "Prosecution for Murder of One Who Pleads Self-Defense: First Speech for the Prosecution," by the Greek orator Antiphon. The online version is available at **www.policing.glencoe.com**.

a. How did Antiphon encourage ancient Greeks to be honest and just?

b. Was murder committed in self-defense treated any differently in ancient Greece than it is now?

c. Explain your answer by referring to the case described in this speech.

13. Sheriffs Then and Now

Research the history of sheriffs in medieval England. Compare this information with what you know about modern sheriffs.

a. What was a sheriff's jurisdiction?

b. Has the concept of a posse changed much since the Middle Ages?

c. What were a sheriff's main duties?

14. The Need for Police

To understand today's police force, you must understand why the first modern one was created. One good online resource on the historical context of London's Metropolitan Police Act can be found at **www.policing.glencoe.com**. Learn why Sir Robert Peel felt that London needed a uniformed police force.

a. What were the conditions in England regarding criminal justice before 1829?

b. Do you feel that a uniformed police force was the best answer at the time?

c. What other options did the city of London have at that time?

Web Patrol

15. Code of Hammurabi

Go to **www.policing.glencoe.com** and use the links provided to read about the Code of Hammurabi in greater detail.

Name similarities between the Code of Hammurabi and American criminal law.

16. Magna Carta

To read the actual text of the Magna Carta, visit **www.policing.glencoe.com** for useful links on the topic.

Which principles set forth in the Magna Carta can be found in the American system of justice?

17. London Metropolitan Police

Go to **www.policing.glencoe.com** and click on the links that offer more information about the historical aspects of the London police.

How does the historic London force compare with today's modern police?

Critical Thinking Exercises

18. Police Resources

You are an Egyptian citizen of the Seventeenth Dynasty, and you must perform public service free of charge. Your assignment is to provide security for tombs in the Valley of the Kings. With several others, you share a 24-hour guard of several tomb openings. You also patrol the area on foot during the day. Like many of the tombs, the one that you are watching also has a secret entrance. This made it easier for those constructing it to enter the deeper sections of the tomb, and it was concealed after the tomb was completed. While on foot patrol, you notice that someone has tampered with the secret entrance. You find out that the thief has been arrested and will be executed, but you worry that others will find the entrance.

Your coworkers and you discuss the situation. Some believe the secret entrance should be guarded to keep it safe, but this will take away guards from both the main entrance and the foot patrol. Others believe this is an unwise use of resources because it will leave the rest of the tomb less protected and draw attention to the secret entrance.

   a. What do you think is the best allocation of police resources? Why?

   b. Name some reasons why it may be unwise to draw attention to the secret entrance.

19. Changing Views of Justice

You are an Athenian widow living at a time of political and legal reform. Politicians are debating how much reform should be implemented and how many crimes should no longer carry the death penalty. Your grandson was recently sentenced to death for stealing goats. Although stealing livestock was a capital offense under the old laws, the law suddenly changed yesterday, about a week before his execution. Now, people who steal livestock have to compensate the victim and perform a year of hard labor for the state.

You go to the city officials and plead for your grandson's life, explaining that even though he has already been sentenced, his punishment should reflect the new laws of the state.

   a. If a law changes after a sentence has been passed, should it affect the sentence? Why or why not?

   b. Should property offenses ever lead to the death penalty? What about violent offenses?

20. Un-Welcoming the Bobbies

It is 1831, and you are a London metropolitan police officer who was been patrolling a working-class London neighborhood. Although this neighborhood has high crime, nobody likes you because they feel that your presence invades their privacy. The individual officers you work with are very patient and professional, but you feel frustrated when citizens refuse to appreciate the work all of you do to apprehend criminals.

You talk with your fellow officers and find out they have similar feelings. You worry that this could lead to serious future problems.

   a. What can the local police do to gain the public's trust?

   b. Based on what you know about community policing, what community-policing principles would have worked in this case?

Endnotes

1. A. C. German, F. D. Day, and R. R. J. Gallati, *Introduction to Law Enforcement and Criminal Justice* (Springfield, IL: Charles C Thomas, 1978).

2. S. N. Kramer, *The Sumerians: Their History, Culture, and Character* (Chicago: University of Chicago Press, 1963).

3. Microsoft® Encarta. CD-ROM [Computer software]. Hammurabi, Code of: Funk and Wagnalls Corporation, 1994.

4. German et al., *Introduction to Law Enforcement.*

5. C. Trojan, "Egypt: Evolution of a Modern Police State," *CJ International 2*, no. 1 (1986): 15.

6. J. M. White, *Everyday Life in Ancient Egypt* (London: B. T. Bastsford, 1963).

7. L. Casson, *Ancient Egypt* (New York: Time, Inc., 1965).

8. German et al., *Introduction to Law Enforcement*, 43.

9. Plutarch, *The Lives of the Noble Grecians and Romans*, Dryden translation (Chicago: Encyclopedia Britannica, Inc., 1952).

10. Ibid.

11. Ibid.

12. Ibid. See also J. Boardman, J. Griffin, and O. Murray, *The Oxford History of the Classical World* (New York: Oxford University Press, 1986).

13. Ibid., 263, 277.

14. R. N. Holden, *Law Enforcement: An Introduction* (Englewood Cliffs, NJ: Prentice Hall, 1992).

15. Ibid., 11.

16. German et al., *Introduction to Law Enforcement*, 45–46.

17. The discussion in the remainder of this section is based on material from German et al., *Introduction to Law Enforcement*, 47–50.

18. German et al., *Introduction to Law Enforcement*, 50.

19. Ibid., 50–54.

20. C. Hibbert, *The English: A Social History* 1066–1945 (New York: Norton, 1987).

21. Ibid.

22. German et al., *Introduction to Law Enforcement*, 54–56.

23. Material in this section is taken from German et al., *Introduction to Law Enforcement*, 53–56.

24. Ibid., 55.

25. Ibid., 56.

26. Ibid.

27. Ibid.

28. Ibid.

29. Ibid., 57.

30. Material in this section was taken from German et al., *Introduction to Law Enforcement*, 57–58.

31. Ibid., 59.

32. E. M. Davis, "Professional Police Principle," *Federal Probation 35*, no. 1 (1971): 29–34.

33. German et al., *Introduction to Law Enforcement*, 59.

34. C. Emsley, *The English Police: A Political and Social History* (New York: St. Martin's, 1991).

35. P. J. Stead, *The Police of Britain* (New York: Macmillan, 1985).

36. German et al., *Introduction to Law Enforcement*, 60.

37. Emsley, *The English Police*, 185.

38. German et al., *Introduction to Law Enforcement*.

39. Emsley, *The English Police*, 190.

40. Stead, *The Police of Britain*, 45.

41. Ibid., 47–49.

Chapter 3

Policing and the American Experience

CHAPTER OBJECTIVES

AFTER COMPLETING THIS CHAPTER, YOU WILL BE ABLE TO:

1. Describe policing during the early era.

2. Compare policing in the East, South, and West.

3. Understand policing during the political era.

4. Discuss the events that changed the police role from service to crime fighting and back to service.

5. Describe policing during the reform era.

6. Explain which police leaders played significant roles in the reform era.

7. Understand policing during the community policing era.

◀ Texas Rangers conduct a raid on Kilgore, Texas oil fields.

3.1 The Early Era (1607–1840)

Any study of modern American policing can be divided into four distinct periods:

1. The early era (1607–1840), in which American cities did not yet have paid, uniformed police forces
2. The political era (1840–1920), in which local politicians created and controlled police agencies
3. The reform era (1920–1980), in which reformers and progressives "got the politics out of policing" and improved police effectiveness
4. The community policing era (1980–present), in which police are learning to become better problem solvers and perform a more service-oriented role

Figure 3.1 on page 75 provides a summary of the four major eras of policing. Some people criticize this outline because the second and third eras apply only to the urban Northeast but ignore developments in the South and West. Although this classification may be limited, remember that municipal agencies throughout the country eventually adopted the policing model that was developed under the political and reform eras in the Northeast. Therefore, this classification provides a clear framework to study organizational differences, the nature of police work, and strategies used during the development of city policing in the United States.[1]

The historical events of the past four centuries have transformed policing from early watch systems to well-trained, high-tech departments in search of new directions. Figure 3.2 on pages 78 and 79 illustrates this shift with a time line of the historical events that have affected American law enforcement.

Colonial Policing

American policing had been evolving for more than 200 years before the political era began. The earliest example is colonial policing. Early English colonists brought customs, laws, and law enforcement systems known in their native land. The early American settlement of Jamestown, Virginia, shows an example of how settlers used law enforcement to establish order.

In 1607, Jamestown became the first permanent English settlement in the New World. Although the harshness of the environment thinned the ranks of the early colonists, petty jealousies and a lack of teamwork almost destroyed the community. Many settlers lacked the strong work ethic necessary to survive. After the first year, only 38 of 144 settlers remained. The future of the settlement was in question. They soon realized that they were

Figure 3.1

The Four Eras of American Policing

Key Factors	Early Era	Political Era	Reform Era	Community Policing Era
The sources from which the police construct the legitimacy and continuing power to act on society	Political	Primarily political	Law and professionalism	Community support (political), law, professionalism, problem solving
The definition of the police or role in society	Order maintenance	Crime control, order maintenance, broad social services	Crime control	Crime control, crime prevention, problem solving
The organizational design of police departments	Decentralized, generally pulled from the military or the citizens	Decentralized and geographical	Centralized, classical	Decentralized, task forces, matrices
The relationships the police create with the external environment	Police generally are members of the external environment.	Close and personal	Professionally remote	Consultative; police defend values of law and professionalism but listen to community concerns
The nature of police efforts to market or manage the demand for their services	Many early police forces operated only when serious problems arose. Night watches detected problems on their own.	Managed through links between politicians and precinct commanders, and face-to-face contacts between citizens and foot patrol officers	Channeled through central dispatching activities	Channeled through analysis of underlying problems
The principal activities, programs, and tactics on which police agencies rely to fulfill their mission or achieve operational success	Night watches, lynch laws, ranging, and slave patrols	Foot patrol and rudimentary investigations	Preventive patrol and rapid response to calls for service	Foot patrol, problem solving
The concrete measures the police use to define operational success or failure	Order maintenance	Political and citizen satisfaction with social order	Crime control	Quality of life and citizen satisfaction

ill prepared to deal with the harsh and life-threatening conditions in the New World.

Captain John Smith brought the discipline and martial law they needed to the settlement. The smallest of infractions, such as a failure to work, could bring harsh punishments such as forced starvation and even banishment. Laws and enforcement in Jamestown were a means to an end—the survival of the colony—and eventually they worked. Under Smith's lead, the town gradually flourished and the population grew.

U.S. Marshal Job Duties

When the U.S. Marshals were created in 1789, their responsibilities included:

- Supporting the federal courts
- Carrying out lawful orders of judges, Congress, and the president
- Serving subpoenas, summons, writs, and warrants
- Making arrests
- Processing the fees and expenses of court clerks, U.S. attorneys, jurors, and witnesses
- Renting courtrooms and jail space in new areas where federal buildings did not yet exist
- Supervising prisoners
- Ensuring that jurors and witnesses were available for trial
- (Until 1870) Conducting the national census every ten years

Policing the Northeast

By the mid-1600s, the seeds of policing were taking root. The watch system developed in the northern colonies, where the population was concentrated in small towns and villages that could be covered by any form of foot patrol. This way of life made the watch system ideal for protecting citizens and property. As in England, however, the watches were not always staffed with the most competent personnel. Often minor lawbreakers were assigned to patrol as punishment.[2]

Night Watches and Lynch Laws In 1636, Boston created a watch system. New York followed suit in 1658 with a nighttime **rattle watch**. Each person carried a rattle to signal to other citizens, announce their location to other watchmen, and call for help. During this era, night watches usually used rattles or whistles rather than weapons.

In less populated areas of colonial America, there was no formal system of justice. Any justice that was rendered was often in the form of **lynch law**, in which a suspected criminal could be caught by a mob and executed on the spot. Although lynching most of the time implies summary hangings, victims could also be beaten or burned to death. Lynch laws were named after Colonel Charles Lynch from Virginia who, during the American Revolution, organized a group of men to track down and confront British sympathizers. The practice quickly evolved into the delivery of punishment, deserved or not, by a mob and over time became strongly connected to American history, particularly on the western frontier, and in the South.[3]

After the American Revolution Following the Revolutionary War, Americans still lacked a formal system of law and government. They appropriated many of England's laws, customs, and police practices. One notable difference, however, was the creation of the first federal law enforcement agency, the U.S. Marshals.

In 1830, the Post Office Inspection system was established to monitor the conditions of the stagecoaches, steamboats, railroads, and horses used to transport mail. It was also responsible for visiting mail distribution offices and examining postal accounts. Its jurisdiction was expanded in 1872 to include mail fraud.[4]

By the 1830s, municipal law enforcement was becoming more structured. In 1833, Philadelphia, which had endured an ineffective night watch since 1700, added a paid daytime patrol. Philadelphia resident Stephen Girard donated approximately $30,000 to get the force started.

Policing the South

Southern policing was an interesting contrast to policing in the North. Unlike the Northeast, the South's population was scattered and rural in nature, making it more suited for the sheriff form of policing. The sheriff patrolled a larger area and would form special posses and patrols as needed. The South had more agriculture, less centralized government, and fewer large cities. Widespread slavery also created different law enforcement issues than those found in the North.

Slave Patrols In the South, **slave patrols** were created to prevent slave rebellions and catch runaway slaves. Communities required that all able-bodied men between the ages of 18 and 50 be available for duty on the patrol. Female heads of household, such as widows, were also summoned but were expected to hire substitutes. Every two weeks the patrol would inspect roadways and inns for slaves who did not have passes to be absent from their master's plantation or for slaves acting in a suspicious or boisterous manner. Violators were apprehended and turned over to a special court consisting of a justice of the peace and two to five landholders.[5] If they were slaves, they were returned to their owners, but freed African Americans were punished or executed.

> **slave patrols** Citizen police patrols that were created in the South to prevent slave insurrections and control crime.

In towns and cities throughout the South, a mutual fear dominated race relations. Even freed African Americans, including the very few who were wealthy and owned slaves (which was legal in Louisiana), were fearful of walking the streets. When it came to community behavior, they adhered to a different set of norms: They had to walk in the gutters of the streets, salute whites they encountered, and never strike a white person, even in self-defense. They could not testify against whites, had to face all-white juries in biased court trials, and had no protection under the law. Their movements were restricted by a strict curfew. On the other hand, southern whites (especially slave owners) were constantly fearful of a violent slave rebellion, such as those that had occurred when Haiti gained its independence in the 1790s.[6]

This constant fear between the races influenced the conduct of business, the architecture of homes, and the administration of the criminal law. Southern homes were heavily secured and guarded with guns to prevent entry at night. Laws were passed that set strict curfews and prohibited selling alcohol to African Americans. To give peace of mind to city residents, communities created walking patrols.

Charleston City Guard One example of an urban walking patrol in the South was in Charleston, South Carolina. In 1806, Charleston established

Figure 3.2

A Timeline of Events in American Policing

Year	Historical Event
1636	Watch established in Boston.
1658	Rattle watch established in New York. ▶
1700	Watch established in Philadelphia.
1776–1783	Lynch law appears in the colonies.
1789	U.S. Marshal's Office established.
1800	Slave patrols used extensively in the South to control slaves.
1823	Texas Rangers established.
1833	Philadelphia creates a paid day police force.
1840	The political era begins.
1844	New York Police Department is established using the Peelian model.
1851	First vigilance committee created in San Francisco.
1865	U.S. Secret Service established.
1868	Internal Revenue Service established.
1870	"Boss" Tweed corruption scandal in New York City.
1871	International Association of Chiefs of Police founded
1881	Wyatt, Morgan, and Virgil Earp and Doc Holiday face the McLaurys and Clantons at OK Corral. ▼

Figure 3.2

A Timeline of Events in American Policing *(continued)*

Year	Historical Event
1883	Civil service established with passage of the Federal Pendleton Act.
1892	Fingerprints become a means of identification.
1893	Appointment of first female police officer, Marie Owens, in Chicago.
1905	Pennsylvania State Police established.
1906	August Vollmer becomes police chief of Berkeley Police Department.
1908	President Teddy Roosevelt establishes the Bureau of Investigations.
1919	Boston police strike.
1920	The Reform Era begins; Volstead Act is passed and Prohibition begins.
1924	The Bureau of Investigationsbecomes the FBI with J. Edgar Hoover as the director. ▶
1931	Wickersham Commission issues report.
1967	Riots in Watts, Newark, and Detroit; Presidential Commission on Law Enforcement and the Administration of Justice issues report.
1968	Kerner Commission Report issued; Omnibus Crime Control and Safe Streets Act passed; LEAA is created; first 911 system established; ATF established.
1972	Kansas City Preventive Patrol Experiment conducted.
1973	DEA is established as the premier drug enforcement agency.
1979	Herman Goldstein publishes landmark article entitled "Improving Policing: A Problem-Oriented Approach."
1980	The community problem-solving era begins. Office of Justice Assistance, Research, and Statistics replaces Law Enforcement Assistance Administration.
1982	James Q. Wilson and George Kelling publish landmark article entitled "Making Neighborhoods Safe," which introduced the concept of "broken windows."
1984	New York City implements community policing.
1994	Community Policing Consortium is established.

the city guard, later known as the city police, along military lines. Privates of the guard carried a musket (an early form of gun that was used in the Revolutionary War), bayonet, ammunition, and rattles. Sergeants, lieutenants, and captains wore swords. Five guards and a sergeant patrolled each district of the city.

Policing the West

As pioneers moved westward in the early 1800s, they encountered a different situation than in the Northeast or in the South. The American West was a wilderness in which settlers quickly filled up large areas. Because of this quick expansion, it was often lacking in law and order. In the early 1800s, western settlements were at the mercy of outlaws and were often in conflict with Indians. Pioneers often found themselves in the company of outlaws who had fled the East to avoid arrest for unpaid debts, family support, or criminal prosecution. Slow communications and isolated land areas offered these individuals anonymity on the frontier.

If the law-abiding pioneers were to survive, they had to protect each other. In the absence of a formal law enforcement function, settlers often resorted to vigilante justice. However, this was not a good long-term solution because vigilantes ignored due process and many of the other procedures that are necessary to ensure guilt in a court of law. Pioneers realized that they needed professional law enforcement that could adapt to the different conditions of the West.

The Texas Rangers In 1823, Stephen F. Austin, in response to the need to protect early settlements, created the Texas Rangers. The first unit of Rangers was ten officers who were ordered to "range" wide areas of the new frontier and stay constantly aware of unwelcome intruders. Rangers were used not just in Texas but also in the isolated regions of Arizona and New Mexico. However, the Texas Rangers are the best known. When Texas was admitted into the union in 1845, the Rangers became the first state police organization in the United States.

Compared to modern-day standards, the selection process to become a Ranger was very simple. Applicants were asked three questions:

- Can you shoot?
- Can you ride?
- Can you cook?

Answering yes to all three questions virtually guaranteed anyone a position as a Texas Ranger.[7] Today the Rangers still perform state policing duties in Texas.

As the territories became more populated and towns appeared, more organized forms of law enforcement appeared. However, many of these early law enforcement officers were no better than the outlaws they policed. In fact, many of the early sheriffs and marshals had been desperadoes prior to entering the law enforcement profession.[8] For example, gunfighter Wild Bill Hickok also served as the town marshal of Abilene, Texas. Wyatt Earp was a deputy town marshal in Wichita, Kansas, and a deputy U.S. Marshal during the shootout in Tombstone, Arizona. He also worked occasionally as a professional gambler.

Researchers have identified four forms of early law enforcement in the West:

1. Extralegal citizen police
2. Formal police
3. Legal citizen police
4. Parapolice

Extralegal Citizen Police Extralegal citizen police operated when no formal criminal justice system was available. This took many forms: self-protection with personal weapons, vigilante justice, and lynching. Although many perceive these early forms of justice as brutal, at the time they were considered a response to real threats to the security and safety of their communities. Many members of these early **vigilante groups**, which were also called

vigilante groups Informal self-protection societies created in the American West; also called vigilance committees or regulators.

Police Procedure

Police Work in the Old West

The everyday duties and actions of police were considerably different in the American Old West. This was mainly due to the West's trademark informality. For instance, arrest procedures were much less formal. Suspects had few due process rights when facing an arrest, and officers were not held responsible for the use of deadly force against armed opponents who resisted them. "If they come along easy, everything will be all right," said Arizona Ranger Captain Burt Mossman. "If they don't, well, we can make pretty short work of them."

Another famous example is the unusual detention of suspects before their trials. Frontier lockups were rarely made of brick and mortar like their eastern counterparts. They included sheds, one-room shacks with tiny barred windows, and other rough accommodations. One sheriff claimed to use a cowhide, which was thrown over a prisoner and pegged to the ground.

Critical Thinking Could the Old West's arrest and detention practices work in today's legal and social climate? Why or why not?

SOURCE: J. Wagoner, *Arizona Territory* (Phoenix: University of Arizona Press, 1970), 374; P. Trachtman, "Frontline Forces of Law and Order," in *Gunfighters* (New York: Time-Life, 1974).

vigilance committees or regulators, were law-abiding citizens. Vigilante groups were sometimes exploited by people who spread false rumors against enemies in order to get revenge. Since they rarely relied on evidence, these groups occasionally killed innocent people.

The first vigilante groups were created in California during the gold rush of the 1840s, when theft was rampant. In San Francisco in 1851, citizens formed a large vigilante group that wrote a constitution and held regular meetings. It was their mandate to arrest, try, and (if necessary) execute those who posed a serious threat to the safety and security of the community. Within months of its creation, the San Francisco committee had publicly executed a number of offenders. The criminals of the city got the message that they were not welcome and departed. Other cities followed this example, and eventually the vigilance committees spread to Arizona, Montana, Colorado, and Nevada.[9]

Formal Police The arrival of formal policing to the West was a significant phase of American law enforcement history. As the West developed into a loose network of towns and trails, three levels of local law enforcement emerged:

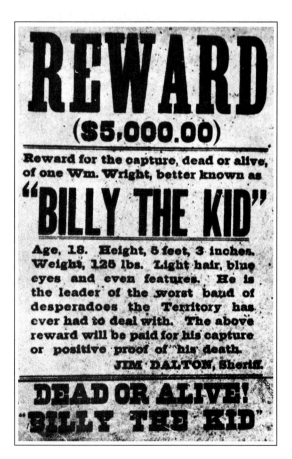

▶ **Old West Wanted Poster for Billy the Kid, circa 1870** Old West vigilance handbills warned criminals that they faced death if they disobeyed the law.
Why were vigilante groups used in the West?

MYTH	FACT
In the Old West, shootouts were everyday events.	A handful of frontier towns, such as Dodge City, Kansas, did encounter periods of frequent violent crimes. However, these periods were always brief. Peaceful homesteaders and Native Americans inhabited most of the West.

1. *Local:* Town marshals acted as chiefs of police do today. They had small forces that usually consisted of an assistant marshal and a few officers. They also had the power to assemble posses when needed.
2. *County:* County law enforcement consisted of the sheriff, under-sheriff, deputies, and posses. The local and county law enforcement performed most of the daily police work.
3. *Federal:* U.S. Marshals and their deputies operated within state, territorial, or regional jurisdictions. Considered a prestigious position, U.S. Marshals were appointed by the president of the United States.

Sometimes these duties overlapped and different levels worked together, as they do today. For example, the U.S. Marshals "were technically in charge of enforcing federal laws and pursuing such criminals as mail robbers and Army deserters, but the deputies often held additional commissions as town or county lawmen and lent a hand—or gun—in support of their local counterparts."[10]

The public's image of the ideal police officer was molded by the way in which sensationalistic eastern newspapers portrayed western law enforcers—an early example of how the media sometimes distort police activities. In the cattle and mining towns of the Old West, law enforcement officers such as Wyatt Earp, Wild Bill Hickok, Pat Garrett, and Bat Masterson became American icons with the help of the press. Their lives and exploits became bigger than life. Eastern newspapers created the image of an ideal western sheriff or officer as one who:

1. Was larger than life
2. Was harsh in attitude
3. Possessed a low point of tolerance
4. Was courageous in the extreme
5. Possessed ample firepower and the will to use it[11]

Legal Citizen Police Although many towns had some type of formal police, private citizens were often called upon to assist the town marshal or sheriff as legal citizen police. This sworn police reserve, sometimes called **casual deputies**, was enthusiastic about serving the community. In many ways, the

casual deputies A sworn police reserve of private citizens who served on posses, guarded jails, and filled in for regular police.

use of deputies was similar to the old tithing system and did much to build cohesiveness in the early frontier towns. As the need arose, citizens were often deputized and asked to:

- Serve on posses
- Guard jails
- Act as replacements when the police were out of town[12]

Parapolice Parapolice were an early form of private security. The majority of western frontier towns lacked the resources to maintain strong and effective police forces. As the frontier expanded, the distance between towns increased. With the growth of the mining of silver and gold, stagecoach lines and railroads faced a whole new set of problems. Because they transported large amounts of gold and silver across vast expanses of desolate territory, they were often the targets of bands of outlaws. In an effort to protect these shipments, special police were hired to ride shotgun. This meant that a private police officer, armed with a shotgun, rode alongside stagecoach drivers and defended the coach from bandits.

Soon private security firms such as Wells Fargo were formed, hiring themselves out to the highest bidder. In the process, the focus turned from prevention to detection and apprehension. Companies such as the Pinkerton Detective Agency not only performed guard services but also pursued and apprehended dangerous outlaws.

These early private police were quite effective. Like today's private security and investigators, they were not bound by the same procedures and laws that restrict public law enforcement. Instead, they knew no jurisdictional boundaries, were not involved in politics, and often ignored legal restraints. This freedom allowed them flexibility in pursuing desperadoes, but it often placed them at odds with the public. For example, Allan Pinkerton's attempts to catch Frank and Jesse James failed because of the public's resentment of his aggressive tactics. Still, although their methods were questionable at times, some considered private police necessary to control violence and lawlessness in the western frontier after the Civil War.[13]

Policing would continue to evolve in the West, but it would eventually be overshadowed by three important factors:

1. The development of municipal policing in the East
2. The development of large cities in the West
3. The beginning of the political era

Self Check 3.1

1. Which police force was to become the first official state police organization in America?
2. What was the role of the casual deputies in the Old West?

POLICING *Online*

Check your answers at
www.policing.glencoe.com

CopTalk

3.2 The Political Era (1840–1920)

Beginning in the 1840s, the **political era** of policing was characterized by political involvement in the administration and operation of police. Although this era was primarily restricted to the Northeast, today its legacy affects policing around the country. This is because of the growth of large cities throughout the United States, all of which adopted the Northeast's municipal policing model when they established their own police departments.

In the political era, politicians were heavily involved in the administration and operation of police. Law enforcement powers came from local leaders and could be taken away for any reason. Politicians helped police chiefs and officers keep their jobs, while the police assisted in keeping the politicians in office. Agencies were divided into precincts. Police managers and local politicians ran each precinct like a small department.

During this period, officers performed the roles of law enforcement, crime prevention, order maintenance, and sometimes social services. The primary tactic of the time was foot patrol. Police effectiveness was measured

political era An era of policing (1840–1920) that was characterized by political involvement in the administration and operation of police.

by the level of crime, the effectiveness of riot control, the maintenance of order, and other problems associated with an industrial society.[14]

In 1844, the New York Police Department (NYPD) was established as the United States' first uniformed law enforcement agency. The NYPD established both a day and night uniform force that was closely modeled after Robert Peel's London police. The first New York police officers were unarmed, but increased assaults on officers in the 1850s raised the question of arming them. Cities were reluctant to give the police guns because of potential for abuse, but the officers felt they needed weapons to protect themselves and the public. It was not until after the Civil War, which saw many advances in the quality and accuracy of handguns, that cities and towns started to authorize the carrying of firearms.

During and after the Civil War, a number of federal law enforcement agencies were created to deal with the crime problems of a growing nation. Also, policing was starting to become more organized, professionalized, and uniformed. For example, amid violence and civil unrest caused by the statewide coal strikes and an ineffective sheriff/constable system, Pennsylvania became one of the first states to establish a uniform state police force in 1905. This new state police force soon proved effective in controlling mob violence, patrolling rural areas, protecting wildlife, and tracking down criminals. From the very beginning, the state police established a reputation of fairness, thoroughness, and honesty. In a short time, the Pennsylvania State Police would become a model for other state police agencies across the nation. (See Figure 3.3 on page 87.)

Another example is the International Association of Chiefs of Police (IACP), which was founded in 1893. The IACP's goal was to develop uniformity in American policing practices. The IACP is credited with several early contributions to law enforcement. The two most important are a centralized clearinghouse for criminal identification records and a fingerprint repository.[15] In the coming years, the IACP would become a dominant force in professionalizing the police.

Politics and Policing

When police agencies began to develop in the nineteenth century, they depended completely on local government. This meant that officers could lose their jobs if the mayor who hired them left office or decided to dismiss them for any reason. Agencies also had to ignore the corrupt activities of the administration that supported them, and this encouraged the spread of corruption among police.

Between the 1830s and early 1880s, local and federal government operated under the spoils system. To the political victors went the opportunity to place their own people in positions of power. Often these politicians were

ETHICS ISSUES

Patronage Jobs

Although the era of patronage is almost over, patronage jobs still exist today in most sheriffs' departments around the country. Most sheriffs are elected and have the power to hire people to whom they owe favors. Patronage jobs are given to such people; they are almost never given to the most qualified applicant. Such jobs generally last as long as the sheriff's tenure.

Patronage jobs can raise concerns about favoritism and the possibility of corruption. *Should sheriffs still be allowed to provide patronage jobs to those who are not always the most qualified for a particular position? Why or why not?*

Figure 3.3

The Pennsylvania State Police, 1905

Pennsylvania's initial state police force consisted of the following positions and salaries:

1 superintendent	$3,000 a year

Four companies, with each company consisting of:

1 captain	$1,500 a year
1 lieutenant	$1,200 a year
5 sergeants	$1,000 a year
50 men or privates	$720 a year

The first applications requested the applicant's name, age, height, weight, birthplace, citizenship, marital status, occupation, and military service. Applicants needed to be between the ages of 21 and 40, but they did not need to be citizens of Pennsylvania. The best chance of selection was for those who had been in the military, were physically fit, and were taller than five foot six.

SOURCE: P. M. Conti, *The Pennsylvania State Police: A History of Service to the Commonwealth: 1905 to the Present* (Harrisburg: Stackpole Books, 1977), 48-49.

incompetent and engaged in widespread corruption, especially in local government. One such corrupt politician was William Marcy "Boss" Tweed, who was involved in New York politics from 1852 to 1871. Tweed created a corrupt administration that controlled a major part of the criminal justice system. Since many officials, policemen, and judges were on his payroll or fearful to defy him, he operated with impunity until he was arrested.[16]

In response to these problems of political patronage and corruption, Congress established the federal civil service system by passing the Pendleton Act in 1883. This meant that government workers were hired based on exams that tested their skills. They could not be arbitrarily removed once a new political party came into power. Many states and cities would eventually adopt the civil service system, and some would even apply it to chiefs of police. In Los Angeles, the chief of police was selected through competitive examination, and in Milwaukee, chiefs were granted lifetime tenure by a commission.

Police Organizations and Unions

Near the end of the nineteenth century, police officers felt the need to organize to protect employee rights. Two important groups that formed were the Police Benevolent Association (PBA) and the Fraternal Order of

Police (FOP). In 1894, a group of New York officers founded the PBA. The primary purpose of the PBA was to address the poor working conditions and welfare of police officers.

The FOP was organized by two Pittsburgh patrolmen in 1915. It differed from a union because it prohibited striking and enrolled both labor and management, so that everyone from patrolmen to chiefs of police could join. The organization worked to achieve many of the same goals as the PBA. Both the PBA and FOP would ultimately become two of the largest and most powerful police organizations in America.[18]

Attempts at Unionization During the late 1800s, big business flourished and grew stronger than ever. In an effort to counter this growing power, labor organizations were created. On numerous occasions, poorly trained, ill-equipped, and outnumbered police were thrust into controversies between industry and labor. Often the results were violent and deadly because strikers resented police interference, and police were under strict orders to suppress the strikers.

One such encounter occurred in 1886 during the McCormack Harvester strike in Chicago. A group of anarchists called a demonstration to protest ongoing police harassment of strikers. When officers arrived on the scene to disperse the crowd, someone in the crowd threw a bomb into the police ranks. It killed eight Chicago officers and injured 67 others. As a result, public opinion turned against labor and in support of the police.

In 1919, police entered the labor movement. During that year at least 33 departments unionized in affiliation with the American Federation of Labor (AFL). This move was fiercely challenged and met with some setbacks.[19] Boston police became the first to unionize after a number of officers grew disenchanted with their outrageous working conditions. Some of the problems that affected their work and morale were:

- Officers were entitled only one day off every 15 days, and even then they were required to have their superiors' permission before leaving the city limits of Boston.
- A typical workweek lasted anywhere from 73 to 98 hours.
- What off-duty time they received was often spent on standby duty in the back of the precinct stations, which were infested with rats and insects.
- Standby officers had to share wobbly old bunk beds—two men to a bed.
- Promotions were often political, and some talented officers were either fired or ignored.
- Officers were often asked to perform nonpolicing duties such as delivering unpaid tax bills or promoting the mayor during elections.

For all of this work, they were paid $1,300 a year (about 25 cents an hour). This salary was one-half of what the average employee made and less than the wages of streetcar operators.[20]

In August 1919, Boston police officers received a union charter from the AFL. The Boston police commissioner was outraged at the officers' attempts to unionize and issued an order for them to disband. The officers refused, and the 19 leaders of the union were disciplined. The mayor, who was working with a citizens' committee to find a solution, delayed their sentencing. The special committee recommended leniency, but the commissioner suspended the 19 officers anyway.

This was the final straw. On September 9, 1,117 of Boston's 1,544 policemen went on strike in protest of the suspensions. When a replacement force could not mobilize the first night of the strike, the city was left unprotected. Crime and violence, which were normally minor, erupted and National Guard troops were sent to Boston. In many cases, the military overreacted in restoring order and even fired indiscriminately at groups of innocent citizens.

The actions of the mayor and National Guard helped to turn public opinion against the striking officers. Massachusetts Governor Calvin Coolidge blamed them for the violence when he issued his famous statement that "there is no right to strike against the public safety by anybody, any time, anywhere." All 1,117 of the striking officers were fired. The actions in Boston, which were a major setback in police rights, became the precedent for dealing with striking officers for the next 50 years.[21] This is still a controversial topic in every jurisdiction today because communities demand effective police services but are often not willing to pay what is needed to provide such services.

◀ **Officers on Strike** National guardsmen keep the peace in front of a store that was broken into and looted of firearms during the 1919 Boston police strike. *Are today's police allowed to strike?*

Moving Toward Reform

Two factors helped move policing out of the political era and into a period of growth and reform: the progressive movement and new technology.

The Progressives In the late 1800s and early 1900s, a political group called the **progressives** emerged with a platform of reform. Progressives were middle-class Americans who advocated efficiency in government operations and involvement in improving the lives of the poor and disadvantaged. Furthermore, they hoped to remove corruption from government by eliminating party politics and patronage. To end the crime problem, progressives called for the professionalization of police, which meant ending the political system and "taking the police out of politics and the politics out of police."[22] The progressive movement set the stage for police to enter the reform era.

progressives A political movement that advocated efficiency in governmental operations and the involvement of government in improving the lives of the poor and disadvantaged.

New Technology Police during the political era experienced a growth in new technologies and inventions. From call boxes to automobiles, policing

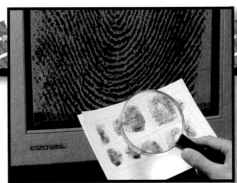

Computer On Patrol

Fingerprinting: The First Technology

Although humans have been fascinated with fingerprinting since prehistoric times, it was not until the 1890s that they were first used for criminal investigation. At that time, Sir Edward Richard Henry created the Henry Fingerprint Classification System, which assigned a numerical value to each fingerprint.

By 1901, Henry had convinced the British government to adopt fingerprint identification in colonial India, then created Scotland Yard's Central Fingerprint Bureau. London was known for its serious crime problem, and investigators were eager to learn this new system. By 1910, the Henry system was in use throughout England and in several other countries. To this day, fingerprinting is a universal form of identification. Its popularity is due to its accuracy and also to the fact that fingerprints are easy and cheap to obtain.

Think About It Can DNA technology ever replace fingerprinting, or should the two be used side by side? Why?

SOURCE: Adapted from Sagem Morpho, Inc., "The History of Fingerprinting." http://www.morpho.com/news_room/library/reference/history.htm.

◀ **The Emergence of Modern-day Police** A Los Angeles policeman detains an offending motorist in a side-car cell (December 20, 1924). By the 1900s most large cities had a regular police force, paid and in uniform.
What effect did this have on American policing?

was presented with opportunities as well as problems. This was because technology has always been a double-edged sword for law enforcement. Although it gives police greater crime-fighting capabilities, it helps criminals equally. One good example is the automobile: It gave police the means to provide more rapid response and greater coverage but also gave criminals greater mobility to evade police.[23]

American law enforcement had come a long way since the colonial night watches and the uniformed police of the early 1800s. The development of police had not been without problems, especially corruption. However, policing, spurred along by the progressive movement, was about to enter a new era—the reform era.

 **3.2 Self Check?**

1. What was the name of first federal law enforcement agency to be created?
2. What was the "spoils system" all about?

POLICING *Online*
Check your answers at
www.policing.glencoe.com

The Reform Era (1920–1980)

reform era An era of policing (1920–1980) that was
characterized by the removal
of politics and corruption
from police.

The relationship between police and politics generated much controversy in the late 1800s and early 1900s. Beginning in the 1920s, the **reform era** was characterized by the removal of politics and corruption from police. This led to the introduction of the professional model of policing, which was supported by new technology in crime control and criminal apprehension.

In the political era, police were seen as an extension of the local government, but in the reform era, they were seen as a component of the criminal justice system. The reform era shifted the focus to crime control and criminal apprehension rather than community service. Police achieved legitimacy through enforcement of the criminal law. During the reform era, the exercise of discretion was discouraged. If police were confronted by a special problem, they would often create a specialized unit (such as vice, juvenile, drugs, or tactical) instead of allowing patrol officers to solve the problem. Police departments emphasized control of their personnel by using bureaucratic methods such as the following:

- Oversupervision, or permitting little autonomy in making decisions
- Limited span of control, or supervising a small number of officers
- Upward and downward flow of communications, which provided a specific chain of command to follow
- The creation of elaborate record-keeping systems, which necessitated more levels of middle managers[24]

These practices made policing even more centralized and authoritarian in nature, giving the officer very little discretion in making street-level decisions on a day-to-day basis. Policing became reactive, rather than proactive, in addressing crime problems.

The relationship between patrol officers and the community was one of neutrality and detachment because police were expected to enforce the law in an impartial manner. Citizens, including victims, had only passive involvement in crime control. They were expected to support police by calling police when a crime occurred, deferring to police actions, and being cooperative witnesses if asked. As a result, police services were developed with little citizen input, which eventually caused friction between the police and the community in the 1960s and 1970s.

The primary focus in the development of police tactics was improving efficiency, and the principal strategies used in the reform era were preventive patrol and rapid response to calls for service. When the 911 emergency system was implemented across the United States at around the end of the reform era, police promoted 911 and rapid response to calls for service as effective policing. The automobile permitted police to appear to be everywhere. This omnipresence, as O. W. Wilson called it, would deter criminals and reassure the community that officers were on patrol. Computer-aided dispatch followed 911 and further improved response time. The major problem, however, was that the police were becoming more detached from the citizens they served.[25] Studies of response time revealed that it is not how fast a police officer responds that affects the likelihood of an immediate arrest but rather how soon victims or witnesses call for help.

Although these characteristics sound rigid and inappropriate now, they were a large improvement over policing of the political era. The reform era was an important step for policing.

Reform at the Federal Level

In the early 1900s, America was experiencing an increased crime rate, especially for white-collar crimes such as medical fraud and monopolies. Many felt that the government needed a professional organization of general investigators. In 1908, President Theodore Roosevelt created the Bureau of Investigations within the Department of Justice. In 1924, this bureau was reorganized and renamed the Federal Bureau of Investigation (FBI), with J. Edgar Hoover as its first director.

Hoover, who embraced the progressive philosophy, was determined to make the FBI an efficient and professional organization. He immediately took the following steps:

- Fired incompetent agents
- Abolished the seniority rule for promotions
- Established a uniform performance appraisal system
- Recognized the need for uniform training and established a formal training course for all new agents[26]

Under Hoover's direction, the FBI also made several important advances in investigation:

- In 1926, the FBI became the national repository for fingerprint cards submitted from law enforcement agencies across the United States.
- The early 1930s saw the bureau's jurisdiction expanded to include interstate crimes such as kidnapping.
- A forensic laboratory was created in 1932.
- In 1935, the FBI National Police Academy was established to train municipal officers in modern investigative techniques.[27]

The Volstead Act The Volstead Act of 1919, a law that prohibited the manufacture, sale, and transportation of alcoholic beverages in the United States, caused drastic changes in policing in the early part of the twentieth century. Congress passed the act as a constitutional amendment in 1919, then repealed it in 1933. During this 14-year era, officers found themselves enforcing an unpopular law, and the relationship between police and community became an adversarial one. Realizing that it was almost impossible to prevent people from making and consuming alcohol, many police officers did not enforce the law and instead took bribes.[28]

During this era, which was known as Prohibition, organized crime discovered that dealing in illegal alcohol was a very profitable business. Prohibition helped organized criminals gain a foothold in the United States. It also created intergang rivalries that resulted in extreme violence on the streets. Between 1923 and 1929, there were 257 gang-related murders in Chicago alone. Gangsters such as Chicago's Al Capone wielded power with an iron fist and terrorized citizens until federal agents arrested him.[29] Federal law enforcement faced many challenges in fighting organized crime, and some of these problems were not resolved until recently.

The Great Depression A second event that transformed the role of the police in this time was the Great Depression, which lasted from 1929 until 1941. During the 1930s, unemployment rose and small gangs and outlaws such as Bonnie and Clyde, Ma Parker, Machine Gun Kelly, Baby Face Nelson, and John Dillinger wreaked havoc across the Midwest and

▶ **Gangsters** This mugshot of Al Capone was taken circa 1925. The 1920s saw a huge increase in gangsterism.
Why do you think this type of criminal activity increased during that era?

Southwest. Local law enforcement was not equipped to fight these gangs, which often outarmed the police with weapons such as the Thompson sub-machine gun and Browning automatic rifles. Many of these gangs would commit crimes in one state and then run to another, hoping to evade pursuing officers.

The ability of the police to effectively combat this new type of crime was questioned, and police had to learn to effectively fight interstate organized crime. Ironically, it was during the Depression years that law enforcement received some of the brightest and most educated officers in the history of policing. With high unemployment, many men entered policing in search of a stable career.

Reform at the Local Level: August Vollmer

August Vollmer was perhaps the best known and most controversial figure of the reform movement. Some of his reforms were so radical that they are still not in widespread use today, such as his belief that all police officers should have a college education. In 1906, Vollmer became chief of police in Berkeley, California. In that position he quickly came to be recognized as an innovator and visionary. He integrated several new technologies into police operations, such as:

- The automobile
- The motorcycle
- Call boxes for citizens to call police for help
- Radios in patrol cars

It was during the 1920s and 1930s that August Vollmer, a progressive, advocated the need for police reform at the municipal level. Vollmer's philosophy of municipal policing, shown in Figure 3.4 on page 96, consisted of 12 elements.

Although the number of arrests, response time, and the number of times a patrol car would pass a given point were measures of police performance during the reform era, the primary measure of effectiveness was the crime rate. Vollmer, in conjunction with the International Association of Chiefs of Police, developed and implemented a uniform system of classifying and reporting crime. Eventually, this reporting system would become the **Uniform Crime Report (UCR)**, which today is administered by the FBI.[30]

Police reformers also called for a professional force that was completely free of political interference and committed to the highest ideals of public service. At the core of the professional model of policing were six elements:

FYI

Well-Armed Thugs

After the deaths of Bonnie and Clyde, an inventory of their bullet-riddled car revealed the following:

- A .45 automatic pistol
- Three Browning automatic rifles
- Nine Colt automatic pistols
- One Colt revolver
- Two sawed-off shotguns
- One hundred 20-round clips of ammunition for the machine guns
- Three thousand rounds of loose ammunition

SOURCE: E. M. Raub, "Bonnie & Clyde: Their Lives and Their Victims—Part III." *Missouri State Trooper's Magazine.* Adapted from http://www.mosta.org/magazine/bnc3.html.

Uniform Crime Report (UCR) A uniform system of classifying and reporting crimes; developed by August Vollmer and the IACP and today administered by the FBI.

1. The police should stay out of politics.
2. Members should be well trained, well disciplined, and tightly organized.
3. Laws should be equally enforced.
4. Police should take advantage of technological developments.
5. Merit should be the basis of personnel procedures.
6. The crime-fighting role should be prominent.[31]

Vollmer did not agree with this last element because he felt that the police role should cover more areas than just crime fighting. He suggested that police needed to take a more proactive role in addressing the root causes of crime. In this respect, his crime prevention approach was far ahead of its time. However, police could not adapt his ideas on proactive preventive policing to their traditional definition of police as crime fighters. The difficulties police had in making this shift, added to the recommendations of the

---

Figure 3.4

Vollmer's Philosophy of Municipal Policing

1. The public is entitled to police services as efficient as budget and manpower permit.
2. Courtesy is of paramount importance in all contact with citizens.
3. Police personnel of the highest intelligence, good education, unquestioned integrity, and with a personal history demonstrating an ability to work in harmony with others are necessary to effectively discharge the police responsibility.
4. Comprehensive, basic, advanced, and specialized training on a continuing basis is essential.
5. Broad responsibilities should be assigned to the beat officer, including the following:
   - A. Crime prevention through effective patrol
   - B. Investigation of all offenses
   - C. Traffic law enforcement
   - D. Juvenile duties
   - E. Public relations
   - F. Report writing
   - G. Witnessing events competently
6. Superior supervision of personnel and effective leadership
7. Good public relations in the broadest sense
8. Cooperation with the press and news media
9. Exemplary official and personal conduct
10. Prompt investigation and disposition of personnel complaints
11. Adherence to the law enforcement code of ethics
12. Protection of individual rights while providing for the security of persons and property

SOURCE: Adapted from W. J. Bopp and D. O. Schultz, Principles of American Law Enforcement and Criminal Justice (Springfield, IL: Charles C. Thomas, 1972), 88-89.

Wickersham Commission, prevented policing from becoming more pro-active than reactive.

Another major contribution Vollmer made was his protégés. A number of officers who worked for Vollmer would ultimately go on to distinguish themselves in American policing. For example, Vollmer recruited O. W. Wilson, who would later become a national authority on police administration, dean of the School of Criminology at Berkeley, and superintendent of police for the Chicago Police Department.

The Wickersham Commission

In 1929, President Herbert Hoover ordered the National Commission on Law Observance and Law Enforcement, also known as the **Wickersham Commission**, to study the increasing crime problem and the quality of the police response. Two years later, it rendered its findings. The commission found that rising crime rates, especially for violent crimes, were a result of police ineffectiveness. They felt that the police needed to place a greater focus on fighting crime and spend less time on ancillary activities such as providing temporary shelter for the needy, escorting drunks home, or dispensing social service moneys.

Again, this crime-fighting approach missed the point that Vollmer stressed repeatedly: that police must also be service oriented in order to be efficient and respected in their communities. Therefore, although the commission's message was strong, the common officer on the street realized that he would still have to perform non-law-enforcement activities such as dealing with domestic disturbances, drunks, vagrants, and troublesome juveniles on his beat. In an effort to make it appear that crime rates were going down, some departments resorted to manipulating crime statistics.[32]

Wickersham Commission
A special commission created in 1929 to study the increasing crime problem and the quality of the police response.

Social Changes in the 1960s and 1970s

During the 1950s, police departments focused on their law enforcement role with little emphasis on community involvement. Training practices reinforced the traditional crime-fighting role. Although this worked for a while, by the 1960s the police faced a number of new challenges, including civil unrest and the antiwar movement, which placed them in roles they were not accustomed to performing. In the mid-1960s, riots in Watts, Detroit, and Newark left police feeling somewhat helpless in preventing severe civil unrest. Confrontations between black residents and mostly white officers often escalated into violence. Once control was lost, city leaders called for the National Guard and, in some cases, federal troops.

In an attempt to help police adapt to these social changes, several commissions and administrations were created during the 1960s and 1970s. Six of the most important ones are covered here.

The 1967 President's Commission on Law Enforcement In the mid-1960s, President Lyndon Johnson, who was facing increasing crime rates, fear of crime, civil disorders, and antiwar demonstrations, moved to establish the **President's Commission on Law Enforcement**. This commission was to examine how effective the criminal justice system was in controlling crime. Some of the commission's more significant recommendations for police included the following:

- Establishing citizen advisory committees in minority group areas
- Recruiting more minority officers
- Providing processes whereby citizens can file complaints against public officials
- Setting the goal of requiring a baccalaureate degree for patrol officers
- Improving screening of candidates for character and fitness
- Requiring a minimum of 400 hours of training
- Establishing police standards commissions in every state
- Involving police in community planning[33]

The 1967 Kerner Commission Stimulated by devastating riots in cities such as Newark, Detroit, and Atlanta, President Johnson established the **Kerner Commission** in 1967 to study these events. The commission found that a deep hostility between police and ghetto communities had been a significant factor in causing the riots. This hostility in some cases was because ghetto residents saw the police as symbols of other problems in the criminal justice system.[34] The commission offered a number of recommendations directed toward police, other components of the criminal justice system, and local and federal government. It was a wake-up call for American police because it clearly showed that the professional policing strategies of the 1940s, 1950s, and 1960s were not effective.[35]

Law Enforcement Assistance Administration (LEAA) In the face of increased crime and violence, Congress in 1968 passed the Omnibus Crime Control and Safe Streets Act, which spawned the creation of the **Law Enforcement Assistance Administration (LEAA)**. The purpose of the LEAA was to provide states and local governments with funds and guidance for crime prevention and reduction. During the life of the LEAA, which was from 1969 to 1982, more than $8 billion was expended on the war on crime, with the majority of funding being directed to law enforcement. After a decade of expenditures, however, the LEAA had made little impact on crime.

President's Commission on Law Enforcement A 1967 commission that examined how effective the criminal justice system was in controlling crime.

Kerner Commission A 1967 commission that found that a deep hostility between police and ghetto communities had been a significant factor in causing inner-city riots.

Law Enforcement Assistance Administration (LEAA) A government agency that provided states and local governments with funds and guidance for crime prevention and reduction; in operation from 1969 to 1982.

Finally, in 1980 Congress replaced the LEAA with the Office of Justice Assistance, Research, and Statistics (OJARS), which functions primarily as a clearinghouse of criminal justice statistics and information. Federal support for criminal justice research and evaluation at OJARS continues under the National Institute of Justice (NIJ) and the Bureau of Justice Statistics (BJS). The NIJ provides grants for criminal justice research, and the BJS collects, collates, and disseminates criminal justice statistics. Although some might view the efforts of the LEAA as a failure, there are two bright notes:

1. Under the LEAA, there was an increased emphasis on research, which produced landmark studies that reshaped the thinking of police administration and established new standards for policing.
2. One major outcome of this emphasis on research was that police management began requiring that policing programs be evaluated. In order to receive an LEAA grant, police departments had to ensure that program evaluation was completed on all funded programs.

The National Advisory Commission In the early 1970s, the National Advisory Commission on Criminal Justice Standards and Goals assembled a task force on police to study the police and make recommendations to improve law enforcement. Its report on the police provided valuable insight into problems of the day and named several standards for police administrators and governmental leaders. Successful programs were studied and then became the foundation for new standards.

Online

Remember, one of your best resources is www.policing.glencoe.com

Bureau of Alcohol, Tobacco, and Firearms (BATF) The year 1968 saw the creation of several federal law enforcement agencies. Following the assassinations of President Kennedy, Senator Robert Kennedy, and Martin Luther King, Jr., Congress enacted stricter firearm laws and created new ways to enforce them. For example, it restructured the Alcohol Tobacco Tax Division. The organization was renamed the Bureau of Alcohol, Tobacco, and Firearms and given jurisdiction over many of the new firearm laws.

The Drug Enforcement Agency (DEA) In the 1960s, America was also experiencing increased drug use. In response to this problem, the Bureau of Narcotics and Dangerous Drugs (BNDD) was formed. However, the BNDD was one of several different federal agencies involved in drug law enforcement. With so many different groups enforcing the law, jurisdictional issues arose and overlaps occurred. By 1972, President Nixon and Congress agreed that there needed to be one unified drug agency instead of many organizations. In 1973, the Drug Enforcement Agency (DEA) was created.[36]

► **Bureau of Alcohol, Tobacco, and Firearms Agents** BATF agents guard a road near the Branch Davidian Compound outside Waco, Texas, in March 1993. The BATF's role has changed drastically over the years. *What do you think their role is today?*

Paradigm Shifts These governmental reports and new agencies would usher in a new era in policing and were the first steps toward the community policing era that began around 1980. What happened was that old policing paradigms, or traditions, started to fade away as researchers found that they were not as successful as people had believed.

The first old paradigm to be challenged was random patrol. In 1974, the Kansas City Preventive Patrol Experiment tested the traditional method of using random, routine, preventive patrol. This experiment found that random preventive patrol did not appear to have an impact on crime. It questioned what had become the main practice of American policing and led to the development of new strategies.

directed patrol Patrol that targets a certain crime hot spot, a certain type of crime (such as drug loitering on street corners), or a certain type of criminal.

One of these strategies was **directed patrol**, which targets a certain crime hot spot, a certain type of crime (such as drug loitering on street corners), or a certain type of criminal. When police departments analyzed their work patterns and workload, they realized that not all officers on a shift were needed to answer calls for service (CFS). Instead, a portion of the force could engage in other directed patrol activities. For example, a community might be experiencing a series of convenience store robberies. Directed patrol would permit those officers not answering CFS to conduct surveillance on local convenience stores. Officers could rotate from answering CFS to directed patrol on each shift or they could be permanently assigned to directed patrol.

team policing A policing strategy that was built on the idea of assigning a group of officers to a geographic area on a permanent basis; used mainly in the 1960s and 1970s.

Another paradigm shift was seen in the development of **team policing** in the 1960s and 1970s. This new policing strategy emerged in a number of large departments across the United States and was built on the idea of assigning a group of officers to a geographic area on a permanent basis. Team policing was attempted in a number of cities, including Los Angeles where it was called the Basic Car Plan. The history of the Basic Car Plan, is covered in Figure 3.5 on page 102.

The rationale for team policing was based on the behavioral principle of **territorial imperative**, which exists when a person defines and defends a geographical territory in which he or she lives and moves. It was thought that by placing teams of officers permanently in an area, they would assume a territorial imperative in that area. In many team policing programs, detectives, juvenile officers, and community relations specialists were assigned to the team. The hope was that the officers would be more aware and responsible for policing their communities.

Unlike directed patrol, team policing never became a widely accepted policing strategy. A major study in the early 1970s found that five major factors appeared to contribute to the failures of team policing:

- Most team policing programs did not adopt the territorial imperative. The result was that their policing differed very little from policing done in the past.
- Decentralization, a key concept in team policing, was never achieved in any of the team policing units.

territorial imperative
When a person defines and defends a geographical territory in which he or she lives and moves.

◀ **Indian Shadow Wolves**
This all-Indian special patrol unit of the U.S. Customs uses ancient tracking skills to apprehend smugglers along the U.S.-Mexico border. This is an example of directed patrol.
How do the Shadow Wolves contribute to localized law enforcement efforts?

Figure 3.5

The Basic Car Plan

LAPD chief Edward Davis first implemented team policing in Los Angeles in the early 1970s. The LAPD's team policing plan, known as the Basic Car Plan, assigned specific patrol cars and officers to specific communities. These teams of officers were in charge of providing all police services to the communities they served. The LAPD also appointed community relations officers to build positive relationships with grassroots leaders in each community.

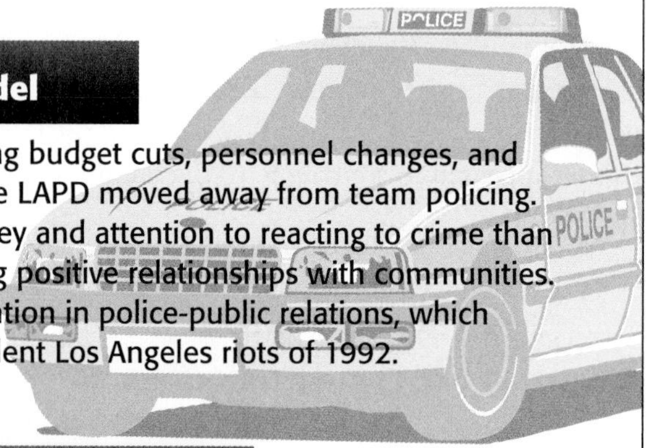

1980s: A New Model

In the 1980s, following budget cuts, personnel changes, and political infighting, the LAPD moved away from team policing. It devoted more money and attention to reacting to crime than to proactively building positive relationships with communities. This led to a deterioration in police-public relations, which culminated in the violent Los Angeles riots of 1992.

1992: The Los Angeles Riots

Following the riots, the LAPD investigated the causes of the unrest and how well it had handled the situation. The department concluded that it had distanced itself from the community it served.

1990s: The Basic Car Plan Returns

As part of its reforms, the LAPD once again assumed a community-oriented approach, reinstituting team policing and the Basic Car Plan. Community-Police Advisory Boards (CPABs) were formed to improve community relations and elicit citizen input, and senior lead officers were appointed to oversee patrol officers in each area of the city. Under the Basic Car Plan, team of officers under the supervision of a basic car coordinator of sergeant rank once again became responsible for crime and problem solving in a specific geographic area. Each officer assigned to a basic car became part of a community-police problem-solving team.

SOURCE: Wellford W. Wilms et al, *The Strain of Change: Voices of Los Angeles Police Officers.* (Los Angeles: University of California, Los Angeles, Graduate School of Education and Information Studies, 2000), pp. 5-9.

- Because team policing required decentralization, police mid-management felt that their power was threatened. In some cases, they actively sabotaged team policing plans in order to maintain their power.
- The dispatching technology did not permit the patrols to remain in their neighborhoods, despite the stated intention of adjusting the technology to the team policing projects.
- The patrols never received a sufficiently clear definition of how their behavior and role should differ from that of a regular patrol. At the same time, they were considered an elite group by their peers, who often resented not having been chosen for the project.[37]

In addition, Roberg and Kuykendall have identified several problem areas. The two most important were that

1. changing from a highly centralized, authoritarian structure to a decentralized, democratic one could not be accomplished in such a short period of time, and
2. no effort was made in these departments to create an organizational climate receptive to innovation.

Despite its overall lack of success, team policing did provide a window to the future of policing. New concepts such as problem-oriented policing and community policing grew out of this period.

The reform era helped remove politics from policing and institute a professional model of policing. As the role of police became more law enforcement oriented and less service oriented, police moved further away from the public they were sworn to protect and serve. The race riots and civil disobedience of the 1960s and the high crime rates of the 1970s cast a dark shadow on American policing, but police had a new opportunity to develop a collaborative relationship with the public and a new era—the community policing era.

3.3 Self Check

1. How did the Wickersham Commission view the role of police?
2. What impact did the LEAA have on crime?

POLICING *Online*

Check your answers at
www.policing.glencoe.com

3.4 Community Policing (1980–Present)

community policing era An era of policing (1980–present) that focuses on police-community collaboration to identify and solve problems that affect the quality of life in a community.

Beginning in the 1980s, the **community policing era** emerged with a focus on police-community collaboration to identify and solve problems that affect quality of life. In the reform era, crime control was accomplished through preventive patrol and rapid response to calls for service. In the community policing era, the role of police expanded beyond merely providing law enforcement and also included the following:

- Order maintenance
- Conflict resolution
- Problem solving
- Provision of services

Problem-Oriented Policing (POP)

problem-oriented policing A policing approach that emphasizes solving problems, not just responding to calls for service.

In 1979, Herman Goldstein introduced **problem-oriented policing**, a policing approach that emphasizes solving problems, not just responding to calls for service. A common complaint among police officers is that they have no control over the causes of the crimes that they must try to prevent and fight. By using a problem-oriented policing philosophy, police departments hoped to change that.[39]

broken windows theory A theory that finds that when citizens allow their communities to deteriorate—such as by allowing broken windows, trash, and abandoned cars to accumulate—they send a silent message to criminals that no one cares about their neighborhood.

The **broken windows theory** gave increased emphasis to the community's role in preventing crime. Researchers have noted that when citizens allow their communities to deteriorate—such as by allowing broken windows, trash, and abandoned cars to accumulate—they send a silent message to criminals that no one cares about their neighborhood. This is an invitation to criminals that they can commit crimes there and nobody will stop them. Therefore, a key to crime prevention is not allowing communities to fall into disrepair.[40]

Problem-oriented policing is characterized by police-community collaboration in solving problems of mutual concern. This was very different from the professional approach of the reform era, in which police remained detached from public contact.

Community Policing

community policing A philosophy and an organizational strategy that promotes a new partnership between people and their police.

The 1980s and 1990s have seen the growth of **community policing**. The creators of community policing, Robert Trojanowicz and Bonnie Bucqueroux of the National Center for Community Policing, have defined community policing as a philosophy and an organizational strategy that promotes a new partnership between people and their police. It is based on the premise that both the police and the community must work together to identify, prioritize, and solve contemporary problems such as crime, drugs, fear of crime, social and physical disorder, and overall neighborhood decay, with the goals of improving the overall quality of life in the area.[41]

Figure 3.6 on page 106 illustrates some of the new tactics used by police departments that practice community policing.

In community policing, success is measured in terms of the quality of life in a community, problem resolution, reduction of fear, increased order, citizen satisfaction with police services, and crime control. Organizational structures are decentralized to allow for greater discretion and tactical decision making. In some departments, the organizational structure has been flattened by removing mid-management layers. This has permitted enhanced communication within the department and a more timely response to community needs and problems.[42]

The Big Six Development and implementation of community policing in any community require extensive planning, collaboration, and coordination among certain stakeholder groups. Trojanowicz referred to these groups as the **Big Six**:

1. **Police** Today police must realize that the traditional incident-driven response to crime, and the dependence on routine patrol and rapid response as deterrents to crime, must be supplemented with a proactive problem-solving style of policing.
2. **The community that they serve** The community, working with the police, must become active in identifying community needs and concerns, then help in finding solutions.
3. **The community's elected officials** Elected officials must walk the beat with community policing officers both to understand the problems that they encounter and to ensure that the community has a clear idea of what police and government officials should be doing.
4. **The business community** Businesses, large and small, must provide volunteer services and resources to community groups and projects. Furthermore, they must form alliances to support good business practices and enhance the quality of life in the community.
5. **Other agencies such as civic, religious, social service, and mental health agencies** Government agencies and private entities must collaborate with police and community in solving local problems.
6. **The media** Finally, the media must become partners with the police in promoting the positive aspects of the police and the public working together.[43]

Big Six The six stakeholder groups in community policing: police, community, elected officials, business community, other agencies (i.e., civic, religious, social service, mental heath), and media.

Police departments in this era focus on community policing. They use tactics such as the following

◆ Foot patrol, which results in increased intimacy between police and citizens
◆ Problem solving
◆ Information gathering
◆ Victim counseling and services
◆ Community organizing and consultation
◆ Education
◆ Regular patrol
◆ Specialized forms of patrol
◆ Rapid response to emergency calls

Public Safety Partnership and Community Policing Act of 1994 An act that emphasized community policing as a crime-fighting strategy and made more funding available for community policing activities.

Advances in Community Policing So great is the promise of community policing for American police that Congress passed the **Public Safety Partnership and Community Policing Act of 1994**, which emphasized it as a crime-fighting strategy and made funding available to local law enforcement agencies to implement its policies. In 1994, the Community Policing Consortium was established as a forum for training and information exchange in community policing.

The philosophy of community policing has shown great promise. More and more departments have embraced community policing and realized that police and public collaboration can make a difference in combating crime. However, there are some concerns:

• Some departments have started bicycle patrols, handed out police trading cards, and held community meetings and call this community policing without understanding its underlying philosophy.
• In some departments, implementation of community policing has been met with resistance. This can be due to a fear of decentralization, or a resistance to the integration of new science and technology that community policing requires.
• Community policing requires a new approach in the recruitment, selection, and training of officers. With it has come a redefinition of police tasks and consequently a different behavioral approach to policing. Police officers who prefer the traditional reactive approach find the new proactive, community-oriented approach a drastic change.

CAREER FOCUS

Domestic Violence Unit Detective

Job Description

Anna T. Pilette, Las Vegas, Nevada Metropolitan Police

One of my main responsibilities is to respond to domestic violence calls. I interview suspects, victims, and witnesses to determine what happened and to write our reports. I teach in our police officers academy, our corrections officers academy, and our citizens academy where people can register and learn about what police officers do. I am also involved in our Safe Nest organization, which assists women, and children who are in domestic violence situations. We have eight detectives, and we get an average of 18,000 domestic violence cases a year, so that's about 200 cases per detective per year.

Las Vegas, NV Metropolitan Police Patch

A challenging aspect of this work is dealing with people who often don't have the ability to help themselves and keep hoping somebody else will solve their problems.

It is particularly rewarding to put a case together and bring the perpetrator to trial. It gives the victim closure and shows that the criminal justice system works. Right now, I have a victim who was stabbed, and we are trying to get who did this to her on attempted murder one. It will be a satisfaction to get him into court.

I would advise young people interested in this line of work to learn as much as possible about different cultures and lifestyles because, as you have to go into people's homes and give them advice about what they could or should do, you need a good deal of life experience.

Employment History

I started out in law enforcement right after high school. I attended the police academy and began as a dispatcher. Next, I was a corrections officer, and a patrol officer. I worked in community policing, in the police employees assistance program, and finally as a detective.

Follow-Up What do you think makes domestic violence cases especially challenging?

Will the police personality of the past function effectively in the community policing context? These concerns and others must be resolved if community policing is to become the new law enforcement philosophy.

Applying Community Policing An excellent example of a police department that has embraced the philosophy of community policing with significant results is the New York Police Department. After experiencing high rates of crime and violence, the NYPD moved to implement community policing in 1984. Between 1993 and 1995, the NYPD saw the following decreases in crime:

- Murder: 39 percent
- Burglary: 25 percent
- Auto theft: 36 percent
- Armed robbery: 31 percent

In 1996, New York City saw a 15 percent decline in its overall crime rate while the rest of the country experienced only a 2 percent decline. New York's success has prompted visits from police officials from other large cities and from foreign countries. But what is causing this phenomenon? Most experts believe it is a combination of reasons, but community policing is the main factor. (See Figure 3.7 for a list of community groups that meet regularly with police forces.)

New York police concentrated on eliminating low-level crimes such as aggressive panhandlers, chronic fare evaders on the subways, drug users, graffiti taggers, and drunks. The NYPD found that many of these perpetrators often engaged in more serious crimes, so by removing these offenders they reduced serious crime. In addition, policing was decentralized so that each precinct commander had the authority to make decisions at his or her level. Finally, policing was tailored to address each community's problems. Community policing in New York City has improved the quality of life and reduced citizens' fear of crime.[44]

Is community policing the cure for crime and social problems in the United States? One research center, which has done extensive research on the effectiveness of community policing in North Carolina, shows cautious optimism:

> Given the relative newness of community policing, its full potential is yet to be known. The early evidence suggests that [community-oriented policing] may be most effective in improving citizen/police relations and in increasing job satisfaction among officers. Its impacts on the fear of crime and crime rates are more uncertain. Based on initial experience in a North Carolina agency, however, the evidence is encouraging that community policing can and will reduce both the fear of crime and actual crime.[45]

Figure 3.7

Definition of Community-Based Crime Prevention

Crime Prevention Is

◆ Everyone's business
◆ More than security
◆ A responsibility of all levels of government
◆ Linked with solving social problems
◆ Cost-effective

Crime Prevention Requires

◆ A central position in law enforcement
◆ Active cooperation among all elements of the community
◆ Education
◆ Tailoring to local needs and conditions
◆ Continual testing and improvement

Crime Prevention Improves

◆ The quality of life for every community

Community policing holds great promise. The partnerships developed between the police and public have the potential to improve the quality of life for all citizens. More important, the responsibility for community crime prevention will be shifted back to where it belongs—the police *and* the community.

History shows that American police evolved in response to societal needs for safety and security. In the future, police will continue to evolve in response to an ever-changing world. The next chapter will look at the development of the modern police role.

3.4 Self Check

1. How does problem-oriented policing work?
2. Why do community-policing experts emphasize the importance of the Big Six?

POLICING *Online*
Check your answers at
www.policing.glencoe.com

Chapter 3

Policing and the American Experience

Summary By Learning Objectives

1. Describe policing during the early era.

The first colonists in America faced adverse conditions. Survival depended on a structured and disciplined lifestyle, which many of the colonists did not possess. In an effort to ensure the survival of the early colonies, such as Jamestown, community leaders passed harsh laws and sometimes imposed martial law. All colonists were expected to conform. Any violations were often addressed by the military leaders of the colony.

2. Compare policing in the East, the South, and the West.

In the early American colonies, two approaches to policing appeared. Northern colonies, where the population was located in small towns and villages, found the watch system suitable to their way of life. In the South, colonists were dispersed about the countryside and found the sheriff form of policing ideal. Southern communities supplemented the sheriff system with slave patrols that provided security against possible insurrections and captured runaways. In the Western territories, there was a lack of a formal criminal justice system. To protect themselves, people often resorted to vigilante justice. Early law enforcement in the West can be categorized into four forms: 1) extralegal citizen police (vigilante groups), 2) formal police (sheriffs and

marshals), 3) legal citizen police (citizen deputies), and 4) parapolice (private security).

3. Understand policing during the political era.

In the mid-1800s, the spoils system dominated government. Policing was characterized by political involvement in the administration and operation of police. The legitimacy and authorization to exercise their police powers came from local political leaders. During this period, police performed the roles of law enforcement, crime prevention, order maintenance, and sometimes social services. Local politicians maintained a reciprocal relationship with police. They helped police chiefs and officers keep their jobs, while police assisted in keeping the politicians in office. Police departments were divided into precincts. Police managers and ward politicians ran each precinct as a small police department. The demand for services came either from the local ward politician or citizen demands directed to the beat officers.

4. Discuss the events that changed the police role from service to crime fighting and back to service.

In the 1920s and 1930s, two events forced a transition of the police role from service to crime fighting:

1. In 1919, Congress passed the Volstead Act, which outlawed the sale and consumption of alcohol. Almost immediately, police found themselves enforcing an unpopular law that often pitted them against friends, neighbors, and relatives.

2. The 1930s saw the Depression devastate the American economy. During the Depression, small gangs of criminals such as Bonnie and Clyde, Ma Parker, Machine Gun Kelly, Baby Face Nelson, and John Dillinger challenged law and order in the country.

In the 1960s and 1970s, antiwar demonstrations and other protests led to police-civilian clashes in which police conduct was called into question. These events, coupled with research such as the Kansas City Preventive Patrol Experiment in 1974, showed that policing needed to return to a more service-oriented role in order to meet the needs of the people. This sentiment led to the development of community policing.

5. Describe policing during the reform era.

Policing in the reform era removed political influence and corruption from policing. The focus of policing was on crime control and the apprehension of criminals rather than on community service. Policing became centralized and authoritarian, discouraging the exercise of discretion in making street-level decisions. When confronted with a special problem, agencies often created specialized units. The relationship between police and community was one of detachment and neutrality, with the community playing a passive role. Rapid response to emergency calls was emphasized. The patrol car provided increased coverage of areas with fewer officers. Police effectiveness was determined by measuring the crime rate.

6. Explain which police leaders played significant roles in the reform era.

A number of law enforcement leaders provided direction for American policing. Most notable is August Vollmer, a progressive, who advocated police reform and professionalization. A protégé of Vollmer, O. W. Wilson, stressed the implementation of a professional model of police that, among other things, emphasized taking politics out of policing, integrating technology, and crime fighting. In the 1920s, J. Edgar Hoover was instrumental in transforming the FBI into one of the premier law enforcement agencies in the world.

7. Understand policing during the community policing era.

In the community policing era, the police role includes not just law enforcement but also order maintenance, conflict resolution, problem solving, and provision of services. The relationship between the police and community is one of collaboration in addressing crime and problems. Community policing involves building partnerships between police and community to address problems that affect the quality of life. There is heavy emphasis on the use of foot patrols, information gathering, problem solving, victim counseling and services, community organizing and consultation, education, regular patrol, specialized forms of patrol, and rapid response to emergency calls.

Key Terms

rattle watch (p. 76)
lynch law (p. 76)
slave patrols (p. 77)
vigilante groups (p. 81)
casual deputies (p. 83)
political era (p. 85)
progressives (p. 90)
reform era (p. 92)
Uniform Crime Report (UCR) (p. 95)
Wickersham Commission (p. 97)
President's Commission on Law Enforcement (p. 98)
Kerner Commission (p. 98)

Law Enforcement Assistance Administration (LEAA) (p. 98)
directed patrol (p. 100)
team policing (p. 100)
territorial imperative (p. 101)
community policing era (p. 104)
problem-oriented policing (p. 104)
broken windows theory (p. 104)
community policing (p. 104)
Big Six (p. 105)
Public Safety Partnership and Community Policing Act of 1994 (p. 106)

Questions for Review

1. What were some differences in the policing styles between the northern and southern colonies?

2. What four categories classified policing in the Old West?

3. How would you characterize the police role during the political era?

4. What were Vollmer's 12 elements of professional policing?

5. What were J. Edgar Hoover's contributions to policing?

6. What federal law enforcement agencies were created during the reform era?

7. What is the difference between problem-oriented policing and community policing?

8. Why is the concept of "broken windows" considered an essential part of any community-policing strategy?

Experiential Activities

9. **Finding Your Local Law Enforcement Roots**

You have been appointed the new public relations officer of your local police department. Your chief has asked you to write a brief summary of the department's history for a new brochure. Possible information sources include your local police department, local college and public libraries, newspaper files, and the Internet.

   a. Research the history of the department and write a brief summary.

   b. Which major events shaped the history of your department?

   c. Which national development in policing influenced your department the most?

Experiential Activities continued

10. History on the Internet
Find out about the history of three departments at any level of government. Try to vary the types of departments (sheriff's department, one state highway patrol, and one federal agency). Find departments from different areas and different jurisdictions (rural, suburban, and urban).
- **a.** Compare and contrast the history of the three departments.
- **b.** Which department has changed the most since its inception?
- **c.** To what can you attribute the differences among these departments?

11. The Police Generation Gap
Interview three people: one age 20 to 25, one age 50 to 55, and one age 70 to 75. Ask them about the views of police officers that were prevalent in their time.
- **a.** What were the differences in how each generation perceived police?
- **b.** Were these differences larger or smaller than what you expected?
- **c.** Which incidents influence the perception of police?

12. Historical Changes
Contact your local historical society. Try to find material that is at least 100 years old. Jot down three to five police duties, procedures, or issues from that time. Next, contact your police department and ask how these duties, procedures, and issues have changed.

- **a.** Do these changes reflect larger shifts in procedural reform and public expectations?
- **b.** Have all of the changes been positive?
- **c.** Give three examples of how police training has changed.

Web Patrol

13. Crime in the Old West
Click on the link at **www.policing.glencoe.com** to learn more about early western officers and outlaws.
Who are some of the lesser-known western law enforcers who died in the line of duty?

14. History of the NYPD
Click on the link at **www.policing.glencoe.com** for an in-depth photographic history of the New York Police Department.
How many officers served in the first NYPD, and how have their duties changed since then?

15. Community Policing Consortium
Click the link at **www.policing.glencoe.com** for additional information on the Community Policing Consortium.
What type of data-sharing resources can be accessed through the consortium?

Critical Thinking Exercises

16. Back to the Future

Compare Vollmer's 12 principles of professional policing, which you read about in this chapter, with Robert Peel's nine organizational principles, which you read about in Chapter 2. While reading both, take notes to compare similarities and differences. Also, keep in mind that each person wrote these sets of principles at different times and different stages of the evolution of policing. When you are done, answer the following questions:

    a. Do you find any similarities or differences? Explain.

    b. If Vollmer and Robert Peel met, what do you think they would discuss, and what would be the opinion of each side?

17. Policing in Transition

The majority of today's law enforcement agencies are uniformed municipal police departments. Officers patrol their jurisdictions by automobile and by foot, and many of their tasks are similar to those performed by the first municipal police departments. Some positive aspects of the job, such as those seen in community policing, have grown considerably. Some negative aspects, such as political influence, have waned.

As you have probably noticed, federal law enforcement agencies operate differently from those at the local and state levels. Based on what you have read about western law enforcement in this chapter, think about this comparison and then answer the following questions:

    a. Are federal law enforcement officers more like today's police departments or the Old West's marshals and sheriffs? Why?

    b. What special challenges do federal law enforcement officers face?

18. Early PBAs

You are a police officer whose department has just formed a Police Benevolent Association (PBA), which has promised to address the problems of low salaries for officers. You and your fellow officers meet to discuss their actions. Many of the others, especially those with families, are excited about the pay raises and are happy with what the PBA is trying to accomplish.

You tell them that you are more worried about the poor quality of service weapons. The guns are old and poorly made, and they fail to fire about 25 percent of the time. Twice your revolver has not fired when you needed it, and you barely escaped serious injury. The others argue that many officers never fire a shot, but all of them need better pay. They also point out that the last officer to die from a faulty revolver was killed by criminals over three years ago.

    a. Based on the circumstances, which argument is more valid and why?

    b. What agreement could be reached to make both sides happy?

Endnotes

1. George L. Kelling and Mark H. Moore, *The Evolving Strategy of Policing* (Washington, D.C.: Government Printing Office, 1988), 2.
2. A. C. German, F. D. Day, and R. R. J. Gallati, *Introduction to Law Enforcement and Criminal Justice* (Springfield, IL: Charles C Thomas, 1978), 64.
3. William J. Bopp and Donald O. Schultz, *Principles of American Law Enforcement and Criminal Justice* (Springfield, IL: Charles C Thomas, 1972), 21–22.
4. History of the U.S. Postal Inspection Service, http://www.usps.gov/websites/depart/inspect/ischrono. htm. Accessed July 7, 1998, pp. 1–2.
5. Herbert A. Johnson and Nancy Wolfe, *History of Criminal Justice*, 2d ed. (Cincinnati, OH: Anderson, 1996), 165–68.
6. Ibid.
7. Bopp and Schultz, *Principles of American Law Enforcement*, 52–53.
8. Ibid., 49.
9. Ibid., 50–51.
10. Paul Trachtman, "Frontline Forces of Law and Order," in *Gunfighters* (New York: Time-Life, 1974), 103.
11. Bopp and Schultz, *Principles of American Law Enforcement*, 51, 53–54.
12. Ibid., 54–55.
13. Ibid., 55–56.
14. Kelling and Moore, *The Evolving Strategy of Policing*, 3.
15. Law Enforcement Assistance Administration, *Two Hundred Years of American Criminal Justice: An LEAA Bicentennial Study* (Washington, D.C.: Superintendent of Documents, 1976), 19.
16. Ibid., 19–20.
17. Kelling and Moore, *The Evolving Strategy of Policing*, 5.
18. Bopp and Schultz, *Principles of American Law Enforcement*, 77.
19. Ibid., 73.
20. Ibid., 73.
21. Ibid., 74–76.
22. George F. Cole, *The American System of Justice*, 6th ed. (Pacific Grove, CA: Brooks/Cole, 1992), 200.
23. Bopp and Schultz, *Principles of American Law Enforcement*, 66–67.
24. Kelling and Moore, *The Evolving Strategy of Policing*, 6.
25. Ibid., 7.
26. "A Short History of the FBI," http://www.fbi.gov/ history/hist.htm. Accessed July 1, 1998, pp. 1–15.
27. Ibid.
28. Merlyn Moore, "The Police: In Search of Direction," in *Managing the Police Organization*, edited by Larry Gaines and Truett A. Ricks (St. Paul, MN: West, 1978), 60–62.
29. Bopp and Schultz, *Principles of American Law Enforcement*, 97.
30. Kelling and Moore, *The Evolving Strategy of Policing*.
31. Cole, *The American System of Justice*, 200–1.
32. Moore, "The Police," 61–62.
33. President's Commission on Law Enforcement and Administration of Justice, *The Challenge of Crime in a Free Society* (Washington, D.C.: Government Printing Office, 1967), 99–123.
34. *Report of the National Advisory Commission on Civil Disorders* (New York: Bantam, 299–322.
35. Ibid.
36. "DEA History," http://www.usdoj.gov/dea/pubs/ briefing/1_2.htm. Accessed July 1, 1998, pp. 1–2.
37. L. W. Sherman, C. H. Milton, and T. V. Kelley, *Team Policing: Seven Case Studies* (Washington, D.C.: Police Foundation, 1973), 107–8.
38. Roy Roberg and Jack Kuykendall, *Police and Society* (Belmont, CA: Wadsworth, 1993), 109.
39. Herman Goldstein, *Problem-Oriented Policing* (New York: McGraw-Hill, 1990).
40. James Q. Wilson and George L. Kelling, "Making Neighborhoods Safe," *Atlantic Monthly* 249 (1982): 29–38.
41. Robert Trojanwicz and Bonnie Bucqueroux, *Community Policing: How to Get Started* (Cincinnati, OH: Anderson, 1994), 2.
42. Kelling and Moore, *The Evolving Strategy of Policing*, 11–13.
43. Ibid., 21–25.
44. Lori Montgomery, "Broken Windows: How a Theory Shook the Foundations of Law Enforcement and Helped Heal a City," http://www.onpatrol.com/cs.brokwin.html. Accessed July 13, 1998, pp. 1–7.
45. William M. Rohe, Richard Adams, and Thomas A. Arcury, *Community Oriented Policing: What It Is, Why It Works, How to Get Started* (Chapel Hill: University of North Carolina at Chapel Hill, Center for Urban and Regional Studies, 1997), 13.

Questions for Review

1. What is the role of the citizen in policing in a democratic society?
2. Explain the conceptual model.
3. describe the use of restitution in England before 1066.
4. Are the goals of police, courts, and corrections related? How?
5. Explain the new paradigm of policing.
6. Explain the concept of system in policing.
7. What is the quiet revolution?
8. Who were the Bow Street Runners?
9. Who was the Provost Marshal?
10. Name Peel's principles of policing.
11. Explain the importance of Peel's principles.
12. How did ancient Greece influence modern law and policing?
13. What was the first federal law enforcement agency in the U.S.?
14. What is the Volstead Act?
15. What did the Wickersham Commission do?

Police Role and Organization

Chapter 4
The Police Role

Chapter 5
The Organization of Policing

The Police Role

CHAPTER OBJECTIVES

AFTER COMPLETING THIS CHAPTER, YOU WILL BE ABLE TO:

1. Gain an understanding of the factors and dynamics that influence the police role.

2. Understand how the police role functions in a democratic society.

3. Identify the factors that account for the responsibilities given police.

4. Describe the essential functions performed by typical police agencies.

5. Distinguish predominant policing styles.

6. Identify the emerging roles of the police.

7. Name factors that shape the new role of police.

◄ NYPD detective and policeman during the September 11, 2001 terrorist attack on the World Trade Center.

4.1 Defining the Police Role

When many citizens think of the goal of policing, they think of law enforcement. The public perceives police in a cops-and-robbers way. This has not only oversimplified the role of the police, but—more important—has also resulted in the police neglecting more important and complex modern police functions.[1]

The fact is that service activities rather than crime-fighting activities occupy the greatest portion of the average patrol officer's time.[2] Why, then, does this cops and robbers misconception exist? This chapter will discuss why there is confusion about the police role, how it impacts the police, and what emerging police roles will stimulate better police-citizen understanding.

The Police Role

Certain terms have both a commonsense and a technical definition. The term *role* is a good example. Technically, a role is a set of standards, descriptions, and names for the behavior of a person or position.[3] What does this mean when applied to policing? The commonsense definition of the **police role** means the customary functions of police such as investigation, arrest, and providing social services. It describes what police perceive as the uses of their authority. It can also mean the ways in which they try to solve problems that they encounter on the job.

police role Customary police functions such as investigation, arrest, and social services; what officers perceive as the uses of their authority; and their problem-solving methods.

The policies and procedures of police departments play a significant part in creating an individual officer's police role. They can also create role behaviors for all of the tasks that police perform. These role concepts affect the relationship between officers and the citizens they serve. Understanding the subtleties of role expectations is also important to individual officers for career development. Officers who understand their roles are often rewarded for performing properly, but those who do not may find that their careers are limited or ended because of confusion about their roles.

Suppose that a young and enthusiastic officer who misunderstands current search and seizure laws apprehends a known drug dealer and illegally seizes evidence from him. Even though he could have seized the evidence legally, he chose to save some time and obtain it illegally because he felt the drug dealer was guilty. The evidence is then ruled inadmissible and the drug dealer, whose charges are dropped due to a lack of admissible evidence, sues the police department because the officer violated his rights.

◄ **Police and Juveniles**
Policeman talks to children during a DARE presentation. Dealing with juveniles is one of many areas in which police get involved.
Why do you think policing the juvenile population would require specific training?

Importance of Understanding the Police Role

A police officer's workday varies between periods of calm and periods of intense pressure and includes contacts in many situations. An officer's personal conception of his or her role may be formed largely from what is observed and heard in the course of daily contacts with the public and peers and not necessarily from direct supervisors. If the officer is not given a clear understanding of what the police agency expects, he or she will be guided by a personal conception of the police role that may or may not be consistent with that of the agency.

Since officers carry out their work without much supervision and must make immediate decisions in many different situations, the manner in which they exercise discretion is critical to effective job performance. A community's conflicting expectations of officers can complicate this use of discretion. For example, Sherry is a community policing officer who correctly perceives her role to be one of providing services and showing restraint in using force and making arrests. When she informally handles a truant juvenile by contacting his school and parents, then returning him to school, most of the community feels that she has acted properly. However, the juvenile's next-door neighbor wanted him arrested because he dislikes the juvenile and his frequent truancy. Regardless of how many times Sherry explains to the neighbor that arrest is not an option in this case, the neighbor is still convinced that Sherry is not fulfilling her police role.

4-100. The basic authority for police officers to make arrests derives from the Wisconsin Statute 62.09(13), which makes it a duty for a peace officer to arrest with or without a warrant and with reasonable diligence to take before the court every person found in the city engaged in any disturbance of the peace or violating any law of the state or ordinance of such city. This authority to arrest is further broadened by State Statute 968.07, which states:

1. **A law enforcement officer may arrest a person when the officer:**
   A. has a warrant commanding that such person be arrested.
   B. believes, on reasonable grounds (also known as probable cause), that a warrant for the person's arrest has been issued in the state.
   C. believes, on reasonable grounds, that a felony warrant for the person's arrest has been issued in another state.

   or

   D. has reasonable grounds to believe that the person is committing or has committed a crime.

2. **A law enforcement officer making a lawful arrest may command the aid of any person, and such person shall have the same power as that of the law enforcement officer.**

3. **Section 175.40(6) of the statutes provides that a police officer outside of his/her jurisdiction may arrest a person or provide assistance anywhere in the state if the following criteria are met:**
   A. The officer is in uniform, on duty, and on official business. If the officer is using a vehicle, that vehicle is marked police vehicle.
   B. The officer is taking action that he/she is authorized to take under the same circumstances in his/her jurisdiction.
   C. The officer is acting to respond to any of the following:
      1. An emergency that poses a significant threat to life or of bodily harm
      2. Acts that constitute a felony

4. **Further, the policy must notify and cooperate with the law enforcement agency having primary jurisdiction.**

The Patrol Officer

No two days are exactly alike for a patrol officer, but each has a common routine: It is shaped by the calls for service to which officers respond. Calls and their outcomes are generally predictable, but there are those rare worst-case scenarios that surprise police with their level of danger.

A typical shift should be described on two levels:

1. That of the first responder, which is the basic patrol unit and will be covered in this section
2. That of shift supervision, which is handled by a field supervisor and a station supervisor and will be covered in the next section

The patrol officer is the first police unit to respond to calls for service. This makes their job predictable in some ways and unpredictable in others. Most calls are unthreatening and easy to resolve, which can make patrol work monotonous. However, a patrol officer does not know whether the next call will involve an argument, arrest, or even gunfire.

This section will cover the typical work shift for patrol officers.

Beginning a Work Shift The patrol officer begins his or her work shift by reporting to a police locker room and changing into his or her uniform. This act constitutes an important stage in the transformation from citizen to officer. Once uniformed, the officer will report to either a roll call room or to a crime analysis office to get an update on the current crime picture. Some roll call rooms have trends, statistics, and wanted suspect posters on their walls. When individual officers who work for a mid- to large-size agency finish reviewing the current crime picture, they take a seat within the roll call room. If they work for a small agency, then a more informal arrangement may prevail.

During **roll call**, a police check-in procedure that ordinarily occurs at least 30 minutes before the start of a shift, officers will receive their duty assignments and briefings on a variety of subjects. Routinely covered subjects include the following:

> **roll call** A police check-in procedure in which officers receive their duty assignments and briefings on a variety of subjects.

- Tactical updates from a previous shift's experiences
- Procedural changes
- Training information
- Special problems
- Descriptions of wanted persons and vehicles
- Miscellaneous announcements

Officers may receive subpoenas for court appearances during this period. Upon conclusion of the briefing, managers may inspect uniforms.

After roll call, officers draw specialized items such as shotguns and radios. Then they get a vehicle and perform checks of its equipment. Often they will also check if any suspects dumped contraband such as drugs or weapons in the back seat of a cruiser. Once the inspection has been completed, officers log on mobile digital terminals, computer terminals that are mounted within their vehicles to receive electronically transmitted calls for service.

Entering the Field As officers leave the safety of their station and go into the field, they take on the heightened awareness of being an official representative of local law enforcement. This sense of responsibility is heightened while the officer mentally transforms to a medium level of personal safety awareness. A high phase, or red phase, is reserved for actual involvement in

perimeter A tactical positioning of police officers to contain someone attempting to escape from the scene of a crime.

a field situation that threatens harm. There are no scripts in policing, so the officer must always be mentally prepared to handle whatever occurs.

For two-person units staffed by officers who have not worked together before, the officers may first determine which tactics they will use in the event of a hazardous or life-threatening confrontation. They may discuss searching protocols or how suspicious persons will be removed from vehicles during traffic stops. This same type of communication occurs between units in agencies and between agencies performing joint law enforcement operations.

Working in the Field Once in the field, the officer's workload is largely dictated by citizens' calls for service. Officers also frequently initiate activities based on their observations of suspicious activity. Veteran officers often develop a sixth sense for spotting criminal offenders. Some become skilled at identifying probable drug abusers, and others display an uncanny ability to detect suspects who are packing guns.

In the course of their shifts, officers will normally issue at least one traffic citation, perform a number of warrant checks on suspicious vehicles or persons, and respond to a wide variety of service requests such as alarm activations, domestic disputes, and theft reports. It is common for officers to arrest someone in the course of their shift. Arrests can result in a significant expenditure of time as officers fill out paperwork. If arrests do occur, officers can most likely expect a court subpoena to soon follow.

In some cases, the status of the arrestee or the nature of the crime can make the paperwork take even longer. For example, juvenile arrests and those for most sexual offenses consume extraordinary amounts of special processing time and paperwork. This is because juveniles have special procedural protections. In most jurisdictions, they cannot be photographed or fingerprinted. In all jurisdictions, jailers must maintain sight and sound separation between juveniles and adult inmates. Sexual offenses require the proper collection and identification of physical evidence, which also involves large amounts of paperwork.

Officers also provide tactical assistance to each other. This can range from assisting in a vehicular or foot pursuit to helping to form a **perimeter**, which is a tactical positioning of police officers to contain someone attempting to escape from the scene of a crime. When needed, officers may back up other jurisdictions' units.

End-of-Watch Duties As the end of the work shift approaches, officers are expected to be especially responsive to calls for service. This is because the watch change is a vulnerable period, since most officers are not dispersed in the field as widely as they should be but instead try to return to the station early. It is important to note that when the next shift is more lightly deployed, which is the case during the change from night shift to the grave-yard shift, a large number of unanswered calls for service can adversely affect the oncoming shift's quality of service and response time.

The Field and Station Supervisors

In mid- to large-size agencies, supervisory assignments for patrol operations normally divide into two tiers: field supervision and station supervision.

The Field Supervisor The **field supervisor** is primarily charged with overseeing the quality of service delivery and supervising demanding tactical situations. He or she is usually a sergeant who roams in the field. The field supervisor's initial responsibility at the beginning of a shift is

field supervisor A police supervisor, usually a sergeant, primarily charged with overseeing the quality of service delivery and supervising demanding tactical situations.

CopTalk

Role Knowledge

The importance of role knowledge to a police officer cannot be overstated because it affects how police perform all of their tasks. Remember that some decisions made by a police officer must be made in life-threatening situations within less than a second's time. Yet the police officer is just as accountable for his or her decisions as is a judge or lawmaker who has deliberated a decision for months.

When a police officer enters an apartment and confronts an enraged, obviously intoxicated husband who is pressing a knife to his wife's throat, the officer's knowledge of his or her role has already formed. He or she must defuse the situation by sub-duing the husband, taking the wife out of danger, and making an arrest. The same is true in any arrest situation or in any case where an officer exercises the discretion to use force. In these cases, an officer must know the police role (and all of the rights and

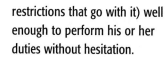

restrictions that go with it) well enough to perform his or her duties without hesitation.

The police role is explained to recruits and officers repeatedly, from the recruit's first police acad-emy classes to officer training ses-sions. These teachings attempt to explain the role of a police officer within the larger societal context, although their value is sometimes underestimated by police who feel they already "know their job." It is wiser to listen to this training and learn something new. Just ask any officers involved in excessive force lawsuits about the results of not learning the correct way to respond to a suspect.

What Do You Think? How should officers deal with the many facets of the police role, which includes activities from community policing to cap-turing violent felons?

to stabilize the call load. If the oncoming watch receives an unusually heavy call load, the supervisor must prioritize the calls while attempting, through the dispatch center, to determine which calls may no longer require police units to respond. The seasoned supervisor routinely handles this with few problems.

When a watch has stabilized, the call load is stable, and there are no exceptional tactical demands on police units, the field supervisor will randomly audit officers' performance as they respond to calls. This means that he or she may check that officers are obeying safety standards, such as having the gun handle facing backward when they interview persons. They may also examine the manner in which they use resources. Some effective uses of resources are the following:

- Use of other units for backup
- Proper use of communications equipment
- Strategic positioning of a police vehicle
- Questioning neighbors adjacent to a disturbance call location before approaching the call site
- Interviewing citizens after officers have left to determine the degree of satisfaction with police services

Regularly, especially in large urban departments, field supervisors will find themselves running tactical field operations involving the deployment of multiple officers. This may involve coordinating the maintenance of a perimeter to contain a suspect. In such circumstances, the supervisor will involve as many resources as appropriate to effect containment. While handling any tactical situation, the supervisor must keep in perspective other calls for service that are being received at the same time. For example, he or she must assess the nature and seriousness of incoming calls against the seriousness of the offense committed by the person who is the subject of a perimeter. Several high-priority calls for service may lead the supervisor to reduce or break up the perimeter, especially if the probability of arrest has diminished.

station supervisor A police supervisor who ensures that activities stay on track within the precinct station; also known as a watch commander.

Station Supervisor

A **station supervisor**, also known as a watch commander, ensures that activities stay on track within the precinct station. The station supervisor is often of a higher rank than the field supervisor and is usually responsible for all matters, including all field activities. Because of this large sphere of responsibility, the station supervisor carries a handheld radio to monitor field operations. In major tactical situations, the shift supervisor may leave the station to respond in the field, after appointing another person to temporarily oversee the station operations.

The shift supervisor has four major responsibilities:

- **Security of arrested suspects** After leading roll call, the station supervisor checks on the status of arrested persons within the station. The supervisor needs to know who is being detained and on what charges. Most arrestees will be confined within lockups, but prebooking arrestees may be waiting outside of the cells. They may pose a security risk even though they are handcuffed, so the supervisor must ensure that they are processed and placed into secure confinement without delay.

- **Project status and paperwork** After checking the status of arrestees, the supervisor completes the next day's assignment board for officers scheduled to work. The next matter is checking all of the administrative matters pertinent to the watch. At times, this can be an extremely arduous task because of all the audits, tactical planning, special reports, training, and personnel complaint investigations that are generated on a shift. A supervisor can find himself or herself inundated with a mountain of paperwork. The station supervisor is also primarily responsible for reviewing and signing all crime reports, arrest reports, and booking approvals. Finally, he or she must review all citations and officer logs (as well as field supervisor logs) from the previous day and the current shift.

- **Interaction with citizens** Throughout the shift, a large number of arrestees, citizens, and officers from other jurisdictions may pass through the station. Each will require a portion of the supervisor's time. Customarily, there are also myriad phone calls to be answered (including citizen and news media inquiries) and official notifications to be made during the course of a shift.

- **End of watch** One end-of-watch responsibility is to ensure that field units remain in the field until the next shift actually begins work. As mentioned earlier, patrol units often try to return to the station early to save time. The shift supervisor works with the field supervisor to ensure that these units remain in the field to handle last-minute calls. Most often the station supervisor is the last member of his or her watch to leave the station when the shift concludes. There is the inevitable paperwork to be finished, and, most important, the supervisor has a responsibility to greet the last unit arriving back from a safely completed shift.

4.1 Self Check

1. What is the police role?
2. Why is it important for an officer to have a clear understanding of the police role?

POLICING *Online*

Check your answers at
www.policing.glencoe.com

Police and their departments developed because community leaders and citizens perceived a need for order maintenance. Although their responsibilities have seldom been clearly defined, they have always been presumed by the public to exist to protect the community. This protection is provided by different units such as patrol, investigations, narcotics, and community policing.

As contemporary urban America grows increasingly diverse, conflicting, and competitive, policing and the police role become more complex. Given these increasing complexities, the police must be ever vigilant in using techniques that maintain order. This should be done in a manner that not only preserves but also extends the precious values of a democratic society.[5]

Social Control

social control All social arrangements that either motivate or compel people to conform to society's rules; a way of maximizing the predictability of social behavior.

At the center of all police systems is the process of social control. **Social control** can be defined as all social arrangements that either motivate or compel people to conform to society's rules. It is a way of maximizing the predictability of social behavior. The police are only one of many social controls that help to maintain order in society. In fact, public policing is a comparatively recent mechanism for attaining social control.[6]

Effective social control results in fewer violations, yet it is not an "all-or-nothing" matter. Every society must be able to tolerate a certain amount of deviation from its norms. For example, many police ignore people who jaywalk or drive less than 10 mph over the speed limit. They may also ignore curfew violations or other minor ordinance violations. What shapes the practice of social control are three issues:

1. Norms of a given community
2. Police use of the rule of law
3. Police use of discretion

norms Principles of conduct that guide acceptable behavior.

Norms of a Given Community Laws are a special form of **norms**, which are principles of conduct that guide acceptable behavior. Laws deal with what society considers the most serious norms, such as those that prohibit murder, rape, and robbery. Consequently, they are the only types of norms whose violations are subject to criminal prosecution.[7]

There are also norms that are specific to the world of policing. Officers may adhere to the norms of the policing subculture more fervently than citizens adhere to those of society at large. This is probably due to the strong rewards and punishments used to encourage conformity to those norms. For example, two of the punishments associated with the rules of firearm safety are injury and death. These are much more severe and memorable than those used to enforce everyday norms.

With this strong adherence to their norms, police departments change slowly and resist new ideas. Policing organizations must be careful, however, to avoid becoming so dependent on their norms and sanctions that their capacity for change is retarded. Police management must be ever vigilant to detect when norms become outdated or when programs and policies are eroded by the police subculture.

Police Use of the Rule of Law Police are required to maintain social order under the principle of legality. This places a constant burden on them to detect and prevent crime. Social order is created not merely by punishing criminals but also by using methods to achieve lawful behavior.

One problem is that actual use of the rule of law and definitions of lawful behavior often vary. Criminal courts try to address this problem by setting standards for police to follow when applying the rule of law. For example, they have ruled several times on laws governing search and seizure practices. These laws are usually developed in narcotics cases, where the evidence is the crime and therefore must be seized legally by police in order for prosecutors to obtain a conviction. As another example, laws that set standards for obtaining legal confessions typically arise from violent crime cases.[8] One such case was *Miranda v. Arizona* (1966), in which a suspect in a kidnapping and rape confessed under police pressure without knowing his rights. Despite this attempt at standardizing laws, the dynamic nature of the American legal system means that laws often change. In other words, what was applicable yesterday may be inapplicable today.

Online

Remember, one of your best resources is **www.policing.glencoe.com**

Police Use of Discretion Although police seem to be entangled by the same body of laws they are sworn to enforce, they are also empowered with considerable discretionary authority. As a general human services agency, the police select from a variety of possible actions to resolve a problem. As noted by one policing expert, "The police function, if viewed in its broadest context, consists of making a diagnostic decision as to which alternative might be most appropriate in a given case."[9]

Discretion is perhaps the most flexible aspect of policing, but it also requires the strongest problem-solving skills and creativity. For example, responding officers can encourage disputing citizens to resolve an argument informally. Neighbors who dispute a property line can hire a surveyor to confirm their legal boundaries, roommates who accuse each other of stealing small items can move apart from each other, and a person with a loud barking dog can be ordered to take the dog to obedience school. Police can also suggest that one or all of the parties involved in disputes should pursue a remedy through the civil courts, where the burden of proof is lower and plaintiffs can receive damages. When the police do not have workable alternatives, or if the situation is too serious to warrant an alternative, they can arrest the suspect.

The concept of police as formal social control agents recognizes that no two cases are alike. Generally, the decisions of officers are guided by community values, and communities that place a higher value on freedom and that expect high levels of individual liberty will narrowly define what kinds of behaviors warrant police attention. A police agency's policies and procedures further instruct officers about how and when to intervene with citizens. Ultimately, the individual officer's personality, the citizen's personality, and both parties' understanding of the police role will shape the final resolution of the problem.[10]

Functional Roles

It is difficult to define the primary policing goals and objectives because their importance and the means for achieving them vary among agencies. Any discussion of goals and objectives must take into consideration the influence of the local community, whose characteristics and expectations are highly influential.[11]

Police and police researchers agree that the police role includes the following essential functions, each of which is linked to the goal of creating an orderly, crime-free environment.

- Crime prevention
- Order maintenance
- Law enforcement
- Criminal apprehension
- Public service
- Traffic control

Crime Prevention Crime prevention has been traditionally accepted as one of the primary objectives of municipal police. Much of the responsibility for crime prevention rests on patrol officers. Departments should designate crime hotspots, which are clusters of crime that should be the focus of targeted patrol. Hotspots can be identified through computer technology for crime analysis, such as crime mapping. In the course of their daily routines, the police routinely process enormous amounts of information, and this information can be analyzed through crime mapping to sort crimes by type, date, and time of occurrence, offender demographics, and any other data elements.

Developing a strong police-community partnership is an essential component of crime prevention. To the extent that police can show the public the importance of having them involved as facilitators and receptors of crime prevention information, crime rates can be lowered. Neighborhood Watch and other community crime prevention programs also hinge on appropriate public participation. See Figure 4.2 on page 132 for a description of police guidelines for a typical Neighborhood Watch program.

It is also important for patrol officers to develop strong links with their agency's investigative unit so that they know what evidence helps investigators and what types of crimes the investigators are able to pursue. Often patrol and investigative units have poor communication, especially in larger departments where many officers do not know each other. Patrol officers should understand that investigators can give them information that will make their targeted patrols even more targeted—and probably more successful in finding criminals.

Order Maintenance Of all policing responsibilities, order maintenance is the most difficult to translate into specific actions and objectives. In most instances, social order is maintained through citizens' acceptance and observance of community values and norms. The police are usually only needed

Computer On Patrol

3-D Crime Scenes

In the past, crime scenes were reconstructed through the use of drawings or other simple devices. Today, computer graphics are used to create a much more sophisticated and detailed version of the scene. By using physical evidence such as bloodstains, dents on crashed automobiles, or bullet holes, these graphics can help piece together the physical evidence of a criminal trial.

"By measuring the location and dimensions of each blood stain," explains Paul Breuninger, creator of 3DCrimeScene.com, "the path of each drop can be represented, thus revealing patterns which can be viewed from any angle." For examples of 3-D crime scene reconstruction, check out this Web site by clicking on the link at **www.policing.glencoe.com**.

Think About It How can crime scene reconstructions help investigators, and how can it be used to help juries understand what happened at the moment of a particular crime?

SOURCE: Paul Breuninger, 3DCrimeScene.com, http://www.3DCrimeScene.com.

Figure 4.2

Neighborhood Watch

LOOK FOR THESE

As a member of the NEIGHBORHOOD WATCH, call the police about all suspicious activity in your neighborhood. You and your fellow members should report any unusual situations, such as:

◆ A stranger entering a neighbor's home or apartment that appears to be unoccupied.

◆ Anyone looking into parked cars, or removing parts, gasoline, or license plates from a car.

◆ Anyone entering or leaving a place of business after hours, or loitering outside.

◆ Breaking glass, gunshots, screams, or abnormally barking dogs.

◆ Anyone loitering around the neighborhood, schools or parks.

◆ Anyone going door-to-door who tries to open a door, or goes into a backyard.

◆ Anyone carrying unwrapped property at any unusual time, or running while carrying property.

◆ Any vehicle cruising slowly back and forth on your street.

◆ Any abandoned vehicle on your street.

◆ Windows or doors broken at a home or business.

◆ Anyone sitting in a parked car, especially at an unusual hour, outside a home or business.

WHAT POLICE NEED TO KNOW

◉ What happened?
Where?
When?
How?
Who did it?

◉ If a vehicle was involved –
what was its license plate?
Color?
Make?
Model?
Year?
Which way did it go?

◉ How many people were in the vehicle?
Were they armed?
What was their sex?
Race?
Age?
Height?
Weight?
Hair color?
Clothing?
Shoes?
Any unusual characteristics?

◉ Did they say anything?

NEIGHBORHOOD WATCH ISN'T JUST RESIDENTIAL

The corner store where you stop for milk and bread should also be part of your NEIGHBORHOOD WATCH program, even if the owner and employees live in other sections of town.

◆ Somebody getting away with the burglary of the liquor store down the street doesn't just mean the store lost money; it means crime has come to your neighborhood.

◆ Invite local business people to attend block meetings and give them the opportunity to voice concerns and offer suggestions for improving the neighborhood security.

◆ By working together with local businesses, you can make your neighborhood a safer place to live and work.

A WORD OF CAUTION

NEIGHBORHOOD WATCH does not mean nosy neighbors trying to stop criminals without the police. As a member, your responsibility is to call the police and report what you've seen – NOT to take action yourself.

SOURCE: Adapted from William K. Muir, Police: *Streetcorner Politicians* (Chicago: University of Chicago Press, 1977), 192.

to maintain social order when the value system fails to operate, which is more often the case in large urban areas with mixed populations, widely different economic levels, and widely differing standards of behavior.

Police provide order maintenance during parades, sporting events, and concerts. Suppose that a small community decides to hold a rock concert on its high school field. Private security is handling crowd control inside the field, but outside the police are handling traffic control, crowd control, and problems resulting from people who are drinking and using drugs.

One fan starts yelling because he does not have a ticket and is not let into the concert, then runs into traffic and almost gets hit. Marcella, who is the sergeant in charge of traffic control, stops and arrests him. Several of his friends start yelling loudly to stir up the other concertgoers. At this point, Marcella can order her officers to approach the others and threaten them with arrest if they continue to be drunk and disorderly, but this could backfire and stimulate riotous behavior. It could also, however, stop the disturbance before it can escalate. In this case, Marcella must call on her experience and read the situation's mix of variables to properly exercise discretion and maintain order.

In practice, successful order maintenance depends largely on officers' experiences and the outcomes they wish to attain in particular circumstances. To ensure that residents are satisfied, the police must understand the norms of that the community. For serious incidents that community members do not want to see repeated, the solution might require an arrest. Less serious matters might result in an informal sanction such as a warning. Problems arise when police encounter unclear areas, such as domestic violence cases where both parties are at fault, or when the community's wishes prove to be unpredictable because of shaky police-community relations.

Law Enforcement Law enforcement can be defined as the police's legal application of the criminal code. The process of enforcing laws is not as clear-cut as might be expected. There are more laws in the criminal code than can be routinely enforced, including outdated statutes that prohibit unusual acts such as spitting on sidewalks or harming birds in cemeteries. One part of the police role is determining which laws are still necessary and should be enforced and which should be ignored.

Online

Remember, one of your best resources is **www.policing.glencoe.com**

Police tend to enforce laws on the basis of what they perceive as organizational priorities. They determine these priorities through 1) agency directives, 2) what they learn from peers, and 3) what their supervisors prefer. At some agencies, supervisors hold monthly recaps of officers' arrest numbers, in which felony arrests earn a much higher point count than do misdemeanor arrests. Because these recaps play a large role in performance evaluations and promotions, they heavily influence officers.

As with other functions in the police role, police often tailor their enforcement actions to community norms. For example, the business community may have certain expectations of officers. For example, shoplifting actions may routinely result in arrests if that is what retailers want.

Criminal Apprehension Criminal apprehension is the arrest of suspects. For the majority of crimes committed, an offender is not apprehended. For example, only about one in five serious crimes will result in arrest, although the arrest rate is much greater for violent crimes than for property crimes. It is much lower overall for less serious crimes.

The apprehension of offenders is largely conducted by first responders, who are usually patrol officers. The probability of arrest is proportionate to the information obtained by patrol officers on their arrival at a crime scene.[12] Detectives can play a crucial role in the apprehension of offenders when a case requires their resourcefulness, zeal, and perseverance to find needed evidence. The differences in quality among investigators can vary greatly and can be the deciding factor in whether a suspect is finally arrested. The apprehension of offenders may also depend on the results of the initial case classification by case screeners. Some police departments classify cases according to solvability factors, which commonly include the presence of an eyewitness, the availability of fingerprints, and whether a suspect has been seen or named.[13]

A key to criminal apprehension is productive teamwork between the officers and detectives. The degree to which patrol officers and detectives interact and train together will in many cases determine the quality of crime scene investigations and resultant suspect apprehension. Detectives should explain to field officers their information needs, and field officers should strive to comply with their requests. For example, if detectives are finding that officers are returning less evidence than seems to be available, they should provide pointers on how to find and collect more types of evidence.

Proactive citizen action can also improve apprehension rates. For example, teaching citizens techniques for detecting clues at a crime scene will increase their usefulness as witnesses and can help the investigator build a much clearer picture of the circumstances of a crime. This will lead to higher arrest rates and more solved cases.

Public Service Public service activities are nonpolicing duties that are performed by officers on an as-needed basis. They routinely include the following:

- Searching for lost persons
- Assisting stranded motorists
- Delivering death notifications
- Providing escorts
- Checking on the welfare of persons at the request of relatives or other concerned persons

These duties fall to the police primarily because of their 24-hour availability and because they are the most visible representatives of government. Also, there is the potential for some public service calls to evolve into criminal matters. For example, a missing person could prove to be a victim of

The Role of Detectives

Except in the case of very serious crimes such as murder, rape, or major robberies, detectives do not respond to the crime scene. Usually, their investigation depends on the physical evidence and the witness or victim statements gathered by patrol officers. Thus, unless photos are taken, the details of a crime scene can be established for future reference only through carefully documented evidence collected by field officers.

◀ **Plain-Clothes Detective** One of the many roles of law enforcement is to blend in with the population in order to make arrests. *How important do you think this role is?*

homicide, kidnapping, or suicide. In such cases, early investigation by police could greatly increase the chances that the offender will be caught.

Providing public services will probably continue to occupy a substantial portion of police officers' time. On one hand, this is good for police-community relations because it contributes to the quality of life in a community and gives officers a chance to build positive experiences with citizens. On the other hand, police must stay aware of budgetary limitations. Because police departments usually have limited staff, they may someday no longer be able to be all things to all people. In such cases, police departments will have to make hard choices and identify those services that are considered essential to the police mission alone.[14]

Traffic Control The police are the leading public safety agency involved in **traffic control**, which involves performing three types of traffic safety functions:

- Enforcement
- Accident investigation
- Parking and intersection control

traffic control Three types of traffic safety functions: enforcement, accident investigation, and parking and intersection control; the first two are performed by the police.

Although parking and intersection control has been successfully reassigned to other municipal agencies, enforcement and investigative functions have remained primary police responsibilities.

The use of motor vehicles by criminals while committing crimes, such as robberies and drug transportation, forces police to be involved in traffic matters. Police can apprehend criminal offenders who are at large in vehicles or who attempt to avoid apprehension by fleeing in vehicles. They are also the best-equipped and best-trained public servants to handle encounters that might develop as a result of traffic stops, such as belligerent drunk drivers, highly aggravated traffic violators, and persons with outstanding warrants. Finally, their investigative skills are helpful in accident investigations because many traffic accidents involve criminal acts such as driving under the influence, hit-and-run, and vehicular manslaughter. Although some police functions are being civilianized to save money, this is why sworn police are always required to perform traffic stops.

Another important issue regarding traffic control is the use of profiling, which is a form of stereotyping in which drivers are judged to be safe or dangerous based on certain characteristics. Racial profiling, where officers use race as a screening factor, has created serious harm to police-community relations. For example, the New Jersey State Police have faced numerous complaints and negative publicity due to their alleged use of racial profiling, which has undermined the public's view of their many helpful efforts.

4.2 Self Check

1. Name the different functional roles of police.
2. What are the factors for and against police playing a greater public service role?

POLICING *Online*

Check your answers at
www.policing.glencoe.com

4.3 Police Responsibilities

By enforcing the laws, police play a vital role in shaping a community's quality of life. The police possess nearly unlimited authority to affect people's liberty through their discretionary powers. The consequences of their actions or inaction, therefore, can be life changing.

State and local governments assign a wide range of tasks to police agencies, mostly without logical planning about the goals and priorities of these responsibilities. Several factors determine the range of tasks and also shape the many roles played by police. The four primary factors involved in delegating these tasks are as follows:

1. Legislative mandates
2. Lawful use of force
3. Investigative capabilities
4. Round-the-clock availability[15]

Legislative Mandates

A **legislative mandate** is a legal requirement that is enacted by government lawmakers, such as three strikes laws that require three-time felony offenders to receive life sentences. A municipality's statutes and ordinances define the duties of the police, which are often defined in phrases such as "to enforce the law" or "to maintain the peace."

The Police Procedure box below gives an example of a city charter's definition of the police role. This broad language provides a legal basis for much of what officers do, and it also provides police with indirect authority for a number of other functions simply because they relate to enforcing the criminal law.[16]

legislative mandate A legal requirement that is enacted by government lawmakers, such as three strikes laws that require three-time felony offenders to receive life sentences.

Lawful Use of Force

Because the police are given authority to enforce the laws, they are the primary coercive force in society. What distinguishes police from citizens is the police officer's ability to resolve problem situations that citizens cannot or will not resolve by themselves. This is the authority to use nonnegotiable coercive force,[17] which means that police may in certain situations use force against another person's will.

Police Procedure

Policing Roles in Statutory Law

To avoid confusion, many jurisdictions provide a written definition of the police role. Typical statutory language can be seen here in the Los Angeles City Charter, Sections 198 and 200:

> The police department shall have the power and duty to enforce the penal provisions of this charter, of the ordinances of the city and of the laws of the state and nation. In the discharge of said powers and duties, the members of said department shall have the powers and duties of peace officers as defined by state laws. The chief of police shall suppress all riots, disturbances, and breaches of the peace, and to that end may call on any person for assistance. He or she may pursue and arrest, within the limits of the city, any person fleeing from justice from any part of the state, and shall forthwith bring all persons arrested before a judge of the proper court for trial or examination. He or she may receive and execute any proper authority for the arrest and detention of criminals fleeing or escaping from other places or states.

Critical Thinking Can you think of anything else that could be included in a statutory definition of the police role? Explain.

SOURCE: Adapted from Los Angeles City Attorney's Office, Los Angeles City Charter (Los Angeles: City of Los Angeles, 1998).

Continuum of Force Police use force to affect citizens' conduct. Officers are trained to employ a **continuum of force**, which is an escalation or de-escalation of force in response to a suspect's actions. An officer should begin by asking a citizen to obey his or her commands and refrain as long as possible from drawing a weapon.

continuum of force An escalation or de-escalation of force in response to a suspect's actions.

The standards for acceptable use of force have been established through court rulings in specific cases where the police used force. Rulings regarding the use of force commonly state that "officers should use no more force than is necessary and reasonable."[18] In *Tennessee v. Garner* (1985), the U.S. Supreme Court found that police unnecessarily used deadly force against a fleeing suspect. The Court used this case to set clear guidelines for the legal use of deadly force.[19] (See Figure 4.3 on page 139)

Four years later, in the case of *Graham v. Connor* (1989), the Court effectively set the standard for judging whether force employed by an officer was reasonable. In that case, the reasonableness of a police officer's use of force "would be judged from the perspective of a reasonable officer on the scene, rather than with the 20/20 vision of hindsight."[20] This means that courts must consider how much the officer could be expected to know about the situation at the time that he or she decided to use force, rather than what is discovered afterward.

Controversy Regarding the Use of Force The subject of use of force by police officers is inherently controversial and has been the subject of in-depth review since the infamous Rodney King beating incident in 1991. In 1994, Congress enacted the Violent Crime Control Act, which required the U.S. Attorney General to collect and study data on the use of excessive force by police. Since then, significant research has "shed light on the factors involved in police-citizen encounters resulting in police uses of force."[21] Two promising strategies for controlling force include 1) strengthening officers' capacities to exercise self-restraint through better training and resources and 2) shrinking the outer limits of discretion to use force, particularly deadly force, through laws, policies, training, equitable disciplinary systems, and the reshaping of police peer pressure.[22]

Investigative Capabilities

criminal investigation The capacity to sift through complex bodies of evidence in order to establish the facts of a case.

Of all the skills that police officers cultivate, **criminal investigation**—the capacity to sift through complex situations in order to verify or establish facts—is among the most important. Criminal investigation is required not only in situations in which a crime is alleged to have occurred but also in numerous everyday occurrences in which something is awry but the officer is still unsure of the exact nature of the situation.

Figure 4.3

Uses of Force Continuum

Each circumstance in a use of force situation is known as a *variable*, and each can work both ways in use-of-force situations. A variable may justify an increase in force in one instance, but may require a de-escalation of force in another. Also, the use of force is often influenced by several variables that are known as the *totality of circumstances*. Some factors affecting the totality of circumstances are:

Officer/Subject Factors	Special Circumstances
Number of Officer(s)/Subject(s)	Proximity to a Firearm
Size/Age/Strength Difference	Position of Disadvantage
Skill Difference	Special Knowledge
Mental State	Imminent Danger

According to the U.S. Department of Justice, the levels of force that should be included in an agency's continuum of force are:

- Verbal commands
- Use of hands
- Chemical agents
- Baton or other impact weapon
- Canine
- Deadly force
- Less-than-lethal projectiles

SOURCE: Adapted from Metropolitan Nashville Police Department Citizen's Police Academy, "Uses of Force Continuum," accessed online at http://www.telalink.net/~police/citizen/kick.html and U.S. Department of Justice, "Use of Force: Continuum of Force," accessed online at http://www.ojp.usdoj.gov/lawenforcement/policeintegrity/chapter1.htm on Dec. 13, 2001

An experienced officer's intuitive sense in such situations undoubtedly develops from his or her mental cataloging of facts, which are accumulated through seeing and investigating countless crime scenes. For example, Vince is a sergeant who is frequently called as a first responder in serious crime cases. When he arrives in response to a couple who says that their child has been kidnapped, he immediately starts to analyze their body language, tones of voice, and what they are telling him. Acting on a hunch, he questions them separately and finds that their stories do not match. At the end of the preliminary investigation, he confides to the lead detective that he considers the parents to be the primary suspects in the kidnap of their child.

The police are also the record keepers for confidential criminal history information. In recent years, the police have adopted technological aids such as automated fingerprint identification systems (AFIS), which can quickly sort through vast numbers of fingerprints, and modus operandi (MO) correlation systems, which link crimes by their similarities. A **modus operandi**, or MO, is a unique identifying action or characteristic of a crime that can identify a particular criminal's involvement in that crime. These automated resources greatly increase police investigative capabilities.

modus operandi A unique identifying action or characteristic of a crime that can identify a particular criminal's involvement in that crime.

► **Report Writing** One of the most unglorified aspects of policing is report writing. *Why do you think that part of the job is crucially important?*

Round-the-Clock Availability

The police are generally recognized as the only government agency that operates 24 hours a day, seven days a week, and that has the capability to respond quickly to wide-ranging requests for assistance. Round-the-clock availability takes on special significance because many of the government and private agencies providing public welfare and utility services are only open during normal business hours. Because of this, their staffers are often unavailable when the need for them may be greatest. Many police precinct lobbies serve as way stations for persons seeking admission to missions or shelters that limit their admission hours. Similarly, it is often the police who erect barriers at street hazards, such as fallen tree branches or missing sewer covers, on weekends or after public works agencies have closed.

Citizens turn to the police for immediate responses to their pressing problems, regardless of whether the police fit their need.[23] Through community policing and its emphasis on reducing the environmental factors that cause crime, the police have encouraged the public to come to them to address quality-of-life issues.

4.3 Self Check

1. What is the legal basis for much of what police do?
2. What factors require police to perform functions other than law enforcement?

POLICING *Online*

Check your answers at
www.policing.glencoe.com

4.4 Operational Role Enactment

The social conduct exhibited by a police officer is called **role enactment**. Researchers have identified four factors that shape the police officer's role:

1. Role expectations
2. Role acquisition
3. Organizational goals
4. Multiple-role phenomenon[24]

An officer's thorough understanding of his or her role is extremely important. Most police academies rarely spend more than a couple of hours on the subject, even though it can affect an officer's actions, use of force, approach to policing, and career advancement. Countless internal investigations have shown that an officer's failure to understand his or her role can lead to police misconduct. Indisputably, role enactment is every bit as important as any other area of the police role. Far too many police officers have positioned themselves in nightmarish predicaments through role failures, often due to their notion that they are owed something because they perform tasks that the majority of citizens cannot or will not do. They rationalize and justify behavior that would be unacceptable if done by a member of the public at large. Such behavior may include violating traffic rules without cause, stealing drug money, and planting incriminating evidence on persons suspected of dealing drugs.

role enactment The social conduct exhibited by a police officer, shaped by four factors: role expectations, role acquisition, organizational goals, and multiple-role phenomenon.

Role Expectations

Role expectations are the rights, privileges, duties, and obligations of any occupant of a social position, as perceived by those occupying other positions in the social structure. To understand role expectations, an officer must take into account the role behaviors of occupants of other positions and understand how his or her behavior fits in. A group of people who perform different roles together are known as a **role set**. For a police officer, the role set includes peers, supervisors, subordinates, the court system, suspects, victims, witnesses, and citizens. Within this role set, an officer is expected to perform actions in specified ways.

The best example of this obligation is the officer's response to procedural law, which is the type of law that governs how police procedures should be performed. For example, if an officer fails to lawfully perform a seizure of evidence, this can result in the exclusion of the evidence seized and the release of a criminal suspect. In such a scenario, the role expectation owed to the crime victim, as well as to the prosecutor, has been jumbled.

role expectations The rights, privileges, duties, and obligations of any occupant of a social position, as perceived by those occupying other positions in the social structure.

role set A group of people who perform different roles together.

Role Acquisition

role acquisition The process of learning one's role, learning one's role set, and knowing how to select a role from one's inventory that is appropriate to the situation at hand.

As an officer becomes knowledgeable about the expectations of others within the role set, he or she acquires the ability to initiate behavior appropriate for a given situation and actor. This process is **role acquisition**, which is the process of learning one's role, learning one's role set, and knowing how to select a role from one's inventory that is appropriate to the situation at hand. The greater the number of roles that an officer can develop, the better prepared he or she is to meet the broad, urgent demands of the job.

Expanding one's inventory of roles is like expanding one's foreign language skills. If an officer can cultivate such versatility, he or she will be able to operate more efficiently in more circumstances. Because police are trained to look for anything unusual or suspicious, their training may prove unworkable in a majority of police-citizen interactions, which require a less confrontational approach. To the extent that officers can expand their role set array and adapt effectively, these interactions can become more productive. For example, an officer who attempts to perform community policing with body language, eye contact, or questioning that seems aggressive will fail in generating the public's trust. Indeed, such an approach can backfire if the public sees such behavior as rude or intrusive.

Organizational Goals

The impact of organizational goals on role enactment can best be determined by officers' perceptions of what is a proper service of the police organization. A large number of police see themselves as crime fighters rather than service providers. If this misconception develops, it can erode vital community links.

In application, the role conception prevalent in a department provides the general framework from which organization goals and citizen demands for services are evaluated as being legitimate or irrelevant. For example, a police agency may only pay lip service to citizens' complaints about chronic disorderly street corner conduct if the agency is focused on dealing with major crimes such as murder, rape, and robbery.

Training and Service Orientation Much of the confusion about the need for police to be client-centered service providers begins at the police academy. Most academies do not provide a sufficient degree of instruction on police role definition, especially the part relating to service orientation. If addressed at all, providing social services is shown as an obligation of police only because of their 24-hour availability. In other words, the service dimension is viewed as something police have gotten stuck with by default, which can encourage officers to resent it.

The scant attention dedicated to role definition in academies does not focus on the daily service and problem-solving activities that make up most of an officer's workload. Instead, academies consistently highlight the danger in police work and the need to remember safety practices. The crime-fighting emphasis is frequently established very early in the recruitment process by police agencies' recruitment brochures, which typically depict police officers engaged in perilous armed confrontations with criminals. This continues through the police selection process and academy training. Although it prepares officers for some circumstances, it leaves them completely unprepared for others.

The Opportunity for Service Work When some officers are given service-oriented work, they complain that they would rather be doing real police work—without realizing that social service *is* real police work. The reality is that police have always been expected to deal with a variety of problems. Police should see service duties as important opportunities to interact with citizens on a positive rather than negative basis. For example, if officers can help a motorist who is locked out of his or her car or can provide directions to a family on an outing, they create and maintain favorable public support and appreciation for the police.

The Need for Public Support The public's support and understanding are essential if police are to carry out their duties and responsibilities effectively. The prevention of crime is undoubtedly not just a police responsibility but also a function that can be performed effectively only with widespread community support. With the shift to the community policing philosophy during the 1980s and 1990s, police management, political leadership, and community activists have helped police departments develop service-oriented mission statements that create a clear sense of purpose and direction.

At the same time, police department policy statements that were revised during the 1980s and 1990s emphasized the complex and diverse nature of the police role in society. For role enactment to focus on the service mission, a police department's organizational rewards and sanctions processes must be in sync. Police administrators must ensure that officers who go the extra mile in furthering their service mission are duly rewarded, and officers who avoid their service responsibilities should be appropriately counseled or sanctioned.

Multiple-Role Phenomenon

The fourth variable that influences an officer's role enactment is termed **multiple-role phenomenon**, which consists of role conflict, role ambiguity, role strain, or any combination of these.

A lack of role understanding by the police can have devastating effects. The worst-case results are death and grievous bodily injury. When the Abner Louima beating occurred, experts realized it was the result of two problems: the blatant abandonment of an appropriate role and a failure to fully understand the role and what was expected from them.

Time and time again, a failure to understand the correct, ethical police role is the cause for countless allegations of misconduct. It is clear that role enactment is every bit as important as any other subject area to be examined in the context of the police role.

What can police management do to prevent role misunderstanding, especially among officers who work in especially high-stress assignments?

multiple-role phenomenon
A variable that influences an officer's role enactment; consists of role conflict, role ambiguity, role strain, or any combination of these.

Role Conflict When an officer encounters two sets of expectations that are inconsistent with each other, **role conflict** arises. Perhaps the most frequent form of role conflict occurs when police officers trained in aggressive policing practices are called on to implement community service functions that rely heavily on open interpersonal communication. Without any training in how to shift between these roles, an officer must rely on his or her social skills and use of discretion.

Frequently in such situations, the pivotal factor that determines whether the officer can resolve the role conflict is the attitude of the citizen. For example, when an officer with a law enforcement orientation is called to deal with a violent parent-child dispute, he or she will probably not be able to defuse the situation if both parties act in an angry and threatening way. However, if the family sets aside their dispute and acts in a peaceful and helpful manner toward the officer, it might be enough to sway him or her to find an appropriate resolution. As another example, an officer must remember his or her role in the enforcement of drug laws. When he or she is in an aggressive crime-fighting role, it can be hard to remember that the same measure of civility is owed the suspected (but not convicted) drug dealer as is owed a respected member of society such as a teacher or doctor.

Role Ambiguity It has long been recognized that **role ambiguity**, which is any uncertainty about one's role, goes along with the police role. This was first noted in 1972 by the American Bar Association (ABA), which developed and published an extensive listing of suggested policing standards. The ABA did this in the belief that greater understanding of the police function would have a direct effect on the systemwide quality of criminal justice administration.

The ABA emphasized that "the police in this country have suffered from the fact that their role has been misunderstood, the fact that demands made upon them have been so unrealistic, and the fact that the public has been so ambivalent about the function of police." It added,

> One of the major complexities in police operations stems from the fact that the police have many responsibilities that extend beyond those which they have in the criminal process; that it is no longer possible to examine police functioning in a meaningful fashion without viewing the police as an agency housing a multitude of varied duties and responsibilities.[28]

Today, role ambiguity has increased further with the growth of community policing. Community policing is a police-community partnership in

role conflict Conflict that arises when an officer encounters two sets of expectations that are inconsistent with each other.

role ambiguity Any uncertainty about one's role; goes along with the police role.

which crime problems are jointly identified, prioritized, and resolved. It requires officers to take on new roles and features a strong community partnership role, which makes the definition of officers' roles a complex—but fully participative—process. This means that officers' roles are now understood to be more complex than before, but many parties—police, politicians, and citizens—help provide these definitions.

Community policing addresses the three most fundamental questions about the police:

1. Who decides what the police role in a community will be?
2. What is that role?
3. What competencies are required to fulfill that role?[29]

Police agencies must make ongoing efforts to minimize role ambiguity, whether its origin is the natural complexity of the police role or results from new policing philosophies such as community policing.

Role Strain Often police officers experience **role strain**, in which their role is limited by what they are authorized to do. Role strain episodes arise from situations in which, regardless of police actions, the outcome will probably fall short of citizen expectations. This is simply because meeting some citizens' needs is beyond the capabilities of the police system, not the fault of the individual officer. One of the distinctive characteristics of role strain is that there is almost no way the officer can resolve it.

role strain In which an officer's role is limited by what he or she is authorized to do.

One important distinction to make is between problems that are truly unsolvable and problems that merely appear to be unsolvable because finding a solution can be difficult. Real cases of role strain can be immensely frustrating. For example, in some cases detectives cannot solve cases because of limits to crime-solving technology or an inability to locate witnesses. Such cases are then closed until a new option arrives. For example, DNA technology has enabled investigators to reopen and solve cases that were previously unsolvable.

Many cases of role strain can be resolved, however, and officers should view these situations as challenges. Officers can overcome traditional police behaviors that have not worked in the past and can change police practices to address this better. One classic example of this is a family disturbance call. Such calls have a high potential for violent confrontation and are difficult to permanently resolve, which explains the average officer's dislike for such calls.

An officer skilled in communication and problem solving can resolve these calls by providing the victim with a shelter or suggesting a self-help approach such as counseling. In some states, those who commit domestic

▶ **Policing the Community**
This can include delicate situations such as domestic violence cases where officers may have to question upset victims and children.
Do you think officers should receive specific training to handle such calls?

violence are separated from their partners and arrested automatically. Those who commit child abuse can be separated from their children. Both types of offenders can face criminal charges, and domestic violence victims can sue their partners in civil court. Therefore, the seemingly unsolvable problem of family violence can have solutions. The challenge for officers is to decide which solutions are likely to work and which are available.

Perhaps the worst effect of strain is when some officers respond to a seeming no-win situation by distancing themselves from the concerned citizens. This can have an enormous negative impact on the citizen-police relationship. Therefore, officers involved in role strain situations must consciously strive to avoid responding to these incidents by distancing themselves. A firm and open manner can often be the most effective in potential strain situations. Officers should demonstrate concern for the disputants and provide referral information if the situation does not warrant an arrest or other direct police action.

4.4 Self Check

1. What are the four factors that shape the police officer's role?
2. What are the differences between role conflict and role strain?

POLICING *Online*
Check your answers at
www.policing.glencoe.com

Policing Typologies

Perhaps the most common type of research on the police role has been the attempt to identify different types of policing styles. Styles are found by observing the attitudes and behaviors of an individual officer: His or her beliefs about the role of the police, the most important police tasks, and manner of interaction with citizens will indicate the policing style that he or she follows.[30]

A number of typologies have been produced for the study of police cultures and management. John Broderick created a typology that has been widely used. He identified four categories of police officers:

1. **Enforcers** Enforcers place a high value on social order and on keeping society safe, while giving due process and individual rights a relatively low value. Officers with this orientation have little tolerance for habitual drug users or for those who show no respect to the police. Conversely, enforcers exhibit compassion for persons they see as merely down on their luck, such as the homeless and the elderly.

2. **Idealists** Idealists place a high value on due process and individual rights while preserving social order and keeping the peace. These officers wholeheartedly embrace the Law Enforcement Code of Ethics. They can be prone to suffer frustration from a lack of adherence to professional standards by fellow officers.

3. **Optimists** Optimists do not define their jobs as simply keeping society safe. They recognize that much of police work does not involve crime fighting and that service obligations occupy much of a police officer's workday. Optimists enjoy helping people and doing what they can to improve community conditions.

4. **Realists** Like optimists, realists also recognize that much of police work does not involve crime fighting and that service obligations occupy much of a police officer's workday. Realists enjoy helping people less than optimists do.[31]

Another typology, created by James Q. Wilson in 1968, is the one most commonly used today. Wilson's typology is less individualized but is highly instructive in illustrating the impact of a prevailing and preferred agency style on the delivery of policing services. Wilson identified three policing styles:

1. The **watchman style** centers on order maintenance. Criminal violations are evaluated in terms of their immediate consequences rather than what the law says about them. The watchman style was most typical of policing's political era (1840–1920).

watchman style A police style that centers on order maintenance; criminal violations are evaluated in terms of their immediate consequences rather than what the law says about them.

legalistic style A style of policing that uses uniform enforcement of codified law with a minimal exercise of discretion.

service style A style of policing that emphasizes enhancement of the quality of life, and informal sanctions are employed in conformance with broad community norms.

2. The **legalistic style** of policing is uniform enforcement of codified law with minimal exercise of discretion. The legalistic style was characteristic of the reform era, which ran from approximately 1920 to 1980.
3. The **service style** of policing emphasizes enhancement of the quality of life, and informal sanctions are employed in conformity with broad community norms. Today's service style is most typical of police agencies that successfully practice community policing.[32]

Broderick's and Wilson's typologies can be used together. Broderick's can be applied to individual officers, and Wilson's to group styles. Just as all of Broderick's typologies can be operative at once within an agency, so can Wilson's. It is also possible for a single agency to have different groups of officers practicing different styles. Often this is a function of local demographics, which require different approaches by officers. For example, research has shown that the service style often works best in relatively homogeneous and middle-class communities. The challenge for police administrators is to match individual policing styles with the communities in which they will be most suitable.[33]

The Watchman Style

In some communities, when dealing with minor crimes, the police focus on maintaining order by dispersing or warning the offenders rather than by taking formal police action. Wilson labeled this the watchman style, a term that accurately described American municipal police before the mid-nineteenth century. All police display this style by showing concern for order maintenance some of the time, but in a few places this style is the operating code of the department.

Under the watchman style, the emphasis is on keeping order in public places. Criminal violations are evaluated more by their immediate and personal consequences (particularly their impact on public order) than by what the law says about them, although felonies are treated more seriously. Administrators influence officers to use their discretion to ignore many common minor violations, particularly traffic and juvenile offenses. Vice offenses are treated as problems only when standards of public order are violated. For example, if an illegal gambling club starts to attract large and unruly crowds of people, order maintenance officers who had previously ignored it will probably start arresting the club's employees and guests.

The watchman style invests the individual police officer with considerable discretionary authority. This can prove to be healthy or problematic for a community's citizens, depending on the judgment of the concerned officer. It is essential that officers using the watchman style be closely monitored by field supervisors who can compare various officers' decisions and create a window of appropriate discretionary practices. Feedback from this process serves to inform officers about the appropriate use of discretion.

This style of policing makes considerable use of informal police intervention such as persuasion and threats. Critics feel that police use this style too often in high-crime communities, even in situations involving a fair amount of violence, because they care less about addressing the causes of crime in such communities. Others, however, point out that by providing order maintenance, police create a stronger sense of community than previously existed. In doing so, they preserve some normalcy in high-crime communities.

Police departments that employ a watchman style will not have identical standards of public order and morality. The quality of law enforcement depends not only on how individual police make judgments but also on the socioeconomic status of the citizens in question, law enforcement standards that are formally or informally set by the political systems, and the special interests and concerns of the police chief. In these cities, the patrol officer is expected to ignore minor crimes but to get tough where it is important. For example, the police may assume a parental posture toward juvenile offenses by choosing to scold a juvenile offender or turn the juvenile over to his or her parents for discipline.[34] On the other hand, an adult committing the same offense may be taken more seriously and arrested. Another example of order maintenance can involve the use of discretion through community mandates. Vagrants may be forced by police to move from a fashionable part of a city, but their presence may be tolerated within that city's slum.

The Legalistic Style

In some departments, police management requires officers to handle commonplace situations as if they were matters of law enforcement rather than order maintenance. This means that officers are encouraged to assume a law enforcement posture by stopping, frisking, and arresting suspects whenever possible. This produces many arrests and citations. When police are called by citizens to intervene in a matter, they will likely make an arrest or urge the person to sign a complaint. Under the legalistic style, citizen arrests are facilitated, prosecution of shoplifters is encouraged, juveniles are handled formally, and drunks are arrested "for their own protection."[35]

Agencies that emphasize the legalistic style commonly have elaborate systems for tracking officer productivity. An officer's contribution to agency goals is assessed through his or her recap, which is a monthly compilation of enforcement efforts that includes the following:

1. Arrests
2. Traffic citations
3. Field interviews
4. Warrant checks
5. Calls handled

It also can include countless other activities such as how many times an officer has used force. Figure 4.4 on page 154 shows a typical use of force report. This bean counting affects officers' semiannual performance evaluation reports. In turn, these reports are a primary decision-making factor for the promotional process.

A legalistic agency measures its officers' success by their ability to invoke the formal legal process to handle crime problems. Officers' informal efforts at affecting crime, such as by providing services or raising the quality of life, are formally unnoticed. It is important to note that strict adherence to this style may often be the result of strenuous efforts to wean police employees from tendencies to under-enforce the law.

The legalistic style can yield both benefits and deficits. Clearly, it provides for uniformity in enforcement. It does provide for discretion, although not nearly as much as the watchman style. In addition, officer productivity can be easily assessed in this style. However, a problem with this style is its de-emphasis on the underlying dynamics of crime issues. Officers' preventive efforts, or any other efforts to uncover the root causes of crimes, are not readily trackable. Therefore, they do not become recappable items and are usually ignored.

The Service Style

In some communities, the police treat all requests for either law enforcement or order maintenance seriously but are less likely to respond by making an arrest or imposing formal sanctions. They intervene frequently, but not formally. This service style is often found in stable, homogeneous, middle-class communities where citizens agree on the need for public order and where there is no crime problem that warrants a legalistic style. In such an environment, the police see their chief responsibility as protecting public order against the minor and occasional threats posed by unruly youth and outsiders.

The service style applies a supply-and-demand philosophy to policing. Community members expect their officers to treat them somewhat deferentially and courteously, much as local merchants and public officials would treat them. Serious police matters such as residential burglaries, violent crimes, or teenage drug use are expected to be taken seriously, and the investigation of such incidents is often handled by specialized police units. With minor infractions, arrests are avoided when possible, but police will frequently use informal sanctions. For example, juveniles might be taken to headquarters for counseling or visited in their homes for lectures.[36]

The contemporary form of this style focuses on enhancement of the quality of life for all community members. Service-oriented agencies are more likely to take advantage of community resources, such as drug treatment programs and family counseling, than are departments that emphasize another style.[37]

4.5 Self Check ?

1. Describe the three police types defined by James Q. Wilson.
2. What are the four categories of police officers identified by John Broderick?

POLICING *Online*

Check your answers at
www.policing.glencoe.com

4.6 Emerging Roles of the Police

Multiple factors shape the emerging role of the police. Among the most significant are the following:

- **Research** Since the 1970s, police researchers have conducted extensive studies that have proven exceptionally informative. The Police Foundation, Police Executive Research Forum (PERF), Bureau of Justice Statistics (BJS), and the National Institute of Justice (NIJ) have made important breakthroughs in policing knowledge. Most important, interdisciplinary partnerships are expected to continue to flourish as we move further into the twenty-first century. The NIJ has established partnerships with both the National Institute of Health and the Centers for Disease Control and Prevention to proactively attack root causes of violence.[38] The public health perspective, unlike the typical law enforcement perspective, is largely preventive and targets both potential offenders and victims through educational and enforcement programs. This approach has proven effective through seatbelt use campaigns, anti-smoking education, and AIDS prevention programs. The same protocol is being examined for application to the subject of handgun violence.
- **Technology** Technology is revolutionizing police work. Technology has altered nearly every aspect of policing, and it continues to fos-ter change at an ever-increasing rate. One impressive

example of technology was New York City's reduction in its crime rate during the mid-1990s. In this case, several factors (including community policing) helped reduce the overall rate, but it was the use of CompStat, a computerized statistics system, that provided the crucial data needed to pinpoint crime hotspots for targeted actions.[39]

- **Accountability** Police accountability, in terms of cost and effectiveness, has become a high priority of the public. Citizens expect quality service and an appropriate return on their tax dollars. The call for police accountability has been further fueled by the increasingly persistent and serious nature of the crime problem. Part of the reason for the rise in community policing has been the need for stronger police-community relations, which help improve accountability.[40]

Community Policing and Holistic Policing

Two new police styles are community policing and holistic policing. Community policing has become an increasingly popular alternative to the apparent failure of traditional policing to deal effectively with street crime, especially violent crimes and drug trafficking. Although community policing is defined in varying ways, it has gained widespread acceptance.[41] It affects the police role because officers are empowered by agency chiefs to enlist and mobilize community members to eliminate crime and the conditions that cause it.

holistic policing Provision of a full array of community treatment regimens to attack crime conditions.

Holistic policing devotes a wider array of resources to crime problems than community policing does. It represents the natural evolution of community policing to full-spectrum services provision. It seeks to attack the conditions that cause crime through a variety of treatments.

MYTH	FACT
Police should prevent crime on their own. After all, that's their job.	A strong police-community partnership is an essential component of crime prevention. To fully exercise the police role, the police must activate the community's support. Neighborhood Watch and other well-established crime prevention programs rely on appropriate public participation, and their benefits can be enormous.

Highway Patrol Officer

Job Description

I ensure the safety of motor vehicle traffic in this area. I deal with collisions, enforce rules of traffic, assist people who are stranded on the highway because of a disabled vehicle, or a problem with tires. I help them deal with what is usually a stressful time.

Speed is the number one problem, and we always try to slow people down. I also deal with drivers who are intoxicated and people who do not have their children in the proper car restraint. I usually work an 8-hour shift. Out of that, I might spend two or three hours on accident investigation, one hour processing an apprehended driver, and maybe another hour promoting safety.

Trooper A.L. Hill, Fayettevi

We run clinics where we inspect car seats for children and teach parents how to properly install and adjust them. We also have classes where we teach people how to handle aggressive drivers (we recommend avoiding confrontation and eye contact, and just staying clear of these drivers).

The most challenging part of this job is definitely when we deal with death in a motor vehicle accident, particularly when the victim is young and engaged in alcohol or drug consumption, and we have to go and tell their parents that they are never coming home. The rewarding part is interacting with people who are glad that you are there, who thank you for what you are doing.

I would advise people interested in this career to be well-rounded, to be disciplined, stay out of trouble, and not experiment with drugs.

Education

I was involved in ROTC in high school and in college, and I always liked being in an environment of discipline. I also like helping people. I went to college and majored in criminal justice with a minor in sociology.

Follow-Up Why do you think it is important to have a well-rounded personality for this profession?

Figure 4.4

Use of Force Report

A. Incident Information

Date	Time	Day of week	Location	**INCIDENT NUMBER**

Type of Incident

☐ Crime in progress ☐ Domestic ☐ Other dispute ☐ Suspicious person ☐ Traffic stop
☐ Other (specify)

B. Officer Information

Name (Last, First, Middle)	Badge#	Sex	Race	Age	Injured Y/N	Killed Y/N
Rank Duty assignment	Years of service		On-Duty Y/N		Uniform Y/N	

C1. Subject 1 (List only the person who was the subject of the use of force by the officer listed in Section B.)

Name (Last, First, Middle)	Sex	Race	Age	Weapon	Injured Y/N	Killed Y/N
☐ Under the influence
☐ Other unusual condition (specify)	Arrested Y/N		Charges			

Subject's actions (check all that apply)
☐ Resisted Police Officer control
☐ Physical threat/attack on officer or another
☐ Threaten/attacked officer or another with blunt object
☐ Threatened attacked officer with knife/cutting object
☐ Threatened/attacked officer or another with motor vehicle
☐ Threatened officer with firearm
☐ Fired at officer or another
☐ Other (specify)

Officers use of force toward this subject (check all that apply)
☐ Compliance hold   Firearms Discharge
☐ Hands/fists   ☐ Intentional
☐ Kicks/Feet   ☐ Accidental
☐ Chemical/natural agent
☐ Strike/use baton   Number of Shots Fired_____
   or other object   Number of hits   _____
☐ Canine   (Use 'UNK' if unknown)
☐ Other (specify)

C2. Subject 2 (List only the person who was the subject of the use of force by the officer listed in Section B.)

Name (Last, First, Middle)	Sex	Race	Age	Weapon	Injured Y/N	Killed Y/N
☐ Under the influence
☐ Other unusual condition (specify)	Arrested Y/N		Charges			

Subject's actions (check all that apply)
☐ Resisted Police Officer control
☐ Physical threat/attack on officer or another
☐ Threaten/attacked officer or another with blunt object
☐ Threatened attacked officer with knife/cutting object
☐ Threatened/attacked officer or another with motor vehicle
☐ Threatened officer with firearm
☐ Fired at officer or another
☐ Other (specify)

Officers use of force toward this subject (check all that apply)
☐ Compliance hold   Firearms Discharge
☐ Hands/fists   ☐ Intentional
☐ Kicks/Feet   ☐ Accidental
☐ Chemical/natural agent
☐ Strike/use baton   Number of Shots Fired_____
   or other object   Number of hits   _____
☐ Canine   (Use 'UNK' if unknown)
☐ Other (specify)

If this officer used force against more than two subjects in this incident, attach additional USE OF FORCE REPORTS

Signature:	Date:
Print Supervisor Name:	Supervisor Signature:

Although the police may never assume responsibility for the direct provision of essential social services, as the only agency of social control open 24 hours daily, they must be able to respond to many types of crisis situations. In the future, "police departments could contribute to the overall performance of municipal government, not only to the just and effective operations of the criminal justice system." In other words, police could become "the agency of government responsible for controlling and preventing crime, reducing fear, and supporting both public and private agencies in their important work."[42] This outlook is not unlike the value-added stance being assumed by corporate security departments seeking to contribute to their organization's bottom line.

Online
Remember, one of your best resources is **www.policing.glencoe.com**

The paradigm shift to holistic policing is well under way. In Los Angeles, which has experienced serious police-community relations problems, holistic policing has become the model of choice in the city's transition to community policing. The Los Angeles Police Department has removed an entire layer of bureaucracy to enable quicker access by field commanders to other city service providers. After removing this bureaucratic layer, LAPD Chief of Police Bernard Parks reinforced the agency's commitment to holistic policing by stating,

> For the first time, geographic commanding officers will be our critical link to other city service providers, as well as in the community, to further our efforts toward a more holistic approach to serving our communities. This is a significant first step toward the realization and coordination of a comprehensive multi-agency approach to reducing crime and improving the quality of life in Los Angeles.[43]

The future form and extent of holistic policing are not yet clear. However, the police have set the trend among criminal justice system components in establishing the worth of the concept. For this accomplishment alone, the police deserve a full measure of commendation. It is hoped that the future evolution will prove equally inspirational.

4.6 Self Check
1. What is the general goal of community policing?
2. Describe the philosophy behind holistic policing.

POLICING *Online*
Check your answers at
www.policing.glencoe.com

The Police Role

Summary By Learning Objectives

1. Gain an understanding of the factors and dynamics that influence the police role.

A prerequisite for effective policing is clear understanding by officers of their role. The policies and procedures of police departments play a significant part in creating role concepts for performing an array of policing activities.

An officer must be able to adapt to the expectations of all those within his or her role set, which is made up of citizens, victims, suspects, court parties, coworkers, and others.

Police officers must realize the complexities of their role. In certain situations role strain, role ambiguity, and role conflict may complicate their role enactment. The practice of discretion, exercised through objective review of the facts at hand in consideration of organizational goals, is the key to successfully handling difficult situations.

2. Understand how the police role functions in a democratic society.

As contemporary urban America grows increasingly diverse, conflicting, and competitive, policing and the police role likewise become more complex.

Given these increasing complexities, the police must be ever vigilant in using techniques that maintain order.

This should be done in a manner that not only preserves but also extends the precious values of a democratic society. Police and their departments developed in response to community leaders and citizens who perceived a need for order maintenance. Although responsibilities of police have seldom been clearly defined, police have always been presumed to exist to protect the community and its basic democratic values.

3. Identify the factors that account for the responsibilities given police.

Four factors account for the responsibilities given police:

1. The police are mandated legislatively to enforce the criminal law and to maintain the public peace.
2. The use of force for the resolution of matters involving a violation of criminal law or a breach of the public peace is a power specifically reserved for the police.
3. The police have cultivated exceptional investigative skills and also have direct access to criminal records.
4. Round-the-clock availability results in the police being assigned myriad public service responsibilities.

4. Describe the essential functions performed by typical police agencies.

Although local community characteristics and expectations shape police functional roles, all typical police agencies perform certain essential functions. These essential functions include the following:

- Crime prevention
- Order maintenance
- Law enforcement
- Criminal apprehension
- Public service
- Traffic control

Each of these functions is linked to the goal of creating an environment free of crime and disorder.

5. Distinguish predominant policing styles.

There are two main classifications of types of police officers and styles of policing. Researcher James Broderick found that police officers fall into one of four categories:

- Enforcers
- Idealists
- Optimists
- Realists

Another researcher and author, James Q. Wilson, created a typolopy of styles. The three predominant policing styles are as follows:

1. The watchman style, which is oriented to order maintenance. In this style, enforcement actions occur when standards of public order are violated.
2. The legalistic style, which is oriented to enforcement of the letter of the law.
3. The service style, which typifies contemporary policing and enlists the community to help enhance the quality of life.

6. Identify the emerging roles of the police.

Accountability, research, and technology are the three main concepts that currently shape the emerging role of the police. In response to public focus on the crime problem, police have become both more client centered and more receptive to research findings and computer-aided crime analysis systems.

Community policing, with its empowerment of line officers and its community partnership, is evolving to holistic policing. Holistic policing musters a wide range of community treatments to attack crime problems.

7. Name factors that shape the new role of police.

The two newest policing styles are community policing and holistic policing. Both styles are increasingly popular because they focus on the roots of crime and bring police officers closer to the communities they work in. The main difference between community policing and holistic policing is that the latter uses a much wider variety of resources to combat community problems and crime.

Many other factors influence the emerging new role of police including:

- Research
- Technology
- Accountability

Key Terms

police role (p. 120)
roll call (p. 123)
perimeter (p. 124)
field supervisor (p. 125)
station supervisor (p. 126)
social control (p. 128)
norms (p. 128)
traffic control (p. 135)
legislative mandat (p. 137)
continuum of force (p. 138)
criminal investigation (p. 138)
modus operandi (p. 139)

role enactment (p. 141)
role expectations (p. 141)
role set (p. 141)
role acquisition (p. 142)
multiple-role phenomenon (p. 143)
role conflict (p. 144)
role ambiguity (p. 144)
role strain (p. 145)
watchman style (p. 147)
legalistic style (p. 148)
service style (p. 148)
holistic policing (p. 152)

Questions for Review

1. How do laws function as a type of social norm, and how do they promote social control?

2. What elements in an officer's organizational environment influence an officer's role acquisition and role enactment?

3. Explain the differences between role expectations, role acquisition, and role enactment.

4. What are the elements of the multiple-role phenomenon?

5. Explain why police should expand their role inventories.

6. Why is the use of force such a controversial subject?

7. What are the pros and cons of the watchman style of policing?

8. Explain how the legalistic style assesses an officer's achievement of agency goals.

9. Which policing style typifies contemporary policing?

10. How does public demand for accountability apply to policing operations?

Experiential Activities

11. Role Expectations
Contact a local sheriff's office and speak to someone in a supervisory role about the training and guidance officers are given?

a. How are the roles of different parts of the sheriff's department different?
b. How are they similar?
c. Name differences between this agency's perception of its role and the public's perception of it.

Experiential Activities continued

12. Multiple-Role Strain

Find a jurisdiction with a very low-crime, middle-class section and a very high-crime, low-income section. Contact the police department and ask how it deals with the different roles the police must play in each community. Ask about the department's overall approach to the two neighborhoods.

   a. How are officers assigned to the different neighborhoods?

   b. How does the department approach the different needs of each neighborhood?

   c. Are the results of policing similar in both neighborhoods?

13. Role Enactment

Find a police department in your region that is known for its success at community policing, then contact the person who is in charge of community policing. Ask him or her to discuss the obstacles they faced when community policing was first introduced.

   a. What kind of obstacles did this department encounter?

   b. Name the problem-solving techniques this officer mentioned.

   c. What was done to help officers take a service-oriented approach?

14. Community Policing

Assess the level of commitment to community policing in your town. Do some research to find out when your community initiated community policing.

   a. What aspects of community policing philosophy do you see in your local policing agency?

   b. Which additional aspects do you think should be implemented?

   c. How has the community improved?

Web Patrol

15. Online Training

Visit the Community Policing Consortium site through the link at **www.policing.glencoe.com**. Look up the training curricula.

Which module is most useful for police trainees?

16. Report-Writing Software

Go to **www.policing.glencoe.com** and find the link for policecomputer.com. Read about automated police incident report-writing software.

Do you think this software makes good writing skills less important?

17. Police Use of Force

Go to the U.S. Department of Justice site through the link at **www.policing.glencoe.com** and read the report on the use of force by police.

What is the difference between use of force and brutality?

Critical Thinking Exercises

18. Attitude Problems

You have just been hired as the chief of a small city and your officers are resisting your authority. Officers are being rough with suspects and are failing to deal with crimes that they do not see as "real crimes" (such as domestic violence cases). You hold small-group discussions with your officers and with different people from your community. You find out that officers feel that their job is to "fight crime" and that they have to "get tough" with suspects in order to gain and keep their respect. Community members accuse the officers of being bullies and say that they do not know or care about the real crime problems.

    a. How can you change the attitudes of your officers?

    b. How can you change recruiting and field training practices so that new officers reflect your ideals?

19. Time for a Role Change

You are a foot patrol officer in a middle-class suburb. Your department is understaffed because city officials will not approve more money for police salaries. As a result, the community policing program is almost nonexistent, and you are expected to focus only on serious crimes. Your community has seen an increasing drug problem among junior high and even elementary school students. Underage drinking and smoking are also problems, but your department does not have the resources to crack down on local liquor and convenience stores. Citizens are worried about the drug problem and feel that the police will do nothing to help.

    a. What police-community efforts could you make that would not ask officers to expend more energy on the job?

    b. How can you mobilize the public to support a larger police budget without making any political enemies?

20. The Role of Order Maintenance

You are a campus police officer at a college where the majority of offenses are drug and alcohol related. Your state has severe anti-drug laws and your department treats drug offenders harshly. In contrast, it treats most alcohol offenders more leniently.

    There have been five DUI-related arrests in the past month, and one involved an accident in which a freshman was nearly killed. The DUI suspects were arrested and are facing trial, but you feel that this could have been prevented if the root of the problem—the rampant under-aged alcohol use—was handled more aggressively. You speak with your chief, and she agrees but explains to you that the local courts are too busy to handle misdemeanor drinking charges.

    a. How do you handle the conflict between the role you would like to perform and the obstacles you have encountered?

    b. How can you focus your efforts on reducing underage drinking?

Endnotes

1. T. A. Johnson, G. E. Misner, and L. P. Brown, *The Police and Society: An Environment for Collaboration and Confrontation* (Englewood Cliffs, NJ: Prentice Hall, 1981).
2. C. D. Hale, *Police Patrol: Operations and Management* (Englewood Cliffs, NJ: Prentice Hall, 1994).
3. Johnson et al., *The Police and Society*, 204.
4. Johnson et al., *The Police and Society*, 16–17.
5. J. D. Lohman, "Human Relations and the Law" (unpublished paper, School of Criminology, University of California, Berkeley, 1968), 9.
6. R. L. LaGrange, *Policing American Society* (Chicago: Nelson-Hall, 1993).
7. Ibid.
8. J. H. Skolnick, *Justice without Trial: Law Enforcement in Democratic Society* (New York: Macmillan, 1994).
9. H. Goldstein, *Policing a Free Society* (Cambridge, MA: Ballinger, 1977).
10. R. H. Langworthy and L. F. Travis III, *Policing in America: A Balance of Forces* (New York: Macmillan, 1994).
11. Hale, *Police Patrol*, 23–25.
12. J. Petersilia, *The Influence of Criminal Justice Research* (Santa Monica, CA: RAND, 1987).
13. Ibid.
14. Hale, *Police Patrol*, 25–49.
15. ABA, op. cit., 46–47.
16. Ibid., 48.
17. E. Bittner, *The Functions of the Police in Modern Society* (Washington, D.C.: National Institute of Mental Health, 1970).
18. J. Skolnick and J. Fyfe, *Above the Law: Police and the Excessive Use of Force* (New York: Macmillan, 1993).
19. *Tennessee v. Garner*, 471 U.S. 1 (1985).
20. *Graham v. Connor*, 490 U.S. 386 (1989).
21. National Institute of Justice, *Police Use of Force* (Washington, D.C.: U.S. Department of Justice, 1997).
22. W. A. Geller and M. S. Scott, *Deadly Force: What We Know* (Washington, D.C.: Police Executive Research Forum, 1992).
23. ABA, 47–51.
24. Johnson et al., *The Police and Society*, 217.
25. T. R. Sarbin and V. Allen, "Role Theory," in *The Handbook of Social Psychology*, edited by G. Lindzey and E. Aronson (Menlo Park, CA: Addison-Wesley, 1968).
26. Ibid., 506–7.
27. Hale, *Police Patrol*, 19.
28. Advisory Committee on the Police Function, *The Urban Police Function* (New York: American Bar Association, 1972).
29. R. R. Roberg and J. Kuykendall, *Police Management* (Los Angeles: Roxbury, 1997), 67.
30. C. Bartollas and L.D. Hahn, *Policing in America* (Boston: Allyn and Bacon, 1999), 46–7.
31. J. Broderick, *Police in a Time of Change* (Prospect Heights, IL: Waveland, 1987).
32. J. Q. Wilson, *Varieties of Police Behavior: The Management of Law and Order in Eight Communities* (Cambridge, MA: Harvard University Press, 1968).
33. D. Carter, *The Police and the Community* (New York: Macmillan, 1994).
34. Wilson, *Varieties of Police Behavior*, 140–45.
35. Roberg and Kuykendall, *Police Management*, 172–75.
36. Ibid., 200–1.
37. M. Hooper, "Police Administration," in *The International Encyclopedia of Public Policy and Administration* (Boulder, CO: Westview, 1998), 1679.
38. National Institute of Justice, *Building Knowledge about Crime and Justice* (Washington, D.C.: U.S. Department of Justice, 1997).
39. H. Safir, "Goal-Oriented Community Policing: The NYPD Approach," *The Police Chief* 64, no. 12 (1997): 37.
40. LaGrange, *Policing American Society*, 360.
41. Roberg, op. cit., 172–5.
42. National Institute of Justice, *Measuring What Matters, Part Two: Developing Measures of What the Police Do* (Washington, D.C.: U.S. Department of Justice, 1997).
43. B. C. Parks, "The State of Community Policing" (management paper, Los Angeles Police Department, 1997).

Chapter 5

The Organization of Policing

CHAPTER OBJECTIVES

AFTER COMPLETING THIS CHAPTER, YOU WILL BE ABLE TO:

1. Name the basic characteristics of American law enforcement.

2. Explain what a jurisdiction is.

3. Understand what local law enforcement does and how this differs from other levels of law enforcement.

4. Distinguish between the centralized and decentralized state police models.

5. Name the different federal agencies and explain their specialized work.

6. List the ways in which community policing can serve as a catalyst for effective organizational change.

7. Name the differences between public policing and private policing.

◀ Police chief briefing officers.

5.1 American Law Enforcement

Although American policing has roots in ancient cultures and in English policing, it has evolved into a unique system. Some basic characteristics of American policing are:

- ***It is large.*** There are over 700,000 police in this country, and more than 400,000 of them are municipal officers.
- ***It is multilevel.*** American police cover municipal, county, state, federal, and sometimes even international crime issues. Their jobs are all slightly different, as you will learn later in this chapter.
- ***It is changing.*** Over the past century, recruitment, training, and police skills have adapted as policing has evolved and crime issues have changed. American police are currently attempting to mobilize community resources for crime prevention through approaches such as community policing.
- ***It shares overlapping jurisdictions.*** Federal police have jurisdiction over the entire country, which includes each state, county, and city. State agencies cover certain geographic areas such as the state's highway system.
- ***It has three distinguishing characteristics.*** These are responsiveness to citizen requests, public accountability, and openness to evaluation.

In the United States anybody can pick up a phone, walk into a police station, or stop a police officer on the street and expect that an armed and uniformed officer, embodying the full authority of government, will attend to the problems of that individual in a humane manner. This is a remarkable development in world government.

Police and Accountability

police operations The preventive, investigative, and crime-fighting work that police do; determined mainly by citizen requests.

American **police operations**, which can be defined as the preventive, investigative, and crime-fighting work that police do, are determined overwhelmingly by requests from individual citizens. Police in the United States often go to great lengths to respond to what individuals want.

The United States makes police accountable through multiple institutions. The best-known examples of these are elected officials, criminal and civil courts, and civilian boards that review complaints. Scholars, management consultants, politicians, and members of the community with a serious interest in policing can gain access to almost any activity of any police force. This is rare in a world where the press is often censored by the government, police misdeeds are subject only to the invisible discipline of the police themselves, and politicians rely on the police to keep themselves in power. Unfortunately, this approach is often the status quo in many countries, particularly those with militarized police forces that focus on enforcing the law through repression. Only a handful of other countries, such as England, France, and Japan, have a system that is open to civilian criticism.[2]

5.1

Self Check

1. What are the characteristics of American policing?
2. How can police operations be defined?

POLICING *Online*

Check your answers at **www.policing.glencoe.com**

5.2 Levels of Law Enforcement

Law enforcement occurs at several government levels. It occurs at the local, county, state, federal, and even international levels. It also occurs in the private sector. Although the various tiers of American law enforcement agencies are similar in a number of ways, they differ somewhat in their responsibilities and activities. This variation in activities and functions is determined, in part, by the agency's jurisdiction and mission.

A **jurisdiction** is the geographic area or type of crime over which a law enforcement organization has authority. When a law enforcement agency is said to have jurisdiction over a geographic area, it means that only they are authorized to perform law enforcement functions in that area. For example, municipal police agencies have jurisdiction within their city's limits. A sheriff's department generally has jurisdiction in a county's unincorporated areas, the county jail, and small towns that are unable to provide their own police services.

When jurisdiction is over a type or class of laws or crimes, that means that a particular agency's goal or mission is to enforce and investigate them. For example, municipal, county, state, and federal police share the geographic jurisdiction over incorporated American cities. However, only the municipal police enforce city ordinances, which are laws that apply within a city's limits and that are enforced by city police. Only the Drug Enforcement Agency (DEA) has jurisdiction over the investigation and suppression of crimes that violate federal drug laws and money laundering laws, as well as related federal crimes within that same city. Although local, county, and state police may help in investigations, the DEA has sole jurisdiction over such crimes. Another example is marine patrols, which are frequently divisions of sheriffs' departments. Because their jurisdiction is over

jurisdiction The geographic area or crime issue over which the authority of a law enforcement organization extends.

the safety and criminal activities on the waterways of the community, they have sole authority over them.

Often two or more agencies will have jurisdiction over the same area or the same general type of crime. One example is drug task forces involving federal, state, and local agencies. Sometimes there are disputes between agencies regarding who should be in charge and which agency should perform various activities. More often than not, though, agencies cooperate with each other.[3]

Another jurisdictional conflict can arise when a suspect is wanted for crimes in more than one geographic jurisdiction. Such matters are often resolved in favor of the agency with the most resources or investigative expertise or the one in which the most severe crime occurred. Police jurisdictions may also share the same prosecuting authority, in which case the various investigators may work jointly in building a case for prosecution.

Different levels of law enforcement can also want the same suspect. A common example is when a drug criminal is wanted for state and federal offenses. These overlapping jurisdictions can cover the same crimes, but in different ways. For example, suppose that Rhonda is pulled over by a state trooper for speeding. It turns out that she is wanted for drug sales in her hometown, which places her in violation of local laws, and for interstate drug transportation, a federal crime. The state officer can turn her over either to federal or local law enforcement. Technically, she could be prosecuted for both violations of local and federal criminal statutes in separate proceedings—and have to pay the speeding ticket.

The following section will break down the different levels of law enforcement to help show their basic duties.

Local Law Enforcement

municipal police City-
based policing agencies; also
known as local police.

sworn officers Officers who
are trained and empowered
to perform full police duties,
such as making arrests and
carrying firearms.

Municipal police organizations are city- or town-based policing agencies. They make up the primary type of policing organizations in the nation and are collectively the largest employers of sworn officers. Municipal agencies in the United States employ more than 410,000 full-time **sworn officers,** who are officers trained and empowered to make arrests and carry firearms. Interestingly, although agencies vary greatly in size and the NYPD employs more than 36,000 sworn officers, the vast majority of agencies employ fewer than 10.[4] In some communities, the force totals one.

There are a number of differences between policing a small town and a large city. The most noticeable ones can be summed up as follows:

- In most small towns across the United States, crime is not as serious a problem as it is in large cities.
- In many small towns, the leading crimes involve thefts, underage drinking, driving under the influence, and, to a considerably lesser degree than in large cities, drug-related crimes.
- Small towns typically are less likely to experience violent crimes such as robbery or murder—although small college towns do sometimes encounter a disproportionate number of sexual assaults.
- Many large cities are likely to experience more violent crimes in a single week than most small towns will in a year.[5]

These differences call for different crime prevention strategies, investigative focus, police-community relations, and policing styles, and organizational structures. Figure 5.1 on page 168 shows how differently a large city's police department is organized from a small town's department.

Crime Prevention Strategies Studies reveal that it is probably true that rural residents seem less fearful of crime than inner-city residents, but how much of the difference is because of survey questions that do not fit rural settings? For example, questions about crime on the respondent's "street" do not reflect the fact that many rural residents live away from residential areas. If a rural resident says that she does not fear street crime, that does not necessarily mean that she does not fear crime. The truth is that rural citizens share many of the same concerns about violent crime, property crime, and drug-related crime as their urban counterparts.

This makes rural crime prevention a paradox: Although rural and small-town residents often have strong interpersonal bonds and patterns of social interaction that help them watch out for each other, they also mistrust outsiders and government representatives such as outside law enforcement. Much of this is because outsiders and government agents are seen as insensitive to local needs. Thus, a key to effective crime prevention programs in

MYTH	FACT
Small-town America shares almost none of the crime problems found in American cities.	Small towns in the United States actually share many of the same common crime problems, such as drug use, DUIs, gangs, and domestic violence. The difference is that they occur less frequently.

Figure 5.1

Small Versus Large

How do small police departments differ in their structure from large ones? One answer is the needs of the communities they serve. A large department in a small town would be wasteful, but a small department in a large city would be unable to adequately protect its citizens. Compare the police services of Chicago, Illinois, and Dyersburg, Tennessee.

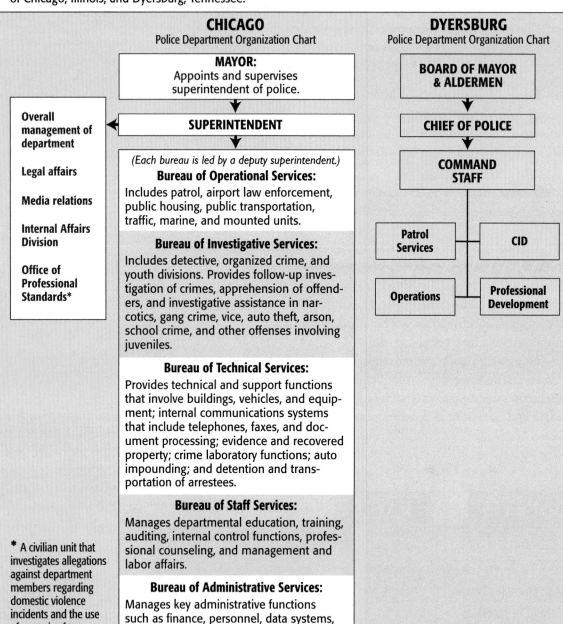

CHICAGO
Police Department Organization Chart

DYERSBURG
Police Department Organization Chart

MAYOR: Appoints and supervises superintendent of police.

SUPERINTENDENT

Overall management of department

Legal affairs

Media relations

Internal Affairs Division

Office of Professional Standards*

(Each bureau is led by a deputy superintendent.)

Bureau of Operational Services:
Includes patrol, airport law enforcement, public housing, public transportation, traffic, marine, and mounted units.

Bureau of Investigative Services:
Includes detective, organized crime, and youth divisions. Provides follow-up investigation of crimes, apprehension of offenders, and investigative assistance in narcotics, gang crime, vice, auto theft, arson, school crime, and other offenses involving juveniles.

Bureau of Technical Services:
Provides technical and support functions that involve buildings, vehicles, and equipment; internal communications systems that include telephones, faxes, and document processing; evidence and recovered property; crime laboratory functions; auto impounding; and detention and transportation of arrestees.

Bureau of Staff Services:
Manages departmental education, training, auditing, internal control functions, professional counseling, and management and labor affairs.

* A civilian unit that investigates allegations against department members regarding domestic violence incidents and the use of excessive force.

Bureau of Administrative Services:
Manages key administrative functions such as finance, personnel, data systems, and records.

BOARD OF MAYOR & ALDERMEN

CHIEF OF POLICE

COMMAND STAFF

Patrol Services

CID

Operations

Professional Development

SOURCE: Dyersburg, Tennessee, Police Department, "Dyersburg Police Dept. Organizational Chart," accessed online at http://www.ecsis.net/cdpd/org3.html on December 13, 2001; and Chicago Police Department, "Overview—Chicago Police Department," accessed online at http://w6.ci.chi.il.us./CommunityPolicing/AboutCPD/Organization/Overview.html on December 13, 2001.

rural regions and small towns is gaining the trust of residents. One method for achieving this is local recruitment. It can help strengthen existing community ties and improve and create partnerships with law enforcement.[6]

Investigative Focus Rural regions and small towns are characterized by informal social controls. Even though police have a unique level of familiarity with citizens, this advantage is often undermined by the same citizens' reluctance to share problems with the police. For example, minor crimes in rural areas are rarely reported to police but instead are handled informally. This is the main obstacle in developing crime prevention programs in rural regions because it prevents any investigative process and also makes it difficult for police to determine criminals' modus operandi (or MO). Detectives often depend on an understanding of MOs to develop case leads.

As is the case with prevention programs, the key to making investigations more fruitful in rural areas is to establish trust among the residents. It is also important to initiate educational programs that show the public the value of reporting crime so that police can compile databases that directly help them prevent crime and arrest perpetrators.[7]

Computer On Patrol

Electronic Facial Identification

Police officers are trained observers. Since much of their work depends on their perceptions, it is important that they learn to look at things objectively. For example, an officer must be able to spot suspicious persons in a crowded area. Police must also be able to remember a criminal's face in case they encounter that person again.

Civilians, however, do not receive the same intensive training that officers do. Often, this makes it difficult to rely on eyewitness testimony. Furthermore, drawing police sketches based on a civilian's memory is often problematic. Using some general descriptive terms, an artist can construct a picture of what a suspect might look like. However, many times, civilians will find that the artist's sketch does not match the image in their heads. This is because a few slight errors in each facial feature can add up to the entire face looking wrong.

These problems may all disappear with the use of a computer program called E-FIT. While it still relies on a witness' clues to construct an image, the program builds this image piece by piece so that each element is more accurate. The program can also disguise and age the faces. In the future, police officials hope to use E-FIT to catch more suspects and to find more missing persons.

Think About It Can you think of other uses for this program?

Police-Community Relations Given the nature of rural culture and of social interactions in rural areas, police-community relations in rural areas vary significantly from those in urban regions. In rural areas, officers are likely to know the offenders and their families. Rural officers are also more likely to know and appreciate the history and culture of an area and to use that information in their work.

Rural officers often find that the level of cooperation they receive is proportionate to the degree of civility given to local citizens. This is in marked contrast to the authoritarian approach often assumed—with frequent success—by urban officers. One rural officer describes his arrest technique in one of his cases: "This summer I encountered a man with maybe 200 plants spread over a small marijuana farm. I informed him that I'd come to get his marijuana." Prior to taking the suspect into custody, the deputy helped him finish unloading a truckload of wood. Then, the officer informed the suspect he was to go down by the pond and verify the presence of marijuana. The potential harvest was confirmed. The deputy said that he avoided an altercation because he didn't say, "You're a marijuana grower and you're worthless." He added, "A lot of times people in these rural areas don't have a problem with being arrested; they just want to be treated like human beings."[8]

Policing Styles Policing styles are partly a reflection of the relationship between police and the community. While police in many urban areas may be detached from their communities, in rural areas they may be an integral part of the community. Studies have disclosed that once police are trusted in rural areas, they get higher levels of public support than their urban counterparts. In many rural areas, police must provide a wide range of services because other social services are either nonexistent or are too remote to provide timely services. In many instances, rural policing responsibilities include the following:

- Firefighting
- Emergency medical services
- Rescue operations
- General public service

Rural police are routinely expected to render services for a wide variety of irregular occurrences, only a few of which are statutorily defined as law enforcement responsibilities. For example, they could be requested to inspect and provide an opinion on a boundary line between two farmers' lands.[9]

County Law Enforcement

county law enforcement
Countywide law enforcement services that are most often performed by a sheriff's department.

County law enforcement is most often performed by a sheriff's department. Although the duties of the county sheriff's department may vary from one jurisdiction to another, the chief officer is almost always an elected official.

The two exceptions to this are the sheriffs of Rhode Island and Hawaii, who are appointed.

One way to distinguish the activities of different sheriffs' departments is to consider the region in which the departments are located. In the South and large portions of the Midwest, Northwest, and Southwest, sheriffs' departments often serve as the principal law enforcement agency in the area. In many smaller communities, the sheriffs' departments also may be responsible for the following:

- Tax assessment and collection
- Patrolling the local bridges and highway extensions
- Serving as jail attendants and courtroom bailiffs
- Executing both criminal and civil processes, which includes serving warrants, subpoenas, and eviction notices

Conversely, sheriffs' departments in the Northeast perform little active law enforcement (although they sometimes travel nationally to locate and apprehend suspects who have jumped bail). Their principal duties entail courtroom security, prisoner transportation, and service of legal notices. Much of this work requires in-depth knowledge of both the criminal and civil law systems.[10]

Sheriffs' departments employ more than 150,000 full-time sworn personnel nationwide. About 37 percent of sheriffs' departments employ fewer than 10 full-time sworn personnel. The largest sheriff's department, the Los Angeles County Sheriff's Department, employs more than 8,000 full-time sworn deputies.[11]

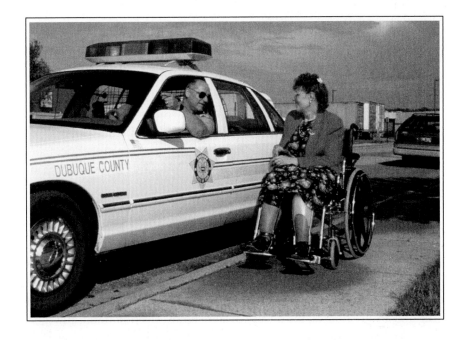

◀ **Rural Policing** Law enforcement in small communities has its specific challenges. *What job skills would you say are important for this type of policing?*

State Law Enforcement

The role of state policing has been controversial in the past. This was because most Americans firmly believed that policing should be handled at local levels such as the city or county. A state police force was unwanted because it seemed to interfere with local autonomy. On the other hand, growing populations and crime problems created the need for state police.[12]

Texas Rangers One historic example of this is the Texas Rangers, who were established by the Republic of Texas in 1835 (and between 1823 and 1834 were known as Ranging Men). Originally the Texas Rangers consisted of three companies of men and operated as a paramilitary force. They defended settlers against marauding Indians and patrolled the border between Mexico and Texas. When Texas became part of the United States, the Texas Rangers began refining their activities and started to investigate crimes statewide. Today the principal tasks of the Texas Rangers are criminal investigation and border patrol.[13]

Pennsylvania State Police The first formal, uniformed state police was the Pennsylvania State Police, which was formed in 1905 after the Great Anthracite Strike. Before the strike, coal mine and steel factory employees worked under deplorable conditions. Miners frequently became ill or died from their work, and both industries hired young children at very low wages. It was similar to the working conditions of Industrial Age England.[14]

Today state police agencies employ more than 55,000 full-time sworn officers nationwide. The California Highway Patrol employs the largest force, with approximately 6,200 sworn personnel. The smallest force is the North Dakota Highway Patrol, which deploys approximately 120 sworn personnel.[15]

State Police Configurations State police departments assume one of two operational configurations: centralized or decentralized. A **centralized state agency** performs a wide spectrum of duties such as enforcing state penal code sections in remote regions and providing supplementary services to other law enforcement agencies. Supplementary services may include laboratory analysis of criminal evidence and air support. Also, centralized agencies handle all highway patrol responsibilities. The Pennsylvania State Police is an example of such a "one-stop" operation (See Figure 5.2 on pages 174–175).

Some states prefer to establish separate state agencies for criminal law enforcement and vehicular code enforcement/accident investigation. The state of North Carolina has a **decentralized state agency**. The North Carolina Highway Patrol enforces the state's traffic laws and assists motorists in distress. The North Carolina State Bureau of Investigation has many enforcement responsibilities, among them original jurisdiction in certain drug and arson offenses, the misuse of state funds, election fraud, and mob violence. It also maintains crime laboratories for use by local agencies.[16]

centralized state agency
A "one-stop" state policing model in which officers have statewide jurisdiction in all typical policing matters, such as criminal investigation.

decentralized state agency
A state policing model in which state law enforcement duties are performed by different divisions, such as a highway patrol.

Federal Law Enforcement

Federal law enforcement agencies, which employ more than 75,000 full-time personnel, are responsible for enforcing federal criminal law statutes. The two largest employers of federal law enforcement officers are both part of the Department of Justice (DOJ): the Immigration and Naturalization Service (INS) and the Federal Bureau of Investigation (FBI). The DOJ also contains the Drug Enforcement Administration (DEA) and the U.S. Marshals Service.[17]

federal law enforcement
Law enforcement agencies that are responsible for enforcing federal criminal law statutes.

The Immigration and Naturalization Service The Immigration and Naturalization Service (INS) was created in 1864 by a law intended to encourage immigration. Under this law, a commissioner of immigration was appointed to regulate the transportation and settlement of immigrants to the United States. The emphasis of the law was then changed to prevent the admission of undesirable aliens and to control contract labor. Currently, nearly half of all 12,403 INS sworn officers are border patrol agents. Border patrol agents intercept undocumented aliens and contraband, including narcotics. The challenge of patrolling 8,000 miles of international boundaries is a formidable one: In recent years, border patrol agents have apprehended a million or more illegal aliens per year.[18]

The Federal Bureau of Investigation Since its founding in 1908, the Federal Bureau of Investigation (FBI) has been the principal investigative arm of the federal government. When the FBI was first formed, its agents investigated violations of some of the comparatively few existing federal crimes, such as

◀ **U.S. Border Patrol** An agent searches a group of illegal immigrants near Brownville, Texas. The role of the Border Patrol is to stem the flow of illegal immigration and deport illegal aliens. *Why is this role so controversial?*

Figure 5.2

Centralized and Decentralized State Police

Some states prefer a centralized state police model that includes a large array of services, but other states prefer to follow a decentralized highway patrol model. Below is the Arizona State Patrol Model.

Arizona Department of Public Safety (decentralized)

The Arizona DPS' four divisions, which are located in over 30 offices across Arizona, are:

◆ *Highway Patrol:*

- ◆ Oversees the functions of the Highway Patrol and related division bureaus
- ◆ Provides specialized training in mitigating hazardous materials incidents
- ◆ Trains internal and external elements in hazardous materials response in conjunction with the Motor Carrier Safety Assistance Program state enforcement plan
- ◆ Conducts hazardous material training for the Department and other agency personnel
- ◆ Oversees the functions of the Duty Office
- ◆ Conducts self-inspection programs for the division
- ◆ Oversees the issuance of school bus driver certifications and inspections of school buses
- ◆ Oversees the state fixed and rotor wing aviation program responsible for emergency medical evacuation, search and rescue, and law enforcement operations statewide

◆ *Criminal Investigations:* The five criminal investigation bureaus are Narcotics, Investigation, Intelligence, Special Enforcement, and the Rocky Mountain Information Network (RMIN). Also provides a Civil Emergency Task Force and Governor's Protection Detail.

◆ *Agency Support:* This division's duties include training, resources, facilities management, and financial services.

◆ *Criminal Justice Support:* This division covers

- ◆ Fingerprint identification
- ◆ Criminal information services
- ◆ Operational communications
- ◆ Scientific analysis
- ◆ Information technology
- ◆ Telecommunications
- ◆ Licensing

Figure 5.2

Centralized and Decentralized State Police *(continued)*

Some states prefer a centralized state police model that includes a large array of services, but other states prefer to focus their state policing efforts on a decentralized highway patrol model. Below is the Minnesota State Patrol Model.

Minnesota State Patrol (centralized)

The Minnesota State Patrol's 11 patrol districts have a total of 61 stations. Their statewide services include

◆ *Highway Patrol:* Provides traffic enforcement on state highways and interstate highways, investigations of crimes occurring on these highways, and accident investigation.

◆ *Flight Section:* Assists the State Patrol and other law enforcement agencies in traffic enforcement, emergency relays, surveillance, search and rescue missions, and photo flights of accident and crime scenes.

◆ *Capitol Security:* Provides security to the governor and his family and at the state capitol complex during various functions including the state legislature and other public events.

◆ *Special Response Team:* Assists the State Patrol in special events such as protests at the state capitol, and helps in search and rescue missions at the request of other agencies.

◆ *Auto Theft:* Investigates crimes relating to motor vehicles such as title fraud, odometer tampering, auto theft, and car dealership violations.

◆ *Criminal Patrol and Canine Unit:* Investigates drug interdiction cases involving motor vehicles and assists other agencies upon request.

◆ *Safety Education:* Safety Education Troopers provide education to the public in the areas of seat belt use, speed, drinking and driving, and general traffic safety.

◆ *Commercial Vehicle Enforcement:* Provides staffing and supports services for weight enforcement through fixed and mobile weight programs, civil weight investigations, commercial vehicle inspections and school bus inspections.

◆ *Training:* Provides continuing education for state troopers and other law enforcement agencies in traffic-related areas such as radar, accident investigation, DWI detection techniques, and drug recognition expert training.

SOURCE: Adapted from Arizona Department of Public Safety, "About the D.P.S.," accessed online at http://www.dps.state.az.us/aboutdps/aboutdps.htm on December 13, 2001; and Minnesota State Patrol, "Information about the Minnesota State Patrol," accessed online at http://www.dps.state.mn.us/patrol/general/patrolinfo.htm on December 13, 2001.

bankruptcy fraud and monopolies. During World War I, the FBI was given new responsibility for investigating draft violations, sabotage, and espionage. Later, the FBI was assigned to investigate the smuggling and violent gang-related crimes that resulted from Prohibition. Today FBI agents have broad investigative responsibilities encompassing more than 250 federal crimes, including bank fraud, embezzlement, kidnapping, and civil rights violations. The FBI is also the lead agency for investigating crimes of terrorism.[19]

Drug Enforcement Administration The Drug Enforcement Administration (DEA) developed from the Federal Bureau of Narcotics (FBN), which was established in 1930. The main priorities of FBN agents were cocaine and opiates. Today's DEA agents primarily investigate major narcotics violators and many other types of drug trafficking prevention and control. They also enforce regulations governing the manufacture and distribution of legal controlled substances. Given the size and scope of the illegal drug problem, the DEA has focused on multilevel (local, state, federal, and international) task forces to better address drug trafficking on regional, national, and international scales.[20]

U.S. Marshal's Service The U.S. Marshals Service is the nation's oldest federal law enforcement agency. The Office of the U.S. Marshal was created under the direction of George Washington by the first Congress in the Judiciary Act of 1789. U.S. Marshals provided local representation for the national government across the colonies and enforced federal laws and court orders across the land. Today the Marshals receive all persons arrested by federal authorities and transfer sentenced federal inmates between facilities. In addition, the Marshals have jurisdiction over the following:

- Federal fugitive matters
- Escaped prisoners
- Violators of probation, parole, and releases on bond
- Persons under DEA warrants

Other responsibilities include managing the Federal Asset Seizure/ Forfeiture and Federal Witness Security Programs, providing security at federal judicial facilities, and escorting missile convoys.

On average, the Marshals Service has in its custody about 20,000 pre-sentence inmates each day. Although this figure is steadily increasing, the flow of resources has not consistently kept up with the workload. In addition, the Marshal's Service is responsible for investigating inmate suicides, arranging for the hospitalization and care of prisoners with terminal or contagious diseases, and finding homes for dependent children of inmates.[21]

The U.S. Treasury Department also houses prominent law enforcement agencies. These include the U.S. Secret Service and the Bureau of Alcohol, Tobacco, and Firearms.

The U.S. Secret Service (USSS) The Secret Service was created in 1865 to prevent counterfeiting. This narrow duty soon expanded to include preventing fraud against the government such as mail robbery, alcohol distilling that did not follow legal guidelines, and land purchase frauds. As a result of the assassination of President William McKinley in 1901, the Secret Service assumed full-time responsibility for protection of the president. Most agents of the Secret Service, which employs 3,185 full-time sworn personnel, still perform duties related to counterfeiting as well as financial crimes, computer fraud, and threats against dignitaries.

The remainder of the Secret Service belongs to the Uniformed Division. This is the most visible branch of the USSS because these officers, who are all categorized under the police response and patrol category, provide protection for the White House complex and other presidential offices; the main treasury building and annex; the president, vice president, and members of their immediate family; and those who attend foreign diplomatic missions.

A major challenge for the USSS is the increasing number of people coming under their protective cloak. A new addition to their workload is the challenge of investigating computer frauds, which continue to increase in number and complexity.[22]

◀ **The U.S. Secret Service**
Uniformed Secret Service officers search the grounds of the White House in February 2001 after a man fired shots outside the fence.
Why do you think this agency is so small?

The Bureau of Alcohol, Tobacco, and Firearms The Bureau of Alcohol, Tobacco, and Firearms (ATF) received its current name in 1972, but its roots date back to 1863, when taxes on distilled spirits were alternately repealed and enacted to meet revenue demands of the Civil War. Congress created detectives to aid in the prevention, detection, and punishment of tax evaders. When the Prohibition Era dawned in 1919, the United States faced unprecedented violence by the gangsters involved in the illicit production and sale of alcohol. Along with expanding the FBI's duties, the federal government also passed gun control legislation aimed at gangster-type weapons and assigned enforcement of these laws to the ATF, then called the Alcohol Tax Unit (ATU). In 1951, tobacco tax duties were also delegated to the ATU.

Currently, the ATF is primarily responsible for investigating the criminal use of firearms and explosives and the use of explosives by both domestic and international terrorists. The ATF also enforces federal laws that tax or regulate alcohol and tobacco.[23] (See Figure 5.3 for a recap of how various law agencies can overlap in one jurisdiction.)

5.2 Self Check

1. What does jurisdiction mean?
2. Name three examples of federal law enforcement agencies.

POLICING *Online*

Check your answers at
www.policing.glencoe.com

5.3 Effective Police Organization

Organization can be defined as arranging and using resources (such as personnel and equipment) in a way that provides the orderly accomplishment of goals.[24] Law enforcement agencies are very similar to other organizations such as universities and corporations in their structure and management processes. A hierarchical structure has evolved to carry out the complex responsibilities of policing. Under community policing, this structure has been moderately transformed to include fewer levels of command.

Organizational Designs and Protocols

hierarchy An organization that is characterized by several levels of command, with authority increasing as the levels reach the top of the pyramid.

The traditional structure of most law enforcement agencies has been a militaristic, pyramid-shaped **hierarchy**, which is an organizational structure with several levels in a chain of command. In a hierarchy, authority starts at the top of the pyramid and decreases as it moves downward. This means that the authority flows from a single leader, the chief or sheriff, down to the broad base of officers.

Chain of Command The **chain of command** is the police department's order of authority. It begins with a single leader at the top of the pyramid and flows downward to the next level, the commissioned ranks in the agency. These ranks may include deputy chief, captain, lieutenant, sergeant, and patrol officer. It is the responsibility of each level to forward communications to the next higher or lower level. Individuals within the agency must be constantly aware of this protocol, as many of their police actions must reflect the preferences of their supervisors and managers. It usually does not take long for officers to learn when they are expected to consult with their immediate supervisors, who are the links just above them in the chain of command.

chain of command A police department's order of authority, which begins at the top of the pyramid with the chief or sheriff and flows downward to the next level or echelon.

Unity of Command Another important part of sound organizational design is unity of command. **Unity of command** means that every individual in the

unity of command A part of sound organizational design, in which every individual in an organization has only one immediate superior or supervisor.

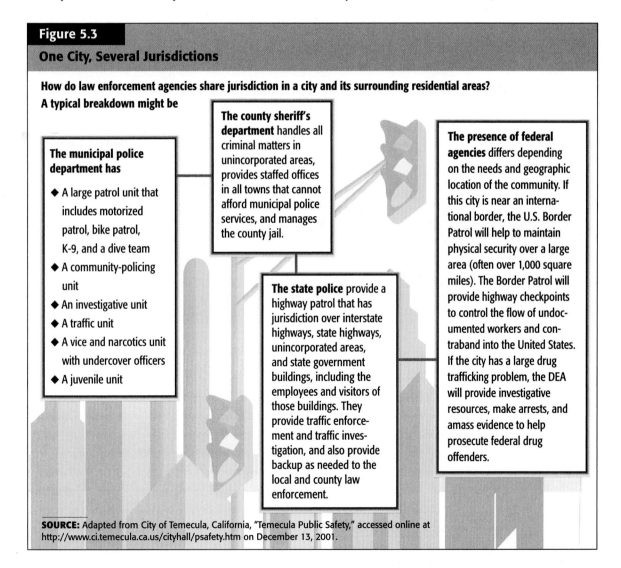

Figure 5.3

One City, Several Jurisdictions

How do law enforcement agencies share jurisdiction in a city and its surrounding residential areas? A typical breakdown might be

The municipal police department has

◆ A large patrol unit that includes motorized patrol, bike patrol, K-9, and a dive team
◆ A community-policing unit
◆ An investigative unit
◆ A traffic unit
◆ A vice and narcotics unit with undercover officers
◆ A juvenile unit

The county sheriff's department handles all criminal matters in unincorporated areas, provides staffed offices in all towns that cannot afford municipal police services, and manages the county jail.

The state police provide a highway patrol that has jurisdiction over interstate highways, state highways, unincorporated areas, and state government buildings, including the employees and visitors of those buildings. They provide traffic enforcement and traffic investigation, and also provide backup as needed to the local and county law enforcement.

The presence of federal agencies differs depending on the needs and geographic location of the community. If this city is near an international border, the U.S. Border Patrol will help to maintain physical security over a large area (often over 1,000 square miles). The Border Patrol will provide highway checkpoints to control the flow of undocumented workers and contraband into the United States. If the city has a large drug trafficking problem, the DEA will provide investigative resources, make arrests, and amass evidence to help prosecute federal drug offenders.

SOURCE: Adapted from City of Temecula, California, "Temecula Public Safety," accessed online at http://www.ci.temecula.ca.us/cityhall/psafety.htm on December 13, 2001.

organization has only one immediate supervisor. Unity of command is extremely important and needs to be firmly in place in most instances. Each individual, unit, and situation should be under the control of one—and only one—person. By ensuring this, police departments can avoid contradictory behavior or a duplication of work.

span of control The number of people or units supervised by one manager.

Span of Control The **span of control** refers to the number of people or units supervised by one manager, which is another critical factor in most law enforcement organizations. Historically, three or four people were considered the maximum that could be effectively managed by a single supervisor. However, because of technological advances and organizational structural changes, this number may rise to 8 to 14 officers reporting to one supervisor. Such changes include digital communications, which afford supervisors enhanced capabilities for monitoring their charges' decisions and actions. Another change is flattening the organization, which means getting rid of extra layers of management to better empower field officers. As levels of management are eliminated to make service delivery quicker and better tailored to clients' needs, the ratio of officers to the supervisory cadre will increase.

The span of control also depends on the department's size, the supervisors' and officers' abilities, crime rates, and community expectations of police services.[25]

Community Policing for Effective Change

Traditional police organizations have followed a hierarchical structure, which aims to control subordinates. This tends to create the following human relations problems:

- It stifles innovation and creativity.
- It promotes alienation and a loss of individual self-worth.
- It emphasizes mediocrity.
- It diminishes the ability of managers to lead.

Community policing requires a shorter and flatter organizational design, in which services are decentralized and community based. This approach is less formalized, less specialized, and less rules oriented. It empowers individual officers with more discretion and more responsibility than traditional policing did, so direction from the organization must emphasize shared values, joint decision making, and a collegial atmosphere. (See Figure 5.4 on page 181.)

Moreover, the organization of community policing is open and sensitive to the environment, with a built-in incentive to interact with members of the wider community. The differences in organizational structure between

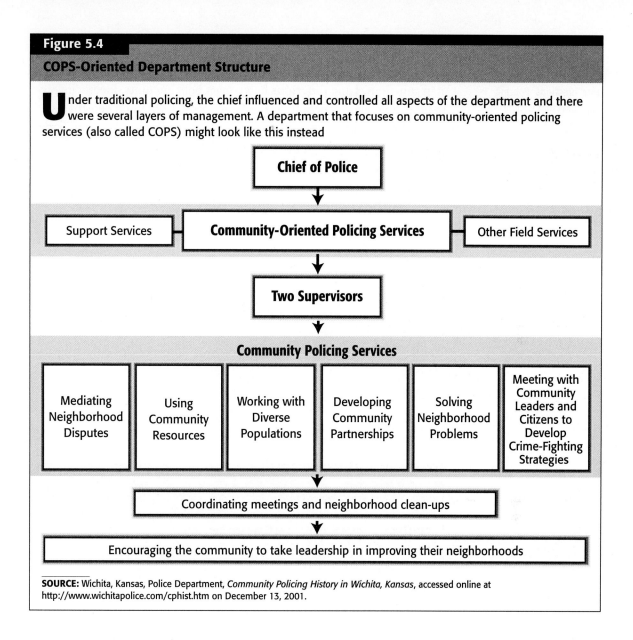

Figure 5.4

COPS-Oriented Department Structure

Under traditional policing, the chief influenced and controlled all aspects of the department and there were several layers of management. A department that focuses on community-oriented policing services (also called COPS) might look like this instead

Chief of Police

Support Services — **Community-Oriented Policing Services** — **Other Field Services**

Two Supervisors

Community Policing Services

| Mediating Neighborhood Disputes | Using Community Resources | Working with Diverse Populations | Developing Community Partnerships | Solving Neighborhood Problems | Meeting with Community Leaders and Citizens to Develop Crime-Fighting Strategies |

Coordinating meetings and neighborhood clean-ups

Encouraging the community to take leadership in improving their neighborhoods

SOURCE: Wichita, Kansas, Police Department, *Community Policing History in Wichita, Kansas*, accessed online at http://www.wichitapolice.com/cphist.htm on December 13, 2001.

traditional policing and community policing are substantial.[26] In the community policing organizational model, the power pyramid is inverted. Power, authority, and responsibility are shifted to field personnel. Police managers assume roles as facilitators, enabling resources from inside and outside the law enforcement agency to be mustered in support of field officers' problem-solving efforts. For example, managers can use their considerable influence to mobilize service organizations and other governmental agency heads to help build youth club facilities or have dilapidated public housing repaired or torn down.[27]

Line Functions

line functions Policing functions that encompass policing units directly involved in the provision of field services.

Many agencies divide their work into two major branches: line functions and staff functions. **Line functions** encompass policing units directly involved in providing field services. These include patrol, traffic, and detective operations. In larger agencies, these functions can include narcotics, vice, and air support operations.

Patrol The patrol function has been dubbed the backbone of policing because patrol officers are the first to respond to citizen requests for service. These incidents may be either criminal (such as a robbery) or ones in which public safety is jeopardized (such as a fallen power line). Patrol officers also perform targeted patrol to prevent crime. Some also still perform random patrol, although this is less effective. When an agency does not have enough staff for specialized traffic, detective, or other units, the patrol unit must perform these functions. (See Figure 5.5 below.)

Traffic Traffic operations include enforcing traffic laws, investigating accidents that occur on roadways, and providing traffic direction. This function may include a substantial amount of public education, in which officers teach traffic safety practices to citizens. In some states, traffic officers also help with drivers' license tests.

Figure 5.5

What Exactly is Patrol?

Patrol units provide some or all of these services
- Animal control
- Bicycle patrol
- Communication
- Dive team
- Field training
- Foot patrol
- K-9 patrol
- Marine patrol
- Mounted patrol
- Reserve patrol officers
- School patrol
- Traffic enforcement

SOURCE: Adapted from City of Naperville, Illinois, *Patrol*, accessed online at http://www.naperville.il.us/patrol.htm on December 13, 2001; and City of Poulsbo, Washington, *Patrol Division*, accessed online at http://www.cityofpoulsbo.com/Departments/Police/policepatrol.html on December 13, 2001.

Detective Operations Detectives conduct follow-up investigations of major crimes that are reported by patrol officers. Major detective activities include locating and interviewing witnesses, narrowing and determining suspects, and preparing cases for presentation to prosecutors.

Narcotics Narcotics units investigate possession and sales of illicit drugs. Much of the workload involves undercover stings in which an officer poses as a drug purchaser, or reverse stings in which an officer offers drugs for sale to anyone interested in purchasing them. Frequently, narcotics units work with other law enforcement agencies in task force operations.

Vice Vice officers enforce laws against prostitution, illegal gambling, and illegal alcohol consumption. They also are often deployed for intelligence-gathering activities, such as when plainclothes officers circulate in crowds where the potential for riots exists. Vice enforcement is normally directed at illegal activities that fit the "three Cs": commercial, conspicuous, and complained about.

Air Support Operations Larger police agencies deploy helicopters and small aircraft to oversee traffic conditions and monitor criminal activity. Airborne units are particularly advantageous in vehicle pursuits because they can communicate with ground units to help them catch suspects. They also help to position ground units that have created a perimeter around a suspect. Aircraft equipped with special night-sight and infrared devices are used for finding missing persons.

Staff Functions

Staff functions are all police activities that support field operations. These include dispatch, records, training, human resources, and property. Each of these units can have several staff assignments, and many of these tasks can be performed by nonsworn (civilian) personnel.[28]

Dispatch The dispatch center is commonly called the nerve center of law enforcement operations. Dispatch involves receiving citizen calls for service, prioritizing them, and then transmitting them to an available police field unit. This is high-stress work that is usually handled by carefully screened and trained nonsworn personnel. The dispatch function is often regionalized, which means that the dispatcher receives and broadcasts calls for service for multiple agencies. This is a cost-cutting measure because communications equipment and dispatchers are expensive.

Records Keeping accurate records is extremely important in police work. Although record keeping does not have the glamour of other police work,

ETHICS ISSUES

You are a new chief and have noticed a strong disparity in the workloads of your two lieutenants. Lieutenant Williams supervises 14 officers, runs the D.A.R.E. program, and is working with the public to found a new community policing program. Lieutenant Moreno supervises five patrol officers and does little else. It becomes clear to you that Moreno was the previous chief's favorite. He resents you because he was expecting to be appointed chief before you were recruited from another jurisdiction. When you give Williams a substantial raise, Moreno threatens to sue you for "being against" him. *What will you say to Lieutenant Moreno to show the ethical justification of your actions?*

staff functions Policing functions that encompass activities provided in support of field operations.

the criminal justice system could not operate without it. Records sections are distribution points and repositories for all criminal incidents that are documented and investigated by police. Prosecutions cannot proceed without records. Records can affect a repeat offender's sentence for new crimes: Often prosecutors are more likely to charge a crime if a suspect has a criminal history, and many jurisdictions require longer sentences for repeat offenders. Record keeping is customarily performed by nonsworn personnel.

Training Training is a vital function within law enforcement agencies. Principal areas of training are recruit training, roll call training, and in-service training. Due to cost considerations, recruit training is usually performed by colleges or training centers that are independent of recruits' parent agencies. Larger agencies such as the FBI and large municipal police departments have in-house training. Trainers may be experienced law enforcement officers or nonsworn technical experts such as psychologists, coroners, or prosecutors.

Roll call training occurs daily, most commonly within patrol divisions, and consists of updates on local crime problems or operational policies. This training also includes critiques of tactical situations. Roll call training is presented by supervisory personnel. The training at smaller agencies is normally less formal than at larger agencies and may consist of tutorials rather than assemblies.

In-service training usually takes the form of extended blocks of instruction that are presented outside the police department, such as at a local college. Topics might include ethics, problem-solving methods, crisis intervention, legal use of force, driver training, or supervisory/managerial skills. Most states have established annual hourly minimums for professional development, which police officers must satisfy to keep their jobs.

Human Resources Human resources divisions communicate with potential future employees and coordinate activities in support of all agency personnel. They ensure that personnel practices are fair and functional, particularly ones related to recruitment, employee reviews, and promotion. The HR division also handles employee benefits and special needs, such as medical/dental coverage or counseling. In small agencies, the local government takes care of HR duties, but large agencies have in-house HR units that are usually staffed by nonsworn personnel.

Property Property really means the evidence that is collected by law enforcement agencies and stored in a secure location. These locations, which are often rooms within a police department, also include found property that was turned in by citizens and is eventually returned to the owners. The most important part of evidence management is maintaining the chain of custody.

◀ **Human Resources** With most large police departments trying to attract the right candidates, this is a key position. *Why else is this role crucial?*

It is absolutely essential that all persons handling evidence be tracked and that evidence be not altered at any point when it is stored, handled, or transferred to court. Much of the evidence stored in property rooms is eventually presented in courtroom proceedings, and its integrity is crucial for successful prosecution. Property rooms may serve one or several agencies, and they are commonly staffed by civilian personnel.

Specialization

As an organization grows in size, specialization develops to meet the needs of the community and the policing organization. The primary policing functions are patrol, investigation, and traffic. **Specialization** is the creation of units that are given specific tasks to perform. Police management decides the extent of specialization for their agency. Typical specialized units include narcotics, vice, internal affairs, and juvenile. Frequently, the tasks performed by specialists are labor intensive or complex in nature, which is why specialized divisions ease the burden for the rest of the police agency. At the same time, specialized units provide higher-quality investigations in critical areas.

Often, when an agency develops specialized units such as narcotics or vice, the detective division also divides its labor. The detective unit personnel may each specialize in specific crime categories such as sex crimes, robberies, burglaries and thefts, auto-related crimes, or computer crimes. The usual effect of this is increased investigative expertise in specialized fields and higher crime clearance rates.

specialization An organizational approach that occurs when an organization's structure is divided into units that are given specific tasks to perform.

Advantages of Specialization Specialization creates a potential for substantially increased levels of expertise, creativity, and innovation. In addition, the more completely any one employee can perform a task or set of tasks, the greater the job satisfaction.

Specialization varies among law enforcement organizations, even of the same size, in different locations. The number of specialized units and the personnel required for each should be based on careful analysis of the local crime statistics and reflect the local crime picture. For example, a relatively low incidence of stolen cars would not the justify the creation of an auto theft unit, but an abundance of gang activity would certainly justify a juvenile unit.

Disadvantages of Specialization There are downsides to specialization. Command among the additional units requires special attention to coordination and communication. Specialization should exist only to the degree that it can help an organization accomplish its work plan without slowing down the total effort. Overspecialization is counterproductive because it prevents agencies from providing courteous, competent, and prompt police services.[29] In addition, employees in specialized divisions may not have as much opportunity for advancement because they are highly trained in a specific area and are thus lacking in mainstream skill areas.

Generalists Officers in the smallest agencies perform virtually all tasks and are considered generalists. They must possess a working knowledge of patrol, investigative, and traffic operations. In a single tour of duty, a patrol officer in a small agency could find himself or herself handling not only the customary preliminary investigation of a convenience store robbery but also an accident investigation resulting from the perpetrator's aborted getaway and a follow-up robbery investigation. The same officer would also prepare the case for filing with the prosecutor.

Accreditation

Whether police agencies specialize or generalize, they need to do so with adequate police skills. A new concept, known as accreditation, has emerged to measure these skills. It emphasizes revamping police organizations as a viable solution to ongoing problems. Standardizing policies and procedures is intended to ensure fair, reasonable, and consistent law enforcement and service delivery.[31] Accreditation differs from **Peace Office Standards and Training (POST)**, which are state programs that ensure that police officers meet minimum standards of competency and ethical behavior. The difference is that accreditation covers the full gamut of agency functions.

Peace Officer Standards and Training (POST) Statewide programs for individual police officers, which ensure that they meet minimum standards of competency and ethical behavior.

Model Minimum State Standards

The International Association of Directors of Law Enforcement Standards and Training (IADLEST) serves all 50 states and the District of Columbia. IADLEST also provides model minimum state standards for academy training, in-service training, training instructors, professional conduct, and peace officer standards and training (POST) administration. Their model minimum state standards influence the standards implemented by state training boards. Some model minimum standards for police officer selection are

◆ **Selection**

Each state commission should prescribe minimum statewide standards that must be complied with by hiring authorities who employ law enforcement and corrections officers and other related public officers.

◆ **Drug Screening**

State law or regulation should require each candidate for an entry level or lateral entry sworn position, to submit to testing to determine if he or she is currently using an illegal controlled dangerous substance.

◆ **Background Investigation**

State law or commission regulation should require each candidate for an entry-level or lateral entry law enforcement or corrections officer position or other related public office, to submit to a thorough background investigation according to protocols developed by the commission, to determine that they have exhibited mature judgment and are of good moral character and reputation.

◆ **Fingerprint Check**

State law or commission regulation should require the hiring authority to conduct a state and national criminal history check, including fingerprinting, and should prohibit the hiring of any person as a sworn police or corrections officer who has been convicted of a felony, or any other crime or series of crimes which would indicate to a reasonable person that the applicant was potentially dangerous, violent, or had a propensity to break the law.

◆ **Education**

State law or commission regulation should require immediately that all persons hired as police or corrections officers possess at a minimum a high school diploma, and should ultimately seek to phase in an entry-level requirement of a baccalaureate degree from a college or university accredited by a regional post-secondary accrediting body. Such college education should include a substantial core of courses in the humanities.

SOURCE: International Association of Directors of Law Enforcement Standards and Training, "IADLEST Model Minimum State Standards," accessed online at http://www.iadlest.org/modelmin.htm on December 13, 2001.

To date, accreditation is a voluntary process, in contrast to state-required POST commissions. (See Figure 5.6)

In 1979, the concept of accreditation was conceived by four leading groups in the law enforcement profession: the International Association of Chiefs of Police (IACP), the National Sheriffs Association (NSA), the National Organization of Black Law Enforcement Executives (NOBLE), and the Police Executive Research Forum (PERF). These groups helped to establish national accreditation by facilitating the creation of the Commission on Accreditation for Law Enforcement Agencies, Inc. (CALEA).[32]

Process of Accreditation As mentioned, seeking accreditation is a voluntary process, and today approximately 20 percent of all U.S. law enforcement agencies use the accreditation process. Accreditation standards address areas such as inmate treatment, complaint review, pursuits, and use of force. The accreditation process has five distinct phases:

1. The application
2. Self-assessment
3. On-site assessment visit
4. CALEA review
5. Maintaining compliance

CALEA awards accredited status to an agency for a three-year period. After each three-year period, CALEA offers the agency the opportunity to become reaccredited. If the agency decides to continue its status, the

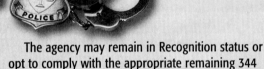

Police Procedure

CALEA Recognition Program

The Program
The Recognition Program may serve as a stepping stone for smaller law enforcement agencies that wish to participate in a professional credentialing program before seeking accreditation. The CALEA Recognition Program is available directly through CALEA or through formal affiliations with selected state/province accreditation programs.

The CALEA Recognition Program identifies 96 standards from the 4th Edition of the *Standards for Law Enforcement Agencies* manual. The standards address 1) Life, Health, & Safety issues, 2) legal & other critical requirements, and 3) conditions that reduce major risk and high liability exposures. Participating agencies comply with those Recognition standards that are applicable to its statutory role or mission. An assessment is conducted and the agency earns the award of CALEA Recognition. The award period is for three years; maintaining compliance, the submission of an annual report, and re-assessment are required to continue the award.

The agency may remain in Recognition status or opt to comply with the appropriate remaining 344 standards and achieve Accredited status, CALEA's highest award.

The Benefits
Support From Government Officials
Recognition provides objective evidence of an agency's commitment to improve resource management and service delivery. Thus, government officials are more confident in the agency's ability to operate efficiently and meet community needs.

Stronger Defense Against Lawsuits and Citizen Complaints
Recognized agencies are better able to defend themselves against allegations of misconduct and lawsuits. Recognized agencies show their professional accomplishments by addressing high liability and critical organizational issues. In doing so, they may be eligible for reduction in costs for liability insurance.

Critical Thinking What can agencies that fail the recognition process do to succeed at it?

self-assessment and on-site assessment phases are initiated once again. Approximately nine of every ten agencies that earn initial accreditation undertake the reaccreditation process.[33]

Benefits of Accreditation The accreditation process provides dynamic and ongoing benefits for police managers, officers, and the community. Managers' benefits include being able to provide norms that can measure agency performance over time. Managers can also get guidance on how to develop and justify stronger police budgets, especially to hire more personnel. Police officers benefit from knowing that organizational processes are in accord with national standards for fair treatment. Finally, the community is assured of a commitment to high-quality service delivery.

The benefits of seeking accreditation and adhering to a professional set of standards have a direct relationship to positively addressing the many significant areas of law enforcement liability. By voluntarily creating policies, procedures, and mechanisms addressing high-risk and high-liability areas such as the use of force, vehicular pursuits, arrest, and search and seizure, a police department can minimize legal vulnerability.[34]

CALCEA summarizes the benefits of seeking and getting accreditation as follows:

1. Providing better public services
2. Controlled liability insurance costs
3. Stronger defense against lawsuits and citizen complaints
4. Greater accountability within the agency
5. Support from government officials
6. verification of excellence

The goals are identified as:

1. Prpmote superior public safety
2. Recognize professional excellence
3. Avoid conflict with technical standards established by authorities

5.3 Self Check

1. How is community policing linked to organizational change within police agencies?
2. What is POST?

POLICING *Online*

Check your answers at
www.policing.glencoe.com

5.4 Private Policing

Private policing, also called private security, consists of any individual, organization, or service, other than public law enforcement and regulatory agencies, that is engaged primarily in the prevention and investigation of crime, loss, or harm to specific individuals, organizations, or facilities.[35] Public safety demands that the police concentrate on crime prevention and criminal apprehension. While these priorities compel federal, state, and local agencies to focus on enforcing the law, they also require them to provide other public services. Some of these do not need to be performed by sworn law enforcement, and some could excessively drain law enforcement resources. Because of this gap in public services delivery, private security forces emerged.

Before the mid-nineteenth century, there was little, if any, private policing, but the need for it was growing. The modern police force became established in the eastern cities and began to spread westward. Not everyone accepted the idea of armed, uniformed policing at public expense. Furthermore, some crimes, especially those that crossed expansive territories and jurisdictions, could not be handled by municipal police. Finally, public police forces were too small to provide protective services for certain projects, such as the building of a transcontinental railroad.

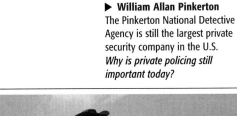

▶ **William Allan Pinkerton**
The Pinkerton National Detective Agency is still the largest private security company in the U.S.
Why is private policing still important today?

▶ **Wells Fargo Security Company** This company started as a uniquely American security service.
How do private police services differ from those of a public police force?

Role Conflicts with Private Policing

With the numbers of private police and security growing constantly, many police are concerned that the actions of this industry will over-shadow the work of public policing. For example, the Canadian Police Association (CPA), which faces a situation very similar to the one in the United States, has "growing concerns over the encroachment of private security on areas of police responsibility."

CPA President Grant Obst states, "If security personnel are acting like the police and looking like the police, then what they do and how they do it can and will impact both the public and the police. Private security is not the police. They are not trained to the same high standard public police services must maintain, they do not have the appropriate status and authority to enforce all aspects of the law, and they are not subject to the public accountability mechanisms the public expects and demands for the police."

What Do You Think? Should police and private security be more clearly separated in the United States, too? Why or why not?

SOURCE: "Canadian Police Association Alarmed about Private Security." From Canada NewsWire, October 6, 1999, http://www.newswire.ca/releases/October1999/06/c1427.html.

In the early days of private security services there were to abuses by untrained and poorly disciplined agents. No licensing standards applied to the private security field, and security personnel sometimes became private goons, thugs that catered only to the wishes of their employers. Many of the persons hired were unfamiliar with citizens' basic constitutional protections and were both legally and physically abusive. In fact, many security personnel could have been arrested for assault and battery had citizens known the criminal statutes and pressed charges.

Another downside to private security was the impact on crime statistics. Very often, criminal perpetrators who faced "street justice" at the hands of security officers were not turned over to the public criminal justice system, which made crime rates seem lower and thus skewed the crime picture.

Private Policing Today

Private security has slowly evolved toward professionalizing its ranks, and it still has far to go before it will match the standards of public policing. Much of the impetus for improving the quality of private policing was due to liability issues. Major corporations employing their own officers were liable for lawsuits due to employee misbehavior. As the demands on public policing increased with the rising incidence of crime, public police often could not provide the level of assets protection that corporate America desired. Given this shortfall, the demand for private-sector services increased—as did the competition. This competitiveness also stimulated them to improve their services.

Training in Private Policing To ensure at least a minimal degree of competence among private security personnel, a number of states now require a licensing process for officers, although a few still require little more than an application and a small fee. Twenty-three states mandate training if the security officer is to be armed, but only 14 require any training for unarmed guards. Most training is relatively simple: Topics typically include fire prevention, first aid, building safety, equipment use, report writing, and the legal powers of private security personnel.

Most private security firms today depend on their own training programs to prevent legally actionable mistakes by employees. Training is also available from a number of schools and agencies. One is the International Foundation for Protection Officers (IFPO). Those who pass the IFPO's home-study course earn the status of Certified Protection Officer. In an effort to increase the professional status of the private security industry, the 32,000-member American Society for Industrial Security (ASIS) was established in 1955. Today ASIS administers a comprehensive examination periodically in various locations across the country. These examinations are very thorough and usually require a combination of experience and study to earn a passing grade. Applicants who pass the ASIS examination earn the coveted title Certified Protection Professional. Examination subject areas include:

- Security management
- Physical security
- Loss prevention
- Investigations
- Internal/external relations
- Protection of sensitive information
- Personnel security
- Emergency planning
- Legal aspects of security
- Substance abuse screening [36]

Growth in Private Policing More than two million persons are employed in more than 4,000 agencies that constitute the private police industry. Private security is estimated to cost American industries in excess of $64 billion

Private Policing Success

Two success stories from early private policing in America were Wells Fargo and Brinks. The Wells Fargo Company was founded in 1852 to supply detective and protective services to citizens living in American states and territories west of Missouri. Because such areas were generally underpoliced, Wells Fargo's services became essential for those handling valuable goods. In 1859, the Brinks Company began as a general package delivery service very similar to the courier services today. By the turn of the century, however, they offered armored delivery for valuable goods. Gradually, they became industry leaders in transporting cash for financial institutions.

CAREER FOCUS

Former FBI Agent

Job Description

New agents usually spend their first assignments doing applicant background investigations for the White House or various government agencies. It is a good way to get experience with the FBI's very meticulous way of getting things done. New agents might also be allowed to work on fugitive cases. A police department might have a fugitive, and they'll call in the FBI for help.

As a rule of thumb, for every hour of investigation (going out, talking to people, conducting surveillance), there are three hours of paperwork. That is a very important part of the job: Once you get in court, you must show analytical and logical thought, and have good writing skills so you come off as professional, otherwise, you will get torn up by defense attorneys. The most rewarding aspect of the profession is working with people from so many diverse backgrounds and yet having everybody mesh together to form a team. On the other hand, you can get into dangerous situations, go in areas that are not friendly to law enforcement, and you have to be aggressive.

Robert J. Golden

Employment History

I was an FBI agent from 1970 to 1988. I started my career in Memphis, Tennessee, after I finished the FBI academy. I was transferred to the Washington, D.C. office and stayed there for several years, and next went on to work in Santa Ana, California. Foreign intelligence was a busy area then because of the Cold War with the Soviet Bloc, but now the emphasis is more on terrorism, bank robberies, and computer crime.

Education

Candidates should have a college degree. Expertise in law, accounting, computers, natural science, biology, physics, foreign languages—any of these can be very good to have. The FBI tends not to hire people right out of college. People should have a little more life and work experience.

Follow-Up Which sounds like the most challenging aspect of this profession? Why?

annually, while public law enforcement expenditures total $40 billion.[37] The private policing field is about three times larger than the federal, state, and local forces combined.[38] (See Figure 5.7.) Major reasons for the quick growth of the American security sector include:

- An increase in crimes in the workplace
- An increase in fear (real or perceived) of crime
- The fiscal crises of the states, which limit public protection and spending
- An increased public and business awareness and use of more cost-effective private products and services[39]

The activities of private security personnel vary widely. Security firms today provide services for hospitals, manufacturing plants, communications industries, retirement homes, hotels, casinos, exclusive communities and clubs, nuclear storage facilities and reactors, and many other types of businesses. Security personnel sometimes work undercover, blending with company

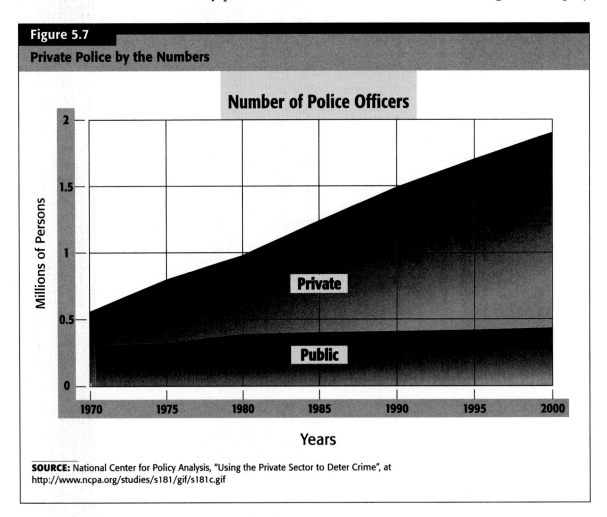

Figure 5.7

Private Police by the Numbers

Number of Police Officers

SOURCE: National Center for Policy Analysis, "Using the Private Sector to Deter Crime", at http://www.ncpa.org/studies/s181/gif/s181c.gif

employees to learn who is pilfering inventory or selling business secrets to competitors. Bodyguards, another area of private security activity, are commonplace among wealthy business executives and celebrities.[40]

Problems in Private Policing The public-private police interface has resulted in a number of positive cooperative efforts involving such tasks as transporting hazardous materials, protecting dignitaries, and controlling crowds. An example is a recent sting operation conducted by the FBI and the security personnel of IBM, involving the sale of computer secrets in California's Silicon Valley. However, this interaction has not been without problems. Lack of communication between public and private policing organizations has resulted in botched investigations, destruction of evidence, and overzealousness by the private police.[41] These problems often surface in the aftermath of burglaries or robberies in the form of contamination of fingerprints or general crime scene disruption.

Private police are less skilled in observing crime scenes and tend to omit important evidence. For example, private police may fail to note the license plates of suspicious vehicles or to accurately describe suspects. Occasionally, security officers jeopardize the safety of police officers by failing to advise them of important information, such as the fact that an armed suspect is at the rear of a building or on a balcony with an unobstructed line of fire toward anyone who approaches.

Private Security/Police Cooperation There is a pronounced, growing interdependence of the private and public protective services sectors. Certainly, law enforcement officials welcome partnerships with private security if it frees up public officers for basic crime fighting. In fact, the National Institute of Justice has identified a number of areas in which private security can assume some of the burden borne by overworked public law enforcement agencies. Services cited include public building security, parking enforcement, animal control, special event security, prisoner transport, courtroom security, and patrol of public parks. Many police departments have been supportive of having the private sector respond to burglary alarms to the private sector. Indeed, numerous law enforcement officials view response to residential burglary alarms as a special consideration for the minority of citizens who can afford such alarm systems rather than as a community-wide police function.[42] Given the steady progression of privatization that has been witnessed to date, the indications are strong for continued effective collaboration for the public good.

5.4 Self Check

1. How is American private policing raising its standards?
2. What are some problems associated with private policing?

POLICING
Online
Check your answers at
www.policing.glencoe.com

Chapter 5

The Organization of Policing

1. Name the basic characteristics of American law enforcement.

Basic characteristics of American policing are:
- It is large.
- It is multilevel, with municipal, county, state, federal, and sometimes even international crime issues.
- It is evolving as crime issues change.
- It shares overlapping jurisdictions.
- It must show responsiveness to citizen requests, public accountability, and openness to evaluation.

2. Explain what a jurisdiction is.

A jurisdiction is the geographic area or crime issue over which the authority of a particular law enforcement agency extends. When a law enforcement agency is said to have jurisdiction over an area, it means that officers are authorized to perform law enforcement functions in that area alone. The issues aspect of jurisdiction represents the subject matter and class of laws or crimes that the agency is responsible for enforcing and investigating. These legal perimeters help to outline an agency's goal or mission. However, only the municipal police enforce city ordinances, which are laws that apply within a city's limits and are enforced by city police.

3. Understand what local law enforcement does and how this differs from other levels of law enforcement.

Local law enforcement, also known as municipal police, is based in cities. Officers enforce city ordinances and state penal and vehicle codes and have special concerns regarding their crime prevention strategies, investigative focus, police-community relations, and policing styles. This differs from other law enforcement agencies because of the other agencies' broader jurisdiction and different focus.

4. Distinguish between the centralized and decentralized state police models.

State police departments are either centralized or decentralized.

Centralized state agencies perform a wide spectrum of duties, which may entail enforcement of state penal code sections in remote regions or provision of supplementary services to other law enforcement agencies.

Decentralized state agencies have separate branches for criminal law enforcement and vehicular code enforcement/accident investigation.

5. Name the different federal agencies and explain their specialized work.

Federal law enforcement agencies are:

- Immigration and Naturalization Service (INS): Nearly half of all INS officers are border patrol agents, who interdict illegal aliens and contraband.
- Bureau of Prisons (BOP): Maintains the security of the federal prison system.
- Federal Bureau of Investigation (FBI): Investigates federal crimes, including bank fraud, embezzlement, kidnapping, and civil rights violations.
- Drug Enforcement Agency (DEA): Investigates major narcotics violators and performs drug trafficking prevention and control.
- U.S. Marshals Service: Receives all persons arrested by federal agencies and is responsible for their custody and transportation until they are sentenced.
- U.S. Customs Service (USCS): Interdicts and seizes contraband, processes persons and items entering through U.S. ports of entry, and administers certain navigational laws.
- Internal Revenue Service (IRS): 89 percent work in criminal investigation and primarily investigate tax fraud, and 11 percent are employed for internal security.
- U.S. Secret Service (USSS): Performs criminal investigation and enforcement duties; provides protection for the president, vice president, and their families.
- Bureau of Alcohol, Tobacco, and Firearms (ATF): Investigates the criminal use of firearms and explosives.

6. List the ways in which community policing can serve as a catalyst for effective organizational change.

Community policing can lead to effective organizational change by:

- Requiring a shorter and flatter organizational design, in which services are decentralized and community-based
- Advocating the empowerment of individual officers with more discretion and more responsibility than in traditional policing
- Showing openness and sensitivity to the environment, with a built-in need to interact with members of the wider community
- Inverting the traditional police hierarchy, giving power, authority, and responsibility to field personnel

7. Name the differences between public policing and private policing.

Private security is engaged primarily in the prevention and investigation of crime, loss, or harm to specific individuals, organizations, or facilities. Private security agencies provide these services for private companies or individuals. Private security forces emerged because of gaps in public services delivery due to limited resources.

Major reasons for the growth of private police include:

- Increase in workplace crime
- Increase in fear of crime
- Fiscal crises which limit state spendings on public protection.
- Increase in business awareness of cost-effective private services

Key Terms

police operations (p. 164)
jurisdiction (p. 165)
municipal police (p. 166)
sworn officers (p. 166)
county law enforcement (p. 170)
centralized state agency (p. 172)
decentralized state agency (p. 172)
federal law enforcement (p. 173)
hierarchy (p. 178)

chain of command (p. 179)
unity of command (p. 179)
span of control (p. 180)
line functions (p. 182)
staff functions (p. 183)
specialization (p. 185)
Peace Officer Standards and Training
    (POST) (p. 186)

Questions for Review

1. How is American policing multilevel?
2. What are some of the typical duties of sheriffs' departments?
3. What is the typical structure of most law enforcement agencies, and how does this affect their chain of command?
4. What are common problems with the traditional structure in police agencies?
5. What are line functions and staff functions, and how do they differ?
6. Name and define the main types of minimum standards for police.
7. How does accreditation differ from Peace Officer Standards and Training (POST)?
8. What is the five-step accreditation process?
9. What are the basic elements of the training of private police?
10. Name some of the typical examination subject areas for American private police candidates.

Experiential Activities

11. Career Choices

You are an academy recruit who is considering offers from a sheriff's department and a local police department. The jobs are slightly different because your county sheriff's department focuses mainly on court processes, maintaining the local jail, and traveling outside of the jurisdiction to apprehend bail jumpers. The municipal agency is located in a small suburb with low crime and a strong focus on community policing; it is clearly more for people who are outgoing and have good communication skills. The municipal agency offers a salary that is $3,000 higher per year and has a higher ceiling, but the sheriff's office offers a one-time $5,000 bonus to officers who successfully complete 12 months of probationary work.

    a. Which job has preferable work duties?
    b. Which job offers more chances to advance your career?
    c. List at least four examples of differences in job responsibilities between the two poistions.

Experiential Activities continued

12. Federal Law Enforcement Online

Select a federal law enforcement agency. It can be one of the several that are listed in your textbook or another, smaller agency. Go online and visit its Web site, then write a one-page report about the following: its founding, history, past and current roles, and any current cases or issues that are worth noting. In addition, answer the following questions:

a. Which agency did you choose, and why?

b. Which current cases and issues interested you, and why?

c. How difficult is this organization's screening process?

13. Differences Between Departments

Research three sheriffs' departments: one from an urban area, one from a primarily suburban area, and one from a rural area. Determine the primary duties, staff size, and staff roles of each one. Find out as much as you can regarding their crime problems and citizen needs.

a. What differences did you find among these three agencies that reflected their different locations?

b. What other differences did you find?

c. How do you think each of these agencies meets the needs of their communities?

14. Mission Statements

Collect the mission statements of three different police agencies. They can be municipal, county, state, or federal agencies of any size, and you may collect these in person, by fax, or online. Compare these statements and note their similarities and differences. Note, also,

what their overall focus seems to be. Although mission statements generally follow the same approach, you should be able to notice some differences.

a. What differences did you find among these three statements?

b. Which statement did you prefer the most, and why?

c. Explain what the common elements of the statements are.

Web Patrol

15. DOJ Online

Visit the U.S. Department of Justice, which oversees the activities of several important federal law enforcement agencies. They can be found online at by clicking the link at **www.policing.glencoe.com**.

What is the mission of the DOJ?

16. World's Most Wanted

Go to **www.policing.glencoe.com** and visit a site showing the world's most wanted fugitives and unsolved crimes. Learn about the most wanted fugitives.

Which cases interested you the most, and why?

17. Racial Profiling

Go to the national Criminal Justice Reference Service site and read the report on racial profiling (both links are available at **www.policing.glencoe.com**).

What have you learned about profiling and police discretion?

Critical Thinking Exercises

18. Organizational Hierarchy

You are a police chief who is trying to determine how many officers can be supervised by one person. You have 3 sergeants, 2 lieutenants, and 48 officers who work mainly in patrol, community policing, and criminal investigation. Draw a chart that breaks down the way that you would organize your agency, and make sure that each supervisor has an appropriate amount of staff. Be sure to also explain all of their duties. In addition, answer the following questions:

   a. Is the span of control appropriate for this department? Why or why not?
   b. What other services could be doubled up on officers? Think of as many as you can and try to distribute them evenly among the officers and their supervisors.

19. College for Officers

You are a police recruiter who has noticed that, in your jurisdiction, candidates with some college education tend to perform better as police officers in many ways. They are also more likely to be promoted and stay with the force for longer periods of time. You suggest to your chief that your department should require a minimum of 30 college credits for all applicants to your department. It will reduce the total number of applicants somewhat but will not reduce the amount of applicants who fit your high standards. Your chief disagrees; since he does not have a college degree, he somewhat resents being told that college education is better for officers, and he always says that there is no proof that they can perform better.

   a. What can you do to convince your chief to see your point of view without offending him?
   b. If your minimum standards reform succeeds, how can you communicate this to new recruits in a way that will entice more college-educated recruits to your department?

20. Problems with Private Security

You are a police officer who is investigating a case of computer theft at a local office building. Evidently, an employee tried to steal several computers and monitors at around 2:00 A.M. this morning. You arrive to lift fingerprints and ask questions. However, the private security staff that already works there tells you proudly that they have all the fingerprints for you. You examine them and find that they were lifted in a very sloppy manner that has smudged all of them beyond recognition. You visit the area in which the computers were stolen and find someone from the cleaning crew wiping down the last of the evidence with a sponge. You ask the security staff if there were any video cameras that show the suspect entering the building, and they say that he entered a door that had a malfunctioning camera.

   a. What has just happened in regard to the private security staff's actions and how it affects this case?
   b. How do the lower standards of private policing create problems for public police?

Endnotes

1. R. M. Shusta, D. R. Levine, P. R. Harris, and H. Z. Wong, *Multicultural Law Enforcement* (Englewood Cliffs, NJ: Prentice Hall, 1995).
2. D. H. Bayley, *Policing in America: Assessment and Prospects* (Washington, D.C.: Police Foundation, 1998).
3. B. L. Berg, *Policing in Modern Society* (Woburn, MA: Butterworth-Heinemann, 1999).
4. B. A. Reaves and A. L. Goldberg, *Census of State and Local Law Enforcement Agencies*, 1996 (Washington, D.C.: Bureau of Justice Statistics, 1998).
5. Berg, *Policing in Modern Society*, 44.
6. National Institute of Justice, *Crime and Policing in Rural and Small-Town America: An Overview of Issues* (Washington, D.C.: Government Printing Office, 1995).
7. Ibid.
8. R. A. Weisheit, D. N. Falcone, and L. E. Wells, *Crime and Policing in Rural and Small-Town America* (Prospect Heights, IL: Waveland, 1996).
9. National Institute of Justice, *Crime and Policing*, 66.
10. Berg, *Policing in Modern Society*, 45.
11. Reaves and Goldberg, *Census of State and Local Law Enforcement Agencies*, 9.
12. F. Schmalleger, *Criminal Justice Today* (Upper Saddle River, NJ: Prentice Hall, 2000).
13. Berg, *Policing in Modern Society*, 48.
14. Official Pennsylvania State Police Web Site [Online]. Available: http://sites.state.pa.us/PA_Exec/State_Police/
15. Reaves and Goldberg, *Census of State and Local Law Enforcement Agencies*, 11.
16. Schmalleger, *Criminal Justice Today*, 181–82.
17. B. Reaves, *Federal Law Enforcement Officers*, 1996 (Washington, D.C.: Bureau of Justice Statistics, 1997).
18. INS [Online]. Available: http://www.ins.usdoj.gov
19. Federal Bureau of Investigations [Online]. Available: http://www.fbi.gov
20. Drug Enforcement Agency [Online]. Available: http://www.dea.gov
21. United States Marshal Service [Online]. Available: http://www.usdoj.gov/marshals
22. United States Secret Service [Online]. Available: http://www.treas.gov/usss
23. ATF [Online]. Available: http://www.atf.treas.gov
24. K. Peak, *Policing America* (Upper Saddle River, NJ: Prentice Hall, 1997).
25. W. W. Bennett and K. M. Hess, *Management and Supervision in Law Enforcement* (New York: West, 1996).
26. C. R. Swanson, L. Territo, and R. W. Taylor, *Police Administration: Structures, Processes, and Behavior* (Upper Saddle River, NJ: Prentice Hall, 1998).
27. R. Trojanowicz and B. Bucqueroux, *Community Policing: How to Get Started* (Cincinnati, OH: Anderson, 1998).
28. W. G. Doerner and M. L. Dantzker, *Contemporary Police Organization and Management: Issues and Trends* (Woburn, MA: Butterworth-Heineman, 2000).
29. Bennett and Hess, *Management and Supervision*, 21–22.
30. International Association of Directors of Law Enforcement Standards & Training, *Model Minimum State Standards* [Online]. Available: http://www.iadlest.org/modelmin.htm
31. Doerner and Dantzker, *Contemporary Police Organization and Management*, 187.
32. R. G. Lynch, *The Police Manager* (Cincinnati, OH: Anderson, 1998).
33. Doerner and Dantzker, *Contemporary Police Organization and Management*, 189–93.
34. Lynch, *The Police Manager*, 200–2.
35. D. Shichor and M. J. Gilbert, *Privatization in Criminal Justice: Past, Present, and Future* (Cincinnati, OH: Anderson, 2001).
36. Schmalleger, *Criminal Justice Today*, 187.
37. Ibid., 190.
38. Ibid., 186.
39. Peak, *Policing America*, 63.
40. Schmalleger, *Criminal Justice Today*.
41. Ibid., 188.
42. Peak, *Policing America*, 64.
43. W. C. Cunningham, J. J. Strauchs, and C. W. Van Meter, *Private Security: Patterns and Trends* (Washington, D.C.: National Institute of Justice, 1991).

Questions for Review

1. Name three stages of a typical day for a patrol officer.

2. What is a first responder?

3. Define the concept of perimeter.

4. What are the responsibilities of a field supervisor?

5. Name the four main responsibilities of a shift supervisor.

6. What are the three issues that shape the practice of social control?

7. List and define the police functions.

8. What is traffic control?

9. Which is most recent, community policing or holistic policing?

10. Why are research and technology key elements of policing today?

11. List and explain the various categories of police officers' personality and the three policing styles.

12. Define chain of command and explain how this concept relates to unity of command and span of control.

13. What is the difference between line of functions and staff functions? Give a few examples in each category.

14. How is rural policing different than policing in large urban centers?

15. Define and contrast a centralized state agency and a decentralized state agency.

The Making of a Police Officer

Chapter 6
Recruitment, Selection, and Training

Chapter 7
Skills for the Successful Police Officer

Recruitment, Selection, and Training

CHAPTER OBJECTIVES

AFTER COMPLETING THIS CHAPTER, YOU WILL BE ABLE TO:

1. Understand what makes a good police officer in the context of modern-day policing.

2. Name the predictors of police success.

3. Understand the recruitment process.

4. Explain all stages of the selection process.

5. List the areas covered by a background check.

6. Distinguish between academy training and FTO training.

7. Discuss current issues in police training.

◀ A potential recruit takes an application for the New york Police Department.

6.1 The American Police Officer

The past two centuries have seen many changes in the role of American policing. Although early American police were modeled after the English bobbies, policing today is quite different. It is easier to understand this transition and its impact on recruitment, selection, and training by comparing the typical officer from the nineteenth century to the officer of the present day.

The Nineteenth-Century Police Officer The first police officers in America were very political in the sense that their appointments were made by politicians. Because of this, officers were forced to waste time catering to these politicians' whims instead of enforcing the law. They had few special skills due to a lack of uniform standards in selection and training. This created police departments that were often dysfunctional and sometimes corrupt.

The Contemporary Officer

The Twentieth-Century Police Officer Policing in the early twentieth century was characterized by an increased interest in reform. Berkeley (CA) Police Chief August Vollmer initiated important changes in a number of areas,

▶ **Police in the New Millennium** Security officer Roger Powell directs Duke to sniff through luggage and locate explosives during a training exercise on January 18, 2002. This is a new era for police, with many more challenges to respond to and expectations to fulfill. *What do you think is the most difficult part of contemporary policing?*

including personnel selection, educational requirements, and training. With the efforts of Vollmer and others, the selection of police officers improved.

During the second half of the century, police agencies raised their standards for hiring and training. In the 1990s, the implementation of problem-oriented and community-oriented policing placed new demands on police officers. Because of these demands, the profile of a typical officer began to change.

The Twenty-First-Century Police Officer The officer of the twenty-first century must be skilled in all of the following areas: problem solving, critical thinking, interpersonal communication, planning and organizing, human behavior, social ecology, and criminal law. Because typical twentieth-century police training standards did not address many of these issues in sufficient depth, many of today's veteran officers struggle with these new skills and expectations.

With such dramatic changes taking place in only a short period of time, recruiting, selecting, and training today's police have become a difficult challenge.

6.1 Self Check

1. How did officers of the nineteenth century differ from contemporary officers?
2. What skills do officers need in the twenty-first century?

POLICING *Online*
Check your answers at
www.policing.glencoe.com

6.2 Recruitment

Recruitment is the use of strategies and benefits to entice people to work as police officers. The quality of services provided by a police department is dependent on the quality of the department's recruits. If a department does not place a high priority on recruitment, there will be fewer candidates in the selection pool and fewer qualified officers on the street.

recruitment The use of strategies and benefits to entice people to work as police officers.

Issues in Recruitment

Today, three issues affect police recruitment: the development of a large enough selection pool, competition with other work fields, and the evolving role of police.

The Selection Pool In the past, departments focused on recruiting enough candidates to fill a **selection pool**, which is all of the candidates from which

selection pool All of the candidates from which a small number of officers are selected.

a small number of officers are selected. It was assumed that most applicants would not survive the selection process because they would be gradually eliminated. For example, a pool of 200 applicants might produce 25 qualified candidates. Most recruiting was conducted within 200 to 300 miles of the department, which provided enough qualified candidates to meet the department's needs.

Today, a shrinking pool of qualified applicants has resulted in departments extending their recruitment areas to cover entire regions and, in some instances, the entire country. A recent survey of police recruiters revealed that the two major problems faced by police recruiters are low entry-level salaries and the inability of applicants to pass the written exam. Approximately 44 percent of applicants felt that the written exams presented the greatest obstacle to becoming a police officer. Their biggest problem areas appeared to be general knowledge and writing.[1]

Outside Competition Another factor that hurts recruiting is the fact that police departments are in competition with every other private business and industry for qualified employees. No longer is entering the police profession a matter of simple idealistic motivation. Rather, candidates are looking at the entire employment package, which includes salary, health care benefits, a retirement package, potential for advancement, and the work environment. To address this, many departments offer incentive pay for education, hazardous duty, merit, shift differential, and language proficiency. For example, candidates for the San Jose (CA) Police Department who speak Spanish, Vietnamese, Chinese, Korean, Cambodian, or Tagalog can receive a biweekly salary incentive for their special language skills.

In addition, police departments offer other benefits such as health care, dental insurance, sick leave, paid holidays, annual leave, pension plans, uniform allowance, and longevity pay. The larger the department, the greater the incentive package offered. One department with excellent benefits is the Fairfax County (VA) Police Department. Employees earn 13 to 40 days of annual leave depending on their seniority, there are 10 paid holidays a year, sick leave may accumulate without limit, and all uniforms and equipment are paid for by the department.[2]

Evolving Role of Police To further complicate matters, the evolving role of police has placed new challenges on police recruiters. Traditional policing in many communities is being replaced with community policing, which requires skills and abilities different from those that are needed for traditional policing. Recruiters must target officers who offer the greatest promise of advancing the ideals and principles of community policing.

Strategies

Successful recruiting requires a number of strategies. A 1994 survey by the Academy of Criminal Justice Science (ACJS) found that the most popular strategy was newspaper advertisements (93 percent), followed by job fairs (81 percent) and radio advertisements (66 percent).[3] Other common strategies include television advertisements, posters, journal ads, and mass mailings. The Internet has provided another means of reaching prospective candidates. Many departments maintain Web sites where candidates can obtain information on hiring criteria, salaries and benefits, and the selection process. Some departments even offer online applications.

What strategies do recruiters use to attract people to policing? Recruiters have to determine what kind of candidates they want and what will make them enthusiastic about policing. Most departments want people who are assertive, willing to take risks, and immersed in police culture. Therefore, they use recruitment tools to project an image of police engaging in dangerous, courageous work such as SWAT, shootouts, and drug busts. Aspects of police work that do not fit the cops-and-robbers image such as community policing usually get less attention. Difficult aspects of policing, such as dealing with gruesome deaths or domestic violence cases, are often left out.

This approach attracts people who are enthusiastic about policing and also helps make policing competitive with other professions that are trying to lure candidates. Still, it has some shortcomings. It sometimes attracts

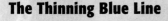

Police Procedure

The Thinning Blue Line

In a tight job market, good cops are hard to find. Detroit's recent recruiting drive yielded 287 viable candidates out of 1,200 applicants. The top disqualification? Prior convictions. The various reasons for disqualification were:

- 324 did not show up for exams.
- 211 had been convicted of felonies or disqualifying misdemeanors.
- 169 flunked a written eighth-grade equivalency exam or an agility test.

- 126 were ineligible for other reasons.
- 66 were disqualified after a background check revealed poor work records or drug use.
- 13 had outstanding arrest warrants for everything from traffic violations to felonies.
- 4 were not U.S. citizens.

Only 287 were left qualified.

Critical Thinking What can recruiters do to attract more qualified applicants?

SOURCE: Lucy Howard, Paul O'Donnell, and Seth Stevenson, "Cop Out: The Thinning Blue Line," *Newsweek* 133, no. 18: 8.

people with aggressive personalities, who can cause liability issues by using excessive force. Furthermore, it might discourage people with the calm and objective personalities needed for successful community policing. Police recruiters need to be aware of this and attempt to attract individuals who are both assertive and approachable.

Regardless of the strategy used, the goal is to produce diversity and quality in the candidate pool. In an effort to increase the quality of the applicant pool, many police departments target special groups such as minorities, women, veterans, college graduates, and those with prior police service. Ninety percent of all departments focus on recruiting minorities, and 52 percent place an emphasis on recruiting women. Only 37 percent target college graduates and veterans, with 20 percent focusing on candidates with prior police experience.[4]

Minimum Standards for Employment

minimum standards
Employment standards such as age, height, weight, education, absence of criminal record, and residency, which are established by the state and the individual police organization.

Any effort to recruit police officers begins with a listing of **minimum standards** for employment. These standards are established by the state and by individual police organizations. Minimum standards ensure a certain level of education and responsibility in policing candidates and help weed out those who are not fit for the job—but do they answer the question of what makes a good police officer? Perhaps not, because police work is so complex and relies on so many different personality traits.

Evolution of Minimum Standards The idea that those who perform the duties of law enforcement should do so in compliance with uniformly applied standards is not really a new concept. In fact, the origin of police standards can be found in the teachings of Robert Peel. He had requirements for his recruits' age, height, and personality. August Vollmer, adopting many of Peel's beliefs, added valuable input about minimum standards to national commissions such as the Wickersham Commission, which used minimum standards to enhance police professionalism.

In 1929, the Wickersham Commission concluded that law enforcement was far too often corrupt, brutal, and composed of unethical and untrained personnel. Its reports formally called attention to these long-standing problems and prescribed corrective action. In 1953, the American Bar Association (ABA) published a "Model Policing Training Act," which outlined broad functions that should be overseen by police regulatory agencies.

In 1967, the President's Commission on Law Enforcement and the Administration of Justice published two reports: *The Challenge of Crime in a Free Society* and *The Police.* Both reports recommended changes to community relations, personnel practices, and operational policies. Finally, in 1973, the National Advisory Commission on Criminal Justice Standards and Goals published its recommendations for improvements. Specific recommendations ranged from proposals for improving recruitment and selection to encouraging the imposition of extensive recruit training and in-service training requirements.

Development of POST The two 1967 reports mentioned above strongly encouraged states to establish Peace Officer Standards and Training (POST) commissions. At that time, 17 states had already established POST bodies; California and New York had established the first POST commissions in 1959. By 1981, all 50 states had POST commissions.

The POST organizations were created out of the crucible of conflict, change, and the demand for professionalism in public officers. POST programs assured citizens that government oversight was in place to ensure that peace officers met minimum standards of competency and ethical behavior. They also ensured that the parent agencies adopted programs that were sensible, effective, and consistent with contemporary notions of what standards should be for all officers.

Scope of Standards Formal standards cover a range of areas. The primary areas of coverage are officer selection, basic recruit and in-service training programs, and instructor development. Selection standards generally require satisfactory completion of a medical examination, criminal history check, psychological exam, physical fitness assessment, and personal interview by the hiring authority. In addition, candidates must satisfy minimum and maximum age requirements, be citizens of the United States, meet educational minimums (usually passing at least a high school diploma), and possess a driver's license.

Basic recruit standards exist to provide a supportive environment that encourages candidates to be empathetic, culturally aware, skilled in the use of discretion, adept at problem solving, and respectful of constitutional limitations on their authority. Curriculum is based on a job-task analysis, which is customarily updated at least every five years. Topics of instruction include criminal law, use of force, search and seizure, defensive techniques, report writing, first aid, pursuit driving, firearms, nonlethal devices, cultural diversity, and traffic accident investigation.

Age, height, weight, education, absence of criminal record, and residency are some of the minimum standards that departments use in the selection process. Applicants are permitted to withdraw if they realize that they do not meet these standards.

Age Police officers are often required to make decisions that can affect the lives of the citizens they serve. Whether an officer makes an arrest or uses deadly force, the consequences are far-reaching. Therefore, most police departments require a minimum age of 21 to ensure that applicants have the maturity to handle the duties and responsibilities of a police officer. As for the upper limit, many departments in the past established a limit of 35 years of age, but federal legislation has forced many departments to remove the maximum age limit.

Height and Weight In the 1960s, most police departments maintained a minimum height standard of 5 feet 8 inches. One state police force required a higher standard of 6 feet. The reasoning was that larger police officers would deter suspects from assaulting the officers and that they would have the advantage in physical confrontations. The reality is that police work rarely requires physical confrontation, because most citizens are compliant when given an order. Instead, officers must be able to give orders to citizens without offending them and causing unnecessary conflicts. Police do not

▶ **Generation Gap** Many older officers face the extra challenge of adapting to the rapidly changing world of policing.
What can be done to help older officers keep up with changes?

need physical strength as much as they need interpersonal communication and critical thinking skills.

In 1994, only 3.4 percent of large police departments still had a minimum height requirement. One reason for this drastic decline was that U.S. courts felt that minimum height standards discriminated against women and certain minority candidates, such as Hispanics and Asians. Today the standard in most police departments is that height and weight must be proportional.

Education Nearly 100 years ago, August Vollmer required a college education for police officers in his department. In the 1960s and 1970s, several national commissions advocated the need for higher educational standards and stressed that all sworn personnel should have bachelor's degrees. In 1997, though, only 1 percent of departments required a four-year degree and 8 percent required an associate's degree. Overall, 31 percent of departments required applicants to have some college education, but the majority of departments required only a high school diploma or general education diploma (GED).

The role of higher education in the police selection process has always been controversial. The key question in the debate is whether people with college degrees make better police officers. Research on this topic has not been able to identify the critical components of a college education that might affect police performance, so the value of college for police officers is still uncertain.

To further complicate the issue, studies on the effect of higher education for police have typically examined two dimensions of measurement—behavior and attitude. Both of these are difficult to measure because of the variable nature of police duties. A positive behavioral outcome of higher education in one situation may be a negative outcome in another. For example, one police chief may want and encourage flexibility in exercising discretion, a quality that is often found in college-educated officers. Another, with a more authoritarian management philosophy, may see such behavior as weak.

Amid uncertainty about the value of higher education, many support the value of a college degree because of the following benefits:

- Greater knowledge of procedures, functions, and principles relevant to the officer's present and future assignments
- Better appreciation of the professional role and its importance in the criminal justice system, as well as in society
- More desirable psychological qualities such as alertness, empathy, flexibility, initiative, and intelligence
- Greater range of interpersonal skills centered in the ability to communicate, be responsive to others, and exercise benevolent leadership

The Minnesota Model

The State of Minnesota has a unique application process for law enforcement officers. It consists of both academic and clinical programs. The academic program requires a two- or four-year degree from one of Minnesota's 20 POST-certified colleges or universities. The clinical program consists of a 9- to 12-week course. Candidates in Minnesota must pay for and complete the program before seeking employment. Candidates must pass a licensing examination in order to receive a temporary license to apply for law enforcement jobs. After an agency hires an individual, POST issues the officer a three-year license to practice in Minnesota. To renew the license, an officer must earn 48 hours of continuing education credit through college courses and agency-sponsored training.

SOURCE: Michael Breci, "Higher Education for Law Enforcement: The Minnesota Model," *The FBI Law Enforce-ment Bulletin* 63, no. 1 (1994): 1.

- Greater ability to analyze situations, exercise discretion independently, and make judicious decisions
- Strong moral character, which reflects a sense of conscience and the qualities of honesty, reliability, and tolerance
- More desirable system of personal values consistent with the police function in a democratic society

Among the perceived disadvantages of college are that college-educated officers are more likely to leave policing, question orders, and request reassignment.[7]

As more and more departments embrace community policing, the need for officers with problem-solving and critical thinking skills becomes essential. These can be found more often in college-educated officers. Furthermore, federal courts have upheld the right of police departments to require higher education in recruits. In the 1985 case of *Davis v. Dallas*, the court upheld the Dallas Police Department's minimum educational entry requirement of 45 college credit hours. The court stated that the nature of policing warranted a higher level of education, even though it limited the number of minority applicants.[8] One state, Minnesota, has taken the lead in establishing a statewide standard by requiring a recruit to complete either a two-year or four-year degree prior to beginning police training.[9] Also, many police departments offer incentives for credits completed or a college degree. The Austin (TX) Police Department pays an additional $50, $100, and $150 a month to holders of associate's, bachelor's, and master's degrees, respectively.

Criminal Record Because integrity is an essential aspect of policing, an applicant with a criminal record is a serious concern to administrators. It indicates an absence of ethical standards, which, if ignored, can have devastating consequences on the street. The 1997 Law Enforcement Management and Administration Survey found that 95 percent of police departments use criminal record checks as part of the screening process.[10]

At the same time, concern about shrinking applicant pools has forced many departments to take a more flexible approach. Many departments now do not automatically reject applicants with criminal records. Instead, they look at whether the crime was a felony or misdemeanor, whether the crime was committed when the applicant was an adult or juvenile, the number of offenses, and when the last offense was committed.

In the past, for example, the Illinois state police automatically denied employment to all candidates with a criminal record. Today, the agency continues to reject candidates who have been convicted of felonies, but it accepts applications from those who have been convicted of misdemeanors.

The California Highway Patrol also accepts applications from candidates who have been convicted of misdemeanors, but its application process includes both a thorough background check and a personal interview during which a candidate must answer questions about his or her personal character. CHP interviewers ask not only about past criminal conduct, but also about the traffic citations, at-fault automobile collisions, and arrests. The CHP also has several automatic disqualification criteria, which are kept secret from applicants in order to ensure their honesty.

Drug Use One of the most difficult ethical areas to judge is drug involvement, because more and more people have used drugs as juveniles. If an applicant has been arrested for a drug offense, it will surface in the criminal record check. Since eliminating every person who has used drugs greatly restricts the applicant pool, the general position today is that experimental use of soft drugs such as marijuana is not a basis for automatic elimination as long as there has been a significant period since the drug was last used. The use of hard drugs such as heroin or crack is not tolerated at all.

Residency In the late nineteenth century, most officers lived in the communities they policed, but by the late twentieth century, many officers lived outside the city and commuted to work. Today, some departments mandate residency within the city limits for several reasons. First, officers living in a community have direct observation of the community on- and off-duty. They also have greater rapport with residents, which results in a better flow of information. Officers who have families and own a home in a particular community are also more likely to be protective of it. Finally, to maintain a racial and ethnic balance between the police and the community it serves, many departments have recruited within its service area where there are often concentrations of various racial and ethnic groups.

Those who oppose residency requirements feel that they limit a department's ability to select qualified officers and require officers to live in less than desirable neighborhoods. In an effort to overcome these objections and entice officers to live in the neighborhoods they police, some departments offer incentives such as housing subsidies. Minneapolis city officials use incentives such as mortgage deals, day care services, discounted bus rides, bonus points on civil service exams, and other preferences for city residents.[11]

6.2 Self Check

1. What are the benefits of a college education for police officers?
2. Name the typical minimum standards for employment in law enforcement.

POLICING Online
Check your answers at
www.policing.glencoe.com

selection The process of testing and interviewing policing candidates to see if they qualify for police work.

Civil Rights Act of 1964, Title VII A federal law that prohibits employment discrimination on the basis of race, color, religion, sex, age, or national origin by employers who employ 15 or more persons and are engaged in an industry affecting commerce; applies to all police departments.

Age Discrimination Act of 1967 A federal law that prohibits employment discrimination against persons older than 40.

Americans with Disabilities Act (ADA) A federal law that makes it illegal to discriminate against qualified individuals with disabilities.

Selection is the process of testing and interviewing policing candidates to see if they qualify for police work. Once a sufficient pool of candidates is created, the selection process begins. Early American law enforcement had an absence of minimum standards. Today, the police officer selection process today can best be characterized as an obstacle course. First of all, any selection process must be conducted according to state and federal guidelines and employment practices. These guidelines include:

- **Civil Rights Act of 1964, Title VII**: This federal law prohibits employment discrimination on the basis of race, color, religion, sex, age, or national origin by employers who employ 15 or more persons and are engaged in an industry affecting commerce. The entire selection process is under the scrutiny of the Equal Employment Opportunity Commission (EEOC), which administers the provisions of Title VII. This law is particularly critical if discrimination exists and a department is struggling with how to develop a selection process that is fair, impartial, and nondiscriminatory.
- **Age Discrimination Act of 1967**: This federal law prohibits employment discrimination against persons older than 40.
- **Americans with Disabilities Act (ADA)**: This federal law makes it illegal to discriminate against qualified individuals with disabilities.

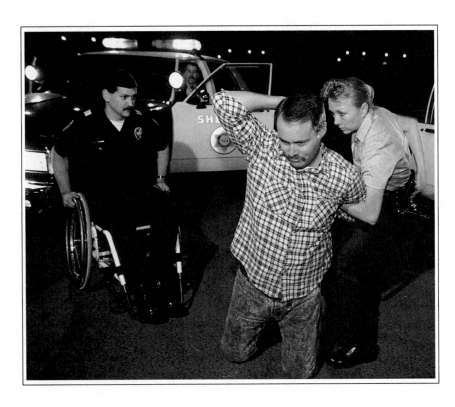

▶ **Equal Opportunity** Chuck Ochoa, a handicapped police officer with L.A. County Sheriff's Star Center (Whittier, CA), observes a policewoman handcuff a suspect. Under federal law, police departments must provide reasonable accommodation to officers with disabilities. *How do you think a department could accommodate an officer who uses a wheelchair?*

Figure 6.1

Minimum Standards for Employment

When recruiting, police departments always measure candidates against minimum standards that must be met for employment. Some typical standards are

- Have a high-school diploma or GED; some agencies encourage applicants to have at least an associate's degree, although most do not require it
- Be at least 21 years old
- Have or be able to obtain a valid drivers license from the appropriate state
- Have not commited or been convicted of any felonies or serious misdemeanors
- Have not been convicted of driving while impaired within a certain time frame
- Be in good physical health
- Be a United States citizen
- Have an honorable military discharge, if applicable
- Pass an entry-level written examination and physical ability test
- Pass an extensive background investigation
- Pass a psychological examination, polygraph examination, medical examination, and drug screening

In addition, state law prohibits discrimination in employment based on race, ethnicity, and gender. More recently, as more minorities have moved up the organizational ladder, the EEOC has changed its focus from discrimination in hiring and testing to a focus on promotions and other personnel actions. The responsibility for overseeing the selection process is normally in the hands of a special commission. All states (except Hawaii) have created a commission that has legislative authority to establish and enforce minimum mandatory standards for law enforcement officers. Candidates in most states are required to be certified by this commission prior to working as law enforcement officers. Figure 6.1, above, lays out the typical minimum standards for police employment. In California, the commission is called the California Commission on Peace Officer Standards and Training (POST). Its mission and vision are:

> To continually enhance the professionalism of California law enforcement in serving its communities ... POST is committed to a vision of the future that ensures quality, integrity, accountability, and cooperation; encourages new ideas; explores and uses appropriate technologies; and delivers relevant, client-based programs and services.[12]

Finally, all employers must consider minimum standards for selelction. Forty-five states mandate that law enforcement officers meet certain minimum standards, which are normally outlined in administrative rules.

Preliminary Examinations

Preliminary examinations consist of the written entrance exam, physical agility test, and polygraph examination. These are relatively inexpensive, so they are placed early in the process. Expensive steps such as the background investigation, oral interview, medical exam, and psychological evaluation are placed later, after the majority of applicants have been weeded out. These will be discussed in later sections of this chapter.

Figure 6.2 on page 219 ("Model for Processing Police Applicants") illustrates the order of steps in ideal selection process.

Written Entrance Exam Any selection process begins with a written examination. Many smaller departments lease their exams from a private contractor who specializes in offering testing services; larger departments may develop and administer their own entrance tests based on their hiring needs. Nearly every department uses a written test, cognitive test, intelligence test, or a combination of these to determine eligibility. Numerous books and workshops are available to aid applicants in preparing for the police entrance examination. If an applicant does not pass the entrance exam the first time, he or she can retake the test.

▶ **Making the Grade** The selection process to become a police officer is lengthy and thorough. *Why are there so many steps in the selection process for police candidates?*

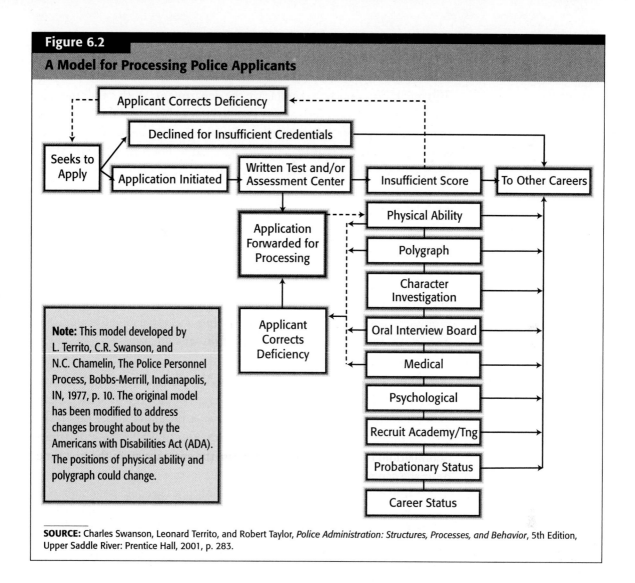

Figure 6.2

A Model for Processing Police Applicants

Applicant Corrects Deficiency

Declined for Insufficient Credentials

Seeks to Apply

Application Initiated

Written Test and/or Assessment Center

Insufficient Score

To Other Careers

Application Forwarded for Processing

Physical Ability

Polygraph

Character Investigation

Applicant Corrects Deficiency

Oral Interview Board

Medical

Psychological

Recruit Academy/Tng

Probationary Status

Career Status

Note: This model developed by L. Territo, C.R. Swanson, and N.C. Chamelin, The Police Personnel Process, Bobbs-Merrill, Indianapolis, IN, 1977, p. 10. The original model has been modified to address changes brought about by the Americans with Disabilities Act (ADA). The positions of physical ability and polygraph could change.

SOURCE: Charles Swanson, Leonard Territo, and Robert Taylor, *Police Administration: Structures, Processes, and Behavior*, 5th Edition, Upper Saddle River: Prentice Hall, 2001, p. 283.

An alternative or supplement to the written exam is the **assessment center,** which provides a series of exercises or simulations. A trained team of evaluators assesses the applicant's behavior and actions in handling the situation. Although expensive in terms of time and manpower, it does provide insight into how a candidate might react on the street. Because this concept is more expensive than traditional written tests, it is often used in selecting mid-management officers but is used less often in the selection of entry-level officers.

assessment center An alternative or supplement to the written exam that provides a series of exercises or simulations.

Problems with Exam Requirements The community-policing movement has highlighted the need for officers who are intelligent and analytical. Unfortunately, many police agencies resist this need in different ways. For example, some departments hesitate to hire officers who are too intelligent.

In 1997, Robert Jordan claimed that the New Haven (CT) Police Department discriminated against him when it denied him employment because his IQ was too high. According to city officials, officers with high IQs quickly become bored and leave the department. With a training price tag of $25,000 per officer, the city decided not to hire candidates who were extremely intelligent.[13] Since Jordan's denial of employment, a federal appellate court has ruled that the city was justified in not hiring Jordan. While his intelligence does not indicate that he would be a poor policeman, Jordan may possess greater flexibility and creativity and might get bored if asked to perform limiting duties such as patrol.

Physical Agility Tests   No one questions the fact that a police officer must be physically fit. The nature of police work often challenges an officer's physical endurance and agility. In police departments, physical fitness is determined by a variety of strategies: Some departments require applicants to run a physical agility course in a prescribed time, and others require applicants to perform certain physical activities within set standards.

Accommodating People with Disabilities   The Americans with Disabilities Act (ADA) has forced law enforcement agencies to reexamine their hiring process as it relates to physical disabilities. A disability is any physical or mental impairment that significantly limits the ability of a person to perform certain functions in life, such as hearing or walking. Public- and private-sector organizations are expected to make reasonable accommodations. For example, an applicant with the use of only one leg could not obtain work as a patrol officer because it would not be reasonable for a police department to modify a patrol car or place a second officer in the car to assist the disabled officer. However, if this disabled applicant applied for a position as a crime analyst, the perspective would change since that job's physical requirements are much less demanding.

polygraph examination
A standard lie detector test that is used in policing to screen applicants.

The Polygraph   Approximately 69 percent of large departments use a **polygraph examination**, which is a standard lie detector test, to screen applicants.[14] Although the polygraph cannot be used in private-sector job screening, governmental agencies such as police departments are exempt. The polygraph offers several advantages to the department. It prompts some applicants to quit the selection process early because they are afraid of disclosing certain prior behavior that might disqualify them from police work. It also conveys a message to the community that the department is employing every means it can to ensure that only qualified individuals are hired.

Before the examination, applicants are presented with a questionnaire that identifies the topics that will be addressed during the examination. These usually include honesty, criminal behavior, sexism, racism,

CopTalk

Physical Exam Tips

The Minneapolis Police Department Training Unit provides helpful online information on how to prepare for the Entry-Level Police Department Fitness Exam. To be considered in the selection process, all applicants must pass each of the events on the day of testing. The tests, minimum passing scores, and tips are as follows:

1. **300-Meter Run (82 Seconds):** The 300-meter run is an anaerobic test. To improve in this event, you should practice sprinting as fast as you can for one-minute periods.

2. **Mile Run (16 Minutes, 15 Seconds):** The 1.5-mile run requires a good level of cardiovascular fitness. To improve in this event, you should be completing 25 to 40 minutes of cardiovascular exercise four or five times per week. You should be exerting yourself to a level equal to at least 70 percent of your target heart rate.

3. **Bench Press (102 pounds or 60 percent of your body weight, whichever is higher, or 25 push-ups):** The upper body (bench press or push-ups) component requires bicep, tricep, and chest strength. To improve in this area, you should be working with free weights or machines or doing such exercises as military presses, bicep curls, tricep extensions, bench press, and rows.

4. **Leg Press (300 lbs., one time) or vertical jump (13.5 inches):** The lower body (leg press) component requires strength in your lower body. To improve in this area, you should use machines or free weights on such exercises as squats, leg extensions, leg curls, lunges, leg press, and dead lifts.

5. **Sit-Ups (30 in one minute):** The sit-up component requires dynamic (endurance) strength in the abdominal area. To improve in this area, you should do several sets of abdominal exercises, such as curl-ups, crunches, or sit-ups four or five times per week.

Finally, if you have access to a health club membership, any personal trainer at that club will be able to provide you with guidance in achieving these goals.

What Do You Think? How much of this test's preparation is physical and how much is psychological?

SOURCE: "Tips for the Physical Fitness Test," Minneapolis Police Department, http://www.ci.minneapolis.mn.us/citywork/police/about/jobs/polap.pdf.

---

aggressive tendencies, motivation for becoming a police officer, and sexual preferences. In recent years, examiners have placed an increased focus on the applicant's involvement with drugs, asking applicants about their recent use of drugs, frequency of use, type of drugs used, and involvement in the sale and distribution of drugs. Many departments have found it difficult to hire officers who are completely drug free. As a result, most permit experimental use of marijuana and even the highly additive drug cocaine, but draw the line with hallucinogenic drugs such

MYTH	FACT
If you become disabled while working as an officer, you will lose your job.	Although some departments dismiss disabled officers (and often lose lawsuits as a result), most departments will find desk jobs or other physically undemanding jobs to help keep them with the department.

as LSD. If an applicant fails the polygraph exam, he or she usually has the opportunity to take a second examination.

As police integrity and ethical conduct are called into question, more and more police departments are using the polygraph. The board of inquiry in Los Angeles' Rampart scandal recommended that all polygraph examinations "should be administered routinely to all police officer candidates prior to conducting their background investigation with a particular emphasis on drug use and integrity issues. The cost associated with this effort will undoubtedly be offset by the reduced costs associated with disciplinary and litigation processes generated by problem officers."[15]

The Background Investigation

background investigation
An extensive investigation of police applicants that examines several prior behaviors, including past drug use, crime record, driving record, and job performance.

More than 95 percent of all police departments use a background investigation as part of their selection process. The **background investigation** is an extensive investigation of applicants that examines several prior behaviors, including past drug use, crime record, driving record, and job performance. The extent of the investigation varies by department. Larger departments have the resources to conduct more extensive checks than smaller departments conduct. A background investigation focuses on a number of areas:

- Verifying all information on the application
- Fingerprinting the applicant
- Checking for a criminal record
- Reviewing the driving record
- Checking military records to verify service
- Interviewing personal references, former employers, and former teachers
- Assessing job and academic performance
- Checking financial stability

The background investigation is normally conducted by a special unit, which approaches the task with the primary goal of verifying that the information provided by the applicant is true. Background investigators must give the same energy and attention to a background check as they would to a major felony case because a minor investigative oversight could result in the selection of an unqualified applicant.

Fingerprinting The applicant who clears the initial written test and physical agility test can expect to be fingerprinted. The fingerprints are then submitted to the FBI for a criminal record check. A failure to conduct this check can have serious repercussions for the department. During a high-profile corruption scandal in the New Orleans Police Department during the 1990s, for example, it was discovered that a number of officers with criminal records were hired because the department did not perform adequate background investigations.

Driving Record Investigators must also check the driving record of applicants. If an applicant has a history of speeding tickets, this indicates a disrespectful attitude toward traffic laws. Even if an applicant meets all other hiring requirements, a poor traffic record could disqualify him or her. When one young applicant applied to a North Carolina police department, he quickly discovered that three speeding tickets within an 18-month period disqualified him. The department told him that his application would be reconsidered after his speeding violations were purged from his record, which takes three years in North Carolina, and if he maintained a clean driving record. He maintained a clean driving record, his speeding violations were purged, and he was eventually hired by the department.

◀ **Background Checks** In one of the worst cases of police corruption Officer Antoinette Frank was convicted of murdering a New Orleans restaurant owner. Several cases point to the importance of thorough checks into the background and character of applicants.
Why do some departments fail to perform adequate background checks?

Military Service If an applicant has served in the military, his or her military service must be verified. Many departments view military service as an advantage for applicants because it provides discipline and structure—as long as the applicant did not have a disciplinary problem while serving and was honorably discharged.

References A major phase of the background investigation is checking personal references, past employers, and former teachers. When it is possible, the best strategy for checking references is to make personal visits. This technique allows the investigator to examine the nonverbal language of the interviewee, which might prompt the investigator to ask more probing questions. Constraints on resources, however, often force departments to check references by telephone.

It should be noted that references listed by the applicant are those chosen by him or her and therefore are most likely to offer a favorable recommendation. A wise strategy is to develop additional references other than those listed by the applicant, especially when it appears that the listed references are providing a rehearsed response.

Job and Academic Performance A check of former employers often offers insight into the applicant's work ethic and ability to work with people. Applicants who have had work-related problems often attempt to conceal this by extending the time periods of former jobs so that there appear to be no gaps in employment. By checking with employers, an applicant's true work history can be verified. If a gap appears, this is a red flag that should prompt further investigation.

Financial Stability Finally, checking an applicant's financial status determines if the applicant has financial problems that could be a liability to the department. An applicant with a good credit rating demonstrates sound financial management skills, responsibility, and self-control. When there is evidence of serious debt or bankruptcy, an applicant is more susceptible to corruption, especially in the form of bribes.

6.3 Self Check

1. What are the federal guidelines that affect police officer recruitment?
2. What areas does a background investigation focus on?

POLICING *Online*

Check your answers at
www.policing.glencoe.com

6.4 Final Selection Stages

Candidates who pass the background investigation stage can expect to have an oral interview. If they pass the oral interview, they will be given medical and psychological examinations. After completing these successfully, the obstacle course of the selection process will be over, and they will be ready for training, which will be covered at the end of this chapter.

Oral Interview Board

The purpose of the oral interview is to evaluate the applicant's overall appearance, demeanor, social skills, interpersonal communication skills, judgment, emotional stability, and suitability for the job. The format of the oral interview differs from department to department. A smaller department may have the candidate interview with the mayor, city council member, or police chief. In larger departments, the candidate may be interviewed by a board consisting of a cross section of government representatives, psychologists, sociologists, community leaders, and police staff officers. In some cases, the entire interview board may be composed of police staff officers or members of a civil service commission.

During the oral interview, candidates are evaluated on their common sense, verbal communication skills, motivation, appearance, thinking skills, compassion, penchant for sexism and racism, and patience. Almost all departments use an identical interview format. Approximately 75 percent have a structured evaluation sheet and provide training to the interviewers. Some departments combine an oral interview with the use of an assessment center.

The Philadelphia Police Department uses the following process:

1. The oral interview begins with an orientation video to help applicants understand the interview process.
2. One candidate at a time enters the interview room for the oral interview.
3. An examiner presents the applicant with four different incident-type scenarios. The applicant is required to develop an effective plan of action and then orally present it to the examiners. The applicant must give satisfactory responses to at least two scenarios.
4. The panel may elect to inquire about the candidate's motivation to become a police officer, previous employment history, goals and objectives, life and professional experiences, aptitudes, and general demeanor.[16]

Interview Tips

- Present a neat businesslike appearance.
- Arrive at least five minutes before your appointment.
- Your conduct, courtesy, alertness, and self-confidence are important.
- Speak in a self-assured tone of voice, smile occasionally, and look the interviewers in the eye.
- Review your application and the job posting before the interview.
- Answer questions truthfully.
- Explain what you have learned from your experiences, good and bad.
- Get your good points across to the interviewers by giving concrete examples.
- Ask questions and take the opportunity to sell yourself at the end of the interview.
- Say thank you and shake hands as you leave.

SOURCE: Adapted from http://www.ci.mesa.az.us/police/hiring/interview.htm

Minnesota Multiphasic Personality Inventory (MMPI-2) A psychological self-test that is used to diagnose mental disorders and select appropriate treatment.

Medical and Psychological Examinations

Because policing work can cause physical and psychological stress, police departments seek candidates who are physically fit and mentally balanced. Medical examinations attempt to determine a candidate's current state of health and medical history, and psychological examinations attempt to determine a candidate's mental stability.

Medical Examination Nationally, 98.3 percent of larger police departments require a medical examination as a prerequisite to employment. The purpose of the medical examination is to determine if an applicant has any physical limitations or diseases that might prevent him or her from performing the various duties, tasks, and responsibilities of a police officer. The medical exam looks not only at diseases but also at physical conditions of vision, hearing, and the cardiovascular and respiratory systems.

Most police departments have established vision standards, but the standards show a lack of uniformity. Some administrators refuse to accept applicants with anything less then 20/20 vision, but the reality is that one does not need perfect vision to be an effective police officer. Most departments will hire candidates whose vision can be corrected to 20/20 by glasses or contact lenses. The rationale for strict vision requirements is that glasses or contact lenses can be knocked off or dislodged during a struggle. Also, poor vision may cause blurring that could have an impact on safety issues such as identifying suspects and dangers at greater distances.[17]

Psychological Evaluation Because of problems with police brutality and misconduct, more and more departments are striving to screen out candidates who are psychologically unfit or emotionally unstable. In large police departments across the country, 55.9 percent use psychometric tests and 91.5 percent conduct psychological interviews.[18] It is important to note that modern-day departments are not only concerned about an applicant's psychological and emotional well-being. They are also concerned about an applicant's interests, critical thinking skills, personality traits, and preferences.

Although psychological exams are important, their accuracy is harder to measure because the tests lack objective standards. Because of this, different agencies use different tests. Some of the most common psychological tests are:

1. The **Minnesota Multiphasic Personality Inventory (MMPI-2)** is one of the most popular personality tests used by police departments. It is a self-report questionnaire that assesses adult psychopathology. Psychologists use it to diagnose mental disorders and select appropriate treatment. The test consists of

567 true or false items and is for individuals 18 years and older. It takes 60 to 90 minutes to complete and requires at least a sixth-grade reading level.

2. The **California Psychological Inventory (CPI)** is a dynamic and objective measurement test that provides an indication of how the applicant compares to the general population on several job-related personality factors. This 434-question test is self-administered and aids organizations in identifying and developing successful employees and leaders. It takes approximately 60 minutes to complete.

3. The **Myers-Briggs Type Indicator (MBTI)** has been one of the most widely used personality inventories for more than 50 years. The MBTI consists of 126 questions that can be administered to individuals age 14 and older. It is written at the seventh-grade reading level and has no time limit. (See Figures 6.3 below and 6.4 on page 228.)

4. The **Watson-Glaser Critical Thinking Appraisal (WGCTA)** is an instrument that assesses an individual's critical thinking skills. It consists of five sections: inference, recognition of assumptions, deduction, interpretation, and evaluation of arguments. The basic test, which has two versions, has 80 items, requires a ninth-grade reading level, and can be completed in 60 minutes.

5. The **Strong Interest Inventory** is an instrument that measures an individual's interest in a broad range of occupations, work activities, leisure activities, and school subjects. The inventory consists of 317 items and is useful in career development.

California Psychological Inventory (CPI) A psychological test that provides an indication of how the applicant compares to the general population on several job-related personality factors.

Myers-Briggs Type Indicator (MBTI) A widely used psychological test that can be administered to individuals age 14 and older.

Watson-Glaser Critical Thinking Appraisal (WGCTA) A psychological test that assesses an individual's critical thinking skills by testing five areas: inference, recognition of assumptions, deduction, interpretation, and evaluation of arguments.

Strong Interest Inventory A psychological test that measures an individual's interest in a broad range of occupations.

Figure 6.3

16 MBTI Personality Types and Their Characteristics

ISTJ: Introverted, Sensing, Thinking, and Judging	**ESTJ:** Extraverted, Sensing, Thinking, and Judging
ISFJ: Introverted, Sensing, Feeling, and Judging	**ESFJ:** Extraverted, Sensing, Feeling, and Judging
INFJ: Introverted, Intuitive, Feeling, and Judging	**ENFJ:** Extraverted, Intuitive, Feeling, and Judging
INTJ: Introverted, Intuitive, Thinking, and Judging	**ENTJ:** Extraverted, Intuitive, Thinking, and Judging
ISTP: Introverted, Sensing, Thinking, and Perceiving	**ESTP:** Extraverted, Sensing, Thinking, and Perceiving
ISFP: Introverted, Sensing, Feeling, and Perceiving	**ESFP:** Extraverted, Sensing, Feeling, and Perceiving
INFP: Introverted, Intuitive, Feeling, and Perceiving	**ENFP:** Extraverted, Intuitive, Feeling, and Perceiving
INTP: Introverted, Intuitive, Thinking, and Perceiving	**ENTP:** Extraverted, Intuitive, Thinking, and Perceiving

SOURCE: Gerald MacDaid, Mary McCaulley, and Richard Kainz, *Atlas of Type Tables,* Center for Application of Psychological Type, Gainesville, Florida, 1986, pp. 324–325.

Figure 6.4

Police Personality Types by Position

MBTI TYPE	Patrol Officer in Urban Community	Police Supervisors in Urban Community	Police Managers
ISTJ	12.77%	14.13%	32.89%
ISFJ	5.67%	10.87%	4.39%
INFJ	1.42%	0%	.66%
INTJ	2.84%	3.26%	4.50%
ISTP	10.645	4.35%	5.37%
ISFP	2.13%	3.26%	1.43%
INFP	3.55%	1.09%	.55%
INTP	2.84%	0%	2.30%
ESTP	7.8%	7.61%	2.41%
ESFP	5.67%	7.61%	1.43%
ENFP	.71%	3.26%	2.74%
ENTP	2.84%	5.43%	2.19%
ESTJ	24.82%	29.35%	26.64%
ESFJ	10.64%	1.09%	3.73%
ENFJ	1.42%	2.17%	1.64%
ENTJ	4.26%	6.52%	7.13%

SOURCE: Gerald MacDaid, Mary McCaulley, and Richard Kainz. *Atlas of Type Tables.* Center for Application of Psychological Type: Gainesville, Florida, 1986, pp. 324–325.

Among the many psychological tests that may be administered during the recruitment process, the MBTI personality type test is very common. Perhaps the main reason for the popularity of the MBTI is its versatility. It can be used in self-understanding and development, communication improvement, problem solving, team-building, better use of learning styles, family counseling, leadership development, understanding of organizational cultures, diversity and multicultural training, career exploration, and counseling. This test and the importance of an officer's personality are further discussed in Chapter 7.

6.4 Self Check

1. What is the MBTI?
2. What does the psychological evaluation part of the selection process try to answer?

POLICING Online

Check your answers at
www.policing.glencoe.com

6.5 Training

Police training is the process of providing recruits with instruction on police work such as police functions, legal limitations, and communication issues. One hundred years ago, police acquired their skills and knowledge from on-the-job training. New officers would often work with veteran officers until they were comfortable with the job—then they were on their own. Today officers are required to complete hundreds of hours of academy training in a wide variety of subjects ranging from defensive tactics to working with special populations. In 1997, the national average for entry-level training was 456.6 hours.[19]

Academy Training

Academy training is referred to as **preservice training**, as opposed to the **in-service training** that the officer receives once on the job. Many states mandate a minimum number of academy training hours in designated topics, and by 1997, 39 states had standardized curricula.[20]

For those applicants who successfully complete the selection process, the police academy is the final major obstacle on their way to becoming a police officer. Some academy training lasts six to eight weeks, but other training programs take as long as six months. The police academy will test the character, intelligence, and endurance of the police recruit. It will also ultimately test the recruit's desire and will to become a police officer.

The Academy Process Every academy starts with an orientation in which the staff familiarizes recruits with the academy, expectations, and an

preservice training
Training in which recruits learn a wide variety of subjects ranging from defensive tactics to working with special populations. Also called academy training.

in-service training Training that the officer receives once on the job, such as field training and professional development.

◄ **Training** Recruits go through physical training session at a Somerset County, New Jersey Police Academy. Part of police training is physical and agility training.
Why are these aspects so important?

overview of the course requirements. At the end of the orientation, recruits know the criteria for successful completion of the academy and the training begins.

Over the past 10 to 20 years, police training has moved away from emphasizing only technical aspects of the job such as firearms training and arrest techniques. Today, instructors spend more time teaching recruits about the legal aspects of policing to ensure that they understand the difference between reasonable suspicion and probable cause. They also teach recruits about behavioral issues, such as learning to identify when a suspect or witness is lying. At the conclusion of academy training, students are required to pass a certification test.

Variations in Academy Training Although much of the police training in large cities is conducted at a departmental police academy, smaller departments often have to rely on training provided by local or regional community college. In Somerset County, New Jersey, for example, the Somerset County Police Academy operates within a local community college to meet the needs of smaller municipal and sheriff's departments that cannot afford to operate their own academies.

Each state has identified certain topics that must be taught for a minimum number of hours in preservice training. Each academy may expand instruction beyond the minimum hours to meet their needs. For example, North Carolina preservice training is a 602-hour course that takes approximately 16 weeks to complete. It is divided into 33 separate blocks of instruction that address topics such as firearms, driver training, motor vehicle law and arrest, and search and seizure. It also consists of practical exercises and an extensive ethics section that is integrated throughout the training experience. The course concludes with a comprehensive state certification exam and a test of specialized skills such as firearms use and defensive driving. After an applicant passes these, he or she is certified to work and is sworn in as a law enforcement officer in North Carolina.

Academy Training Standards While virtually every state's oversight body has a process for certifying recruits who undergo academy training and officers who take in-service training, there is much less quality control for instructors. Some states still do not certify their instructors, although a comprehensive instructor development course is necessary for instructors to provide a consistent curriculum. Unless the instructional staff members know the purpose of performance objectives, how they are measured, and how to write proper test questions and demonstration scenarios, their ability to teach effectively is diminished. The International Association of Directors of Law Enforcement Standards and Training is currently strongly encouraging all states to certify its law enforcement instructors.

Field and In-Service Training

Once the recruit completes basic training, he or she begins a probationary period that averages about 13 months. It begins when the new officer is assigned to a **field training officer (FTO)**, who becomes a mentor to the new officer by teaching him or her to apply academy training to situations on the street. The average length of time that an officer spends with a FTO is approximately four months, but it varies by department. Based on the FTO's evaluation of the probationary officer's progress, he or she may be recommended for assignment to patrol duty, recommended for additional training in deficient areas, or terminated.

field training officer (FTO)
An experienced officer who becomes a mentor to a new officer by teaching him or her to apply academy training to situations on the street.

Role of the FTO The role of the FTO is a critical one in the development of competent police officers. Much of the learning that a new officer acquires is through experience, so it isn't surprising that about 91 percent of FTOs allow the new officer to take the initiative. However, learning from experience is impossible without feedback from the FTO. About 85 percent of FTOs spend the majority of the training time giving feedback to the new officer,[21] as well as modeling and teaching behaviors and high conduct standards.

Figure 6.5

Training Curricula

Training curricula vary from state to state; however, a typical curriculum might include

1. Course Orientation (2 hours)
2. Physical Fitness Training (54 hours)
3. Ethics for professional law enforcement (4 hours)
4. Arrest, Search and Seizure/Constitutional Law (28 hours)
5. Elements of Criminal Law (24 hours)
6. Communication skills for law enforcement officers (8 hours)
7. Law Enforcement Radio Procedures and Information Systems (8 hours)
8. Field Notetaking and Report Writing (12 hours)
9. Interviews: Field and In-Custody (16 hours)
10. Subject Control/Arrest Techniques (40 hours)
11. Juvenile Law and Procedure (8 hours)
12. Fingerprinting and Photographing Arrestees (6 hours)
13. Dealing with Victims and The Public (10 hours)
14. Firearms (48 hours)
15. Criminal Investigation (32 hours)
16. ABC Laws and Procedures (4 hours)
17. Motor Vehicle Law (20 hours)
18. Law Enforcement Drive Training (40 hours)
19. Crime Prevention Techniques (6 hours)
20. First Responder (40 hours)
21. Domestic Violence Response (12 hours)
22. Controlled Substances (10 hours)
23. Techniques of Traffic Law Enforcement (24 hours)
24. In-Custody Transportation (8 hours)
25. Traffic Crash Investigation (20 hours)
26. Explosives and Hazardous Materials Emergencies (12 hours)
27. Individuals with Mental Illness and Mental Retardation (8 hours)
28. Crowd Management (12 hours)
29. Preparing for Court and Testifying in Court (12 hours)
30. Patrol Techniques (20 hours)
31. Sheriff's Responsibilities: Detention Duties (4 hours)
32. Sheriff's Responsibilities: Court Duties (6 hours)
33. Civil Process (24 hours)

SOURCE: Adapted from North Carolina Justice Academy, *BLET Lesson Plans*, July 19, 2001, http://www.jus.state.nc.us/NCJA/lessons.htm.

Experience Levels of FTOs One would think that FTOs are the most experienced officers on the force, but this is not the case. From 1990 to 1994, the average FTO's job experience as a police officer decreased from 2.6 years to 1.9. One explanation for this decrease might be that the demand for FTOs increased as the time spent with them also increased. This may have prompted departments to lower their eligibility requirements in order to have a larger pool of officers for FTO positions. The effect of this on new officers is not yet clear, but it could pose future risks for police efficiency and safety.

In-Service Training The nature of policing requires that police become life-long learners. With the emergence of new technologies and new crimes, police are constantly striving to stay current. Most police departments require some minimum in-service training for their officers. A number of colleges, universities, and private companies also offer ongoing training for police officers. Some notable examples are the Northwestern University Traffic Institute and Center for Public Safety, the University of Northern Florida, and the Southern Police Institute.

The purposes of in-service training are as follows:

- To ensure that perishable skills such as pursuit driving, defensive techniques, and first aid are refreshed
- To update officers on evolving issues such as problem-solving methodologies, identity theft, and computer crimes
- To instruct newly promoted employees
- To instruct those transferred to special assignments such as vice and narcotics
- To satisfy legislative requirements, such as instruction on racial profiling or domestic violence
- To communicate what police managers have learned from recent conferences or police research

Many states require that officers receive a specified number of hours of specialized training on an annual or biennial schedule. POST commissions often assume an integral role in the content and approval of in-service training courses.

Current Issues in Training

In 1994, an Academy of Criminal Justice Science survey on American police departments identified three primary police training issues:

1. Training assessment
2. Training methods
3. Liability in police training[22]

Academy Stress

You are a police recruit in your first week of academy training. Three people have already dropped out, and you are worried that you will not make it either. This morning, the drill instructors are hollering at some of the recruits for their sloppy appearance. One of them yells at you because your belt looks wrong. Afterward, in the locker room, you feel depressed and want to quit. Another recruit is threatening to complain because he feels that the instructors' remarks were harassing and uncalled for.

When drill instructors verbally attack recruits, how does this fit the context of police training? Can this be an ethical issue?

CAREER FOCUS

Police Officer Trainee

Job Description

David Perez, South Bay Regional Public Safety Training Consortium San Jose, CA

The training here is very intense. We are in class three days a week for seven hours, plus one hour a day of physical training. We have shooting practice (getting familiar with your weapon, how to shoot, accuracy shooting, day and night combat course), arrest control practice for four hours a week each. We also just started driving practice once a week to learn various techniques for patrol. Every Thursday, we have eight hours of class when we focus on a different learning domain: arrest, custody, search and seizure, etc. For each area, we have a lot of information to understand and memorize about laws and procedures. When we complete one segment, we have a test on that content. On Fridays, we have four hours of report-writing instruction. We cover everything—different styles we can use, how to condense, how to avoid jargon, correct grammar, and spelling tests—which we might need to write reports that can be used in court.

Seal of South Bay Regional Public Safety Training Consortium

I love going to arrest control or shooting practice, but I find the class work very intense and challenging.

Education

I have an Associate's degree in liberal arts and a Bachelor's degree in criminal justice. While I was still in high school, a volunteer position came up for community service in the Los Gatos Police Department. I applied and got the position. I continued as a paid community service officer while I was in college. The work included taking reports on burglaries, theft, and dealing with abandoned vehicles. This is the path I have wanted to take ever since I was little.

Follow-Up What differences do you perceive between this type of academy training and the training a student might get from a college program in criminal justice?

Training Assessment Any training process requires an evaluation phase to determine if the training is meeting the needs of the officers on the street. Training research generally states that evaluation improves training and thus helps officers carry out their policing duties. One of the strategies presently used to evaluate and improve training is job analysis, which is the process of analyzing current police practices and duties to determine if training is preparing officers for the job. Programs are often revised or modified to match training with the tasks reflected in the police job description.[23] In recent years, this strategy has been questioned.

Training Methods

Once the appropriate training needs are identified, methods must be developed that provide for effective learning. The move from traditional policing to community policing has created the need for a new set of job skills. The problem has been that police training has retained the same focus on **task-oriented training** for the past 20 years.

task-oriented training Training that focuses on developing repetitive skills and conditioned responses in recruits, such as by training them in defensive tactics, firearms, and writing traffic citations.

Task-Oriented Training In this type of training, recruits develop repetitive skills and conditioned responses such as defensive tactics, firearms, and writing traffic citations. Task-oriented training reflects both the reactive and reform models of policing.[24]

cognitive training Training focuses on developing critical thinking, problem-solving, and decision-making skills, all of which are necessary for successful community policing.

Cognitive Training Another method, **cognitive training** stresses developing critical thinking, problem-solving, and decision-making skills, all of which are necessary for successful community policing. A study of training syllabi and curricula in 22 states found that less than three percent of basic academy time was spent on cognitive training, with the remaining time dedicated to task-oriented training. Community policing requires skills that are therefore not currently considered in the selection process or taught in the academy.

If departments are to meet these new demands, researchers believe that departments must recruit and select candidates based on the knowledge, skills, attitudes, and other characteristics associated with effective community policing. Furthermore, police academies must develop and implement curricula that place a great emphasis on cognitive training. Recognizing the need to design a curriculum with a greater emphasis on cognitive training, the state of Massachusetts developed a curriculum in 1997 with a cognitive focus. This curriculum still teaches task-oriented skills, but from a cognitive point of view.[26]

A good example of this training style can be seen in the way in which officers are trained in patrol procedures. In a task-oriented curriculum, objectives are tasks that the recruit must accomplish, such as identifying effective field interview techniques or the proper procedure for executing a stop-and-frisk. Training with a cognitive focus emphasizes the use of interpersonal communication skills and critical thinking in conducting an effective field interview or stop-and-frisk. This approach provides the officer with skills to manage a variety of problematic situations that might be encountered on the street. Procedure and tactics are still taught, but are secondary to the primary goal of using effective interpersonal communications skills and critical thinking. This approach prepares the officer to be proactive instead of reactive on the job, a trait essential to community policing.

Training with Computers In recent years, the use of computers, lecture techniques, and stress training has been a topic of debate. Computers offer a cost-effective alternative to traditional classroom training, and software programs that allow officers to learn new skills at their own pace are now available. Their greatest potential now lies in online training courses. In recent years, there has been a proliferation of online courses offered by colleges, universities, and private companies. For example, the American Institute of Applied Science offers a variety of forensic courses online, including fingerprint classification and identification, firearms identification, and document and voice examination.

Training by Lecture In police academies across the country, lecturing has been a primary instructional strategy for years. This has been widely criticized, because lecturing has some possible limitations:

- It limits feedback from the student to the instructor.
- Information learned in a lecture may be difficult to apply on the job.
- Some instructors believe that lecture is not an efficient means of transferring knowledge over time.

New methods of instruction are clearly needed. One promising strategy is **problem-based learning (PBL)**, which fosters many of the skills necessary for effective community policing:

- Critical thinking
- Team building
- Interpersonal communication
- Leadership
- Readiness for lifelong learning

problem-based learning Recruit training that fosters the skills necessary for effective community policing, such as critical thinking, team building, interpersonal communication, and leadership.

high-stress training A widely criticized training method that places officers in a very stressful training environment similar to that of military boot camp.

High-Stress Training Another type of instructional strategy that has drawn criticism is the use of **high-stress training**, a technique that places officers in a very stressful training environment. This training resembles military

Computer On Patrol

SEARCH National Technical Assistance and Training Program

The National Technical Assistance and Training Program, administered by SEARCH, The National Consortium for Justice Information and Statistics, offers on-site, no-cost technical assistance to justice agencies across the country in the development, management, improvement, acquisition, and integration of automated information systems. In addition, in-house services are offered through the program at the National Criminal Justice Computer Laboratory and Training Center.

Technical assistance activities, services, and products are designed to assist state and local justice agencies in determining system needs, establishing system requirements, and designing or procuring cost-effective, integrated information and workload management systems. Technical assistance projects include working with law enforcement agencies to implement mobile computing, computer-aided dispatch, mugshot and fingerprint identification, and records management system technologies; assisting prosecutors, public defenders, and court officials with case management information systems; and working with jails, corrections, and probation and parole agencies to implement offender tracking programs. SEARCH training courses focus on justice agency use and implementation of information technology to investigate and prosecute computer-related crime and the increasing number of crimes perpetrated over the Internet.

Through lectures, discussions, exercises, and hands-on computer use, trainees learn the skills necessary to deal with the application of computer technology to criminal justice. Most courses run from three to five days. Onsite training is provided at SEARCH's National Criminal Justice Computer Laboratory and Training Center in Sacramento, California. The training center, equipped with state-of-the-art training technology, serves as a hands-on resource for criminal justice practitioners to learn and evaluate computer technology.

SEARCH offers training courses to local, state, and federal agencies on such topics as:

- Seizure and examination of microcomputers
- Investigation of computer crime
- Internet crime investigation
- Investigation of online child exploitation
- Basic local area network investigations
- Child pornography and the Internet (provided to the U.S. Customs Service)

Think About It What other technical training opportunities could you take advantage of in your area?

SOURCE: SEARCH at www.search.org U.S. Department of Justice, Office of Justice Programs, Bureau of Justice assistance at http://www.ncjrs.org

boot camp, where the strategy is to break a person down and rebuild him or her to the specifications of the organization. In the military context, such training is logical because the military wants soldiers who do not hesitate when given an order, especially in a combat situation.

High-stress police training can create problems in recruits such as low self-esteem, poor coping skills, and the inability to make independent decisions. Officers who lack these traits will not succeed in a community-policing context.

Liability in Police Training Poor or inadequate training can create a liability for departments, because citizens who are injured or harmed by police as a result of such training can seek compensation under both federal civil rights laws or state negligence laws. Under federal law, a plaintiff may sue the police when it can be shown that the failure to train reflects an indifference to the rights of the citizens they police. The plaintiff must show that police administrators made a deliberate effort to not fully train officers and that the consequence of inadequate training was a denial of the citizen's civil rights. In state negligence cases, the requirement for guilt is actions or behavior that fall below that expected from a person in the same or similar circumstances.

In 1999, Amadou Diallo, a West African immigrant, was killed by 19 of the 41 bullets fired at him by undercover officers of the Street Crimes Unit (SCU) of the New York Police Department. Diallo was shot as he reached for his wallet and turned toward police, who had been searching for a serial rapist when they noticed Diallo acting suspiciously. Many of the members of the SCU had received as little as three hours of intensive training.[29] During the subsequent investigation and trial, it became evident that inadequate training may have been a major factor that led to Diallo's unnecessary death.

High-profile cases such as this one raise questions about police competency and training. As juries award large sums of money to victims of police misconduct or incompetence, police administrators are placing a greater emphasis on training as a strategy to reduce a department's liability. On the other hand, as more and more departments move to community policing, they are placing a greater emphasis on recruiting and hiring highly qualified candidates and on more comprehensive education and training. Police academies must develop training techniques and curricula that will prepare the officer for community policing in the twenty-first century.

6.5 **Self Check**

1. What are the various methods of training police officers?
2. How are academy training standards established?

POLICING *Online*

Check your answers at
www.policing.glencoe.com

Chapter 6

Recruitment, Selection, and Training

Summary By Learning Objectives

1. Understand what makes a good police officer in the context of modern-day policing.

Although minimum standards are important in the selection process, they do not predict or guarantee success. In today's policing environment, a successful police officer must be defined within the context of community policing. Community officers today must be creative problem solvers and effective communicators and be skilled in conflict resolution and crisis intervention. They must exhibit sound critical thinking skills in a policing environment framed by the highest standards of ethical conduct. A study of personality attributes is useful in matching police personalities with job assignments.

2. Name the predictors of police success.

The key to successful recruitment and selection is to find candidates that exhibit traits that promote the delivery of effective police services. Apart from basic qualities such as ample physical strength, integrity, and basic intelligence, departments define effective policing within the context of community policing. The community police officer must be proficient in effective communication skills (verbal and written) and interpersonal skills (multicultural communication, collaboration and creativity, conflict resolution, and crisis intervention).

3. Understand the recruitment process.

Recruiters use a variety of strategies, including newspaper advertisements, job fairs, radio and television ads, posters, journal ads, and mass mailings. In an effort to increase the quality of the applicant pool, many police departments target special groups such as minorities, women, veterans, college graduates, and those with prior police service. Applicants to policing jobs must meet several minimum standards, such as clean driving and criminal records and U.S. citizenship. Of these standards, education is the most controversial. There is, however, strong support among police executives to increase educational requirements for officers. All departments require a minimum of a high school education, and some departments now require a minimum of 60 semester hours of college credit. One state, Minnesota, requires that all applicants obtain either an associate's or bachelor's degree prior to entering police training.

4. Explain all stages of the selection process.

The selection process is designed to screen out applicants who are not suitable for policing. It normally consists of a series of steps, or hurdles, that the applicant must overcome. Although each department has its own selection process, an ideal model would begin with the written test, physical agility test, and polygraph test. The rationale for this is to position the steps in an order that maximizes efficiency in screening while minimizing the expense to the department. Candidates who pass the background investigation stage can expect to have an oral interview. The purpose of the oral interview is to evaluate applicants' overall appearance, demeanor, social skills, interpersonal communication skills, judgment, emotional stability, and suitability for the job. If they pass the oral interview, they will be given medical and psychological examinations. The purpose of the medical examination is to determine if applicants have any physical limitations or diseases that might prevent them from performing the various duties, tasks, and responsibilities of a police officer. Psychological examinations help to screen out candidates who are psychologically unfit or too emotionally unstable to serve as police officers.

5. List the areas covered by a background check.

A background investigation usually focuses on the following areas:

- Verifying all information on the application
- Fingerprinting the applicant
- Checking for a criminal record
- Reviewing the driving record
- Checking military records to verify service
- Interviewing personal references, former employers, and former teachers
- Assessing job and academic performance
- Checking financial stability

6. Distinguish between academy training and FTO training.

Today, police officers are required to complete hundreds of hours from a standardized curriculum covering topics such as firearms, driver training, motor vehicle law, arrest, and search and seizure. In many states, officers must successfully pass a certification exam at the end of their training. Once hired, an officer is on probation and often under the supervision and mentoring of a field training officer (FTO). The FTO teaches the officer to apply the concepts learned in the academy to police work and instructs the new officer in proper police practices and the importance of high conduct standards. The average time with an FTO is approximately four months.

7. Discuss current issues in police training.

Training issues have been categorized into three groups: 1) training assessment, 2) training methods, and 3) liability in police training. One of the strategies used to assess police training is job analysis, which involves analyzing current police practices to determine if current training is preparing the officers for the job. In the past, much police training focused on task-oriented training. Today, there is a new emphasis on increasing cognitive training, which focuses on developing critical thinking, problem-solving, and decision-making skills. Computerized instruction, lecture techniques, and stress training have become important policing issues. Problem-based learning (PBL) is based on experiential learning theory and emphasizes hands-on experiences from which the trainee learns and solves problems. High-stress training has been criticized for diminishing recruit self-esteem, coping mechanisms, and autonomy.

Key Terms

recruitment (p. 207)
selection pool (p. 207)
minimum standards (p. 210)
selection (p. 216)
Civil Rights Act of 1964, Title VII (p. 216)
Age Discrimination Act of 1967 (p. 216)
Americans with Disabilities Act (ADA) (p. 216)
assessment center (p. 219)
polygraph examination (p. 220)
background investigation (p. 222)
Minnesota Multiphasic Personality Inventory
   (MMPI-2) (p. 226)

California Psychological Inventory (CPI) (p. 227)
Myers-Briggs Type Indicator (MBTI) (p. 227)
Watson-Glaser Critical Thinking Appraisal
   (WGCTA) (p. 227)
Strong Interest Inventory (p. 227)
preservice training (p. 229)
in-service training (p. 229)
field training officer (FTO) (p. 231)
task-oriented training (p. 234)
cognitive training (p. 234)
problem-based learning (p. 235)
high-stress training (p. 235)

Questions for Review

1. Give an example of a minimum standard required for employment as a police officer.
2. What are the skills necessary to become a successful community police officer?
3. Why are medical and psychological examinations necessary in police selection?
4. Compare the different types of psychological tests.
5. What strategies are used to recruit police officers?
6. What are the stages in the ideal selection process?
7. What are the different types of training?
8. What is the role of the field training officer?
9. Why should police departments be concerned about the quality of their training?
10. Why is problem-based learning an effective strategy for training police officers?

Experiential Activities

11. Comparing Hiring Standards
Visit a police department in your state; then, using the Internet, find the Web sites of three other departments in different regions of the United States. One helpful resource can be found through **www.policing.glencoe.com**.

a. Compare hiring standards, salary, and benefits. What differences did you observe?
b. What differences did you find among requirements for qualifications and training?
c. How do advancement opportunities differ among the departments?

Experiential Activities continued

12. Mock Interview Board
One class member will be a job applicant, and three others will be a local citizen, a veteran police officer, and a city manager who make up the police oral interview board. Interview the applicant using questions formulated from the perspective of each member of the board.

   a. What were the hardest questions for the applicant to answer?

   b. What were the similarities and differences between the applicant's view of policing and the oral board's?

   c. What did you learn about the selection process from this exercise?

13. Review Training Curriculum
Contact your local police department and obtain their training curriculum and lesson plans. If your local department uses academy training, visit the nearest police academy and ask for this information. Analyze the curriculum to determine how many hours of the training are task-oriented and how many are cognitive.

   a. How much training was task-oriented?

   b. How much was cognitive?

   c. Does this curriculum promote community policing?

14. Academy Tour
Contact your local academy and ask if they offer any tours, informational lectures, or the like in which prospective recruits can see how the academy operates and ask questions. Your instructor can arrange for a class tour.

   a. What questions did you ask, and how were they answered?

   b. What did you like the most and the least about academy training?

   c. Which aspect of training seemed most challenging?

Web Patrol

15. Policing Careers
Click on the link at **www.policing. glencoe.com** to learn about careers and personality types.

How might your personality type be best put to use in a police department?

16. Psychological Evaluations
For more information on preparing for a psychological evaluation, visit the site through the link at **www.policing. glencoe.com**.

What kinds of questions are usually asked, and in what frame of mind should you approach this test?

17. U.S. secret Service
Go to the U.S. Secret Service Web site through **www.policing.glencoe.com** and click on the "opportunities" link to read about current openings.

What did you learn about job requirements for this arm of law enforcement?

Critical Thinking Exercises

18. The History of Training

Go to your library or search the Internet for information about historical changes in police training throughout the twentieth century. Pick one issue of your choice, such as August Vollmer's reform of the Berkeley (CA) Police Department or the cause and impact of the Miranda warning on police arrest techniques. Write a one-page report on how policing was before this reform was implemented, what brought the change, and how police training is different today. In addition, answer the following questions:

a. What topic did you choose, and why?

b. What was the most important thing you learned from it?

19. Applicant Drug Use

You are in charge of the unit in your department that conducts background investigations. Your department has a zero-tolerance drug policy, which means that applicants with any history of drug use are disqualified. Recently, your chief has become concerned about the number of applicants who are disqualified due to drug use. Your records show that out of the 74 who were disqualified for drug use, 52 used marijuana alone, 9 used powder cocaine, 4 used LSD, 8 used other hard drugs such as heroin and crack cocaine, and 1 was addicted to legal diet pills for

almost three years and spent a month in rehab. Answer the following questions:

a. If you could rewrite the policy, would you consider any of these applicants for employment?

b. Which would you not consider under any circumstances, and why?

20. Applicant Ethics

You are a veteran officer who is part of the oral interview board for all applicants to your police department. Those who reach the oral interview stage have already passed the written, polygraph, and physical exams, as well as an extensive background investigation. You are interviewing a candidate who has a very clean record with no drug use or traffic violations. During the oral interview, you ask him about dealing with people who try to avoid arrests and ticket writing. He replies, "I'll know how to handle them; I've talked my way out of it at least a dozen times," then laughs. The others assume he is joking and also laugh, but you are concerned.

a. What are some of the concerns you might have regarding this applicant's prior behavior?

b. What are the ethical implications of this person becoming a police officer?

Endnotes

1. U.S. Bureau of Statistics, *Local Police Departments*, 1997 (Washington, D.C.: Government Printing Office, 1997).

2. San Jose Police Department Home Page, "Police Salaries" [Online]. Available: *http://www.sjpdjobs.com/lateral.htm*; Fairfax County Police Department, "Employment Fairfax County Police Officer" [Online]. Available: *http://www.co.fairfax.va.us/ps/police/police4a.htm*

3. R. Langworthy, T. Hughes, and B. Sanders, *Law Enforcement Recruitment, Selection and Training: A Survey of Major Police Departments in the U.S.* (Highland Heights, KY: Academy of Criminal Justice Sciences, 1995).

4. Ibid., 23.

5. U.S. Bureau of Justice Statistics, *Local Police Departments 1997* (Washington, D.C.: Government Printing Office, 1997).

6. J. Hudzik, "College Education for Police: Measuring Component and Extraneous Variables." *Journal of Criminal Justice 6*, no. 1 (1978): 69–81.

7. J. Sterling, "The College Level Entry Requirement." *The Police Chief* 41, no. 8 (1974): 28–31.

8. *Davis v. Dallas*, 777 F.2d 205 (5th Cir. 1985), cert. Denied, 106 S. Ct. 1972 (1986).

9. M. Breci, "Higher Education for Law Enforcement: The Minnesota Model," *The FBI Law Enforcement Bulletin* 63, no. 1 (1994): 1.

10. B. A. Reaves and A. L. Goldberg, *Local Police Departments–1997* (Washington, D.C.: Government Printing Office, 2000).

11. "City Workers: Let Them Live Where They Choose," *Minneapolis Star Tribune*, 1 January 1999, 18A.

12. California Peace Officer Standards and Training, *Mission Statement* [Online]. Available: *http://www.post.ca.gov/newindex.htm*

13. "How Smart Is Too Smart," *Washington Post*, 31 May 1998.

14. Langworthy, Hughes, and Sanders, *Law Enforcement Recruitment*, 26.

15. B. Parks, *Los Angeles Board of Inquiry into the Rampart Corruption Incident: Public Report* (Los Angeles: City of Los Angeles).

16. Philadelphia Police Department Homepage, *Police Officer Selection Process* [Online]. Available: *http://www.ppdonline.org/ppd5_processtxt.htm*

17. T. Cox, A. Crabtree, and A. Millett, "A Theoretical Examination of Police Entry-Level Uncorrected Visual Standards," *American Journal of Criminal Justice* 11, no. 2: 199–208.

18. Langworthy, Hughes, and Sanders, *Law Enforcement Recruitment*, 26.

19. IADLEST, A Sourcebook: Standards and Training Information in the United States (Richmond, VA: CJ DATA/Flink and Associates, 1997)

20. Ibid., 25.

21. Langworthy, Hughes, and Sanders, *Law Enforcement Recruitment*, 40.

22. Ibid., 17.

23. G. Cordner, "Job Analysis and the Police: Benefits and Limitations," *Journal of Police Science and Administration* 8: 355–62.

24. D. Bradford and J. Pynes, "Police Academy Training: Why Hasn't It Kept Up with Practice?" *Police Quarterly* 2, no. 3 (1999): 283–301.

25. Ibid., 288.

26. Ibid., 289.

27. Ibid., 289.

28. S. Smith, "Lectures Aren't Enough: How to Achieve More Learning in Your Academy," *Law and Order*, March, 40-43.

29. "Black and" Blue: The Four Cops Who Killed Amadou Diallo Are Acquitted, but the Case Will Go On Raising Questions about Race and Crime Fighting, Sending Tremors Right through the November Elections," *Time*, 6 March 2000, 24.

Chapter 7

Skills for the Successful Police Officer

CHAPTER OUTLINE

7.1 TRAITS OF A GOOD POLICE OFFICER
PREDICTORS OF SUCCESS

THE POLICE PERSONALITY

7.2 CRITICAL THINKING
A CLOSER LOOK AT CRITICAL THINKING

BENEFITS OF CRITICAL THINKING

DEVELOPING CRITICAL THINKING SKILLS

7.3 PROBLEM SOLVING
POP AND SARA

PROBLEM SOLVING IN POLICING

DEVELOPING STRONGER PROBLEM-SOLVING SKILLS

7.4 INTERPERSONAL COMMUNICATION
UNDERSTANDING NONVERBAL COMMUNICATION

ROADBLOCKS TO EFFECTIVE COMMUNICATION

7.5 POLICE AS LIFELONG LEARNERS
IMPORTANCE OF LIFELONG LEARNING IN POLICING

WHAT IS LIFELONG LEARNING?

IN PURSUIT OF LIFELONG LEARNING

CHAPTER OBJECTIVES

AFTER COMPLETING THIS CHAPTER, YOU WILL BE ABLE TO:

1. Understand the factors that predict success in policing careers.

2. Explain the process of critical thinking and its application in policing.

3. Name the six stages of developing critical thinking skills.

4. See how creativity can be used in effective policing.

5. Explain the process of problem solving and its application in policing.

6. Develop and use tools to solve problems in police work.

7. Name the guidelines that lead to a better understanding of nonverbal communication.

8. Understand lifelong learning and its application in policing.

◀ Boston police officers console and help the wife of a shooting victim in a Charlestown neighborhood.

7.1 Traits of a Good Police Officer

Some of the traits of a good officer were summed up by August Vollmer. He said that citizens expect police officers to have "the wisdom of Solomon, the courage of David, the strength of Samson, the patience of Job, the leadership of Moses, the kindness of the Good Samaritan, the strategic training of Alexander, the faith of Daniel, the diplomacy of Lincoln, the tolerance of the Carpenter of Nazareth, and finally, an intimate knowledge of every branch of the natural, biological, and social sciences. If he had all these, he might be a good policeman!"[1]

Although Vollmer made this famous statement in the early twentieth century, it is still an accurate reflection of the expectations and demands placed on police today. Furthermore, it implies that the nature of policing demands special skills and abilities.

Predictors of Success

The key to successful recruitment and selection is to find candidates who exhibit traits that promote the delivery of effective police services. In the past, having the physical ability and stamina to walk a beat was essential. One nineteenth-century police department's only qualifications were that the applicant provide character references and pass a running test. Some of the qualities required today are similar, such as ample physical strength, integrity, and basic intelligence.

Today, however, effective policing is defined within the context of community policing. The community police officer is required to demonstrate more than physical abilities. He or she must be proficient in effective communication skills (oral and written) and interpersonal skills (multicultural communication, collaboration and creativity, conflict resolution, and crisis intervention).[2] Within the context of community policing, these skills are essential. They are discussed in greater detail below.

Oral Communication Skills An officer's ability to communicate with citizens is essential to the acquisition of timely and meaningful information. He or she must be able to communicate with people on almost any topic and in stressful situations when people are angry or fearful.

Written Communication Skills Police need to be able to complete accurate reports because they are essential in the prosecution of offenders. Officers without sound grammatical skills will produce reports that cannot withstand the scrutiny of prosecutors, defense attorneys, and judges. In community policing, officers are often involved in preparing and writing documents and

Figure 7.1

Distant Early Warning Signs (DEWS) System

Indicators Used to Assess the Potential for Racial Tension in a Community

Consider Changes and Trends in the Following Items

◆ Increased disturbance calls in particular areas
◆ Increased number of interracial assaults
◆ Increased number of assaults against police
◆ Increased citizen complaints of police excessive use of force, racial profiling, and discourtesy
◆ Decreased levels of community involvement with local police department and officers
◆ Presence of or increase in hate group activity
◆ Scheduled major events likely to attract protesters (opening of a controversial movie, music concert, athletic event, etc.)
◆ Media reports exacerbating racial issues, tensions, conflicts, or incidents
◆ Increased school-based racial incidents
◆ Increased incidents of racial graffiti
◆ Major racial or ethnic population changes in makeup of communities
◆ Harsh weather conditions creating racially disparate hardships and stress
◆ Unusual and racially disparate crowding in housing, schools, and community facilities
◆ Critical, polarizing, or provocative comments from community leaders and public officials that heighten racial tension
◆ Layoffs, company closings, and other developments that cause racially disparate unemployment and underemployment
◆ Perceived racial and ethnic disparities in the administration of healthcare, welfare, and social services
◆ Demonstrations that reflect racial and ethnic polarization
◆ History or presence of unresolved racial conflicts
◆ Perceived racial or ethnic disparity in rationing of gas, food, water, or electricity

SOURCE: Adapted from www.ojp.usdoj.gov

reports outside the police department. Often, they are required to write articles and announcements for community newsletters. The community's perception of the officers' professionalism is therefore often gauged by their verbal and written communication skills.

Multicultural Communication The social fabric of America is changing. As minority groups account for larger proportions of the American population and communities become more ethnically and racially diverse, officers face challenges in their interactions with the public. (See Figures 7.1 above and 7.2 on page 248 to learn about racial tension and conflict resolution.) In addition, any discussion of diversity must also address the issues of gays, lesbians, and women, who have struggled to receive fair and equal treatment from police.

Multicultural communication overlaps somewhat with oral communication while adding another dimension to it. Officers who speak foreign languages and understand the different norms, values, and beliefs of other cultures will be able to interact with the public more effectively.

Collaboration and Creativity It has been said that teamwork is the fuel that allows common people to achieve uncommon results. In today's policing environment, collaboration and creativity are essential to the success of community policing. Officers are asked to forge relationships with citizens to solve problems and improve the quality of life in the community.

Conflict Resolution and Crisis Intervention Today's police have to deal with many situations that have the potential for violence. From domestic disturbances to convenience store robberies, police are often the first on the scene. How they respond will frame the public's perception of them. Police in

---

Figure 7.2

Racial Conflict Resolution: A Training Scenario

A white and an Asian American family are neighbors. Both have lived in their adjoining houses for three years without any problems. One Saturday, the father of the Asian American family cuts down an oak tree located on the property of the white neighbor's house, mistakenly believing it is on his side of the property line. The father of the white family observes this, runs out, yells racial epithets, and punches the Asian American man in the face.

1. Are there bias indicators present? (Yes) What are they? (Different races, use of racial epithets)

2. What do you believe was the motivating factor(s) for this incident? Was there more than one? (Cutting down of tree, possible underlying bias against Asian Americans)

3. How can you determine whether bias motive was involved? (Investigator needs to determine perpetrator's attitude toward neighbors and the nature of their relationship prior to this dispute. Were they social friends or did they exchange few words over the years? Did perpetrator ever express unhappiness with having Asian American neighbors?)

4. Does this conduct constitute a violation of any State or Federal criminal law or criminal civil rights law? Which ones? Assuming that you conclude there are mixed motives that led to the incident or contributed to its seriousness (i.e., the tree cutting and anti-Asian bias) does that make a difference as to whether or not one can prosecute under your hate crime statute?

5. Does bias motivation need to be the sole or primary motivation for conduct, or can it be one of the motivating factors in order to prosecute under your State statute?

6. Could a person be prosecuted under your State's statute if you conclude the incident became more violent because of bias, even though the catalyst for the initial dispute was based on race-neutral factors?

7. Would you still consider it as a bias crime under the Hate Crime Reporting Act?

SOURCE: Adapted from www.ncjrs.org

---

recent years have learned the benefits of conflict resolution and crisis intervention strategies. These skills can be taught to any new officer, but it is important that he or she have an open mind and a willingness to be flexible.

Identifying all of these personal attributes and skills is a challenge, because there are many necessary skills other than those that a recruit can demonstrate in an interview or develop during training.[3] To understand how police officers can meet these new demands and roles, a study of personality characteristics and attributes is useful. By understanding officers' personalities, police departments can assign officers to roles and tasks that complement their personalities and can answer the question, "What is the relationship between personality and job assignments?"

The Police Personality

The term *personality* refers to the various personal characteristics that make up each individual. It can describe values, attitudes, motivations, and other personal characteristics. This section will discuss the personality characteristics that are common to many police officers.

Past discussions of police personality examined two perspectives. The first was that police have a certain personality disposition because of the nature of policing. This implies that officers acquire police personality traits after entering the profession. The second was is that those who become police officers already have a police personality. Therefore, those who enter policing already share personality traits common to police officers.[3]

Even with these perspectives, police administrators still struggle to understand the personalities of the department's officers. Some common questions that arise among administrators include:

- Why do certain officers resist change?
- Why are some apparently mismatched to their jobs?
- Why do some have difficulty relating to and interacting with people?
- Why are some teams or task forces unable to solve problems creatively?
- Are certain personality types more compatible with police work than others?

The Myers-Briggs Type Indicator attempts to provide that explanation.

Myers-Briggs Type Indicator The Myers-Briggs Type Indicator (MBTI) was developed in the early 1940s to make psychological theories of human personality understandable and useful in people's lives. In World War II, the MBTI was used to place factory workers in jobs that matched their personality types. It has undergone decades of rigorous scientific validation and today is the most widely used personality indicator.

The MBTI consists of eight preferences organized into four dimensions that describe how people function in the everyday world.[4] These dimensions include:

Scale	Refers to
1. Extraversion (E) or Introversion (I)	How a person is energized
2. Sensing (S) or Intuition (N)	What a person pays attention to
3. Thinking (T) or Feeling (F)	How a person decides
4. Judging (J) or Perceiving (P)	Lifestyle a person adopts

Each dimension has unique preferences. The extraverted person draws energy from the outside world of people, activities, or things, while the introverted person draws energy from his internal world of ideas, emotions, or impressions. Taking in information through the five senses and noticing what is actually happening characterizes the sensing person, while the intuitive person takes in information through a sixth sense and by noticing what might be. The thinking person organizes and structures information to decide in a logical and objective way, while the feeling person organizes and structures information to decide in a personal, value-oriented way. Finally, the judging person prefers a planned and organized life, while the perceptive person prefers a spontaneous and flexible life.[5]

In none of the dimensions are the preferences evenly distributed. The dimension of thinking versus feeling is the only dimension in which there is a gender difference. Females have a greater orientation for feeling, while males have a greater preference for thinking. The eight preferences when organized into the four dimensions produce sixteen MBTI types. Each type has unique characteristics that set it apart from the others.

With the MBTI, the police personality could be analyzed by how police share common personality traits. A study of police officers in Michigan and Florida in the 1970s revealed that two MBTI personality types are most common in policing. Hanewicz found that ESTJ (20.7 percent) and ISTJ (14 percent) comprised over one-third (34.7 percent) of all police personality types. Furthermore, he found that the ST (Sensing and Thinking) combination accounted for over 50percent of the personalities.[6] Research by Hennessey found:

- 70 percent of police are Sensing-Thinking (ST), compared to 32 to 42 percent of the general population.
- 14 percent of police are Intuitive-Thinking (NT), compared to 15 to 22 percent of the general population.
- 11percent of police have the combination of Sensing-Feeling (SF), compared to 31–41percent of the general population; and
- 5percent of police have the combination of Intuitive-Feeling (NF), compared to 15–21percent of the general population.[7]

Clearly, there is a difference between the personality types of police and the general population, especially ST, SF, and NF types. The impact of this on the quality of policing services is significant. For example, police officers of the Sensing-Thinking (ST) orientation:

- Approach decision making by first processing information through their five senses, then applying analytical reasoning to reach a logical decision
- Use sequential thinking
- Have a high level of structure in their jobs (e.g., policy, procedures, and rules)
- Act brief and businesslike in their encounters with the public
- Choose truthfulness in situations where they must choose between tact and truthfulness

STs may lack compassion or sensitivity when dealing with the public and may also seem blunt. Although STs dominate policing, being an ST does not automatically make a person a good officer.

Intuitive-Thinking (NT) occurs in police at roughly the same proportion in which it appears in the general population. The major difference between the NT and ST personality types is that NTs use intuitive decision making instead of relying solely on fact gathering through the senses. Police officers with this orientation tend to:

Online

Remember, one of your best resources is www.policing.glencoe.com

- Have global perspectives on issues and problems
- Be challenged by the complexity in situations and always look for possibilities, rather than trying to categorize cases, suspects, or victims
- Move often from one task to another without bringing closure to the preceding task
- Think about the future, not the present

They do not like detail and routine and often become easily bored. Because they generally use intuition and logic in their decision making, they can also appear to be blunt and insensitive. For example, they do not enjoy dealing with personal problems.

The next two combination types, SFs and NFs, have the smallest distribution among police officers. The SFs process information through their five senses , but consider the impact of their decision on the people that will be affected. Clearly, feeling is a major factor in their decision making. Officers with the SF personality orientation:

- Are more focused on the task
- Are practical, observant, and structured and are very adept at using common sense in dealing with people in practical situations
- Give the appearance to other officers of not being tough minded because of their orientation toward people and human values

Finally, NFs have the smallest distribution of the four combinations. NFs process information through intuition and make decisions based on feeling. Officers with a NF personality orientation:

- Are people oriented and approach issues and problems from a global perspective, but have a dislike for routine and detail.
- Enjoy addressing long range issues and conceptualizing.
- Are often perceived by other officers as very different.

It is NFs who have the highest dropout rate after entering the police occupation. Why? The job does not live up to their expectations of helping people and providing services. When they find themselves in an environment dominated by structured, pragmatic, practical, logical, decisive, traditional, and impersonal individuals, they leave policing. Sometimes NFs will attempt to perform as STs; however, this often results in internal and job-related stress. Clearly their strength is working with people, and they thrive in situations where they can work with the community.

Traditional policing is characterized by reactive policing such as responding to incoming 911 calls, with a focus on random routine preventive patrol. This type of policing is well suited to the ST personality type. Community policing, on the other hand, emphasizes collaborative problem solving to address the factors that contribute to social disorder and crime. Its goal is to improve the quality of life for all citizens, which requires that police officers interact with the community from a position of sensitivity and concern. It is obvious that STs and NTs would find such interaction uncomfortable, but SFs and NFs would flourish in such an environment.

Importance of MBTI in Policing Because different types of policing require different types of personalities, a balance of these types is necessary for a successful police department. An understanding of them is therefore useful to police officers and administrators in five important ways:

1. The MBTI can work as an aid in team building because those who understand various personality preferences are able to recognize and accept differences in communication styles.
2. It helps officers look at issues from different perspectives.
3. It helps officers understand why they may feel uncomfortable in certain job situations but excel in others.
4. It can be used during recruitment, not to screen out those types uncommon to law enforcement but to help understand an applicant's personality strengths and possible weaknesses.
5. It may help applicants understand the policing culture.

With the increased emphasis on community policing, the nature of policing is changing. The traditional aspects of policing will continue to exist and will require STs and NTs, but SFs and NFs will play an ever-increasing role. Although STs might prefer traditional patrol, SFs and NFs work well with informants and in community policing. The key is to provide all officers with a self-awareness of their strengths and weaknesses. As officers realize their weaknesses, they can focus on strategies to minimize the impact of their weaknesses. Supervisors gain a greater understanding of police officer behavior on the street and also gain knowledge that can be used in job assignments and team building.

7.1 Self Check?

1. On what is the MBTI based?
2. For what purpose was the MBTI developed?

POLICING *Online*
Check your answers at
www.policing.glencoe.com

7.2 Critical Thinking

Some believe that law enforcement is entering an age of enlightenment, in which police leaders can take unprecedented steps in improving the overall approach to crime and the community. New policing philosophies such as community policing require that police officers possess a new set of skills to adapt to these changes.

Police officers are continuously confronted with situations that require **critical thinking**, which can be defined as the analysis of ideas in the process of solving a problem or formulating a belief. In community policing, "the officer becomes a thinking professional, utilizing imagination and creativity to identify and solve problems."[8] To develop the skills needed for community policing, officers must demonstrate proficiency in several areas: problem solving, creativity, empathy, and an understanding of community values. To have skills in these areas, they must first possess the ability to think critically.

critical thinking The analysis of ideas in the process of solving a problem or formulating a belief.

A Closer Look at Critical Thinking

When thinking critically, a person first determines the best solution or most reasonable belief, then evaluates and refines it. For example, Lora is a criminal justice student who is trying to decide whether to finish college before entering the police academy. Although her jurisdiction does not require a college degree, she knows from what others have told her that officers with degrees get promoted more quickly. Furthermore, all of the officers in management have at least a bachelor's degree. Since Lora wants to be a career officer and eventually a chief, this appeals to her. She knows that she could resume school after completing the academy and starting work, but that might be more tiring because it would take so much longer. She decides to complete her remaining three semesters and earn a degree before entering the academy.

Another perspective comes from psychologists Goodwin Watson and Edward Glaser, who view critical thinking as a composite of attitudes, knowledge, and skills that includes:

1. Attitudes of inquiry that involve an ability to recognize problems and accept the need for evidence in support of what is asserted to be true. This is crucial for criminal investigation, which requires the ability to search for and detect clues and evidence.
2. Knowledge of the nature of valid inferences, abstractions, and generalizations in which the weight or accuracy of different kinds of evidence is logically determined. This is important when talking to suspects, witnesses, and victims, who each give different perspectives of the same situation and sometimes lie to sway an officer's beliefs.
3. Skills in employing and applying the above attitudes and knowledge.[9] This means that along with being able to deduce and analyze, an officer must know the correct police procedures for handling such situations.

inference An intellectual act by which one concludes that something is so in light of something else's being so, or seeming to be so.

Recognition of Assumptions An **assumption** is "a statement accepted or supposed as true without any proof or demonstration; an unstated premise or belief."[11] This can be seen in many negative police-citizen interactions, such as when an officer decides that a rape victim is not telling the truth because of her clothing or behavior. It can also be seen in positive situations, such as when an undercover officer sees a suspicious-looking stranger in an area known for drug crimes. After watching and waiting, the person reveals himself to be a drug dealer, which confirms the officer's assumptions that he seemed suspicious.

assumption A statement accepted or supposed as true without any proof or demonstration; an unstated premise or belief.

Inference An **inference** is "an intellectual act by which one concludes that something is so in light of something else's being so, or seeming to be so."[10] For example, if an officer sees a suspicious-looking person carrying a television from a dark house at night, he or she will infer that the person stole it. Inferences are often, but not always, correct.

Deduction Deduction involves the determination of whether certain conclusions necessarily follow from information derived from given statements or premises. Suppose that a homicide detective finds a knife at a murder scene that perfectly matches the knives of a cutlery set that the victim's business partner owns. Is this particular knife missing from the business partner's cutlery set? Did the business partner replace the missing piece with a new knife to mask the disappearance? Is this cutlery set owned by many people in this area, including other witnesses? An investigator must determine all of this before trying to reach a conclusion.

Interpretation Interpretation involves weighing the evidence and deciding if generalizations or conclusions based on the given data are warranted. If this same detective finds that the business partner has a complete set of knives that look equally worn and aged, but a clerk at a nearby department store verifies that the victim's ex-husband recently purchased similar knives, the detective may wish to focus the investigation on the ex-husband rather than the business partner—at least until further evidence points back to the business partner.

Evaluation of Arguments Finally, evaluation of arguments involves distinguishing between arguments that are strong and relevant and those that are weak or irrelevant to a particular question at issue. If an officer is talking to two neighbors who crashed cars while getting out of their driveways on the way to work, he or she may find that some of the arguments and finger-pointing have nothing to do with the car accident. Neighbors often squabble about each other's children, property lines, pets, and other issues that may come out when the officer is trying to collect information about the accident. It is important not to be swayed by irrelevant information. Paul and Elder have identified a specific process involved in critical thinking. The process, referred to as the universal structures of thought, includes eight steps. Whenever we think we think:

1. for a purpose
2. within a point of view
3. based on assumptions
4. leading to implications and consequences
5. using data, facts, and experiences
6. to make inferences and judgments
7. based on concepts and theories
8. to answer a question or solve a problem[11]

Skills Involved in Critical Thinking Researchers emphasize the need for officers to develop critical thinking skills to help them exercise discretion wisely.

They see critical thinking as involving a number of special skills. The most important ones are the following:

- Problem solving: the ability to analyze a problem and develop several possible solutions
- Identifying perceptions: the ability to detect and analyze the perspective of each member of a criminal act (including victims and witnesses); the ability to know one's own perceptions and keep them neutral
- Generating concepts from observations: the understanding that certain social environments, individuals' behaviors, and other indicators can show whether there is an increased or decreased likelihood of criminal activity
- Applying concepts to police problems: the ability to know when one is making assumptions, inferences, or evaluations, then act on them appropriately
- Designing systematic plans of action: understanding what one needs to achieve (such as find more evidence or talk to more witnesses) and determining how to accomplish it[12]
- Addressing societal problems from different perspectives: Criminals are as diverse as the general population, which creates special issues when dealing with various crime problems. For instance, there are significant procedural differences in how juvenile and adult offenders are handled. There are also different issues relating to the emotional and psychological maturity of young offenders, which require special critical thinking skills.

Police officers with critical thinking skills will be more adept at solving problems, especially within the context of community policing. The basic critical thinking skills, such as exploring and evaluating alternatives, challenging assumptions, detecting bias, and recognizing inconsistencies in reasoning, will enhance the ability of police officers to make sound decisions within an ever-changing environment.

Benefits of Critical Thinking

Research has established a direct link between critical thinking and the following benefits:

- Reflective thinking and the ability to empathize
- The ability to accurately evaluate situations and information
- The ability to solve problems
- Awareness and personal meaning
- The ability to lead a self-fulfilling and morally satisfying life

In addition, many feel that a reduced level of critical thinking negatively influences the capacity for individuals to apply information to which they are exposed.[13]

Intelligent decision making may be the most important benefit of improved critical thinking because the decisions that officers make have the potential to affect people's lives for years to come. Many of the decisions that officers make can deprive citizens of their liberty, reputation, material possessions, and even their lives.[14] These choices often must be made instantly. Furthermore, critical thinking is not the only factor that affects the decision-making process. Other factors such as stress and situational circumstances also affect the decision-making process.

Consider the awesome responsibility placed on an officer in the following situations:

- A decision made at a domestic disturbance, which may mean the difference between life or death for the battered spouse
- A decision made during a child abuse investigation, which may have lifelong consequences for the child
- A decision made when faced with an opportunity to commit corruption
- A decision made to spend time with a troubled youngster, which may make the difference in that youth's life

Critical Thinking and Discretion Police with critical thinking skills offer hope of a fair and just use of discretion. Consequently, bias and discrimination can be reduced. This has several benefits for officers and their departments:

- Higher levels of officer integrity and ethical conduct
- Lowered risk of liability due to misuse of force
- Improved police-community relations
- Police decisions that are more likely to be upheld by courts

Critical Thinking in Community Policing There are other implications of critical thinking for policing, especially community policing. First, the current job design of traditional policing does not encourage critical thinking by officers. To address this, police departments must redesign the jobs of community police officers to meet the needs of the community policing concept. The work environment must encourage and promote critical thinking by encouraging rather than ignoring new ideas and suggestions for improvement. If officers' new ideas and desire for change are ignored, they will become bored and frustrated. As a result, they will either leave the department or become unenthusiastic about their duties.

Other implications relating to critical thinkers in the criminal justice system include:

- Police critical thinkers will improve the quality of criminal investigations. Because critical thinkers are more receptive to new ideas, such officers will be able to embrace new technologies and thus improve the clearance rates of crimes once thought to be unsolvable.
- Police critical thinkers will be able to make more informed decisions when they act as first responders to crime and human suffering and better choices that can make the difference in the lives of victims. In doing so, they can help to restore respect for the policing profession and the administration of justice.
- Police critical thinkers will be able to see the criminal justice system from a holistic perspective, which will allow them to have a more sensitive understanding of how their actions will affect the rest of the system. This will make them more careful during arrest and search procedures and evidence collection, because they will realize that any carelessness in these procedures can result in dismissed cases.

When police agencies have master thinkers on the beat—those who exercise better problem solving, interpersonal communication, empathy, open-mindedness, and decision making—they will greatly improve the delivery of all policing services. Consequently, the police will be able to improve community co-operation and collaboration and build strong partnerships in fighting crime and solving problems in the community.

Developing Critical Thinking Skills

If critical thinking is so important to the police officers of tomorrow, how can recruits and in-service officers develop it? This is easier said than done because one is born with a predetermined critical thinking level. Rather, a person will, over a period of time, progress through various levels of thinking and reasoning. The types of thinking skills that one uses in kindergarten are much different from those used at age 30. Indeed, it appears that age and education are the only factors that affect the development of critical thinking.

In *How We Think*, psychologist John Dewey outlined the journey that a person takes in the development of thinking skills, which evolve through childhood from concrete to abstract. Only when a child moves to the abstract can he or she enter the realm of critical thinking. This transition is critical in a young person's development, and a failure to complete this transition can result in an inability to form intelligent judgments and solve problems.[15]

Six Stages of Development The key to thinking critically lies not in concrete knowledge of a concept and its process, but in understanding how to evaluate one's own thinking while evaluating information and forming solutions. The development of critical thinking requires movement through a number of stages:

CopTalk

Basic Law Enforcement Supervisor Training Program (BLESTP)

The Federal Law Enforcement Training Center is an example of the in-service training resources for new and experienced law officers. It offers courses such as:

- Understanding Behavioral Diversity
- Communication Skills
- Conflict Management
- Introduction to Briefing Skills

- Computer Skills Workshop
- Networking
- Workplace Stress Issues
- Values & Ethics
- Performance Management
- The One-Minute Manager
- Supervisory Legal Topics
- Paradigms and Technical Change
- Problem Solving
- Law Enforcement Leadership

What Do You Think? Why are these courses so important to police success?

SOURCE: Adapted from Federal Law Enforcement Training Center at www.fletc.gov/fmi/blestp2.htm

1. Most people begin as unreflective thinkers, who are unable to recognize flaws in their thinking.
2. Challenged thinkers realize that they have problems in their thinking.
3. Beginning thinkers attempt to develop critical thinking skills but on an inconsistent basis.
4. Practicing thinkers realize that their critical thinking will only improve with regular practice.
5. Advanced thinkers experience improvement and develop proficiency in their thinking.
6. When skilled and insightful thinking becomes second nature, one has attained the level of **master thinker**. Master thinkers possess a number of "qualities of mind." They are conscious of the workings of their minds and are highly integrated, rationally powerful, logical, far-sighted, deep, self-correcting, and emancipated in their thinking. Few people ever become master thinkers; however, it is a goal worthy of pursuit.[16]

master thinker People who are master thinkers are at the highest level of critical thinking because they are conscious of the workings of their minds.

For example, Officer Smith is on patrol when he notices Jennifer, a local prostitute, running toward him. From past experience, a number of prostitutes have filed false complaints in an effort to get revenge on clients who did not pay. Officer Smith assumes prostitutes are not to be trusted. Jennifer informs him that she was abducted and raped. Officer Smith infers that Jennifer is lying. Based on this assumption and previous knowledge, he makes the judgment that Jennifer may be trying to get revenge on a client who didn't pay.

To avoid the mistake of assuming that his first judgment must be correct, Officer Smith remains objective as he reinitiates the critical thinking process. He listens as Jennifer explains what happened and processes her information. He notices that her report is being stated with more emotion and sincerity than in the past. He also observes that she has a bruise on her left cheek, which coincides with her story that the rapist hit her. In addition, recent training in detecting deception leads Officer Smith to believe that Jennifer is being truthful. He files a report based on her claims and drives her to a hospital emergency room. In this case, his awareness of to his own assumptions and the use of the critical thinking process allowed him to reach a sound decision.

Effects of College Education Research indicates that higher education improves critical thinking levels. One review of 27 studies from 1950 through 1985 found that students' critical thinking abilities generally increased during four years of college, even though the use of special instructional techniques or courses had no impact on improving critical thinking levels.[17] Even one year of college can improve critical thinking levels.[18]

Benefits of College Education The benefits of higher education have been known for years. Another review of the research literature found that officers with a college education are:

- Better at performing the tasks of policing than non-college-educated officers
- Better communicators
- Better at exercising flexibility in difficult situations
- Better at interacting with persons of different cultures, lifestyles, and races
- More professional and dedicated to policing
- Better able to handle organizational change
- More open-minded to alternative approaches to policing
- More holistic in their views of the criminal justice system[19]

Recruiting College-Educated Officers To enhance critical thinking, police departments need to place emphasis on recruiting college-educated officers and incorporating better instructional techniques in both preservice and in-service training. Greater use of simulations, case studies, and role-plays in academy training can enhance critical thinking. Veteran officers without college degrees need to return to the classroom, and those who already have graduated should pursue graduate degrees.

Problems with Egocentrism It is necessary to recognize one of the greatest inhibitors of sound critical thinking—**egocentrism**. By their nature, humans are irrational at times. They often view and react to events from

egocentrism A way of thinking that chooses to see the world from a very narrow and self-serving perspective, which can lead to manipulative and self-serving behavior.

Police Procedure

Hiring Educated Officers

Although police executives still disagree about the value of higher education in policing, they generally see more advantages than disadvantages in a police officer with a college degree. It is not only the knowledge gained from education that makes a better police officer, but also the influence on the officer's critical thinking skills. Higher education involves more than the acquisition of knowledge. It also involves learning how to think and how to solve problems.

If only one strategy were to be identified for improving critical thinking among police officers, it would be higher education. Prospective recruits and working officers can improve their critical thinking levels. Embracing the concept of police as master thinkers has a number of implications for policing.

Critical Thinking What controversies might erupt if preference is given to college-educated applicants for policing jobs?

an egocentric frame of reference that is devoid of rational thinking. A person who exercises egocentric thinking sees the world from a very narrow and self-serving perspective. In turn, this perspective can make such a person manipulative and self-serving, believing that their egocentric thinking is rational.[20]

Police are susceptible to egocentric thinking. The influences an officer's feelings, emotions, and actions. Egocentric thinking may be the most significant barrier to critical thinking. As a solution, sound critical thinking principles can eradicate the egocentric thinking process.

7.2 Self Check

1. What is critical thinking?
2. What are the benefits of critical thinking?

POLICING *Online*

Check your answers at
www.policing.glencoe.com

7.3 Problem Solving

problem solving The act of recognizing and solving a problem; an essential part of effective policing.

Problem solving has always been a key part of policing, even though the ways by which police have approached it have varied over time. The most common problem-solving model consists of the following steps:

1. Recognize that a problem exists
2. Define the problem
3. Generate possible solutions to the problem
4. Evaluate alternative solutions
5. Choose a decisive course of action
6. Take action to implement your decision
7. Establish controls and follow up to make sure the problem is solved[21]

POP and SARA

problem-oriented policing (POP) A problem-solving process that helps officers identify and solve persistent problems on their beats; central to this process is SARA.

With the advent of 911, police became more reactive in their response to crime. They also became frustrated with their inability to address the underlying causes of many crime problems, especially domestic disturbances that never seemed to be resolved. In 1979, Herman Goldstein presented a new approach to this problem: **problem-oriented policing (POP)**.[22] If officers could identify and solve persistent problems on their beat, they could reduce the number of 911 calls and improve the quality of life in their communities.

At the center of POP is the problem-solving process know by the acronym **SARA**—*scan, analysis, respond,* and *assess.* The process requires analytical and problem-solving skills not possessed by many officers. For officers to succeed in implementing SARA, they first need to understand what problem solving is. One way to define it is in the context of experiential learning, the major means by which officers learn policing.

SARA An acronym that stands for the analytical and problem-solving process of *scan, analysis, respond,* and *assess.*

Problem Solving in Policing

Experiential learning as problem solving is best illustrated by David Kolb's model (see Figure 7.3 below). Experiential learning is best characterized as an experience-based process of feeling, watching, thinking, and doing, which everyone uses in the process of solving problems and learning.

When individuals learn, they move from concrete experience to reflective observation to abstract conceptualization to active experimentation. In more simple terms, individuals feel, watch, think, and do. As a result of his research, Kolb identified four styles of learners, each represented by a quadrant of the circle.[23] Figure 7.4 on page 264 profiles Kolb's Learning Styles. Although each person has a preferred learning style, all four styles are essential in day-to-day functioning.

Figure 7.3
Kolb's Experiential Learning Model

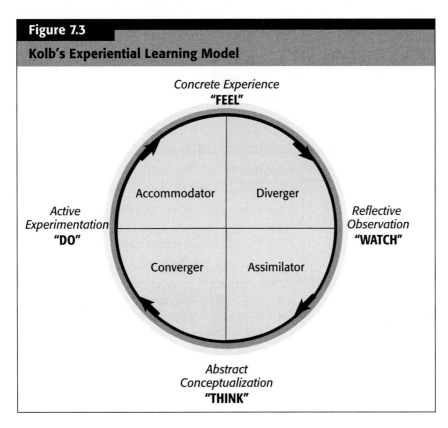

Concrete Experience
"FEEL"

Active Experimentation
"DO"

Reflective Observation
"WATCH"

Accommodator   Diverger

Converger   Assimilator

Abstract Conceptualization
"THINK"

Figure 7.4

Four Styles of Learning: Profile of Kolb's Learning Styles

Concrete Experience

ACCOMMODATOR 4

Strengths:	Getting things done
	Leadership
	Risk Taking
Too much:	Trivial improvements
	Meaningless activity
Too little:	Work not completed on time
	Impractical plans
	Not directed to goals

To develop your Accommodative learning skills, practice:
◆ Commiting yourself to objectives
◆ Seeking new opportunities
◆ Influenceing and leading others
◆ Being personally involved
◆ Dealing with people

DIVERGER 1

Strengths:	Imaginative ability
	Understanding people
	Recognizing problems
	Brainstorming
Too much:	Paralyzed by alternatives
	Can't make decisions
Too little:	No ideas
	Can't recognize problems
	and opportunities

To develop your Divergent learning skills, practice:
◆ Being sensitive to people's feelings
◆ Being sensitive to values
◆ Listening with an open mind
◆ Gathering information
◆ Imagining the implications of uncertain situations

Active Experimentation ← → *Reflective Observation*

CONVERGER 3

Strengths:	Problem solving
	Decision making
	Deductive reasoning
	Defining problems
Too much:	Solving the wrong problem
	Hasty decision making
Too little:	Lack of focus
	No testing of ideas
	Scattered thoughts

To develop your Convergent learning skills, practice:
◆ Creating new ways of thinking and doing
◆ Experimenting with new ideas
◆ Choosing the best solution
◆ Setting goals
◆ Making decisions

ASSIMILATOR 2

Strengths:	Planning
	Creating models
	Defining problems
	Developing theories
Too much:	Castles in the air
	No practical application
Too little:	Unable to learn from mistakes
	No sound basis for work
	No systematic approach

To develop your Assimilative learning skills, practice:
◆ Organizing information
◆ Building conceptual models
◆ Testing theories and ideas
◆ Designing experiments
◆ Analyzing quantitative data

Abstract Conceptualization

Each of the four styles of learning is indicative of how each person perceives and processes information:

Divergers **Divergers** perceive information concretely and process it reflectively. Their favorite question is, "Why?" This is because they are interested in personal meaning and need to be personally involved in the learning experience. They learn best by listening and sharing ideas and excel when they are able to view direct experience from a variety of perspectives. Their goal is harmony, and their behavior reflects thoughtfulness and enjoyment in observing others.[24]

divergers People whose learning style involves perceiving information concretely and processing it reflectively.

Assimilators **Assimilators** perceive information abstractly and process it reflectively. Their favorite question is, "What?" They acquire facts and information to enhance conceptual understanding. Details are essential to the thinking process, as are the views of experts. Their thinking process can best be characterized as sequential and analytical, because they seek certainty. If a situation is perplexing, they will reexamine the facts until the situation becomes clear. Intellectual competence and personal effectiveness are important to them.

assimilators People whose learning style involves perceiving information abstractly and processing it reflectively.

Convergers **Convergers** perceive information abstractly but process it actively. Their favorite question is, "How does this work?" They are effective at integrating theory and practice. In their learning, they love to experiment, need to understand how things work, and constantly edit reality. They value strategic thinking and are pragmatic in their view of learning. If it works, they use it. In their relationships with other people, they may appear bossy and impersonal at times.

convergers People whose learning style involves perceiving information abstractly but processing it actively.

Accommodators **Accommodators** perceive information concretely and process it actively. Their favorite question is, "What if?" because they are enthusiastic about new things. Their strength is integrating experience and application. Engaging in trial and error allows them to learn. They are intuitive and believe in self-discovery; because of this, they are adaptable and flexible to ever-changing situations. In their relationships with others, they are people oriented, but they may be perceived as manipulative or pushy.

accommodators People whose learning style involves perceiving information concretely and processing it actively.

To be effective in solving problems, all four learning styles are necessary. The key is to develop skill in all four quadrants by identifying one's weak areas and practicing those skills until they appear to be balanced. The next section will provide other approaches to developing better problem-solving skills.

Developing Stronger Problem-Solving Skills

Much criticism has been directed toward police academies and institutions for their inability to nurture and develop problem-solving skills. In the academy, case studies, simulations, and well-constructed role-plays can assist officers in developing problem-solving strategies. One promising instructional strategy is problem-based learning (PBL).

Most important, officers must know their strengths and weaknesses. Figure 7.4 on page 264 identifies ways that each person can develop skills in each of the four learning styles. Remember that problem solving is maximized when all four styles are employed. When forming a task force, it is critical that the composition of the task force has representation from each of the four styles so that each member is equipped to address different types of problems.

Problem Solving and Discretion How does problem solving work for police officers who use discretion to solve a problem? It can help them to explore options more open-mindedly and develop more creative solutions. An officer who can solve problems thoroughly and with a minimum of police resources will be highly valued by his or her department.

Imagine being a community police officer assigned to a business district in a large city. You have heard from a number of business owners and local residents that there is a problem with older teenagers hanging around the pay telephones at several convenience stores. They are there at all hours of the day and night. Recently, vandalism, littering, and assaults have increased in the area. Residents are concerned about the safety of their children walking to a nearby school and are afraid to go to the convenience stores at night. They also worry about the safety of their homes. In addition, a large number of merchants feel that the problem is keeping customers away.

You decide to investigate by staking out the areas for several days and nights. You observe a large number of older teenagers and adult males loitering in the parking lots of these convenience stores. It appears that they are using the telephones to answer calls on their pagers. Shortly thereafter cars will pull up to the curb, at which time a drug transaction appears to take place.

The local merchants inform you that the phones are operated and maintained by the local telephone company. You brainstorm with them at a meeting and come up with several solutions: more active patrolling of the areas, an undercover operation (which might take months to conclude), posting "No Trespassing" signs, and asking the local phone company to remove the pay telephones. You decide to try removing the telephones because it is the quickest and least expensive.

After the telephones are removed, you observe the area for the next week and notice that the group of adults and teenagers are no longer in the area after dark. You conclude that the solution of removing the pay telephones was the main factor in solving the problem. Within days the loitering and vandalism complaints from local business owners have dwindled to zero. In solving this problem, you have just demonstrated experiential learning by using what you have seen and heard to develop and implement solutions. In the future, you will have this experience to draw on in similar situations.

7.3 Self Check ?

1. What is SARA?
2. What are the main styles of learning?

POLICING *Online*

Check your answers at
www.policing.glencoe.com

7.4 Interpersonal Communications

One of the most prominent characteristics of successful police officers is their ability to effectively communicate and interact with people. As community policing becomes more dominant, the need for effective interpersonal communication skills is critical. How do police officers compare to the general population in the area of interpersonal communications? The reality is that they are no different from the rest of the population. As a rule, the average person doesn't communicate well, and everyone, including police officers, can benefit from learning better people skills.

Developing a personal strategy of effective interpersonal communications can only improve the relationship between police officers and the community. In the past, little attention has been given in academy training to developing good interpersonal communication skills. If community policing is to realize its full potential, the police-community relationship must involve effective two-way communication.

Understanding Nonverbal Communication

Much of the interaction that a police officer has with residents involves listening to complaints or problems. How the officer listens will determine how he or she responds. There is a major difference between hearing and listening. An officer may hear what someone is saying, but does he or she understand it? The effective use and understanding of nonverbal communication involve three primary skill clusters: attending, following, and reflecting skills.[25] The next sections will discuss attending, several issues related to attending, and then following and reflecting.

▶ **Body Language** Many clues to a person's state of mind are unspoken. Here a sullen-looking teenager is under arrest. *How do you think this person feels toward the officer? Why?*

attending Giving your attention to another person with a strong focus on nonverbal communication.

Attending Giving your attention to another person with a strong focus on nonverbal communication is called **attending**. A study by Albert Mehrabian found that nonverbal communication accounts for 93 percent of the social meaning in a message: 55 percent of this nonverbal communication is attributed to expressions of the eyes and face, and 38 percent is attributed to the tone and pitch of the voice.[26] Every day, police officers must attempt to read nonverbal language in victims, suspects, and witnesses. At first, officers struggle to read nonverbals, but practice will help them see their true meaning. Nonverbal communication can be a clear yet confusing language. The police officer can become more effective in dealing with nonverbal communication by using five guidelines:

1. Make a conscious effort to focus on those cues that might be useful.
2. Look at each nonverbal in the proper context.
3. Look for incongruities when they exist.
4. Be aware of one's feeling during an interaction involving nonverbal communication.
5. Where appropriate, reflect back one's interpretation of the nonverbal message to the speaker for confirmation or correction.

In attending, one uses appropriate body motion and maintains eye contact but avoids distracting motions or gestures such as talking with the hands. Effective attending also minimizes environmental distractions.

Paralanguage By focusing attention on auditory and visual cues, an officer can gain greater insight into the meaning of the message. Cues can include specific words that are spoken; the sound of the voice; and how fast the person is speaking, the frequency and length of pauses, and how often the speech is disrupted with words like "aah" and "mmm." these cues are known as **paralanguage**, which has seven different categories:

1. **Monotone:** Boredom
2. **Slow speed, low pitch:** Depression
3. **High voice, emphatic pitch:** Enthusiasm
4. **Ascending tone:** Astonishment
5. **Abrupt speech:** Defensiveness
6. **Terse speed, loud tone:** Anger
7. **High pitch, drawn-out speech:** Disbelief [27]

> **paralanguage** Auditory and visual cues such as specific words, voice tone, voice speed, frequency and length of pauses, and the use of words like "aah" and "mmm."

Visual Cues: Body Language A person's facial expression, posture, and gestures clearly show a person's hidden feelings. One old saying states that "the eyes are the window to the soul." Research tends to support this: When an individual is interested or receptive to what another person is saying, the pupils in the eyes dilate while disinterest or boredom brings a constriction of the pupils. By observing facial expressions, one can also note reactions to words and comments spoken.

A person's posture and body movements also reflect much about feelings, self-image, and energy level. People who lean back in their chairs and lock their hands behind their heads may be communicating authority and power. A person who walks backwards while being addressed by a superior indicates inferiority on the part of the employee and superiority on the part of the superior. In addition, people may stretch their legs, straighten papers on their desk, or close a briefcase to indicate the need to terminate a conversation.

Whenever possible, remove obstacles such as loud noises or physical barriers such as desks. Getting up and coming around a desk and sitting at an angle fosters a closer person-to-person relationship, while sitting behind a desk gives the impression of authority. Most individuals have a specific technique unique to themselves. If you observe closely enough, it will become obvious and you will be able to understand that person better as a result.

Body Language: Appearance and Environment Additional visual cues can be revealed in a person's clothing, grooming, and environment. Appearing clean-shaven and dressed in a suit communicates a different lifestyle than a beard and faded blue jeans. Where one lives, and in what type of house, communicates something about that person. A person's office often reflects his or her attitudes, beliefs, values, and priorities. An office organized around a computer workstation with minimal seating for visitors might indicate a task-oriented person, and an office with sofa and chairs might indicate a people-oriented person.

Misleading Signals Sometimes nonverbal communications can be confusing and misleading. This is because all nonverbal cues have multiple meanings and may be different within the context of different situations. For example, crossed arms is often seen as indicating defensiveness, but it could also mean that a person is cold. Always try to read nonverbals in the context of the situation.

Proxemics If an officer is using attending skills, he or she inclines slightly toward the speaker, with his or her right shoulder near the other's left shoulder. He or she maintains an open position and does not cross the arms or legs, which might indicate defensiveness. Also critical to attending skills is knowing how to keep an appropriate physical distance from the speaker. The study of personal space and how it is used is called **proxemics**. Edward Hall, a famous anthropologist, has identified four proximity zones:

proxemics The study of personal space and how it is used.

Intimate distance	Up to 18 inches is reserved for intimate and private conversation, such as two close friends discussing a sensitive matter in public.
Personal distance	From 18 inches to 4 feet is for personal conservation, such as personal friends talking.
Social distance	From 4 feet to 12 feet is for social conversation, such as mingling at a party.
Public distance	Beyond 12 feet is considered public space, such as yelling to a person across the street.[28]

The normal distance in American society is about 3 feet. When arriving on a scene, an officer must assess the situation and decide how far to enter into the other person's space.

following skills Listening skills that focus on staying out of the speaker's way so that the listener can discover how the speaker views his or her situation.

door openers A process one uses to initiate communications.

Following Skills The second skill cluster involves **following skills**, which focus on staying out of the speaker's way so that the listener can discover how the speaker views his or her situation. Four tools for developing one's following skills are door openers, minimal encouragers, infrequent questions, and attentive silence. **Door openers** may be the most important way to initiate communication. As a rule, they have four elements:

1. the other person's body language
2. to talk or continue talking
3. which gives the other person time to decide whether to talk and what to say
4. Attending with eye contact and a posture of involvement that demonstrates your interest in and concern for the other person

After door openers, the listener must use **minimal encouragers** such as "Tell me more" or "Go on" to keep the speaker active in the process. Try to use questions infrequently, if at all, since questions from the listener often focus on the intent, perspective, and concerns of the listener and not the concerns of the speaker. If questions are used, avoid closed-ended questions since they restrict open communication. Finally, use attentive silence. This strategy allows the speaker to think, feel, and express himself or herself. The benefit to the listener is a better understanding of the speaker's concern.

One problem that occurs with door openers is that people are prone to initiate communication with judgmental statements such as, "What did you do, lose your best friend?" instead of an effective door opener such as, "Looks like you are having a rough day. I have the time if you would like to talk."

Reflective Listening The final listening skill is **reflective listening**, which is listening to the speaker and repeating the feeling and content in the message back to the listener to demonstrate understanding and acceptance. Special skills within this cluster include paraphrasing, reflecting feelings, reflecting meanings (tying feelings to content), and summative reflections. A listener uses **paraphrasing** to restate the essence of the speaker's content in the listener's own words. The listener reflects feeling by mirroring back to the speaker the emotions of his or her message.

> **minimal encouragers** Phrases such as "Tell me more" or "Go on" to keep the speaker active in the communication process.

> **reflective listening** A listening skill that involves listening to the speaker and repeating the feeling and content in the message back to demonstrate understanding and acceptance.

> **paraphrasing** Restating the essence of the speaker's content in the listener's own words.

MYTH	FACT
Police can always tell a criminal by his or her behavior.	Although most criminals show their guilt through their behavior, many intelligent criminals can use deceptive nonverbal communication. Sometimes they also know how to fake eye-accessing cues to fool officers skilled in this. Therefore, an officer needs to be aware that a suspect may be lying and try to look for inconsistent signals.

To reflect feeling, do the following: 1) focus on feeling words, 2) note the general content of the message, 3) observe the body language, and 4) ask yourself, "If I were having that experience, what would I be feeling?" When reflecting feelings, it is essential to reflect meaning also. To accomplish this, try telling the person, "You feel (insert the feeling word) because (insert the event or content that is associated with the feeling)."

The final stage of reflective listening is summative reflections, in which the listener states the main points or feelings expressed by the speaker throughout the conversation. Summative reflections not only give the listener an understanding of the problem, but also give the speaker an integrated picture of what has been said.

Figure 7.5 below lists some of the guidelines for when to use or not use reflective listening. The degree of success that an officer experiences when using these listening skills is dependent on how often he or she uses the skills. In this case, practice makes perfect, and officers who do not work on these skills will lose them.

Nonverbal Communication and Police Discretion When police are interviewing suspects or possible suspects, they look for several signals to determine probable cause. What a suspect actually says is a small part of the picture. All of the other clues that an officer receives will probably be nonverbal. Shifty eye contact, an attempt to conceal something, or a nervous tone of voice all may indicate that a suspect is hiding something, which can raise police suspicions and may lead to an arrest.

Because nonverbals cannot be evaluated objectively, all officers need to know the difference between suspicious behavior and fearful or anxious

---

Figure 7.5

Use of Reflective Listening

When to use reflective listening	When not to use reflective listening
◆ Before you act	◆ When you are not able to be accepting
◆ Before you argue	◆ When you do not trust the other person
◆ When the other person experiences strong feelings or wants to talk over a problem	to find his or her own solution
◆ When the other person is speaking in a code	◆ When you are not separate from the other
◆ When another person wants to sort out his or her feelings and thoughts	◆ When you use listening as a way of hiding yourself
◆ During a direct mutual conversation	◆ When you feel very pressured, hassled, or depleted
◆ When you are talking to yourself	
◆ When encountering new ideas in a book, lecture, or at work	

behavior that many people experience when talking to police. Some people are nervous around the police for no reason, and this may lead them to act in ways that are misleading. Also, officers need to realize how their own non-verbal behavior affects citizen responses.

Suppose that Craig is a rookie officer who wants to make a strong impression on the public. To show others that he is firm and authoritarian, he stares at people so persistently that he frequently "stares them down." Most prefer to avoid eye contact with him and seem to be shifty-eyed when he talks to them. Also, because of his style of eye contact, citizens are less willing to talk to him and cooperate as witnesses. If he interprets this citizen behavior as "proof" that they must be guilty of a crime, he can face a serious backlash when he realizes that his own behavior caused it.

Roadblocks to Effective Communication

In today's policing environment, officers must be effective communicators if they are to achieve the goals of community policing. An understanding of interpersonal communication begins with understanding the three categories of roadblocks to effective communication:

- Judging involves criticizing, name-calling, diagnosing, and praising in an evaluative manner
- Sending solutions encompasses behavior such as ordering, threatening, moralizing, excessive or inappropriate questioning, and advising
- Avoiding the other's concerns is illustrated by such behaviors as diverting, logical argument, and reassuring

Yet another roadblock is telling others that they are sending communication roadblocks.

Obstacles to Effective Policing It is also important to understand the roadblocks that directly affect policing. Some of these are:

1. Failure to practice active listening
2. Status differences that make it difficult to achieve effective communication
3. Feelings of inferiority or superiority
4. Noise such as psychological stress, not listening actively, or environmental distracters that make it harder to listen
5. Communication barriers that occur when individuals do not express themselves clearly, concisely, or in a manner that is understandable to others

Body Language

You are a desk sergeant who just got an anonymous complaint from a local resident regarding the behavior of a local officer. You ask the complainant several questions, but he is not able to give you any specific reasons for the complaint except that that officer "had an attitude." You talk to the officer, but he seems genuinely surprised because he thinks that he gets along well with everyone. Ever since you hired this officer, you have been concerned that he would encounter prejudicial behavior because he is a member of an ethnic minority. *How can you ensure that this complaint is handled in a way that gets to the root of the problem and does not cause unnecessary punishment for the officer?*

6. Fear of criticism, which often occurs because of a lack of confidence; sometimes it causes individuals to not make positive declarations

7. Jumping to conclusions, which is reaching a conclusion without enough information

8. Filtering, which occurs when information is lost as a message is passed from one person to another

9. Individual sentiments and attitudes

10. Intentional suppression or manipulation of communication, which occurs most often between subordinate and supervisor

11. Complexity of communication channels, which means that the more people involved in the interpretation of a message, the greater the likelihood of distortion

12. Overloading the listener with too much information

13. Overstructuring of communication channels and overreliance on using formal communication channels[29]

Officers sometimes judge, threaten, moralize, and even avoid citizens' concerns. Policing relies heavily on the communications process in conducting day-to-day law enforcement activities. Effective communication, on the other hand, is the responsibility of both the individual officer and the police organization. See Figure 7.6 below for ideas on how to improve your listening skills.

Figure 7.6

Improve Your Reflective Listening Skills

To improve your listening, try the following:

1. Do not fake understanding.
2. Do not tell the speaker you know how he or she feels, because this is a cliched response.
3. Vary your responses.
4. Focus on the feelings.
5. Choose the most accurate feeling words.
6. Develop vocal empathy.
7. Listen with your heart as well as with your head.
8. Strive to make statements that are concrete and relevant.
9. Provide nondogmatic but firm responses.
10. Give the speaker resources that will help him or her handle the problem.
11. Reflect the feelings that are implicit in questions.
12. Accept that many interactions will be inconclusive.

SOURCE: R. Bolton, *People Skills: How To Assert Yourself, Listen To Others & Resolve Conflicts*

Police Sergeant

Job Description

I am a shift supervisor. I am responsible for officers out on patrol and for my own calls, too. I answer for officer behavior on the street, I track patrols on the radio, answer officers' questions and requests for help. Policing is a very independent activity, and because we have to use force sometimes, supervision is very important. You have to know that your officers are trained to your standards because if something goes wrong, your career can be on the chopping block. The most challenging thing is to find the right balance between supervision, support, and micromanagement. You have to know your people's personalities, what motivates them, and you also have to be willing to stand by your officers when they are right, even if it is politically incorrect.

Karen J. Finkenbinder, Carlisle, PA police

A military experience is very important for law enforcement officers. It forces you to be physically fit and teaches you to work in a structured environment. Plus, veterans get preference at hiring time. Education develops a different set of skills and expands your cultural horizon. College educated officers are less likely to resort to force and have better communication skills.

Employment History

In 1976, I went into the army as a military policewoman, and I became a probation officer for juveniles at an army post. After college graduation I taught criminal justice to American students enrolled at a state agency on a military base in Germany. Next, I went to the Persian Gulf as an intelligence officer in a prisoner camp.

Education

I have completed my M.A. in criminal justice and I am working on my Ph.D. in public administration, with an emphasis on criminal justice, at Temple University.

Follow-Up What is the most important skill for this position? Why?

In Pursuit of Lifelong Learning

After graduation, some active-duty officers continue their education by enrolling in college courses or attending law enforcement training sponsored by major colleges and universities. A number of colleges and universities have developed nontraditional programs for police officers.

For example, in the mid- and late 1970s, Fayetteville (NC) Technical Community College offered a "flip-flop" arrangement on a number of its criminal justice courses, which allowed local officers to move between day and night classes as their working schedules changed. Also, the University of South Carolina offered a weekend graduate program that permitted criminal justice practitioners to attend classes on selected weekends throughout the semester. Today, distance learning, in which individuals can take courses online, has provided officers the opportunity to enroll in college courses anywhere and at anytime.

Although there are many opportunities for formal learning, police officers also need to engage in self-directed learning, which is learning outside the formal setting of a college or university. By establishing self-directed learning projects each year, officers can develop critical thinking and problem-solving skills in ways that are not covered by colleges or academies. For example, an officer might decide to read several recognized books on interpersonal communication to improve his or her abilities as a community police officer. As another example, a police sergeant might create a learning project on how to develop a more effective leadership style. Still another officer may decide to subscribe to and read professional magazines such as the

Computer On Patrol

In Pursuit

Visit TraceIt4U.com, a British Web site helping people who have experienced burglary. TraceIt4U can be visited online by clicking the link at **www.policing.glencoe.com**. Read the main page and "About Us" to learn about their services.

Think About It Why was TraceIt4U created? How does it help police and victims recover stolen property?

Figure 7.7

Why a Learning Organization?

- Because we want superior performance and competitive advantage
- For customer relations
- To avoid decline
- To improve quality
- To understand risks and diversity more deeply
- For innovation
- For our personal and spiritual well being
- To increase our ability to manage change
- For understanding
- For energized committed work force
- To expand boundaries
- To engage in community
- For independence and liberty
- For awareness of the critical nature of interdependence
- Because the times demand it

SOURCE: Leeds School of Business, University of Colorado at Boulder, at http://www.bus.colorado.edu/faculty/larsen/learnorg.html

FBI Law Enforcement Bulletin or *Police Chief* to learn new ideas and techniques in policing.

Regardless of the rank, commitment to lifelong learning is necessary if police departments are to become learning organizations. With lifelong learning, officers can be certain that their communication, critical thinking, and problem-solving skills will increase steadily over time. In addition, this effort will make them more professional, as well as justifiably proud of the work that they do. Such efforts will improve the confidence that the public has in their police and will improve relations on all levels.

7.5 Self Check

1. Explain the concept of lifelong learning.
2. How can officers find time to pursue lifelong learning?

POLICING *Online*

Check your answers at
www.policing.glencoe.com

Chapter 7

Skills for the Successful Police Officer

Summary By Learning Objectives

1. Understand the factors that predict success in policing careers.

Effective policing is defined within the context of community policing. Therefore, successful officers possess physical abilities, effective oral and written communication skills, and interpersonal skills such as multicultural communication, collaboration and creativity, conflict resolution, and crisis intervention.

2. Explain the process of critical thinking and its application in policing.

The police officer of today must use sound critical thinking skills, because they are essential to effective interpersonal communication and decision making. they also help eliminate egocentric thinking. There is evidence that higher education and critical thinking are related; four years of college can significantly improve an individual's critical thinking levels.

Police departments can also emphasize critical thinking in simulations, case studies, roleplays, and problem-based learning conducted as part of preservice and in-service training. When officers become aware of the critical thinking process and evaluate how they think, especially in making assumptions and drawing inferences, their effectiveness increases greatly.

3. Name the six stages of developing critical thinking skills.

The six stages of developing critical thinking skills can be defined by the six general stages of thinkers:

1. Unreflective thinkers
2. Challenged thinkers
3. Beginning thinkers
4. Practicing thinkers
5. Advanced thinkers
6. Master thinkers

4. See how creativity can be used in effective policing.

Creative thinking is a state of mind in which people manipulate knowledge to create new ideas and look for new experiences in order to find more new ideas. It is required in problem-oriented and community policing, which focus on quality-of-life issues and emphasize finding creative, long-term solutions. Some ways to promote creativity include looking for the second answer, looking for ideas outside of standard logic, questioning how things have been done in the past, asking "what if" often, using humor to develop a creative state of mind, accepting failure as a stepping stone to a solution, playing with ideas, hunting for new ideas in all disciplines, avoiding putting down other's ideas, and believing you can be creative.

5. Explain the process of problem solving and its application in policing.

Problem solving has been an essential part of policing over the years. The process involves recognizing that a problem exists, defining it, generating possible solutions, evaluating the alternatives, choosing a course of action, implementing those actions, and developing a means to evaluate it. The SARA (scan, analyze, respond, and assess) process simplifies these steps. There are four general types of learners: divergers, assimilators, convergers, and accommodators. Although each person tends to have a preferred learning style, true effectiveness comes from developing abilities in all four styles, because each style brings strength to the learning and problem-solving process. Furthermore, when problem solving is seen as learning, the officer develops an experiential learning process that will aid him or her in future problem-solving situations.

6. Develop and use tools to solve problems in police work.

One of the most prominent characteristics of successful police officers is their ability to effectively communicate and interact with others. There are three categories of roadblocks to effective communications: judging, sending solutions, and avoiding the other's concerns. Other barriers include a failure to listen, status differences, inferiority or superiority complexes, language barriers, fear of criticism, and filtering. Listening skills involve three primary skill clusters: attending, following, and reflecting skills. A useful model for good listening is neuro-linguistic programming (NLP). Through NLP, the police officer can build rapport with citizens and improve the quality of interpersonal communications.

7. Name the guidelines that lead to a better understanding of nonverbal communication.

Nonverbal communication can be clear or confusing, depending on the officer's experience in dealing with it and the situation in which it occurs. There are five basic guidelines for becoming more effective in dealing with nonverbal language:
1. Make a conscious effort to focus on those cues that might be useful.
2. Look at each nonverbal in the proper context.
3. Look for incongruities when they exist.
4. Be aware of one's feelings during an interaction involving nonverbal communications.
5. When appropriate, reflect back one's interpretation of the nonverbal meaning to the speaker for confirmation or correction.

8. Understand lifelong learning and its application in policing.

Lifelong learning is continuous learning, either formal or informal, that is directed toward personal enrichment, professional development, or both. It is an important component of all learning organizations, which are organizations that continually expand their capacity to shape their own future.

As police departments begin moving in this direction, some must try harder than others to develop critical thinking, creativity, and problem solving. Individuals can become lifelong learners by enrolling in college courses that expand their knowledge. They must also be receptive to innovative training opportunities. Finally, they must become self-directed learners who create their own learning experiences based on their personal needs.

Key Terms

critical thinking (p. 253)
inference (p. 254)
assumption (p. 254)
master thinker (p. 260)
egocentrism (p. 261)
problem solving (p. 262)
problem-oriented policing (POP) (p. 262)
SARA (p. 263)
divergers (p. 265)
assimilators (p. 265)
convergers (p. 265)

accommodators (p. 265)
attending (p. 268)
paralanguage (p. 269)
proxemics (p. 270
following skills (p. 270)
door openers (270)
minimal encouragers (p. 271)
reflective listening (p. 271)
paraphrasing (p. 271)
lifelong learning (p. 276)

Questions for Review

1. What traits are sought in recruiting and selecting police officers?

2. Which MBTI personality type makes up 70 percent of police? Why do you think that is?

3. What is critical thinking, and how is it used by police officers?

4. What are the benefits of critical thinking in policing?

5. Why is the problem-solving process important to police officers?

6. What are some of the roadblocks to effective communication?

7. What are the three skills necessary for effective listening?

8. Why is an understanding of nonverbal communication important to police?

9. What is lifelong learning?

10. What are some of the ways that police officers can become lifelong learners?

Experiential Activities

11. **Focus on Modes of Perception**
Engage a friend or classmate in conversation. Be aware of both your modes of perception the whole time. Use a mode of perception that is different from the one used by the other person. Then, switch to use the same mode as he or she is using.

    a. What was the other person's mode of perception?

    b. What happened when you chose a different mode of perception?

    c. What did you learn about relating to other people?

12. **Talk to a Police Officer**
Schedule an interview with a police officer in your area. Ask the officer to describe how he or she makes decisions. Ask for real-life examples.

Experiential Activities continued

a. Does he or she apply the critical thinking process in making decisions?

b. At which of the six stages of the thinking process does this officer operate? Explain.

c. Does the officer observe nonverbal cues when on duty? Which ones?

13. Use Your Critical Thinking Skills

Get a copy of an article that covers a recent crime. Use critical thinking to write a one-page plan explaining how you would investigate this crime.

a. How did critical thinking help you determine a plan for this case?

b. Is your plan similar or different from typical police procedure?

c. What recommendations would you make to the investigators in the case?

14. Response to a Theft Report

A local resident calls your police department to say that his television was stolen. The television was left on the curb the previous night with the trash. The owner explains that the trash service does not pick up furniture and that the TV was left out for a friend to get it in the morning. The owner wants you to find the thief who took his television.

a. Do you attempt to find the person who took this television?

b. Would you charge him or her with a crime?

c. How would you handle the owner?

15. Handling a Domestic Disturbance Call

You are answering a complaint about a family who is frequently warned for disturbing the peace. The mother tells you her children are out of control. She smells of alcohol and does not look you in the eye as she speaks. Both daughters, 11 and 15, accuse her of beating them and not leaving any food in the house. They look pale and unwashed.

a. What follow-up questions would you ask?

b. What legal action should be taken?

c. Outline what you will cover in your report.

Web Patrol

16. Improve Your Cross-Cultural Communication

Review the recommendations of the US Department of Justice for police officers dealing with multicultural issues at **www.policing.glencoe.com**.

Which piece of advice do you find most applicable to your own community and its racial/ethnic makeup?

17. What Is Critical Thinking?

Visit "Mission: Critical," to explore critical thinking through tutorials. It can be accessed online at **www.policing. glencoe.com**. Read the first page, then take the tour.

Select a tutorial and apply it to a policing situation of your choice.

18. Exploring Nonverbal Behavior

Visit "Exploring Nonverbal Communication" through the link at **www.policing.glencoe.com**. Click on two or three of each section and read the different articles.

What have you learned about nonverbal communication?

Critical Thinking Exercises

19. Reviewing a Citizen's Complaint

You are working for the internal affairs division of a metropolitan police department. You have received a complaint from a 50-year-old motorist who claims that one of your officers was rude and disrespectful during a traffic stop. The officer denies the allegations vehemently. He claims that when he tried to cite the motorist, the motorist became belligerent and vulgar. You feel the matter will quickly be settled since the officer videotaped the incident with his vehicle-mounted video recorder.

The tape starts with the officer approaching the stopped motorist and saying, "Sign at the 'x.' I cited you for doing 65 in a 45-mph zone." You hear the motorist reply, "But when you stopped me, I was only going 50." The officer shakes his head and responds, "I don't think so." Immediately, the motorist begins to curse and for the next five minutes directs a total of 25 obscene words toward the officer. The officer is very relaxed and polite to the motorist. After several minutes, the motorist tears up the ticket in frustration and drives away. A review of this officer's record indicates that he has had numerous verbal abuse complaints from stopped motorists.

- **a.** Consider the officer's possible nonverbal communication. What could have made his behavior seem rude to motorists?
- **b.** What will you do to resolve this complaint and the previous ones?

20. Nonverbal Communication

You are a patrol officer who has pulled over a young man for swerving on the road. He does not appear drunk or drugged but is acting strange and distant. You ask him where he has been, and he says that he is driving home from a prayer group and that he is tired from working long hours.

As he speaks to you, he does not look at you, but his eyes shift down, then up and to the right. He mumbles a lot and seems uncertain, then gets defensive when you try to question him further.

- **a.** What nonverbal signals is this person giving you, and how do they affect the sincerity of his message?
- **b.** What can you do to further investigate the situation?

21. Interviewing a Suspect

You and your partner are patrolling a quiet, low-crime area when you see a man running from his house and waving his arms at you. He screams that his wife has been kidnapped. He seems distraught, and you feel that he is sincere after you walk through the house and see broken glass and other signs of a struggle.

As you write a report, he tells you how much he loved her and how upset he is. Then he tells both of you that his wife and he never had an argument. Your partner asks him to come to the station for questioning, and you can tell from his tone of voice that he now considers the husband a suspect.

- **a.** What triggered this response from your partner? Why?
- **b.** Do you agree? Explain.

Endnotes

1. August Vollmer, The Police and Modern Society, Berkeley, CA, University of California Press, 1936, p. 222.
2. Robert Trojanowicz and Bonnie Bucqueroux, *Community Policing: How to Get Started,* 2nd ed., Anderson Publishing, Cincinnati, 1998, p. 65.
3. Wayne B. Hanewicz, "Police Personality – Jungian Perspective," *Crime and Delinquency,* 24(2), 159.
4. Stephen M. Hennessey, *Thinking Cop: Feeling Cop: A Study of Police Personalities,* 3rd Edition, (Scottsdale, AZ: Leadership, Inc., 1999), 19–21.
5. Sandra K. Hirsh and Jean M. Kummerow. *Introduction to Type in Organizations,* (Palo Alto, CA: Consulting Psychologists Press, Inc, 1990), 4.
6. Wayne B. Hanewicz, "Police Personality – Jungian Perspective," *Crime and Delinquency,* 24(2), 159.
7. Hennessey, op. cit., pp. 13–22.
8. Edwin Meese, *Community Policing and the Police Officer: Perspectives on Policing,* (Washington, DC , National Institute of Justice, 1993), p. 1.
9. G. Watson and E. Glaser, *Critical Thinking Appraisal: Manual* (San Antonio, TX: The Psychological Corporation, 1980).
10. R. Paul, *Critical Thinking: What Every Person Needs to Survive in a Rapidly Changing World,* 2d ed. (Santa Rosa, CA: The Foundation for Critical Thinking, 1992), 651.
11. Richard Paul and Linda Elder, *Critical Thinking: Tools for Taking Charge of Your Learning and Your Life* (Upper Saddle River, NJ: Prentice Hall, 2001), 52.
12. Karen M. Hess and Henry M. Wrobleski, *Police Operations* (St. Paul, MN, West Publishing Company, 1993), 27.
13. E. Garver, "Critical Thinking, Them and Us: A Response to Arnold B. Arons's 'Critical Thinking' and the Baccalaureate Curriculum." *Liberal Education* 72 (1986): 245–49; S. Tanner, "Education by Criticism." *English Journal* 75, no. 6 (1986): 26; K. Vandergrift, "Critical Thinking Misfired: Implications of Student Responses to the Shooting Gallery." *School Library Media Quarterly* 15, no. 2 (1978): 86–91; A. Sharp, "What Is a 'Community of Inquiry'?" *Journal of Moral Education* 16, no. 1 (1987): 37–45; and E. Glaser, "Critical Thinking: Educating for Responsible Citizenship in a Democracy." *National Forum: Phi Kappa Phi Journal* 65, no. 1 (1985) : 24–27.
14. C. Bartollas and L. Hahn, *Policing in America* (Boston: Allyn & Bacon, 1999), 348.
15. J. Dewey, *How We Think* (Boston: D. C. Heath, 1933).
16. Richard Paul and Linda Elder, *Critical Thinking: Tools for Taking Charge of Your Learning and Your Life* (Upper Saddle River, NJ: Prentice Hall, 2001), 22.
17. J. McMillan, "Enhancing College Students' Critical Thinking: A Review of Studies." *Research in Higher Education* 26(1) (1987): 3–29.
18. E. Pascarella, *The Development of Critical Thinking: Does College Make a Difference?* (ERIC Document Reproduction Service No. ED 292417, 1987).
19. D. Carter, A. Sapp, and D. Stephens, *The State of Police Education: Policy Direction for the 21st Century* (Washington, DC: Police Executive Forum, 1989).
20. Paul and Elder, op. cit., 214–215.
21. D. Umstot, *Understanding Organizational Behavior,* 2d ed. (St. Paul, MN: West, 1988), 344.
22. H. Goldstein, Improving Policing: A Problem-oriented Approach, *Crime and Delinquency* 25 (1979), 236–258.
23. David Kolb, *Experiential Learning : Experience as the Source of Learning Development* (Englewood Cliffs, NJ: Prentice Hall, Inc., 1984), 25–60.
24. B. McCarthy, *The 4MAT System: Teaching to Learning Styles with Right/Left Mode Techniques* (Barrington, IL: Excel, 1987), 37.
25. R. Bolton, *People Skills: How to Assert Yourself, Listen to Others, and Resolve Conflicts,* (New York, NY: Simon and Schuster, 1979).
26. A. Mehrabian, "Communication without Words." *Psychology Today,* September 1968, 53.
27. Len Sperry, *Developing Skills in Contact Counseling* (Reading, MA: Addison Wesley, 1975), 40.
28. Joseph DeVito, *The Interpersonal Communication Book* (New York, NY: Harper and Row, 1989).
29. N. F. Iannone, *Supervision of Police Personnel,* 4th ed. (Englewood Cliffs, NJ: Prentice Hall, 1987), 107–114.
30. P. Senge, *The Fifth Discipline: The Art and Practice of the Learning Organization* (New York: Currency Double Day, 1990), 14.
31. William Geller, "Suppose We Were Really Serious About Police Departments Becoming 'Learning Organizations'?" *National Institute of Justice Journal* December (1997), 2–6.

Part 3

Questions for Review

1. Explain and define the concept of jurisdiction.
2. What are three characteristics of American policing?
3. What is the difference between a centralized and a decentralized agency?
4. What are four major federal law enforcement agencies?
5. What is the chain of command?
6. Define the expression span of control.
7. What are three examples of line functions?
8. What are minimum standards?
9. What does POST stand for?
10. Name three laws that affect the selection process during recruitment.
11. How many tests are included in the selection process of officer recruitment? What are they?
12. What are the benefits of critical thinking?
13. What is the MBTI?
14. How can you use MBTI results to improve your learning skills and your performance?
15. Why is lifelong learning important?

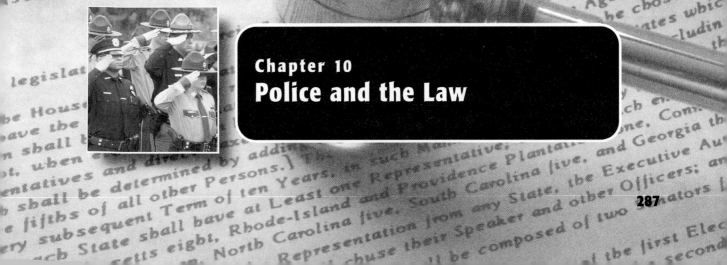

Police Behavior, Attitudes, and Stress

CHAPTER OBJECTIVES

AFTER COMPLETING THIS CHAPTER, YOU WILL BE ABLE TO:

1. Understand the police subculture and its effects on officers.

2. Analyze the dynamics that shape the police personality.

3. Explain the similarities and differences between eustress and distress.

4. Discuss the main symptoms of police stress.

5. Name the five primary sources of police stress.

6. Describe strategies for controlling stress.

7. Explain the importance of support systems.

◀ Police officer stands watch on a police line in Washington D.C.

8.1 Police Behaviors and Attitudes

Police behavior has always been shaped by its environment. Patrol units developed to monitor large urban or residential areas, investigative units developed to solve crimes, and community policing units developed to strengthen police-community relations. As police departments evolved, they developed particular behaviors and attitudes that strongly influenced new officers. Usually, rookies had to adapt to their agency's subculture to succeed, and they also had to develop a distinct working personality that reflected the goals of police management.

The Police Subculture

police subculture The meanings, values, and behavior patterns that are unique to those in policing.

Each occupation has its own subculture. A **police subculture** can be defined as the meanings, values, and behavior patterns that are unique to police officers. Police organizations, especially larger ones, may have several subcultures. There might be one at the patrol level, another at the supervisory level (such as sergeants and lieutenants), and another at the management level. There also might be different subcultures in different units, especially when these units are relatively large and independent. Some attitudes and values will be common at all levels, some will differ, and some will conflict.[1] The police subculture is mainly composed of:

- Cynicism
- Solidarity
- Authoritarianism
- Isolationism
- Conservatism
- Siege mentality

cynicism Distrust of human nature and motives.

Cynicism Distrust of human nature and motives is called **cynicism**. It is easy to see how police officers can feel this way. Their constant exposure to crime suspects, weak or unfair court decisions, plea bargaining, and perjury on the witness stand—even by their police peers—can distort their view of human nature. One classic study of the New York Police Department identified five stages of cynicism:

1. Cynicism begins during academy training when instructors tell recruits their war stories, or police experiences, which compare the innocence or ignorance of citizens with the special knowledge possessed by police. This comparison can lead officers to believe that the police are in some ways superior to citizens, which may sometimes lead to arrogant behavior.

CopTalk

War Stories

Police war stories, which are the work-related experiences of police officers, usually emphasize encounters with suspects or other individuals who fail to meet police expectations of appropriate conduct when encountered in the street. Perhaps they don't look normal according to the individual officer's judgment, or they do not act afraid or respectful toward the police. Police may be generally hostile and sometimes harass these individuals.

One researcher traced the origin of this to the widespread belief by the police that they are primarily law enforcers—perpetually engaged in a struggle with those who would disobey, disrupt, do harm, agitate, or otherwise upset the status quo. This can include

anyone from murderers to teenagers with strange clothing. The police in these cases believe that they and they alone are the most capable of sensing right from wrong and deciding what to do about it. They consistently deny anyone that they consider disruptive the opportunity to provide a different set of beliefs to support his or her actions, insisting that the individual's behavior is understandable *only* as something abnormal. At the same time, they ignore beliefs that are different from theirs, and they consistently dislike those who would dare question their activities.

What Do You Think? What are some liability issues that may result from police actions toward those they do not consider normal?

SOURCE: Adapted from Arthur Neiderhoffer, *Behind the Shield* (Garden City, NY: Doubleday, 1969); P. K. Manning and John Van Maanen, eds., *Policing: A View from the Street* (Santa Monica, CA: Goodyear, 1978), 221–38.

---

2. Cynicism increases sharply after recruits graduate from the police academy. This results from a combination of what they learned in the academy and what they are witnessing in the field. In addition, senior peers often emphasize the worst aspects of the job to ensure that rookie officers show appropriate caution.

3. Between two and six years of service, cynicism increases at a much slower rate as officers become more mature and comfortable with the job.

4. At about mid-career, or after 8 to 13 years of service, officers' cynicism begins to decline. The mid-career officer has most probably attained a promotion and improved salary and benefits and has come to the realization that he or she is about halfway to retirement.

5. Toward the end of the career stint, the officer accepts the flaws of the system, and his or her cynicism reaches its lowest level in years.[2]

Cynicism has always been a part of the police officer's working persona—and will continue to constitute a part of the police personality. Some cynicism is desirable: Police should not be gullible but should recognize and inquire into suspicious actions. Still, their cynicism must be balanced with good judgment, realism, and perspective.

Involving the police and the public in community policing and problem solving has the positive effect of reducing officers' alienation and withdrawal. At the patrol level, where studies have revealed the highest incidence of cynicism, community policing can provide an outlet for accomplishment and build employees' self-esteem. With realistic expectations, strong and compassionate leadership, and ongoing training on the symptoms of cynicism, officers can avoid the conditions that lead to extreme cynicism and can maintain their ideals and values.[3]

Solidarity Although many groups other than police, such as firefighters and medical professionals, also work with the community and uphold social values, policing is different because its subculture seems to have a stronger solidarity. All occupational groups share some inclusiveness, but police exhibit an unusually high degree of occupational solidarity.

Some police departments show extreme cases of solidarity, especially when they face charges of police abuse or have to combat major civil disorder. The Webster Commission, which convened after the 1992 Los Angeles riots, found that the professional model of policing created an emphasis on command and control, which can increase police solidarity but can also encourage confrontations. This us-versus-them mentality was cited as creating a climate of distrust between the police and the public.[4] (See Figure 8.1 on page 293 for data on the code of silence.)

Research conducted by the National Association for the Advancement of Colored People (NAACP) found the same thing. They reported that the police subculture is drilled into officers and that many subcultural beliefs "encouraged police behavior that ranged from the insensitive to the brutal and promoted institutional insularity and detachment." They strongly advocated replacing these subcultural beliefs with more productive values, "which must be at the heart of any reform strategy."[5]

Another factor that creates police solidarity is a lack of public support. Although the police see themselves as specialists in dealing with violence, they do not want to fight alone. They find a lack of public support for several reasons:

1. The popular view that police officers are merely robots. Once the officer's humanity is recognized, the citizen is forced to recognize that police work is often dirty and dangerous.

Figure 8.1

Code of Silence

	Strongly Agree	Agree	Disagree	Strongly Disagree
The code of silence is an essential part of the mutual trust necessary to good policing.	1.2%	15.7%	65.6%	17.5%
Whistle blowing is not worth it.	3.1%	21.8%	63.5%	11.7%
An officer who reports another officer's misconduct is likely to be given the cold shoulder by his or her fellow officers.	11.0%	56.4%	30.9%	1.8%
It is not unusual for a police officer to turn a blind eye to improper conduct by other officers.	1.8%	50.6%	43.3%	4.4%
Police officers always report serious criminal violations involving abuse of authority by fellow officers.	2.8%	36.2%	58.5%	2.5%

SOURCE: Adapted from www.ncjrs.org/pdffiles1/nij/181312.pdf

2. There is an appearance or existence of prejudicial behavior toward women, minority groups, or other population groups.
3. Past police-citizen encounters in which police arrogance or carelessness either appeared to exist or actually existed.

Authoritarianism The conspicuous exercise of legal powers constitutes **authoritarianism** and is a factor that is sometimes desirable in a police officer. Just as suspiciousness is a desirable trait in an officer, officers should be able to assert their authority during crisis situations. The balanced application of authority is critical to successful policing practice. For example, an officer should use his or her authority to protect others, but an officer should not use authority to intimidate or harass people.

Authority has many forms, such as the officer's right to arrest suspects, the right to search persons or property, and the right to seize evidence. Another form of authority is the right to use deadly force when necessary. These rights separate police officers from citizens, because officers are required to enforce laws that regulate the flow of public activity and morality. The police officer's uniform and equipment are symbols of authority that identify the police to the public.

authoritarianism The conspicuous exercise of legal powers.

isolationism The effect of exclusion from mainstream society from being a police officer.

symbolic assailant Someone whose gestures, language, or attire signify to police a capability of being dangerous.

Isolationism In policing, **isolationism** is exclusion from mainstream society as the result of one's status as a police officer. Isolation may be traced to two aspects of policing:

- **The element of danger** Police training cautions officers to constantly be aware of suspicious circumstances and persons. This apprehension and sensitivity set police apart and tend to isolate them from those who are being policed. In response, police develop perceptual shorthand to identify certain kinds of people as symbolic assailants. A **symbolic assailant** is anyone whose gestures, language, or attire signal to a police officer an individual who has or may be identified as being potentially threatening or dangerous.[6] Veteran officers may see the signs of a symbolic assailant when they spot someone who turns out to be carrying drugs or weapons. The problem with perceptual shorthand, however, is that it can be basically the same as stereotyping or profiling, and inexperienced officers may misuse the concept.

- **The element of authority** The element of authority also adds to police isolation. For example, this is commonly seen when police enforce traffic laws. People can be resentful and even hostile to police who give them citations. Police involvement in regulating public events and public morality creates further isolation.

Computer On Patrol

The Mobile Digital Terminal

Instead of police radios, more and more patrol cars are being equipped with computerized mobile digital terminals. At the beginning of a shift, officers log onto their terminals for two reasons:

1. **To receive calls for service:** Dispatchers send out calls for service in typed messages that the police read, then respond to. Such messages include the crime, address, and any other pertinent information that officers should know (such as whether the suspect is armed).

2. **To query automated databases for criminal records checks:** When an officer pulls over a car or stops to question a suspect, he or she can type in that person's personal or automobile information to see if that person has any outstanding warrants or criminal record. If he or she does, a routine questioning can lead to an arrest.

Think About It What other information might be helpful for police to have online?

◀ **Solidarity** Police officers who feel a strong sense of solidarity may sometimes isolate themselves from other elements in society.
How can police solidarity have both positive and negative effects?

Conservatism A mind-set that supports the status quo and does not want rapid change, particularly in regard to laws and customs, is called **conservatism**. Historically, police have held the conservative belief that the justice process should be retributive, or punishment oriented, rather than rehabilitative, or treatment oriented. Their feelings toward constitutional law are also often narrow, as are their attitudes toward welfare and social assistance.

Some research has found that minority officers are more liberal than nonminority officers when they start working at a police department but become more conservative during their years of service. This illustrates how deeply these minority officers a socialized into the police subculture: Even officers with more liberal attitudes gradually change them to fit in with their fellow officers.

conservatism Supportive of the status quo, particularly regarding society's laws and customs.

Siege Mentality A **siege mentality** is a state of mind characteristic of a group that has a strongly antagonistic relationship with the rest of society and sees the world as "us" versus "them." In this case, "us" is the police and "them" is everyone who is not a police officer. The mere fact that the police are engaged in enforcing a set of rules implies that they also support them, sometimes in conflict with the rest of society. Prohibition is an example of the type of long-term unpopular law that can create a siege mentality among officers.

The police subculture is not as strong in service-oriented departments as in departments that still follow the reform-era style of policing.[7] This is an important point to remember, because the reform era is sometimes

siege mentality A police mind-set that groups people into two categories: "us" (police) and "them" (everybody who is not a police officer).

believed to have created a siege mentality among police. Departments that follow this traditional style of policing emphasize a law-and-order approach to the public, find it difficult to adapt to more flexible styles of policing and communication, and often behave with a heightened sense of drama.

The Working Police Officer Personality

The police officer's working personality is the personality that he or she shows while in uniform. It is developed within the police subculture and is a mixture of the demands of that subculture and the individual's personality. This role contains two principal variables: danger and authority.

- **The element of danger** makes the officer especially attentive to signs indicating a potential for violence and lawbreaking. As a result, the officer can become suspicious and cynical. This element socially isolates the police, both from the dangerous segment of society and from law-abiding citizens who are perceived as unwilling to fully support the police. For example, police officers may feel that the public will criticize them for using strict measures to control crime in a high-crime inner city but would never visit that neighborhood themselves or do anything to help solve the crime problem.
- **The element of authority** reinforces the element of danger in further isolating the police. Typically, the police are required to enforce moral laws such as those prohibiting drunkenness in public and laws regulating the flow of public activity, such as traffic laws. Because enforcing these laws makes the police unpopular, police tend to feel further isolated.

For example, suppose that local police have to close down a bar because there have been too many resident complaints about noise and fighting. They close it down on a Wednesday morning when there are only three customers in the bar, but bar patrons are outraged and several call the police station to complain. A local newspaper criticizes the police for being puritanical, even though they were only responding to resident complaints. The sides of the police and the residents near the bar are never heard, but the public's opinion of the police ends up being slightly more negative.

These behaviors and attitudes can make it difficult for officers to handle the high stress of police work with flexibility and open communication. The next section examines the capabilities of officers to handle the extreme demands of policing.

8.1 Self Check

1. How does cynicism usually develop throughout a police officer's career?
2. What specific elements characterize the subculture that develops among police officers?

POLICING *Online*

Check your answers at
www.policing.glencoe.com

8.2 Stress and Policing

Police officers are constantly exposed to situations that are uncertain, unpredictable, and dangerous. These situations can create high levels of stress in any officer. In turn, stress can cause the following:

- Physiological problems such as coronary heart disease, ulcers, and cancer
- Psychological problems such as depression and suicidal tendencies
- Problems with the cognitive (or thought) processes, especially decision making and problem solving

Police stress is a topic that needs more research, more instruction time at training academies, and more attention in police departments. Most police departments are unequipped to deal with job-related stress and do not provide adequate resources for officers who need help. Also, the police subculture discourages officers from showing their emotions or admitting to any thoughts or feelings that might be seen as weak.

The Nature of Stress

Stress can be defined as any situation—whether an event or a state of mind—that requires the body to adapt in some way. Stress research expert Hans Selye defines stress as "the body's non-specific response to any demand placed on it."[8] To many police officers, stress is often a confusing and misunderstood concept. This is because most people think that stress is only negative, but stress can also be positive. Positive stress is called **eustress**. It can include falling in love, getting a new job, or going on vacation. To eliminate *all* of your stress would take the spice out of life because eustress makes people happy and motivated. Negative stress is **distress**, which is stress caused by an unpleasant situation or state of mind. Distress can linger if a person has sad or regretful memories.

A **stressor** is any event that triggers a response from the **autonomic nervous system (ANS)**, which is the part of the nervous system that sends impulses to the heart, muscles, and glands. The ANS controls a number of bodily functions:

- Gland responses
- Circulatory functions
- Respiratory functions
- The digestive system
- Uro-genital functions
- The involuntary muscles associated with these systems
- The involuntary muscles associated with the skin

stress Any event that requires a person to adjust in some manner; the body's nonspecific response to any demand placed on it.

eustress Stress that results from positive events.

distress Any type of negative or unpleasant stress.

stressor Any event that elicits a response from the autonomic nervous system (ANS).

autonomic nervous system (ANS) A system that supplies impulses to the heart, muscles, and glands.

The ANS can be divided into two systems: the sympathetic and the parasympathetic. The role of each system is different, but both constantly interact to create a balance in the body. When faced with danger, the **sympathetic system** accelerates the function of the heart and lungs and slows down the digestive organs. On the other hand, a period of relaxation prompts the **parasympathetic system** to slow down the heart and lungs but stimulate the digestive system.

Three Stages of Reaction The body reacts to stressors by passing through three stages of physiological reaction.[9] These stages include:

1. **Alarm** In the alarm stage, the body is confronted with a stressor and mobilizes to meet the threat. For example, suppose that you are investigating a dark area where you just heard a struggle. Suddenly someone fires three bullets at you; two miss and one hits your protective vest. Your ANS reacts with alarm.

2. **Resistance** In the resistance stage, the body operates at an optimal level to resist the stressor. This is when the body releases adrenaline to give itself energy. The stressor may remain, but the symptoms that appeared in the alarm stage disappear as the body reacts to the stressor. After being fired upon in the last stage, you now grab your service weapon and place yourself behind a car while trying to determine who fired the shots. You also call for backup.

3. **Exhaustion** Under extended periods of stress, the body may not be able to resist stressors any longer. If the body reaches the exhaustion stage, the immune system is weakened, and many of the emotions experienced in the alarm stage may reappear with greater force. Continued exposure to the stressors can lead to exhaustion and ultimately death.

It is during the exhaustion stage that the body becomes vulnerable to numerous diseases, which Selye called diseases of adaptation. These can include ulcers, high blood pressure, coronary disease, and cancer. Indeed, stress is cumulative in most cases. Minor stresses may add up to produce a major stress that leads to a physical or mental breakdown. Prolonged emotional stress—the kind that is a part of the everyday work environment, especially in policing—can wear down the immune system in ways that may become irreversible. Some of the symptoms of stress include increased heart rate and blood pressure, perspiration, dry mouth, and increased blood sugar.

Stress Tolerance Levels Many experts agree that stress, like beauty, is in the eye of the beholder. This means that what causes stress for one person may not cause it for others. For example, some officers thrive on dangerous police work and volunteer for challenging units such as SWAT and hostage negotiation. Others are overwhelmed by patrol duty and burn out quickly, then change professions.

Stress tolerance levels vary from person to person, but anyone can become overstressed if they are not careful. The question is, how much stress is too much? The amount of stress that an individual can manage effectively is referred to as his or her **zone of stability**. In the zone of stability, stress is measured not only in terms of excitement and arousal but also in terms of boredom. Each officer must strive to find his or her zone of stability, which is necessary to succeed in policing and avoid burnout. For example, some officers find boredom very stressful and seek excitement in the field. On the other hand, some do not want to face danger on the street but instead work at desk jobs and enjoy the excitement of talking to their colleagues in the field.

zone of stability The amount of stress that a person can effectively manage.

Measuring Stress

Each individual has limits to his or her ability to take stress. When do you know that you have exceeded your limit? To answer this, stress researchers T. H. Holmes and R. H. Rahe developed a social readjustment rating scale to measure the impact of major life events on an individual. This scale ranks major life events with a certain amount of points for each one. By figuring out which events apply and adding up the points, an individual can learn his or her stress limits. Figure 8.2 on page 300 shows the scale with assigned values.

Anyone who scores over 300 has reached a critical stress level. This person has an 80 percent chance of developing stress symptoms such as ulcers and high blood pressure within one year. If the score is between 150 and 300, there is a 50 percent chance, and a score of less than 150 indicates a 30 percent chance or less. A quick review of this list reveals that a number of the events are positive eustress events such as vacation, marriage, and outstanding personal achievement. If a person is not careful, even too much of a good thing can cause a high level of stress.

The Costs of Stress

The cost of stress to police officers can be seen in several ways:

- *Lowered productivity* Stress reduces a person's ability to perform efficiently.
- *Poor morale* When an officer realizes that he or she cannot meet the expectations of the job, he or she becomes frustrated and demoralized.
- *Alcoholism* Alcoholism affects police about three times more often than it does the rest of the American population.

Figure 8.2

The Social Readjustment Rating Scale

Life Event	Mean Value
1. Death of spouse	100
2. Divorce	73
3. Marital separation from mate	65
4. Detention in jail or other institution	63
5. Death of a close family member	63
6. Major personal injury or illness	53
7. Marriage	50
8. Being fired at work	47
9. Marital reconciliation with mate	45
10. Retirement from work	45
11. Major change in the health or behavior of a family member	44
12. Pregnancy	40
13. Sexual difficulties	39
14. Gaining a new family member, such as through birth or adoption	39
15. Major business readjustment, such as a merger, reorganization, or bankruptcy	39
16. Major change in financial state—a lot worse or a lot better than usual	38
17. Death of a close friend	37
18. Changing to a different line of work	36
19. Major change in the number of arguments with spouse—either a lot more or a lot less than usual	35
20. Taking out a mortgage or loan for a major purchase, such as for a home or business	31
21. Foreclosure on a mortgage or loan	30
22. Major change in responsibilities at work, such as a promotion, demotion, or lateral transfer	29
23. Son or daughter leaving home, marrying, or attending college	29
24. Trouble with in-laws	29
25. Outstanding personal achievement	28
26. Spouse beginning or ceasing work outside the home	26
27. Beginning or ceasing formal schooling	26
28. Major change in living conditions, such as building a new home, remodeling, or the deterioration of one's home or neighborhood	25
29. Revision of personal habits like dress, manners, or associations	24
30. Trouble with the boss	23
31. Major change in working hours or conditions	20
32. Change in residence	20
33. Changing to a new school	20
34. Major change in usual type and/or amount of recreation	19
35. Major change in church activities—a lot more or a lot less than usual	19
36. Major change in social activities like clubs, dancing, movies, or visiting	18
37. Taking out a mortgage or loan for a lesser purchase such as a car or a college education	17
38. Major change in sleeping habits—a lot more or a lot less sleep, or change in part of day when asleep	16
39. Major change in number of family get-togethers—a lot more or a lot less than usual	15
40. Major change in eating habits—a lot more or a lot less food, or very different meal hours or surroundings	15
41. Vacation	13
42. Christmas	12
43. Minor violations of the law such as traffic tickets, jaywalking, or disturbing the peace	11

SOURCE: T. H. Holmes and R. H. Rahe, "The Social Readjustment Rating Scale," *Journal of Psychosomatic Research* 11 (1967): 213–18.

- **Drug abuse** Drug abuse can involve legal prescription drugs or illegal ones. Corrupt officers can easily obtain drugs in the field.
- **Marital problems** This can include spousal abuse, separation, and divorce.
- **Depression** This is another sign of poor morale and can be long lasting.
- **Suicide** More officers die by suicide than by street violence.

How do some of these outcomes appear in real life? Suppose that Larry is a two-year veteran of a department that polices a fast-growing large city. Crime is growing, too, especially gang- and drug-related offenses. Larry finds that many of his colleagues start ignoring crime in lower-income areas because they find it is not worth the trouble. His management and the local courts reinforce this by discouraging him from overloading the courts with too many suspects. This lowers his morale, which is further lowered when he realizes that some of the other patrol officers are taking bribes from small-time drug dealers. Since Larry does not feel comfortable about turning in a fellow officer, he watches the corruption with growing uneasiness.

One night he is performing patrol alone when he sees one of the bribing drug dealers selling cocaine. He pulls over and arrests him, and when the dealer resists, Larry suppresses him too roughly and breaks his wrist. The suspect is eventually charged and convicted of dealing drugs, but not after Larry is reprimanded by his supervisor for excessive use of force, the dealer threatens to sue the department, and Larry's patrol buddies get angry at him for arresting someone who was bribing them to not be arrested. One year later, a burnt-out and depressed Larry leaves policing.

Some of the most serious and controversial problems among police officers revolve around police alcoholism, drug abuse, divorce, domestic violence, post-traumatic stress disorder (PTSD), suicide, stressors for female officers, and stressors for minority officers.

Police Alcoholism Alcohol abuse is a significant problem among police officers, who may find themselves drinking to deal with their daily exposure to death, crime, and human misery. Because police see events that can make them very angry, afraid, or depressed, they sometimes try to relax and forget about it by drinking. To complicate the situation further, the police subculture encourages officers to be very close-knit. After a shift, they will often gather at a local bar to drink, share war stories, and find relief from the trauma and stress of their jobs.[10]

There are some experts who believe that alcoholism among police is a result of more than just trauma exposure. There is the belief that in the first five years of policing, officers are attracted to the excitement, camaraderie, and intensity of being a street cop. When off-duty, officers drink to regain the high of being a cop. When this turns into alcoholism, they become detached and apathetic. This transition to alcoholism can destroy their marriages and lead to domestic violence and divorce.

Police alcoholism is a dark secret that some police departments do not want to reveal. This leads to **denial** on the part of the officer, his or her family, and the police department. Denial can be a serious obstacle when police are trying to find help for their problems. It can also be seen in official responses to many other police stressors. When police find that they have alcohol problems, they may not find help within their departments. Fellow officers may do more harm than good by 1) denying that there is a problem or 2) distancing themselves from someone they perceive as weak. Until police departments provide better resources and can communicate more openly with their officers about substance abuse, officers are usually better off seeking private counseling.

Police Drug Abuse Although alcohol abuse is a known problem among American police, the use of drugs is less obvious. Considering the impact that stress has on police officers, it is not unusual that some resort to illegal drug use. Although the police are expected to enforce the law, the nature of policing produces stressors that can make officers susceptible to drugs. The problem of police drug abuse must not be ignored if the integrity of the police is to be maintained. Researchers state that police drug abuse is a result of three factors:

1. Police exposure to the drug-using element of society
2. Almost constant exposure to drugs
3. The opportunities provided to engage in such behavior[11]

The exact number of officers who use illegal drugs is not known. However, if results from mandatory drug testing are any indication, the problem is significant. For example, the Boston Police Department initiated an annual drug-testing program in January 1999. The Boston PD conducts random hair analysis. It prefers hair to urine because a hair analysis gives a more comprehensive picture of the officer's drug use. Hair analysis allows detection of drug use within the past three months, while urine indicates drug use only within the past four days. Any officer who refuses drug testing is automatically terminated.[12]

MYTH	FACT
If an officer says he or she has no problem with alcohol, it is best to believe it.	**Denial is a major characteristic of the disease of addiction and is to be expected.**

denial A means of avoiding a problem by pretending that it does not exist; common among alcoholics and substance abusers.

Between January 1999 and October 1999 1,200 officers were tested; 23 tested positive for drug use, mainly cocaine and marijuana. Most were patrol officers with between 10 and 20 years of experience on the police department. The Boston Police Department dealt with the problem with a mixture of discipline and rehabilitation. In an effort to allow officers to become drug free, they established a second chance program. Officers in this program are given suspensions and drug rehabilitation and undergo monitoring by the department. If they fail to become drug free, they are terminated.

Divorce in Police Families Police families have high rates of divorce, and families of male officers have very high rates of domestic violence. Although the national divorce rate is 40 percent, the rate for police families is estimated to be somewhere between 60 and 75 percent. Married officers who cannot communicate with their spouses will find that their marriage will be strained and will probably end in divorce. Worse yet, officers who go through a divorce are five times more likely to commit suicide.[13]

Part of the reason for marital difficulties such as separation and divorce is that officers have trouble communicating their stress level to their spouses. The world of the police officer can be difficult, if not impossible, to describe to a spouse. This is because officers see events that most people never experience. How does someone explain to his or her spouse the murders, suicides, and accidental deaths that an officer may see every week? One officer may arrive at a scene to find that an elderly man, terminally ill with cancer, has committed suicide by placing a shotgun in his mouth. The next week, he may feel the anguish of responding to a traffic accident where a young mother and child survive a head-on collision only to burn to death before they can be extracted from the car. Two months later, he may find the decomposing body of a young woman on a hot summer afternoon. All these experiences will be etched in the memory of the officer but may be difficult to describe to a spouse. Add to these experiences the stress of rotating shifts, low pay, and dangerous encounters on the street, and an officer will find himself or herself emotionally and physically drained.

Online

Remember, one of your best resources is **www.policing.glencoe.com**

Domestic Violence in Police Families In recent years, a new problem has appeared—domestic violence committed by police officers. Although about 10 percent of families in the general population experience domestic violence, one research study found that four times as many police officers had exhibited physical aggression toward a spouse in the past year.[14] Also, these are only the reported incidents. The actual number of cases of police domestic violence is unknown because police domestic violence incidents often go unreported. Victims often feel that departments will side with the officer and ignore their complaints.

Traditionally, this fear has been justified: When domestic violence is reported, the departmental strategy is often to handle it internally with no criminal sanctions against the abusive officer. To complicate matters further, police departments today have been slow to enact policies to address this problem. In 2000, the International Association of Chiefs of Police (IACP) addressed the problem directly and announced it was taking a leadership role in drafting a policy to deal with officers committing domestic violence. The IACP believes that any policy on police domestic violence must stress zero tolerance.

In 1996, a major victory against domestic violence was accomplished with the passage of the Domestic Violence Offender Gun Ban. This federal law prohibits those convicted of misdemeanor domestic violence or child abuse crimes from buying or owning a firearm. For officers convicted of domestic violence offenses, this law meant the end of their policing careers.[15]

The problem of police domestic violence has implications beyond the police department. The National Center for Women and Policing feels that police who fail to recognize and address police spousal abuse within their departments cannot effectively respond to domestic violence in the community.[16] Other experts agree and believe that the key to preventing police domestic violence is to identify problems early, then provide counseling and support services to police families. Assistance can come in the form of police chaplains, police psychologists, employee assistance programs, or peer counseling programs.[17] Groups such as Spouse Abuse by Law Enforcement (SABLE) maintain Web sites that offer guidance and resources for victims of police domestic violence.

Post-Traumatic Stress Disorder (PTSD) In policing, a single traumatic event can lead to severe stress-related problems. For example, an officer who is wounded in a shooting in which he also shoots and kills a suspect can develop **Post-Traumatic Stress Disorder**. PTSD is a strong physical, emotional, and cognitive reaction to a traumatic event that threatens a person's ability to function normally. Although PTSD is more commonly associated with soldiers and victims of violent crimes, police frequently develop it too. Officers with PTSD may experience symptoms such as those listed in Figure 8.3 below.[18]

The figures on police with PTSD are not conclusive, but as many as one-third of all officers may be suffering from untreated PTSD. What is stopping many of these officers from seeking treatment? The same problems that are seen with alcoholic or drug-addicted officers: denial, an organizational culture that supports keeping quiet about an officer's personal problems, and the proud nature of many officers. As a result, many officers neither seek treatment nor demand that departments provide treatment. This is a dangerous mistake, for until PTSD is recognized by police departments, "police officers will continue to suffer and a number will die by their own hand as a result of their untreated symptoms."[19]

Post-Traumatic Stress Disorder (PTSD) A psychological condition that sometimes occurs after an individual has been exposed to a traumatic experience.

Police Suicide The ultimate cost of police stress is suicide. It is estimated that the police suicide rate is about twice as high as among the general population. Worse still is the fact that police suicides outnumber police murders: In 1994, the number of documented police suicides was 300, and the number of officers killed in the line of duty was 137. Today the number has risen, so that one officer commits suicide approximately every 24 hours. The number

---

Figure 8.3

Symptoms of Post-Traumatic Stress Disorder (PTSD)

Physical Reactions	Emotional Reactions	Cognitive Reactions
◆ Headaches	◆ Anxiety	◆ Debilitating flashbacks
◆ Muscle aches	◆ Fear	◆ Repeated visions of the
◆ Sleep disturbances	◆ Guilt	incidents
◆ Changed appetite	◆ Sadness	◆ Nightmares
◆ Decreased interest in	◆ Anger	◆ Slowed thinking
sexual activity	◆ Irritability	◆ Difficulty in making
◆ Impotence	◆ Feeling lost and	decisions and solving
◆ Withdrawal	unappreciated	problems
	◆ Disorientation	◆ Lack of concentration

SOURCE: Arthur W. Kureczka, "Critical Incident Stress," *FBI Law Enforcement Bulletin* 65, no. 2/3 (February–March 1996): 15.

of undocumented suicides is unknown, and it is difficult to acquire accurate statistics on police suicides because most departments do not maintain or release data on officer suicides. As with alcoholism and drug abuse, many departments are embarrassed about these problems and often prefer to stay in denial about them.

To officers who cannot cope with the hopelessness, emotional pain, and stress of their jobs, suicide provides a way out. Police officers are taught to take control of a situation: They start with verbal control, and if that does not work they use physical control. When all else fails, they use their weapons. It is fitting that when they ultimately lose control in their lives, the gun becomes the final solution. Most often the officer uses his (or, less often, her) own weapon.

Many stress factors in policing are interconnected. Therefore, it is not surprising that alcohol is a key factor in most police suicides. The suicide rate among alcoholics in the general population is 270 per 100,000. In more than half of police suicides, the officer was drinking heavily at the time of the suicide. A Detroit Police Department study also states that approximately 42 percent abused alcohol and 33 percent were diagnosed with a psychosis. In this study, the most significant problem was marital problems. The vast majority of suicides in this study were young white males, married, and high school educated.[20]

suicide by criminal An indirect form of police suicide, in which officers place themselves in unsafe situations or ignore standard safety precautions out of indifference for their own lives.

Although most police kill themselves with their own weapons, some use an indirect way out known as **suicide by criminal**, in which officers place themselves in unsafe situations or ignore standard safety precautions out of indifference for their own lives. As one former sheriff's deputy described it, "I began to ignore my training and was exposing myself to dangerous situations that could have easily turned fatal. I had chased people into their homes without backup and chose not to draw my weapon when the situation clearly called for doing so." He did this to give them "more than ample opportunity to kill or hurt me."[21]

One would think that with the seriousness of the problem, police departments would offer recruits some training in preventing suicide. This is not the case. Despite the need for change in many areas of policing and the need for a new breed of officer to enact these changes, many police administrators still cling to outdated beliefs that a macho, emotionless officer is the best officer.

Stress Among Female Officers Female officers are not immune from police stresses but must cope with a number of barriers within police departments that create potentially harmful stressors that male officers do not face. These include male chauvinism, lack of support and respect, negative attitudes from the public, high turnover, and sexual harassment. In some cases, male officers refer to women as ladies or girls, which implies they need protection.

The use of profanity often creates tension between male and female officers. Male officers do not want to be inhibited in expressing themselves, but female officers who curse offend many officers. Furthermore, women officers who are inhibited in using profane language often find their words have an almost hollow meaning, which hinders their ability to be taken seriously on the street. When men tell sexual jokes, female officers often withdraw to avoid any interaction that might be construed as improper or sexual in nature. The result is that women officers do not develop the close relationships with fellow male officers that are necessary for officer teamwork and support.

Not until the early 1970s did women begin to enter law enforcement in increasing numbers. During this time, female officers were scrutinized by their male counterparts. In the minds of many male officers, including administrators, they were not capable of performing the duties of a police officer. In the past and even today, many females enter policing with less preparation to perform the traditional roles of policing. Men are encouraged to have numerous opportunities to develop police skills, such as through military experience, playing team sports, and firearms training. Women, however, are less likely to engage in these activities. In addition, many girls are still taught to play support roles rather than leadership ones. When this is combined with sexism in a police department, female officers face an uphill struggle to gain respect and credibility.[22]

In the new millennium, the situation may be improving. Research indicates that the gender-related stressors associated with earlier times may be diminishing in some departments. The reason may be that males and females

◄ **Women Police Officers**
Washington D.C. officers converse before searching Rock Creek Park for missing intern Chandra Levy on July 16, 2001. While female officers have made great progress in recent years, work relations can sometimes still be tense.
What do you think police departments could do to improve male-female relations?

are assuming equal roles in everything from raising families to participating in sports and serving in the military. The acceptance of women into policing is also made easier by the fact that as the number of female officers increases, so does the number of top-level female administrators. Female officers today have more female role models within their departments who can offer mentoring and career guidance. Women have proven they can perform as well as men. They are gaining respect and, consequently, eliminating the stressors that once plagued them.

Stress Among Minority Officers Minority officers in a department can experience stress beyond that experienced by other officers. In many departments, minority officers find themselves under the scrutiny of the majority. Researchers note that:

1. Minority officers are expected to be more tolerant of community problems within their minority population, yet are also expected to enforce the law impartially.
2. Minority officers may be expected to join a minority organization within the department, separating them from the majority of the force.
3. Plainclothes minority police are at greater risk of being mistaken for criminals by other officers in large departments, where officers in one precinct do not necessarily know officers in other precincts.[23]

In the past, minority officers struggled to gain credibility in policing. Prior to the 1960s, discrimination in hiring, job assignment, and promotion was very evident in police departments across America. Although discrimination issues still arise in some police departments, more and more evidence reveals that minority officers are gaining acceptance within their own departments and the public they serve. A 1999 study found that minority officers report experiencing job-related stress at rates similar to white officers.[24]

The work environment for minority officers is also improving. Increasing numbers of minorities in top-level management positions have provided needed role models for aspiring minority officers entering the law enforcement occupation. Minority officers are becoming more self-confident and unwilling to tolerate discrimination in the workplace. The stress that minority officers will experience in the future will be experienced by all officers, regardless of their race or ethnic origin.

8.2 Self Check

1. What are eustress and distress?
2. What are the typical signs and symptoms of stress?

POLICING Online

Check your answers at
www.policing.glencoe.com

Most police applicants do not know much about stress except for what they have seen in movies or on television. This is often inaccurate, because movies and television shows about police are written to entertain audiences and portray police work as something that is constantly exciting and adventurous. Each movie or TV episode shows numerous gun battles and high-speed pursuits in a short period of time, but the public never sees or feels the real emotional strain that policing has on the police officer. They never experience the feeling of shooting and killing a suspect, telling a mother and father that their 15-year-old son was just killed in a traffic accident, or responding to a scene where a two-year-old baby has been beaten to death.

The reality is that police officers must confront high-risk and emotionally charged situations that are not entertaining but deeply disturbing. What an officer sees in a single year, the average citizen may not experience in a lifetime. In addition, police are exposed to numerous other stressful events in their lives such as seeing fellow officers get injured or killed, having to use deadly force, and dealing with ongoing stressors of department politics. Some of these stressors can be devastating. Figure 8.4 on page 310 lists 25 of the most stressful events in a police officer's life. Five main sources of stress experienced by police officers are the nature of police work, police organizations, the individual officer, the criminal justice system, and the media.

Police Work

Policing is very high risk by nature. Some stressors that occur directly from police work are burst stress, suicide by cop, stress from the use of discretion, and stress from facing death or injury. Change in work conditions and special assignments can also lead to stress.

Burst Stress Headlines on the evening news tell the public of murder-suicides, hostage situations, armed robberies, high-speed pursuits, and shoot-outs—all of which involve the police. When an officer goes on duty, he or she has no way of predicting what the shift will bring. A police officer can spend hours in boredom, then suddenly face several minutes of stark terror.[25] This is known as **burst stress**, which is stress caused by important single events (such as a shootout) rather than continual low-grade stressors (such as departmental politics).

Suicide by Cop One severe single-event stressor is **suicide by cop**, which is when citizens act in ways that endanger life, forcing police to respond with

burst stress Stress that is caused by important single events (such as a shootout) rather than continual low-grade stressors (such as departmental politics).

suicide by cop A severe single-event stressor that occurs when citizens act in ways that endanger life, forcing police to respond with deadly force.

Figure 8.4

The 25 Most Stressful Life Events in Law Enforcement

1. Violent death of a partner in the line of duty
2. Dismissal
3. Taking of a life in the line of duty
4. Shooting someone in the line of duty
5. Suicide of an officer who is a close friend
6. Violent death of another officer in the line of duty
7. Murder committed by a police officer
8. Duty-related violent injury to another officer
9. Violent job-related injury to another officer
10. Suspension
11. Passed over for promotion
12. Pursuit of an armed suspect
13. Answering a call to a scene involving the violent nonaccidental death of a child
14. Assignment away from family for a long period of time
15. Personal involvement in a shooting incident
16. Reduction in pay
17. Observing an act of police corruption
18. Accepting a bribe
19. Participating in an act of police corruption
20. Hostage situation resulting from aborted criminal action
21. Response to a scene involving the accidental death of a child
22. Passed over for promotion by inexperienced or incompetent officer
23. Internal affairs investigation against self
24. Barricaded suspect
25. Hostage situation resulting from domestic disturbances

SOURCE: Adapted from James D. Sewell, "Police Stress," *FBI Law Enforcement Bulletin*, April 1981, 9.

deadly force. Suicide by cop is not common, but its effects can be devastating. On top of forcing police to use deadly force, it is a manipulative act that can make an officer feel angry and resentful. Imagine that you are driving a car, then someone jumps in front of you to commit suicide. The shock, anger, and sadness that you would feel for being forced to participate in such an event are similar to what police feel when they are provoked into a suicide by cop scenario.

Correct Use of Discretion   The very nature of policing involves discretionary power. Every day, police officers are pressured to make the right decisions when handling interactions with suspects and the public:

- Should they question a person?
- Should they search a person or a place?
- Should they arrest a person?

Apart from the fact that police work is scrutinized by police management and the public, there is also the moral obligation to make the right decision. Many officers enter policing with a strong sense of right and wrong. When they realize that they have made a wrong decision, or that the system encourages or forces them to make wrong decisions, they experience stress. This can be extremely frustrating to officers who see such mistakes as giving ground to the other side. Although the implications for questioning a suspect are not as strong as they are when using force, officers know that every police action—correct or otherwise—can have repercussions. Experienced officers deal with this by simply doing the best that they can and knowing that nobody is perfect.

Facing Death or Injury Another stressor is facing any scene of death or serious injury. To observe a dead person in a funeral home is quite different from an officer's experience at the scene where death has actually occurred. Officers encounter death on a regular basis. From the drunk driving fatality to the murder-suicide, the officer often sees scenes that will be forever etched in his or her mind. One of the most memorable experiences an officer will have is the first time he or she encounters a dead body. This is especially true if the body is decomposing or mutilated, or if the death resulted from a very traumatic event such as a mass murder or disaster. Particularly distressing is any scene involving the abuse or death of a child. An officer may experience feelings of numbness or shock, and in later years a particular sound, smell, or image may trigger a flashback.

The World Trade Center Attack On September 11, 2001, the world was stunned after terrorists flew two large airliners into the Twin Towers of the World Trade Center (WTC) in New York City. That day would forever change the lives of thousands of police and firefighters in the New York City area. The extent of the emotional toll would not be known for weeks, months, or even years. When the first airliner struck 1 WTC, scores of police officers and firefighters responded quickly and were followed by more when the second airliner struck 2 WTC. As they entered the Twin Towers, they knew the risks and dangers; however, their focus was clear—rescue those people trapped in the floors above. As the towers collapsed, two billion pounds of steel, glass, and concrete were compressed into a pile of rubble nine stories high. The missing persons included 23 New York City police officers, 35 New York Port Authority officers, and more than 300 New York City firefighters—all of whom are now presumed dead.[26]

The grim reality was that few, if any, of those trapped in the WTC would survive the collapse. As rescuers began recovering the dead, they quickly realized that in many cases, few intact bodies would be found.

Many had been incinerated by the inferno, while others were pulverized as the towers collapsed. Rescuers found 256 body parts, including fingers, arms, legs, toes, one head, and numerous pieces of unrecognizable human flesh. As the body parts were recovered, they were tagged and placed in refrigerated vans at the recovery site. Handling this human carnage posed both health and mental health dangers for police, firefighters, and rescue workers. As rescuers recovered more and more bodies and body parts, many became overcome with emotion. One rescuer became very emotional after finding a dead infant strapped in a car seat of a driverless vehicle.[27]

If the emotion and trauma of searching the WTC site were not enough, the debris was hauled to the city dump and reexamined by 400 NYPD detectives, along with FBI agents, National Guardsmen, and other federal investigators who combed through this looking for evidence and body parts. This task was nothing short of gruesome: The workdays were long with workers staying at the site for up to 18 hours a day. To add to the trauma and stress, many of the police and firefighters who arrived after the collapse learned that many of their friends and even family were missing in the WTC.

Officers who arrived after the collapse could take solace in the fact that those who died were heroes. There is the case of John Perry from the 40th Precinct who was in Manhattan to file his retirement papers. When he saw the burning towers, he ran to offer assistance and eventually died in the collapse. As friends noted, he could have gone home and pursued his dream of becoming a lawyer, but he responded to those in distress.[28] He truly was the embodiment of the ideals and values of the New York City Police Department.

Police Organizations

organizational stressor
Any factor within an organization that can contribute to a police officer's stress.

Another police stressor is the officer's police organization. An **organizational stressor** is any factor within an organization that can contribute to the police officer's stress. This can include:

- A quasi-militaristic model of policing, in which officers are treated harshly and discouraged from voicing their opinions
- A rigid bureaucratic structure, in which communication and change are discouraged by unnecessary rules and layers of management
- Poor supervision, which can lead to poor officer conduct or to the development of police subcultures that do not reflect the agency's mission

- Lack of employee input into policy and decision making, which can lead to inefficient and unpopular policies
- Excessive paperwork, which keeps officers away from their beats
- Lack of administrative support, which can cause poor morale
- Divisive or petty department politics, which can lead to excessive or unjust discipline, performance evaluation, and promotions
- Role conflict and role ambiguity, which can lead to conflicting organizational missions, values, goals, and objectives
- Inadequate pay, which can cause poor morale
- Poor equipment, which can cause unsafe work conditions: Although officers do not know what will happen on their shifts, they do expect to leave the shift alive. When their safety is challenged, officers rely on their equipment and training. A lack of proper equipment such as bulletproof vests, radios, computers, and weapons can increase an officer's anxiety. It may also make him or her feel that police management or the general public does not care.
- Adverse work schedules that are unpleasant or disrupt an officer's health
- Understaffing, in which police departments with high turnover rates have difficulties remaining at full strength. As a recent example, in November 1997, the Atlanta Police Department had 193 vacancies, which meant that ten percent of all police positions were vacant. The result was that fewer officers were handling the same urban areas and doing more police work. The consequences can be slower response times, longer shifts, unpatrolled areas, and some service calls answered by phone calls instead of police visits.
- Boredom[29]

All of these factors can contribute to an officer's frustration and lower his or her morale. The officer may feel that he or she is being treated like a robot. Unlike a robot, however, the officer is suffering from stress due to these organizational stressors.

The Individual Officer

Police officers can develop conditions that create lowered immunity and stress tolerance. These factors include poor nutrition, poor physical fitness, problems with an officer's marriage or family relations, and personality characteristics.

Poor Nutrition The officer who is constantly under stress will probably change his or her eating habits. Some of the noticeable changes will include a loss of appetite, eating at irregular times or in irregular quantities, and eating poor-quality foods such as sugar, caffeine, and fried foods. A combination of these factors can reduce physical performance in any profession, but especially one that requires quick thinking and stamina such as policing does. During stressful periods, vitamins B and C are depleted and fewer digestive enzymes are produced, which means that fewer nutrients are absorbed into the body. Considering that the average daily calorie requirements are 1,800 for men and 1,400 for women, imagine the requirements that are needed under stressful conditions.

When a person combines poor eating habits with poor-quality foods, he or she will be unable to produce adequate energy levels. If the body has to endure stress for 24 hours or more, it will enter the exhaustion stage. The body will experience low blood sugar levels, resulting in feelings of depression and fatigue; higher blood pressure; and susceptibility to infections and injuries that will take longer to heal.[30] This situation can become a vicious circle when injuries seem to take forever to heal, which reduces an officer's physical effectiveness and thus makes him or her more likely to get injured again.

Poor Physical Fitness Another key factor is physical conditioning. Policing by nature is sedentary, and contrary to what people see in movies and television, most of a police work shift is spent sitting in a patrol car or at a desk. Therefore, a police officer must exercise regularly to avoid gaining weight. If he or she gains weight, the body is forced to carry this additional weight and produce more blood vessels, which forces the heart to work harder. In fact, each additional pound of fat requires an additional 2,300 feet of blood vessels for proper circulation. Add to this the fact that for every decade over age 30, the heart's ability to pump blood decreases six to eight percent and blood pressure increases five to six percent. Obviously, the older, overweight officer with high levels of stress is at a high risk for heart problems.

Personality Characteristics Finally, a police officer's personality can influence his or her adaptation to police work. Five personality traits are necessary for the successful performance of diverse police duties:

1. Emotional restraint, which is the officer's ability to control his or her anger in confrontations with a suspect, especially when a suspect is verbally abusive
2. Emotional expressiveness, which is the use of interpersonal communication to avoid physical confrontation, make chaotic situations calm, and relax nervous citizens

Figure 8.5

Contradictions in Policing Personalities

The five personality characteristics discussed below can be self-contradicting. However, these contradictions are a part of policing.

On the one hand	On the other hand
1. Stick to your responsibility.	You are a crime fighter, psychiatrist, social worker, minister, doctor—and you're the only one around.
2. Don't cover a job alone.	Handle your own load and avoid making unnecessary calls to other officers for help.
3. Deter the incidence of crime.	Don't jack up the neighborhood.
4. Don't get involved.	You gotta have empathy.
5. Don't turn in an officer to Internal Affairs.	Don't do anything illegal or wrong.
6. Be firm; don't lose face.	The first thing is to be nice.
7. Don't break the law to enforce the law.	Use your discretion.

SOURCE: Adapted from William K. Muir, *Police: Streetcorner Politicians* (Chicago: University of Chicago Press, 1977), 192.

---

3. Group cohesiveness, which involves following group norms and the concept of teamwork

4. Independent style, which involves being self-sufficient and autonomous

5. Realistic orientation, which means that officers must be logical and analytical instead of emotional and impulsive in their decision making

Although these five personality characteristics are essential to effective policing, each can also be contradictory. These contradictions are summarized in Figure 8.5 above.[31] These paradoxes often create a stressful situation for the police officer, such as the following: What action should I take? Will it be successful? Is it ethical?

The Criminal Justice System

The criminal justice system contributes to the stress of policing in different ways than do experiences on the street. Stress from the criminal justice system comes from several sources:

1. **Frustration with having to rearrest the same offenders** More and more arrests involve repeat offenders, which raises questions about the effectiveness of the correctional system and court sentencing.
2. **Frustration with the use of plea bargaining and other court procedures** Sometimes an officer prepares a strong case against a defendant, only to see a prosecutor plea bargain for a lenient sentence instead of going to trial. In other cases, a minor technicality can exclude a case from trial or dismiss it on appeal. Even when a strong case goes to trial, it may be thrown out due to a procedural error committed by the prosecutor. An officer has no control over any of these situations, and it is frustrating to see defendants who are probably guilty going free.
3. **Testifying in court** Another source of stress is testifying in court. Experienced officers enter the courtroom after preparing themselves for questioning by the prosecutor and intense cross-examination by defense attorneys. When officers are on the witness stand, they may have to defend their judgment, competency, and integrity. When officers internalize sarcastic comments or questions by defense attorneys, they can carry grudges that create stress. They must realize that these remarks are not personal but only part of the adversarial process of a criminal trial.

The Media

In recent years, the media have become a major source of stress for many police departments. Press scrutiny during lawsuits and trials against police is almost always negative. While the criminal justice system is expected to treat any defendants as innocent until proven guilty, the media are not bound by this doctrine. This creates stress among officers, and an entire department can feel stress from a lawsuit against a single officer. A department may even experience stress from police trials that affect other jurisdictions, due to police solidarity and the feeling that such negative publicity can affect police everywhere.

Another problem is that headlines can be misleading. A headline such as "Suspect Dies in Police Custody" leaves the impression that the suspect died *due* to police custody, not from something unrelated such as a health

◀ **High-Publicity Cases** A New York police officer holds back protesters on Fifth Avenue, on February 26, 2000, during a demonstration against the acquittal of four officers in the shooting death of Amadou Diallo. Cases of police brutality attract a high level of negative publicity.
How do you think these cases affect the rest of the police force?

condition. Finally, the rise of investigative reporting has also resulted in public relations problems for police. Although some of these stories are accurate, others are not, and certain camera angles and edited interviews can leave the viewer with a biased perspective.

The police response to media attacks has been to limit press access to the police, but this is a double-edged sword. It can limit negative press, but it can also make police look secretive. The American public may wonder what a department is hiding by avoiding the press. Furthermore, accountability requires that police explain their actions thoroughly to the general public, even if they have made a mistake. This can be a challenge when police departments feel that the media will distort their messages. To deal with this complex issue, many large departments have public relations departments, and smaller ones may have a public relations representative.

8.3 Self Check

1. What is burst stress?
2. Name five personality characteristics that are necessary for the successful performance of police duties.

POLICING *Online*
Check your answers at
www.policing.glencoe.com

Police officers will always be exposed to job-related stressors. Some of these, such as inadequate equipment or training, can be eliminated. Others, such as murders, rapes, and deadly traffic accidents, will never go away but will remain a permanent part of policing.

The question is not really how an officer can eliminate stress but rather how to cope with unavoidable stressors. The Central Florida Stress Unit offers the six Rs for **stress management**:

stress management
Reducing or eliminating unhealthy stress in order to lead a balanced lifestyle.

- Responsibility: You are in control of your life, so establish priorities and keep it simple.
- Reflection: Know what causes you to have stress, be aware of stress symptoms, and check periodically to make sure your life is balanced.
- Relaxation: Do something good for yourself, schedule yourself worry time to work out personal problems (such as through counseling or talking to a family member), and schedule time out.
- Relationships: Maintain supportive relationships, manage your relationships, and improve your relationship with yourself.
- Refueling: Eat a balanced diet with high fiber and low cholesterol; avoid poisons such as caffeine, fats, nicotine, and fast food; and drink lots of water.
- Recreation: Learn how to have fun with your family and friends, enjoy your life, and treat others the way you want to be treated.[32]

Stress Inoculation

stress inoculation
Developing a lifestyle that makes one resistant to the effects of stress.

Stress inoculation is a detailed stress-management strategy in which an officer develops a lifestyle that makes him or her resistant to the effects of stress.[33] Some ways to accomplish this include relaxation techniques, exercising frequently, eating a regular, balanced diet, getting enough sleep, and establishing a network of friends and family for support.

Developing Support Systems

Any stress management program requires an officer to have strong support systems from both family and fellow officers. Support systems may come in the form of the following:

- Family stress reduction training for police families
- Peer counseling
- Department psychological services
- Early warning mental health programs
- Police stress units

Police Family Stress Reduction Units In November 1997, the National Association of Police Organizations (NAPO) started stress reduction training for police families in the Dallas Police Department. The training is covered by a National Institute of Justice grant. The purpose of the training is to give police families an increased awareness, understanding, and solutions to personal and organizational stressors experienced by police officers and their families. It addresses stress management strategies and resources, burst stress, the police subculture, and the police working personality.[34]

Peer Support Another means of coping with effects of stress is peer support. Officers who experience a traumatic event such as a shooting are quick to seek out fellow officers for support. This can be comforting, because fellow officers know what they have experienced and can often give helpful advice and support. On the other hand, it can sometimes backfire when fellow officers are reluctant to offer support. In these cases, they become more of a problem than a solution. There are a number of reasons why officers sometimes avoid offering support to each other:

- A need to protect their unemotional image
- An egotistical tendency to want to top each other's war stories
- Police training to ask questions and not get entangled in emotions
- Uncomfortable feelings of tension and anxiety
- A sincere need to support the rightness of what another officer has done by avoiding feelings such as guilt, sadness, or frustration[35]

Critical Incident Stress Debriefing Teams It is essential that every officer receive counseling services whenever he or she needs them. Many departments do maintain psychological services, such as **Critical Incident Stress Debriefing Teams (CISDTs),** for their officers.[36] Although a burst stress incident (such as a shooting) is traumatic for an officer, the period following it may cause even greater stress. A CISDT will debrief the officer, which means that it will question him or her to learn useful information about the incident. After that, it will provide emergency counseling services as needed.

An excellent example of a CISDT is one offered by the Boston Police Department. Formed in 1973, it is staffed by three full-time police officers

Critical Incident Stress Debriefing Team (CISDT)
A unit that provides emergency counseling services to officers experiencing PTSD.

and six volunteer officers. All of them have suffered stress trauma and resolved it. They are trained as certified employee assistance professionals and as drug and alcohol counselors.

Participation in this CISDT is voluntary but highly recommended to avoid the consequences of unresolved stress. Officers who participate are treated with complete confidentiality, and nobody learns any information except for the participant, counselor, and program director. Over the years, the program has proved to be a valuable asset to the Boston Police Department.

A number of years ago, a detective in a medium-size urban police department accidentally dropped his weapon and killed a fellow officer. The officer was told by his supervisors to go home and take a few days off. One can imagine what must have been going through the mind of this officer. If there was ever a time that counseling was needed, it was then, but he did not receive immediate counseling because the department offered no psychological services to its officers.

Early Warning Mental Health Programs A pioneer in police psychological services was Martin Reiser of the LAPD. As early as 1970, Reiser established an **early warning mental health program** for police sergeants. Since sergeants are the first-line supervisors, which means that they are the lowest level of police supervisors, they have daily contact with officers and are best qualified to detect mental health problems among them. Reiser worked with sergeants to prevent major emotional crises in police officers and to increase supervisors' human relations skills. Police supervisors were given 12 hours of training that covered the following:

1. Emotional development, stress, and personality
2. Early warning signs of emotional upset
3. Crisis intervention techniques
4. Referral criteria, counseling limits, and referral resources

Police Stress Units Although psychological services are necessary for police, many departments cannot afford such a unit. Worse, those that do provide services find that many officers are reluctant to seek assistance because they are afraid of being stereotyped as weak and unreliable. In response to both these concerns, an alternative has evolved. A **police stress unit** is a nonprofit organization that is not affiliated with any law enforcement agency but provides specialized and confidential help for officers and their families.

The units are typically staffed with peer support volunteers and licensed mental health counselors. They provide services in areas such as marital or family problems, post-shooting trauma, financial problems, alcoholism, drug abuse, gambling, and retirement issues. What makes these programs

early warning mental health program An in-house police mental health program in which sergeants are taught to detect early symptoms in officers.

police stress unit A nonprofit organization that is not affiliated with any law enforcement agency but provides specialized and confidential help for officers and their families.

Police Psychologist

Job Description

I am the NYPD's uniformed psychologist. Currently, there are only 12 law officers who are police psychologists nationwide. There are no career lines mapped for this job, but I would encourage people who are interested to go for it.

Gregory I. Mack, New York PD

I conduct fitness for duty evaluations and I am also a liaison for the department's confidential peer support program. Because of the nature of job, I work in a non-police office at John Jay College so patients can see me in privacy.

Some of the officers I see either called the hotline number or are on sick leave. When an officer identifies a problem and comes in voluntarily, he or she is motivated to get better and problems are very treatable. Following 9-11, a lot of officers experienced difficulty sleeping, others had acute anxiety, and I have seen a 200 percent increase in cases.

I also have cases where therapy has been mandated, and it can be very difficult to get information out of officers who do not want to "open the door."

The stressors in this job are powerful and range from working long hours to seeing people victimized or die. What I like the best is that, as an officer, I can help my colleagues and understand what they go through. The hardest part is when an officer with a severe problem does not make progress, medication does not work, and they have to retire.

Education

I have a B.A. in criminal justice, and an M.A. and a Ph.D. in clinical psychology. Officers are more and more accepting of psychological problems; confidential programs are also becoming more common, so clinical psychologists are needed.

Follow-up Why do you think there are so few uniformed psychologists?

so attractive to police officers is that they are not affiliated with their police department. If an officer is having a problem, he or she can seek out counseling without his or her peers or department knowing about it.

The success of police stress units depends on building trust with the officers. Once they realize that they can talk openly and find solutions to their problems, other officers will come forward. In Connecticut, a special counseling unit with more than 100 hundred members from EMS, police, and emergency room personnel provides 24-hour on-call counseling services to officers who have experienced traumatic incidents. To reach as many officers as possible, including those whose departments do not offer services, units such as the Central Florida Police Stress Unit offer full-service Web sites.

Organization-Centered Stress Management

Most strategies for reducing stress focus on the individual, not on the organization. Although this is necessary for one-on-one counseling for personal issues, it does not solve many of the underlying organizational problems that cause police stress. Even small changes in organizational structure and operations can reduce stress throughout an entire department. These changes can affect supervisory style, field training officer programs, critical incident counseling, command support after critical incidents, shift work, and job assignment. Their benefits can include enhanced departmental image, cost savings, improved morale and efficiency, and reduced stress.[37]

Some organizational stressors that should be addressed in all departments are the roles of management, negative publicity, the loss of an officer to violence or accidents, and shift rotation. (See Figure 8.6 on page 324 about organizational stress management options.)

Roles of Management Several key figures in policing can affect stress levels: police management, sergeants, and FTOs. First, police management needs to monitor management decisions for possible stress impact. They must search for strategies to reduce or lessen stress, and they must keep their managers advised.

Sergeants who are skilled in problem solving, interpersonal communication, conflict resolution, and leadership are critical to any organizational effort to reduce stress. In the Michigan State Police, sergeants are trained to manage stress among their officers. This training enables them to become more sensitive to how their own management style affects their subordinates.

One of the earliest experiences that affects an officer's attitude and view of policing, positively or negatively, is his or her time with the field training officer (FTO). Today, many departments hire private counselors to train

FTOs in how to interact with trainees most effectively. In addition, departments are encouraged to use only volunteers for FTOs. With positive mentoring early in a police officer's career, he or she can develop a less cynical—and less stressful—view of the world.

All law enforcement managers, supervisors, and instructors must be actively involved in developing strategies that reduce or eliminate police stress. Creating a healthy workplace should be the goal of every police organization. Police executives can achieve this goal by implementing the following strategies:

1. Examining the workplace for problems
2. Believing in the mission
3. Living the organizational values
4. Encouraging upward communication
5. Discouraging autonomy
6. Ensuring fairness
7. Caring about people[38]

Another police department commissioned a study to identify organizational stressors and suggest strategies for eliminating or reducing them. The study found that both the formal and informal organizational structures—in other words, the formal chain of command and the informal peer groups and subcultures—were contributing to poor communication and strained relationships. A management consultant and mental health specialist were hired to design and implement an 18-month program to reduce organizational stress. Using a variety of techniques, officers were taught effective interpersonal communication and problem-solving skills. The program was so successful that the department still uses it.

Negative Publicity Every department is concerned about poor police-community relations and negative press. Again, organizational stress management can help. For example, one North Carolina sheriff's department had a reputation for being inefficient and political. After a new sheriff was elected, he restaffed all top-level management positions with experienced law enforcement managers and developed a community policing program. His department soon acquired a positive image of being an innovative and progressive agency. Deputies started to take pride in their work, and in 1996 and 1997, the department received the North Carolina COPS Links Award for its outstanding community policing program. Today the department is recognized as one of the top sheriff's departments in the state.

Violence or Accidents Affecting Officers Every police chief and commander dreads the announcement that one of his or her officers has been

Figure 8.6

Advantages and Disadvantages of Two Basic Organizational Options

Advantages	Disadvantages
In-House Programs	
◆ As department employees, staff more likely to have long-term commitment to agency and law enforcement community.	◆ Clients more likely to view program as a tool of management and to be worried about confidentiality, and hence may be less likely to use program services.
◆ Staff more likely to be viewed by officers and other clients as part of the law enforcement community.	◆ Typically a more expensive option because of the cost of office space, equipment, and staff benefits.
◆ Staff more likely to be knowledgeable about general law enforcement stresses, those particular to the agency, and the structure of the agency (facilitating efforts to address organizational sources of stress).	◆ Risk of conflict in duties to client and agency.
◆ Staff more likely to become personally familiar with officers, non-sworn employees, and family members (prior to any services being rendered) and have greater visibility and accessibility.	◆ Staff's authority may be limited by departmental supervision.
◆ Easier to obtain logistical and management support from the department (e.g., to conduct training and allow officers to take time to be peer supporters or go in for counseling).	◆ Staff may be pressured to conduct activities outside of what they consider to be their scope of work.
◆ Greater chance of institutionalizing the program.	
External Programs	
◆ Officers and other clients less likely to view staff with suspicion, offering a greater chance of building trust.	◆ Greater chance of program being isolated and officers and other clients viewing staff as inaccessible, not part of the law enforcement community, and unfamiliar with law enforcement work and stress.
◆ Typically less expensive than an internal arrangement because of: — reduced overhead and staff benefits — competitive bidding, which may lower prices for program services.	◆ Competitive bidding process causes uncertainty and can be time-consuming and stressful for both staff and clients.
◆ Greater autonomy in program operations.	◆ Program less likely to become institutionalized and therefore more vulnerable to budget cuts.
◆ Less chance for dual relationship problems and pressure to be all things to all people.	

SOURCE: http://www.ncjrs.org/pdffiles/163175.pdf

shot or seriously injured in an accident. It is during this time that the injured officer doubts his or her judgment and abilities as a police officer. Police executives and commanders need to personally visit the injured officer and his family. Nothing does more to increase morale than to know that the chief cares.

Shift Rotation Another stressor in policing is shift work. Michigan State Police officers were originally allowed to determine the frequency of their shift rotation and have the option to change it at least annually. When research by the trooper's association found that rotating shifts present a number of health and safety risks, officers were given the option of permanent shifts. The association demonstrated that officers on permanent shifts were more productive and enacted change from cooperation, not confrontation.

A new approach to job assignment has been implemented in the San Antonio Police Department. The psychologist for the department convinced administrators that by matching officers' capabilities with the requirements of the job, the result would be more motivated, more competent, and less stressed officers. Every position in the department was analyzed to identify the requisite skills necessary to perform each job. Today, hiring and promotions are based not only on civil service exam scores but also on matching an officer's current skill level with the position. Even the training curriculum has been modified to include instruction in problem solving, critical thinking, and stress prevention and management—skills that are necessary for successful performance and reduced stress levels in any profession.

Policing is changing. Changes in organizational structure, limited resources, new technologies, and new policing strategies are presenting officers with new challenges—and new stressors. By emphasizing efficiency and effectiveness, police administrators can find ways to minimize the stress associated with these changes.

8.4 Self Check

1. What are some of the components of developing a stress-resistant lifestyle?
2. What are the benefits of looking at organizational problems in relation to stress management?

POLICING *Online*
Check your answers at
www.policing.glencoe.com

Police Behavior, Attitudes, and Stress

Summary By Learning Objectives

1. Understand the police subculture and its effects on officers.

The police subculture consists of attitudes and behaviors that are unique to police work. This subculture is characterized by cynicism, solidarity, authoritarianism, isolationism, and conservatism.

Officers first experience the subculture when they begin police training, and they continue internalizing it upon assignment to field duties. As police officers continue in their duties, they often become convinced that the public, as well as higher-ranking police officials and city officials, do not support them. This tends to heighten the intensity of the subculture. Community policing philosophy tends to weaken the police subculture because it requires officers to work closely with the community and develop mutual trust.

2. Analyze the dynamics that shape the police personality.

The police officer's working personality is mainly shaped by the elements of danger and authority. The element of danger makes the officer especially attentive to signs indicating a potential for violence or law breaking. Police officers show authority by their uniforms, equipment, attitudes and behaviors, and the nature of their job.

3. Explain the similarities and differences between eustress and distress.

Positive stress is called eustress. It can include falling in love, getting a new job, or going on vacation. Negative stress is distress, which is stress caused by an unpleasant situation or state of mind. Distress can linger if a person has sad or regretful memories. Both types of stress can cause long-term physical, emotional, and cognitive problems such as headaches, anxiety, and debilitating flashbacks.

4. Discuss the main symptoms of police stress.

Police officers are routinely exposed to high-risk situations that can cause both physical and psychological problems. The cost of stress takes its toll in lowered productivity, poor morale, alcoholism, and sometimes suicide. In biological terms, stress is caused when a stressor elicits a response from the autonomic nervous system (ANS). The body reacts to stressors by going through three stages: alarm (fight or flight), resistance (body actively resists the stressor), and exhaustion (occurs when the body can no longer resist the stressors). It is during exhaustion that physiological problems (ulcers, high blood pressure, and coronary disease) appear.

5. Name the five primary sources of police stress.

There are five categories of sources of stress for police:

1. **The nature of police work** The nature of the job brings with it discretionary power, death, injury, dangerous situations, changes in work conditions, and special assignments.

2. **The police organization** Organizational stress can result from autocratic models of policing, hierarchical structures, poor supervision, lack of administrative support, role conflict and ambiguity, inadequate pay and resources, adverse work schedules, boredom, and unfair discipline.

3. **The individual officer** Police officers' nutrition, poor physical condition, and personality can also be sources of stress.

4. **The criminal justice system** The criminal justice system can also contribute stress when the officer believes that actions of courts and corrections are unfair.

5. **The media** Finally, the media can give police departments an unfavorable image that harms the relationship between police and the public.

6. Describe strategies for controlling stress.

Police officers will never eliminate all the stress in their lives. They can, however, develop strategies for coping with stress. There is no single strategy that will reduce all stress. Instead, a comprehensive approach is most effective. One of the most effective comprehensive approaches is stress inoculation, which is developing a lifestyle that offers resistance to the effects of stress. An effective strategy includes relaxation, exercise, good nutrition, adequate sleep, mental discipline, self-regulation, good self-esteem, support from family and peers, career clarity, time management, mental stimulation and creativity, recreation, giving meaning to your life, and humanness.

7. Explain the importance of support systems.

No stress management system can be complete without the support of officers' families and fellow policemen and women. The National Association of Police Organization (NAPO) started stress reduction training in 1997 in Dallas, Texas. The purpose of the training is to give families an awareness and understanding of personal and organizational stressors, and to offer them solutions.

Critical Incident Stress Debriefing Teams (CISDTs) also provide departmental psychological services and debriefing in cases of burst stress incidents.

Key Terms

police subculture (p. 290)
cynicism (p. 290)
authoritarianism (p. 293)
isolationism (p. 294)
symbolic assailant (p. 294)
conservatism (p. 295)
siege mentality (p. 295)
stress (p. 297)
eustress (p. 297)
distress (p. 297)
stressor (p. 297)
Autonomic Nervous System (ANS) (p. 297)
sympathetic system (p. 298)
parasympathetic system (p. 298)

zone of stability (p. 299)
denial (p. 302)
Post-Traumatic Stress Disorder (PTSD) (p. 305)
suicide by criminal (p. 306)
burst stress (p. 309)
suicide by cop (p. 309)
organizational stressor (p. 312)
stress management (p. 318)
stress inoculation (p. 318)
Critical Incident Stress Debriefing Team (CISDT) (p. 319)
early warning mental health program (p. 320)
police stress unit (p. 320)

Questions for Review

1. Explain the five stages of police cynicism.
2. How does the police subculture affect individual officers' attitudes and behaviors?
3. What are stress and stressors?
4. What are some physiological, emotional, and cognitive symptoms of stress?
5. Explain the autonomic nervous system (ANS).
6. How does alcohol and drug abuse play a role in police stress?
7. How can police stress play a role in officers family problems?
8. What stress issues concern female officers? Minority officers?
9. Of the five categories of sources of stress to police officers, which has the greatest impact on officers and why?
10. Which of the 14 components of stress inoculation seem to be the hardest for police to implement, and why?

Experiential Activities

11. Stressors
Using the Social Readjustment Scale, calculate your level of stress.

    a. Does your score reflect the level of stress that you are feeling?

    b. If you score is under 300, what stressors concern you and how you can deal with them? If your score is 300 or above, develop a stress management strategy.

    c. How can you use this scale to cope with stress?

Experiential Activities continued

12. Exploring the Police Subculture

Ask to visit a law enforcement agency during a shift change to interview a few police officers and learn more about how they deal with stress in their off-duty time.

  a. What are some of the ways that they deal with stress, and which ways seem most effective to you?

  b. How much off-duty time do they spend with other officers and their families?

  c. What does this mean in terms of emotional support and social isolation?

13. Test the Stress Scale

With another student, go over Figure 8.4 (25 Most Stressful Life Events in Law Enforcement) on page 310. Figure out which events you think would be the most stressful in your career and why. Next, reorder the items on the list according to how stressful you believe they would be for you. Compare your results with your partner's.

  a. Which were your top 5 stress factors?

  b. How did your list compare with Figure 8.4?

  c. How did your list differ from your partner's list?

14. Police and the Media

Find a recent case where the police have come under media scrutiny. You might select a case in which police have been accused of using excessive force, in which officers have been tried for drug dealing, corruption, or perjury, or in which police-community relations have been examined. Try to find articles and reports that present varied viewpoints.

  a. Describe the details of the case as objectively as you can.

  b. How do different news organizations present the same story in different ways?

  c. Do you notice any bias against or for the police? If so, give examples of this bias.

Web Patrol

15. Police Domestic Abuse

For more information on the increasing problem of police domestic abuse, click on the link at **www.policing.glencoe.com**.

What are some solutions to officer domestic violence that every agency should implement?

16. Stress Test

Take the Stress Test, which can be accessed online by clicking on the link at **www.policing.glencoe.com**. As you take the test, put yourself in the shoes of a police officer.

What can you do to reduce distress in your life? Increase eustress?

17. On the Street

Go to "On the Street," which can be accessed online through **www.policing. glencoe.com**, to gain knowledge and insights into the world of the street cop. As you visit this site, try to understand the stressors that occur during typical (and less typical) police work shifts.

What are some of the more challenging personal and professional aspects faced by the typical street cop?

Critical Thinking Exercises

18. You Be the Chief

You are the newly appointed police chief for the police department of a city of 300,000. From the time that you applied for the job, you knew that the department had serious problems among its rank and file.

You learn quickly that this police subculture focuses on prejudice, protecting other officers (even corrupt ones) at all costs, and ignoring crimes that the officers have deemed unimportant, such as family violence cases. The officers are very stubborn and tell you very little.

a. Name some things that you should do to establish your authority and make officers understand that they must follow your directives.

b. What other steps might you take to begin to move the rank and file in a positive direction?

19. Understanding the Stages of Stress

You are a counselor at a police stress unit. Since you have spent 14 years as a municipal police officer and have a degree in psychology, you are highly qualified to help other officers with their stress issues, and officers frequently request you to be their counselor.

Today you are having an initial consultation with a young officer who is finding herself unable to sleep because of stress. She encounters stressful situations and deals with them, but the adrenaline rush does not go away for hours and she ends up feeling depleted. This is beginning to wear her down physically, and she is worried that she will not be able to do her job well enough to keep herself and her partner safe.

a. Describe how Hans Selye's three stages of physiological reactions to stress apply to this case.

b. What can you do to help her calm down and reduce her stress level?

20. Severe Stressors

You work in a high-crime area, and in the past six months you have seen many traumatic and stress-causing events. First, your longtime partner died in a shootout. About two months later, you were involved in another shootout in which you shot three people and killed one. You were dismissed because your chief believed that you used excessive force, then brought back when he realized that your actions were just. The people who did your re-employment paperwork forgot to state that you were a former employee, and you are in danger of losing six years' seniority, which would affect your salary and your retirement date. You have been very depressed, and you are fighting with your spouse.

a. Name all of the stressors in your life.

b. Name different options that you have to find relief from this chronic stress.

Endnotes

1. Radelet and Carter, *The Police and the Community* (New York: Macmillan College, 1994), 189–90.
2. Arthur Neiderhoffer, *Behind the Shield* (Garden City, NY: Doubleday, 1969).
3. Wallace Graves, "Police Cynicism: Causes and Cures," *FBI Law Enforcement Bulletin*, June 1996, 16–20.
4. Special Advisor to the Board of Police Commissioners on the Civil Disorder in Los Angeles, *The City in Crisis* (Washington, D.C.: Police Foundation, 1992), 168.
5. National Association for the Advancement of Colored People, *Beyond the Rodney King Story: An Investigation of Police Conduct in Minority Communities* (Boston: Northeastern University Press, 1995), 17–19.
6. Jerome H. Skolnick and James J. Fyfe, *Above the Law: Police and the Excessive Use of Force* (New York: Free Press, 1993), 97.
7. Radelet and Carter, *The Police and the Community*, 192.
8. Hans Selye, *Stress without Distress* (Philadelphia: Lippincott, 1974)
9. Hans Selye in Leonard Territo and Harold J. Vetter, *Stress and Police Personnel* (Boston: Allyn & Bacon, 1981), 3.
10. Skolnick and Fyfe, *Above the Law*, 43.
11. P. Kraska and V. Kappeler, "Police On-Duty Drug Use: A Theoretical and Descriptive Examination," *American Journal of Police* 7, no. 1 (1988): 1–28.
12. F. Latour, "23 Officers in Boston Test Positive for Drug Use," *Boston Globe*, 21 October 1999, A1.
13. J. Raymond, *American Demographics* 23, no.2 (2001): 60; see also D. Goldfarb, *The Effects of Stress on Police Officers*, retrieved November 12, 2001, from the Web: http://www.thinblueline.com/polstress.htm
14. *Understanding and Preventing Violence* (Washington, D.C.: National Academy of Sciences, 1993); see also P. Neidig, H. Russell, and A. Seng, "Interspousal Aggression in Law Enforcement Families: A Preliminary Investigation," *Police Studies*, Spring 1992, 30–38.
15. D. Wetendorf, *The Impact of Police-Perpetrated Domestic Violence*, retrieved November 12, 2001, from the World Wide Web: http://www.policedv.com/fbispeech.html; *Representative Bob Barr (R-GA) to Offer Amendment to Put Guns Back Into the Hands of Wife Beaters and Child Abusers*, retrieved November 12, 2001, from the Web: http://www.vpc.org/press/9705barr.htm.
16. Feminist Majority Foundation and the National Center for Women and Policing, *Police Family Violence Fact Sheet*, retrieved November 14, 2001, from the Web: http://www.feminist.org/police/pfvfacts.html.
17. L. Lott, "Deadly Secrets: Violence in the Police Family," *FBI Law Enforcement Bulletin*, November 1995, retrieved November 14, 2001, from the Web: http://www.fbi.gov/publications/leb/1989-1995/leb89-95.htm.
18. Arthur W. Kureczka, "Critical Incident Stress," *FBI Law Enforcement Bulletin* 65, no. 2/3 (February-March 1996): 15.
19. Carl von Czoernig, "Police Officers in Trouble: PTSD, Stress, Anxiety and Depression within the Law Enforcement Community" [Online]. Available: http://www.help4cops.netheaven.com/index2.html.
20. B. I. Danto, "Police Suicide," *Police Stress* 1 (1978).
21. von Czoernig, "Police Officers in Trouble."
22. Susan Martin, "Women Officers on the Move: An Update on Women in Policing," in *Critical Issues in Policing*, edited by R. Dunham and G. Alpert (Prospect Heights, IL: Waveland, 2001), 409–11.
23. Bennett and Hess, *Management and Supervision*, 448.
24. R. Haarr and M. Morash, "Gender, Race, and Strategies of Coping with Occupational Stress in Policing," *Justice Quarterly* 16 (1999): 303–36.
25. "Choir Practice and Its Effects on The Law Enforcement Family," Central Florida Police Stress Unit, Inc., retrieved November 3, 2001, on the Web: http://www.policestress.org/choir.htm.
26. "A New 'Date Which Will Live in Infamy': 60 Cops Could Be among the Dead and Missing from Terrorist Attacks on the Trade Center, Pentagon," *Law Enforcement News* 27, no. 561 (2001): 1.
27. J. Marzulli and C. Siemaszko, "Sad and Slow Sifting," *New York Daily News*, 19 September 2001, 66; see also J. Stein, "Digging Out," *Time Magazine*, 24 September 2001, 62.
28. Marzulli and Siemaszko, "Sad and Slow Sifting," 66.
29. J. Marzulli and L. Standora, "Kerik Tells Troops of NYPD's Great Tragedy Says the List of Officers Missing Grows to 23," *New York Daily News*, 15 September 2001, 45.
30. Basic elements of this list, and some of the examples, were adapted from Richard Ayres, *Preventing Law Enforcement Stress: The Organization's Role* (Alexandria, VA: National Sheriff's Association, 1990), 11.
31. Anderson et al., *Stress Management*, 40.
32. William K. Muir, *Police: Streetcorner Politicians* (Chicago: University of Chicago Press, 1977), 192.
33. Central Florida Stress Unit, http://policestress.org/six.htm.
34. "NAPO to Host Police Stress-Reduction Awareness Training for Police Families in Dallas" [Online]. Available: http://www.napo.org/napo_stress.htm.
35. Anderson et al., *Stress Management*, 252.
36. Bill Clede, "Stress, Insidious or Traumatic, Is Treatable," *Law and Order*, January 1994.
37. Peter Finn, "Reducing Stress: An Organization-Centered Approach," *FBI Law Enforcement Bulletin*, August 1997.
38. Ayres, *Preventing Law Enforcement Stress.*

Components of Police Integrity

CHAPTER OBJECTIVES

AFTER COMPLETING THIS CHAPTER, YOU WILL BE ABLE TO:

1. Define integrity and its primary components.

2. Understand the meaning of professionalism.

3. Recognize how community policing is a catalyst for professionalism.

4. Explain the factors that influence discretion.

5. Identify methods for appropriately limiting discretion.

6. Understand the importance of ethics in law enforcement.

7. Recognize the standards of ethical conduct.

8. Identify the dynamics of corruption.

9. Learn how to prevent corruption.

◀ Sergeant Denise Valentin shakes hands with Police Commissioner as she receives the police medal of honor.

ethics Study and analysis of what constitutes good or bad conduct, addressing specific moral choices an individual makes in relating to others.

This chapter examines the core concepts of professionalism, discretion, and ethics. These three concepts are primary ingredients of policing integrity and are examined together because of their integral relationship to one another. For example, the **ethics** concept is a core component of professionalism. It is the analysis of what constitutes good conduct and the study of moral choices. Similarly, ethical conduct is essential in the exercise of discretion.

In selecting the term *integrity* as the umbrella term for discussing professionalism, discretion, and ethics, we follow the lead of the National Institute of Justice and the Office of Community-Oriented Policing Services. In 1996 these two prestigious organizations combined to assemble a premier group of law enforcement practitioners and researchers for the National Symposium on Police Integrity. The symposium was intended to discuss the same matters that are the subject of this chapter. In the words of the symposium's planners:

> Perhaps the most important aspect of the endeavor was selecting a key word title for the symposium since language often determines direction. Terms such as officer discretion and police accountability were considered. However, when the term 'police integrity' was put forth, all members concurred that this was the most appropriate language for the issues at hand. A focus on 'police integrity' opened a whole new domain.[1]

P.I.G.

Municipal law enforcement officers have through the years deflected their detractors' "pet" name for them, "pig ," by interpreting the i in pig as "integrity." The p represents pride and the g stands for guts. While "pig" is now somewhat passe in its use as a derogatory term by detractors, police officers continue to use "pig" as symbolic of their collective "pride, integrity, and guts."

Police integrity guided the focus to a broader goal of developing a healthy organization that would serve to reinforce and maintain the good character and constructive motivations of many of the individuals joining the ranks of law enforcement. Recognize that within the ranks of America's most prestigious law enforcement agency, the FBI, the I in FBI implies foremost to agents integrity—not "investigation." The F represents fidelity and the B connotes bravery. The bureaucratic meanings of the initials F, B, and I are secondary to the rank-and-file's interpretation.

Components of Integrity

Integrity is defined as the integrated collection and application of virtues that bring about the goals of an organization. A person of integrity has a reasonably coherent and stable set of core moral virtues. The person's acts and speech tend to reflect those principles. Desirable virtues include the following:

- Prudence
- Trust

- Courage
- Honesty
- Justice
- Responsibility
- Self-Effacement (putting others' needs before one's own needs)

In short, a police officer of **integrity** is one who has incorporated these seven virtues into his or her duty performance to the extent of routinely exhibiting traits of character that make clear the organizational goals of protection and service.[2] In practice, these seven virtues are exhibited through officers' professional conduct, exercise of discretion, and adherence to ethical standards.

The following sections will discuss professionalism, discretion, and ethics separately. Keep in mind that in practice the concepts overlap. Remember, too, that the term "integrity" is the applied outcome of the combination of the three concepts. The essence of policing is integrity. To most police officers, nothing is more sacred than their respective integrity levels.

integrity Integrated collection and application of virtues that bring about the goals of an organization. It is the applied outcome of the combination of the concepts of professionalism, discretion, and ethics.

9.1 Self Check ?

1. What three core concepts are used to define integrity?
2. How do police officers show integrity?

POLICING *Online*

Check your answers at
www.policing.glencoe.com

9.2 Professionalism

Professionalism has long been an elusive goal of American law enforcement. By policing professionalism, we mean assigning professional status to those practitioners empowered to enforce the criminal laws of our society. Policing has traditionally been considered an occupation or a craft—not a profession like the practice of medicine, law, or accountancy. **Professionalism** implies preparation for work in accordance with standards that include advanced education, demonstrated familiarity with the field's core body of knowledge, accountability through peer review, and a code of ethics.[3]

A task or a job does not suddenly become a profession. In tracing the history of several professions, definite patterns can be established. Certain elements precede others. A job begins to take shape as the need for someone to perform various duties is recognized. Law enforcement history reflects this, for as society began to regulate itself through law, it became evident that the laws were of little value without a person to enforce them. It was up to the early policing practitioners to define tasks and training needs. Training then customarily proceeds through a process of apprenticeship.

professionalism
Preparation for work in accordance with standards that include advanced education, demonstrated familiarity with the field's core body of knowledge, accountability through peer review, and a code of ethics.

Persons on the job during its formative stages begin to develop and collect a common body of knowledge. Education soon begins to play an important role in teaching new and improved methods for performing job tasks. As a result of society's increased recognition of the job, the quality of recruits is established as a primary concern. Usually an organization or association is formed to restrict entry into the ranks of practitioners. In 1852, lawyers began restricting entry into their ranks via the Council of Legal Education, requiring that individuals pass examinations held by that body before being called before the bar and accepted to practice law. Today, state policing commissions perform a similar function, establishing performance standards that limit access into the field of policing. A final stage in the evolution of a profession is development of a code of ethics for ensuring quality of service rendered.[4]

Evolution of Professionalism

▲ **Chief August Vollmer**
Vollmer laid the groundwork for the professionalization of policing.
Do you think Vollmer's achievements still influence policing today? How?

The foundation of a professional status for American police was provided by the father of modern police administration, August Vollmer. He developed the first formal training school for police officers in 1908, reaching an agreement nine years later with the University of California in which on-the-job experience could be combined with an academic education. The curriculum included technical subjects along with liberal arts classes, leading in 1933 to creation of a criminology major.[5]

Need for Professionalism Vollmer had reasoned that the police officer required significantly special skills to perform the tasks of policing, skills that could not be learned and ingrained on the beat by a recruit who was indifferent to the higher purposes of policing. It was inconceivable to him that a police officer should become identified with workers whose sense of occupational purpose extended only so far as a decent wage and adequate conditions on the job.

For the police in those early years, professionalism meant control of their work world without interference from corrupt politicians who appointed unqualified patrolmen and interfered with or controlled hiring, firing, and assignment. It held the promise of scientific policing, which emphasized a style of policing that was both detached and objective and adopted techniques that took advantage of the latest scientific advances in detecting and solving crimes, as well as in personnel management. For Vollmer, the professional model meant all the foregoing, plus much more. He was experimenting with the prototype of a genuinely professional model of policing, one that would reach to the higher purposes of policing. He advocated higher education, peer review, collaboration with other professions, and numerous other classical professional practices.

Scientific Management Soon after Vollmer appeared on the scene, other policing reformers adopted and incorporated the term professionalism into their definition of the scientific approach to policing. Their adaptation was fashioned largely along the lines of an emerging scientific management style of the era. This scientific management style, developed by Frederick Taylor, emphasized efficiency in operations and urged centralization of authority, task specialization, and layers of control. This style was easily assimilated by police agencies (See Figure 9.1 on page 338 for a current inventory of law enforcement agencies), which were already highly structured organizationally. So, in the spirit of increased efficiency, even more control mechanisms were put into place: extensive rules and regulations, span of control (a specific ratio of supervisory personnel to line officers—often 1 to 7), unity of command (each employee had a predesignated person to whom he or she was reportable), specialization of work, and reduction in discretion.[6]

▲ **Frederick Taylor**
Taylor was the co-developer of the Taylor-White process for treating high-speed tool steels. Author of *The Principles of Scientific Management. How do you think Taylor's principles apply to policing?*

To a majority of police practitioners professionalism meant the use of technology, task specialization, and rigid organizational controls to enhance policing. This meaning of professionalism became the predominant meaning to most practitioners and led many of them, to believe that the policing occupation was on the verge of attaining professional status in the primary sense of the word.

The misconception about policing's near-professional status continued as prestigious federal commissions convened to study the police. Many practitioners and observers seemed to believe that the mere convening of prestigious bodies added to the degree of professionalism that was being attained by the police. While, indisputably, the principal federal commissions had good intentions, it was often the case that standards imposed by the commissions contained no sanctions for non-compliance. A classic

Figure 9.1

Numbers of Law Enforcement by Agency, 1996

Type of agency	Number of agencies	Number of full-time sworn officers
Total		738,028
All state and local	18,769	663,535
Local police	13,578	410,956
Sheriff	3,088	152,922
Primary state police	49	54,587
Special police	1,316	43,082
Texas constable		1,988
Federal*		74,493

Note: Special police category includes both State-level and local-level agencies. Five consolidated police-sheriffs are included under local police category.
*Non-military federal officers authorized to carry firearms and make arrests.

SOURCE: U.S. Department of Justice. Bureau of Justice Statistics, Washington, D.C.

example was the set of educational standards imposed by the 1973 National Advisory Commission on Criminal Justice Standards and Goals. The National Advisory Commission established educational standards that were to have required all police officers to possess a baccalaureate degree as a condition of initial employment. The effective date of this standard was 1982.[7] All of us can readily recognize today the extent to which this standard failed (and continues to fall short).

Continuing Struggles for Professionalism From the 1930s to well into the 1970s, the reform model of policing masqueraded as the professional style envisioned by Vollmer. This is not at all to deny the invaluable contributions of the reform era model toward depoliticizing policing and reducing corruption. However, upon the widespread application of a community policing model in the 1980s and 1990s, it became obvious that the professional model of the reform era did not contain the core elements of true professionalism that were required for success in the broad-based community policing model. For what was sorely needed in the application of the community policing philosophy was a broad-minded, problem-solver who could be relied upon to empower and mobilize citizens in a partnership campaign against crime. This type officer was best cut from the fabric of the true professional police officer, following the ideal of August Vollmer.

Community Policing as a Catalyst for Professionalism

Policing in the 21st Century requires a broad-based individual who is highly public-centered and communicative. Additionally, it is important for the officer to be constantly vigilant to improve methods for building trust among his or her community constituency. To the extent officers can research methods for building community cohesion and participation, they will enjoy success in problem-solving. Community partnership also means adopting a policing perspective that exceeds the conventional law enforcement emphasis. The broadened outlook recognizes the worth of activities that contribute to the orderliness and well-being of a neighborhood. Such activities include dispute resolution services and family violence counseling, as well as a wide array of other social services. Importantly, too, police officers must cultivate a worldly perspective that enhances cultural awareness and sensitivity toward all persons, regardless of the socio-economic climate.

Policing and Values Community policing is ultimately about values. It relies heavily on values that stimulate citizen involvement in matters that directly affect the safety and quality of neighborhood life. Some of the community policing tasks that cultivate such values are listed in Figure 9.2. These values, in the form of agency goals, give direction to agency employees and link values to behaviors.[8] Note how community policing aligns with the spirit of integrity, as defined near the beginning of this chapter.

Figure 9.2

Community Policing Tasks

- Learn community characteristics
- Become acquainted with leaders in area
- Make residents aware of who officer is and what he/she is trying to accomplish
- Identify area problems
- Communicate with supervisors, other officers, and citizens about the nature of the area
- Do research to determine sources of problems
- Provide citizens information about the ways they can handle problems (educate)
- Help citizens develop appropriate expectations about what police can do
- Teach citizens how to interact effectively with police
- Develop resources for responding to problems
- Implement problem solution
- Assess effectiveness of solution
- Keep citizens informed

SOURCE: Timothy N. Oettmeier and Mary Ann Wycoff, *Personnel Performance Evaluations in the Community Policing Context*, Police Executive Research Forum, Washington, D.C., 1997, p. 22.

Interviewing Victims

The U.S. Department of Justice (DOJ), Office of Justice Programs, offers a variety of resources to law enforcement personnel. Here are several pointers for law enforcement officers on how to approach victims of crime:

"As soon as the most urgent and pressing tasks have been addressed, officers will focus their attention on the victims and their needs. At this point, how the officers respond to the victims, explain the competing law enforcement duties, and work with the victims is very important. By approaching victims appropriately, officers will gain their trust and cooperation. Victims may then be more willing to provide detailed information about the crime to officers and later to investigators and prosecutors, which, in turn, will lead to the conviction of more criminals."

"Remember that you are there for the victim, the victim is not there for you. You can help victims by understanding the three major needs they have after a crime has been committed: the need to feel safe; the need to express their emotions; and the need to know what comes next' after their victimization."

Now go to **www.policing.glencoe.com** for a link to the U.S. Department of Justice site, where you can read the full 20-point approach to communicating effectively with victims of crime.

What Do You Think? After reading everything, find a recent newspaper story about a violent crime. Write out a list of questions that you would ask the victim(s), showing how you would follow the guidelines.

Thus it does appear that we may now be at a point where the quest for professionalism in policing may soon be realized. Community policing has proved to be the catalyst because of the degree of mutual trust that must be sustained for its optimal operation. Professionalism inspires confidence and respect because it means to the public that the practitioners have internalized values of service, self-control, and commitment to high ideals of behavior. In short, community policing requires its practitioners to possess the same attributes found among other client-centered service providers who meet the criteria for professional status in their respective fields.

Impediments to Professionalism

Many in law enforcement believe that the best hope for achievement of professionalism in policing rests in pursuing community policing. Others insist that professionalism is an impossible dream, even through this avenue. From the community's standpoint there is too little cohesion or ability to respond to police initiatives; from the police standpoint, the requisite skills are difficult to obtain and require mid-management support that to date in many departments has been notably lacking. Also, there is the question of availability of resources in the community for problem solving.[9]

Education and Professionalism One factor that will aid in the success of both community policing and police professionalism is the growing recognition that a college education benefits police officers. Because college develops critical thinking and mental self-discipline, it produces officers who can apply such helpful traits on the job. In community policing, creative problem-solving skills that are encouraged in college are essential and win the respect of the public.

Today, it is common for officers to have some college education, and many high-ranking officers have advanced degrees. Some police agencies now require that applicants possess a minimum number of college credits, but there is still no uniform policy on this issue.

Self-Regulation Policing expert Richard Lumb believes that the difficulty in achieving professionalism among police is because police cannot regulate themselves. Established professional fields such as law and medicine are self-regulated by the American Bar Association and American Medical Association, respectively. Although not perfect, these associations are accepted by the American public as adequate monitors of the behavior of

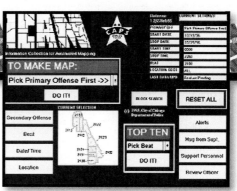

Computer On Patrol

What Is ICAM?

Information Collection for Automated Mapping (ICAM) is an easy-to-use computerized mapping program designed to help Chicago police officers in analyzing and solving neighborhood crime problems.

With ICAM, beat officers and other police district personnel can quickly and easily generate maps of timely, accurate crime data for their beats, sectors, or districts. Using this information, the police can target hot spots of criminal activity.

The system also makes it easier for the police to share crime information with the community as they work together as part of the Chicago Alternative Policing Strategy (CAPS). ICAM is operational in all 25 Chicago districts.

Think About It What do you think are the top three greatest advantages of ICAM?

individual practitioners. On the other hand, external review of the police is a right that is fiercely held by citizens and governmental figures. Since police departments are a branch of government, total autonomy is not possible because of the public nature of government work. However, avoiding political control is possible, and is universally considered a positive policing goal.[10]

Online

Remember, one of your best resources is **www.policing.glencoe.com**

Limited Resources Limited resources often create dilemmas in small-town police departments that wish to implement community policing. For example, Troy, the police chief of a small town in northern Florida, wants to help the mayor make the town more attractive to newcomers and tourists. They agree that community policing is long overdue, although the police already have a friendly relationship with most of the locals. However, as soon as they begin a problem-solving dialogue with the townspeople and shopowners, they find that everyone has completely different agendas regarding crime prevention. The townspeople are worried about controlling delinquents and drunken tourists. The shopowners are upset about homeless people who live around the main shopping area and engage in aggressive panhandling. The police department is most concerned about more serious offenses, such as problems with drug dealing and family violence. However, officers do not know how to talk with community members to make them understand the department's priorities, or to enable them to address the community's priorities. More training and resources are needed for your community policing program, but money is not available for it.

The Bottom Line on Professionalism

The preceding discussion of police professionalism was intended to provide a picture of the concept within the context of police integrity. This expanded discussion was important in order to identify the defining characteristics of the true professional, as well as to point out the dual meaning of the often used descriptive term. Professionalism has only rarely been practiced by police in a manner recognizable as such by professionals outside the field of law enforcement. It is important that the policing practitioners of the 21st Century persevere in the attempt to attain professional status. Some obstacles have been cited, but also cited have been the advantages afforded by implementation of the community policing model. The discussion of professionalism will be concluded by a detailing of what professionalism normally entails. It is hoped that you will embrace these key elements and strive vigorously to cause their realization within the field of policing. (See Figure 9.3). Admittedly, there are impediments, but through creativity and focused effort they can be overcome. The efforts expended will be well worth the enormous gains obtained.

> **Figure 9.3**
>
> **Elements of Professionalism**
>
> ◆ A transmittable body of knowledge that is constantly growing and being refined
> ◆ A code of ethics defining relations between members of the profession and the public, including an obligation to render services exclusive of any other considerations
> ◆ High standards for membership, often including higher education and training
> ◆ Accountability through peer review and, therefore, continous evaluation and improvement through research of professional practices
> ◆ At some point in the evolution of the occupation, acknowledgement from outsiders that the occupation is a profession
>
> **SOURCE:** Adapted from Barbara Raffel Price, "Police and the Quest for Professionalism," *Law Enforcement News*, John Jay College of Criminal Justice, June 15, 1995.

9.2 Self Check

1. Why has professionalism been difficult to establish in policing?
2. What are the key elements of police professionalism?

POLICING *Online*

Check your answers at **www.policing.glencoe.com**

9.3 Discretion

Discretion is a vital component of policing integrity. It is an indispensable tool for individualization of justice, and it is the principal source of creativeness in law.[11] Police officers employ it constantly in their capacities as the initial decision makers within the criminal justice system, determining the work load of the system by making the primary arrest decision. Interestingly, the quest for professionalization of policing is due in large part to the desire to ensure the proper exercise of police discretion.[12]

discretion The autonomy or freedom an officer has in choosing an appropriate course of action. A police officer has discretion whenever the effective limits of the officer's power leave him or her free to make a choice among possible courses of action or inaction.

Definition of Discretion

The term discretion refers to the autonomy or freedom an officer has in choosing an appropriate course of action. A public officer has discretion whenever the effective limits of the officer's power leave him or her free to make a choice among possible courses of action or inaction.[13] This definition was coined by Kenneth Culp Davis in his classic book entitled

Discretionary Justice. In his book Davis provided an extended explanation of the phrase "effective limits." He emphasized that "effective limits" encompassed both illegal and marginally legal exercises of power. As an example, he cites the fact that officers frequently do not make an arrest when technically they should. This set the stage for Davis's book-long discussion on how to eliminate unnecessary discretion and how to control necessary discretionary power.

Factors That Influence Discretion

The concept of discretion within a statutorily based law enforcement function might appear to be contradictory. It would seem that laws are to be enforced as written. However, upon closer analysis it may be observed that multiple variables operate to stimulate discretion in law enforcement. These variables include the following:

- Limited resources
- Ambiguity within criminal statutes and procedures
- Informal expectations of legislatures and the public
- Situational expectations

The next sections will discuss each of these variables in great detail.

Limited Resources

There are far more criminal law violations occurring than the police, as resourced, could ever cope with. Provision of policing services to handle merely the most visible and serious offenses is highly labor- and equipment-intensive. One must realize, first, that policing occurs around the clock every day, and just one position staffed by a single individual on a daily basis requires 4.8 officers per year.[14] Variables such as regular days off, vacation days, and sickness and injury must be factored in. Of course, the specialized vehicles and communications equipment necessary to support just one 24-hour position can be extremely expensive.

Using Civilian Resources The police are constantly under the gun to devise ways to do more work with fewer resources. Some cities, for example, no longer dispatch police units to take property-damage-only traffic accident reports. Others take crime reports telephonically for specified crimes. Of course, too, a number of municipalities have civilianized functions that can be performed by employees without sworn peace officer status. Some departments, such as the Jefferson County Police Department in Kentucky, have taken unprecedented steps to perform important investigative tasks without increasing their patrol or detective staffs. Jefferson County has established a partnership with its media outlets to broadcast at no charge fugitive information throughout the county. The "Citizens Arrest" program call-ins have been so great that nearly half of those wanted persons featured on the program soon find themselves behind bars. Thus a department of 450 personnel, serving a population of 650,000, has developed an impressively effective method for eliminating a multitude of "door knocking" excursions while at the same time enhancing its arrest rate—both at a cost savings.[15]

Arrest Procedures The resource crunch is most apparent in the heart of the policing process, i.e., suspect apprehension. While some of the tasks associated with the pursuit and detection of a suspect can be delegated to the citizenry, the labor-intensive and non-delegable tasks arise upon the apprehension of a suspect. The evidence continuity and chain of custody protocols of the criminal justice system require that sworn employees (detectives and patrol officers) participate actively in all phases of in-custody procedures. The time-intensive process commences with physical apprehension of the criminal suspect in the field by patrol officers and transportation for booking into the nearest police facility. This transportation phase can be extended considerably if the arrestee sustained injuries or if special circumstances exist, e.g., a female arrestee, in which case a single male officer might request a female officer to handle the transportation to prevent accusations of improprieties. The booking process at the station is time-consuming, as officers must prepare detailed arrest reports and assist in the booking of the suspect. If the arrest is for a serious offense or for a complicated offense detectives might be called to the station and/or legal consulting with the prosecutor's office might be required. As may be seen, the resource drain can be substantial. Thus there must be appropriate decision making in consideration of the potential resource drain each time an arrest situation arises.

Perimeters and Call Loads Another common situation in which consideration must be accorded to resource use is in the course of a field tactical situation. Major depletion of resources results frequently from incidents that require establishment of perimeters to contain suspects who may still be lurking in the vicinity of a crime scene. A **perimeter** is the arrangement of police officers and equipment for the purpose of encircling a suspect's presumed location to prevent escape or to prevent harm to passersby. A minimum of four police units are required to secure a perimeter, and many more may be required in expanses larger than a square block. Another common source of resource depletion is crime scene preservation. In any crime scene requiring the dispatch of criminalists or detectives, the evidence at the scene must be protected from contamination. The greater the seriousness of the

perimeter The arrangement of police officers and equipment for the purpose of encircling a suspect's presumed location to prevent escape or to prevent harm to passersby.

offense or its newsworthiness, the greater the number of personnel required at the scene for security purposes. Again, the impact on resources must be considered each time a field tactical situation is encountered, and the appropriate degree of discretion must be exercised in allocating resources.

Another variable that cannot be overlooked in considering maintenance of resources is the call load. The volume of calls coming into a communications center in the course of each hour is generally predictable, with some variance between weekends and the weekdays and during the staging of special events. Normally, the second thought that crosses the mind of a field supervisor or watch commander upon the onset of a major field incident, or upon the sight of an arrestee being escorted into the police station, is the status of the call load (the first thought is the disposition of the situation at hand). Certainly, the decision to maintain or dismantle a perimeter will be made in consideration of both the likelihood of imminent apprehension of a suspect and the effect of the incident on the call load, i.e., the nature and number of calls queued for eventual dispatch. Discretion must be considerate of both the call load factor as well as the nature of a field incident or the time required to process an arrestee. In an arrest situation, it is not uncommon for arresting officers to temporarily confine an arrestee in order to briefly return to the field to "knock down" the call load. Such an option would normally be chosen close to the time of a shift change, because the fresh and unencumbered new shift could clean up the call load.

▶ **Communication Centers and Call Load** Calls that are made into police stations reach communication centers first.
Why do you think the volume of calls affects police discretion?

Police Procedure

Responding to Community Pressure

A group of business owners, for a variety of reasons, were upset about waves of young people who crowded into their compact urban district on Friday nights to engage in "vehicular cruising." The effects of the street cruising extended to the streetside metered parking accommodations and to the sidewalks. In response to this business group's concerns, the police closed a number of streets to traffic and restricted turning from others. At the same time, they gave specialized traffic units with instructions to concentrate on double-parking and turning violations. The policing objective was to keep traffic moving along a designated corridor. However, the policing measures incensed the vast majority of the business community. The president of the business owners association paid a visit to the office of the Chief of Police to present him with an estimate of the dollars lost on Friday evenings due to the policing "blockade."

Critical Thinking What do you think the moral of this field situation is? Which procedural step did the officers skip?

Vague Criminal Laws and Procedures

The nature of the criminal law itself is a major stimulant for discretionary enforcement. Definitions of many crimes are inherently vague in their application. For example, the Uniform Crime Reporting Program defines burglary as the unlawful entry of a structure to commit a felony or theft. Within this particular statute exist two elements that can be subject to interpretation, "entry" and "structure," and thus can prove vague to the police officer attempting to align the facts of a particular situation with the burglary statute's elements. Just what constitutes an "entry" can be subject to interpretation. If one uses a drill to bore a hole into the side of a grain elevator, such action can be considered a constructive entry, even though no part of the burglar's body was inside the grain elevator. In some jurisdictions, e.g., California, the entry can occur during normal business hours, through the regular customer doors, and the entry can be considered unlawful if it can be shown a perpetrator possessed an intent to commit theft upon entry. Usually this is accomplished by showing that the suspect had on his or her person a concealed bag or coat with special oversized inner pockets. Of course, determining just what constitutes a structure for purposes of burglary can be challenging on occasion. Generally, a structure must have four sides and a roof. In some states, however, vehicles can be considered structures for purposes of burglary, provided their doors are locked (if unlocked, the crime can be judged a theft). Just by examining the common crime of burglary one can readily see just how complicated interpretation of statutory criminal law can be.

Vagueness of Criminal Procedures It is important to recognize that because of the vagueness of criminal procedures, police are regularly used as a resource to achieve some larger purpose, often described as peacekeeping. Police officers frequently use the threat of arrest, e.g., for violation of disturbance ordinances, to gain compliance. In fact, for loud parties or disturbance calls not involving threatened or actual harm, a warning is the most commonly used action. If disturbance calls are unabated, then the arrest sanction can be imposed, but it is rarely required.[16]

criminal procedure The regulatory guidance for officers' actions in matters involving the criminal law, including the rules governing matters such as search and seizure and field detentions and arrests.

The ambiguity within the various criminal statutes is compounded by the nature of criminal procedure. **Criminal procedure** is the regulatory guidance for officers' field actions in matters involving the criminal law. Criminal procedure includes the rules governing matters such as search and seizure and field detentions and arrests. It is interesting to note in this context the distinction that Jerome Skolnick makes between criminal law and criminal procedure. His view is instructive as to the mindset of police officers in their exercise of discretion in the two areas. Skolnick views the police as making a moral distinction between criminal law and criminal procedure. "The substantive law of crimes, e.g., robbery, theft, burglary, etc., is intended to control the behavior of people who willfully injure persons or property, or who engage in behaviors eventually having such a consequence, e.g., narcotics use. Criminal procedure, by contrast, is intended to control enforcement authorities, not criminals. As such, in the eyes of police, criminal procedure does not fall into the same moral class of constraints as substantive criminal law. Further, Skolnick suggests that police tend to believe that as specialists in criminal investigation they have cultivated the ability to distinguish between guilt and innocence, i.e., they do not charge innocent parties.[17]

Court Decisions Although police officers are not lawyers, they are held accountable for complete knowledge of the law of criminal procedure. If they fail to understand or properly apply the legal principles set forth in appellate court decisions, cases are dismissed and resources are wasted. Courts generally are more concerned with the rights of individual defendants than with the effect their decisions will have on law enforcement operations. Moreover, court decisions are rarely structured to provide significant guidance to officers in the infinite variety of complex situations that might in some way be affected by a particular court decision. Nevertheless, police are schooled in the fundamentals of procedural law and are expected to keep current with evolving procedural decisions. Usually, individual police departments or local prosecutorial offices provide officers with updates on key changes. Additionally, officers may subscribe individually to professional publications that regularly issue procedural changes.

What often results from the combination of the officer mindset (as previously described) and "Monday morning quarterbacking" by courts is reliance by officers on criminal procedures that less prone to change over the long term. For example, a less knowledgeable police officer may be much more comfortable conducting a frisk search on a detained pedestrian than examining the contents of a container within a vehicle. Vehicle search guidelines seem to be constantly changing, while the basic "patdown" has remained relatively unchanged in its general application. Thus, certain officers may be less anxious to encounter suspects in vehicles and prefer to "take them down" while they are on foot or in less protected environments. Another stimulus for a less restrained discretion in the area of procedural matters stems from the lack of sanctions invoked against officers for procedural transgressions. A sizable percentage of officers see getting suspects off the streets and confiscating their contraband, without regard to the period of confinement, as a desirable end. Of course, the better officers realize such an imperfect exercise of discretion is only a short-term fix to a chronic problem.

Informal Expectations of the Legislatures and the Public

Enforcement of certain laws under some circumstances would be contrary to legislative intent, just as would be the case with underenforcement of laws in specific situations. The law covers many aspects of morality, including behaviors that some people regard as immoral but that others view as legitimate recreation. These morality-based offenses are among the crimes in which discretion is most often exercised. Such offenses include a number of vice offenses, e.g., gambling, pornography, and certain forms of sexual behavior. These conflicting expectations encourage discretion. In practice, the general enforcement guidlines in the area of these vice offenses is known as the "3 Cs":

- Commercial
- Conspicuous
- Complained of

As a result, a Saturday evening poker game for low stakes in a private home would not receive any enforcement action (nor would enforcement occur if it were outside in one's backyard). Of course, the commercial book-making operation that employs multiple phone lines and full-time employees would be a target of enforcement action.

Socially and medically based offenses, such as alcoholism and mental illness, comprise another category of offenses in which discretion is exercised extensively, often for reasons of social control. Samuel Walker ably makes the point in his assessment of this offense category. In his extensive analysis of

ETHICS ISSUES

ACLU

Go to **www.policing. glencoe.com** for a link to the ACLU Web site. Read the section on law enforcement matters and the "What To Do If You're Stopped By the Police?" card that the ACLU makes available for downloads. *Do you think law enforcement brutality and/or breach of ethics are considerable issues in the U.S.? Why or why not?*

arrest records, he has recognized that alcoholism problems account for a huge volume of arrests. However, he has observed too that officers often use their arrest powers in alcohol-related matters for reasons other than prosecution and punishment. An intoxicated person may be arrested because he or she has no place to stay and the temperature is expected to plummet to below zero. Similarly, a mentally ill person may be arrested for a minor offense in order to remove him or her from a chaotic scene in order to restore order.

Online

Remember, one of your best resources is **www.policing.glencoe.com**

Public Expectations In some situations, the public mandate for vigorous enforcement and the legislative mandate coincide in time, and discretion is only rarely exercised. A clearcut example of such a situation occurred with the enactment of car-jacking legislation introduced during the mid-'90s. A collective sense of outrage and concern mushroomed as the media highlighted an increase in the number of vehicles stolen at gunpoint. This non-controversial crime topic garnered support from all political constituencies, and, as a result, legislators wasted no time in getting legislation drafted and into the penal codes for this particular offense. Similarly, the Mothers Against Drunk Drivers (MADD) group has been successful in gathering widespread community and political support for its cause. Given the universal disdain for drunken driving, most police agencies exercise minimal discretion in the arrest and prosecution of offenders who violate driving-under-the-influence laws.

We have covered examples of situations in which the public and legislative mandates both encourage and discourage discretion. In practice, it is always a challenge to read these unspoken political and community imperatives with 100 percent accuracy. The key is to be as attuned as possible to community sentiment. Of course, the best way to accomplish this is for field officers to maximize their public interaction. If an ear is constantly attuned to community sentiments, and those interests are communicated throughout the police agency, the chances for the proper exercise of discretion are maximized. Most assuredly, the public will express the same sentiments to its political representatives. By listening to the community at large, the police can parallel the waves of public opinion as they cascade—and, hopefully, not crash—upon the political shores. Such a proactive approach is extremely beneficial for the appropriate exercise of discretion.

Situational Expectations

The characteristics of any given situation in which citizens and officers interact exert considerable influence on the outcome of a police encounter. These circumstances can include the physical environment, seriousness of an offense, strength of the evidence, victim/offender dynamics, and the characteristics of the individual officer.

MYTH	FACT
White officers are more likely to use physical force against members of another race.	Author and researcher Albert Reiss found that African-American officers were slightly more likely to use physical force than white officers, but that all officers were more likely to use force against members of their own race.

Physical Environment Officers making a pedestrian stop or vehicle pullover in a suburban middle-class neighborhood environment are likely to feel less threatened by onlookers than if they were in a depressed, gang-infested neighborhood. As a result, they might take more time to conduct their field investigation. This extra time can translate into a wider array of options for handling a situation. Conversely, police who perceive a hostile environment might be inclined to handle matters quickly. Often this results in either the suspect being arrested outright or detained and transported to downtown headquarters for continued interviewing. Of course, both these options result in a trip downtown as opposed to a field release (which could occur, but is unlikely due to the threatening environment). Certainly, too, persons detained in an area notorious for drug activity may have to work harder to earn a discretionary release from the police than persons detained in an area of low drug trafficking.

Severity of the Offense The seriousness of an offense is always a major determinant of the amount of discretion to be exercised. Actually, there is a practical reason behind this that goes to the nature of the classifications of crimes. More serious offenses are usually classified as felonies while lesser offenses tend to be misdemeanors or infractions. With felonies there is actually more latitude for arrest decision making since the victim does not actually need to personally observe the accused person committing a crime; the evidence can "tell the tale," and the police can make a decision based upon the sufficiency of the evidence. With regard to misdemeanors or infractions, usually the victim must have actually seen the suspect commit an offense. Thus, with misdemeanors, the situation offers far less discretion for an officer; the citizen witnessing an offense either decides to make an arrest or decides not to make an arrest. All an officer does is transport the arrestee for the arresting citizen. Furthermore, felonies, because of their higher order, often permit a reduction in grade to a lesser offense (e.g., "grand theft auto" reduced to "joyriding"), while misdemeanors rarely permit reductions; it is either arrest for the misdemeanor or release. It should be kept in mind, though, that, generally, the more serious the crime the greater the likelihood of an arrest (for some offenses).

Strength of the Evidence The presence (or lack) of evidence is a crucial factor in discretion. The stronger the evidence in the field situation, the more likely an arrest. Rarely do police confront persons as suspects without some evidence.

It is important to recognize that the strongest evidence may not always be physical residue. In many instances, witness testimony is the primary or only evidence available. Such evidence often challenges police officers to call upon their experience and "third sense" as aids in decision making. Multiple witnesses enhance decision making, particularly when they are independent, i.e., have no prior relationship with the accused party.

Victim-Offender Dynamics The dynamics involving victims and offenders are as pivotal as any other factor when it comes to the exercise of discretion. Arrest practices sharply reflect the preferences of citizen complainants. The police are an instrument of the complainant in two ways: generally they handle what the complainant wants them to and they handle the matter in the way the complainant prescribes.[18] It is important to recognize too that the nature of the relationship between the victim and suspect is influential in decision making. Arrests tend to be less common among persons related intimately. The police often regard these incidents as private matters. They are normally more likely to make arrests for crimes involving strangers. Of course, some domestic violence legislation compels arrests when injuries are visible or other critical factors are present.

Discretion and the Use of Force

Interestingly, research has shown that characteristics of officers themselves do not appear to be generally influential. Walker made the point in his review of studies examining race, sex, and education as causal factors in the exercise of discretion. James Fyfe found that white officers were no more likely to use physical force or lethal force, or to make arrests, than were African American or Hispanic officers.

Studies comparing male and female officers have found both to be similar in crucial field situations involving application of control techniques and arrests. Studies attempting to identify differences in performance on the basis of educational levels have to date not yet found significant differences. Something to keep in mind in this regard, though, is that most measures used were "traditional" indicators of performance and decision making (e.g., type of crimes arrested for and number of field interviews, warrant checks, etc.), as compared to the indicators used to assess performance in the course of community policing (e.g., problem solving, team building, or mobilization of resources, etc.).

While studies of race, gender, and education have not demonstrated very much influence of these factors on decision making, some studies have revealed that suspect or victim characteristics can actually impact officers' discretion. The demeanor of a suspect has been shown to be consistently influential in arrest decision making. An arrest is far more likely if a suspect is antagonistic or disrespectful to police.[19] A few studies have shown that officers' moral judgments about victims can cloud credibility. Gary LaFree conducted studies that disclosed substantial evidence that police officers discount the allegations of rape victims whose lifestyle they view as non-conformist.

Controlling Discretion

Both Kenneth Culp Davis and Samuel Walker, as well as other experts on the subject of discretion, agree on the need to control police discretion. As long ago as 1973, the National Advisory Commission on Criminal Justice Standards and Goals decreed the necessity for establishing standards for controlling discretion. In fact, the Commission was quite specific as to the areas in which standards should be established. The areas included arrest, investigations, and recurring peacekeeping activities. In another proactive vein, the Commission expressed a need for agencies to review all existing criminal statutes for their practicality of enforcement and to advise states' legislatures of any statutes' impracticality of enforcement.[20] Indisputably, discretion needs to be "reined." Uncontrolled discretion can create serious problems, including denial of due process and denial of equal protection, ineffective personnel supervision (since the bounds of discretion are not clearly specified in order for supervisory oversight to properly operate), and inability to plan (planning requires some degree of predictability, and non-conforming discretion frustrates opportunities for predictability).

Need for Honesty The first step toward confining and structuring the discretionary power of the police is to bring to the surface, community-wide, the fact that the police use as much discretion as they do. Traditionally, the police tend to deny the extent to which they engage in discretionary action and often claim publicly that they fully enforce all laws.

The myth of full enforcement exists for several reasons. First, the police seek to maintain an image of authority so as to prevent the undermining of their authority in encounters with citizens. Second, for the police to admit that they do not arrest everyone would expose them to liability for constitutionally based equal protection violations. Finally, most states' legislatures require full enforcement of the laws. In fact, many states have penal code sections containing sanctions for police and other officials who do not enforce the law.

Policy Creation Written policies have a strong influence in enhancing consistency when using discretion. Written policies are all the more important given the wide extent of discretion used by the police. When Kenneth Culp Davis completed his examination of discretionary justice, he learned that the police made far more discretionary determinations in individual cases than any other class of administrators (1969). He calculated at that time that the amount of governmental activity through the police was 40 times as much as the amount of governmental activity through all the federal regulatory agencies.[21] Considering the growth in the number of police officers since 1969, the amount of discretionary opportunity has mushroomed. Davis cited the Internal Revenue Service as a preeminent example of a government agency that has "pulled toward uniformity" in its decision making policies by issuing precise and detailed rules.

Pros and Cons of Rulemaking

Administrative rulemaking by a police department offers several advantages. Such directives are written and as such are circulated to all individuals within the organization. This wide distribution promotes consistency of performance, which by its very nature guards against constitutional abuses, e.g., equal protection of the law. Simply put, the real value in rules is not to eliminate discretion but to narrow the number of situations in which the police officer has to make a decision. Davis refers to this as confining discretion.

How Rules Get Created The development of rules of operation for police departments is uneven across agencies. Some are active participants in the process, while others only seem to do so when necessary, e.g., when a lawsuit looms as a result of failure to regulate conduct that can imperil the citizenry or suspects. Several attempts have been made to encourage systematic rulemaking. A number of those attempts have failed largely because of the voluntary nature of the compliance. The Commission on Accreditation for Law Enforcement Agencies (CALEA) has been the most successful to date in guiding discretionary actions. The hundreds of CALEA agency accreditation standards require a written directives system that covers a multitude of field operational procedures. Agencies seeking accreditation by CALEA must demonstrate by-the-letter conformance with the standards. Since the standards are applied nationally, as more and more agencies seek accreditation the level of guided discretion should increase markedly across the country.

Reactive Rulemaking When it comes to rulemaking, all too often agencies engage in the process reactively. Rules are routinely created in the wake of incidents for which policing agencies have incurred substantial civil liability. (See Figure 9.4 on page 356.)

Common incidents that prompt reactive policy making include

- Vehicular pursuits
- Use of force
- Domestic violence
- Custody (of prisoners)

It is important for all police personnel to understand the purpose of rules and to embrace their value. Very often, police officers fail to comprehend the clarifying value of rules and react defensively. Those who react defensively assume the perspective that rulemaking makes it easier for oversight authorities to "burn them to learn them" (common police slang for the initiation of formal misconduct allegations by higher authorities). Officers with this mindset need to recognize that the presence of rules gives them something to "hang their hats on." It is far better to be able to cite a concrete rule to support one's actions than to have to undergo post-incident scrutiny that is not rule-based. Most agencies are conscientious in taking the initiative to inform employees of rules, so it is not difficult at all to be fully informed on operational rules. In fact, in a lot of cases employees are bombarded with rules and this can dampen the receptivity of employees to rules generally.

The very nature of policing necessarily involves some amount of discretion. Full enforcement across the board would prove unfair to certain individuals in certain situations.

9.3 Self Check
1. What factors influence the exercise of discretion?
2. What are some methods for controlling discretion?

POLICING *Online*
Check your answers at
www.policing.glencoe.com

9.4 Ethics

The point was just made that discretion is essential in order to guard against unfair treatment of individuals. We also stated that well reasoned rules were important for channeling discretion, i.e., ensuring the presence of some "boundary markers," to ensure optimal uniformity in outcomes. As we progress now, we want to provide further guidance for ensuring fair and impartial treatment of the police clientele. The discussion will now proceed from the ethical perspective. Shortly, we will discuss discretion and professionalism in the context of ethics, but first we need to define ethics and explain its importance in policing. Ethics refers to the study and analysis of what constitutes good or bad conduct. It addresses the specific moral choices an individual makes in relating to others.

Figure 9.4

Federal Court Decisions in Cases of Police Brutality

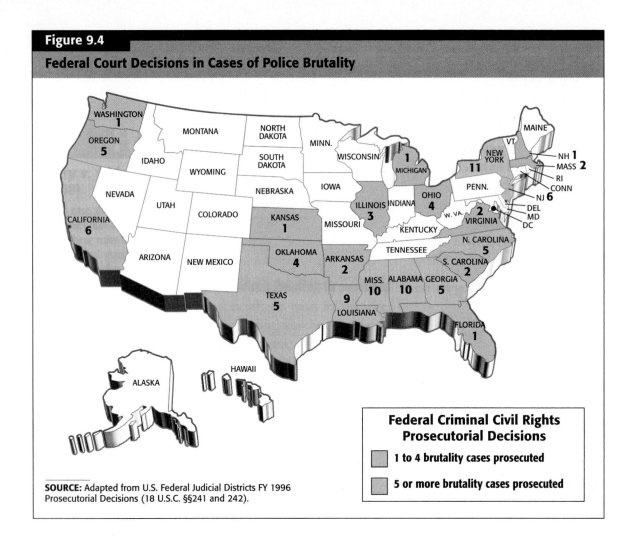

Federal Criminal Civil Rights Prosecutorial Decisions

☐ 1 to 4 brutality cases prosecuted

☐ 5 or more brutality cases prosecuted

SOURCE: Adapted from U.S. Federal Judicial Districts FY 1996 Prosecutorial Decisions (18 U.S.C. §§241 and 242).

The Need for Ethics

The necessity for the practice of ethics in law enforcement springs from the central nature of the position. Ethical considerations are central to decisions involving force and due process, routine and extremely important experiences for police.[22] Public confidence in the ability of police officers to ethically discharge their duties is integral to social order. The police are the most visible symbol of government, a point that cannot be overstated. Citizens view the quality of police service as an indicator of the quality of government. Any decline in the trust citizens have in their police as impartial agents of justice can translate into dire consequences for government.

Twice in recent history, the police have caused the public to question government processes and controls. In the late '50s and '60s the police were viewed as a tool of the white majority population in violating rights of minorities. Again in the late '60s and early '70s, college students, draft age individuals, and others viewed the police as the arm of an "establishment" that was rendering decisions they perceived favored a military industrial complex. A substantial segment of society perceived that police had no regard for the welfare of all citizens and projected this perception on government.[23]

In the '80s with the advent of the crack epidemic and the proliferation of gangs, the police were perceived as critical to the security of citizens. Their relative lack of success in curtailing the drug problem spoke poorly of the effectiveness of the police-government alliance in its attempt to eradicate illegal drugs. In the '90s local militias, citizens courts, and national publicity on the "weakness" and questionable practices of law enforcement, as in the Rodney King and Waco cases, arose as an expression of skepticism about the total justice system.

Just as the actions of the police can affect people's view of government as a whole, unethical actions of individual officers can effectively contaminate an entire agency. Each employee must possess an internal moral compass that distinguishes between right and wrong. Agency management must ensure that employees' perceptions of right and wrong are not in conflict with those of the organization.

Standards of Ethical Conduct

Many organizations have either a value system or a code of ethics to guide the behavior of those who work within the organization. Police departments have both. The organizational values are instilled via the organizational value system. The values can be found within an agency's mission statement. Typical values include the following:

- Service to the community
- Reverence for the law
- Respect for people
- Quality through continuous improvement

These four values would be representative of a police department committed to a community policing philosophy.

Codes of Conduct and Ethics A code of ethics is a **code of conduct** specific to the behavior of individual officers. Generally, these codes are aspirational. An **aspirational code of conduct** implies adherence to ethics that would exemplify the "perfect" professional. In practice, the code represents a goal to work toward. It is motivational because of its articulation of the highest standards of policing; all officers can improve because no officer is perfect. To the extent agencywide values match those practiced by the rank and file, the police organization will be high performing. This meshing of values can yield extraordinary performance; however, there are many authorities who

code of conduct A code of conduct specific to the behavior of individual officers.

aspirational code of conduct Implies a type of code of ethics that motivates adherence to the highest standards of policing.

Figure 9.5

Law Enforcement Code of Ethics

As a law enforcement officer, my fundamental duty is to serve mankind; to safeguard lives and property; to protect the innocent against deception, the weak against oppression or intimidation, and the peaceful against violence or disorder; and to respect the constitutional rights of all men (and women) to liberty, equality, and justice.

I will keep my private life unsullied as an example to all; maintain courageous calm in the face of danger, scorn, or ridicule; develop self-restraint; and be constantly mindful of the welfare of others. Honesty in thought and deed in both my personal and official life, I will be exemplary in obeying the laws of the land and the regulations of my department. Whatever I see or hear of a confidential nature or that is confided to me in my official capacity will be kept ever secret unless revelation is necessary in the performance of my duty.

I will never act officiously or permit personal feelings, prejudices, animosities, or friendships to influence my decisions. With no compromise for crime and with relentless prosecution of criminals, I will enforce the law courteously and appropriately without fear or favor, malice or ill will, never employing unnecessary force or violence and never accepting gratuities.

I recognize the badge of my office as a symbol of public faith, and I accept it as a public trust to be held so long as I am true to the ethics of the police service. I will constantly strive to achieve these objectives and ideals, dedicating myself before God to my chosen profession . . . law enforcement.

SOURCE: International Association of Chiefs of Police.

view this as the greatest challenge the police administrator faces.[24] It is a lot easier said than done. All agency employees do need to consciously strive for this outcome.

The International Association of Chiefs of Police has created the most widely used code of ethics.[25] The principles of fairness and justice are the dominant themes in the code shown above in Figure 9.5. A second theme is that of service to the community. Another theme is reverence for the law, and what is stressed here is that their exercise of the law must be totally within the bounds set for them by the law. The final theme is one of behavior; this demands a higher standard of behavior in their professional and personal lives than expected from the general public.

In addition to the formal organizational value system and the code of ethics, all police departments have an oath of office that is often a shorthand version of either or both of these. The oath usually briefly expresses a moral obligation to the community and to the sacred trust it entails for the individual officer.[26]

Ethics and Professionalism As a concept, ethics is closely associated with professionalism. Codes of ethics are vital to guide behavior of practitioners of the learned professions. For peace officers such codes promote self-regulation and discipline within a law enforcement agency. In the best sense professionalism implies having more than technical skills and refers to the moral contributions that professionals make in a complex, democratic society—the ethic of the calling. The ethical person is perceived as someone who has courage and integrity and is willing to resist corruption and unprincipled people by upholding humanity, justice, and civility. Such a peace officer tries to be loyal to his or her conscience and avoids unprofessional behavior (e.g., use of excessive force, expressions of bias and bigotry, or acceptance of bribery).

In addition to all the foregoing benefits from embracing a code of ethics, the quest for professional status for police officers literally demands a code of ethics. You will recall from Figure 9.3 (Elements of professionalism) that one of the five elements was a code of ethics. Therefore, a code of ethics is a central feature of the truly professional law enforcement officer.

Ethics and Discretion A major ethical concern in policing practice involves the use of discretion in the performance of duty. As has been established, discretion is a necessary element in law enforcement. Law enforcement professionals have a great deal of discretion regarding when to enforce a law, how to enforce it, how to handle disputes, when to use force, and so on. The need for discretion, however, leads to a greater dependence on individual ethical codes. Most ethical dilemmas that police officers face derive from their powers of discretion.

Ethical dilemmas are relative to the particular police function in which they arise. Patrol officers may have to make ethical decisions pertinent to defining crimes and initiating the formal criminal justice process. Patrol officers are also subject to the temptations of gratuities. Follow-up investigators must be concerned with the propriety of evidence collection, both physical and testimonial. Undercover officers have special ethical concerns relevant to informants, deception, and target selection. Supervisors and managers have ethical quandaries unique to being responsible for others.

Regardless of their agency role, police employees must approach their decision making with appropriate beliefs about their mission and their role in society. That is why it is so important for organizational values to mesh with codes of ethical conduct. This process of goal and ethical code integration must begin in the police academy and continue throughout an officer's career. This places the burden on agency management to ensure officers are informed on and fully involved in shifts in organizational philosophies. If an agency is oriented toward a neighborhood policing concept, then service and partnership values must be instilled in officers. Modernly, many police chiefs have been met with resistance in their efforts to convert senior officers from their '70s outlook to that required of the contemporary cop. Training is vital in this regard and will be discussed subsequently in the context of corruption prevention.

In situations involving the exercise of discretion in the line of duty, there are three questions that each officer must ask himself or herself:

1. What does the law require?
2. What does departmental policy dictate?
3. What do individual ethics dictate?

Addressing discretion by posing these three questions provides a structural framework for decision making that is consistently considerate of law, policy, and ethics.[26] The more articulated and compelling the applicable law and policy, in all probability the less the reliance on the code of ethics for decision making. Conversely, the less the clarity of the law or policy on a subject (or their absence altogether), the greater the reliance on the code of ethics.

Corruption

Of all the problems in the realm of policing, none is more damaging than corruption. Eradicating the scourge of corruption is one of the most critical internal issues police face if they are to maintain the public trust and support. Corruption occurs in the gap of the ethical standards promoted by the police agency and the ethical standards held by individual officers. The relation of police integrity to corruption can be regarded as a continuum, with integrity on one end and corruption on the other. Along the continuum, proceeding from integrity to corruption, may be violations of administrative procedures, deceptive or false testimony, or abuse of force.

corruption Acting on opportunities created by virtue of one's authority, for personal gain, at the expense of the public one is authorized to serve.

Recent Examples of Corruption While not subject to a one-size-fits-all definition, **corruption** may be defined as acting on opportunities, created by virtue of one's authority, for personal gain at the expense of the public one is authorized to serve.[27] The infamous 1991 Rodney King beating incident is probably one of the most devastating acts of police malfeasance in the history of American policing. While this single action led to demoralization of the LAPD, the act of perjury by Detective Mark Fuhrman during testimony in the spectacular O.J. Simpson trial almost dealt the death blow to this agency's standing in the law enforcement community, as well as in the eyes of the public it served. It took the live telecast of heroics of officers involved in a perilous 1997 shoot-out with bank robbers (North Hollywood shoot-out) to begin to restore the stature of the agency.

CAREER FOCUS

Internal Affairs Investigator

Job Description

I address citizens' complaints, check daily on the status of current internal investigations, and also follow up on allegations of misconduct that are reported within our department.

Most complaints are related to some sort of communication issue. People call in because they feel they did not do what the officer say they did, or they think they have been racially profiled.

A citizens' review committee looks at every complaint, and if it is deemed valid, the complaint is sent to the internal affairs department, assigned a number, and investigated. The reasons to decline a complaint can be that the police report clearly shows evidence that there is no ground to the complaint, or it is a dispute over a ticket that can and should be solved in court.

Darrel Schenck, Portland PD

Depending on the results of the investigation, a supervisor can meet with the officer to review and critique the officer's behavior so there is a chance to learn from the experience. The officer's commander recommends disciplinary action if necessary. We also often mediate complaints with citizens.

The most challenging thing is to identify clearly which practices are positive, ethical, and responsible. While it is easy to define in words, it is sometimes hard to apply in practice, especially when there are so many different views about what policing should "look like today." It is very rewarding to have the citizens involved in the review of complaints, it reinforces the principles of community policing.

Education

I have a B.A. in sociology and an M.A. in criminal justice. If young officers do not have a college degree, I would recommend that they make it a number one goal.

Follow-Up What do you think might be a stressful aspect of this job? Why?

Forms of Corruption Corruption takes many forms. It is not limited to monetary gain. Traditionally, it is thought of as criminal violations committed by police officers for the purpose of personal gain such as:

- Accepting bribes
- Selling confidential information
- Tampering with evidence
- Failing to respond to calls for service
- Withholding information from police reports
- Failing to bring forth firsthand knowledge of wrongdoing by other officers

Establishing the boundaries of corruption is difficult. Acceptance of a gratuity is a prime example. A **gratuity** is something given freely to a police officer, which may or may not be in return for a favor or in expectation of a future favor. Some maintain that a gratuity is only a token of appreciation from a merchant. Others argue that petty favors and gifts may leave an officer vulnerable to more serious transgressions. Regardless of the level, there can be distinctions drawn between magnitudes of misconduct and any appropriate sanctions imposed.

gratuity Something given freely to a police officer, which may or may not be in return for a favor or for an expectation of a future favor.

Causes of Corruption

Theories of corruption are as controversial as they are numerous. Frequently cited causal factors include:

- Political influences
- Dilution of hiring standards
- Economic necessity
- Unclear (or lacking altogether) agency policies
- Changing social values
- Poor supervision

Author Edwin Delattre's hypotheses about police corruption include three elements:

- Blaming society at large in that citizens provide gifts and gratuities that can lead to bribes and ultimately aggressive criminal activity by officers
- Police cynicism based on a loss of faith in humankind; ultimately, misconduct becomes acceptable within a police department
- The "rotten apple" phenomenon, which results from poor recruitment[28]

The International Association of Chiefs of Police has conducted extensive research on the causes of police corruption and has fashioned two schools of thought to explain the formative process of corruption: structural and individual explanations.[29] The structural school focuses on the organization. Structural explanations have shown dramatically that corrupt behavior arises through the development of an informal structure within the police department, an infrastructure that provides an officer with the opportunity to not only break the rules but also a transgression that is encouraged and supported by a subcultural code of beliefs. Studies have repeatedly shown the power of the policing subculture to adversely influence behavior. Figure 9.6 on page 364 shows an example of a formal organizational structure within an internal affairs department.

Individual explanations acknowledge the presence of a deviant subculture but point toward a predisposition on the part of the officer as pivotal, rather than the officer being lured into wrongdoing. Whether a police officer chooses to engage in corrupt behavior has more to do with his or her personal benefit from an act than a submissive affinity for the deviant infrastructure. In other words, the corrupt officer consciously exercises discretion to engage in prohibited conduct. In the context of the individual explanation, questions have been raised concerning the different values recent recruits have brought to policing. Some police officials believe that changing societal values will encourage more independent officers to adopt a diminished standard of integrity.

Prevention of Corruption

When devising strategies to prevent corruption, it must be recognized at the outset that no prototype corruption blueprint exists. There are, however, five critical components to a prevention program: recruitment, a comprehensive code of ethics, ethics training, sound disciplinary apparatus, and proactive policy making. To the extent these components are in place, the greater the immunity to corruption.

Recruitment Policing responsibilities must be carefully researched and the recruitment focused accordingly. Years ago, much police recruiting was done at military installations. This was intended to recruit an officer who would be readily adaptable to the policing style of that era. In recent years, the demand is for a problem-solving, interactive individual who can be relied upon to take the initiative in forging an alliance with the community. This target candidate may very well still be found in a military uniform, but this individual is as likely to be found on a college campus.

A vital part of the recruitment process includes the background examination. Research continues to support the fact that maximum attention should be allotted to the background investigation.

Figure 9.6

An Internal Affairs Organizational Chart

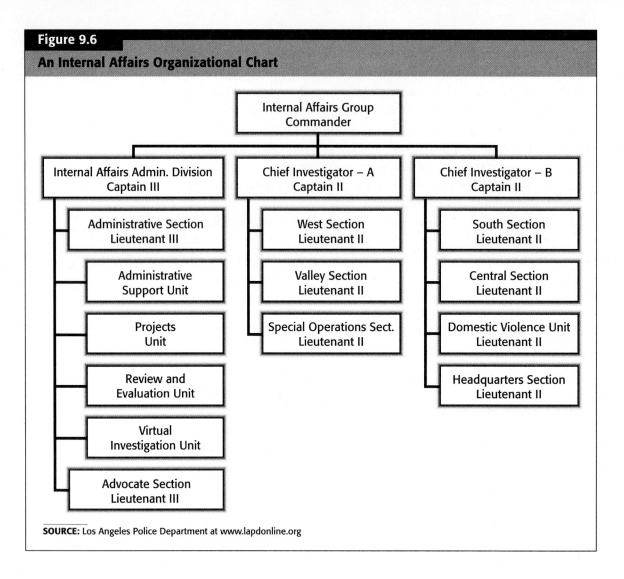

SOURCE: Los Angeles Police Department at www.lapdonline.org

Code of Ethics It is absolutely essential that all officers operate from a common ideology that provides guidance for conduct in situations they are likely to experience in the field. The IACP advocates both a general code of ethics as well as a detailed listing of prohibited activities that will not be tolerated. Both the code of ethics and the listing of prohibited actions should be published and distributed to each agency member. The two items should be routinely reviewed and reinforced at roll call briefings.

Ethics Training Ethics training is the police department's chance to establish the difference between legal behavior and ethical behavior, and to stress the importance of ethical behavior as it relates to public confidence. This has become most important in the transition to community policing, in which public trust is a preeminent goal. An ideal program should encompass historical and social aspects of the corruption problem, practical exercises, and review of the agency code of ethics. It is extremely important that ethical training begin at the police academy for the potential result of a uninformed recruit is uneducated discretion in the field. Aside from recruit training, follow-up in-service training courses are essential to provide a continuum of ethics training.

Disciplinary Apparatus A variety of mechanisms for handling reported or detected misconduct exist:

- Sworn department employees in all aspects of the complaint adjudication process
- Citizen review boards
- Oversight authority to ensure the complaint process is functioning optimally

Regardless of the methodology—and all the systems have weaknesses and strengths too numerous to detail here—the key to a successful apparatus is the ease with which complaints can be registered. This is the crucial initiating step in the complaint process. The other crucial component in the complaint process is speedy and fair resolution of complaints.

Proactive Policy Making This is a subtle but highly effective preventive strategy. The key here is to constantly evaluate policies and rules to eliminate vulnerability points. This is most applicable to narcotics operations, a notorious source of scandalous conduct. There are numerous points of vulnerability that can be literally "sealed" off—a play on words that relates to the tamperability of evidence seals—by effective policies. One of this textbook's authors spent four years streamlining a police department's evidence processes because of an instance of missing narcotics evidence. Other areas for proactive policy attention include:

- Body searches
- Informant control
- Prisoners' money counts
- Use of force
- Vehicular pursuits
- Use of intoxicants
- Vice protocols
- Financial obligations

1. Why is the practice of ethics in law enforcement important?
2. What is the connection between ethics and professionalism?

Check your answers at
www.policing.glencoe.com

Components of Police Integrity

Summary By Learning Objectives

1. Define integrity and its primary components.

Integrity is police officers' application of core moral virtues, e.g., trust, courage, and honesty, in their duty performance. Actually, we are talking about three concepts when we speak about integrity. These three concepts are professionalism, discretion, and ethics. They all work in unison in igniting the spirit of integrity.

2. Understand the meaning of professionalism.

In policing, professionalism has taken on a dual meaning. In the context of policing integrity, it alludes to performance of policing by officers whose qualifications include the following: advance education, familiarity with the field's body of knowledge, and adherence to a code of ethics. Additionally, the professional police officer's performance is subject to peer review for purposes of accountability. This form of professionalism is akin to that which is characteristic of the medical and legal professions. The outcome sought through professionalization is improvement in the quality of law enforcement services.

3. Recognize how community policing is a catalyst for professionalism.

Community policing is a boost for professionalism because its demands require a police officer who possesses qualities that are a by-product of professionalism. Community policing requires a highly interactive and worldly officer who can inspire the level of trust necessary for mobilizing the community toward a policing partnership. Additionally, community policing is centered on a problem solving approach that can best be executed by an officer who has been adequately schooled on the criminal justice body of knowledge.

4. Explain the factors that influence discretion.

Discretion is a vital component of policing integrity. It is constantly employed by police. Principal factors that influence the exercise of discretion are as follows: amount of resources, ambiguity in the criminal law and criminal procedure, informal expectations of legislators and the public, and dynamics of a particular situation. Personnel and equipment limitations simply do not permit full enforcement of the criminal law. The ambiguous nature of the criminal law compounds the difficulty of enforcement of its provisions. Therefore, officers frequently "wing it" in an effort to effect street justice. Informal expectations of legislators and the public play a role in an officer's exercise of discretion. Some laws are expected to be enforced to the "letter of the law," e.g., carjacking, while others such as vice laws are not expected to be enforced unless violations are commercial in nature. Finally, situational factors, such as the seriousness of an offense, the nature of the evidence, victim-offender dynamics, and the characteristics of the concerned officer, can exert a pronounced influence on the nature of decision making.

5. Identify methods for appropriately limiting discretion.

The 1973 National Advisory Commission on Criminal Justice Standards and Goals decreed the necessity of establishing standards for controlling discretion and identified areas in which standards should be established. These areas include: arrests, investigations, and recurring peacekeeping activities. The first step toward structuring police discretionary power is to acknowledge to the community the police's wide use of discretion. Secondly, discretion is limited or controlled principally through the creation of written rules. Rules provide parameters for decision making. Once all employees are informed of rules, the outcome can be a more consistent exercise of discretion. The Commission on Accreditation for Law Enforcement Agencies (CALEA) has created accreditation standards that require a written directives system covering many operational procedures.

6. Understand the importance of ethics in law enforcement.

Public confidence in the ability of police officers to ethically take care of their duties is integral to social order. Any decline in the trust citizens have in their police as impartial agents of justice can translate into dire consequences for government and provoke public unrest and affect an entire police department or police at large. It will notably impair the perception of police officers as professionals with a strict code of ethics.

7. Recognize the standards of ethical conduct.

Standards of ethical conduct are normally contained in a formal code of ethics. It is most important that this code be practiced in conformance with the police department's expressed organizational values. Typical values include: service to the community, reverence for the law, respect for people, and quality through continuous improvement. To the extent agencywide values match those practiced by the rank and file, the police agency will be high performing.

8. Identify the dynamics of corruption.

Corruption occurs in the gap of the ethical standards promoted by a police agency and the ethical standards held by individual officers. Corruption occurs when officers act on opportunities created by virtue of their position for the purpose of personal gain. The formation of corruption may occur both at the organizational level and the individual level. At the individual level, corruption frequently springs from a predisposition on the part of an officer, rather than being lured into it.

9. Learn how to prevent corruption.

There are five components to a corruption prevention program: recruitment, code of ethics, training in ethics, discipline system, and proactive policy making. The key to effective recruitment is a comprehensive background investigation. An appropriate code of ethics and recurrent training on ethics are crucial preventive actions. An efficient complaint system that facilitates intake of complaints and provides for speedy and fair adjudication is vital. Proactive policy making is a subtle but highly effective method for eliminating vulnerabilities that can lead to misconduct.

Key Terms

ethics (p. 334)
integrity (p. 335)
professionalism (p. 335)
discretion (p. 343)
perimeter (p. 345)

criminal procedure (p. 348)
code of conduct (p. 357)
aspirational code of conduct (p. 357)
corruption (p. 360)
gratuity (p. 362)

Questions for Review

1. What are the primary components of integrity?
2. Cite the five elements of classic professionalism.
3. Distinguish the two main ways the term professionalism is used.
4. How does community policing serve as a catalyst for the development of the true policing professional?
5. Cite an inherent impediment to attainment of policing professionalism.
6. Identify the four principal factors that influence discretion.

7. Which of the four categories is the most important to the exercise of discretion, i.e., which is the most frequently invoked?
8. How does increased rulemaking improve the exercise of discretion?
9. What is a key reason for the necessity of ethical conduct in law enforcement?
10. Should a code of ethics contain standards reflective of the "average" officer or the "perfect" officer? Why?
11. Cite the IACP's two schools of thought on the formative process of corruption.
12. List the five components of a corruption prevention program.

Experiential Activities

13. Solve an Ethical Dilemma
This exercise can be done in small groups of four or five, in pairs, or alone. Pick one of the ethical dilemmas listed below. Discuss your selection in the context of the law enforcement code of ethics. You may create laws or policies as necessary. If you are working with a group, develop a consensus on the best solution to the ethical dilemma.

a. You are offered a large cash bribe to "lose" evidence for trial.
b. You cite a man for assault and battery, but are asked by a city councilman to "let it go" because the man is his nephew.
c. You need an informant's help in apprehending a drug dealer, but find out that she is involved in other criminal activities that will be completed before you are able to bust the dealer.

Experiential Activities continued

14. Explore Police Professionalism

Contact a nearby law enforcement agency at the local, county, state, or federal level and ask them how they ensure that employees possess the following qualities:

  a. Advanced education

  b. Familiarity with the field's body of knowledge

  c. Adherence to a code of ethics

Be prepared to discuss the question: Which of these qualities is the most important to you? The least?

15. Defining Integrity

This exercise can be done alone or in a group of three or four. Interview 2 or 3 people and ask them these questions:

  a. How do you define *integrity*?

  b. How do you define *police integrity*?

  c. Do you feel that police should be held to the same standards, or to higher standards, as others? Why?

16. Ethics among Coworkers

The sense of solidarity among police officers is a strong and fulfilling one, but it does have a negative side. Police sometime choose to not report corrupt fellow officers, and even lie to protect each other. This side of police corruption can be extremely frustrating for police management. Contact a police academy and ask them the following questions:

  a. How do they instruct recruits to handle such situations?

  b. If they offer instruction on the issue, what are recruits taught?

  c. How is the issue addressed?

Web Patrol

17. Police and Personal Integrity

Go to **www.policing.glencoe.com** for links to sites dealing with police integrity. Try to get a sense for the type of training law enforcement practitioners are attending to enhance their integrity levels.

How might some of the concepts discussed be applied to your personal life?

18. Education and Law Enforcement

Go to **www.policing.glencoe.com** for a list of progressive agencies that have fully embraced the spirit of education in law enforcement.

How have these agencies fully embraced education?

19. Police and Ethics

Go to **www.policing.glencoe.com** and check out Web sites that explore strategies to enhance the ethical climate in policing.

What strategies do you think might be most effective in improving ethics in policing?

Critical Thinking Exercises

20. Lobby Cruising

At approximately 3:00 A.M., you are flagged down by two security officers at the main entrance to a five-star hotel. The security officers point to an individual standing next to his motorcycle outside the hotel's entrance doors. They inform you the individual has refused to identify himself after his detention for driving his motorcycle inside the hotel's lobby and dropping off someone (literally) at the front desk. You observe black rubber marks on the lobby's glass doors and carpet, and a tire mark on one of the doors.

You then ask the suspect for identification. He slurs, "Okay," and hands you a police identification card that resembles him perfectly. When the security officers see it, they say in unison, "Forget it—no problem."

a. What is your personal "gut" response to this, and what is the proper organizational response? Are the two the same? Why or why not?

b. What, if any, ramifications may result from releasing the off-duty officer?

21. Bowling for Dollars

You are an investigator for a suburban police department. One Monday morning, an anonymous caller tells you that someone is "sharking" at the local bowling alleys. He is a teenaged boy who pretends to be an average bowler, but who managed to win over $700 in bets over the last weekend at one of the town's two bowling alleys. On Sunday afternoon, the owner told him to get out, but the caller says that he just saw him at the town's other bowling alley, using the same ruse. He says that the bowler is very deceptive and always wins his games by just a few points, which makes it harder for people to believe that they are being sharked—but, the caller insists, they are.

Your department is currently shorthanded and is committing most of its investigative resources to a more serious numbers operation that is run by a local crime family. You are planning to interview a low-level informant later this morning, and the booking and paperwork of the bowling shark could take a few hours. If he is a juvenile, it will take longer because you will be responsible for taking him to an intake center.

a. What could be some of your options for using your department's limited resources?

b. Which is the best option, and why?

22. Arrest the Victim?

You are answering a call for an alleged aggravated battery that occurred near the local campus. When you arrive, you find a young man who has been severely beaten up by his next-door neighbor, who is clearly on drugs. You arrest the assailant, but as you take a report from the victim you notice a small amount of marijuana, wrapped in a baggie, in his kitchen. In your state, nonviolent drug offenders can receive harsh sentences, and the jails and prisons are also extremely overcrowded. Nevertheless, your chief zealously endorses a "zero tolerance" anti-drug policy.

a. Do you arrest the victim for his drug possession? Why or why not?

b. If you do not make an arrest, is there any other action that you can take? If so, what? If not, why?

Endnotes

1. National Institute of Justice and Office of Community-Oriented Policing Services, Police Integrity: Public Service with Honor, U.S. Government Printing Office, Washington, D.C., 1997, p. 1.

2. Ibid., pp. 14–15.

3. Barbara Raffel Price, "Police and the Quest for Professionalism," *Law Enforcement News*, John Jay College of Criminal Justice, June 15, 1995.

4. Richard V. Mecum, *The Police Chief*, August, 1979

5. Harry W. Moore, Jr., *Critical Issues in Law Enforcement*, Anderson Publishing Co., Cincinnati, 1981, p. 289.

6. William Geller and Hans Toch, *Police Violence*, Yale University Press, New Haven, Connecticut, 1996, pp. 194–206.

7. National Advisory Commission on Criminal Justice Standards and Goals, *Police*, Government Printing Office, Washington, D.C., 1973, p.369.

8. Bureau of Justice Assistance, *Understanding Community Policing*, U.S. Government Printing Office, 1994, p. 24.

9. Price, op. cit.

10. Richard C. Lumb, "Standards of Professionalization: Do the American Police Measure UP?," *Police Studies*, Vol. 17, No. 3, 1994, pp. 1–19.

11. Kenneth Culp Davis, *Discretionary Justice*, Louisiana State University Press, Baton Rouge, Louisiana, 1969, p. 25.

12. Bureau of Justice Statistics, *Report to the Nation on Crime and Justice*, U.S. Department of Justice, Washington, D.C., March 1988, pp. 56–60.

13. Davis, op.cit., p. 4.

14. National Advisory Commission, op. cit., p. 204.

15. Community Policing Consortium, *Community Policing Exchange*, July/August, 1998, p. 4.

16. Steve Herbert, "Police Subculture Reconsidered," *Criminology*, Volume 36, No. 2, 1998.

17. Jerome H. Skolnick, *Justice Without Trial: Law Enforcement in Democratic Society*, Macmillan College Publishing Company, New York, 1996, pp. 191–192.

18. Donald J. Black, "The Social Organization of Arrest," *Stanford Law Review*, Vol. 23, 1971.

19. Geller and Toch. op. cit., p. 24.

20. National Advisory Commission, op. cit., p. 21.

21. Davis, op. cit., p. 223.

22. George Felkenes, "Ethics in the Graduate Criminal Justice Curriculum," *Teaching Philosophy*, Vol. 10, No. 1, 1987, pp. 23–36.

23. NIJ and COPS, op. cit., p. 82.

24. Robert Wasserman and Mark H. Moore, "Values in Policing," *Perspectives on Policing, National Institute of Justice*, No. 8, November 1988.

25. Michael Davis, "Do Cops Really Need a Code of Ethics?" *Criminal Justice Ethics*, Vol. 10, No. 2, 1991, pp. 14–28.

26. Joycelyn M. Pollock and Ronald F. Becker, "Ethics Training Using Officers' Dilemmas," *FBI Law Enforcement Bulletin*, Vol. 65, No. 11, 1996.

27. Howard Cohen, , "Exploiting Police Authority," *Criminal Justice Ethics*, Volume 5, No. 2, 1986, pp. 23-31.

28. Edwin J. Delattre, *Character and Cops: Ethics in Policing*, Enterprise Institute for Public Policy Research, Washington, D.C., 1989.

29. International Association of Chiefs of Police, *Corruption Prevention*, IACP National Law Enforcement Center, Alexandria, Virginia, 1996.

Chapter 10

Police and the Law

CHAPTER OBJECTIVES

AFTER COMPLETING THIS CHAPTER, YOU WILL BE ABLE TO:

1. Explain how the U.S. Constitution, Bill of Rights, and U.S. Supreme Court relate to law enforcement.

2. Understand the various types of law.

3. Distinguish between the exclusionary rule and good faith exception.

4. See the differences in mere suspicion, reasonable suspicion, and probable cause.

5. Explain the requirements for a legal stop and frisk, search and seizure, and arrest.

6. Understand the concept of custodial interrogation.

7. Comprehend the legal principles that apply to identification procedures.

8. Explain how civil liability applies to policing.

◀ Officers salute the flag at the Vermont Police Day ceremony at the Statehouse in Montpelier.

10.1 Police and the Constitution

American police are required to enforce the laws of their jurisdictions. The rule of law, used to ensure social, economical, and political stability in the United States, defines the legal limits of human behavior and actions. Whether a law prohibits murder or sets a speed limit on local highways, laws are essential in maintaining effective law enforcement while respecting individual rights. If an officer is to provide fair and equal treatment to all citizens under the law, he or she must first understand the legal principles that influence any law enforcement decisions.

To understand the role of the police and the law, one must first understand the U.S. Constitution. The goal of those who wrote the Constitution in 1787 was to create a government with power, but not enough power to become capricious or cruel toward its citizens. The U.S. Constitution illustrates "perhaps the most successful example in history of a legal instrument that has served both as a safeguard of individual freedom and as a ligament of national unity."[1]

The U.S. Constitution consists of three articles, which identify and define the three branches of government:

- Article I outlines the powers of the legislative branch, which is responsible for making the laws.
- Article II outlines the powers of the executive branch, which is responsible for enforcing the laws.
- Article III outlines the powers of the judicial branch (including the Supreme Court), which has the primary responsibility of interpreting the laws.

The Bill of Rights

Bill of Rights Ten amendments to the Constitution that protect American citizens from government abuses.

As the Constitution was being written, early American citizens and politicians were deeply concerned about the federal government abusing its powers. To prevent this, a **Bill of Rights** was created and passed after the U.S. Constitution was ratified. The Bill of Right's original ten amendments gave American citizens protection from government abuses. Amendments were added over time to address additional issues, and today there are 27. The amendments that have the most relevance to policing are the First, Fourth, Fifth, Sixth, Eighth, and Fourteenth Amendments. Figure 10.1 on page 375 lists each of these amendments.

After the ratification of the Constitution and the Bill of Rights, citizens were protected from abuses by the federal government, but not from abuses by state governments. Not until the passage of the Fourteenth Amendments, which was ratified after the Civil War, did citizens gain constitutional protection in state matters.

Figure 10.1

Selected Amendments to the U.S. Constitution

Amendment I

Congress shall make no law respecting an establishment of religion, or prohibiting the free exercise thereof; or abridging the freedom of speech, or of the press; or the right of the people peaceably to assemble, and to petition the Government for a redress of grievances.

Amendment IV

The right of the people to be secure in their persons, houses, papers, and effects, against unreasonable searches and seizures, shall not be violated, and no warrants shall issue, but upon probable cause, supported by oath or affirmation, and particularly describing the place to be searched, and the persons or things to be seized.

Amendment V

No person shall be held to answer for a capital, or otherwise infamous crime, unless on a presentment or indictment of a Grand Jury, except in cases arising in the land or naval forces, or in the militia, when in actual service in time of war or public danger; nor shall any person be subject for the same offense to be twice put in jeopardy of life or limb; nor shall be compelled in any criminal case to be a witness against himself, nor be deprived of life, liberty, or property, without due process of law; nor shall private property be taken for public use, without just compensation.

Amendment VI

In all criminal prosecutions; the accused shall enjoy the right to a speedy and public trial, by an impartial jury of the State and district wherein the crime shall have been committed, which district shall have been previously ascertained by law, and to be informed of the nature and cause of the accusation; to be confronted with the witnesses against him; to have compulsory process for obtaining witnesses in his favor, and to have the assistance of Counsel for his defense.

Amendment VIII

Excessive bail shall not be required, nor fines imposed, nor cruel and unusual punishments inflicted.

Amendment XIV

All persons born or naturalized in the United States, and subject to the jurisdiction thereof, are citizens of the United States and of the State wherein they reside. No State shall make or enforce any law which shall abridge the privileges or immunities of citizens of the United States; nor shall any State deprive any person of life, liberty, or property, without due process of law; nor deny any person within its jurisdiction the equal protection of laws.

The Fourteenth Amendment

The Fourteenth Amendment established the dual citizenship clause, which means that it gave American citizens constitutional protection in both state and federal criminal cases. To activate this protection in a state case, a citizen had to claim that his or her individual constitutional rights had been violated.

Suppose that Frank, a resident of St. Louis, Missouri, is accused of robbing a local convenience store. He is convicted by a Missouri state court and appeals his case while in prison. His case ends up before the U.S. Supreme Court. His lawyer explains to the Court that his Fourth Amendment rights, made applicable to state cases through the Fourteenth Amendment's due process clause, have been violated because police searched his home and person unlawfully. It is important to understand that because this is a state case, he *has* to first state that Frank's Fourth Amendment rights have been violated through the Fourteenth Amendment. If this were a federal case, he could simply say that Frank's Fourth Amendment rights had been violated.

The U.S. Supreme Court

U.S. Supreme Court The "court of last resort" for all cases that it hears, which means that all cases decided by the Supreme Court cannot be appealed again; the final interpreter of all constitutional matters.

The court that has the greatest impact on law enforcement is the **U.S. Supreme Court**, which is the "court of last resort" for all cases that it hears. This means that cases decided by the Supreme Court cannot be appealed again. In *Marbury v. Madison* (1803), the U.S. Supreme Court ruled that it was the final interpreter of all constitutional matters.

Because the Court is very selective in deciding the cases it will hear, an appeal to the U.S. Supreme Court does not automatically guarantee that the Court will hear it. Many criminal cases heard by the Court start when a defendant has been convicted and is incarcerated in a state prison. The U.S. Supreme Court requires that inmates must exhaust the state appeal process before appealing to the Court. This means that the state courts must deny the inmate's appeals until the inmate cannot appeal to them anymore. If the appeals are denied, the inmate can then petition the U.S. Supreme Court for a **writ of certiorari**, which is a written request to the Court asking it to review the case. If certiorari is granted, the case is heard before the entire Court in brief oral arguments by the prosecution and defense.

writ of certiorari A written request to the Supreme Court asking it to review a particular case.

Types of Law

There are three types of law in the United States but many different ways in which law can be categorized. What they have in common is that they all are written law that is enforceable by the American court system.

1. **Criminal law**, also called *penal law*, defines crimes and their punishments. Criminal law takes the form of either statutory law or procedural law, which are discussed below.
2. **Civil law** provides a means of controlling the noncriminal relationships between individuals, businesses, or organizations. It defines the rules for divorce, libel, creation of wills, defective consumer goods, and contracts.
3. **Administrative law** provides the rules and regulations that are established by governments to control the actions of industry, business, and individuals. One example is state law that outlines procedures for electing or appointing judges to state courts.

In all types of cases, the law is an adversarial process, which means that the two sides fight each other to try to obtain the outcome they desire. The defendant is innocent until proven guilty. Guilt must be established, or found and proven, through an adequate amount of evidence to support the court's burden of proof.

In addition, there are two types of criminal law, and officers must understand their differences:

1. *Substantive law* defines offenses and their elements, as well as the punishments that are allowed for those convicted of particular offenses.
2. *Procedural law* defines the methods for handling violations of the substantive law by focusing on the rights of suspects or defendants in criminal cases. Examples of procedural law are rules of evidence, guidelines for conducting lineups, and procedures for arresting a suspect.

Finally, there are two different ways in which laws are made:

1. *Statutory law* is created through American state and federal legislatures. All states, as well as the federal government, have a set of criminal statutes.
2. *Case law* is law that develops from court decisions. When judges decide on a particular case, this sets a **precedent**, which means that past judicial decisions are followed in making future decisions. Precedent is based on *stare decisis*, which means "let the decision stand" from previous cases and apply to similar ones that are tried in the future.

These types of law overlap in many ways. For example, case law often affects procedural law. For instance, the U.S. Supreme Court decision in *Miranda v. Arizona* illustrates case law. This case eventually influenced the creation of procedural law in establishing the guidelines for administering the Miranda warning.

criminal law The branch of law that defines crimes and punishments; also called *penal law*.

civil law The branch of law that provides a means of controlling the noncriminal relationships between individuals, businesses, or organizations.

administrative law The branch of law that provides the rules and regulations established by governments to control the actions of industry, business, and individuals.

precedent Past judicial decisions are followed in making future decisions; based on *stare decisis*, which means "let the decision stand."

Another example can be found in cases involving criminal and civil charges. The next section will cover the little-understood topic of civil law and explain why it is important for police officers to understand.

A Closer Look at Civil Law

Police are usually trained in the basics of criminal law, but they usually do not learn about civil law until hearing about a department that is facing a lawsuit. It is important for officers to understand civil law because lawsuits are expensive, embarrassing, and generally avoidable if officers are first trained in citizens' civil rights. Also, since the burden of proof is lower in civil courts than in criminal ones, it is easier for lawsuits to succeed than for criminal charges in the same case.

Civil cases are different from criminal cases in several ways. Criminal cases are represented by prosecutors, who work on behalf of the state. Civil cases are represented by plaintiffs, who are individuals seeking redress against any person, government entity, or (increasingly) corporation. In criminal cases, the wrong charged against the defendant is called a crime, which is an offense against the criminal law. In civil cases, the wrong charged against defendants is called a **tort**. Perhaps the most important difference is the fact that criminal convictions can lead to a loss of liberty or life through incarceration or execution. Civil judgments, on the other hand, do not punish defendants but only require them to provide money or property as compensation.

tort The wrong charged against defendants in civil cases.

Torts can be classified in three categories:

1. *Strict liability torts* involve behavior that is so dangerous that one who engages in it can expect to inflict harm or injury on another. One example might be where police purposefully use a harmful chemical to eradicate marijuana, and the subsequent use of treated marijuana results in serious physical injury by those who smoke it. Normally, however, strict liability torts are not associated with police but with commercial products.
2. *Intentional torts* occur when an officer engages in a dangerous, purposeful behavior that was foreseeable on the part of the officer. Police behavior that would fall under intentional torts would be wrongful death, assault and battery, false arrest, and false imprisonment.
3. *Negligence torts* occur when an officer engages in deliberate behavior that can result in damage or injury. The burden of proof for convincing a court that an officer foresaw the danger is lower in negligence torts than it is for intentional torts. Therefore, it is easier to prove the officer's awareness of danger under a negligence tort.

Police negligence can take one of four forms: negligent operation of emergency vehicles, negligent failure to protect, negligent failure to arrest, and negligent failure to render assistance.[2] To prove negligence in any of these areas, the plaintiff must prove the following elements:

1. *A legal duty*, which is two-dimensional because officers are required to take certain actions but not take others. Suppose that a police officer fails to follow departmental policy by administering a field sobriety test to a suspected drunk driver, then that driver kills someone in an accident ten minutes later. This officer has failed in his or her legal duty.

2. *Proof of a breach of duty* requires proving that an officer violated his or her duties to a citizen, based on the facts of the situation. For example, a homeowner calls the police to inform them that someone has threatened to break into his house. A break-in then occurs without any police action. In this case, the police may be found in breach of duty.

3. *Proximate causation* is showing that the officer's conduct resulted in the plaintiff's injuries. For example, if an officer is chasing a suspect and an innocent bystander is killed due to the officer's negligence, proximate cause can be established.

4. *Actual damage or injury* must be shown. Suppose that a domestic violence victim tells police that her ex-husband is defying a restraining order and has threatened to return and try to kill her, but police refuse to respond by arresting him. As a result, she sustains injuries and is hospitalized. In this case, the damage and injury requirement has been established.

Online

Remember, one of your best resources is **www.policing.glencoe.com**

All torts can apply to policing, and negligent police work can create several liability issues for police. This applies not only to police-citizen interactions but also to how police handle evidence. The next section will discuss the rules that police must follow to legally perform searches and seize both evidence and suspects.

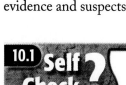

10.1 Self Check

1. Which type of tort seems easiest to prove, and why?
2. Define probable cause.

POLICING *Online*

Check your answers at **www.policing.glencoe.com**

The Exclusionary Rule

exclusionary rule A rule of evidence that does not allow any court to use evidence that is obtained in violation of a defendant's constitutional rights.

When police search for evidence and seize it in ways that are illegal, they violate the Fourth Amendment. A major consequence of this is that courts will dismiss such evidence according to the **exclusionary rule**, a rule of evidence that does not allow any court to use evidence that is obtained in violation of a defendant's constitutional rights.

The modern exclusionary rule was defined by the case *Weeks v. United States* (1914). In *Weeks*, the U.S. Supreme Court stated that federal law enforcement agents could not illegally seize evidence and use it against a defendant in a federal case. The original exclusionary rule did not apply to state cases. In fact, state law enforcement agents continued to illegally seize evidence and were allowed to present it to the federal courts. In 1960, with *Elkins v. United States*, the Court ruled that presenting illegally seized state evidence in federal courts was unconstitutional.[3] Still, the matter of introducing illegally seized evidence in state courts had not been resolved. This changed with the landmark case of *Mapp v. Ohio* (1961), in which the Court stated that any evidence seized in violation of the Fourth Amendment could not be admitted into any court, state or federal.[4] Finally, an exclusionary rule that was applicable to all courts in America had been established. (See Figure 10.2 on page 381 for exceptions to the exclusionary rule.)

The exclusionary rule also applies to evidence that is found as an indirect result of illegal searches. Suppose that police are illegally searching for drugs but accidentally discover illegal weapons. In this case, both the direct

▶ **Exclusionary Rule** Police search a crack house in Broward County, Florida. Some very strict rules dictate how a search can be conducted.
Why do you think these rules were established?

Figure 10.2

Exceptions to the Exclusionary Rule

There are three exceptions to the exclusionary rule:

1. ***The Good Faith Exception:*** This was created by the U.S. Supreme Court cases *U.S. v. Leon* (1984) and *Massachusetts v. Sheppard* (1984). Suppose that an officer receives a search warrant and uses it to seize evidence, but later finds that the warrant was not valid because of technical reasons or incorrect information. Under the good faith exception, the search is still legal if it can be proven that the officer acted *in good faith* to obtain and use a legal warrant. This exception does not apply if the defense proves that the officer lied or "showed a reckless disregard for the truth."

2. ***The Inevitable Discovery Doctrine:*** This exception developed from *Nix v. Williams* (1984). If evidence is seized illegally, but legal searches already in progress would have eventually found this evidence anyway, the seizure becomes legal because it becomes "inevitable" that it would be discovered. In proving this doctrine, the prosecution's burden of proof is a *preponderance of the evidence* (a majority of the evidence, which is any amount over 50 percent) that the seized evidence would eventually be discovered by legal means.

3. ***The Independent Source Doctrine:*** This exception developed from the Supreme Court case of *Segura v. U.S.* (1984). If evidence that is first seized illegally is again seized with a proper warrant, it becomes legally admissible evidence. "For example, if one were to photo-copy financial records without a warrant of someone suspected of embezzlement, but then later returned with a warrant and recopied the information, that evidence would be allowed."

SOURCE: Michael Cooke, *Evaluation of the Exclusionary Rule,* accessed online at http://sc.essortment.com/exclusionaryrul_rmlx.htm on December 14, 2001.

---

goal of the search (the drugs) and the indirect discovery (the weapons) will be considered inadmissible in court. This secondary evidence is called the fruit of the poisonous tree.[5] Although the fruit of the poisonous tree doctrine originally applied to illegal searches, courts have also applied it to other constitutional violations such as illegal arrests, illegal identification procedures, and involuntary confessions.[6] It is crucial that officers exercise sound decision making in considering searches or interrogations so that evidence and criminal cases are not thrown out on the basis of technicalities.

The courts do acknowledge that police sometimes commit accidents when trying to obey procedural laws. Since *Mapp*, the Court has established the **good faith exception** for searches pursuant to a warrant. In *United States v. Leon* (1984), the Court ruled that evidence obtained from a warrant that is properly prepared, but later determined to be invalid for reasons that police did not foresee, does not make the evidence legally inadmissible.[7] The officer still has a responsibility to ensure that the affidavit presented to a magistrate or judge is accurate to the best of his or her knowledge.

good faith exception An exception to the exclusionary rule that holds that evidence is admissible when obtained from a seemingly acceptable warrant that is later determined to be invalid for reasons that police did not foresee.

10.2 Self Check

1. What is the exclusionary rule?
2. What is the fruit of the poisonous tree?

POLICING *Online*

Check your answers at **www.policing.glencoe.com**

10.3 Search, Seizure, and Arrest

Some of the greatest powers that police possess are those of search, seizure, and arrest. An officer's decision-making process in any of these actions must reflect a complete understanding of the laws that determine what he or she can and cannot do in these situations. If officers do not fully understand these laws, they can face criminal charges or lawsuits, can see evidence dismissed against defendants who are clearly guilty, or all of the above.

Among other things, officers must have an understanding of mere suspicion, reasonable suspicion, and probable cause:

mere suspicion The "gut feeling" that officers have when they suspect that something is wrong but have no proof; cannot be used to justify legal action.

reasonable suspicion The amount of knowledge necessary to make an ordinary and cautious person believe that criminal activity is occurring; necessary for a stop and frisk.

stop and frisk An action in which police stop, briefly detain, and frisk individuals in the course of a field interrogation; requires reasonable suspicion.

probable cause A level of suspicion, based on evidence, that can lead a reasonable person to believe that a suspect has committed or will commit a specific crime; required for an arrest or to obtain a legal arrest warrant or search warrant.

- **Mere suspicion** is the lowest level of suspicion and can be compared to the gut feeling that officers have when they suspect that something is wrong but have no proof. Mere suspicion is not enough to justify any legal action against individuals. For example, if an officer merely claims that someone needed to be stopped and frisked because he looked suspicious, the officer has only mere suspicion, not reasonable suspicion.
- **Reasonable suspicion** is the amount of knowledge needed to make an ordinary and cautious person believe that criminal activity is occurring. This knowledge must be specific and concrete, and the officer must be able to explain it clearly. Reasonable suspicion is necessary for a **stop and frisk**, in which police stop, briefly detain, and frisk individuals in the course of a field interrogation. It is not enough to conduct searches, seizures, or arrests.
- **Probable cause** occurs when evidence can lead a reasonable person to believe that a suspect has committed or will commit a specific crime. It is required for an officer to make a legal arrest or to obtain a legal arrest warrant or search warrant.

Probable cause may be based on the following:

1. *Observation by officers*, which is based on evidence detected by the officer's sense of sight, hearing, or smell, is considered the strongest form of probable cause.
2. *Officer expertise and circumstantial factors* combine the officer's knowledge and experience to piece together circumstantial evidence to determine a criminal's behavior. This type of evidence is often combined with observations by officers.
3. *Information communicated to officers* can be received from official sources, crime victims, informants, and witnesses.[8]

The transition from reasonable suspicion to probable cause can occur very quickly if an officer finds evidence that indicates criminal behavior or if the suspect says anything that is self-incriminating. Decisions are made quickly and can have far-reaching consequences as it relates to the safety of the officer and the public. Officers need to realize that the law, as it pertains to arrest, search, and seizure, allows them to use discretion and reasonable actions to protect themselves. Figure 10.3 on page 384 illustrates the amount of information needed for a stop and frisk, arrest, and conviction.

In what circumstances does an officer determine mere suspicion, reasonable suspicion, and probable cause? When an officer determines these levels of suspicion, how does he or she apply this to legal actions? The next two sections will discuss how officers can apply levels of suspicion to pre-arrest measures and to arrest.

Prearrest Measures

Officers can take many actions to build evidence and confirm suspicions to develop probable cause, which is required for an officer to make a legal arrest. The primary encounters are voluntary encounters, stop and frisks, searches, and seizures of evidence.

Voluntary Encounters The majority of police-citizen encounters are voluntary in nature. In such encounters, people willingly talk to police and give them information. An officer may have mere suspicion toward the person being interviewed but sometimes will gather evidence by talking to witnesses or victims. When a voluntary encounter begins to raise the officer's suspicions, the overall tone of the encounter can move from mere suspicion to reasonable suspicion, justifying the use of a stop and frisk within seconds.

Stop and Frisk In high crime areas, police routinely stop and briefly detain individuals to conduct a field interrogation. If these individuals act in a suspicious or threatening manner, officers will frisk them. In *Terry v. Ohio* (1968), which is discussed in the FYI box on page 388, the Court offered guidance on when stop and frisks are legal.

Searches and Seizures Search and seizure laws regarding people and automobiles are very complex and have changed frequently over the past three decades. Because searches and seizures require probable cause, and because officers may be legally liable when they perform searches and seizures without adequate probable cause, the best thing for officers to do is to use Court decisions "as a learning tool and continually educate themselves."

A **search** occurs when police examine a person, object (such as a vehicle or package), or location (such as a business or residence) to find evidence of criminal activity. To perform searches, police must generally have a search

search Occurs when police search a person, object (such as a vehicle or package), or location (such as a business or residence) to find evidence of criminal activity; generally requires a search warrant.

warrant. In some circumstances, they can perform searches on the spot without a warrant.

As you will read later on in this section, the circumstances of warrantless searches have been well defined by the courts. This type of search can happen if it is deemed reasonable, in most cases this involves a situation where there can be no expectation of privacy. These cases include among others:

- Consent searches
- "Search" for items that are in plain view
- Emergency exceptions when public safety is in jeopardy

seizure Occurs when police take physical evidence or property to help build a case.

A **seizure** occurs when police take physical evidence or property to help build a case. For example, drugs, weapons, fingerprints, and other evidence

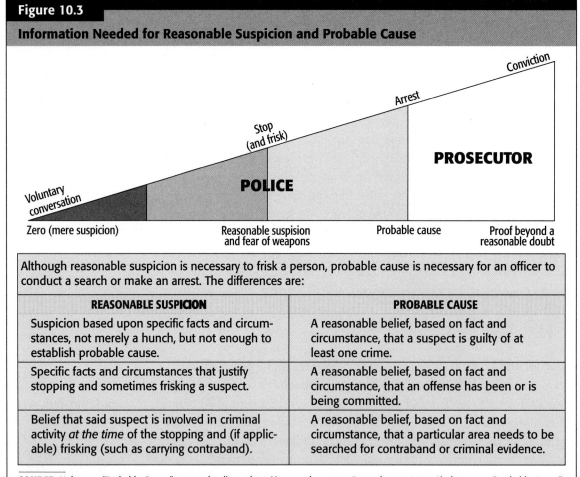

Figure 10.3

Information Needed for Reasonable Suspicion and Probable Cause

Although reasonable suspicion is necessary to frisk a person, probable cause is necessary for an officer to conduct a search or make an arrest. The differences are:

REASONABLE SUSPICION	PROBABLE CAUSE
Suspicion based upon specific facts and circumstances, not merely a hunch, but not enough to establish probable cause.	A reasonable belief, based on fact and circumstance, that a suspect is guilty of at least one crime.
Specific facts and circumstances that justify stopping and sometimes frisking a suspect.	A reasonable belief, based on fact and circumstance, that an offense has been or is being committed.
Belief that said suspect is involved in criminal activity *at the time* of the stopping and (if applicable) frisking (such as carrying contraband).	A reasonable belief, based on fact and circumstance, that a particular area needs to be searched for contraband or criminal evidence.

SOURCE: Nolo.com, "Probable Cause," accessed online at http://www.nolo.com on December 13, 2001; FindLaw.com, "Probable Cause" and "Reasonable Suspicion," accessed online at http://www.findlaw.com on December 13, 2001.

Knowing the Law

Police attorney Carl Milazzo, who is also chair of the International Association of Chiefs of Police (IACP) Legal Officers Section, gives officers this advice on knowing the law:

Officers must understand the entire body of case law governing their safety, because tactical training is less effective if an officer hesitates out of legal ignorance. The law requires less justification when looking for a weapon than when searching for evidence. Some officers dangerously learn to hold themselves to a higher standard on the street because of ignorance or negative reinforcement in the courtroom.

What Do You Think? How can you balance your rights and limitations as an officer?

SOURCE: Carl Milazzo, "Supreme Court Emphasizes Significance of Officer Safety," *The Police Chief*, October 1998, 151.

---

can be "seized." To seize personal property such as cars or items inside of a home, the police usually have to obtain a search warrant. A **search warrant** is a document that is prepared by an officer, sworn to be true and accurate by the officer, and then issued by a judicial official. It states the circumstances and facts that support probable cause.

Searches and seizures are performed together. If a search is performed in accordance with the law, any property seized during that search will be legal, admissible evidence. Therefore, this section will discuss what qualifies as a legal search. The seizure of persons is actually arrest, which will be discussed in the next section.

search warrant A document that is prepared by an officer, sworn to be true and accurate by the officer, and then issued by a judicial official in order to support the probable cause required for a search.

Types of Searches Searches can be either warrantless or with a warrant. In either case, the police are intruding on a citizen's privacy, so the courts have identified three principal types of legal searches:

1. **Searches with Warrants** If a warrant is to be issued, it must describe the exact location to be searched and the exact items to be seized. Simply stating the location as a white house on Oak Street and the item as a television is insufficient. The police need to provide an exact street address and a detailed description of the items to be seized.

   There are also limitations in the type of search that officers can perform for the items named in the warrant. For example, if a search warrant specifies a 41-inch television, officers may not look in desk or dresser drawers because these are too small to hold an object that size. If, however, they find other evidence such as drugs or weapons in places large enough to be searched, this is admissible evidence. Figure 10.4 on page 387 shows a sample search warrant form.

2. **Searches Incidental to Arrest** Searches that are incidental to a lawful arrest are also legal. They must occur at the time the arrest is made and must be restricted to the immediate area of the arrest. In *Chimel v. California* (1969), the Court stated that a search incidental to arrest can be conducted only on the suspect's person and in the area within his or her immediate control or reach. This means that items such as the suspect's clothing, purse or wallet, backpack, or baby stroller may be searched when the suspect is arrested.

3. **Consent Searches** The third type of search is the consent search, in which a person willingly allows an officer to search a specified area. To conduct a search properly, the officer should first ask for permission, such as by saying, "Can I search your gym bag?" If the officer instead orders, "Open your gym bag," this is not a consent search but one that the officer has coerced through his or her officer's authority, which is illegal.

▶ **Seizure** Police are allowed in certain circumstances to take items from the scene they have searched.
How do you think this can affect court procedures?

Figure 10.4

Sample Search Warrant and Affidavit

Affidavit

SEC. 99-25-15. Affidavit to obtain search warrant.

"State of Mississippi, _____ County.

"Before me, Andrew Sims, a justice of the peace of said county, Edward Nolly makes oath that, on or about the _____ day of _____ 2002, in the said county, a box of lightbulbs and a case of work boots, the property of affiant, of the value of seven hundred dollars were feloniously stolen, taken, or carried away; and affiant suspects Samuel Miller as the person guilty of said crime, and has reason to believe and does believe that the said stolen articles, or some of them, are now concealed in or about the dwelling house, or outbuildings connected therewith, of the said Samuel Miller, in said county; and affiant prays a search warrant to search said premises, and seize the said goods if found, and also the body of said Samuel Miller, to be disposed of according to law.

"Edward Nolly.

"Sworn to and subscribed before me, the ___day of _____, 2001.

"Andrew Sims, J.P."

Search Warrant

SEC. 99-25-17. Search warrant and capias.

"The State of Mississippi.

"To any lawful officer of _____ County:

"Oath having been made before the undersigned, a justice of the peace of said county, that a box of lightbulbs and a case of work boots, the property of Edward Nolly, on or about the _____ day of _____ 2002, in said county, were feloniously taken, stolen, and carried away and that suspicion rests on Samuel Miller as guilty of said crime, and affiant has reason to believe and does believe that the said stolen articles, or some of them, are concealed in or about the dwelling house, or outbuildings connected therewith, of the said Samuel Miller, in said county:

"We command you, with the necessary assistance, to enter into the said dwelling house of Samuel Miller, and the outhouses connected therewith, and there diligently search for the said goods and chattels; and if the same, or any part thereof, be found, that you bring them, and also the body of said Samuel Miller, forthwith before the undersigned, or some other justice of the peace, to be disposed of according to law.

"Andrew Sims, J.P."

SOURCE: State of Mississippi, "Affidavit to obtain search warrant," accessed online at http://www.mscode.com/free/statutes/99/025/0015.htm on December 14, 2001; Codes, 1892, Sec. 1497; 1906, Sec. 1569; Hemingway's 1917, Sec. 1331; 1930, Sec. 1357; 1942, Sec. 2604. Also State of Mississippi, "Search warrant and capias," accessed online at http://www.mscode.com/free/statutes/99/025/0017.htm on December 14, 2001; Codes, 1892, Sec. 1498; 1906, Sec. 1570; Hemingway's 1917, Sec. 1332; 1930, Sec. 1358; 1942, Sec. 2605.

In addition to these three traditional searches, police also use the following three types of legal searches for special circumstances:

1. **No-knock search warrants** On television, officers often announce their presence prior to executing the warrant. In reality, this is not always the best approach. For example, in drug or gambling investigations, an officer's hesitation gives the suspects time to destroy or remove evidence. In this situation, officers can get permission from a judge to perform a no-knock search warrant, which allows them to enter a location before announcing that they have a search warrant.

plain view doctrine A doctrine that allows officers who observe evidence in plain view to seize it without a warrant or probable cause.

Terry v. Ohio (1968)

In this case, the U.S. Supreme Court established these rules for constitutional searches:

1. Where a police officer observes unusual conduct that leads him or her to reasonably conclude that criminal activity may be occurring
2. and that the person with whom he or she is dealing may be armed and dangerous
3. and in the course of investigating this behavior states that he or she is a policeman
4. and asks reasonable questions to help determine probable cause
5. and where nothing in the initial stages of the encounter serves to dispel a reasonable fear for safety
6. that officer is entitled to ensure the protection of him or herself and others by conducting a carefully limited search of the outer clothing of such person in an attempt to discover weapons.

SOURCE: *Terry v. Ohio*, 392 U.S. 1, 88 S. Ct. 1868 (1968).

2. **Seizure or securing of dwellings** If officers have probable cause and are in the process of securing a warrant, the dwelling may be secured to prevent the removal or destruction of evidence. The U.S. Supreme Court has ruled that this is a reasonable seizure of the dwelling or its contents.

3. **Anticipatory search warrants** An increasing trend in the use of search warrants has been the use of the anticipatory search warrant, which specifies a place to be searched and an item or items to be seized that have yet to arrive at the location of the search. For example, this type of warrant is used to seize items being shipped through the mail. The U.S. Supreme Courts have stated that if properly prepared, it does not violate the Fourth Amendment.[11]

Legal Doctrines Relating to Searches There are general legal doctrines, or rules, that officers must follow when conducting searches. Although the details regarding searches change frequently and are beyond the scope of this book, the basic rules will be covered here. Officers should have a full understanding of these before attempting to understand more detailed legal issues.

- The **plain view doctrine** was established in *Harris v. United States* (1968), in which the Court decided to allow officers who observe evidence in plain view to seize it without a warrant or probable cause. The following requirements must be met to justify the plain view doctrine:

  1. The officer, as a result of a prior valid intrusion, must be in a position in which he or she has legal right to be.
  2. The officer must not unreasonably intrude on any person's reasonable expectation of privacy.
  3. The incriminating character of the object to be seized must be immediately apparent to the officer.
  4. The discovery of the item of evidence by the officer need not be inadvertent.[12]

Several situations allow the legal use of a plain view search. These include making an arrest, performing a search that is incident to an arrest, conducting a stop and frisk, executing a search warrant, making controlled deliveries, pursuing a fleeing suspect, or responding to an emergency.[13] If there is no expectation of privacy, there is no violation of the Fourth Amendment.

The Plain Feel/Touch Doctrine A similar concept is the plain feel/touch doctrine, which was established in *Minnesota v. Dickerson* (1993). In Dickerson, the Court held that police may seize nonthreatening contraband such as drugs that are detected during the type of protective patdown search permitted by *Terry*, as long as the search stays within the guidelines established in *Terry*.[14]

The Open Fields Doctrine In the open fields doctrine, a police officer not only may seize items in open view but also may search for and seize items that may be concealed.[15] The difference between the open fields and plain view doctrines is that open fields are not constitutionally protected.

Determining where Fourth Amendment protection ends and open fields begins is a key concern in open fields doctrine. The answer has come from the courts' broad definition of the word *house*. The Fourth Amendment protects persons in homes regardless of whether the homes are owned, rented, or leased. This definition also includes permanent or temporary accommodations such as apartments, hotel and motel rooms, and hospital rooms.

The Inevitable Discovery Doctrine The inevitable discovery doctrine holds that illegally obtained evidence is admissible in a criminal trial *if* the prosecution can show that it would have been discovered anyway by legal police activity.[16]

In addition, police need to be aware that there are special legal considerations when searching vehicles or private property outside of the home.

Vehicle Searches In the case of vehicle searches, a major concern today is the use of vehicles to carry and conceal evidence. Vehicle searches have been addressed by the Court several times, with the following outcomes:

- Police may search an automobile without having to first arrest the driver or passenger if the officer has probable cause to believe that 1) the automobile contained illegal items and 2) it would it leave the scene before a search warrant could be acquired.[17]
- Officers with probable cause to search a car can take it to the police station to be searched.[18]
- The principle of mobility applies *only* if there is a chance that the car will be moved.[19] It is important to remember, however, that cars that appear unable to move (such as inoperable ones) can be towed.
- If a driver or passenger is arrested, the interior and all contents of the car can be searched *only if* the search follows the arrest.[20]
- Officers who have legitimately stopped an automobile and have probable cause to believe that contraband is concealed somewhere within it may conduct a warrantless search of the vehicle and all of its contents and containers.[21]
- Pretext stops, which involve stopping a vehicle for reasons other than a specific violation, do not justify a subsequent search of that vehicle.[22]

ETHICS ISSUES

Search and Arrest

Tom is patrolling a strip mall when he notices a shadowy figure behind a store that has been burglarized several times in recent months. It is 2 A.M. and there is no reason for anyone to be there at this hour. Tom calls for backup, then approaches the rear of the store. When he sees a person attempting to hide in a dumpster beneath some boxes, he tells him to show his hands slowly and climb out of the dumpster. The person tells Tom that he was looking for empty boxes. He is very nervous and keeps moving his hand toward a rear pocket. At this time fearing for his safety, Tom orders him to place his hands on the dumpster and frisks him. Tom feels what appears to be a small caliber handgun and retrieves a .32 automatic, then arrests the suspect. *Were Tom's actions justified? Why or why not?*

▶ **Car Search** In the wake of anthrax scare, police search a car before it enters the Capitol area in Washington D.C. The right of police to search a car on suspicion has been under debate many times.
Why do you think this is a controversial issue?

- On the other hand, police agencies can spot-check vehicles, such as with police sobriety checkpoints. For example, one program in Michigan established clear guidelines for operations, site selection, and publicity. In addition, the checkpoints did not allow unbridled officer discretion and was not in violation of the Fourth Amendment.[23]
- For reasons of safety and to avoid the destruction of evidence, an officer may order all occupants to exit a vehicle until the completion of a traffic stop.[24]

curtilage The area and outbuildings surrounding a house that are considered private property.

Searches on Private Property When dealing with private property, the courts have further expanded coverage to include **curtilage**, which is the area and outbuildings surrounding a house that are considered private property. How have federal courts defined curtilage issues? Some findings are as follows:

- **A residential yard is curtilage** The courts have held that the yard is always within the curtilage of a house and receives Fourth Amendment protection from warrantless searches. The only exception is when it is obvious that the owner has permitted public access to the yard and had no expectation of privacy.
- **Yard fences define the perimeter of the curtilage** If a fence defines the perimeter around a house, the area within is normally considered curtilage. In contrast, fenced areas outside of the curtilage do not create the expectation of privacy or bring the area within the curtilage.

- **Garbage on the curb is not curtilage** In *California v. Greenwood* (1988), the Court held that the Fourth Amendment allows the warrantless search and seizure of garbage left for collection outside the curtilage of a home.
- **With businesses, curtilage applies only to areas not open to the public**

Arrest

Arresting a suspect is not a simple process. The authority and conditions under which an officer can arrest a suspect are outlined in state statutes that cannot violate the Fourth Amendment. Typical elements of an **arrest** include:

1. The officer's authority to arrest
2. The officer's intent to arrest
3. An understanding by the suspect that he or she is being arrested
4. A seizure of the suspect by the officer

Arrests have different legal requirements depending on whether the officer has an arrest warrant. When an officer has a warrant, he or she may arrest the suspect at any time within his or her jurisdiction. If a warrant has been issued but is not in the possession of the officer, often the officer may still arrest the suspect as long as the warrant is served as soon as possible.

To obtain a warrant, an officer must provide a statement of the crime for which the suspect is accused. The officer must show probable cause through either a sworn affidavit or sworn oral testimony to a magistrate

arrest A seizure of a suspect by an officer; requires probable cause.

Computer
On Patrol

Aerial Searches

What are law enforcement agencies' legal rights in the case of aerial searches, in which officers fly over an area (usually in a helicopter) to find suspects? Since the technology used to find suspects could also invade the privacy of innocent people, it may seem that officers need a search warrant. In fact, the

U.S. Supreme Court held in *California v. Ciraolo* (1986) that police do not need a search warrant if they are observing an area open to observation from the air, even if it is within the property lines of a home.

Think About It Why do you think a search warrant is unnecessary for aerial searches?

SOURCE: *California v. Ciraolo*, 476 U.S. 207 (1986).

MYTH	FACT
Police can perform a warrantless search on anything outside, since this fits the open fields doctrine.	**Many private areas are considered to be curtilage, which is private property that is under a home's umbrella of protection in the following four ways:** **1. The proximity of the area to the home** **2. Whether the area is within an enclosure surrounding the home** **3. The nature and uses to which the area is put** **4. The steps taken by the resident to protect the area from observation by passersby** **SOURCE:** *United States v. Dunn,* 480 U.S. 294 (1987), 300.

or judge. In some jurisdictions, the officer can provide sworn oral testimony by teleconferencing.[28]

Most arrests are performed *without* a warrant. To arrest a suspect without a warrant, the officer must have probable cause to believe a crime has been committed in his or her presence. Under certain circumstances, an officer may also arrest a suspect who has committed a crime outside of the officer's presence. In North Carolina, any of these circumstances apply:

- There is probable cause to believe the suspect has committed a felony or a misdemeanor.
- The suspect will not be apprehended unless immediately arrested.
- The suspect may cause physical injury to himself or herself or to others.
- The suspect will cause damage to property unless immediately arrested.

Unless special circumstances exist, an officer needs an arrest warrant to enter a house in order to arrest a suspect. If officers have a legal justification to be in a residence, they can arrest a suspect without a warrant. For example, if an officer is in hot pursuit of a robbery suspect who enters a private house, the officer may enter the house without a warrant. If the officer does not have a warrant and is not in hot pursuit, he or she cannot force the suspect to come outside to be arrested.

10.3 Self Check

1. Why do vehicle and curtilage searches have detailed restrictions?
2. Why do arrests inside of a house usually need a warrant?

POLICING *Online*
Check your answers at
www.policing.glencoe.com

10.4 Custodial Interrogation

The next step after an arrest is often police interrogation. **Custodial interrogation** happens when an officer interrogates a person who is under arrest or whose freedom to leave is restricted in some significant manner. (Figure 10.5 on page 394 lists landmark cases related to evidence gathering an interrogation) From 1936 until 1966, the Court made the following decisions on this issue:

- In *Brown v. Mississippi* (1936), the Court prohibited convictions that were obtained solely on confessions that police gained by using brutality and violence.[31]
- *Mallory v. United States* (1957), held that any confession obtained during an unnecessary delay in arraignment was inadmissible. A confession obtained during a lawful delay before arraignment was admissible.
- In *Malloy v. Hogan* (1964), Fifth Amendment protection against self-incrimination became applicable to the states.[32]
- In *Escobedo v. Illinois* (1964), the Court ruled that police must provide counsel to defendants in their custody if those defendants are being interrogated. This is in accordance with the Sixth Amendment requirement to provide counsel.
- In the landmark decision *Miranda v. Arizona* (1966), the Court greatly expanded a defendant's rights during interrogation.

custodial interrogation
When an officer interrogates a person who is under arrest or whose freedom to leave is restricted in some significant manner.

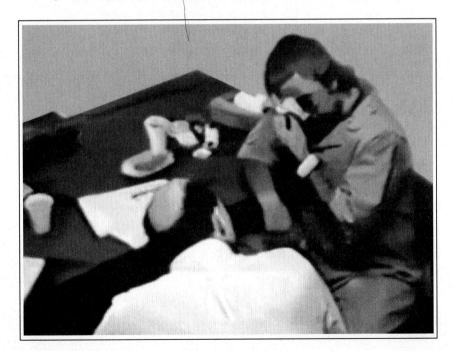

◀ **Custodial Interrogation** This video tape still of Richard Allen Davis (accused of the murder of 12-year-old Polly Klaas) shows him crying during an interview with Petaluma, California Sergeant Mike Meese. Interrogation procedures are strictly regulated.
Why do you think the courts worry about that aspect of the procedure?

Figure 10.5

Landmark Fourth and Fifth Amendment Cases Related to Law Enforcement

Fourth Amendment	Fifth Amendment

Fourth Amendment

"The right of the people to be secure in their persons, houses, papers, and effects, against unreasonable searches and seizures, shall not be violated, and no Warrants shall issue, but upon probable cause, supported by Oath or affirmation, and particularly describing the place to be searched, and the persons or things to be seized."

◆ *Boyd v. United States* (1886): This case widened the scope of the Fourth Amendment and the right to privacy. It stated that a warrantless search is "the invasion of [a citizen's] indefeasible right of personal security, personal liberty and private property."

◆ *Weeks v. United States* (1914): The U.S. Supreme Court found that evidence gathered in an illegal manner, without probable cause or without a search warrant, should be ruled inadmissible in court.

◆ *Olmstead v. United States* (1928): In this case, the Court ruled that a FBI wiretap was not a search and seizure within the meaning of the Fourth Amendment, and therefore did not require a search warrant.

◆ *Mapp v. Ohio* (1961): This case led to the creation of the *exclusionary rule*, which holds that criminal evidence that is seized in violation of defendant's constitutional privacy protection is inadmissible in court.

◆ *Katz v. United States* (1967): In this case the Court reversed its findings in *Olmstead* and found that unwarranted wiretapping violates a citizen's right to privacy.

◆ *Terry v. Ohio* (1968): The Court found that a stop and frisk performed by officers is legal if the officers observe suspicious behavior and have reason to believe that the suspect(s) may be armed and dangerous.

Fifth Amendment

"No person shall be held to answer for a capital, or otherwise infamous crime, unless on a presentment or indictment of a Grand Jury, except in cases arising in the land or naval forces, or in the Militia, when in actual service in time of War or public danger; nor shall any person be subject for the same offence to be twice put in jeopardy of life or limb; nor shall be compelled in any criminal case to be a witness against himself; nor be deprived of life, liberty, or property, without due process of law; nor shall private property be taken for public use without just compensation."

◆ *Malloy v. Hogan* (1964): This case found that the Fifth Amendment protection against self-incrimination is applicable to the state cases as well as federal ones.

◆ *Miranda v. Arizona* (1966): In this case the U.S. Supreme Court greatly expanded a defendant's rights during interrogation so that arresting officers must inform defendants of their rights immediately.

◆ *Williams v. Florida* (1970): The Court decided that a law requiring a defendant to provide witnesses to his or her alibi did not violate Fifth Amendment protections against self-incrimination.

◆ *Waller v. Florida* (1970): This case protects citizens against double jeopardy, and found that defendants can't be retried for a different crime related to one on which they've been acquitted with the same evidence.

◆ *Doyle v. Ohio* (1976): Defendants who take the stand and provide an alibi that they refused to provide to police or prosecutors (because of their right to remain silent) may not be convicted if the alibi they provided was sufficient to acquit them.

SOURCE: Leming, Robert S., "Teaching about the Fourth Amendment's Protection against Unreasonable Searches and Seizures," accessed online at http://www.ed.gov/databases/ERIC_Digests/ed363526.html on December 14, 2001; "Landmark Cases," accessed online at http://www.billofrightsinstitute.org/pdf/landmark-cases.pdf on December 14, 2001; and Cornell Legal Information Institute, "Historic Supreme Court Decisions: Fifth Amendment," accessed online at http://www2.law.cornell.edu/cgibin/foliocgi.exe/historic/query=[group+f_fifth+amendment:]/doc/{@1}/hit_headings/words=4/hits_only? on December 17, 2001.

The Miranda Warning

Today, any interrogation of a suspect must start with the Miranda warning. Without it, a confession will be ruled inadmissible and a case may be thrown out of court. The **Miranda warning** is a result of *Miranda v. Arizona*, in which the Court ruled that police must advise a suspect of his or her constitutional right to remain silent and request the assistance of counsel. As the Court stated,

> The person in custody must, prior to interrogation, be clearly informed that he has the right to remain silent, and that anything he says will be used against him in court; he must be clearly informed that he has the right to consult with a lawyer and to have the lawyer with him during interrogation, and that, if he is indigent, a lawyer will be appointed to represent him.[33]

Officers must first understand the concepts of interrogation and custody. When an officer approaches a person suspected of committing a crime, his or her intent is to interrogate the suspect. If the officer finds probable cause and does not want the person to leave his or her custody, the officer must give the Miranda warning. It is important to remember that Miranda warnings are required only if the suspect is being interrogated. Officers must ensure that the following statements are made to the suspect:

1. You have the right to remain silent.
2. Anything you say can and will be used against you in a court of law.
3. You have a right to talk with a lawyer and have a lawyer present with you while you are being questioned.
4. If you cannot afford to hire a lawyer, one will be appointed to represent you before any questioning if you wish.

Miranda warning A rule that police must advise a suspect of his or her constitutional right to remain silent and request the assistance of counsel; a result of *Miranda v. Arizona* (1966).

Police Procedure

Informant Exceptions to Miranda

When an undercover officer poses as an inmate to obtain a confession from another inmate, he or she need not give a Miranda warning. Miranda seeks to protect suspects from police coercion, and that coercive atmosphere is not present when an incarcerated person speaks freely to someone who is (1) believed to be a fellow inmate and (2) assumed to not be anyone having authority. In such circumstances, Miranda does not forbid mere strategic deception by taking advantage of a suspect's misplaced trust.

Critical Thinking Should other types of undercover officers be exempt from Miranda? Why or why not?

SOURCE: *Illinois v. Perkins*, 496 U.S. 292 (1990).

5. You can decide at any time to exercise these rights and not answer any questions or make any statements.

6. Do you understand each of these rights I have explained to you?

7. Having these rights in mind, do you wish to talk to us now?

If a defendant asks for a lawyer, the police are prohibited from any further interrogation until the lawyer is present.[34] If the suspect decides to talk with officers without having a lawyer present, the officers must ensure that the waiver is voluntary and the suspect is aware of the consequences of his waiver. When possible, officers may have the suspect sign a rights waiver form.

Since the *Miranda* decision, numerous appeals have made their way to the U.S. Supreme Court. In *Dickerson v. United States* (2000), it was challenged by a plaintiff who stated that a federal statute created by Congress in 1968 required only that a confession admitted into trial be given voluntarily. In a strongly worded decision, the Court ruled that *Miranda* and related court decisions since then "govern the admissibility of statements made during custodial interrogation in both state and federal courts." Therefore, Congress could not create a statute to overrule a decision of the U.S. Supreme Court.

10.4 Self Check

1. What is the Miranda warning?
2. What is custodial interrogation?

POLICING Online

Check your answers at
www.policing.glencoe.com

10.5 Identification and Surveillance

Identification procedures such as police lineups can violate a suspect's rights if not performed properly. (See Figure 10.6 on page 397) Surveillance procedures, such as those governing wiretaps and eavesdropping, are even more restricted. This is because they can be misused, thus creating serious infringements of innocent people's rights to privacy.

Identification Procedures

A key element of effective criminal investigations is the use of three types of pretrial identification:

- In a **lineup**, several persons appear before a victim or witness for the purpose of identification.
- In a **showup**, one suspect appears before a victim or witness for the purpose of identification.
- In a **photo lineup**, a victim or witness views several photographs of possible suspects for the purpose of identification.

lineup Having several persons appear before a victim or witness for the purpose of identification.

showup Having one suspect appear before a victim or witness for the purpose of identification.

photo lineup Having a victim or witness view several photographs of possible suspects for the purpose of identification.

Figure 10.6

Guidelines for Pretrial Identification Procedures

◆ Before conducting an identification procedure, officers should not tell a witness that they have a suspect in custody or that a suspect will be among the people or photographs the witness is about to view.

◆ After the procedure, they should not tell the witness whether the witness identified the "right" suspect.

◆ If two or more witnesses are to participate in an identification procedure, they should do so separately and should not be allowed to discuss their identifications with each other.

◆ There should be several persons in a lineup or several photos in a photo lineup, and the people should look as similar as possible (in appearance, dress, and the like) under the circumstances.

◆ There is no legally required minimum number of people or photos to constitute a proper lineup or photo lineup.

◆ If a second identification procedure is to be conducted, an officer should avoid a situation in which only one person appears in both procedures.

SOURCE: Robert Farb, *Arrest, Search, and Investigation*, 2d ed. (Chapel Hill: Institute of Government, University of North Carolina, 1992), 226.

Constitutional Guidelines The courts have scrutinized each of these techniques to ensure that they are conducted within constitutional guidelines. Officers who conduct lineups and other identification procedures must adhere to two constitutional provisions. First, they must conduct identification procedures but not violate the defendant's due process rights. In some cases, they must also provide the defendant with counsel during the identification procedure unless a waiver is obtained.[36]

One of the greatest concerns to the courts has been the suggestive nature of some lineups. In *Stovall v. Denno* (1967), the Court ruled that any lineup identification procedure that denies a suspect due process of law is unconstitutional. The Court also noted that the totality of the circumstances must be considered. In this case, a witness who had been hospitalized with a life-threatening injury could not go to the police station for a lineup. Police brought the key suspect to the hospital, and the victim identified him. The Court stated that the circumstances of this case made this approach necessary and that the police actions were feasible within the totality of circumstances.[37]

Right to Counsel In the matter of counsel at a lineup, the Court ruled in *Kirby v. Illinois* (1972) that a person at a lineup or showup is entitled to a lawyer if the procedure is held at or after the time that criminal proceedings have started.[38] If it is held before the beginning of criminal proceeding, a suspect is not entitled to a counsel. Counsel is not required at photographic lineups.

A defendant who wishes to waive the right to counsel at a lineup or showup may do so orally or in writing. Any waiver should include the following statements:

1. You are going to be placed in a lineup (or showup) so that a witness to a crime may attempt to identify the suspect.
2. Do you understand what a lineup or identification procedure is? (If not, explain it.)
3. You have the right to have an attorney represent you during this lineup (or showup) if you wish.
4. If you cannot afford to hire an attorney for this purpose, one will be appointed for you before the lineup (or showup) is conducted.
5. Do you understand the rights I have explained to you?
6. Do you wish to have an attorney represent you during the lineup?[39]

If the officer has any doubt about the right to counsel, the officer should resolve it by either providing counsel or obtaining a signed waiver from the suspect. A failure to do so can result in the identification being declared inadmissible.[40]

Avoiding Misidentification The possibility always exists that a lineup will result in a misidentification. In 1972, the Court identified five factors that need to be considered to detect misidentification. They are the opportunity of the witness to view the criminal at the time of the crime, the witness' degree of attention, the accuracy of the witness' prior description of the criminal, the level of certainty demonstrated by the witness at the confrontation, and the length of time between the crime and the confrontation.[41]

Figure 10.6 on page 397 lists some of the guidelines that need be followed when conducting an identification procedure.

Wiretaps and Eavesdropping

Today, numerous technologies move human communications around the world. From the cell phone to the Internet, the world has become smaller. With a smaller world have come problems of international fraud and terrorism. Police face new challenges as they attempt to monitor criminal activity and threats to American security, both at home and overseas. A key strategy in solving and prosecuting crimes and acts of terrorism has been the use of wiretaps and electronic eavesdropping.

wiretapping Secretly listening to telephone conversations for investigative purposes.

electronic eavesdropping Surveillance over computers and other electronic devices.

Legal Restrictions on Surveillance The modern use of **wiretapping**, which is secretly listening to telephone conversations for investigative purposes, and **electronic eavesdropping**, which is surveillance over computers and other

◀ **Listening In** Developments in electronic transmission of information and the use of encryption have reopened the debate on privacy and police surveillance.
What do you think is a legitimate reason for electronic surveillance?

electronic devices, was established with *Lee v. Florida* (1968). In *Lee*, the federal government decided that evidence obtained from a telephone wiretap without a warrant was inadmissible.[42] Recording devices concealed on an officer's or informant's body carry similar restrictions. In *Berger v. New York* (1967), the Court approved the state use of wiretaps and bugs where probable cause had been established and a search warrant obtained.[43]

At the same time as *Berger*, the Court also ruled that a public telephone booth is a constitutionally protected area. Therefore, any electronic eavesdropping at a phone booth requires probable cause and a search warrant.[44] This was clarified in *United States v. White* (1981), in which the Court ruled that a warrant is not necessary if one of the parties in a communication gives consent.[45] In *United States v. Karo* (1984), which affected police investigative powers in drug cases, the Court decided that placing a location beeper in a barrel of ether (used in processing cocaine) to track the ether to the manufacturer's home required a search warrant.[46]

When conducting electronic eavesdropping, how much of the conversation does an officer record? In *United States v. Scott* (1978), the Court established the minimization requirement, which stated that the recording of communications must be restricted to that related to criminal activity. When it becomes obvious that a conversation shows no sign of relating to criminal activity, officers must cease their monitoring.[47]

The Electronic Communications Privacy Act of 1986 In 1986, Congress passed the Electronic Communications Privacy Act (ECPA), which resulted in new guidelines and requirements for police in using wiretaps. The ECPA provides guidelines on gathering records, including stored records, in three areas of electronic communications:

1. *Wiretaps and bugs* Currently, law enforcement is required to obtain court orders to eavesdrop on ongoing electronic communications.
2. *Pen registers* Devices that record numbers dialed from a telephone. The use of pen registers does not require a court order.
3. *Tracing devices* To identify the origin of a telephone call.

Stored communications can include computer backup files, faxes, and archives. Electronic information stored less than 180 days requires a search warrant, but information stored more than 180 days requires only a court order showing why police need the information.[48]

More recently, the FBI unveiled its brand new software program, *Carnivore*, which is designed specifically to conduct electronic surveillance of e-mail and Internet communications at Internet Service Providers (ISP) facilities following a court order.

Communications Assistance for Law Enforcement Act (CALEA) With advances in telecommunications technology and the increased use of this technology in criminal endeavors, the Communications Assistance for Law Enforcement Act (CALEA) of 1994 became necessary, allowing police and telecommunication companies to work together so that police can use new telecommunication technologies in effective wiretapping. In the area of wireless communications, such as cell phones, CALEA is allowing law enforcement to be able to legally track the location of any wireless communications user.[49] This has led to criticism that American citizens will eventually be under continuous surveillance, a harbinger of George Orwell's "Big Brother" scenario. However, in light of the September 2001 terrorist attacks on New York and Washington, D.C., further restriction of law enforcement access and monitoring of electronic communications may become a moot point.

10.5 Self Check

1. In what surveillance situations are warrants needed?
2. How does CALEA help law enforcement use surveillance procedures?

POLICING *Online*

Check your answers at
www.policing.glencoe.com

10.6 Police Liability

In recent years, many police actions have resulted in civil lawsuits against police departments, and some have resulted in criminal charges. In some cases, police have been charged with criminal offenses. More and more departments are placing increased emphasis on strategies to reduce liability to the department. Still, the potential for civil suits exists.

Civil Liability

Today, police departments cannot escape **civil liability**, which is liability for civil action that is taken by private citizens against police misdeeds. Civil action is any action brought to enforce, redress, or protect private rights. The number of civil suits against police has been increasing since the 1970s. In 1976, there were 13,400 lawsuits filed against police, but current estimates place the number of lawsuits at more than 30,000 a year. Between 1978 and 1995, the average award in federal police lawsuits was over $134,000, but in recent years departments have sought out-of-court settlements instead.[51] Figure 10.7 on page 402 shows the cost of police lawsuits in major American cities.

Police win about 92 percent of all civil suits filed, but the legal costs can be severe. Costs can include liability insurance, litigation expenses, out-of-court settlements, and punitive damages. Departments now carry expensive liability insurance, but insurance costs can become too expensive if the department faces several expensive lawsuits. Sometimes insurance companies may refuse to insure a department.[52]

Damage to public relations can also be serious. When police departments face frequent lawsuits, their integrity is questioned and their ability to achieve effective policing, especially community policing, is jeopardized. As Sir Robert Peel made clear in his principles of policing, the focus of police is to build collaboration and respect, not confrontation and disrespect. To provide high-quality services within ethical standards, police must develop strategies to prevent and reduce their liability.

To compound this problem, police defendants are rarely disciplined. Although lawsuits against police totaled nearly $92 million between 1986 and 1991, only 8 of the 185 officers involved in these lawsuits were disciplined, 17 were promoted, and the remaining 160 had no action taken against them.[53]

civil liability In policing, liability for civil action that is taken by private citizens against police misdeeds.

Figure 10.7

The Cost of Police Civil Lawsuits in Major U.S. Cities

CITY	YEARS	PAYMENT	AVERAGE PER YEAR
New York	1994–1996	$70 million	$23.3 million
Los Angeles	1991–1996	$79.2 million	$13.2 million
Detroit	1987–1994	$72 million	$9 million
Philadelphia	1993–1996	$32.6 million	$8.1 million
Washington, D.C.	1993–1995	$4 million	$1.3 million
Atlanta	1994–1996	$1 million	$333,333
New Orleans	1994–1996	$1 million	$333,333
Indianapolis	1994–1996	$750,000	$250,000

SOURCE: Human Rights Watch, *Civil Remedies*, retrieved September 10, 2001, from the World Wide Web: http://www.hrw.org/reports98/police/uspo30.htm.

Protection under Section 1983

Title 42 of the United States Code Section 1983 An act passed by Congress in 1871 to ensure that the civil rights of men and women of all races were protected.

Numerous civil suits are being filed under **Title 42 of the United States Code Section 1983**, an act passed by Congress in 1871 to ensure that the civil rights of men and women of all races were protected. It states the following:

> Every person, who under color of any statute, ordinance, regulation, custom, or usage, of any State or territory, subjects, or causes to be subjected, any citizen of the United States or other persons within the jurisdiction thereof to the deprivation of any right, privileges, or immunities secured by the Constitution and laws, shall be liable to the party injured in an action at law, suit in equity, or other proper proceeding for redress.

Despite this, police departments were not liable for lawsuits for over a century because of the concept of sovereign immunity. Under sovereign immunity, citizens could not bring lawsuits against federal, state, or municipal government agencies, although individual officers could be sued. This precedent changed in 1978, when the Court stated in *Monell v. New York Department of Social Services* that municipalities can be sued under Section 1983 when their employees have committed constitutional violations toward citizens.[54]

In police-related cases, municipalities can be sued if an officer's misdeeds followed official departmental policy or organizational custom. Suppose that Asian American citizens complain that local police officers customarily use prejudicial language when stopping them in their cars. If it can be shown that this follows departmental policy or organizational custom, they can file suit under Section 1983.

Section 1983 has been become a major vehicle for suing the police. When confronted with a Section 1983 suit, police departments have four possible defenses:

1. **Absolute immunity** is immunity from civil liability. Most often reserved for judges, it also applies to police officers who commit perjury or offer incorrect information at a criminal trial. Such an officer cannot be sued because the courts believe that a threat of civil liability for police testimony may lessen officer cooperation and openness.

2. **Qualified immunity** is a lesser form of immunity. It applies to officers performing discretionary duties, which require deliberation and judgment on the part of the officer. Although qualified immunity is often restricted to policy decisions by administrators, it can also apply to an officer's discretion to arrest or not arrest.

3. **Probable cause** applies to false arrest or unlawful searches. If an officer can show that probable cause was present at the time of the arrest or search, he or she is immune from liability.

4. **Good faith** applies to officers who can demonstrate that they could not have known that a particular police action was either unconstitutional or unlawful. For example, an officer who executes a search warrant that is later declared invalid has a defense of good faith.[55]

To establish a good faith defense, the courts need to see one of four justifications:

- The officer's actions were based on departmental policy and regulations.
- The officer was acting pursuant to a law that was valid at the time.
- The officer was acting on supervisor orders that he or she believed to be legal.
- The officer was acting on advice of legal counsel that he or she felt was valid.[56]

Common Exposures to Liability

Individual officers must constantly attempt to minimize civil liability to their departments. High liability areas include everything from the negligent operation of police emergency vehicles to the use of deadly force. Some of the more common areas that officers are at risk for civil liability are false arrest, use of excessive force, and hot pursuit. (See Figure 10.8 for a liability assessment guide.)

False Arrest To prove false arrest against a police officer, plaintiffs must show all of the following elements:

1. The police willfully detained them.
2. Their detention was against their will.
3. The detention was made without authority of law.[57]

Often a false arrest is the result of a lack of probable cause, which officers can avoid by first obtaining an arrest warrant. However, if an officer provides a judicial officer with false information in obtaining the warrant, then he or she is still liable for false arrest.

Use of Excessive Force Cases of police use of force can be divided into those involving lethal force and those involving nonlethal force. Lethal force is any type of force that officers use to cause death or serious injury. Nonlethal force is any force that does not result in death or serious injury. Depending on the circumstances, both categories may or may not be categorized as excessive.

The federal standards for the use of lethal force were established in *Tennessee v. Garner* (1985). In *Garner*, the Supreme Court stated that two important criteria must be met for officers to legally exercise lethal force:

1. Where the officer has probable cause to believe that the suspect poses a threat of serious physical harm, either to the officer or to others
2. If the suspect threatens the officer with a weapon, or there is probable cause to believe that he or she has committed a crime involving the infliction or threatened infliction of serious physical harm[59]

In the matter of nonlethal force, the Court noted that four factors must be considered. An officer must consider "the severity of the crime at issue, whether the suspect poses an immediate threat to the safety of the officers or others, and whether he is actively resisting arrest or attempting to evade arrest by flight."[60]

Hot Pursuit Each year, hundreds of accidents result from the practice of pursuing criminal suspects in police vehicles, often at high speeds. In determining whether an officer is negligent in a hot pursuit accident, the courts do not focus on the officer's decision to pursue but rather on whether his or her operation of the vehicle was careful and reasonable or negligent. State courts have identified four zones of negligence. The more factors that a court finds, the more likely that unreasonable behavior will be established.

FYI

The Price of Brutality

New York City and its police union paid brutality victim Abner Louima $8.75 million four years after he was beaten and sodomized while in police custody. One officer was convicted of assaulting and sodomizing Louima with a broken broomstick in a station house bathroom. Three other cops were tried for attempting to cover it up; Louima claimed the police union aided in that effort. The settlement is the largest the city has ever paid in a brutality claim and appears to be the first in which a police union was involved.

SOURCE: Kit R. Roane, "Brutality's Hefty Price," *U.S. News & World Report,* 23 July 2001, 28.

CAREER FOCUS

Legal Counsel

Job Description

I am the Assistant Executive Director for AELE (Americans for Effective Law Enforcement) a Chicago-based national nonprofit legal training organization. I am also involved with the IACP (International Association of Chiefs of Police) as the Chair of the Legal Officers Section. The Section writes a column in *Police Chief* magazine every month, and I participate in training, reviewing model policies and statutes, arranging workshops, and doing a lot of consulting and networking at the national level.

Carl Milazzo, Police Legal Counsel

AELE is a resource center for police and law enforcement that publishes a monthly report and provides seminars on civil liability, internal affairs, and employment law. What I do now is a fraction of what I did as a police attorney and legal advisor in Fayetteville, North Carolina. I did in-service training for officers, and I took a lot of time to make sure our department knew the law well. We helped officers learn how to write and review search warrants or how to obtain evidence.

Administratively, legal counsels review all high-risk policies such as policy on pursuit, use of force, use of restraint. Many policies vary greatly because the state laws vary, and it is very important for departments to evaluate their rules and regulations and make sure that they are in line with federal and state laws.

I worked on internal investigations and internal discipline. Sometimes you get criticized on both ends—the community and officers—but it is a necessary function of police management.

Education

I majored in Law Enforcement Administration went to law school, and earned a Juris Doctor. Right after that I joined the U.S. Army and became a legal advisor for various units at Fort Bragg, North Carolina. I also graduated from the FBI National Academy.

Follow-Up What seems to be the most difficult aspects of this profession? Why?

Figure 10.8

Police Liability Assessment Guide

This document is a summary of many law enforcement practices and procedures that are necessary to reduce a municipal officer's exposure to liability.

1. All officers and reserve officers should be fully trained and certified by the State before they go on the street.

2. Reducing the risk of police civil liability should be a priority for all police departments in America.

3. It is flawed thinking to operate under the assumption that policing is by its very nature a high-liability occupation and there is little that can be done. Police departments can use high standards to reduce liability.

4. All officers should undergo annual re-qualifications in critical tasks and in their competency with weapons.

5. All instructors in critical tasks should be fully trained, certified and have sufficient qualifications to instruct.

6. All trainers and instructors should receive annual or recent upgrading of their training.

7. Records of all training and qualifications should be maintained.

8. Attendance records should be maintained for all training activities.

9. Police departments should have policies or procedures on critical tasks, such as the use of force, emergency driving, pursuit driving, off-duty employment, carrying off-duty weapons, use of force reports and review process, domestic violence, and dealing with infections diseases.

10. There should be policies, procedures, and training for special units, such as SWAT, TAC, hostage rescue, K-9s, and bomb squads.

11. Basic training for officers should exceed the state minimum.

12. All officers should have annual requirements for in-service training.

13. All agencies should have a Field Training Officer (FTO) program.

14. All agencies should require probationary periods for young officers, with a written policy and procedures.

15. All agencies should have psychological evaluations for recruits.

16. All agencies should have psychological services for all officers.

17. All officers should have adequate basic and annual legal training.

18. All municipal attorneys should periodically review existing and new court decisions concerning all police liability issues.

19. All officers should be made aware of recent court decisions and new statues.

20. All major policies and procedures on key issues should be reviewed and approved by legal counsel familiar with police operations for your city.

21. All officers should have complete copies of all policies and procedures.

22. All supervisors should have adequate pre- and post-promotional supervisory training and some form of supervisory in-service training on a regular basis.

23. All officers should be knowledgeable of the policies and practices of their department.

24. All supervisors should examine these policies in the light of court decisions, new research, and new thinking in the police profession.

25. All supervisors should develop comprehensive data on previous and current lawsuits, judgments, complaints, in order to recognize their causes.

26. A complaint investigation procedure should be incorporated and strict follow-up should be performed.

SOURCE: Public Risk Management Association, *Police Liability Assessment Guide*, retrieved September 6, 2001, from the Web: http://www.primacentral.org/resorce/pfile/docs/DR10891.html.

Reducing the Risk of Police Liability

It is inevitable that police will be sued, and police officers and departments cannot control the flow of civil lawsuits. Furthermore, citizens in a democratic society should have the right to sue government agencies that fail to protect and serve the people. The problem is that the economical and social costs associated with police civil liability can create additional taxpayer burdens such as the following:

- Higher liability insurance costs
- Increased use of limited city and county legal resources

The issue is not whether civil liability can be eliminated but how the risk of it can be reduced. Police departments can reduce civil liability by following a number of steps:

1. Acting within their official scope of authority
2. Knowing the laws of police liability
3. Keeping abreast of the changing laws of liability
4. Reading and following departmental rules and regulations
5. Keeping and maintaining adequate records and documentation on police operations
6. Seeking the assistance of the county attorney or other counsel on liability matters
7. Implementing and providing continuing training for police liability
8. Selecting officers with higher education and recruiting officers who adhere to and respect the rule of law
9. Maintaining good community relations and advising citizens of drastic changes in police policy or operations

To help reduce police liability, many administrators are taking proactive steps to enforce these principles. Figure 10.8 on page 406 depicts one department's guidelines to help officers understand how to avoid such problems.

10.6 Self Check

1. How can officers protect themselves and their departments from liability?
2. Name three common exposures to liability.

POLICING *Online*
Check your answers at
www.policing.glencoe.com

Chapter 10

Police and the Law

1. Explain how the U.S. Constitution, Bill of Rights, and U.S. Supreme Court relate to law enforcement.

The U.S. Constitution was created to ensure that America had a strong government but did not act in a capricious or cruel manner toward its citizens. It consists of three main articles that outline the responsibilities of the three branches of government: legislative, executive, and judicial. The Bill of Rights originally included ten amendments to the Constitution that clarified individual rights for Americans. The ones that are most applicable to policing are the First, Fourth, Fifth, Sixth, Eighth, and Fourteenth Amendments. The U.S. Supreme Court is the final interpreter of the Constitution.

2. Understand the various types of law.

There are three types of law in the United States: criminal law, civil law, and administrative law. Criminal law involves criminal offenses and their punishment, which could result in loss of liberty or life. Civil law involves personal wrongs that are noncriminal and may be compensated with financial damages. Administrative law deals with guidelines and regulations for business, industry, and government.

3. Distinguish between the exclusionary rule and good faith exception.

The exclusionary rule states that evidence obtained in an unlawful manner is inadmissible in both federal and state courts. An extension of the exclusionary rule is the fruit of the poisonous tree doctrine, which states that any evidence obtained directly or indirectly *as a result of* evidence obtained in an illegal search is inadmissible. The good faith exception holds that evidence obtained with a warrant that is later determined to be invalid is not automatically inadmissible. If examination reveals that the warrant was obtained in good faith with no intent to circumvent the requirements of the Fourth Amendment, the evidence remains admissible.

4. See the differences in mere suspicion, reasonable suspicion, and probable cause.

Mere suspicion is an officer's gut feeling that something is wrong and should be investigated. At this stage, there is no hard evidence and the officer cannot do more than engage in voluntary conversation. Reasonable suspicion is the amount of knowledge needed to make an ordinary and cautious person believe that criminal activity is occurring. Probable cause is the requirement for making an arrest, obtaining a search warrant, and conducting a warrantless search. Exercising the powers of arrest, search, and seizure occurs when the officer is in the field, and the escalation from mere suspicion to reasonable suspicion to probable cause can happen in seconds.

5. Explain the requirements for a legal stop and frisk, search and seizure, and arrest.

Reasonable suspicion is needed for making a stop and frisk and was clarified in *Terry v. Ohio*. Searches may be conducted with or without a warrant, but in either case, probable cause is required. For example, searches incident to an arrest, plain view searches, or certain emergency situations do not require a warrant, but probable cause must be present. An arrest may occur with or without a warrant. To make an arrest without a warrant, an officer must have probable cause that the suspect has committed a felony or a misdemeanor. Without probable cause, the suspect will not be apprehended unless he or she damages property or causes physical injury to himself or herself or others.

6. Understand the concept of custodial interrogation.

When officers are conducting an interrogation and the suspect is not free to leave, this is considered by the Court to be a custodial interrogation, and the officer must advise the suspect of his or her Miranda rights. These rights include the following:

1. The right to remain silent
2. Anything the defendant says can and will be used against him or her in a court of law
3. The right to talk with a lawyer and have him or her present with the defendant being questioned
4. The right to appointed counsel if the defendant cannot afford one
5. The right of the defendant to stop answering questions at any time

The officer must also ask the defendant if he or she understands each of the rights explained and wants to talk to the officer. In certain situations, such as when an officer is working undercover or when public safety is at stake, officers do not need to issue the Miranda warning.

7. Comprehend the legal principles that apply to identification procedures.

A lineup consists of having the victim or witnesses view a group of individuals (suspect included) in an effort to identify the perpetrator. A showup is having one suspect appear before a victim or witness. Counsel is required if the lineup or showup is held after the beginning of criminal proceedings against the suspect. A photo lineup consists of showing a victim or witness a series of photos with the suspect included. Photo lineups do not require the presence of counsel.

8. Explain how civil liability applies to policing.

In recent years, police actions have come under increased scrutiny. Many civil lawsuits against the police have resulted in settlements in excess of one million dollars. The cost in economic and social terms is significant. There are a number of high liability areas, but some of the more common ones are false arrest, use of excessive force, and hot pursuit. Although police departments will never totally remove the risk of liability, they can take steps to reduce the risk. Police departments need to constantly assess high liability areas. Police departments that display a commitment to high standards of performance within a framework of high-quality training and professionalism can reduce the risk of liability within their departments.

Key Terms

Bill of Rights (p. 374)
U.S. Supreme Court (p. 376)
writ of certiorari (p. 376)
criminal law (p. 377)
civil law (p. 377)
administrative law (p. 377)
precedent (p. 377)
tort (p. 378)
exclusionary rule (p. 380)
good faith exception (p. 381)
mere suspicion (p. 382
reasonable suspicion (p. 382)
stop and frisk (p. 382)
probable cause (p. 382)
search (p. 383)

seizure (p. 384)
search warrant (p. 385)
plain view doctrine (p. 388)
curtilage (p. 390)
arrest (p. 391)
custodial interrogation (p. 393)
Miranda warning (p. 395)
lineup (p. 396)
showup (p. 396)
photo lineup (p. 396)
wiretapping (p. 398)
electronic eavesdropping (p. 398)
civil liability (p. 401)
Title 42 of the United States Code Section 1983
(p. 402)

Questions for Review

1. What is the role of law enforcement within the framework of the law?

2. What are the protections provided by the First, Fourth, Fifth, Sixth, Eighth, and Fourteenth Amendments?

3. Explain the differences between statutory law and case law, as well as between substantive law and procedural law.

4. How are mere suspicion, reasonable suspicion, and probable cause related?

5. What are the differences between searching a house, car, and open field?

6. What is the Miranda warning, and what are the exceptions to the Miranda rule?

7. What are some guidelines officers should follow when preparing a lineup?

8. What is the difference between wiretapping and electronic eavesdropping?

9. Explain Title 42 U.S. Code Section 1983.

10. What are some of the common areas of risk for police civil liability?

Experiential Activities

11. Decision to Stop and Frisk
Your instructor will invite police officers with different levels of experience to talk to your class. Ask them how they make decisions regarding reasonable suspicion and performing stop and frisks.

a. Do they use the same or different reasoning in conducting stop and frisks?
b. If their reasoning is different, explain.
c. How do they report their decision to stop and frisk at the end of their shift?

12. Debating Miranda

This exercise can be performed in pairs or in groups of four or six. Divide each group into two, and then debate against each other to determine whether the Miranda warning is valid. Does its guarantee of constitutional rights work, and does it unnecessarily hamper police efforts? Debate your side for five minutes, then switch sides and debate the other side for another five minutes.

    a. Do you feel that the Miranda warning is an effective way to safeguard constitutional rights? Why or why not?

    b. Does it hamper police efforts in any way? Why or why not?

    c. If you find flaws in the Miranda warning, how could it be improved?

13. Wiretapping

Go to your library or search the Internet and find a recent case on wiretapping. Be sure to learn about the case, why the wiretapping was performed, if it was effective, and if it was admissible as evidence in a criminal trial.

    a. How was wiretapping used in this case?

    b. Explain why or why not the evidence was considered admissible.

    c. Do you think evidence could have collected otherwise?.

14. Electronic Eavesdropping

Find a recent case on electronic eavesdropping. This can include e-mail accounts that are secretly monitored. Be sure to learn about the case, why the eavesdropping was performed, what legal hurdles law enforcement faced to perform the eavesdropping, if it was effective, and if it was admissible as evidence in a criminal trial.

    a. What circumstances led law enforcement to feel that electronic eavesdropping was a good approach?

    b. Was the evidence admissible? Why or why not?

    c. What issues have arisen with electronic eavesdropping that are not issues in wiretapping?

Web Patrol

15. Miranda Warning

Learn more about the case behind the Miranda warning, *Miranda v. Arizona.* Information can be found online by clicking on the link at **www.policing.glencoe.com**.

What element of this case surprised you the most, and why?

16. Effective Law Enforcement

Visit the Americans for Effective Law Enforcement Web site by clicking on the link at **www.policing.glencoe.com** for case summaries on current litigation issues.

What seem to be the recurring issues in civil cases against police?

17. Search and Seizure

Read "Effective Search and Seizure," which can be viewed online by clicking on the link at **www.policing.glencoe.com**.

Which legal issue is often at the core of search and seizure, and why?

Critical Thinking Exercises

18. Responding to a Burglary Call

Two police officers are on patrol when they receive a radio call regarding a burglary. The officers respond and meet with the complainant, who says that two males tried to kick in his front door, and that one of them—a bald male wearing a gray sweat suit—ran east down the street. The officers drive down the street and soon spot a bald male wearing a gray sweat suit and carrying a blue gym bag. He is running west toward the scene of the crime. He makes no attempt to flee. Without questioning him, the officers pat him down and then search his opaque, zippered gym bag. Inside the bag they discover a loaded .32 revolver.

   a. Was the pistol legally seized? Why or why not?

   b. What should the officers do next?

19. Negligent Conduct

You are an officer driving through snowy and icy conditions in February. You are used to driving in such conditions and know that the patrol cars have good snow tires. You attempt to pull over someone who runs a red light in an area with no pedestrian traffic, but the driver speeds up. When you try to chase the car, your car spins out of control and hits a car parked on the sidewalk. The other car gets away because you did not have time to get the license plate number.

   a. Explain which factors contribute to negligence, and which do not.

   b. Explain why or why not this is negligent police conduct.

20. Probable Cause and Wiretapping

You are an investigator who would like to perform a wiretap on a suspected group of terrorists. It appears that the group is responsible for several local bombings, but the snag is that they seem to do their meeting and planning at a local religious center. You are worried that wiretapping any type of religious structure will not be considered acceptable by the judge, however you feel you have established probable cause.

   a. Should you pursue this wiretapping or not? Why?

   b. Suppose that you do request to wiretap this institution. What will you say to the judge to justify your position?

Endnotes

1. Saul Padover, *The Living Constitution* (New York: Mentor Books, 1968), 15–16.
2. Victor Kappeler, *Critical Issues in Police Civil Liability*, 2d ed. (Prospect Heights, IL: Waveland, 1997), 19–27.
3. *Elkins v. United States*, 364 U.S. 206 (1960).
4. *Mapp v. Ohio*, 367 U.S. 643 (1961).
5. John Ferdico, *Criminal Procedure for the Criminal Justice Professional*, 7th ed. (St. Paul, MN: PUBLISHER, 1999), 81.
6. Ibid.
7. *United States v. Leon*, 104 S.Ct. 3405 (1984).
8. Henry Wrobleski and Karen Hess, *Introduction to Law Enforcement and Criminal Justice*, 6th ed. (Belmont, CA: Wadsworth-Thomson Learning, 2000), 326–27.
9. Patrick Fagan, "Effective Search and Seizure," retrieved October 4, 2001, from the World Wide Web: http://www.fsu.edu/~crimdo/fagan.html.
10. *Chimel v. California*, 395 U.S. 752 (1969).
11. Fredico, *Criminal Procedure*, 176–77.
12. Ibid., 358–59.
13. Ibid., 359-64.
14. *Minnesota v. Dickerson*, 508 U.S. 366 (1993).
15. *Hester v. United States*, 265 U.S. 57 (1924).
16. *Nix v. Williams*, 467 U.S. 431 (1984).
17. *Carroll v. United States*, 267 U.S. 132 (1925).
18. *Chambers v. Maroney*, 399 U.S. 42 (1970).
19. *Coolidge v. New Hampshire*, 403 U.S. 443 (1971).
20. *New York v. Belton*, 453 U.S. 454 (1981).
21. *United States v. Ross*, 456 U.S. 798 (1982).
22. *United States v. Millan*, 56 CrL 1057, 9th Cir. (1994).
23. *Michigan Dept. of State Police v. Sitz*, 496 U.S. 444 (1990).
24. *Maryland v. Wilson*, 117 S.Ct. 882 (1997).
25. *United States v. Van Dyke*, 643 F2d 992, 4th Cir. (1980); see also, Fredico, *Criminal Procedure*, 411.
26. *United States v. Swepston*, 987 F.2d 1510, 10th Cir. (1993); Oliver v. U.S., 466 U.S. 170 (1984).
27. *California v. Greenwood*, 486 U.S. 35 (1988).
28. North Carolina Statute, § 15A-304.
29. North Carolina Statute, § 15A-401.
30. *Payton v. New York*, 445 U.S. 573 (1980).
31. *Brown v. State of Mississippi*, 297 U.S. 278 (1936).
32. *Malloy v. Hogan*, 378 U.S. 1 (1964).
33. *Miranda v. Arizona*, 384 U.S. 436 (1966).
34. *Minnick v. Mississippi*, 498 U.S. 146 (1990).
35. *Dickerson v. United States*, 000 U.S. 99-5525 (2000), 2.
36. Robert Farb, *Arrest, Search, and Investigation*, 2d ed. (Chapel Hill: Institute of Government, University of North Carolina, 1992), 225.
37. *Stovall v. Denno*, 388 U.S. 293 (1967).
38. *Kirby v. Illinois*, 406 U.S. 682 (1972).
39. Farb, *Arrest, Search, and Investigation*, 227.
40. Ibid., 227.
41. *Neil v. Biggers*, 409 U.S. 188 (1972).
42. *Lee v. Florida*, 392 U.S. 378 (1968).
43. *Berger v. New York*, 388 U.S. 41 (1967).
44. *Katz v. United States*, 386 U.S. 954 (1967).
45. *United States v. White*, 401 U.S. 745 (1971).
46. *United States v. Karo*, 468 U.S. 705 (1984).
47. *U.S. v. Scott*, 436 U.S. 128 (1978).
48. Electronic Communication Privacy Act of 1986.
49. CALEA Implementation Section Federal Bureau of Investigation, *Communications Assistance for Law Enforcement Act (CALEA)*, retrieved September 11, 2001, from World Wide Web: http://www.cybercrime.gov/usamay2001_4.htm.
50. Henry Campbell Black, *Black's Law Dictionary*, 6th ed. (St. Paul, MN: West, 1991), 167.
51. Victor Kappeler, S. Kappeler, and Rolando del Carmen, "A Content Analysis of Police Liability Cases: Decisions of the Federal District Courts, 1978-1990," *Journal of Criminal Justice* 21, no. 4 (1993): 325-37; Rolando del Carmen, *Criminal Procedure for Law Enforcement Personnel*, 3d ed. (Monterey, CA: Brooks and Cole, 1995).
52. I. Silver, *Police Civil Liability* (New York: Matthew Bender, 1996); Kappeler et al., "A Content Analysis," 325-37; both cited in Victor Kappeler, *Critical Issues in Police Civil Liability*, 2d ed. (Prospect Heights, IL: Waveland, 1997), 4, 8.
53. Ibid.
54. *Monell v. New York City Dept. of Social Services*, 436 U.S. 658 (1978).
55. Kappeler, *Critical Issues*, 414; Larry Gaines, Victor Kappeler, and Joseph Vaughn, *Policing America*, 3d ed. (Cincinnati, OH: Anderson, 1999), 413.
56. del Carmen, *Criminal Procedure*.
57. Kappeler, *Critical Issues*, 22.
58. Ibid., 22-23.
59. *Tennessee v. Garner*, 471 U.S. 1 (1985).
60. *Graham v. Connor*, 490 U.S. 386 (1989).
61. Gaines et al., *Policing America*, 415.

Part 4

Questions for Review

1. Define professionalism and explain how the concept applies to policing.
2. What is integrity?
3. Why does scientific management apply to policing?
4. Who was August Vellmer and what did he contribute to the field of law enforcement?
5. Which parts of the body does stress affect?
6. How can police corruption be prevented?
7. Write out the basic text of the Miranda Warning.
8. Name the three stages of the body's reaction to stressor.
9. What is discretion?
10. Should police officers be familiar with the exclusionary rule? Why or why not?
11. What is probable cause?
12. What is eustress?
13. Explain the importance of the Code of Ethics.
14. Name three types of pretrial identification procedures.
15. Why is the reading of the Miranda Warning required before an interrogation?

Patrol: The Backbone of Policing

CHAPTER OBJECTIVES

**AFTER COMPLETING THIS CHAPTER,
YOU WILL BE ABLE TO:**

1. Identify the basics of traditional patrol.

2. Understand which options are available for concentration on special crime problems.

3. Explain police methods for prioritizing service delivery.

4. Learn about the value of foot patrol.

5. Describe the problem-solving approach to policing.

6. Learn the principles of community policing.

◀ Female officer on horse patrol in Venice Beach, California.

11.1 Traditional Patrol

Most police services are delivered by uniformed police officers who are readily identifiable as government agents charged with protecting the public. To the members of the general public, officers who respond to their calls for service may all appear to practice identical service delivery methods, particularly since all that citizens see is a uniformed officer standing before them after their calls for services have been dispatched. What citizens may not recognize is that a police agency's patrol operations have a substantial influence over crime prevention, perpetrator apprehension, and officers' response time. There are actually many different approaches to patrol, and some work better than others.

The following discussion of service delivery will show its evolution from traditional random routine patrol to contemporary community policing.

Understanding Patrol

patrol To walk or drive through an area to ensure public order.

The word **patrol**, which means to walk or drive through an area to ensure public order, is believed to be derived from the French word *patrouiller*, which originally meant "to walk or paddle in mud or dirty water." This definition captures the essence of police patrol, which can be tiring, difficult, and performed in dirty or unsafe conditions. Patrolling is traceable to Robert Peel's London police. The mission of Peel's bobbies was to walk the streets of London, assist citizens, and serve as deterrents to criminals. This early form of random patrol was adopted in the United States. When police agencies introduced the automobile, they adopted them for patrolling. Automobiles not only afforded much greater mobility but also proved useful in transporting arrestees, inmates, and evidence.[1]

The patrol function, commonly referred to as the backbone of policing, is the primary framework for agency operations. Without patrol, there would be no police because patrol officers are the key individuals in providing police services. Either a dispatcher or citizen begins the process of service delivery by alerting the patrol officer, or a patrol officer can initiate service delivery on his or her own if he or she notices something suspicious. In extreme situations, such as when a patrol officer comes upon a violent crime in progress, the officer can be the originator of law enforcement activity as well as the adjudicative agent.

The following sections examine two of the principal duties performed by a patrol officer: preventive patrol and service activities. The third key duty, the preliminary investigation, will be discussed with other types of investigations in the next chapter.

Preventive Patrol

Preventive patrol has a twofold meaning: It deters crime through a visible police presence while enabling police to detect potential criminal incidents. Deterrence of crime by a visible police presence was one of Robert Peel's requirements for effective police work. Peel required officers to maintain a visible presence in the community by continuously patrolling fixed beats.

One pioneer in preventive patrol was O. W. Wilson, former chief of police in Berkeley and Chicago and a strong believer in the philosophy of August Vollmer. Wilson expanded the concept of preventive patrol to create an impression of **omnipresence**, in which police strategized their patrol so that it appeared as if they were "always there." In such circumstances, criminals simply could not operate because they would fear getting caught. Wilson also pioneered methods by which the patrol unit's focus on crimes, the amount of time spent on different tasks, and the nature of the patrol functions were allocated in the most effective way. For example, these methods examined the ways in which foot patrol, automobile patrol, canine units, or accident investigation units could be used most wisely.

All successful patrol officers develop special observational skills, enabling them to detect potential criminal incidents in the course of performing patrol work. Because they are continually exposed to crimes and criminals, an intelligent officer can cultivate these skills, drawing on his or her own experience to make deductions and detect crimes. In the course of preventive patrol, officers constantly look for telltale signs that could lead to detection of a potential crime or someone who has already committed a crime. At any given time, patrol officers may have around a half-dozen wanted persons descriptions or mug shots in their heads as they make their rounds.

One drawback does occur when officers are less experienced and able in their observational skills: They may engage in profiling. Profiling, which is discussed throughout this text, is the unethical use of stereotyping to assume that a person's looks or behavior make him or her suspicious. This commonly occurs against racial minorities, although it can happen against any group that an individual officer finds suspicious, such as juveniles, women, or those of lower economic status. Since officers who commit profiling can be a liability to a police department, police management should be alert to this problem and encourage officers to develop more sound intuitive skills.

Service Activities

Service activities, while not as visible or as glamorous as other police functions, cannot be ignored. Uniformed officers must respond to missing persons calls, deaths where a physician was not present, injuries occurring

preventive patrol A type of patrol that deters crime through a visible police presence while enabling police to detect potential criminal incidents.

omnipresence A characteristic of successful preventive patrol that creates the impression that the police are always present.

ETHICS ISSUES

First Responders

The patrol officer is the first to respond to any incident that is suspicious or needs further investigation. The importance of conducting a thorough preliminary investigation cannot be overstated. Both witnesses and evidence can be lost forever if patrol officers do not work quickly and thoroughly. This is true in many different situations: If a tornado wrecks homes and people have to evacuate, police need to estimate the damage, report any problems with utility lines or city structures, and guard against looting. *Should the ethical need to provide prompt service apply equally to crime scenes and to non-crime situations?*

▶ **Police Services** Assisting disabled motorists is a common service function performed by police. *What are other types of common police services?*

under suspicious circumstances, loud parties, landlord-tenant disputes, traffic jams, and myriad other incidents in which the police are the only public agency available to respond.

To what extent do patrol officers perform service activities? Numerous studies indicate that patrol officers spend at least ten percent of their time performing service activities. Between 1976 and 1978, researchers of the Police Services Study analyzed patrol service in 60 neighborhoods within 24 jurisdictions in Rochester (New York), St. Louis, and Tampa–St. Petersburg. In the 60 neighborhoods studied, 18 percent of police-citizen encounters dealt with service activities. Service encounters included medical assistance, provision of information, dealing with dependent persons, and other general assistance.[2] Approximately ten years later, researchers studied a full year's worth of dispatch data for the Wilmington, Delaware, Police Department. An analysis of this study revealed that 12 percent of officers' time was spent on service activities (including medical assistance).

One of the most troublesome problems in studying the service workload is the diversity of situations in which police must act. A standard definition of what constitutes service activities has not been developed because it covers such a wide area. Regardless of the definition, it is well documented that police contribute a substantial amount of their patrol time to non-enforcement activities.

11.1 Self Check ?

1. What are the principal duties performed by the uniformed patrol officer?
2. What are service activities?

POLICING *Online*

Check your answers at **www.policing.glencoe.com**

11.2 Hybrid Patrol Strategies

Prior to the 1960s, there was little study of the police patrol function. For years the writings of O. W. Wilson were the standard for patrol strategies. The omnipresence of patrol officers through routine preventive patrol, and by a mix of motorized patrol and foot patrol, exemplified the spirit of professional policing. In 1968, however, the Omnibus Crime Control and Safe Streets Act inspired change in patrol procedures by providing massive funding for criminal justice research and technology. As a result, traditional policing assumptions were challenged scientifically; one initial focal point of research was the value of preventive patrol.

The 1972 Kansas City Preventive Patrol Experiment was one of the most important examples of police research to result from this movement. Sponsored by the Police Foundation, the experiment tested the value of preventive patrol. Three controlled levels of police presence were employed:

1. One area received no preventive patrol at all.
2. Another area experienced double and triple increases in police patrol presence.
3. A third area received the normal level of preventive patrols.

Online

Remember, one of your best resources is **www.policing.glencoe.com**

In its final analysis of findings, which were published in 1974, the Police Foundation reported no significant differences in the level of crime, attitudes toward police services, fear of crime, police response time, or citizen satisfaction with police response time.[3]

The Kansas City study shocked many people—the conclusions differed from all the assumptions that had long been held regarding preventive patrol. This caused many knowledgeable practitioners to caution against taking the study results to imply that the experiment proved more than it did. Joseph McNamara, who became police chief of the Kansas City Police Department after the study, stressed that the experiment did not show that a visible police presence had no impact on crime in certain circumstances. What it actually revealed was that police officers' uncommitted time—time in which police were not responding to calls or were otherwise engaged—could be used more effectively, such as for focused crime suppression. Clearly, the experiment showed police chiefs that they could try alternative patrol tactics without fearing that a reduced random routine patrol would result in a calamity.

The Kansas City experiment was only one experiment that occurred during the 1970s. On the patrol front, four concepts evolved during this period. These were team policing, split-force patrol, directed patrol, and differential response to calls for service.

Team Policing

team policing Combining officers who perform different duties such as patrol, investigative, and traffic into teams assigned to specific geographic regions, with primary responsibility for all policing within a team's geographic region.

In **team policing**, persons performing line-operational functions (patrol, investigative, and traffic) would be grouped into teams and assigned to specific geographic regions. Each team would then have primary responsibility for all policing within its geographic region.[4] Multiple teams were formed within each precinct when resources permitted.

Team policing emerged in the United States during the late 1960s and early 1970s as an attempt to reduce isolation and involve community support in the war on crime. The strategy encouraged public cooperation but did not depend on it. The cooperation was primarily a means for the police to gain more and improved information about a neighborhood and its problems. The strategy shared some aspects with problem-oriented policing and community policing as practiced currently, but in reality it was not a police-community partnership.

Pioneer Programs The Syracuse, New York, Police Department pioneered team policing in 1968. The crime control team was led by a lieutenant team leader and operated independently from the rest of the agency. The rest of the team consisted of a deputy leader and eight police officers. The team focused on controlling serious crime, apprehending offenders, and conducting investigations in selected high-crime areas within Syracuse.

The 1973 National Advisory Commission on Criminal Justice Standards and Goals described the value of team policing:

> Once a crime is committed and prevention has failed, the police must switch their tactical emphasis from prevention to interception. Police must depend to a great extent on information supplied by the public to increase their chances of intercepting a criminal while the crime is in progress or during flight from the immediate scene. Once prevention and interception have failed, the only tool left to the police is investigation. But like prevention and interception, investigation requires cooperation from the public in apprehending the suspect and providing testimony in any subsequent court proceeding.[5]

All team policing experiments had one common variable: The team had complete jurisdiction over its assigned geographic area. Patrol units from other areas or precincts could enter the team area only for backup purposes when in pursuit of a suspect. On the other hand, steps were taken to ensure that the team members did not have to respond to calls outside their jurisdiction.[6] Some agencies prepared elaborate crossover reports to document the instances when nonteam units came into the team area or when team units went outside their area.

The team policing strategy was short-lived and was practiced primarily between 1970 and 1974. One leading criticism of the strategy was that the costs incurred in the course of creating separate crime units proved too high for municipal budgets. In New York City, which experimented with team policing, the teams failed to change the role of the patrol officer or increase his or her job satisfaction. In other cities that experimented with team policing, such as Los Angeles and Cincinnati, the evaluations showed no change in officer job satisfaction or community attitudes toward the police.[7]

Split-Force Patrol

Split-force patrol involves assigning the largest portion of a patrol force the responsibility of responding to calls for service, while a smaller group of officers, often termed the special problems unit, is responsible for attending to preventive patrol or special crime problems. Split-force patrol was developed in the 1970s as a means of satisfying the needs of both preventive patrol and the demands imposed by calls for service. The theory behind the split-force concept is that by allowing one part of the patrol force to focus exclusively on preventive patrol, this duty can be performed more effectively than if it were simply one of many tasks expected to be performed.

split-force patrol Assigning most of a patrol force to respond to calls for service while assigning a smaller special problems unit to give attention to preventive patrol or special crime problems.

The Wilmington, Delaware, Police Department was one of the first agencies to implement split-force patrol on a widescale basis, and much that is known about this patrol tactic was learned through the Wilmington experiment. The initial evaluation of the program indicated that several objectives were achieved, and the three most important were:

- An increase in patrol productivity
- Increased accountability of the officers
- A reduction in the rate of certain crimes[8]

In 1991, the Houston Police Department, faced with a spiraling crime rate, implemented a form of split-force patrol called *High Intensity Patrol (HIP)*. The program was funded from an overtime account and had as many as 35 officers working on their days off. The HIP officers performed highly visible patrol in specific areas to emphasize the police presence. They were specifically directed not to answer 911 calls. Although HIP did provide a larger police presence, its overall performance received mixed reviews because the call load continued to pile up while the HIP officers were restricted from helping out.

Minimizing Negative Effects For the split-force concept to be effective, police departments must use it in a manner that minimizes potential adverse effects, such as a swollen call load and animosity from the regular patrol units. The Houston experiment showed how both of these problems can result through inflexibility. Ideally, departments using a split-force technique should identify situations when special problems units should pick up radio calls so that call loads stay manageable. Another effective measure for preventing internal problems is to set up a regular rotation of officers to work in the special problems unit. In this way, all officers can work on special problems and gain insights about how a special problems unit can best complement the regular patrol force.

Directed Patrol

directed patrol A patrol strategy that provides dedicated patrol units to special problems as time allows during the course of a shift.

In contrast with the concept of split-force patrol, **directed patrol** allows dedicated patrol units to devote their efforts to special problems as time allows during the course of a shift. With directed patrol, there is generally no shift-long dedication of time to a problem. Preventive directed patrol activities are designed on the basis of the following:

- Detailed analyses of crime incidents
- Offender characteristics
- Methods of operation (MO)
- Locations of crimes

In essence, directed patrol attempts to identify certain crime trends and then develop targeted patrols to interrupt those patterns.

A Combination of Detail and Deterrent Directed patrol goes beyond traditional patrol techniques in the way that it identifies and analyzes crime problems. Under traditional forms of patrol, information about a series of thefts from vehicles in a shopping mall parking lot might be given out at roll call so that police will be aware of the problem, but no specific instructions to solve the problem would be provided. Under directed patrol, however, more detailed information about the time of day, day of the week, and type of cars being attacked might be provided. In addition, specific deterrent strategies would likely be formulated, such as, "Patrol south and east lots for 20 minutes every hour between 1600 hours and 1900 hours, alternating routes of travel."[9] These instructions would most probably be in written form, and officers assigned to this patrol area would be required to document in their daily patrol logs the times the area received directed patrol.

Often the directed patrol requests evolve from citizen complaints about disorderly conditions or street corner drugs sales. The officers who receive directed patrol requests through citizen complaints are instructed to contact the complainant to learn more about the problem's specifics and to express to citizens that requests for service are being acted on.

In any situation, the effectiveness of directed patrol really depends on the amount of time that officers have to address a specific problem. Also, officers must prioritize such problems so that more serious matters get resolved first. In some instances, officers will ignore the directed patrol requests in favor of their personal preferences, such as looking for stolen cars or drunk drivers. Field supervisors and watch commanders must reinforce attention to duty in this area to ensure that officers are pursuing the mandate of the directed patrol request. The best way to do this is to assign a due date for completion of the directed patrol and to track the assignment in a master project file.

Differential Response

Differential response to calls for service is a policy that abandons the traditional practice of responding to all calls for service. In **differential response**, responses to citizens' calls for service are matched to the importance of each call, and a police unit is either assigned or not assigned accordingly.

differential response
A dispatch method in which responses to citizens' calls for service are matched to the importance of each call, and a police unit is either assigned or not assigned accordingly.

Immediate Response Reports of crimes in progress, the at-scene presence of a suspect, life-endangering incidents such as suicide attempts or traffic accidents, or serious crime scenes require an immediate response by police. With such situations, response time can literally mean the difference between life and death. In these cases, it is vital that police respond rapidly for obvious reasons. A quick response can also ensure preservation of the crime or accident scene for subsequent investigations. It is really not possible to enumerate specific incidents that qualify for immediate dispatch. In certain circumstances, even missing persons calls, in which suspicious circumstances are evident or a child is missing, can result in immediate response. The decision to immediately dispatch a police unit is a function of both agency policies and the interpretation of an incoming call's contents by the dispatcher. As a result of constant training and experience, dispatchers develop a sixth sense for how to assign and prioritize calls.

Delayed Response Conditions for which delayed or alternative responses are appropriate include:

- Past burglaries or thefts
- Annoying phone calls
- Traffic accidents in which only property has been damaged
- Noisy parties

Differential response alternatives can include delaying a police unit for these matters until the call load permits, or it can result in dispatching a civilian employee or a telephone report. Some jurisdictions employ police reserve officers, part-time police who handle certain calls such as abandoned vehicle recoveries or other "stale" incidents. Some police agencies no longer take traffic

Incoming Calls to Cincinnati Police Dispatcher, January–December 2000

Incoming Telephone Calls

Total Calls	715,095
Emergency Calls	555,272
Percentage of Emergency Calls that are 911 Calls	65.7 percent
Percentage of 911 Calls Answers in 20 Seconds	93.8 percent

Radio Dispatches

Total Radio Dispatches	285,685
Emergency Calls Dispatched	2,425
Emergency Calls and Average Response Time (minutes)	3.4
Code "9" (violent and nonviolent mental) calls	4,639
Dispatches for Burglar Alarms	27,034

Telephone Crime Reporting Unit

Offense Reports Taken	11,148
Other Reports	1,152
Persons Advised (nonpolice, civil matters, etc.)	2,728

SOURCE: Adapted from Cincinnati Police Department, "Cincinnati Police Division Operations," accessed online at http://www.cincinnatipolice.org/stats/eis98-00.pdf on December 18, 2001.

accident reports in which there are no injuries. Also, a number of departments provide for telephone reporting of minor crimes such as car stereo theft. In such instances, the value of an item stolen was below a specified minimum amount, a suspect was not seen, or there was no detectable evidence at the crime scene.

Differential response is designed to better manage the workload of patrol personnel, allowing officers more time to conduct essential preliminary investigations and perform directed patrol. Research also supports the effectiveness of the differential response, concluding that rapid response is often unnecessary because calls are placed by citizens long after crimes have been committed. In addition, research has revealed the value of call-screening procedures to first determine whether a rapid response is necessary. Other studies have shown that community residents would accept responses other than the presence of police immediately on the scene if they were well informed about the nature of alternatives, such as the dispatch of a report unit (with an estimated time of arrival) or a telephone report.[10]

11.2 Self Check

1. What is the common feature that is found in all team policing applications?
2. What is meant by "differential response"?

POLICING Online

Check your answers at
www.policing.glencoe.com

Interactive Patrol

New developments, insights, and research during the 1970s accelerated the growing awareness of the limitations of traditional patrol procedures. They also stimulated experimentation with new approaches to preventing crime and improving police-community liaisons.

What Is Foot Patrol?

As may be seen in the Newark and Flint foot patrol experiments, foot patrol has considerable merit. In recent years, it has regained acceptance as a viable patrol procedure. The foot patrol officer is usually more able than the patrol car officer to develop a closer relationship with the people who reside, shop, or work on the beat. Foot patrol officers can identify with people on the beat since they have direct interpersonal contact with them. The various roles of an officer—information provider, assistance giver, law enforcer, apprehender of lawbreakers, counselor, and friend—are facilitated by this contact.

Foot beat officers have additional advantages, as compared with officers who use motorized vehicles. They are in a better position to do the following:

- Manage their beats
- Understand what constitutes threatening or inappropriate behavior
- Initiate measures to repair conditions of disorder

◄ **Benefits of Foot Patrol** City of Poughkeepsie police officer talks with a business owner as part of the community policing program which keep police informed on what is happening in the city. Foot patrol affords an up-close and personal involvement with community members. *What are some of the other benefits of foot patrol?*

Foot patrol officers are likely to pay more attention than other officers to derelicts, petty thieves, disorderly persons, panhandlers, noisy juveniles, and aggressive or unstable street people who cause concern and fear among many citizens.

Size and Boundary A beat's size and boundaries have an impact on foot patrol officers' effectiveness. The beat should not be so large an officer cannot cover it effectively and it should not be so small that resources are wasted or officers get bored. This must be considered when beats are created and staffed. Boundaries should be determined according to a community of interest that bases itself on concerns about crime and disorder. Often a public housing tract forms an entire beat because this neighborhood area will provide sufficient work for patrol officers. In other cases, it is surrounding a school or an ethnic or racial enclave that exhibits some cohesiveness. If an area is densely populated, the beat might include only a block or two. It is difficult to generalize about the optimal size for every beat because size is dependent on the following variables:

- Population density
- Amount of crime and disorder
- Number of perpetrators frequenting an area
- Number of businesses
- Cohesiveness of the community
- A number of other factors such as police-community relations, individual officer experience, and police management philosophies

One useful guideline for determining a beat area is that the officer should be able to knock on every door in the area, for the purpose of establishing contact, within an eight-month period, recognizing that not everyone will be home at the time of the attempted contact. Another helpful guideline is to understand the limitations of foot patrol. Although it has many advantages, it must be recognized as a support service for motorized patrol. The speed of motorized response in serious situations and the automobile's ability to cover more area are indispensable to contemporary policing.[11]

The following sections cover experiments and research conducted in San Diego, California; Newark, New Jersey; and Flint, Michigan.

San Diego Community-Oriented Policing

The San Diego Police Department conducted several significant research studies during the 1970s. These included a community-oriented policing project, which became the first of its type to undergo scientific evaluation. The community-oriented policing style required patrol officers to become knowledgeable about their beats through beat profiling activities. **Beat profiling** entails the study of beat topographics, demographics, and call histories; it required beat officers to develop tailored patrol strategies to address the types of crimes and citizen concerns pertinent to the beat.

The San Diego project demonstrated what other interactive patrol experiments found—that interaction with the community could improve the attitudes of officers toward their jobs and toward the communities they served. It also revealed that such specific beat knowledge could encourage officers to develop creative solutions to complex crime and delinquency problems.[12]

beat profiling Study of beat topographics, demographics, and call histories to develop tailored patrol strategies to address the types of crimes and citizen concerns pertinent to the beat.

Newark Foot Patrol Experiment

During the mid-1970s, the Police Foundation sponsored a study of foot patrol effectiveness in Newark, New Jersey. While popular with citizens and politicians at the time, foot patrol was viewed by most police executives as a waste of valuable resources that could be better used for policing by automobile. Because of foot patrol's popularity with citizens, however, the state of New Jersey funded foot patrol as part of its Safe and Clean Neighborhoods Program. Grudgingly, city police accepted the money, largely for the additional jobs and funding it provided.

Police Foundation researchers studied closely the effects of the foot beats. Researchers found that the officers, even though they had received only minimal training and guidance, immersed themselves in the neighborhoods in which they worked. Foot patrol officers kept abreast of local problems; assumed special responsibility for particular locations or people; developed regular sources of information such as apartment managers, merchants, and street people; became regulars at local restaurants; checked bars; and in other ways came to know and to be known on their beats.

Citizen responses to the foot patrols were uniformly positive, even in predominantly African American neighborhoods that were patrolled by white officers. Perhaps this is because of traditional feelings among African American communities that police are usually unresponsive to their needs. Although foot patrol did not appear to be any more effective in reducing crime levels, surveys did reveal substantial declines in citizens' fear levels and soaring increases in citizen appreciation. Foot patrol officers, in turn, had more positive attitudes toward citizens and experienced higher morale than did officers who patrolled in cars.[13]

Flint Foot Patrol Experiment

In 1979, the Neighborhood Foot Patrol Program (NFPP) was launched in Flint, Michigan. The Mott Foundation provided a $2.6 million, three-year grant to put 22 foot patrol officers into base stations (many in schools) within 14 neighborhoods that contained 20 percent of the city's total population. The program was designed to address three long-standing problems:

1. Lack of citizen involvement in crime prevention
2. Depersonalization of interactions between officers and residents
3. Lack of comprehensive neighborhood organizations and services

Among the program's ten basic goals were to decrease crime and enhance community awareness of crime problems and crime prevention strategies. The NFPP officers provided full law enforcement services as well as social service referrals.

Highlights of the neighborhood foot patrol program were as follows:

- Targeted crimes decreased almost nine percent.
- Citizens felt safer.
- Crime reporting by citizens increased.
- Citizens saw foot patrol officers as more effective than motorized patrol officers in preventing crime and working with juveniles.

Although the Flint foot patrol was disbanded in its original form due to unexpected economic and political circumstances, such as large layoffs at nearby General Motors plants, the foot patrol effort in Flint was a remarkable success.

An important finding from the Flint experiment was that fear reduction was linked to the order maintenance activities of foot patrol officers. Subsequent experimentation in other cities disclosed that even tactics other than foot patrol, which also emphasized increasing the quantity and improving the quality of police-citizen interactions, had outcomes similar to those of foot patrol. The findings of the foot patrol and fear reduction experiments, when coupled with the research on the relationship between fear and disorder, have created new opportunities for police to work with citizen groups and understand their increasing concerns about disorder.[14]

11.3 Self Check

1. What problems did the Flint foot patrol experiment address?
2. What were some positive outcomes of the foot patrol studies?

POLICING *Online*

Check your answers at
www.policing.glencoe.com

11.4 Problem-Oriented Policing

In 1979, Herman Goldstein developed and advanced the concept of problem-oriented policing, which encouraged police to begin thinking differently about their purpose.[15] **Problem-oriented policing (POP)** involves concentrating police resources on the underlying dynamics of a problem to find a lasting solution. Goldstein undertook his work in the area of problem solving because he saw police administrators preoccupied with striving to enhance administrative competency. What was troubling to him was that these administrators did not concern themselves (as they should have) with whether their streamlined organizations provided better police services. As a result, he sought to create more systematic concern for the result of police efforts and encouraged police managers to break down problems in as much detail as possible. He encouraged analysis of all the variables pertinent to a crime problem and saw the detailed analysis of problems leading to important revelations for response. In fact, problem analysis could even lead to curing multiple dimensions of a problem, such as recurring purse snatches and a neighborhood's fear level. Goldstein identified three primary aspects of a problem-solving approach:

problem-oriented policing (POP) The concentration of police resources on the underlying causes of a problem in order to find a lasting solution.

- **Problem definition** In the area of problem definition, it is as important to be precise about locale, time of day, type of perpetrators, and type of victims as it is to be knowledgeable about motive and crime scene qualities.
- **Problem analysis** In performing an analysis of a problem, Goldstein encouraged officers to draw on their unique understanding of the various aspects of problems that frequently come their way.
- **Exploration of resolution alternatives** Experienced officers develop a feel for what, under given circumstances, constitute the most effective responses. Goldstein encouraged officers to make a fresh, uninhibited search for alternative responses. He even fashioned a list of categories of alternatives to stimulate fresh thinking. These categories are listed in Figure 11.2 on page 432.

Newport News Experiment

In 1983, following a pilot test of the concept, the National Institute of Justice (NIJ) funded the POP program in Newport News, a mid-sized coastal city in Virginia. The Newport News program was unique in that from the outset, the objective was to make problem solving the focus of the daily operation of the entire agency. The department concentrated on three major community problems: burglaries in a low-income, government-subsidized housing project; thefts from automobiles parked in downtown parking lots; and robberies related to prostitution in the downtown area. In addition, it addressed chronic problems such as disturbances at convenience stores, drug dealing at specific locations, and robberies in the central business district.

In each case, the particular problem was solved not only by solving the crimes and arresting perpetrators, or by increasing levels of patrol (though both were done), but also by thoroughly analyzing the immediate conditions that were contributing to the offenses. The problem-solving approach viewed police incidents as symptoms of underlying problems, which could be resolved by dissecting problems to identify their components in order to fashion a customized, effective response. Systematic inquiry into problems was a joint venture of the police and concerned community members.

The problem analysis process yielded an important four-step problem-solving technique, commonly referred to as SARA. **SARA** is an acronym for the elements comprising the problem-solving technique: scanning, analysis, response, and assessment. Figure 11.3 on page 433 shows the basics of SARA.

SARA An acronym for the elements comprising the problem-solving technique: scanning, analysis, response, and assessment.

Scanning In the initial stage of the technique, officers are encouraged to see individual related incidents that come to their attention as collective

---

Figure 11.2

Exploration for Alternatives

The following can stimulate the quest for alternative methods for solving problems:

◆ Can the problem be reduced or eliminated through physical or technical changes such as target hardening?

◆ Can the problem be alleviated by changes in other government services such as poor housing conditions because of lax building code enforcement?

◆ The best response the police can make to many requests for help is to provide accurate, concise information, such as whether a person who has a missing license plate can drive a car until the plate is replaced.

◆ The greatest way to improve the handling of some problems is by providing police officers with new forms of specialized training, such as skills required to deescalate family quarrels.

◆ Do the police need a specific, limited form of authority that they do not presently have? For example, can the police take the keys from a person who is not sufficiently intoxicated to be arrested for public drunkenness but is definitely unfit to drive?

◆ Analysis of a problem may lead to the conclusion that assistance is needed from another government agency. One example is the development of shelters for domestic violence victims.

◆ Can the problem be handled through a tightening of regulatory codes such as improved locking systems or more soundproofing?

SOURCE: Herman Goldstein, "Improving Policing: A Problem-Oriented Approach," *Crime and Delinquency 25*, no. 2 (1979): 236–58.

Figure 11.3

SARA

Scanning: Identifying and selecting a problem.

Analysis: Analyzing the problem.

Response: Responding to a problem.

Assessment: Assessing the impact on the problem.

problems, then define these problems in more useful terms. A problem eventually means a cluster of similar, related, or recurring incidents rather than isolated incidents. The assumption is that few incidents are isolated, as all are part of a wider set of social phenomena. For instance, an incident classified as a robbery might be seen as part of a pattern of muggings occurring near bus stops and other transit points.

Analysis In performing an analysis of the robberies, officers collect information from a variety of public and private sources, not just traditional police data such as criminal records and past offense reports. Officers rely on problem analysis guides that direct them to examine offenders, victims, the social and physical environment, and previous responses to the problem. The goal is to understand the scope, nature, and causes of the problem and formulate a variety of strategies for its resolution. To understand a problem, problem solvers have found it useful to visualize a link among three elements required to constitute a crime in the community: an offender, a victim, and a crime scene or location. As part of the analysis phase, it is important to find out as much as possible about all three legs of the triangle. One way to start is by asking who, what, when, where, how, and why (and why not) about each leg of the triangle.

Response and Assessment The knowledge gained in the analysis stage is problem response and problem assessment, which are then used to develop and implement solutions. Officers seek the assistance of citizens, businesses, other police units, other public and private organizations, and anyone else who can contribute toward developing an effective action plan. Solutions often go well beyond traditional police responses. Following implementation of a problem-solving strategy, the problem area is monitored and assessed to determine the effectiveness of the strategy.[16]

Broken Windows Theory

broken windows theory
An analogy employed to describe the relationship between disorder and crime; for example, if a window in a building is broken and left unrepaired, this sends a signal that no one is in charge of the street.

Closely associated with the problem-driven approach to policing is the broken windows concept. **Broken windows theory** is an analogy employed to describe the relationship between disorder and crime. For example, a building with broken windows sends the message that no one cares about the building or the neighborhood. It can also imply that nobody is in charge of the street.

This concept evolved from researchers James Q. Wilson's and George Kelling's observations of the results of the Newark foot patrol experiment previously discussed. They observed in the Newark experiment, as well as other similar experiments, the significance of order

CopTalk

Problem Solving in Action

Although the SARA problem-solving method has often been challenged when introduced into a police department, it has proved highly useful to law enforcement agencies that have employed it. For example, in early 1993, the Seattle suburb of Redmond, Washington, faced a citywide graffiti problem. The 42,000 residents of the city were filing more than 60 graffiti-related complaints per month. At first, police officers employed traditional approaches to the problem, such as by organizing cleanup work parties and increasing enforcement patrols in the locations with the most graffiti. It didn't work.

In the problem analysis phase, officers interviewed a number of youths who they believed were associated with the graffiti. They learned that some people considered the vandalism a form of hip-hop art. In addition, after an officer analyzed the case reports and researched the origins of graffiti more

deeply, it became clear to him that the Redmond problem did not involve gangs. This was because its content was generally not violent. On the other hand, gang graffiti can include code references to murder and other acts of violence.

Next, the officer met with teen-aged taggers to find a solution to the problem. The taggers suggested establishing a legal place to paint in return for a tagging "cease fire." The officers helped the taggers obtain permission from the city council to erect a graffiti wall and worked with the taggers to obtain donations from local businesses for materials needed to construct it. Since the wall was constructed, monthly complaints about graffiti have decreased from more than 60 to about 4 per month.

What Do You Think? In what kinds of other crime situations could a compromise like this be appropriate, and when would it be inappropriate?

SOURCE: Office of Community-Oriented Policing Services, *Problem-Solving Tips* (Washington, D.C.: U.S. Department of Justice, 1998), 22.

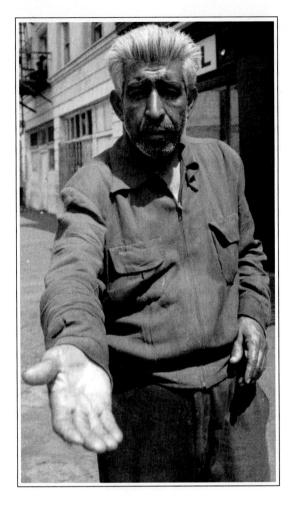

◄ **Broken Windows Theory**
A neighborhood's appearance and the presence of panhandlers can actually affect its crime rate. *Do you agree? Why?*

maintenance activities by the police and attempted to bring the concept before the public in 1982.

Wilson and Kelling believed strongly that serious crime flourished in areas in which disorderly behavior was unaddressed. In real life, "broken windows" are not just windows—they can be entire buildings, situations, conditions, or even people.

For example, an unchecked panhandler who pesters passersby and blocks doorways to businesses could be the first of several broken windows in a neighborhood. Muggers and robbers, whether opportunistic or professional, would then see their chances of being caught, or even identified, reduced on streets where potential victims were already intimidated by prevailing conditions of disorder.

Wilson and Kelling reasoned that if a neighborhood could not keep a bothersome panhandler from annoying passersby, the robber may reason that someone would be even less likely to call the police to identify a potential mugger or to intervene if a mugging were to actually occur.[17]

Today, the broken windows theory has proven to be a highly viable concept in the quest to restore order along urban streets. Four elements of the strategy explain its impact on crime reduction:

1. Dealing with disorder and low-level offenders both informs police about, and puts them into contact with, those who have also committed serious crimes, including the hard-core six percent of youthful offenders. This was a major factor in turning around New York City's formerly dismal crime picture. The NYPD aggressively targeted quality-of-life violators. It was learned in that city that a large proportion of persons who engaged in minor offenses such as "fare beating" on the subway system or who provided unsolicited and often harassing "squeegeeing" services to motorists had lengthy criminal records for serious offenses.

2. The high visibility of police actions and the concentration of police in areas characterized by high levels of disorder protect "good kids," while sending a message to "wannabes" and those guilty of committing marginal crimes that their actions will no longer be tolerated. Both these two actions ultimately bring greater control to bear to prevent crime.

3. Citizens themselves begin to assert control over public spaces by upholding neighborhood standards for behavior and ultimately move onto center stage in the ongoing processes of maintaining order and preventing crime.

4. Finally, as problems of disorder and crime become the responsibility not merely of the police but of the entire community, including agencies and institutions outside but linked to it, all mobilize to address them in an integrated fashion. Through this broadly based effort, a vast amount of resources can be marshaled and, through problem solving, targeted at specific crime problems.[18]

11.4 Self Check

1. What does SARA stand for?
2. Can you explain the broken windows theory?

POLICING Online

Check your answers at
www.policing.glencoe.com

11.5 Community Policing

Programs and experiments such as those implemented in the cities of Flint, Newark, and Newport News demonstrated that the community could be an important partner in dealing with the problems of crime and fear of crime. The stage was set for the introduction of a policing approach that would fully involve the community in policing. This policing approach is called **community policing**, which is an organizational philosophy based on a set of values emphasizing problem-solving partnerships between community members and their police. In community policing, both work together to identify, prioritize, and solve crime problems to attain improved quality of life in their community.[19]

community policing An organizational philosophy based on a set of values emphasizing problem-solving partnerships between community members and their police in which both work together to identify, prioritize, and solve crime problems to attain improved quality of life in the community.

What Is Community Policing?

Community policing is based primarily on two social science themes: normative sponsorship theory and critical social theory. Normative sponsorship theory declares that most people are of good will and willing to cooperate with others to satisfy their needs. It proposes that a community effort will only be sponsored if it is normative (within the limits of established standards) to all persons and interest groups involved. For a community to unite and actively support a program of community policing, the major groups in the community must agree that a project is worthy of undertaking in the context of their attitudes, values, norms, and goals.

The Big Six Community-policing pioneers Robert Trojanowicz and Bonnie Bucqueroux identified the **Big Six** groups, or stakeholders, that must be identified and must work together to ensure the success of community-policing efforts:[20]

1. Police department
2. General community
3. Businesses
4. Civic officials
5. Media
6. Public and nonprofit agencies

Big Six Principal groups that must work together to ensure the success of community policing efforts: police, general community, businesses, civic officials, media, and public and nonprofit agencies. Also called *stakeholders*.

The community-policing officer assumes a key leadership role in stimulating community groups to implement community policing. This frequently involves substantial information gathering as the community-policing officer must be prepared to fully inform the citizenry on the subject of local crime, encouraging the formation of coalitions with shared social values to control and prevent criminality.

Computer On Patrol

Technology and Community Policing

Technology and community policing sound like an unusual mix. After all, isn't community policing supposed to consist of low-tech activities such as meeting the public and performing foot patrol? Actually, technology can be used to provide vital police-community connections and to deliver police services to the community.

For example, most police departments are online and have Web sites. On these sites, community-minded departments post many resources for crime prevention. These can include the following:

- Home safety tips to prevent burglary or arson
- Child safety tips to avoid sexual abuse or kidnapping
- Travel safety tips (both for yourself and for your home while you are away)
- School and work safety issues

In addition, all Web sites offer phone numbers and, sometimes, Internet-based forms that people can use to report crimes.

Think About It Check out your local police department's Web page. What can it do to improve its community crime prevention pages?

Principles

Understanding the essence of community policing is a challenge, and ten principles should be included in all policies, procedures, and practices associated with community policing. These ten principles are change, leadership, vision, partnership, problem solving, equity, trust, empowerment, service, and accountability.

Change Change is a constant factor that drives a police organization and its individual officers to view the transition to community policing not as an unwelcome change but as an opportunity to improve the way police services are delivered. Because it requires proactive change, community policing is a significant departure from traditional policing. It also requires forging new partnerships with the community and implementing changes within the department that maximize opportunities for everyone to participate in community building and community-based problem solving.

Leadership In community policing, leadership involves constantly emphasizing and reinforcing community policing's vision, values, and mission within all levels of an organization. This means that everyone within a police department must support and promote the commitment to community building and community-based problem solving as the primary police activities. Leadership also implies serving as role models for taking risks and building collaborative relationships to implement community policing, inside and outside the organization. Everyone must exhibit leadership within the opportunities and limits of his or her role and position to influence and educate others about community policing.

Vision How does a police agency improve public safety and quality of life through community policing? It does so by envisioning what it can do for the community. This vision, which should include the core values of police personnel and citizens, should provide the inspiration and motivation to achieve short-term and long-term goals to implement community policing. The vision of community policing is an entirely new philosophy and management approach that influences organizational policies, procedures, and practices.

Online

Remember, one of your best resources is **www.policing.glencoe.com**

Partnership Equal partnerships need to be developed among all groups within the community to promote collaboration and consensus. Developing community-policing partnerships is an organizational philosophy and strategy for community building and problem solving.

Problem Solving Problem solving is an analytical process and strategy for identifying and pinpointing, in a collaborative manner, specific community situations/events and their causes, so that tailor-made responses may be designed. Problem solving involves an organization-wide commitment to go beyond traditional police responses to crime and to address a multitude of problems that adversely affect quality of life.

Equity In police service, equity ensures that all citizens will receive effective, respectful police service regardless of race, gender, ethnicity, religious belief, income, sexual preference, and other differences. Community policing also recognizes the special concerns of specific populations, such as women, the elderly, and juveniles. Moreover, it recognizes that providing equitable service does not always mean providing the same amount or level of service but that which is necessary for the individual situation.

Trust Trust is the conviction that people mean what they say. A community policing organization must demonstrate that it has integrity and will follow through on its promises to the community. Trust reduces mutual suspicions between police and residents, providing the foundation that allows the police and community to collaborate. Trust can have long-term stability only if it is based on mutual understanding and respect.

empowerment is the act of creating an opportunity for expressions of power and ownership, such as over a community.

Empowerment Through **empowerment**, an opportunity for expressions of power and ownership, such as over a community, can be created. Community policing creates a shift within the police organization, giving officers and the community greater freedom to make decisions. Empowering nonsupervisory police personnel is designed to encourage and support them in collaborative community building and problem solving to assist the community in empowering itself.

Service Community-policing officers are committed to providing decentralized and personalized police service to neighborhoods, with the intensity and type of services dictated by the needs of the neighborhood. In the service-oriented style of policing, police should view citizens as customers. By viewing the citizens as their clients, police can learn, through actively listening to citizen comments, which services are most needed and when.

Accountability With mutual accountability, the community holds the police accountable for their actions. At the same time, the police hold the community accountable for shouldering its share of the responsibility in promoting and maintaining public safety and the overall quality of life.[21]

Implementation

Developing and implementing community policing in any community requires extensive planning, collaboration, and coordination among Big Six stakeholders:

1. The police must realize that the classic incident-driven response to crime and the dependence on routine patrol and rapid response as deterrents to crime must be supplemented with a proactive problem-solving style of policing.
2. The community, working with the police, must become active in identifying community needs and concerns and finding solutions.
3. Elected officials must walk the beat with community officers to understand both the problems that the community officers encounter and the community's clear view of what police and government officials should be doing.

Patrolman

Job Description

I spend about 80 percent of my time out in the field and 20 percent preparing reports. I am usually on call doing neighborhood checks, dealing with shoplifting, burglaries, family disturbances, and traffic control.

Since this is a small community, everybody knows me, they understand what I do, and they try to help out if I am looking for somebody or investigating a case.

Another advantage of working for a small department is that I get to work in many different fields: I work on patrol, I do detective work, and I also function as an instructor in the department and in the community.

Victor H. Gonzalez, Humble

The most difficult part of my job has to be when I have to do a death notification, but the best aspect is being able to help people out.

The advice I would give to young people interested in this line of work is first to do it because they want to, not because of the money. They also should be careful not to get into trouble and avoid being involved with drugs because that would bar them from a career in law enforcement.

Education

Since I was very young, I have always wanted to be a police officer. In 1990, I was in private surveillance, and I went through basic academy training at Houston Community College.

Follow-Up Compare this job profile to that of a patrolman in a large urban center. Which do you prefer? Why?

4. Businesses, large and small, must provide volunteer services and resources to community groups and projects. Furthermore, they must form alliances to support good business practices and enhance the quality of life in the community.

5. Government agencies (such as mental health, social sciences, and public works) and private entities (such as local businesses) must collaborate with police and the community in solving local problems.

6. Finally, the media must become partners with the police in promoting the positive aspects of the police and the public working together.

Models for implementing community policing may differ among communities, but they often have common components: grassroots support, strategic planning, managing resistance, institutionalization, and full implementation.

Police Procedure

Goal-Oriented Community Policing

The case of Officer Michael Kelley of the NYPD is an excellent example of what can be accomplished through goal-oriented community policing. Kelley, a beat officer, earned accolades from both his department and the media for his central role in the indictments and arrests of 35 gang members in the No Fear Gang on murder, narcotics, and weapons charges. These gangsters earned up to three million dollars annually in drug sales. Upon assignment to Harlem's 28th Precinct, Kelley quickly learned that this violent drug gang controlled the neighborhood through intimidation.

Kelley's initial approach to the problem was the traditional solution of arresting the dealers one by one. He soon realized that this had little impact. He then approached the precinct commander, who provided the support for a multifaceted attack on the problem. With Kelley as the spearhead, a task force of uniformed and narcotics officers, as well as personnel from the district attorney's office, focused on eradicating the gang. Patrol officers aggressively enforced quality-of-life violations in the neighborhood and determined whether offenders had outstanding warrants; those who did were taken into custody. Confidential informants were developed and controlled buys were made. Also, patrol officers with close ties to the community and its residents provided additional intelligence.

As a result of this coordinated approach, the entire gang was broken up in a matter of months, and control of the neighborhood returned to law-abiding residents. Equally as important, community members witnessed police taking decisive action against those who had violated their rights through fear and intimidation.

Critical Thinking How can police help communities such as this try to avoid having the same problem again?

SOURCE: Howard Safir, "Goal-Oriented Community Policing: The NYPD Approach," *The Police Chief*, December 1997, 38.

Grassroots Support An agency lays the foundation for community policing by obtaining grassroots support. Target groups are local politicians, businesspeople, and police associations, all of whom have influence over large groups of people and can help influence them in getting more involved in fighting crime within their communities.

Strategic Planning A second step is developing a strategic plan along with action steps. Strategic planning is an ongoing effort that responds to organizational and environmental changes. The recommended time frame for this plan is five years, during which time the stakeholder groups are incorporated into the implementation process. The stakeholders clarify agency values, rewrite mission statements to conform to the philosophy of community policing, identify community needs, convert needs to goals, establish objectives for each goal, formulate action plans to achieve objectives, and identify evaluation strategies. Evaluation is a critical component.

Also during strategic planning, the stakeholders redefine the role of the community police officer from specialist to generalist and reengineer the organization to deliver community police services. The agency's mission and organizational structure must provide for deploying resources in response to emergencies but also direct a preponderance of resources toward preventing crime and solving community problems that generate exhausting demands on the police.

Reengineering involves establishing community police stations, among other tasks. The decision to establish a station in a neighborhood should be the result of an agreement between the law enforcement agency, the governing body, and the community. Once a community police station is operational in a neighborhood, it sends a strong message of commitment. It brings police service directly to the community, where that service is needed most.

Managing Resistance As law enforcement agencies shift their emphasis from overdependence on the formal criminal justice system to the establishment of programs such as community action groups and youth activity teams, some officers and police management show classic signs of resistance to change. In this respect, law enforcement is no different from any other profession that must cope with change: Like other professionals, police get set in their ways and find it difficult to see the wisdom of doing things differently.

One strategy to reduce resistance is to implement community policing in small steps, rather than attempting a major change all at once. Small steps will have an immediate impact on the community. Another strategy for managing change is to celebrate success at each stage of implementation. In the process, the agency should emphasize collaboration among the six stakeholder groups.

Community Network Centers

The Lumberton Police Department in North Carolina reengineered its community policing efforts by making its substations "community network centers" that also provide social, mental health, and various other city services.

Institutionalization The next stage is institutionalization. At this point, the agency has accomplished the transition. Goals and objectives reflect the mission, vision, and core value statements of community policing. Job descriptions, performance evaluations, and recruitment, selection, training, and promotion criteria are all oriented toward community policing as are operational policies and procedures.

Although community-policing programs have been in place in some agencies for a decade, it is becoming uncomfortably clear that law enforcement agencies are not consistently recruiting officers who are adept at performing community-policing tasks. Moreover, they are slow to adopt and use uniform criteria for selecting persons for community-policing assignments. Most new officers entering the profession want to help people. However, they tend to prefer general patrol duties over public speaking, creative problem solving, and networking with community and government organizations. Newly appointed officers who do not possess personal traits and characteristics compatible with community policing quickly grow frustrated, causing resistance.

Recruiting and selecting the right people create fertile ground for training. Training itself must focus on the skills critical to successful community policing: planning and organizing, problem solving, critical thinking, and interpersonal communication.

Full Implementation of Community Policing Citizens realize that the community-policing philosophy has been implemented when they witness the placement of police substations in their neighborhoods, designed to deliver personalized police services. At this stage, citizens assist in setting priorities through regular dialogue and participation with community police officers and the local management team. The clearest indication that community policing is working is when citizens, elected officials, the business community, helping agencies, and the media are accepting individual and collective responsibility for the plight of their neighborhoods.[22]

Houston Experiment

In 1982, the Houston, Texas, Police Department adopted a set of values that emphasized problem solving and collaboration with the community. For a period of five years, Houston steadily implemented changes designed to provide the public greater accessibility to participating in policing efforts. Principal program elements included the following:

1. A police community newsletter
2. A citizen contact program that kept the same officers patrolling the same beats to facilitate individual contacts with citizens in the area

3. Recontacting victims of crime in the days following their victimization to reassure them of a police presence

4. A police community contact center within which a truancy reduction program and park program operated

In addition, the department reconfigured its patrol beats to reflect natural neighborhood boundaries.

At the end of the five-year evolutionary period, the police department became fully involved in a partnership with the community. Pursuant to this commitment, the department effected sweeping changes in its policing style to implement a fully interactive process between the police and the community to mutually identify and resolve community problems. The elements of this process, which embodied the essence of community policing, included the following:

- An orientation toward problem solving and empowerment of beat officers to initiate creative responses to problems
- Accountability to the community for crime control and prevention activities
- Decentralization of organizational authority and structure
- Responsibility for decision making shared by the police and the community
- Permanent beat assignments for officers
- Revised training and personnel evaluation practices to reflect a community policing orientation

By achieving these goals, the Houston experiment successfully implemented a comprehensive program of community policing that was fully functional within a major urban environment.[23]

A Tale of Two Cities: Lumberton, North Carolina, and New York City

How does community policing actually operate in a community? Perhaps the best answer is provided by examining two community-policing programs in two very different jurisdictions: the small city of Lumberton, North Carolina, and the metropolis of New York City. This extreme contrast shows that community policing is an exceptionally adaptive framework—it can work in a city of 20,000 just as effectively as it can in the nation's largest city.

Lumberton Lumberton, North Carolina (population 20,000), is a good example of a small city that has reengineered the delivery of police services to make successful use of the community-policing model. In Lumberton, the push for community policing came in 1990 after the city experienced a riot. Many citizens accused the police department of not being responsive or sensitive to community concerns and needs. Local politicians and community leaders reacted by supporting a movement to community policing. In 1992, to ensure that the transformation would take place, the city hired a police chief who embraced the community-policing philosophy.

Making the Change Happen The transition began with a redefinition of the Lumberton Police Department's mission, vision, and core values to ensure compatibility with the philosophy and the principles of community policing. To empower officers, the chief provided training in community-policing philosophy and procedures. All officers received training because the first community police officers were from the department itself. It is important to note that in Lumberton, community-policing officers added to but did not replace traditional patrol officers. The police chief made several organizational and personnel changes:

1. To alter its management structure, the police department created a quality improvement team to recommend improvements in police services and resolve conflicts in the implementation process and a management team consisting of department managers and supervisors to focus on current problems and long-range planning.

2. In an effort to decentralize operations, the department created four substations that were opened between December 1993 and November 1996. The commander of each substation was a lieutenant who in many ways became a mini-chief. Community policing started with seven officers assigned to public housing areas within the territory covered by the four substations. Later, five more officers were added, one assigned to each of the four substations and one to a special downtown office.

3. Management delegated day-to-day planning to the individual community police officers at the substations. Decision making thus became decentralized.

4. The community police officers, including detectives, juvenile officers, vice officers, and narcotics officers, were organized into teams, with four officers providing service to one community beat (the area served by a substation). Officers assigned to a team took special pride in their beat, becoming concerned and protective of it. The team interacted regularly and held periodic meetings with residents to discuss community problems, concerns, and solutions. Communication among officers increased because they were permanently assigned to a substation and thus had the opportunity for more interaction.

MYTH	FACT
Most officers, especially older ones, dislike community policing.	At first, about 80 percent of officers opposed or were ambivalent about community policing. Now about 70 percent support it.

Initially, community police officers were primarily assigned to community-policing duties, and patrol officers responded to 911 calls. Today, the two types of officers are beginning to work together, both answering calls for service and performing community-policing duties.

Despite the success of community policing in Lumberton, some traditional officers still express resentment of community police officers. When they see an officer sitting on a porch drinking tea with a citizen, they perceive the officer to be nonproductive instead of building rapport and a foundation for future cooperation with the community. Still, although some veteran officers still harbor negative attitudes toward community policing, attitudes are changing. This is attributed primarily to the recruitment of new officers who are open to community policing, as well as a deeper understanding and appreciation of community policing among experienced officers.

Success Factors Community policing requires community involvement to succeed. In Lumberton, residents have participated in activities such as the citizen police academy and organized community watch programs, block parties, community cleanups, and a Police Explorer Scout Program. The police department also created a citizens' advisory committee for each of the four substations to assist the substation commander in prioritizing local programs.

The police department uses a number of strategies to keep the public informed: community meetings, local newsletters, and a locally produced television show called *Lumberton Police Chronicle*. In addition, the citizen police academy offers an excellent opportunity to educate the community about police work. Residents routinely visit their neighborhood stations because the substations provide the same services as police headquarters.

The implementation of community policing in Lumberton presented several challenges to police and government leaders, including officer resistance, significant resources, and decreased power over officers by command staff. Amid all the challenges, the community-policing experience in Lumberton has proved rewarding. While a significant component of service will necessarily always be dedicated to emergency response, Lumberton fully recognizes the special value of community policing in improving the quality of society overall.[24]

New York City Community policing eventually succeeded in New York, but only after overcoming some mistakes. When the New York Police Department (NYPD) initiated community policing in 1984, it did so by taking a bottom-up approach to the traditional pyramid-shaped police hierarchy. Beat officers in community police units were empowered as chiefs of their beats and were given great discretion in taking the lead in determining and delivering necessary police services. For a number of reasons, including resistance to change by senior officers, the community-policing units were staffed with an abundance of younger, inexperienced officers. This approach resulted in supervisors, commanders, and members of specialized units being cast in support roles, with their activities largely determined and directed by a cadre of relatively inexperienced beat cops. This arrangement effectively challenged the authority of ranking officers and seasoned investigators and seemed a complete reversal of the agency's rank and power structure. More important, it also flew in the face of sound management theory; it was impractical to expect that the resources of so large a police agency could be effectively marshaled and directed by almost 3,000 chiefs.

The bottom-up style of management created other difficulties as well. Although the NYPD expended considerable effort and resources in attempting to design community beats whose boundaries matched the contours of definable neighborhoods, the reality of crime patterns and hot spots often crossed neighborhood and beat lines. To be effective, officers would have to construct cross-beat strategies. Although some officers were able to organize and coordinate resources to accomplish this complex task, the unfortunate truth was that the process typically placed a severe burden on inexperienced beat officers.

Facing the Challenges and Creating Solutions To address these early problems, in the mid-1990s, the NYPD took a bold move toward accountability by placing the responsibility for problem solving squarely on the shoulders of middle managers and precinct commanders. (See Figure 11.4 on page 448.) Beat officers were still responsible for achieving results, but the responsibility for identifying and addressing problems through a coordinated strategic process went to the managerial corps. Vesting the lion's share of responsibility for addressing crime and quality-of-life conditions in its 76 precinct commanders has proved highly effective. Because precincts are composed of multiple beats, their commanders have a broader view of the precinct's crime and quality-of-life picture. Precinct commanders also control personnel and have the formal rank to obtain additional resources from specialized units. The NYPD has implemented a number of crime-specific strategies, including:

- Getting guns off the streets
- Curbing youth violence
- Driving drug dealers out of New York City
- Breaking the cycle of domestic violence
- Reclaiming the city's public spaces
- Building organizational integrity

Designed to give all members of the department a standardized and coordinated blueprint for action, they are still flexible enough to be adapted to meet the particular needs of specific communities. Taken collectively, the goal of these interlocking crime control and quality-of-life strategies is to create a seamless and comprehensive plan for action, using every available department resource.

Accountability of precinct commanders is achieved in large measure through the CompStat (Computerized Statistics) process. Using CompStat, precinct commanders meet with top agency executives to review and discuss their problem-solving efforts and activities. CompStat's technological capabilities enable computerized pin mapping so that high-crime areas can be clustered and highlighted. The comprehensive CompStat database can be accessed on a map depicting any geographic area of the city, instantly projecting relevant information. These projections permit precinct commanders and members of the executive staff to rapidly identify patterns, as well as solutions.

The importance of the CompStat process lies not only in its ability to identify hot spots where crime and quality-of-life problems exist but also in its capacity to share this information throughout the agency and across organizational lines. Through information sharing, as well as the efficient and economic use of personnel and resources, every member of every operational unit in the NYPD is ultimately empowered to put his or her best efforts toward resolving problems.[25]

Imperatives

All the benefits that can be derived through community policing do not come without a substantial cost. It is a complex enterprise with heavy demands in a large number of areas. The successful mobilization of a community by the police does require a special type of front-line officer: one who is both a problem solver as well as an interactive individual.

In addition, to ensure optimal functioning of such personnel, an employee evaluation system must be in place that continues to reward and empower highly performing individuals. Of course, the importance of targeted recruiting and selection cannot be minimized, nor can the necessity for training all personnel in the community-policing role.

The Need for Support The front-line officers must receive the organizational support that is essential to their duty performance. This organizational support has a dual meaning.

First, direct supervisors must provide their officers the measure of trust they have earned and the green light to continue their productivity. This usually translates into ongoing flexibility in resources provision.

The second aspect is that from agencies outside the police department, the importance of addressing quality-of-life matters must be understood by all municipal entities.

For example, the environmental conditions that lead to fertile habitats for narcotics traffickers must be recognized by all members of the city workforce—not just the police. Police requests for trash removal or repair of street lighting must be seen as important to public safety as replacing a knocked-down stop sign.

The Role of Top Command Much of the success (or failure) of community policing will rest with the decisions of the agency's top command. These leaders must be able to translate their visions into practice and create a structure to allow new ideas from all levels of the organization to surface to the top.

Most importantly, management must devise ways to sustain momentum toward a constantly enriched partnership in service of community building and problem solving.

What the police have done to date through the community-policing vehicle has been exceptional. Perhaps the gains can be applied conceptually to other institutions perceived as losing touch with the community.

The rise of the militia movement reflects a loss of faith in state and federal governments by many blue-collar workers and rural residents who see their way of life threatened by the global economy. There is a growing sense that we have not kept pace in developing mechanisms that allow the voices of average citizens to be heard.

The principles embodied in community policing point the way toward a total community approach where partnership with the community becomes the cornerstone for broad-ranging public reform.[26]

11.5 Self Check

1. What are the ten principles used in fashioning community policing?
2. What is the clearest indication that community policing is working?

POLICING *Online*

Check your answers at
www.policing.glencoe.com

Chapter 11

Patrol: The Backbone of Policing

Summary By Learning Objectives

1. Identify the basics of traditional patrol.

Police patrol is a multifaceted concept that involves a visible police presence for the purpose of deterring crime, observing conditions that might lead to crime occurrence, and apprehending people who have committed crimes or who might be about to commit crimes. In the course of their exposure to crimes, intelligent patrol officers draw on their experience to develop strong observational skills. In addition to maintaining a deterrent presence, officers perform a wide variety of noncriminal service functions.

2. Understand which options are available for concentration on special crime problems.

A routine demand faced by police departments is how to address special crime problems. Special crime problems can range from a rapist or a burglar on the prowl within a residential community to late-night drag racing or after-hours drinking parties in public areas. Two customary methods for addressing these types of problems with existing resources are split-force patrol and directed patrol. In the split-force approach, a few members of the patrol force are formed into a team with shift-long dedication to the special

problem at hand. This team of officers does not respond to routine citizen calls for service; the remaining members of the patrol handle all the calls for service. In a directed-patrol scheme, no officers are assigned shift-long responsibility for a special crime problem. Instead, officers are requested to spend any available time in the special crime problem area.

3. Explain police methods for prioritizing service delivery.

To better manage the workload of patrol officers, calls for service are prioritized, and differential response is used so that responses to citizens' calls for service are matched to the seriousness of the situation. Reports of incidents in progress that are life threatening are given the highest level of dispatch priority. Delayed or alternative responses are fashioned for calls of lesser urgency. Conditions for which delayed responses are appropriate could include past burglaries or thefts. In certain specified situations, dispatch of a police car may be eliminated altogether. Such incidents could include annoying phone calls or abandoned vehicles; these types of matters might be handled by phone, or the caller might be referred to another government agency.

4. Learn about the value of foot patrol.

Foot patrol has enjoyed a resurgence in the era of community policing because it has been shown to be highly effective for reducing fear levels among neighborhood residents. It is also an ideal vehicle for stimulating the police-citizen interaction essential for mobilizing the community. Also, the nature of foot patrol enables police officers to treat conditions of disorder that have been shown to foster crime occurrence. While there are many advantages to foot patrol, it does need to be recognized as a support service for motorized patrol.

5. Describe the problem-solving approach to policing.

The problem-solving concept has had a pronounced influence on policing. More than any other factor, it has stimulated proactivity in policing. In addition to getting at the root causes of problems, this approach can result in a reduction of repeated calls for service at the former problem location. The reduction permits officers to spend more time on newly emerging problems. A problem-solving strategy, referred to as SARA, has emerged in the course of widespread experimentation with problem solving. SARA is an acronym for a standardized problem-solving technique: scanning, analysis, response, and assessment. In scanning, officers are encouraged to assume a wide perspective in clustering incidents according to shared characteristics. The next step is to analyze aspects of the cluster to understand the scope, nature, and causes of the problem. Once the problem has been analyzed, a response to the problem may be formulated. Following implementation of a problem-solving strategy, the problem area is monitored and assessed to determine the effectiveness of the strategy. Closely associated with the problem-driven approach to policing is the broken windows theory. This concept is an analogy to describe the relationship between disorder and crime. The originators of the broken windows concept believed strongly that serious crime flourishes in areas in which conditions of disorder have been unaddressed. Broken windows has proven to be a viable concept in the quest to restore order along urban streets through the problem-solving approach.

6. Learn the principles of community policing.

Community policing is an organizational philosophy based on a set of values emphasizing problem-solving partnerships between community members and the police. Both the community and the police work together to identify, prioritize, and solve crime problems to attain improved quality of life in their community. The community-police partnership is the essence of the concept of community policing. For a community to unite and actively support a program of community policing, the major groups in the community must agree that a project is worthy of undertaking in the context of their attitudes, values, norms, and goals. Like a marriage, both partners must be prepared and committed toward the endeavor. Six key groups have been identified as crucial for community policing to be successful. These are referred to as the Big Six: police department, citizenry, businesses, civic officials, media, and public and nonprofit agencies. The beat officer assumes a key role in mobilizing the community and sustaining its zeal toward successful implementation of the community-policing philosophy.

Key Terms

patrol (p. 418)
preventive patrol (p. 419)
omnipresence (p. 419)
team policing (p. 422)
split-force patrol (p. 423)
directed patrol (p. 424)
differential response (p. 425)

beat profiling (p. 429)
problem-oriented policing (POP) (p. 431)
SARA (p. 432)
broken windows theory (p. 434)
community policing (p. 437)
Big Six (p. 437)
empowerment (p. 440)

Questions for Review

1. Why is patrol referred to as the backbone of policing?

2. What is the twofold purpose of preventive patrol?

3. Discuss the relative importance of the preliminary investigation conducted by patrol officers in the context of the total criminal investigation.

4. What is a key factor distinguishing the split-force concept from directed patrol?

5. What is differential response, and how does it operate?

6. What are the unique benefits of foot patrol?

7. Briefly describe each stage of the SARA problem-solving technique.

8. How does the broken windows theory contribute to the problem-solving approach?

9. Identify the key elements that constitute community policing.

10. Which groups comprise the Big Six?

Experiential Activities

11. Using SARA

Your city has seen convenience store robberies increase over the past five years. Since the problem began, 45 of 47 San Luis convenience stores have been robbed at least once. Nearly half were robbed five or more times. Convenience stores account for only 18 percent of small service businesses, but they account for 50 percent of the robberies. The police have also learned that 75 percent of the convenience store robberies have taken place between the hours of 7:00 P.M.

and 5:00 A.M. One clerk was present in 92 percent of the crimes. In addition, 24-hour convenience stores were robbed 77 percent more than ones that closed by 11 P.M. Perform a SARA-method analysis of the situation.

a. What will be your first steps in solving this problem?

b. At what point will you consider this crime problem resolved?

c. How would you determine whether this is a specific crime trend?

Experiential Activities continued

12. Involving the Community
Using the scenario in exercise 11. Consider what convenience stores could do, or what a city ordinance could require in order to make conditions safer between 7:00 P.M. and 5:00 A.M.
  a. Can changes in working conditions of convenience store employees help reduce crime?
  b. How can the employees help you in preventing further crime and in arresting suspects?
  c. What do you think you could learn from community group discussions?

13. Causes of Crime
Your police department has been unable to stem your city's increasing drug-dealing problem. The narcotics division is convinced that if more resources were allocated to fighting the drug problem, other crime problems such as robberies would be resolved. Your chief cannot do so without reducing the patrol division. This would make residents feel less safe.
  a. Do you agree with the narcotics division's belief?
  b. Devise a way in which the narcotics division can get more resources without depleting the foot patrol.
  c. How would you present your decision to citizens?

14. A Virtual Visit
Tune in to PoliceScanner.com (click on the link at **www.policing.glencoe.com**). Listen to at least three police departments' communications centers and jot down the first ten calls monitored for each agency.

  a. Which call suits a problem-solving approach?
  b. Which call requires a split-force approach?
  c. What difficulties did you encounter during decision making?

Web Patrol

15. Crime Prevention
Visit an officer's crime prevention page for the Cook College Community Policing Unit (of Rutgers University, NJ) by clicking on the link at **www.policing.glencoe.com**.
  How do sites like this help serve the community and improve the quality of life?

16. Community-Oriented Policing
Visit the U.S. Department of Justice's page for Community-Oriented Policing Services by clicking on the link at **www.policing.glencoe.com**. Read about the grant funding and training services.
  What kind of training and grants does this government service provide to police departments?

17. Safety House
Go to **www.policing.glencoe.com** and read about the Safety House Programme, an Australian community-based crime prevention program that provides safe refuge for anyone in the community.
  How could this program be used in the United States?

Critical Thinking Exercises

18. Underaged Drinking in the Park

You are a police officer assigned to a patrol unit. Your patrol beat includes a popular park, which is open daily from 6:00 A.M. until 10:00 P.M. After closing, particularly on weekend evenings, the quiet park is used extensively by local teenagers who drink and use drugs in the parking lot.

When the problem involved only local juveniles, your department chose to ignore it because they were not making noise or committing other crimes. Recently, juveniles from other communities have been joining the locals. The average number of cars has increased from 3 to nearly 20. The juveniles are loud and unruly, and leave a large amount of broken bottles behind. Homeowners who reside near the park have delivered a petition to your chief, demanding immediate action.

   a. As a night watch officer, whose shift begins at 4:00 P.M. and ends just after midnight, how would you handle the problem on the night shift?
   b. What can you do to communicate to the homeowners that the problem is not being resolved?

19. Mobilizing the Big Six

If you had been assigned a specific beat as a community-policing officer, how would you sustain the interest and active involvement of the Big Six, especially other municipal departments, in the community-policing concept?

   a. Identify strategies that could be employed to maintain zeal on the part of each of the Big Six entities.
   b. Which of these six entities, other than the police, seems most likely to support community policing? Least likely?

20. Broken Windows

You are a foot patrol officer in a low-income neighborhood that consists primarily of elderly people and young (often one-parent) families on public assistance. The neighborhood is rundown, and the crime problem has grown worse over the three years in which you have worked here.

You believe that the neighborhood's deterioration makes it look less protected and more receptive to crime. Drug dealers loiter there often. Arresting them one by one has not solved anything; sting operations have helped the problem more but do not focus on the underlying problem.

In your opinion, the neighborhood needs to be cleaned, painted, repaired, and kept that way for people to respect it and feel that it is worth defending. The elderly residents agree with you wholeheartedly, but they do not have the money to paint their homes. The younger residents are not interested in doing anything that resembles what they call "working for free."

   a. Does the broken windows theory apply to this neighborhood?
   b. Do you think that the community could be rallied to clean up the physical appearance of their neighborhood and maintain it?

Endnotes

1. Kenneth J. Peak, *Policing America: Methods, Issues, and Challenges* (Upper Saddle River, NJ: Prentice Hall, 1997).

2. Gordon Whitaker, Stephen Mastrofski, Roger Parks, and S. Percy, *Basic Issues in Police Performance* (Washington, D.C.: U.S. Department of Justice, 1982).

3. George L. Kelling, Anthony M. Pate, Duane Dieckman, and Charles E. Brown, *The Kansas City Preventive Patrol Experiment: A Summary Report* (Washington, D.C.: Police Foundation, 1974).

4. National Advisory Commission on Criminal Justice Standards and Goals, *Police* (Washington, D.C.: Government Printing Office, 1973), 156.

5. Ibid., 160.

6. Edward A. Thibault, Lawrence M. Lynch, and R. Bruce McBride, *Proactive Police Management* (Upper Saddle River, NJ: Prentice Hall, 1998), 198.

7. Ibid., 198-99.

8. Charles D. Hale, *Police Patrol: Operations and Management* (Englewood Cliffs, NJ: Prentice Hall, 1994), 254.

9. Hale, *Police Patrol*, 252.

10. John E. Eck and William Spelman, "A Problem-Oriented Approach to Police Service Delivery," in *Police and Policing: Contemporary Issues*, edited by D. J. Kenney (New York: Praeger, 1989), 101.

11. Hale, *Police Patrol*, 191–92.

12. John E. Boydstun and Michael E. Sherry, *San Diego Community Profile: Final Report* (Washington, D.C.: Police Foundation, 1975).

13. George L. Kelling, *The Newark Foot Patrol Experiment* (Washington, D.C.: Police Foundation, 1981). [Author Question?—See 17]

14. Robert Trojanowicz, *An Evaluation of the Neighborhood Foot Patrol Program in Flint, Michigan* (East Lansing: Michigan State University, 1982).

15. Herman Goldstein, "Improving Policing: A Problem-Oriented Approach," *Crime and Delinquency* 25, no. 2 (1979): 236–58.

16. William Spelman and John E. Eck, *Problem-Oriented Policing* (Washington, D.C.: National Institute of Justice, 1986).

17. Wilson, [Author Question?] ; Kelling, *The Newark Foot Patrol Experiment*.

18. George L. Kelling and Catherine M. Coles, *Fixing Broken Windows* (New York: Simon & Schuster, 1996), 242–43.

19. Robert Trojanowicz and Bonnie Bucqueroux, *Community Policing: How to Get Started* (Cincinnati, OH: Anderson, 1998), 6.

20. Ibid.

21. Ibid., 8–10.

22. Darl H. Champion, "The Police Are the Public: Community Policing in North Carolina," *Popular Government*, Summer 1998, 24-26.

23. Mark H. Moore, *Perspectives in Policing* (Washington, D.C.: National Institute of Justice, and Cambridge, MA: John F. Kennedy School of Government, Harvard University, 1993).

24. Champion, "The Police Are the Public," 19–22.

25. Howard Safir, "Goal-Oriented Community Policing: The NYPD Approach," *The Police Chief*, December 1997, 31–58.

26. Trojanowicz and Bucqueroux, *Community Policing*, 96.

Chapter 12

The Expanded Police Response

CHAPTER OBJECTIVES

AFTER COMPLETING THIS CHAPTER, YOU WILL BE ABLE TO:

1. Understand what dynamics initiate the police response to crime.

2. Describe the differences between preliminary and follow-up investigations.

3. Gain insights into the police investigative process.

4. Explain the different types of undercover operations.

5. Appreciate the preventive orientation of juvenile services.

6. Identify the three principal domains of traffic operations.

◀ Police stand guard during a protest in Philadelphia at the site of the Republican Convention in July 2000.

While the patrol officer is often on the front line of police response to crime, several other police units are commonly involved in crime-fighting or service activities:

- Investigation
- Undercover work, including narcotics and vice
- Juvenile services
- Traffic operations

How Does the Police Response Begin?

Before focusing on the role of each unit and analyzing how they interact, it is important to gain an understanding of how the police response usually begins: A citizen requests service over the telephone. Upon receiving a call for service, a dispatcher quickly attempts to obtain sufficient information to categorize the call as routine, urgent, or emergency and determine the priority of police unit dispatch. The police dispatcher may also choose to contact other resources, such as a rescue ambulance or animal control services.

▶ **Evidence** Investigators place the bicycle belonging to a missing five-year-old into a plastic bag to preserve it as evidence. Gathering evidence in a thorough and legal manner is a crucial step that can affect an entire case.
Why do you think evidence-gathering is governed by so many rules?

In addition to placing phone calls, citizens can also contact the police in person, either at the local station or in the field. Except for the smallest agencies, police routinely provide counter service for walk-ins. Sometimes, citizens also flag down officers on motorized patrol or approach officers assigned to foot patrol.

Routine Patrol and Response to Crime In the course of performing patrol, detective, traffic, or other field duties, officers routinely approach suspects or other persons. Many of these incidents originate during traffic stops in which officers either have observed a violation of traffic laws or have other probable cause for a vehicle pullover. Often, police officers recognize persons or patterns of conduct that pique their interest during their regular patrols. For example, while patrolling near a convenience store, an officer may observe a parked vehicle, its engine running, that matches the description of a car used in a local hold-up. The officer has two choices: initiate a field interview of the driver or merely observe the vehicle and record its license plate number while surveying the scene.

Preliminary Investigation and Response to Crime When calls are dispatched to the police, the initial responding unit is usually a patrol officer. Depending on what is learned through the patrol officer's preliminary investigation, additional resources may be deployed, such as the following:

- A traffic unit or traffic accident investigator
- A narcotics officer or other undercover officer
- A detective
- A criminologist or forensic specialist from a local crime lab

Resources and Skill Levels An agency's size and mission will affect the nature and variety of resources deployed. Larger municipal agencies may be able to provide an enormous array of in-house specialists for important cases. In smaller agencies, however, patrol generalists may have to wear several specialist "caps," handling as much of an investigation or tactical situation as their skills permit. Although demanding, detectives in smaller departments benefit from having more control over investigations from beginning to end. If required expertise cannot be found within a police department, then resources must be requested externally.

Self-Motivation

Officer-initiated activity is generally highly praised and encouraged within police organizations. The number of documented field interviews and warrant checks conducted by officers is usually included in monthly recaps of officers' field activities.

12.1 Self Check

1. What is the most common form of police response?
2. Which units may be deployed in response to a crime?

POLICING *Online*

Check your answers at
www.policing.glencoe.com

12.2 Preliminary Investigation

preliminary investigation Encompasses the evidence-gathering activities that take place at the scene of a crime immediately after the crime has been reported to or discovered by the police.

A patrol officer is often the one who performs the preliminary investigation, regardless of how a crime or suspected criminal activity comes to the attention of the police. During the **preliminary investigation**, evidence-gathering activities take place at the scene of a crime (or suspected crime) immediately after it has been reported or is discovered by police officers.[1] Because this task consumes a large amount of a patrol officer's time, it is important to fully understand the steps involved in the preliminary investigation.[2] (See Figure 12.1 below.)

The patrol officer is the first to respond to any incident that is of suspicious origin or for which further detailing is required. This is the case no matter what the incident—from natural disasters, such as the touching down of tornadoes, to catastrophic events, such as the horrific terrorist attacks on Oklahoma City in 1995 and New York City/Washington, D.C. during 2001. The importance of conducting a thorough preliminary investigation cannot be overstated. Both witnesses and evidence to crimes can be lost forever if patrol officers do not exercise diligence at the outset.

Figure 12.1

Preliminary Investigation Responsibilities

P roceed to the crime scene with safety and dispatch

R ender assistance to any injured persons

E ffect the arrest of any suspected perpetrator(s)

L ocate and identify witnesses

I nterview complainants and witnesses

M aintain and protect the crime scene

I nterrogate suspects

N ote all conditions, events, and remarks

A rrange for the collection of evidence

R eport the incident fully and accurately

Y ield responsibility to detectives

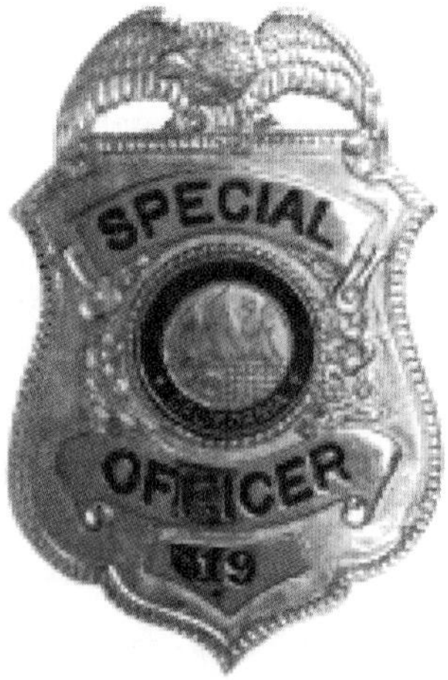

SOURCE: O. W. Wilson, *Police Administration* (New York: McGraw-Hill, 1963), 282.

Officers conduct preliminary investigations for three reasons:

1. Determine if a crime has actually occurred
2. Gather evidence to identify a criminal suspect
3. Document the crime scene for the benefit of follow-up investigators and prosecutors

Figure 12.1 on page 462 contains a list of patrol officers' responsibilities during the preliminary investigation. This conception of patrol officers' crime scene responsibilities has remained essentially the same since the beginning of modern policing. With the exception of rendering assistance and arresting suspected perpetrators(s), most of these responsibilities involve securing the crime scene and gathering information. An officer must act swiftly to locate and identify complainants, witnesses, and suspects. If he or she fails to question all relevant parties at the scene, or does not arrange for the proper collection of evidence, valuable clues can be lost and evidence can be tainted or even destroyed.

Depending on the size and structure of a law enforcement agency, the preliminary investigation can include investigations beyond traditional criminal misconduct. A patrol officer could be the routine preliminary investigator for traffic collisions. Similarly, the first responder could be charged with maintaining and protecting the scene for a hazardous materials incident or even a bombing incident. No matter what the situation might be, the initial actions by the first patrol officer to arrive at the scene can set the tone for the quality of the outcome of the investigation.

Importance of the Preliminary Investigation

By their nature, crime scenes change quickly. Evidence is cleaned up and thrown away, or it disintegrates or decomposes. The more rapidly patrol officers get to a crime scene, preserve evidence, and collect it, the greater the opportunity to solve the crime by obtaining valuable clues. An officer's role at a crime scene extends beyond merely providing security; he or she must be proactive in locating witnesses and gathering physical evidence.

A landmark 1975 study showed that well-handled preliminary investigations make an enormous contribution in solving crimes ultimately handled by detectives. What determines, more than anything else, whether a case is solved is the nature of information recorded by the patrol officer first on the scene, including:[3]

- Amount and quality of evidence
- Number of witnesses and their level of cooperation
  whether possible suspects were determined
- General understanding of the crime scene as a whole—especially if the officer is going to describe it in court

The largest issue relative to the initial investigation is the competency of the preliminary investigators. Patrol officers must be well trained in the fundamentals of recognizing and preserving physical evidence at the crime scene. The mishandling of evidence following the murders of Nicole Brown Simpson and Ron Goldman, for example, highlighted the need to adhere to appropriate protocols in crime scene investigations at the preliminary stages.

Another key factor that determines whether or not a case will be solved is the case's solvability. Cases should be screened at the outset to determine their potential solvability. Research has revealed **solvability factors,** which are reliable indicators of the potential for solving a particular case.[4] Figure 12.2 above provides a list of solvability factors. the preliminary investigator should determine the answer to each of these questions. the more accurate answers he or she collects, the more likely the case is to be solved. A case in which the witness can name and describe a suspect and a suspect vehicle, for example, is much more likely to be solved that a case in which a witness can provide only a suspect description.

solvability factors Reliable indicators of the potential for solving cases.

12.2 Self Check

1. What are the three basic reasons for doing a preliminary investigation?
2. What are the officer's investigative responsibilities during the preliminary investigation?

POLICING Online

Check your answers at
www.policing.glencoe.com

12.3 Follow-Up Investigation

The **follow-up investigation**, which is a continuation of the preliminary investigation, focuses on reconstructing the circumstances of (1) an illegal act or failure to act when legally required to do so and (2) the mental state accompanying it. The combination of these two elements is what defines a crime, and investigators must establish both in order to ask a prosecutor to file charges.

The problem with the follow-up portion of the investigative process, however, is that it has traditionally lacked systems for assigning, coordinating, directing, and monitoring the continuing investigative effort. This frequently results in inequitable caseloads, improper assignments and priorities of cases, lateness of investigator responses, and a lack of investigative continuity. To cure these deficiencies, those who supervise an investigative unit will often employ the following techniques:

- *Centralized filing of all investigative folders* This ends a tradition of officers' exclusive retention of their own case folders. It enables all investigative personnel and supervisors to review the folders and obtain (and furnish) relevant information when necessary. One drawback is that keeping track of all materials is more difficult, and some documents can be lost or stolen more easily when accessible to an entire department.
- *Mandatory review dates* They serve as "ticklers" for detectives to stay on track on all their cases.
- *Extensive use of investigative checklists* This ensures that steps are not missed in the investigative process and providing a common format across all cases. This uniformity also enables persons other than the assigned investigator to quickly obtain information from a case folder if needed.[5]

The Role of the Police Detective

How does one become a police detective? Detectives are police officers who work in entry-level units, such as patrol, until they are selected to be detectives. On average, officers who become detectives work in patrol for four to eight years before being promoted. This position is generally held in very high status within agencies, with many patrol officers aspiring to become detectives someday.

Detective Units Police agencies need to ensure that the necessary time and qualified personnel are available for in-depth investigations, so they usually designate a detective unit, or *detective bureau*, as the organizational entity

follow-up investigation
Continuation of the preliminary investigation conducted by patrol officers in an attempt to reconstruct the circumstances of an illegal act.

The Expanded Police Response **CHAPTER 12** 465

responsible for criminal investigation. In medium- and large-sized police agencies, this segment generally is divided into two functional units:

1. A property crimes unit that investigates burglaries, thefts, and related crimes
2. A crimes against persons unit that investigates crimes such as homicides, sex crimes, assaults, kidnappings, and robberies.[6]

Online

Remember, one of your best resources is **www.policing.glencoe.com**

Investigative Duties Although detective work is given high status, it is still very hard and unglamorous work. The detective assigned to a case has four main responsibilities, and each is time-consuming and difficult:

1. Develop evidence that will further the investigation, lead to the identification and apprehension of the offender(s), and assist in the prosecution of the perpetrator(s)
2. Bring an investigation to a successful conclusion
3. Exonerate innocent persons involved in the case
4. Focus the investigation on the culpable person(s)

In other words, detectives must evaluate the evidence for a case, find and investigate leads, and find and interrogate suspects in order to determine who is guilty and innocent. In addition, detectives must juggle several cases at once.

Traits of Successful Detectives Most detectives must work with heavy workloads that cover only the most serious cases. Therefore, they see far more death, sex offenses, and serious assault and abuse cases than most other police personnel do. This can cause stress, burnout, and even substance abuse or suicide. Police management often tries to avoid this problem by selecting individuals whose personalities are best for detective work. Some traits will help a detective stay effective and avoid burnout:

- A thorough understanding of different types of evidence and what evidence is required to establish guilt or innocence
- An extensive knowledge of criminal law and rules of evidence
- An excellent memory that can recall crime scenes and interviews in great detail
- Strong critical thinking skills
- Creative problem-solving skills
- Patience
- A capability for observation and objective perception
- An ability to organize evidence and small details
- Emotional stability
- The ability to interact with fellow detectives in an information-sharing capacity

Career Paths for Detectives Many detectives prefer to stay in their positions for the duration of their careers because detective work can be very fulfilling. Also, detective work can be fairly independent and free of departmental politics. As agencies grow, detectives may choose to focus on developing their experience in specialized areas such as homicides, arsons, or sex crimes. This enables the department to provide a higher level of expertise during criminal investigations.

Successful detectives may also be promoted to chief of police or get elected as county sheriff. Often a detective who is well known and liked by the community can be elected sheriff, especially when a community feels that law enforcement needs to take a stronger crime-fighting focus.

Crime Clearance

A primary purpose of the investigative process is to identify, arrest, and prosecute law violators. A successful outcome of this purpose is **crime clearance**, which occurs when a detective has solved the crime and has taken all possible, appropriate action against at least one suspect. Case clearance requirements are based on FBI Uniform Crime Reporting (UCR) guidelines. While interpretation of these guidelines may vary, the requirements are not subject to revision or alteration on a local basis. (See Figure 12.3 on page 469 for crime clearance rates.)

crime clearance The status assigned to a case when the concerned detective has solved the crime and has taken all possible, appropriate action against at least one suspect.

Crime clearance is often categorized as follows:

- Cleared by arrest
- Cleared other
- Report unfounded

Cleared by Arrest The classification *cleared by arrest* is assigned when a person has been arrested and charged with an offense and the matter is set for a prosecutorial hearing. This classification may also be used when a felony warrant based on the crime report has been served and the named suspect has been booked.

Cleared Other The classification *cleared other* indicates when a case has progressed to a point where further action cannot be reasonably taken and all four of the following circumstances exist:

1. The identity of the perpetrator has been established.
2. The detective knows a location where the perpetrator could be arrested.
3. There is sufficient evidence to support arresting and turning the perpetrator over to a court for prosecution.
4. The case is outside of police control.

In addition to these circumstances, a case may be "cleared other" when a suspect in custody confesses to crimes that are similar to crimes for which criminal complaints were issued. In such instances, additional evidence or specific admission must substantiate a suspect's confessions for each crime. For example, additional evidence or specific admissions would include the suspect's specific knowledge of the method of entry, the layout of the crime scene, and/or the property taken—details that could only be known by a person who participated in the crime.

Report Unfounded A *report unfounded* classification occurs when the crime or incident alleged in the original report did not occur, the same crime has been reported more than once, or *specific intent* to commit the crime is a necessary element for prosecution but investigative efforts have failed to

MYTH	FACT
Once a crime is cleared, the detective's work is done.	The fact that a crime report is cleared does not relieve the detective of the responsibility to investigate co-suspects or to recover property.

Figure 12.3

Example of Crime Clearance Rates

Indexed Crimes	2000	1999
Criminal Homicide/Murder	86.7 %	92.0%
Forcible Rape	59.4%	46.6%
Robbery	33.0%	34.4%
Aggravated Assault	65.1%	63.1%
Burglary	14.7%	10.4%
Larceny/Theft	26.6%	28.2%
Motor Vehicle Theft	29.8%	22.7%
Overall Clearance Rate	27.6%	27.7%
Other Crimes of Interest	**2000**	**1999**
Criminal Homicide/Negligent Manslaughter	100.0%	0.0%
Simple Assault	84.6%	82.3%

SOURCE: Colorado Springs Police Department, "2000 Statistical Annual Report: Clearance Rates for Indexed Offenders," accessed online at http://www.springsgov.com/Page.asp?NavID=2051 on December 18, 2001.

prove that specific intent existed. For example, in many bad check cases, insufficient funds on deposit at the time a check was written cannot prove specific intent because bank records do not indicate histories of overdrafts.[7]

Enhancing the Investigative Process

In the wake of extensive federal-sponsored research on the investigative function, improvements in the criminal investigation arena have been concentrated in four general areas:

1. Managing investigations
2. Enhancing police-prosecutor relations
3. Targeting investigations
4. Scientific investigation

Managing Investigations In the literature of the field, a collection of scientifically tested suggestions for improving the investigative process is called **managing criminal investigations (MCI)**.[8] Under MCI, four considerations apply to any assessment of the investigative function:

managing criminal investigations (MCI) An array of scientifically tested suggestions for improving the investigative process such as case screening.

1. Number of arrests
2. Number of cases cleared
3. Number and percentage of cases accepted for prosecution
4. Number of convictions

The first two items, basic to the control of criminal investigations, are the responsibility of the detective and police supervisors. The third item depends on the standards set by the prosecutor and the ability of the detective to meet them. The final consideration involves the jury, judge, and prosecutor. To some degree, a detective's performance on a particular case can affect the outcome of all four.

Under MCI, four elements are critical in the management of criminal investigations, three of which were discussed earlier: the preliminary investigation, case screening, and controls such as investigative checklists. The final element is police-prosecutor relations.

Police-Prosecutor Relations Outsiders may be unaware that police-prosecutor relations are often rocky. Seasoned investigators frequently look upon prosecutors as people who do not understand the reality of a given case (especially when it is plea-bargained instead of brought to trial) or who are inept in presenting a case. The prosecutor, often beset with a staggering caseload, may not have the opportunity to analyze every aspect of a case. The

CopTalk

Outside of Police Control

The phrase *outside of police control,* which is one of the reasons for a classification of *clearance other,* can mean any of the following:

1. The prosecutor does not believe that the probability of conviction is high enough.
2. The perpetrator is serving time in another jurisdiction, and his or her release cannot be obtained.
3. The perpetrator is offered immunity.
4. The perpetrator is charged with a more serious offense in another jurisdiction and is released to that jurisdiction.

5. The prosecutor decides to refer the perpetrator to a public social service agency for counseling or other services that are deemed necessary.
6. The victim refuses to prosecute or cooperate, and the victim's testimony is essential in substantiating the elements of the crime.
7. The perpetrator has died.

What Do You Think? Can any of these obstacles be overcome by a persistent arresting officer? Which ones, and why?

situation may be compounded by a case folder that lacks the organization and level of detail needed to plan the prosecution effectively.

Poor police-prosecutor relations can be disastrous. One famous example is the relationship between detectives and the prosecutor in Boulder, Colorado, during the JonBenet Ramsey case which still has not been prosecuted. Some detectives handling that case felt that the prosecutor's ambition to be promoted led him to refuse to press charges against JonBenet's parents, John and Patsy. The result of this friction was bad publicity, the resignation of the case's lead detective, and—worst of all—an unsolved case.

Perhaps the best specific action steps that can be taken to improve communications between both parties are the following:

- Increased dialogue between supervisory personnel from both departments
- Use of liaison officers to communicate to police officers the investigatory techniques and evidence standards that are required by the investigator to file a case
- Development of a system of formal and informal feedback to the police on case dispositions (dismissal, continuance, or other outcomes)

Targeting Investigations When investigators attempt to move a criminal investigation from a reactive mode to a more proactive and focused strategy. One form of targeting is to concentrate on high-rate offenders. Investigators narrow their attention to these repeat offenders through surveillance, informants, stings, and enhanced prosecution. Another way to target criminal activity is to use task forces to zero in on major crimes or specific types of offenses, such as drug trafficking, instead of relying solely on the efforts of individual detectives. Finally, targeting investigations can focus on nontraditional but insidious offenses such as domestic violence, hate crimes, corruption, or white-collar crime.[9]

Scientific Investigation Although prevalent from the beginning of the twentieth century, scientific criminal investigation did not become vital until the due process revolution of the 1960s and 1970s, when the U.S. Supreme Court outlawed many questionable police techniques and specified restrictive guidelines for searches, seizures, and interrogations. Changes in criminal procedure forced the police to do a better job of "making" cases, as opposed to depending on coerced confessions or questionably obtained evidence to obtain convictions.[10]

Modern technology has dramatically altered the nature of detective work and the effectiveness of criminal investigation. One line of development has been in the area of information technology. For example, computer-assisted information sharing between jurisdictions on homicides and rapes has facilitated identification of serial killers and rapists. Crime analysis systems also have provided valuable relational data to identify crime "hot spots." The other principal type of technology development influencing criminal investigation has been in the area of forensic science.

Technological advancements continue to improve the police's ability to find and analyze physical evidence. Recent innovations in DNA and automated fingerprint identification systems (AFIS) have allowed criminal investigations to become far more exacting. DNA and AFIS facilitate investigations by identifying specific suspects.[11] Psychological profiling has brought the social sciences into the crime lab as an indispensable tool for identifying a suspect's personality and emotional characteristics.

DNA testing Technology that identifies offenders and corpses by testing biological evidence to find its DNA sequence.

DNA Testing One of the most powerful investigative tools available is **DNA testing**. DNA testing has proven to be one of the most important advances in crime lab technologies because the technology is reliable, it can accurately identify certain contributors of biological samples, and only a minute amount of sample DNA is needed for analysis. DNA is a molecule that is present in all life forms and different for each person (except identical twins). The order of a person's DNA sequence makes that person unique and determines his or her physical makeup. For almost all of us, some areas along the DNA strand are going to be the same, such as having two legs and two eyes. Other areas, such as eye color and hair color, will have slightly different orders along the DNA at those locations. There are also millions of genetic traits that people cannot see (such as blood type), but they will appear on DNA tests. Forensic scientists compare areas along DNA strands to determine differences among individuals.

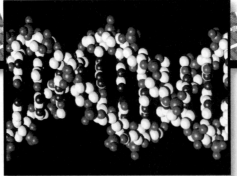

Computer On Patrol

Forensic Science

Forensic science is a field that has benefitted from many technological developments, and greatly influenced and helped criminal investigations. Advancements continue to improve the police's ability to find and analyze physical evidence. Recent innovations in DNA (deoxyribonucleic acid) and AFIS (automated fingerprint identification system) testing have allowed investigations to become far more precise. DNA and AFIS facilitate investigations by identifying specific suspects with high accuracy.

Think About It Which technological approach sounds more flexible for investigators, DNA or AFIS?

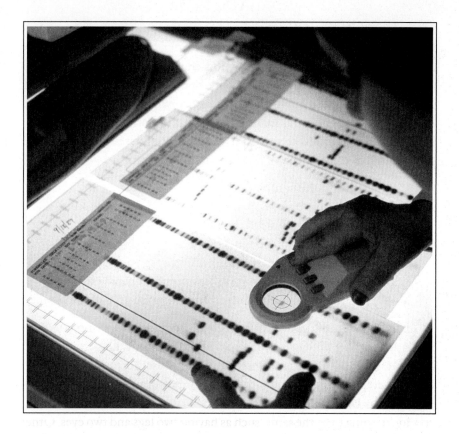

DNA is the same in any cell in the body, so a mouth swab that contains saliva can be equally effective as a blood test. Many types of evidence may have traces of saliva or blood on them, such as straws, cigarette butts, eating utensils, or toothbrushes. Saliva containing DNA has been found on a bite mark that had been submerged underwater and on a victim's ear that had been chewed. Skin tissue with DNA can be found on earrings, hats, clothing, gloves, and eyeglasses.

AFIS Technology Unquestionably, computer technology has significantly improved many aspects of police work. Among the most important advances is **automated fingerprint identification system (AFIS)** technology. This computer technology uses a mathematically created image of a fingerprint and identifies up to 250 characteristics for each print. Standard 10-print cards, which in the past had to be searched by hand, are now scanned electronically, digitized, and made readable by the computer system to create the database of fingerprints for comparison.

Once the AFIS creates a live digital fingerprint, images of the prints can be generated and transmitted for identification. Thus, a networked AFIS can allow an agency to compare a suspect's fingerprints with thousands or even millions of data bank prints in a matter of minutes. The same search might take weeks or months if done manually.

automated fingerprint identification system (AFIS) A computer-based fingerprint technology that uses a mathematically created image of a fingerprint that identifies up to 250 characteristics for each print.

psychological profiling A method of suspect identification that seeks to identify an individual's mental, emotional, and personality characteristics as manifested in things done or left behind at a crime scene.

Psychological Profiling One method of suspect identification is **psychological profiling**, which seeks to identify an individual's mental, emotional, and personality characteristics as manifested in things done or left behind at a crime scene. Profiling is most often employed when there is a series of crimes or when there are crimes of violence with no apparent motive. Profiles are not as specific as DNA or fingerprints. Rather, they point to the type of individual most likely to commit the crime under investigation. The process used to create a profile typically has seven steps:

1. Evaluation of the criminal act
2. Comprehensive evaluation of the specifics of the crime scene
3. Comprehensive analysis of the victim
4. Evaluation of preliminary police reports
5. Evaluation of the medical examiner's autopsy protocol
6. Development of profile with critical offender characteristics
7. Investigative suggestions predicated on construction of the profile

The person preparing a criminal personality profile uses a process similar to that used by clinicians to make a medical diagnosis. Data are collected and assessed, the situation is reconstructed, hypotheses are formulated, a profile is developed and tested, and the results are reported back. Profiling has been used by law enforcement with success in many areas, and it is a useful way for an officer to narrow the scope of the investigation.

12.3 Self Check

1. What are the primary job responsibilities of a police investigator?
2. What criteria are used to assess the investigator function?

POLICING *Online*

Check your answers at **www.policing.glencoe.com**

12.4 Undercover Operations

undercover investigation An investigation in which an investigator assumes, for organizationally approved purposes, a different identity to obtain information or achieve another investigative purpose.

In an **undercover investigation**, an officer assumes, for purposes approved by his or her superiors, a different identity to obtain information or achieve another investigative purpose.[12] During undercover investigations, officers gather evidence on criminal activities for the subsequent disruption of illicit activities. The focus of these investigations is often on drug trafficking and sales, vice activities, buying and selling stolen property, and white-collar crime. Often, investigators work undercover as decoys to apprehend muggers and other dangerous street criminals. The following sections address important aspects of undercover operations and some specific undercover applications.

Selection

The selection process for undercover officers varies depending on the nature of the assignment. In deep cover assignments, police supervisors usually select and place officers immediately after they graduate from the police academy. In some jurisdictions, persons with no police training or affiliation are hired as undercover officers. There are three main reasons for doing this.

1. Sometimes it may be necessary for the officer to have a youthful appearance, such as when an investigation requires undercover work on a high school or college campus.
2. In many instances, inexperienced officers are selected simply because undercover operatives must not have had prior contacts with the group to be infiltrated (which could have resulted in the course of extensive police service).
3. Inexperienced officers have not yet acquired typical police mannerisms or jargon that would give them away in undercover assignments. For example, police officers habitually use the term vehicle instead of car or automobile, and they frequently refer to people as persons. They often hook their thumbs over the front of their belts or place their car keys in or near their belt buckles.

Whenever possible, an officer selected for undercover work is placed on a loan period of about 30 days in order to evaluate his or her effectiveness as an investigator. Such a period provides supervisors with an opportunity to observe an officer under actual field conditions.

The job also demands certain qualifications and personality traits such as emotional stability, maturity, creative problem-solving skills, personal integrity, agency loyalty, the ability to make appropriate decisions on the basis of available data, and self-discipline. Self-discipline is essential because an undercover operative will be continually exposed to temptations.

Undercover Levels

Light Cover According to George Miller, there are two levels of undercover work: light cover and deep cover.[13] **Light cover** is of comparatively short duration, often lasting for only a single work shift. Such officers often depend on the assistance of informants who provide introductions or pass information while going about their everyday business, which is frequently of a criminal nature. An example of a light cover assignment would be decoy work, in which an officer may don a disguise during an evening shift to mask his or her identity as a police officer. Another example is the typical drug sting, in which an officer poses as a drug buyer for a brief period to fool a drug dealer into making a transaction.

ETHICS ISSUES

Undercover Assignment

You are a police supervisor who is in charge of assigning five new officers to assignments. You would like to assign two of these five to undercover work. Considering the personality traits that you know an undercover officer should have, write an evaluation of the ideal undercover officer. *Which of these traits do you think is most important, and how do all of them overlap?*

light cover An undercover assignment of very short duration, such as stings or decoy work.

deep cover Submersion in a false identity for an extended time period, sometimes months.

Deep Cover In contrast to light cover, **deep cover** entails submersion in the false identity for an extended time period, often lasting months (and sometimes years). The ultimate power of the deep cover disguise is that an officer is able to circulate and gather evidence in areas and within groups the police could not otherwise infiltrate. Such assignments could include infiltration of a cocaine smuggling ring or an "outlaw" motorcycle gang.

Vice and Narcotics Enforcement

Vice and narcotics enforcement represent the most common deployment of undercover officers. Therefore, examination of these criminal enterprises yields insights into the nature of both undercover operations and vice and drugs netherworlds.

vice investigation Investigation that focuses on crimes against the morals of a community.

Vice Examples of vice offenses include gambling, prostitution, illegal sale of alcohol, and pornography. **Vice investigation** generally deals with crimes against the morals of a community. Vice control has historically been a province of police because of public clamor. Often these crimes are considered victimless; however, analysis of vice-related offenses clearly reveals that victims do exist, even though the participants engage in such conduct with mutual consent. (See Figure 12.4 on page 477 for an example of a vice division organization.)

▶ **Undercover Work** A member of the Detroit Gang Squad, an undercover group focused on juvenile gangs, speaks with a man under arrest. Most commonly, undercover officers are employed in the enforcement of narcotics and vice laws. *Why do you think undercover police is better suited to this work than uniformed officers?*

Vice divisions enforce state laws and city ordinances against illegal gambling, prostitution, alcohol distribution, and pornography. They may also be in charge of providing permits to those wishing to open sexually oriented businesses (such as adult bookstores) or dance clubs.

◆ **Administrative Squad** This squad conducts vice-related computer investigations and is responsible for day-to-day administrative duties and investigative hold authorizations.

◆ **Organized Gambling Squad** This unit investigates illegal gambling with an emphasis on bookmakers in sporting events on a year-round basis. It also investigates the use of video poker machines in local bars and areas of entertainment. Investigation of illegal card games and carnivals are also the responsibility of this unit.

◆ **Organized Prostitution Squad** This unit investigates escort services, massage parlors, modeling studios, and topless clubs that are suspected of fronting prostitution. They are also responsible for conducting street prostitution stings in conjunction with the appropriate Division Tactical Unit.

◆ **Pornography Squad** This unit investigates all forms of pornography in the city. They are also responsible for enforcing and investigating the city's Sexually Oriented Business Ordinance (SOB.) This ordinance controls the placement of various businesses in the city that require SOB permits.

◆ **General Vice Squad** These units are assigned to the night shift and are responsible for vice-related crimes that occur at night, with an emphasis on liquor licensed establishments. They are also responsible for conducting reverse prostitution stings with the appropriate Division Tactical Unit.

SOURCE: Adapted from City of Houston, Texas, *Vice Division*, accessed online at http://www.ci.houston.tx.us/departme/police/vice.htm on December 18, 2001.

Vice offenses present the police agency with a host of problems. Beyond the offense, a variety of secondary effects can occur. Customers can be "rolled" (robbed), other crimes may be committed, and the area where all this happens can undergo an economic decline. Vice activity that operates without interference by the police may give the impression that the police are being paid to look the other way.[14]

Because of the covert nature of vice activity and the monetary incentives provided, no other criminal activity lends itself so readily to organization. The term organized crime denotes an organized effort by persons who, in varying degrees, supply illegal services that cater to the weaknesses of individuals. The ultimate objective of organized crime syndicates is accumulating financial power and influence within legalized government to make more money.[15]

Criminals within these syndicates do not limit themselves to activities connected with consensual crimes. Their activities encompass every conceivable type of criminal scheme, including extortion, loan sharking, and murder.

The direct links between vice activity and organized crime groups are frequently difficult to detect. The undercover investigator is relied on as a principal investigative tool in the development of intelligence that ultimately leads to the detection and prosecution of perpetrators of vice offenses.

Narcotics Undercover work related to drug trafficking generally occurs along two paths (see Figure 12.5 below). The first one is infiltrating the criminal organization that sells large quantities of drugs.[16] In such an operation, the undercover officer buys larger and larger quantities of drugs to reach as high as possible into a targeted organization's hierarchy. To gain access to an illicit organization's upper echelon, the investigator must gain the trust of someone of influence within the organization. This level of operation generally requires sophisticated electronic surveillance measures and

---

Figure 12.5

Want to Work as a Narc?

A narcotics agent enforces the Uniform Controlled Dangerous Substance Act. His or her typical job functions are:

◆ Investigates violations of state (or federal, depending on the agency) laws concerning narcotics, dangerous drugs, or other controlled substances

◆ Participates in undercover operations, raids, and surveillance of persons or targeted locations or where it is believed that the law is being violated

◆ Operates and monitors electronic surveillance equipment

◆ Infiltrates illicit drug channels

◆ Works closely with and interviewing confidential informants

◆ Establishes and maintains cooperative relationships with municipal, state, and federal law enforcement organizations

◆ Identifies and arrests drug traffickers

◆ Confiscates illegal drug supplies

◆ Develops evidence to seize financial assets gained from the proceeds of drug trafficking

◆ Searches for and gathers physical or documentary evidence or clues, interviews witnesses, interrogates suspects, and presents findings in reports

◆ Assists prosecutors in filing charges, appears as a witness in criminal and administrative court proceedings, and drafts and executes legal documents such as subpoenas for evidence, search warrants, arrest warrants, and affidavits

◆ Participates in in-service training: learns new investigative procedures and techniques, studies legal materials relating to court rulings and state and federal law, and attends training sessions to acquire new skills

SOURCE: Adapted from State of Oklahoma, *Law Enforcement Narcotics Agent*, accessed online at http://www.opm.state.ok.us//jfd/g-specs/g24.htm on December 18, 2001; Drug Enforcement Administration (DEA), *Criminal Investigator—Special Agent*, accessed online at http://www.usajobs.opm.gov/wfjic/jobs/IK7325.HTM on December 18, 2001.

---

a significant time period. Activities such as locating key figures in the drug distribution network and collecting incriminating evidence against them are the essence of deep cover work.

The second principal method of interrupting drug trafficking is the undercover **buy and bust** or *sting*, an operation in which an undercover police officer purchases a quantity of drugs from a narcotics suspect and shortly thereafter arranges for the apprehension of the seller by police cohorts positioned nearby. The "buy and bust" is generally used in low-level drug sales activities that have become the object of community complaints. A closely related technique is the **reverse sting**, in which an officer poses as a seller of drugs, rather than as a purchaser. As mentioned earlier, sting operations frequently employ officers in light cover capacities.

Performing in either deep cover or light cover roles, undercover drug investigators face many risks, including increased exposure to weapons wielded by drug dealers, increased violence by foreign nationals involved in drug trafficking, and the risk of handling informants whose allegiance may be confused.[17] The dollar amounts involved in the drug trade are so enormous that human life is often viewed as insignificant in contrast and undercover officers must exercise extreme caution.

buy and bust An operation in which an undercover officer purchases a quantity of drugs in order to arrest the seller; also called a sting.

reverse sting An undercover officer poses as a seller of drugs for the purpose of arresting a predisposed purchaser of drugs.

Decoy Operations

Decoy operations are effective in combating the crimes of robbery, purse snatching, and other thefts from the person. They have also been employed to combat burglaries and thefts of and from vehicles. As a **decoy**, an officer dresses as and assumes the role of a potential victim and waits to be the subject of a crime. A backup team of officers is positioned nearby to apprehend any violator in the act of committing an expected crime. As is the case with all undercover operations, service as a decoy is inherently dangerous.

Blending is a technique akin to decoying, but in employing this strategy, officers do not pose as potential victims. In **blending**, officers assume the roles and dress of ordinary citizens (e.g., construction workers, bicyclists, or disabled persons) so that without being recognized, the officers can be close enough to observe and intervene should a crime occur. In employing blending, officers may target areas where a substantial amount of crime occurs, or they may follow particular people who appear to be potential victims or offenders.[18]

decoy An undercover operation in which an officer dresses as and assumes the role of a potential victim and then waits to be the subject of a crime.

blending An officer assuming the role and dress of an ordinary citizen in order to remain undetected in an area of high crime potential.

Surveillance

Discussion of undercover operations would be incomplete without mention of surveillance. **Surveillance**—the observation of a person, place, or thing in an unobtrusive manner—is seldom performed exclusively from a fixed position. As the subject of surveillance moves about, so too must the officer

surveillance Observation of a person, place, or thing in such a manner that the observer is undetected.

technical surveillance The use of electronic and visual enhancement devices to overhear or view suspects in the conduct of their affairs.

performing the surveillance, unless the observation goal is a very limited one. As necessary, technical surveillance is employed. **Technical surveillance** involves the use of electronic and visual enhancement devices to overhear or view suspects in the conduct of their affairs. It should be noted that the use of electronic devices is fraught with legal impediments, so these devices are not used without appropriate legal guidance.

Surveillance is seldom the task of a single person; it usually employs at least one other person and a variety of resources. Vehicles equipped with direct intercommunications are generally essential. Less expensive equipment, such as infrared optical devices and high-quality binoculars, may suffice to locate suspects from afar. The objectives of surveillance can be realized without elaborate resources and staff. For more elaborate investigations, surveillance may require helicopters or fixed wing aircraft. In such instances, state-level law enforcement agencies are usually brought into the investigation since they may possess the specialized equipment essential for the elaborate surveillance.[19]

While it may appear that investigators must be extraordinarily careful if they are to go undetected during their covert observations, in reality a large number of suspects really do not want to discover that they are the objects of surveillance. Oftentimes, persons engaged in criminal activities are concerned about whether the police are watching them, yet at the same time they are reluctant to face the fact that they are the object of surveillance. This conclusion was reached after analyzing a series of ongoing "heavy-footed" surveillance outside

Police Procedure

Extreme Surveillance

Since 1965, the LAPD has deployed a surveillance squad that not only practices covert observations of suspected criminals but also monitors them as they commit crimes. The 20-member Special Investigation Section (SIS) is called into service when other LAPD detectives believe that they have identified a suspect but cannot prove it. It then becomes the job of SIS to confirm whether the person is a suspect and to gather more evidence until probable cause can be established. The SIS detectives spend long hours "shadowing" suspected individuals, waiting for them to commit crimes. If the suspect commits a crime, the detectives close in with overwhelming force *after* the crime's commission. In recent years, SIS has been the target of numerous lawsuits stemming from a series of controversial shootings. Critics call the SIS a "death squad," citing that the unit has killed 34 suspects since its inception in 1965. These deaths often have resulted from officers' use of the "jam" technique, which encourages shootouts by pinning a suspect's getaway car with police vehicles.

Critical Thinking Do you feel that the current SIS approach is appropriate, or is there a better approach to handling such situations? Explain.

SOURCE: Matt Lait, "SIS: Stormy Past, Shaky Future," *Los Angeles Times*, 29 November 1998, 1.

the meeting places of known hoodlums and gang members in the New York area. Similar conclusions have been reached through the experiences of state and federal agents performing stakeouts at major U.S. airports.[20]

Of course, a number of persons are still vigilant for law enforcement "tails" and cause authorities to undertake special measures to avoid being "burned" in the course of surveillance. In such circumstances, surveillants work in two- or three-person teams. **Leapfrogging** is a technique used to rotate surveillance team members into a close contact position with an individual being watched. The particular value of this technique is that the chance of being detected by the suspect is diminished because the same person is not following the suspect continuously. With the leapfrogging technique, the suspect just about makes an identification when a new member (or vehicle) of the surveillance team moves up into contact, and the other team member(s) drops back into a position well to the rear or across the street. All that is required of the personnel who drop back is to keep the contact position investigator in sight. When vehicles are used as "leapfrogs," such contact can be maintained by radio.[21]

Informants

An **informant** is a person who informs against another person who is suspected of violating some penal statute. While anyone can technically qualify as an informant (e.g., victims, witnesses, and civic-minded citizens), the term usually describes criminals or persons directly associated with individuals engaged in criminal activity. The assistance of informants is generally sought to uncover primary or secondary leads, initiate the ritual of "making buys" to justify the arrest of drug dealers, acquire current information on the operations of criminal groups, and provide meaningful evidence in a criminal trial.

Most police and citizens view informants as immoral and untrustworthy. This can be an important consideration when a case is going to trial because the defense attorney may try to convince a jury that the informant is lying for the police. This sometimes occurs when informants give police false or unsubstantiated information to escape punishment. Still, informants are necessary for some types of criminal investigation because they allow police to gather evidence of criminal enterprises—without requiring an officer to risk his or her life by going undercover.

When employing informants, the investigator may be viewed as relinquishing his or her basic responsibility in collecting objective evidence (see Figure 12.6 on page 482). The use of informants also reflects negatively on detectives because it brings them into close contact with persons who are "street-smart" and have low thresholds for moral and criminal misconduct. To counteract informant problems, investigators must verify any information

Decoy Innovations

The New York City Police Department (NYPD) is known for its innovations in decoy operations. Each of the NYPD's precincts has its own decoy unit, which is staffed with experienced decoys. Officers have donned a variety of disguises, including posing as McDonald's employees and cab drivers, to combat assaults against such employees.

The Miami Police Department has also employed decoys to reduce crime against tourists. At the height of a series of robberies of tourists, Miami police posed as tourists and sat in rental cars parked in crime-prone areas.

leapfrogging A technique used to rotate various surveillance team members into a close contact position with an individual being watched.

informant A person who informs against another suspected of violating some penal statute.

Figure 12.6

Skills for Managing Informants

Informants can be unpredictable, unreliable, and untruthful. On the other hand, they are sometimes the only people who can provide crucial evidence needed to solve criminal cases. Some of the skills needed to manage informants are:

◆ Understanding the rewards and incentives that motivate informants

◆ Classifying different types of informants based on the quality and quantity of their evidence

◆ Avoiding manipulation by informants

◆ Successful recruitment techniques

◆ Turning a one-time informant into a long-term source of information

◆ Effectively preparing informants to look for evidence

◆ Interviewing informants to retrieve all available information

◆ Avoiding unethical "deals" with informants

◆ Avoiding unnecessary risks to the detective's or department's security

◆ Sharing informants with other detectives or agencies

◆ Protecting informants under the law

SOURCE: Adapted from Beacon Analysis, "Informant Skills Training," accessed online at http://members.tripod.com/~BeaconAnalysis/html/body_informant_skills.html on December 18, 2001.

received from informants, maintain nonsocial relationships with them, and keep informants' identity secret unless it is vital to the prosecution's case or a trial court orders disclosure of identity. All of these strategies will help ensure that informants stay relatively trustworthy. Ideally, the function of an informant is investigative only; it is hoped that compelling evidence of a defendant's guilt can be obtained through other sources.

If informants are used, the relationship between them and the investigators must be controlled. Controls are essential for protecting the integrity of investigators and the police unit. At the heart of the control process is agency registration of informants. Through registration, informants' actual names, code names, and other data are placed in confidential records. The officer in charge of the investigative unit oversees informant files through the registration protocol. As a result of the registration process, "snitches" are no longer the exclusive property of any one investigator. This expands the use of the information provided by informants and allows others to evaluate its credibility and value.[22]

12.4 Self Check

1. What are the two levels of undercover work?
2. What are the pitfalls of undercover work?

POLICING
Online

Check your answers at
www.policing.glencoe.com

12.5 Juvenile Services

I n the recent past, police have had to become more and more involved with juvenile offenders. Very high juvenile crime rates in the United States have made increasingly stringent policing actions necessary. Although the police response to juvenile crime used to be less formal and delinquents were more likely to be handled through social services than through a correctional system, police today are more likely to treat juvenile offenses the same way as the ones committed by adults.

Specific Duties of Juvenile Units

Many police agencies have separate juvenile units, but smaller departments may instead have one or two juvenile crime specialists. As a general rule, the juvenile detail is a specialized unit within the detective division. The responsibilities of juvenile officers typically include handling any case that relates to persons 17 years or younger, whether suspects or victims. Juvenile delinquency specialists provide a police department with expertise in juvenile court procedures and juvenile offenses that are normally handled differently than adult offenses. These officers place special emphasis on gang and drug eradication and work closely with other agencies in suppressing such activities. In addition, they understand the special procedural laws surrounding the arrest, booking, and detention of juveniles who have special protection rights that adults do not.

In addition to being active enforcers and investigators in violations of juvenile laws, juvenile officers also give preventive programs a sizable portion of their available time. Many police precincts have established Law Enforcement Explorer Posts for juvenile explorers who eventually might choose to become police officers. Explorer programs are designed to allow youths to gain firsthand insights into law enforcement operations and career possibilities. They can provide an opportunity for positive police-youths interaction, giving young persons opportunities for community service by supplementing police at parades and other public events. School liaison programs and Drug Abuse Resistance Education (D.A.R.E.) are additional programs that make a positive police presence at schools possible.[23]

Online

Remember, one of your best resources is **www.policing.glencoe.com**

12.5 Self Check

1. What juvenile crime prevention programs have proven to be most effective?
2. What are the duties of a juvenile unit officer?

POLICING *Online*

Check your answers at **www.policing.glencoe.com**

12.6 Traffic Operations

Traffic enforcement has always been a police function in the United States because of its relationship to the police role of protecting life and property. The streets and roadways of America are inextricably linked both to automobiles and the crimes connected with cars. Police involvement in traffic operations occurs in three principal domains:

1. Traffic law enforcement
2. Accident investigation
3. Traffic direction and control

As increasing emphasis has been placed on the quality of service delivery, law enforcement has added a service component to its traffic operations. It accentuates assistance to disabled vehicles, public information provision, motor vehicle theft prevention, and other activities vital to the safe and efficient movement of traffic.

Traffic Law Enforcement

traffic law enforcement
The total police effort directed toward obtaining compliance with traffic movement regulations after programs of education and engineering have failed to reach this goal.

The inclusion of the term *movement* within the definition of **traffic law enforcement,** is crucial. Its implication is enforcement of vehicle code sections regulating moving vehicles, as opposed to stationary (parked) ones. Officers customarily issue citations for moving violations and deal with drivers directly instead of issuing absentee citations as is done for parking violations. Sometimes, traffic law enforcement includes detaining a moving vehicle or confronting the vehicle operator.

Enforcement of traffic laws encourages drivers to obey those laws. This is necessary because most traffic laws have no social stigma attached to their violation. Violations such as speeding or running a stop sign are not considered offenses of "natural law," as are violations of laws prohibiting rape, robbery, or murder. Therefore, people regularly and without consciousness of wrongdoing violate laws created to effect safe use of the roadways. By issuing citations and warnings, police endeavor to create an awareness of the consequences of violating traffic laws.

selective enforcement
Concentrating enforcement action on those motorists who are violating the laws that contribute most often to injurious accidents.

Ideally, traffic enforcement is accomplished through the selective enforcement strategy. In **selective enforcement**, action is concentrated on those motorists who commit traffic laws violations that most often cause injurious accidents. Besides concentrating on specific violations, selective enforcement also requires a location orientation (i.e., officers should practice selective enforcement in locations that have a high accident incidence as a result of identified primary causes).[24]

CAREER FOCUS

Senior Detective Supervisor

Job Description

I work as a senior detective in the LAPD robbery and homicide division. Along with my caseload, I am responsible, citywide, for robberies and homicides that affect business conveyances such as taxicabs, couriers, bank depots, bars, etc. I deal with any kind of serial crime and cases involving kidnapping for extortion.

My duties also include work in the witness protection program and, as a domestic violence expert, I have developed policies and procedures to reorganize that unit of the LAPD.

Timothy T. Williams, Jr., Los Angeles PD

About 80 percent of my work is investigative and 20 percent administrative. I also teach a class in police administration at a local community college. I think almost 90 percent of law enforcement relates to writing, and it's important to master this skill.

Investigative work is pretty involved. For example, I had a case of a 5-year old kid who was kidnapped and left to die in the Griffith Park area. It was very rewarding to see that, through the coordination of efforts from law enforcement and the community, we were able to apprehend the suspect, and that he has just received a sentence of life without parole.

Education

I was a pre-med student and went on to major in liberal arts. I also graduated from West Point's leadership program and I am a musician. I think it's important to be a well-rounded person to be a good officer, and to be able to think outside the box.

Follow-Up Why do you think a detective needs a diverse and well-rounded background?

Accident Investigation

accident investigation
Collection and assessment of facts surrounding vehicular collisions.

In an **accident investigation**, officers collect and assess the facts surrounding traffic collisions. Accident investigations are conducted for three basic reasons:

1. Most important, investigations can preserve human life by collecting information that can be used to prevent similar accidents in the future.
2. Investigations can determine if there is criminal wrongdoing on the part of any involved motorists.
3. Investigations are useful to insurance companies in determining fault and liability.[25]

The lifeline of a good accident investigation program is report writing. The finest possible investigation is useless if not accurately and completely reported. Reports must be accurate, clear, and as concise as possible.[26] (See Figure 12.7 below about technology and accident report writing)

Figure 12.7

How Technology Can Help Collision Reports

Streamline report writing and improve data collection for traffic collisions through the use of electronic technology at the scene.

Background
The substantial volume of paperwork that must be completed for traffic collision reports consumes a significant amount of a patrol officer's time with a resulting loss of proactive enforcement and in-view patrol. Historically, all forms and reports prepared by the patrol officer have been completed manually, an inefficient and error-prone method. Automating the patrol officer's environment to allow on-the-spot information gathering and reporting will improve officer efficiency, improve service to the public, and improve the reliability and timeliness of the data.

Actions
◆ Deploy traffic data collection devices (laptops or other devices)
◆ Improve network transmission capability
◆ Reengineer traffic data collection systems
◆ Seek support and funding from the private sector to promote this technology

Benefits
◆ Enhance public and officer safety
◆ Minimize report writing time.
◆ Improve data quality
◆ Reduce the time required to make data available for traffic analysis
◆ Increase amounts of time officers have for patrol and enforcement

Other Considerations
◆ Cost of the technology
◆ Increased skills, expertise and training for personnnel to support and operate

SOURCE: Adapted from http://www.nhtsa.dot.gov/people/injury/enforce/Millennium/strategy_55.htm

---

An efficient traffic records system complements a quality reporting system. The data that are taken from reports and, in turn, entered into records systems lead to a variety of follow-up activities. Information from accident reports is forwarded to transportation departments so that any required changes to control devices or roadways can be made. Police departments routinely use data from reports to identify accident patterns and develop enforcement priorities. Municipal law enforcement agencies with substantial accident investigation details and state traffic agencies use their accident databases for a number of investigative uses, such as locating vehicles involved in hit-and-run accidents.

Traffic Direction and Control

The expeditious and safe movement of traffic is a focal point of traffic operations. While accidents occur intermittently, the responsibility for the safe movement of traffic is constant and is the domain of **traffic direction and control**. Personnel assigned to this function are also responsible for impounding vehicles and directing traffic at special events.

Nonsworn personnel often perform traffic direction and control duties. There is little need for trained police officers to be solely involved with issuing parking tickets or directing traffic. These functions are, for the most part, mechanical and do not require the broad training and experience base of a sworn police officer.

In an ideal division of labor, civilian traffic control officers are present and are primarily responsible for routine traffic management activities. In such configurations, the civilian traffic contingent works closely with police officers. The radio frequencies are shared so that sworn officers can respond rapidly to any assistance requests broadcast by civilian personnel. Similarly, civilian personnel should be poised to relieve police officers from routine tasks such as impounding a stolen vehicle that had been the object of a police pursuit. Such teamwork maximizes the amount of available time that can be dedicated to primary safety objectives.

traffic direction and control Entails actions taken to ensure the expeditious and safe movement of traffic, as well as the enforcement of laws regulating parking.

12.6 Self Check
1. Why is selective enforcement in traffic situations sometimes a positive thing?
2. What is the lifeline of good accident investigation?

POLICING *Online*
Check your answers at
www.policing.glencoe.com

<table>
<tr><td>

Chapter
12

</td></tr>
</table>

The Expanded Police Response

Summary By Learning Objectives

1. Understand what dynamics initiate the police response to crime.

Most commonly, the police response begins with a citizen request for service, which is usually communicated via telephone. Also, officers routinely initiate encounters with suspected law violators. Often these originate via traffic stops. Frequently while patrolling, officers recognize patterns of conduct (a car left running outside a bank) or persons (a known narcotics dealer) that pique their interest. Regardless of how a police response is stimulated, the initial responding unit will more often than not be a uniformed patrol officer. An agency's size and mission will determine the impact and nature of resources deployed.

2. Describe the differences between preliminary and follow-up investigations.

The preliminary investigation is all of the evidence-gathering activities that take place at the scene of a crime (or suspected crime) immediately after it has been reported or is discovered by police officers. There are three basic reasons for conducting a preliminary investigation:

1. To determine if a crime has actually occurred

2. To gather evidence in order to identify a criminal suspect

3. To document the crime scene for the benefit of follow-up investigators and prosecutors

The follow-up investigation is a continuation of the preliminary investigation. It focuses on reconstructing the circumstances of 1) an illegal act or failure to act when legally required to do so and 2) the mental state accompanying it. The combination of these two elements is what makes a crime, and investigators must establish both in order to ask a prosecutor to file charges.

3. Gain insights into the police investigative process.

Police investigation is a two-phase process. In the preliminary investigation, a patrol officer usually determines whether a crime has been committed, gathers evidence, and documents the crime scene. The follow-up investigation is a continuation of the preliminary investigation. In larger agencies, detectives usually conduct the investigation, focusing on in-depth reconstruction of the circumstances of the crime. The detective assigned a case is responsible for bringing an investigation to a successful conclusion, exonerating innocent persons involved in a case, and focusing the investigation on the culpable person(s). In the wake of extensive federal-sponsored research, improvements in the investigative process have been concentrated in four areas: (1) managing investigations, (2) police-prosecutor relations, (3) targeting investigations, and (4) scientific investigation.

4. Explain the different types of undercover operations.

The primary objective of undercover operations is gathering evidence through covert methods. The focus of these operations is often on drug trafficking, vice activities, buying and selling stolen property, and white-collar crime. Often, investigators work undercover as decoys to apprehend dangerous street criminals. In the course of undercover investigations, officers frequently cultivate informants to further their information- and evidence-gathering activities. Surveillance is an important aspect of many undercover operations, and the activity often involves the use of electronics and visual enhancement devices to view or overhear suspects in the conduct of their affairs.

5. Appreciate the preventive orientation of juvenile services.

The enormity of juvenile crime has necessitated the development of units specifically addressing criminality among youth. The responsibilities of juvenile officers typically include handling any case that involves suspects or victims age 17 years and younger. Most juvenile details place special emphasis on gang and drug eradication and work closely with other agencies' personnel in suppressing such activities. In addition to being vigilant enforcers and investigators, juvenile officers also dedicate a large percentage of time to preventive strategies. These strategies include school liaisons and police-sponsored explorer programs.

6. Identify the three principal domains of traffic operations.

Police involvement in traffic operations occurs in three domains:

1. Traffic law enforcement

2. Accident investigation

3. Traffic direction and control

As the emphasis on service delivery has increased, law enforcement traffic operations have added a service component that accentuates assistance to disabled vehicles, public information provision, and motor vehicle theft prevention.

Key Terms

preliminary investigation (p. 462)
solvability factors (p. 464)
follow-up investigation (p. 465)
crime clearance (p. 467)
managing criminal investigations (MCI) (p. 469)
DNA testing (p. 472)
automated fingerprint identification system
   (AFIS) (p. 473)
psychological profiling (p. 474)
undercover investigation (p. 474)
light cover (p. 475)
deep cover (p. 476)
vice investigation (p. 476)

buy and bust (p. 479)
reverse sting (p. 479)
decoy (p. 479)
blending (p. 479)
surveillance (p. 479)
technical surveillance (p.480)
leapfrogging (p. 481)
informant (p. 481)
traffic law enforcement (p. 484)
selective enforcement (p. 484)
accident investigation (p. 486)
traffic direction and control (p. 487)

Questions for Review

1. Provide an example of a situation in which an officer might be the initiator of police response to suspected criminal activity.

2. Who most frequently conducts the preliminary investigation of crimes?

3. What term describes the situation in which a detective has solved a crime and has taken all possible action against at least one suspect?

4. What are the four main duties of a detective?

5. What are three reasons why police departments often assign inexperienced officers to undercover work?

6. Distinguish light cover from deep cover and provide examples of each.

7. Why is the use of informants by the police often viewed with disfavor by the public?

8. What are the differences between decoys and blending?

9. Provide an example of a juvenile delinquency prevention program.

10. What is the dual focus of selective enforcement, as practiced in traffic operations?

Experiential Activities

11. Case Solvability
Create a crime narrative or take one from the news. Review it for its case solvability and give it a total score. For each factor, count its point value (1 through 8).

a. Which factors are easiest to find?
b. Which are the most difficult?
c. Which factors were you lacking in your case, and why?

Experiential Activities continued

12. Police Scanner
Visit PoliceScanner.com through the link provided at **www.policing.glencoe.com**. Listen for requests for additional police cars or for other special services. If a supervisor, detective, or crime lab unit has been requested, a serious crime has probably been committed.
  a. What was the normal police response?
  b. What was the most interesting crime that was dispatched?
  c. What was the most interesting police response to a given crime?

13. Doing It Right
You are working in a light undercover operations known as the "buy and bust." Lately, drug pushers have refused to sell to you. You wonder if they know you are a police officer. You go to your supervisor in your undercover clothing and ask what you are doing wrong. He points out your walk and straight posture, your steady eye contact. "The combination gives you away in a minute," he explains.
  a. How can you change your appearance?
  b. How can you prevent this in the future?
  c. Can you return to your assignment and be effective?

14. Blending Too Well?
You are working undercover and posing as a sidewalk florist near a busy liquor store and street corner. Several suspicious-looking youths gather at this corner. When they start selling drugs you notify your station, and officers come out to arrest them. One youth grabs a passer-by and threatens to shoot her. They are very close to the booth, and the assailant has his back turned to you. You move out of the booth to draw your gun on him, but a customer tries to stop you.
  a. How do you handle the customer?
  b. How do you handle the assailant?
  c. Since you are about to blow your cover, should you explain who you are?

Web Patrol

15. Communities and crime-solving
Visit the Web sites of community organizations such as Partners Against Violence, Domestic Violence Information Center, and FBI Hate Crime Information. These links are available at **www.policing.glencoe.com**.
  What expertise do you think these organizations bring to help police in their work?

16. Compare organizational Structures
Go to **www.policing.glencoe.com** to view the Des Moines, Iowa, Police Department's Web site.
  Compare the Des Moines organizational structure to that of your local police department, which elements are unique to each and why?

17. Newest Forensic Techniques
Go to **www.policing.glencoe.com** for links to comprehensive information on the latest scientific advances and other news in forensics.
  What current developments in forensics do you think will be most valuable in investigating crime?

Critical Thinking Exercises

18. Crime Scene Integrity

In recent years, the media have exposed some prominent "snafus" within high-profile cases. Two famous examples, which hindered the successful prosecution of the crimes' chief suspects, were the murders of Nicole Brown-Simpson and Ron Goldman and JonBenet Ramsey. Examining each of these cases, you can see that the improper handling of evidence was crucial to the Simpson case, and the improper handling of the crime scene was crucial to the Ramsey case.

Refer to preliminary investigation responsibilities listed by O. W. Wilson under the acronym PRELIMINARY (see Figure 12.1) and answer the following questions:

   a. In each case, which of the responsibilities appear to have been violated?

   b. How do you believe this can occur, given the training and experience of most police officers?

19. "Civilianizing" Traffic Enforcement

After reading this chapter, you now understand a number of the most common components of the police response to crimes. Among the components discussed were those dedicated to traffic operations. Traditionally, sworn law enforcement officers are the only ones authorized to work in traffic enforcement. This includes writing parking tickets, issuing citations for moving violations, and investigating traffic accidents. Nonsworn personnel can be used for traffic direction and control functions. Based on what you have read about the duties performed by sworn personnel, answer the following questions:

   a. Could nonsworn personnel work in other traffic functions? If so, which ones? If not, why?

   b. What obstacles could result from nonsworn personnel trying to work in certain traffic functions, especially if they are not uniformed?

20. Deciding Whether to Share Files

You are an investigator working for a precinct that fired many people for corruption two years ago. These detectives were being paid by suspects to steal case folders from other detectives' offices and then "lose" this evidence by throwing the files into the garbage chute, where they were incinerated. This went on for two months until a janitor found some files and went to the supervisor, who began a secret investigation that resulted in seven people getting fired and three going to prison. Now, each investigator keeps his or her files locked up and hidden.

Two weeks ago, your department got a new supervisor from a quiet, low-crime precinct. One of the first things that he wanted to implement was the centralized filing of all investigative folders, so that all personnel can access the information as needed. When the staff hears this, they create an uproar and explain what happened two years ago. They do not want to share their files and risk having them stolen again. The supervisor is surprised but still wants the information to be available to everyone.

   a. Who do you agree with—the supervisor or the investigators? Explain.

   b. Name at least one compromise that will allow the files to stay secure but will also allow for information sharing.

Endnotes

1. Bruce L. Berg and John J. Horgan, *Criminal Investigation* (New York: Glencoe/McGraw-Hill, 1998), 20.

2. Joseph C. DeLadurantey and Daniel R. Sullivan, *Criminal Investigation Standards* (New York: Harper & Row, 1980), 38.

3. Peter W. Greenwood and Joan Petersilia, *The Criminal Investigation Process: Summary and Policy Implications* (Santa Monica, CA: RAND, 1975), vi.

4. James W. Osterburg and Richard H. Ward, *Criminal Investigation: A Method for Reconstructing the Past* (Cincinnati, OH: Anderson, 1997), 638.

5. Edward A. Thibault, Lawrence M. Lynch, and R. Bruce McBride, *Proactive Police Management* (Upper Saddle River, NJ: Prentice Hall, 1998), 171–72.

6. Paul B. Weston and Kenneth M. Wells, *Criminal Investigation: Basic Perspectives* (Upper Saddle River, NJ: Prentice Hall, 1997), 2–3.

7. Investigative Analysis Section, Los Angeles Police Department, *Detective Operations Manual* (Los Angeles: Los Angeles Police Department, 1986).

8. Ellen Greenberg and Robert Wasserman, *Managing Criminal Investigations* (Washington, D.C.: National Institute of Law Enforcement and Criminal Justice, 1979).

9. Gary W. Cordner, Larry K. Gaines, and Victor E. Kappeler, *Police Operations: Analysis and Evaluation* (Cincinnati, OH: Anderson, 1996), 243.

10. Ibid., 242.

11. Ibid., 244.

12. George I. Miller, "Observations on Police Undercover Work," *Criminology* 25, no. 1 (1987): 27–46.

13. Ibid.

14. Thibault et al., *Proactive Police Management*, 150.

15. DeLadurantey and Sullivan, *Criminal Investigation Standards*, 300.

16. Dempsey, *An Introduction to Policing*, 189–90.

17. Berg and Horgan, *Criminal Investigation*, 535.

18. Dempsey, *An Introduction to Policing*, 185.

19. Osterburg and Ward, *Criminal Investigation*, 269–84.

20. Weston and Wells, *Criminal Investigation*, 166.

21. Ibid., 165.

22. Weston and Wells, *Criminal Investigation*, 149–59.

23. Thibault et al., *Proactive Police Management*, 153–61.

24. National Advisory Commission on Criminal Justice Standards and Goals, *Police* (Washington, D.C.: Government Printing Office, 227.

25. Bruce L. Berg, *Policing in Modern Society* (Boston: Butterworth-Heinemann, 1999), 106.

26. National Advisory Commission on Criminal Justice Standards and Goals, *Police*, 228.

Chapter 13

Police-Community Relations

CHAPTER OBJECTIVES

AFTER COMPLETING THIS CHAPTER, YOU WILL BE ABLE TO:

1. Understand the dynamics of a productive police-community relationship.

2. Know how public relations and community relations help to create a positive police-community relationship.

3. Recognize how attitudes form and can affect the quality of police work.

4. Know how prejudice can form and cause problems in police-community relations.

5. Understand how the public's constant interactions with the police affect their relationship.

6. Explain the different methods by which citizen complaints can be handled.

7. Understand the main problems and solutions to improving police-community relations.

8. Know how to implement a cultural awareness program at a local police academy.

◀ Officers on bike patrol in Bernards, New Jersey.

Law enforcement agents are the primary public contact in the criminal justice system. Each interaction an officer engages in has the potential for misunderstandings and altercations. All of an officer's tasks are under public scrutiny, from the pursuit of suspects and the use of force to car and body searches, and each carries its own potential for controversy. In addition, courts and administrators pressure police to perform their tasks correctly. It is of little surprise, therefore, that law enforcement officers may become defensive about how to serve the public.

Law enforcement has unique organizational challenges because each officer must be equipped to handle both criminal and noncriminal matters. Law enforcement agencies are called to handle nonviolent family disputes, barking dog complaints, scuffles between schoolchildren, and other actions where there is not always a clear solution.[1] Given the complexities of this role, police need to maximize the quality of their interactions to avoid public criticism.

The Police-Community Relationship

police-community relations
A relationship based on public relations, community service, and community participation.

Police-community relations are based on three equal components:

1. Public relations
2. Community service
3. Community participation

When departments pay equal attention to these three components, the police-community relationship can improve. Under these circumstances, police agencies will find it easier to work with the community to anticipate and prevent problems and find solutions before a crisis occurs. When these components are not present, conflict will likely occur.

In the Los Angeles County Sheriff's Department, for example, three cases helped fuel poor police-community relations. One deputy shot and killed a pedestrian under unusual circumstances. Another person was arrested for selling cocaine after being observed by two deputies for half an hour. The deputies had no training or experience in surveillance, however. In the third case, 13 deputies killed an incarcerated man with schizophrenia by piling on him while trying to restrain him. Each of these cases sparked citizen discontent and lawsuits that cost the county $2 million. That discontent was further fueled by the sheriff's refusal to admit to any wrongdoing on the part of his department. By not making efforts in the areas of public relations and community policing, the department added to the public's discontent.

Police-community relations, properly understood, involve **proactive policing**. Successful police-community relations programs state that the best way to control a riot is to prevent it from occurring in the first place. Indeed, the best way to control any crime is to prevent it. This is the opposite of reactive policing, which entails fighting crime while it is happening or after it has occurred.

The need to improve police-community relationships has been recognized for some time. The intense rioting and social unrest of the 1960s, and the mass destruction caused by it, forced American police agencies to strengthen relations between the police and community. The riots and firestorms that occurred in various cities during this time marked a turning point in police-community relations programs. Suddenly the nation was jolted into realizing the intense racial and social divisions among its people. The assumptions of goodwill and fair treatment of others that had motivated earlier police-community relations programs were abruptly called intoquestion.[2] After this era, police agencies devoted substantial energy toward alleviating some of these problems. Today's concepts of the proactive problem-solving process and the police-community alliance developed in response to the social turmoil of the 1960s. (See Figure 13.1 on page 499 for a comparison of relations in different periods of policing.)

proactive policing Policing that acts on the belief that the best way to control crime is to prevent it from occurring in the first place.

Public Relations

Virtually every organization that provides a product or service finds it necessary to provide **public relations**, which is an agency's efforts to communicate

public relations A police department's efforts to communicate with the public about the work it does.

with the public about what it does. In policing, which serves and protects the public, these communications have two different but related aims. The first aim is to inform the public about the availability of its services, using resources such as community policing and crime prevention education. The other aim is to increase the demand for police services.

In the for-profit business world, this activity is called advertising or marketing, and the operative assumption is that higher demand is good. In the not-for-profit public-sector world in which policing operates, matters are more complex. There are some occasions when police agencies clearly do want to advertise their services and persuade the public that the demand for their services is growing. They can achieve this by publicizing increasing crime rates or warning the community about an impending threat, such as the appearance of a new drug that has caused recent deaths.

Public Education At other times, the demand for police services is too much for police departments. In these cases, they must manage the overload through public education. A typical example of this would be a crime prevention program that provides tips on how to avoid common property crimes or how to prevent violent crime by following personal safety guidelines. Providing useful and accurate information to the public, especially during times of crisis, is an important function of police public relations efforts.

For example, suppose that Cheryl is a police investigator working in a small town about 400 miles north of the U.S.-Mexican border. Over recent years, a highly dangerous form of heroin called chiva has been smuggled into the United States with greater frequency. It has caused several deaths around the country, but many young people continue to use it. Until now, chiva has not affected her town, but she just learned that someone died using it only 20 miles away. She immediately puts together drug information packets for local schools, updates the department's Web site to reflect the same information, and begins to work with the public to educate them about this danger. Her high school classroom talks focus on the tragic deaths of the people who used this drug. Over time, she is pleased to see that although chiva eventually reaches their area, most of the community avoids it.

Communication The second aim of an agency's communication with its public is to establish and maintain a good organizational reputation. The quality of one's product or service is, of course, the most crucial factor for accomplishing this goal, but organizations can seldom rely on this alone to bolster their public image. Politicians, community leaders, or others who are critical of police activities may be engaged in an effort to influence public opinion with a different image of the police. To deal with this criticism, police agencies plan and implement a variety of activities to help create a favorable image of themselves and defend their image when it is attacked.

Founder of Police-Community Relations

In 1947, Joseph Lohman, a former sheriff of Cook County, Illinois, and a former dean of criminology at the University of California, Berkeley, published the first textbook on the topic of enhancing police-community relations. It was for academy recruits of the innovative Berkeley Police Department. Because of his efforts, Lohman has been dubbed the "father of police-community relations."

SOURCE: Joseph D. Lohman, *The Police and Minority Groups* (Chicago: Chicago Park Police, 1947).

Figure 13.1

Police-Community Relations 1950–2000

	Police Attitudes	Citizen Attitudes	Major Influences	Outcome
1950s	◆ Upholding the law ◆ Maintaining order ◆ Greater focus on street crimes and on quality-of-life violations (such as panhandling) than on family violence	◆ Among many White Americans: Desire to maintain postwar prosperity ◆ Among many African-Americans: Growing resentment of unfair treatment	◆ Beginning of civil rights movement ◆ Growth of American cities such as Los Angeles creates beginning of sharp increases in urban crime	◆ Relatively stable period for police-community relations ◆ Civil rights clashes set the stage for further dissent in the 1960s
1960s	◆ Overreaction among some officers to those considered "different" ◆ Realization among policing experts that selection and management must be reformed	◆ Outrage at unfair and sometimes violent treatment of antiwar and civil rights protesters ◆ Simultaneous concern about police ethics	◆ Vietnam antiwar protests ◆ Civil rights protests ◆ Inner-city riots and high crime rates ◆ Increase in experimental drug use	◆ Police-community relations at an all-time low ◆ Poor media relations ◆ Several commissions study American policing and recommend changes
1970s	◆ Police management begins to implement reform in hiring practices ◆ Overall frustration about spiraling drug crimes and crime rates ◆ Uncertainty about level of public support	◆ General feeling that crime (especially urban crime) is uncontrollable ◆ Mixed feelings about reliability of police, but less hostility than in 1960s	◆ Racketeering Influenced and Corrupt Organizations (RICO) Act passed to combat organized crime ◆ Frank Serpico reveals serious corruption problems within the NYPD ◆ Kansas City Preventive Patrol Experiment questions traditional patrol practices	◆ Police selection process greatly expanded ◆ Police pre-service (academy) training greatly expanded ◆ Police research receives greater funding and support than ever before
1980s	◆ Police face new challenges with sharp increases in drug and drug-related crimes ◆ Serious gang problem creates new law enforcement obstacles, especially regarding juveniles	◆ Dependence upon police to resolve high crime rates ◆ Relatively high faith that police will be able to combat new crime problems ◆ Continuing concern that American crime rates are uncontrollable	◆ War on Drugs ◆ Crack epidemic begins 1986–1987 ◆ Explosion of gang-related crime, which leads to overall increase in juvenile and drug crimes	◆ Policing experts begin to see need for community partnerships to restore peace and order ◆ Lawmakers see that current laws and procedures are not adequate to fight new crime problems
1990s	◆ Mixture of enthusiasm and resistance toward community policing ◆ Expansion of recruitment territory and use of aggressive recruitment strategies ◆ Mixture of enthusiasm and resistance toward growing numbers of female and minority officers	◆ Public feels that War on Drugs was lost ◆ Concern about treatment of female and minority victims of crime ◆ Outrage toward police brutality ◆ Optimism about crime reduction in urban centers	◆ Community policing introduced by Robert Trojanowicz in 1990 ◆ Rodney King beating, riots resulting after first trial of officers ◆ Racial profiling ◆ Domestic violence awareness and prosecution ◆ Proliferation of television cop shows, which glamorize law enforcement	◆ Community policing slowly becomes widespread ◆ Experiments with different community-oriented efforts, such as foot patrol ◆ Sharp decrease in long-term crime problems in New York City ◆ More police agencies obtain liability insurance
2000s	◆ Widespread desire to create uniform standards for professionalism ◆ Overall acceptance of community policing ◆ Lingering mixed feelings about resolving racial conflicts	◆ Support of law enforcement to fight terrorism and protect national security ◆ Increased desire to be involved in police activities through community policing, independent monitors, and lawsuits	◆ Heroic police response to World Trade Center attack ◆ Increased police presence at airports and other areas prone to terrorist activity ◆ RICO charges against LAPD Rampart Street Division set a new precedent in police liability	◆ Community policing a mixed success due to inconsistent use among agencies ◆ Improved media relations ◆ Increased reliance on police to help maintain domestic security

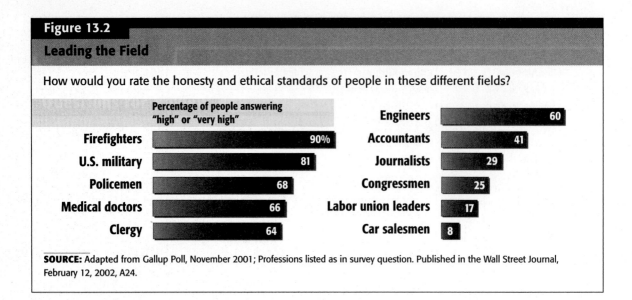

Figure 13.2

Leading the Field

How would you rate the honesty and ethical standards of people in these different fields?

Percentage of people answering "high" or "very high"

Field	%	Field	%
Firefighters	90%	Engineers	60
U.S. military	81	Accountants	41
Policemen	68	Journalists	29
Medical doctors	66	Congressmen	25
Clergy	64	Labor union leaders	17
		Car salesmen	8

SOURCE: Adapted from Gallup Poll, November 2001; Professions listed as in survey question. Published in the Wall Street Journal, February 12, 2002, A24.

Community Relations

community relations The relationship that a department and its individual staff have with the public; it may be either positive or negative.

The combined effects of public relations and human relations are known as **community relations**. Police-community relations involve an entire police department and groups in the community. They may be either positive or negative, depending on the quality of officer interactions with community members, which is the human relations aspect, and the collective images that each group holds of the other, which develop from both public and human relations. (See Figure 13.2 above)

Among the potential benefits for police that come from improving community relations are:

- Greater personal safety
- Increased citizen cooperation during investigations and adjudication (leading to higher crime clearance rates)
- More credibility in addressing community issues and problems
- Enhanced respect from citizens
- Job satisfaction and self-esteem
- Reduced job-related stress
- More budgetary and moral support from the community

The benefits for citizens include, but are not limited to, safer communities, less fear of crime, and a stronger trust that their families and homes are safe.[3]

13.1 Self Check

1. What are the three components of police-community relations?
2. How can police improve public relations and community relations?

POLICING Online

Check your answers at **www.policing.glencoe.com**

13.2 Attitude Formation and Prejudice

It is a natural human trait to seek consistency, stability, and predictability in one's self-image and in one's image of others. **Stereotyping** is a form of perceptual shorthand in which a person categorizes someone or something before fully understanding it. For example, an officer may assume that any young person wearing certain colors in a certain neighborhood is a member of a gang. Or police may think that a man wearing a suit and tie must be an office worker and could not be a shoplifter. Although it is more convenient to stereotype people, this tendency needs to be controlled.

A large problem in improving police-community relations is that sometimes individual community members and entire groups of people stereotype police negatively. They choose to see all of them as brutal, racist, corrupt, or possessing other negative traits.[4]

Stereotypes can be positive but still inaccurate. If a police officer unlocks a door for someone who locked his or her keys in the car, that person will tell everyone that cops are marvelous people. If, on the other hand, a person is stopped and harassed for being African American, for being female, or for any other inexcusable reason, that person will tell everyone about the prejudice and unprofessional behavior of police. Likewise, if police start a community-policing program in a neighborhood that already likes police and is eager to help, whatever stereotypes they may form will likely be more positive than those formed by officers who work in fragmented and apathetic communities with high crime rates.

stereotyping A form of perceptual shorthand in which a person categorizes someone or something before fully understanding it.

Attitudes

Perceptions are the ideas of an individual, which may or may not have been thought out but still form the basis for a person's opinions on any given subject. These are ideas that are open to dispute and can be subject to change, but some remain with people for a long time. They take deeper root, which makes the individuals holding such perceptions less willing to change them. Such deeply held opinions can eventually become convictions, which are moral principles on which a person is prepared to act. These convictions show themselves in everyday behavior as attitudes.

Attitudes develop primarily from individuals' choices to align themselves with groups that they feel will help them attain important goals. Thus, the choices a person makes, such as to affiliate with a particular organization, prefer a political party, and read a particular newspaper, are often decisions based on a certain set of attitudes. The average person's attitudes, beliefs, and values tend to be self-insulating and reinforcing because they shut out contrary or opposing evidence.[5]

attitudes Behavior that a person chooses to align himself or herself with that the person feels will help him or her attain important goals.

What does this mean for policing? It can mean that officers who do not control their individual tendency to form attitudes will form them unknowingly. When an officer first encounters a crime scene, he or she needs to maintain an open mind to properly assess the situation and evaluate all possible evidence. If an officer instead forms an attitude toward a crime, victim, or suspect—whether this is positive or negative—it will affect the integrity of the investigation. The ideal approach to policing is to analyze each crime situation individually.

In addition, all police align themselves strongly with the attitudes of one particular organization: the police organization, along with the sense of brotherhood that comes with it. This creates a strong and positive sense of unity among police officers. They know that they will look out for each other and support each other. On the other hand, such an attitude can also lead to officers reinforcing each other's stereotypes and prejudices.

Prejudice

prejudice A type of attitude that is formed regarding objects, persons, groups, or values on the basis of limited information, association, or experience.

Prejudice is a type of attitude that is formed regarding objects, persons, groups, or values on the basis of limited information, association, or experience. The word *prejudice* means to prejudge, and prejudice is the act of judging something before understanding it well enough to do so. Studies have indicated that prejudicial attitudes are acquired at an early age.

Stereotyping or overcategorization is one of the working tools of prejudice. It is a sweeping generalization regarding an entire group or category, such as when a person says, "Police officers are corrupt." Stereotypes are often socially supported by the mass media, such as in literature, journalism, movies, radio, and television.

Another tool of prejudice is projection, or scapegoating. It means that people tend to look for the causes of their failures outside themselves. Minority groups are often society's favorite scapegoats.[6]

Prejudice harms the effectiveness of police work and can seriously erode the quality of police-community relations. For example, if a person feels that a police officer is prejudiced against her, she may be less likely to report a crime out of fear of being harassed or harmed.

13.2 Self Check

1. What can an officer do to stop himself or herself from stereotyping others?
2. What can happen when the public detects prejudice in a police officer?

POLICING *Online*

Check your answers at
www.policing.glencoe.com

13.3 Police-Citizen Interaction

Effective policing requires that police officers work closely with citizens in designing and implementing a variety of proactive crime prevention and control measures.

To accomplish these initiatives, officers must do the following:

- Be closely integrated with the majority of citizens in the community
- Share important community values and beliefs
- Feel confident of community support in the decisions they make[7]

The quality of the police-citizen relationship, which must be high for such actions to take place, must be considered by all agencies. It is an often overestimated factor in the quality of provision of law enforcement services because many police agencies mistakenly assume that police-community relations are better than they actually are.

Prevalence of Citizen Contact with the Police

The Bureau of Justice Statistics (BJS) has developed the most extensive database and analysis of the prevalence and nature of police-citizen contacts. Since 1996, it has annually surveyed the public on their interactions with police. In 1999, the BJS interviewed more than 80,000 individuals age 16 or older about the quality of their relationships with law enforcement.

The results of these interviews revealed that approximately 21 percent of all persons age 16 or older (43.8 million) had at least one face-to-face contact with a police officer.[8] About 50 percent said that the reason for the contact was a motor vehicle stop in which they were either a passenger or an operator of a motor vehicle. About 20 percent of the remaining respondents said that they had contacted the police to report a crime, and about 3 percent said the contact occurred because the police suspected them of involvement in a crime. The rest reported miscellaneous events that brought them in contact with law enforcement.

The single most important factor affecting the rate of contact between residents and the police was age, and this was mainly due to the high number of young drivers pulled over for a motor vehicle stop. The rate of traffic stops among those ages 18 to 24 was more than double that of persons age 40 or older.[9]

Traffic Stops In 1999, an estimated 10.3 percent of licensed drivers were pulled over by police one or more times in a traffic stop. That percentage represents 19.3 million drivers. Of the 19.3 million, the breakdown by gender and ethnicity was as follows:

- An estimated 60.8 percent (11.7 million) were male and 39.2 percent (7.6 million) were female.
- An estimated 77 percent (14.9 million) were white, 11.6 percent (2.2 million) were black, 8.4 percent (1.6 million) were Hispanic, and 3 percent (0.6 million) were drivers of other races, such as Asian, Pacific Islander, or Native American.

Perhaps the most positive finding of the statistics, both for police and for the general public, was that most respondents felt that the police had acted fairly in traffic situations. The vast majority of drivers stopped by police (84 percent) said they had been stopped for a legitimate reason. An even larger majority (90 percent) felt police had behaved properly during the traffic stop.[10]

Use of Force The use of force is a different matter. During 1999, approximately 422,000 persons age 16 or older experienced a police officer who threatened to use force against them. The estimate of the number of persons experiencing force or the threat of force equaled about one percent of the nearly 44 million people reporting face-to-face contact with police.

▶ **Relationship with the Community** Police Community Affairs Sergeant Delacy Daris, leader of Black Cops Against Brutality, talks to a community member in East Orange, New Jersey. A key ingredient of community policing is that the citizens' concerns are heard even when complaints do not involve a specific crime.
What do you think the difference might be between responding to a crime and responding to a concern?

Overall, 57 percent of persons involved in a police force incident reported that they argued, disobeyed, or resisted the police or that they had been drinking or using drugs at the time. This provides an excellent example of how police and citizen attitudes can clash. A sober person arguing with or resisting police may have a perfectly legitimate reason to do so. However, most officers will see this as a challenge to their authority and respond to that challenge instead of the issue about which the person is arguing. On the other hand, a drunken, drugged, or belligerent person may feel that his or her behavior is justified, but police will know that it is not and threaten to use force to help control the situation.

Other findings regarding the use of force are as follows:

- An estimated 75 percent of the 422,000 persons involved in a use of force incident characterized the force as excessive.
- The vast majority of people experiencing the threat or use of force (92 percent) said the police acted improperly.
- Whites were as likely as blacks to describe the use of force as excessive.
- Younger persons ages 16 to 29 with police contact were significantly more likely than those older than age 29 to have had force used against them.[11]

Rapport

If a citizen perceives a police-citizen contact as coercive or as a restraint on his or her freedom, the possibility of citizen hostility increases, and the officer's chance of obtaining useful information diminishes. When police-citizen contacts are handled properly, they can stimulate cooperation, useful information, and citizen goodwill, which will in turn improve the departmental image.

Officers initiating citizen contacts should work to establish a **rapport** with the public, which is the process of establishing open communication by acting in a courteous and restrained manner at all times. Before anything else, they should first introduce themselves and explain the reason for making the contact. While this may seem obvious, some officers do not begin their interactions this way. Instead, they adopt an authoritative persona that may or may not be effective for these types of interactions. Even when a citizen is hostile and uncooperative, a professional approach should be used for as long as possible. Getting tough with someone is sometimes necessary and effective, but in the majority of cases it will merely escalate the situation into an unneeded confrontation.

Some police officers may feel that asserting authority is necessary in all situations to maintain control and preserve their dignity and authority.

rapport A friendly relationship that results from establishing open communication by acting in a courteous and restrained manner at all times.

The fact is that such attitudes merely offend people and induce them to be uncooperative or resentful. Indeed, one of the most important principles of modern police work is something that brings success to any aspect of life: Be nice to people, unless there is a clear need to assert authority. Officers should attempt to view the contact from the citizen's perspective and treat the citizen in the same manner as the officer would like to be treated if the roles were reversed.[12]

Research conducted by the Police Foundation found that Americans associate six characteristics as absolutely essential in policing for people:

- Attentiveness
- Reliability
- Responsiveness
- Competence
- Manners
- Fairness[13]

Online

Remember, one of your best resources is www.policing.glencoe.com

Attentiveness Americans want their service providers to pay attention to them and understand their needs. When citizens call 911, for example, they expect a response. Furthermore, when citizens complain about policing problems, they expect a solution. The reason community policing is so appealing to the public is that it increases police-citizen contact, thereby increasing police attentiveness.

Reliability Reliability is another important element of policing for people. People expect a degree of predictability in what police do and want service that is timely and error free. In comparison, McDonald's succeeds not because the cuisine is exciting and inventive but because the restaurant is reliable and consistent. When a system of police service works well, it is like McDonald's. Citizens can depend on their police on a consistent basis.

Responsiveness Americans expect more of their police than officers who merely follow bureaucratic rules. They also want responsive and client-centered good-faith service. A good-faith effort by an officer to resolve a situation is often appreciated as much as a favorable outcome. Citizens are delighted when their police see a job through to completion, then check back later to see how things worked out. Even when they cannot attain closure on a matter or when they deny a citizen's request, police can be responsive by explaining the outcome in a way that shows they tried to resolve the issue.

Competence The public wants competent service providers who can get the job done. When you get your car repaired, you expect the mechanic to know what he or she is doing. When you call the police to report a theft, deal with a domestic disturbance, or quell a noisy party next door, you expect the responding officer to know how to deal with the situation. The public judges police competence primarily in terms of the tangible things they can readily observe by watching the officer at work and making judgments about his or her ability to get the job done.

How the average citizen defines police competence may be different from how an experienced and skilled police officer defines it. Most often, citizens may overestimate officers' capacities, both in terms of their legal authority and their ability to mobilize resources. For instance, a burglary victim may be outraged when a police department does not send a detective to investigate. This is because he does not understand that most departments only have enough detective staff to cover serious violent offenses such as murder, rape, and kidnapping. Another area in which people misunderstand police resources is in relation to the type of resources used to fight crime. For example, some departments may allocate more resources toward crime prevention education than toward bringing offenders to justice. Citizens may not agree with this use of resources.

Manners An essential element of quality service is having polite manners.[14] Studies show that a bad manner is among the most frequent complaints citizens have about their contacts with police. Studies also show that the most powerful predictors of citizen satisfaction with the police have more to do with how police treated the citizen than what the police accomplished.[15] A number of studies show that citizens are more likely to obey the law and less likely to be disorderly or violent in the future when police enforce the law in a respectful manner.[16]

Fairness The final element of policing for people is fairness.[17] In studies, it has been found that citizens who perceive that they were treated fairly by legal officials, such as the police, also report a stronger inclination to obey the law in the future. The factor having the greatest impact on people's feelings about legal authority is their perception of a fair procedure. The impact on citizens is even greater than that of the citizens' sense of the favorableness or fairness of the outcome.[18]

13.3 Self Check

1. Why are traffic stops less likely to cause citizen dissatisfaction than incidents involving the use of force?
2. How could police use force against suspects in a less offensive manner?

POLICING *Online*
Check your answers at
www.policing.glencoe.com

13.4 Addressing Citizen Concerns

Despite the widespread growth in community policing and the multitude of exemplary police-citizen interactions, one might be hard-pressed to describe current police-citizen relationships as friendly. Although the disharmony of police-citizen relationships in the 1960s was more obvious, relationships today are still strained.

Episodes of abuse that did surface in the 1990s revealed police-community strain of a shocking magnitude. Although the 1991 Rodney King beating was an extremely excessive use of force, that incident paled in comparison to the severity of harm inflicted on Abner Louima by the New York City Police Department. In 1997, Haitian immigrant Louima was arrested in a brawl outside a Brooklyn nightclub. An officer, mistakenly believing that Louima had punched him, sought revenge by arresting Louima, then sodomizing him with a broomstick at the police station.[19] A few years later, in 2000, this event was eclipsed by scandals involving the Los Angeles Police Department's Rampart Patrol Division. In this situation, an LAPD officer admitted that he and several others were involved in numerous widespread episodes of flagrant civil rights violations, including the unprovoked shooting of unarmed suspects.[20] (See Figure 13.3 below for a listing of the major incidents of police brutality in the 1990s.)

When situations like this occur and the police are accused of exceeding their authority and violating the public trust, police agencies must ensure the public that they will swiftly and thoroughly investigate the

---

Figure 13.3

How Police-Community Relations Work

Share important community values and beliefs	Build community confidence
1. Determine which offenses affect the community most	**1.** Support an independent monitor or auditor to evaluate citizen complaints
2. Develop increased interaction between children and police	**2.** Develop community notification procedures
3. Expand information sharing between police and community	**3.** Address allegations of racial profiling
4. Find whether or not aggressive police practices will help or hurt the community	**4.** Address concerns that victims of crime are not being treated consistently
5. Conduct community satisfaction surveys	**5.** Involve community in ongoing discussions about how police-community relations can be improved

SOURCE: Adapted from "Mike Bloomberg Discusses Police-Community Relations As He Announces Next Part of Public Safety Plan," accessed online at http://www.mikeformayor.org/News/0827200188.shtml on December 18, 2001; and Center for Excellence in New York City Governance, "Public Safety Checklist," accessed online at http://www.nyu.edu/wagner/excellence/htm/reports/papers/publicsafety/ checklist.htm on December 18, 2001.

matter. The relationship between the police and the community requires that the police accept that they are accountable and never above the law. Swift and unwavering disciplinary action by police executives against corrupt officers demonstrates to the community and to other officers that corruption will be punished.[21]

Formalized Complaint Review

A **formal disciplinary system** is necessary for reinforcing public trust and organizational policies.[22] The complaint process may take a variety of forms, depending on the individual agencies' preferences. Complaints are different from inquiries, which are citizen comments, compliments, or suggestions regarding issues that are resolved to the citizen's satisfaction.

> **formal disciplinary system** A system by which complaints are processed and resolved; a necessity for reinforcing public trust and organizational policies.

Generally, all complaints should be documented when they are received from citizens. Complaints are categorized for statistical purposes, and such categories may include the following:

- Improper tactics
- Discourtesy
- Unnecessary force
- Discrimination/harassment

Ensuring that the discipline matches the offense is a rule of good disciplinary practice. All acts of misconduct are different, as are the complaint histories of different individual officers. It would not make sense for every act or omission to carry the same penalty because some are much more serious than others are. Also, unless the offense is serious, it would not make sense for an officer with a spotless record to be treated the same as one with a lengthy disciplinary history.

Somewhere between the gravity of the offense and the disciplinary record of the officer lies the concept of **progressive discipline**. This concept recognizes that repeated minor disciplinary offenses deserve increasingly serious punishment. Progressive discipline calls for increasing the severity of punishments as an officer's transgressions become more frequent. When practiced correctly, it can lead to the reform of a good officer who has made mistakes—or can lead to the dismissal of a bad one who should not be involved in police work.[23]

> **progressive discipline** A type of officer discipline that calls for increasing the severity of punishments as an officer's transgressions become more frequent.

Methods of Handling Complaints

Citizen complaints against police misbehavior can be a frustrating experience for everyone involved. Citizens become frustrated because they feel their complaints are not taken seriously or are not thoroughly or objectively investigated. Officers become frustrated because they feel the public does not understand police work. Local officials become frustrated because they feel uncertain about how best to hold departments accountable for officer behavior.

When personnel complaints are received from citizens, they are either processed internally or externally. The most common internal methods are investigation and adjudication by an offending officer's supervisors or by an internal affairs unit. External processes include citizen review boards, mediation, or outsourcing. A hybrid (combination internal/external) that has evolved in recent years is the independent monitor or auditor.

Supervisor Investigation Complaints are customarily investigated by a supervisory-level officer, who may be the direct supervisor of the employee against whom a complaint has been lodged. The results of the investigation against this officer are forwarded through the agency's hierarchy, along with recommendations for discipline if the supervisor feels they are warranted. If misconduct has been substantiated, corrective action will be imposed and may range from an official reprimand to suspension or termination.

In communities where police-community relations are good and the level of police integrity is high, this system can often work well. In addition, this method is the easiest for a police department to administer. It can be less successful in other circumstances, such as when supervisors personally like the officer against whom the complaint was filed or share the same attitudes or prejudices that led to the complaint. Citizens in jurisdictions with poor police-community relations often prefer one of the following internal or external methods instead.

internal affairs division A section of a police agency that handles citizen complaints or initiates investigations of officers who are committing crimes or misusing their authority.

Internal Affairs A police agency's **internal affairs division** handles citizen complaints or initiates investigations of officers who are committing crimes

MYTH	FACT
Internal affairs units treat officers as guilty until proven innocent.	Internal affairs units tend to be one of the most thorough investigative bodies found in law enforcement agencies. Assignment to this unit is coveted and is often viewed as a baptism for the upper-management promotional track.

SOURCE: M. L. Dantzker, *Police Organization and Management* (Woburn, MA: Butterworth-Heinemann, 1999), 256.

or misusing their authority. Larger departments have separate internal affairs divisions that receive complaints and conduct investigations. In smaller agencies, the chief of police or a designated officer may comprise the entire internal affairs unit. It is important to note that usually only serious complaints become the province of internal affairs. Minor transgressions, such as failure to appear at a court proceeding or failure to pass a firearm qualification test, are handled on an informal basis by immediate supervisors or peer groups.[24]

Citizen Review Boards When police-community relations are poor and citizen distrust is high, a **citizen review board** might entirely displace internal affairs. Review boards exist when public procedures by presumably unbiased citizens are considered preferable to private internal procedures by law enforcement officials who are considered incapable or unwilling to police themselves.

Review boards perform the following tasks:

- Subpoena police officers and witnesses
- Make requisite factual findings
- Recommend or even determine appropriate discipline

The concept of a citizen review board springs from a community's distrust of police self-regulation. Some citizens feel that police credibility has been so eroded that they cannot convincingly assert that they are policing themselves. The individual community's depth of skepticism will drive the degree to which citizen participation replaces departmental decision making. If the skepticism and distrust are mild, then one citizen might sit with two sworn executives on a fact-finding review board that is subject to limited review by the police chief thereafter. If the distrust is severe, citizens may comprise the entire board and can have considerably more powers.

Citizen review boards provide a link for necessary police-community communication when distrust is high. Department officials should view these boards as vehicles to help them better understand the public they serve. Review boards also have shortcomings, which have been well noted:

- They often do not receive the training or resources to competently perform an investigative function.
- They often begin to identify with the police department and agree with the police in nearly every situation, which causes them to quickly lose credibility.
- When not provided with adequate resources, they fall behind in their workload.

ETHICS ISSUES

Internal Affairs

You are your municipal police department's internal affairs officer, and you handle all of the complaints for your department. Recently, an officer with three spotless years of work with your agency was accused of fatally shooting an unarmed suspect without adequate provocation. The evidence against her is quite strong, and you are fairly sure that she will be convicted. Although this is the only problem she has ever had on the job, it is quite serious and you are under public pressure to fire her.

How would you handle this delicate situation? For what types of offenses should first-time offending officers be suspended? Terminated?

citizen review board A method for processing citizen complaints that consists of citizens who subpoena officers and witnesses, find facts, and recommend or determine discipline.

- Since their focus (such as on the merits and demerits of a given complaint) is so narrow, their wider impact on police policy and practice is minimal.[25] Police personnel usually write their own policies, and if they are not integrally involved in the complaint adjudication process, they may not grasp the need for policy changes. On the other hand, if a department is unable to police itself, it may also be incapable of writing new policies based on the review board's findings. Therefore, the solution to this problem may be increased police involvement with review boards, or it may be increased citizen involvement in policy writing.

Mediation The process of mediation involves negotiation that brings together two or more interested parties to reconcile seemingly unsolvable differences and to reach a voluntary agreement or settlement. In some police complaint cases, mediation is informal: A supervisor arranges for the officer and complainant to talk in private, and the matter can sometimes be resolved. More typically, the process involves a trained mediator who runs a formal session at a neutral location.

▶ **Independent councils and monitors** In some cases, police departments can turn to the objective analysis of a qualified outsider. Warren Christopher ran the Christopher Commission which investigated police conduct surrounding the Rodney King beating.
What do you think is the main benefit of independent councils?

The process generally begins with the police department, sheriff's department, or citizen oversight body asking the complainant if he or she is willing to mediate the complaint. If the person is willing, the department or oversight body finds out if the officer is also willing. If both parties agree, the mediator works first to help the parties clarify the underlying issues or points of disagreement. Once the mediator and the parties have a clear understanding of the incident, they focus on reaching a positive resolution.

Mediation can have positive outcomes and result in improved police-community relations, but it can also cause serious dissatisfaction if not handled correctly. If the complainant expresses to the mediator satisfaction with the result, the case is considered closed and the content of the mediation remains confidential. If not, a complainant may refile the complaint and seek other methods of resolution. In some jurisdictions, however, complainants may not be able to take any further action against officer misconduct. This lack of recourse can further frustrate discontent citizens.

Outsourcing Some agencies, particularly smaller ones, have turned to outsourcing their complaint investigations to private investigators. This practice, though costly, offers many advantages:

- It enables agencies to maintain their field strength by not enlisting supervisors to handle complaint investigations.
- The level of objectivity is much higher when an outsider handles the investigation.
- Having an outsider conduct a personnel investigation can prevent the occurrence of awkward, unfriendly, or even vengeful relationships between the investigator and the accused officers, which can arise after an investigation conducted by an agency supervisor.

Independent Monitors/Auditors Informed members of the general public have shown strong doubt that law enforcement agencies are capable of self-regulation. There has been sustained public interest and healthy experimentation in giving independent **monitors** or other public representatives unprecedented access to law enforcement files, records, and personnel. This enables the monitors to review and comment publicly on police agency performance. These new models for outside involvement and oversight enhance police responsibility and accountability. They accomplish these ends by critiquing the rationality and integrity of the decision-making process.[26] (See Figure 13.4 on pages 514–515 for an independent auditing operation organizational chart.)

The independent monitor or auditor's primary objective is to provide independent civilian review of an agency's citizen complaint process.[27]

Independent Police Auditors

The office of the Independent Police Auditor (IPA) in San Jose, California, has been exceptionally proactive in conducting community outreach. Its 31 referral sites are stations located in community centers or other locations frequented by the public. Each referral site includes a staff person who provides orientation on the services and functions of the IPA. Also, the sites contain binders with information about the IPA, the complaint process, and contact numbers for social and legal services. The IPA also receives assistance from 18 local libraries, each of which displays IPA brochures at their information counters.

SOURCE: Teresa Guerro-Daley, *Independent Police Auditor 2000 Year-End Report* (San Jose, CA: City of San Jose, 2001), 35.

monitors Public representatives who are given unprecedented access to law enforcement files, records, and personnel to review agency performance.

Figure 13.4

Selected Police Brutality and Misconduct Cases, 1991–2001

When considering these cases and their outcomes, police officers and management should avoid rushing to judge the individual victims or officers. Instead, they should consider how these incidents negatively reflect departmental policy and harm police-community relations.

Incident	What Happened	Investigations & Reform	Discipline Implemented
Rodney King	A police car chase in March 1991 led to the brutal beating of Rodney King, who suffered skull fractures, brain damage, and kidney damage. The incident was videotaped.	The Christopher Commission examined police brutality and accountability within the LAPD, then published its findings in July 1991.	All four officers involved were originally acquitted. In a later trial two officers were convicted and two were acquitted of civil rights violations. All were fired from their jobs.
Randy Weaver/ Ruby Ridge	In August 1992 a standoff between Randy Weaver and the FBI ended in the deaths of Weaver's wife, his 14-year-old son, and a deputy marshal.	A Justice Department task force concluded that the FBI overreacted, violated bureau guidelines, and violated the Fourth Amendment.	The FBI disciplined 12 agents and employees. Weaver was convicted of two minor charges and served two months of an 18-month sentence.
Branch Davidians/ Waco	A botched ATF raid on the Branch Davidian compound in February 1993 led to a 51-day standoff between the compound and the FBI. Negotiations failed and the Branch Davidians appeared to set their compound on fire and die in the flames.	A federal investigation questioned the use of teargas and why negotiations failed. The Texas Rangers provided evidence that questioned federal government claims that the FBI had not contribute to the Waco fire.	The FBI, ATF, and Attorney General Janet Reno (who was sworn in during the standoff) were criticized for the mishandling and aggressive tactics of the federal government.
Kim Groves/ Len Davis	New Orleans police officer Len Davis ordered the October 1994 murder of Kim Groves "after he learned she had filed a brutality complaint against him."	None.	Davis was convicted of murder and sentenced to death. He also received a life sentence plus five years for unrelated federal drug charges.
Abner Louima	In August 1997 Abner Louima was arrested, then beaten and sodomized by police at the station house. Louima was hospitalized for 63 days for internal injuries.	A 28-person task force studies problems with police brutality and makes recommendations, some of which were refuted or ignored by then-New York Mayor Rudolph Giuliani.	All four officers involved were fired for participating in a cover-up. Justin Volpe received a 30-year sentence and Charles Schwarz received a 15-year sentence for their role in beating and torturing Louima. Louima also won a $8.7 million civil judgment.
Jenni Hightower	14-year-old Jenni Hightower was killed in March 1998 in Trenton, New Jersey, after police fired 20 shots into a stolen car in which she was a passenger. The 16-year-old driver was critically injured.	None.	A state grand jury declined to file criminal charges against the officers when they argued that the teen-agers had tried to run them down. (One officer was hit by the stolen car when it swerved after police had fired into it.)

Figure 13.4

Selected Police Brutality and Misconduct Cases, 1991–2001 *(continued)*

Incident	What Happened	Investigations & Reform	Discipline Implemented
Pedro Oregon	In July 1998, six Houston police officers conducted a no-knock search in the home of unarmed Pedro Oregon, who died in his bedroom from 12 gunshot wounds.	None.	Originally, one officer was indicted on a criminal trespass charge, but after a public outcry, the officers were found guilty of "egregious misconduct" and fired.
Donta Dawson	In October 1998, 19-year-old Philadelphian, Donta Dawson was fatally shot by a police officer who approached him after seeing him sitting in a car with the engine running. The officer fired after Dawson leaned forward and raised his arm.	None.	The officer was twice charged with manslaughter (voluntary and involuntary) but acquitted each time. In July 1999 the City of Philadelphia agreed to pay Dawson's family a settlement of $712,500.
Amadou Diallo	In February 1999, Guinean immigrant Amadou Diallo was fatally shot 19 times after plainclothes NYPD police officers fired at him 41 times.	None.	All four officers were acquitted and will not face federal civil rights charges. A $61 million lawsuit by Diallo's parents is still pending.
Mario Paz	In August 1999, an El Monte (California) SWAT team of about 20 officers fatally shot an unarmed elderly man, Mario Paz, twice in the back. No drugs were found in the raid, and there was no evidence that anyone in the Paz family was involved in any crime.	None.	No charges have been filed at this time.
Timothy Thomas	In April 2001, unarmed Timothy Thomas was shot and killed by Officer Steve Roach while fleeing arrest for misdemeanor charges.	None.	Roach was acquitted of two misdemeanor charges.

SOURCE: Adapted from American Civil Liberties Union, "Police Practices," accessed online at http://www.aclu.org/issues/ policepractices/ispolice.html; *Department of Justice Report Regarding Internal Investigation of Shootings at Ruby Ridge, Idaho, During Arrest of Randy Weaver,* accessed online at http://www.byington.org/Carl/ruby/ruby1.htm; Rights for All, "Police Brutality: A pattern of abuse," accessed online at http://www.rightsforall-usa.org/info/report/r03.htm; "Police Shootings," accessed online at http://www.amnesty-usa.org/rightsforall/police/brutality/brutality-4.html; Human Rights Watch, "Shielded from Justice: Police Brutality and Accountability in the United States," accessed online at http://www.hrw.org/reports98/police/ uspo94.htm; Michael Perlstein, "Officer had a history of complaints," Times-Picayune, December 7, 1994; Human Rights Watch, "Case of Abner Louima," accessed online at http://www.hrw.org/reports98/police/uspo102.htm. All sources accessed on December 18, 2001.

There are three primary functions:

1. It serves as an alternate office where people may file a complaint.
2. It monitors and audits the investigations of citizen complaints conducted by the local agency.
3. It promotes public awareness of a person's right to file a complaint.

Every aspect of the complaint process is closely examined by the monitor, from the initial interaction between the internal affairs investigator and the complainant to the conclusion of the investigation. All findings are examined to ensure that they are supported by the evidence. Also, an examination of the process used to communicate the results of the investigation to the complainant is conducted.

13.4 Self Check

1. What is progressive discipline?
2. What is the role of independent monitors?

POLICING *Online*

Check your answers at
www.policing.glencoe.com

13.5 Cultural Awareness

Culture is the social environment that people create to cope with their physical or biological environments. Customs, traditions, and taboos for survival and development are passed down generations among a particular people. Culture embraces what people believe in, value, fear, and exclude; how they learn and work; and how they create families and institutions to facilitate their lives. It preserves a group's security, but also its prejudices.

cultural awareness A level of understanding that enables one to comprehend characteristics of culture in general and apply them to specific cultures.

Law enforcement officers need to possess **cultural awareness** to comprehend characteristics of culture in general and apply them to specific cultures, such as that of a foreign country, a minority group, or an organization. Officers who are able to achieve this will have a much better understanding of cultural themes and diversity. Sensitive peacekeepers translate awareness into effective relationships with people who are different, whether in their own agency or in the community.

Cultural insensitivity by agents of the criminal justice system has, unfortunately, been commonplace. It often has led to tragic consequences: unjust harassment, civil disturbances, and even death.[28] There has been much difficulty in developing and maintaining a stable alliance between the police and the community.

One tragic example of cultural insensitivity occurred in the summer of 1993. A plainclothes Dallas, Texas, police officer responded to a call at an apartment complex. There were reports that a man had fired shots. It was dark when the officer arrived, but he saw a man with the end of a pistol sticking out of the waistband of his pants standing about 50 feet away. The officer told the man to put his hands in the air. Instead of complying, the man drew his gun and moved it toward the officer. The officer fired his weapon and killed the man.

Later, it was revealed that the victim was a Mexican citizen who spoke no English and probably did not realize that the plainclothes officer was a policeman. Members of the Hispanic community protested that officers should be more culturally aware and should know enough Spanish to communicate commands. While the officer was exonerated, the chief of police increased the amount of time that officers would spend learning Spanish.

Problematic Issues

There are many problematic issues that are natural to the police-community relationship. These include the use of force, corruption, discourtesy, and authoritarianism, which are covered below.[29]

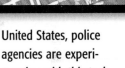

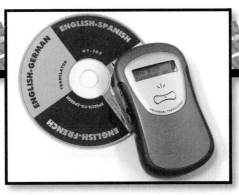

Computer On Patrol

Voice Translators

One of the biggest hurdles to building police-community relations is language. Language differences make it difficult to interrogate witnesses and suspects, communicate with citizens, and receive calls for service. Many public and private organizations are working on devices that can translate spoken languages instantaneously. Researchers hope that this technology will one day make the language barrier virtually disappear. Today, however, the most sophisticated devices can only translate key phrases. In the United States, police agencies are experimenting with this technology in schools and in multilingual communities. European police officials are also studying this technology as their governments relax their border controls, making it easier for criminals to cross from country to country. The European police hope that translation technology will simplify communications between police of different countries.

Think About It What potential uses can you imagine for voice translators?

SOURCE: www.nlectc.org/virlib/InfoDetail.asp?intInfoID=408 and Ectaco, Inc. for the UT-103.

Use of Force There is, perhaps, no single issue that stirs emotion in the police-citizen relationship as much as the use of excessive force. The community wants the police to be more proactive in dealing with crime problems such as drugs and violence but also strongly feels that this proactivity *must* be tempered by constitutional controls.[30] The use of force commonly leads to community dissatisfaction. Flagrant episodes of brutality—even though such episodes are rare—can sometimes lead to full-scale riots. In fact, their rarity is precisely what makes them front-page news.

The most dangerous situation for police-community relations is when an incident of excessive use of force by police occurs when the community already has several other grievances, even if the majority may be unrelated to policing. Such unrelated issues could be unemployment, high drug use, a high prevalence of gang violence, resentment toward the court system for perceived instances of unequal justice, and deficient local schools.[31] Such a community may already be a tinder box, and the spark that ignites a furious riot may be a single incident of excessive use of force by the most visible representative of government, a uniformed police officer, toward an uncooperative arrestee.

Corruption Law enforcement has a notorious legacy of corruption. Although the movement to professionalize policing, particularly in the 1970s, addressed the issue of corruption by aggressively upgrading internal

▶ **Community Policing in Action** A group of concerned citizens meet with their local police officers in Austin, Texas. Town meetings and other types of gatherings allow citizens to meet the officers in charge of protecting their community and develop with them a common plan of action.
How common do you think these meetings are?

investigations, hiring practices, job performance standards, supervision, and the quality of management, law enforcement has experienced a new generation of corruption. This new generation has resulted largely from the vast amount of money in the illicit drug trade.

When corruption occurs, there is a loss of public confidence in the police because officers have violated their oath of office. Efforts to bolster the police-community alliance may be met at first with cynicism and skepticism because the public has been betrayed. Fortunately, serious cases of corruption are not widespread, and ongoing good-faith efforts by police agencies will usually restore trust.

Discourtesy One of the most common complaints against officers is rudeness. Officers must understand their obligation to explain their actions and tolerate when citizens question it, particularly when some type of official action is being taken against the citizens. Rudeness is a universal problem in policing because it is magnified by the nature of the police-citizen relationship. Small, seemingly inconsequential moments of rudeness can create grudges on both sides and maintain conflict that will serve as an obstacle to building a police-community alliance.

Authoritarianism Some research indicates that police work attracts people with authoritarian and sometimes angry personalities. Other research suggests that these personality characteristics are produced by occupational socialization, which means that police learn to be authoritarian as a result of job standards and organizational values.[32]

Authoritarianism does have some beneficial effects, such as when it is used during the following police activities:

- Interrogating a suspect
- Handling a crime scene
- Conducting an investigation
- Maintaining control at a traffic accident

This characteristic becomes a problem if it emerges too strongly in situations requiring communication, cooperation, and compromise. Dealing with the community requires **tempered authoritarianism**, which means authoritarianism that is used only when needed. Officers do need to maintain an authoritative personality, but they also need to let go of this characteristic appropriately. Many officers are able to accomplish this quite easily, but some have greater difficulty.

Uncontrolled authoritarianism is a major impediment to police-community relations. This is because inappropriately authoritarian behavior toward citizens is interpreted as arrogance and as a demonstration of the

Diversity Training

Since the early 1990s, the state of California has mandated training on racial and cultural awareness. It states that "the course or courses of instruction and the guidelines shall stress understanding and respect for racial and cultural differences, and development of effective, noncombative methods of carrying out law enforcement duties in a racially and culturally diverse environment."

SOURCE: California Penal Code, Section 13519.4.

authoritarianism A personality trait that favors obedience over freedom, which is often found in police officers.

tempered authoritarianism Authoritarianism that is used only when needed, such as in situations requiring the use of force.

police's ability to restrict the public's freedoms. Since such behavior conflicts with American ideals of freedom, it creates a serious obstacle to stable community interaction. Moreover, extreme authoritarianism can lead to conflict and have a debilitating effect on community relationships.[33] (See Figure 13.5 below for a comparison of authoritarianism and tempered authoritarianism.)

Enhancing Police-Community Relations

Just as there are clearly identifiable problems that prevent healthy police-community alliances, there are identifiable elements that, if present, can greatly enhance them. These five elements are trust, communication, respect, accountability, and freedom from fear.[34]

Figure 13.5

Authoritarianism Versus Tempered Authoritarianism

Situation	When to Use Authoritarianism	When to Use Tempered Authoritarianism
Motor vehicle stop	When the driver is aggressively unco-operative or when it is clear that a crime is occurring (such as illegal weapons or drug offenses)	When the driver is cooperative, passively resistant, or mildly uncooperative
Arresting drunken suspect	When the suspect behaves in a violent or threatening manner	When the suspect lacks self-control but is otherwise not harming anyone
Arresting resisting suspect	When the suspect shows physical resistance	When the suspect shows verbal resistance, such as by trying to talk the officer out of making the arrest
Breaking up a fistfight	Until the fighting is stopped and under control	When questioning participants and witnesses about what happened
Interviewing a witness	When the witness is clearly uncooperative or committing perjury	When the witness is unsure, scared to talk, or intoxicated
Interviewing a victim	Never, unless the victim is lying to protect the assailant or to cover other crimes (such as an abused spouse lying to con-ceal her husband's child abuse crimes)	When the victim is unsure about whether to provide information because he or she "doesn't want to get involved"
Interviewing a cooperative suspect	Rarely, unless the suspect shows signs of becoming uncooperative	Throughout the interview, in order to keep the suspect focused
Interviewing an uncooperative suspect	Until the suspect shows a willingness to become cooperative	As a positive reinforcement when the suspect shows signs of behaving in a cooperative manner

Community Policing Officer

Job Description

I am currently "on loan" from the San Diego police department to head the community policing training institute. We train police officers and citizens. There are eight community policing institutes across the US which provide no-cost training. In San Diego last year, we trained 2000 people. About 70 percent were police officers.

Basically, you get two things out of community policing: the community recognizes and takes responsibility and interest in problem solving, and citizens learn to use resources other than the police. Police become more effective and better able to look at long-term solutions.

Unlike law enforcement actions portrayed on television, the vast majority of the work requires the

Lt. Margaret Schaufelberger, San Diego PD

ability to reaosn, to write, and to relate to others the facts of an arrest. This job demands good public speaking skills and computer literacy.

Employment History

I have been with San Diego PD for 24 years. In my career, I enjoyed the active phases of law enforcement, the change from day to day. I did patrol, training, worked as a detective in the burglary unit, a sergeant downtown and a lieutenant watch commander.

Education

I graduated with a B.A. in physical education.

Follow-Up What do you think is a difficulty in starting a community policing program?

Trust Trust is the ability to put confidence in someone or something. A law enforcement agency must earn trust by demonstrating that it has integrity, which means that it will follow through on its promises to the community. Trust reduces mutual suspicions of police and residents, and it provides the foundation that allows the police and community to collaborate.[35] In a recent poll, police officers were rated as one of the most honest and ethical of a number of professions.

Communication Lack of effective communication is a major source of tension between police and citizens. Language and cultural differences, especially among immigrant and refugee communities, can prevent the development of effective relationships. Since information exchange is vital to the police-community partnership, the flow of information cannot be blocked due to language barriers. To remedy this, police should find and use citizen translators to increase communication between police and non-English-speaking people. It is important that police take the initiative to learn about the various cultures in the community and that citizens try to understand more about police work in their community.

Respect Many community members, and even entire communities, feel that police show a lack of respect toward people, especially toward women, minorities, and those with lower socioeconomic status.[36] Police officers must take the initiative to dispel this widely held belief. Not only is according respect and dignity to all persons the right thing to do, but it also makes police work safer and easier for officers, since mutual respect leads to increased communication and security.

Accountability Just as the community holds the police accountable for its actions, the community is mutually accountable to the police for its quality of citizenship and contributions to public safety. Another important aspect of this social contract is the level of police responsiveness to citizen service requests and complaints. If this crucial information channel stays open, the police will be able to maintain the public's trust.

Freedom from Fear In many communities, fear of encounters with the police has made neighborhood residents unwilling to interact with police. This creates an us-versus-them attitude on both sides, which is unacceptable for successful policing.

This attitude of fear and resentment has been well documented in research on Hispanic cultures. The research indicates that the public's positive image of the police drops as their fear of crime increases, as frequency of contact with the police increases, and as victimization increases. Many Hispanic citizens feel that the police routinely discriminate against them. This feeling of discrimination is based on the belief that the police will do little or nothing to deal with victimization or to help resolve conflicts. In fact, a notable number of Hispanic crime victims said they did not report crimes to the police because their previous experience with the police was bad and they were afraid of the police.[37]

Ideally, no victims of crime should feel afraid to contact the police to report a crime. When crimes are not reported due to poor police-community relations, any other police efforts to fight crime may be pointless because the police are not being informed of the entire crime problem. Police training that emphasizes the need to treat all victims equally is crucial, and professional police behavior must reflect this training.

CopTalk

Dealing with Distraught Witnesses

Witnesses of crimes that involve injury or death are sometimes distraught and unable to communicate clearly, but it is important for officers to build a rapport with these witnesses to gain accurate testimony. While it is important to get the facts, an intelligent officer will use tact in obtaining testimony. Witnesses

should be treated sympathetically but should also be gently kept on track in providing a factual account of the crime incident.

What Do You Think? What should you do if a witness is too upset to provide testimony?

Cultural Awareness Program Implementation

To facilitate greater cultural awareness, police agencies can create and implement programs addressing this issue. The action plan must also contain a method for assessing success or failure. (See Figure 13.6 below for rate of contact with police by race.) There are four critical components of a **cultural awareness program**:

cultural awareness program A program for improving police-community relations that consists of active support by the agency head, self-assessment by the police agency, community assessment, and development of a training plan.

1. active sponsorship by the agency head
2. self-assessment by the police agency
3. community assessment
4. development of a training plan

Active Sponsorship A law enforcement agency's chief executive officer not only must set the tone for accepting a formal program of cultural awareness

Figure 13.6

Rate of Contact with Police by Race

Reason for contact with police	Number of respondents who had contacts with police per 1000 residents age 16 or older				
	Total	White	Black	Hispanic	Other race
Contact with police: Any reason	209	221	189	167	161
Respondent contacted police:					
Report a crime	40	41	39	32	35
Witness to a crime	7	7	8	5	7
Ask for Assistance	25	27	21	17	18
Report a neighborhood problem	19	21	15	13	7
Witness to an accident	8	9	5	4	4
Other reasons	19	21	16	11	14
Police contacted respondent:					
Motor vehicle stop	109	113	107	90	83
Involved in accident	16	18	12	10	10
Witness to accident	4	4	2	2	1*
Victim of crime	4	4	5	5	3*
Witness to crime	7	7	6	6	4*
Suspect in crime	6	6	8	8	5
Serve Warrant	2	1	5	1	2*
Crime prevention	3	3	3	2	1*
Other reasons	25	27	25	19	17

Note: Respondents may have described more than one reason for a contact.

*Estimate was based on 10 or fewer sample cases. Includes persons who were either passengers or drivers.

SOURCE: Adapted from Contacts Between Police and the Public. Findings from the 1999 National Survey at www.ojp.usdoj.gov

but also must prepare the organization for change and understand potential resistance. Internally, some officers may foster an attitude that the agency has chosen to give special treatment to certain groups of citizens or offenders. At the same time, there may be increased service requests from minority groups. If a police agency is not ready to deal with these groups in a fair manner, any cultural awareness efforts may backfire.

Self-Assessment Following enunciation of active support by the agency head, the agency must engage in some pointed self-assessment. Key in this regard is the evaluation of existing policy statements on community relations and the analysis of the type and extent of training on the subject. Police departments must take the necessary steps to overcome shortfalls in these two areas.

Community Assessment To address specific cultural needs accurately, a police agency must conduct a community assessment. A community's level of ethnic diversity may be determined through review of census data. In addition, key social leaders and groups such as churches and service organizations need to be identified.

Developing a Training Plan The final step is the development of a training plan. First, a training needs assessment of the agency must be conducted. Existing cultural training must be compared with the community demographics and recent history to determine training gaps. After this is determined, community-training mentors must be selected and schooled in agency policies.

When implemented correctly, such a program will have many positive effects. Victims will feel comfortable and safe with police. Police will find that the community is more responsive and helpful in solving crime problems. Citizens will be more likely to obey the law. Such police-community relations, though understated in today's media, are the backbone of American policing.

13.5 Self Check

1. Which behavior do you think is most important in building police-community relations?
2. Which component of the cultural awareness program do you feel is most important, and why?

POLICING *Online*

Check your answers at
www.policing.glencoe.com

Police-Community Relations

Summary By Learning Objectives

1. Understand the dynamics of a productive police-community relationship.

Police-community relations are based on three equal components: public relations, community service, and community participation. When these three components work together, they help to prevent crime by focusing on anticipating problems, preventing them, and doing something constructive about them before a crisis occurs. When they are not present, conflict will likely occur. Because the policing role is so complex, police need to maximize the quality of their interactions to avoid becoming prime recipients of public criticism.

2. Know how public relations and community relations help to create a positive police-community relationship.

In policing, public relations has two different but related aims: (1) to inform the public about the availability of its services and sometimes to increase the demand for it and (2) to establish and maintain a good organizational reputation. Community relations, which is a combination of public relations and human relations, involves a police department and all individual personnel at all levels, as well as other individuals and groups in the community. They may be either positive or negative, depending on the quality of officer interactions with community members and the collective images that each group holds of the other.

3. Recognize how attitudes form and can affect the quality of police work.

Attitudes develop primarily from an individual's choices to align himself or herself with a group that the person feels will help him or her attain important goals. This is because people tend to prefer what coincides with what they already believe. In policing, it means that officers who do not control their individual tendency to form attitudes will form them unknowingly. This affects the quality of their work because the ideal approach to policing is to analyze each crime situation individually, rather than to stereotype it and then form an attitude.

4. Know how prejudice can form and cause problems in police-community relations.

Prejudice is a type of attitude that is formed regarding objects, persons, groups, or values on the basis of limited information, association, or experience. Another type of prejudice is scapegoating, which occurs when people look for the causes of their failures outside of themselves. Prejudice in any form harms the effectiveness of police work. People cannot trust an officer to be fair and impartial if his or her prejudices are apparent to the general public. This can seriously erode the quality of police-community relations.

5. Understand how the public's constant interactions with the police affect their relationship.

Since the police and public constantly interact, there are several ways in which conflict and altercations can occur. This can lead to positive outcomes or to negative ones that create grudges and resentment—even over seemingly minor incidents. The quality of the outcome varies depending on the type of interaction. Most drivers who were pulled over for moving violations reported that the officer's treatment of them was fair, but most who encountered police use of force did not.

6. Explain the different methods by which citizen complaints can be handled.

Citizen complaints should be processed and resolved in a uniform, objective, and timely matter. A formal disciplinary system by which complaints are handled may take a variety of forms, depending on the individual agencies' preferences. Generally, all complaints should be documented and categorized when they are received

from citizens. There are several types of methods for processing citizen complaints. Some are external to the police agency and some are internal. There are investigations by the following:

- Agency supervisors
- Internal affairs divisions
- Citizen review boards
- Mediation
- Private investigators to whom the matters are outsourced by the police agency
- Independent monitors or auditors

7. Understand the main problems and solutions to improving police-community relations.

The main problematic issues that are natural to the police-community relationship are the use of force, corruption, discourtesy, and authoritarianism. Likewise, the main elements that lead to healthy police-community alliances are trust, communication, respect, accountability, and freedom from fear.

8. Know how to implement a cultural awareness program at a local police agency.

To successfully implement a cultural awareness program, a police agency must include four components:

1. Active sponsorship by the agency head
2. Self-assessment by the police agency
3. Community assessment
4. Development of a training plan

Key Terms

police-community relations (p. 496)
proactive policing (p. 497)
public relations (p. 497)
community relations (p. 500)
stereotyping (p. 501)
attitudes (p. 501)
prejudice (p. 502)
rapport (p. 505)
formal disciplinary system (p. 509)

progressive discipline (p. 509)
internal affairs division (p. 510)
citizen review board (p. 511)
monitors (p. 513)
cultural awareness (p. 516)
authoritarianism (p. 519)
tempered authoritarianism (p. 519)
cultural awareness program (p. 524)

Questions for Review

1. What is proactive policing, and how does it differ from reactive policing?
2. What are some examples of police efforts at public relations?
3. What benefits can a police department realize from improving community relations?
4. What is stereotyping?
5. What six characteristics are essential in "policing for people"?
6. What is progressive discipline?
7. What are the pros and cons of a citizen review board?
8. What are the three primary functions of an independent monitor?
9. What are the pros and cons of authoritarianism?
10. What is the desired outcome of a cultural awareness program?

Experiential Activities

11. Police-Community Relations
Call a municipal police department and speak to the person who answers the phone. Ask this person to define police-community relations.
   a. What is the biggest challenge in maintaining police-community relations?
   b. How do the police want to be perceived?
   c. Does this person think that police-community relations are good?

12. Police-Citizen Conflict
Find a recent case of a police-citizen conflict. It can be anything from harassment to a riot, but it should have occurred in the past two years.
   a. Summarize the events and their aftermath (trials, arrests, etc.).
   b. How did public relations and community relations fail?
   c. What can be done to restore police-community relations?

13. Positive Relations

Find a recent example of positive police-community relations. It can be a school program, an example of community policing, or a traditional crime-fighting activity that was successful and was appreciated by local citizens.

  a. What was done correctly in regard to public relations and community relations?

  b. How did this specific event help police-community relations?

  c. What can the police do so that police-community relations remain positive?

14. Citizen Complaints

Contact a local police department and find out which methods they use to resolve citizen complaints. Ask them how they chose these methods, what they used before, and what results they have observed recently. Next, contact a much larger department. Ask the same question.

  a. Which method does each department use and why?

  b. Do you feel that this method is the best choice?

  c. Explain any differences in the departments' choices.

Web Patrol

15. Ask a Cop

Learn about the San Marcos (TX) Police Officers' Association, an officer-run organization that works to improve police-community relations through the link at **www.policing.glencoe.com**. Read the first page, then click on "Ask a Cop."

What has this organization accomplished since its inception?

16. K-9s in the Community

Read about the Waupun (WI) Police Department's K-9 Unit and its police-community efforts by clicking the link at **www.policing.glencoe.com**.

How do these demonstrations help citizens understand K-9 work? Why is it good to bring such demonstrations to schools?

17. G.R.E.A.T. in Philadelphia

Read about Philadelphia's chapter of the Gang Resistance, Education And Training program by clicking on the link at **www.policing.glencoe.com**.

How does this program help build community relations?

Critical Thinking Exercises

18. Dealing with Drunk Driving

You are the chief of a town that has recently boomed into a small city. The main reason for this change is the opening of three large camp-grounds and resorts, which bring in tourists for a long summer season. The main crime problems during the summer are theft and drunk driving. This year, your town has seen an upsurge in the amount of drunk drivers, and your officers have arrested them accordingly. This has brought two completely different reactions from the city's permanent residents. Most of the residents resent the wealth and rudeness of the tourists and applaud your actions because they want public safety. A small, very vocal group of shop-owners resents your actions because your city is getting a reputation for being tough on drunk drivers, which is scaring away tourists from the new pubs and restaurants that have opened to accommodate the tourist season.

    a. Did your department do the right thing by cracking down on drunk drivers? Why or why not?

    b. To what extent can you encourage tourism without allowing crime to proliferate?

19. Progressive Discipline

You are a police lieutenant who is the internal affairs officer for your small municipal police department. In recent months, your department has had problems with new officers who are causing discontent among local citizens with their rude behavior. They did not engage in bru-tality or other forms of corruption but were authoritarian when it was not necessary and caused unnecessary arguments and complaints with their behavior. One officer, James, has had five written complaints lodged against him in the past 18 months. You have tried speaking to him, engaging him in mediation with the com-plainant, and giving him written warnings, but now he has incurred a sixth complaint.

    a. At this point, what should you do to deter James's impolite behavior?

    b. What can you do to ensure that this problem does not damage police-community relations?

20. Responding to Domestic Disturbances

You are a patrol officer who is responding to a call for a domestic disturbance. When your partner and you arrive, a married couple answers the door. Both have bruised faces and cut lips, and when you walk inside you see that they are both drunk. You explain that, according to local laws, you will have to arrest both of them for domestic violence. The wife starts screaming at you, but you stay calm. Finally, she pushes your arm, and you restrain her. This makes the hus-band angry, and to defend her he shoves you hard on the chest and kicks your partner. Your partner hits him with a billy club, bruising his head severely. The husband immediately threat-ens to sue your department for brutality and use his wife as a witness.

    a. What can you say or do to help calm this situation?

    b. Explain whether or not you feel that your partner's actions were correct.

Endnotes

1. Denny F. Pace, *Community Relations Concepts* (Placerville, CA: Custom Publishing, 1991), 48.
2. Louis A. Radelet and David L. Carter, *The Police and the Community* (New York: Macmillan, 1994), 21–34.
3. Steven M. Cox and Jack D. Fitzgerald, *Police and Community Relations* (Dubuque, IA: Brown and Benchmark, 1996), 8–10.
4. Radelet and Carter, *The Police and the Community*, 262–67.
5. Ibid.
6. Ibid.
7. Robert C. Ankony, "Community Alienation and Its Impact on Police," *The Police Chief* 66, no. 10 (1999): 150.
8. Patrick A. Langan, Lawrence A. Greenfield, Steven K. Smith, Matthew R. Durose, and David J. Levin, *Contacts between Police and the Public* (Washington, D.C.: U.S. Bureau of Justice Statistics, 2001).
9. Ibid.
10. Ibid.
11. Ibid.
12. International Association of Chiefs of Police, *Police-Citizen Contacts* (Alexandria, VA: International Association of Chiefs of Police, 2000).
13. Stephen D. Mastrofski, *Policing for People* (Washington, D.C.: Police Foundation, 1999).
14. Ibid.
15. Wesley G. Skogan, *Contacts between Police and Public: Findings from the 1992 British Crime Survey* (London: Her Majesty's Stationery Office, 1994).
16. Raymond Paternoster, Robert Brame, Robert Bachman, and Lawrence W. Sherman, "Do Fair Procedures Matter? The Effect of Procedural Justice on Spouse Assault," *Law and Society Review* 31, no. 1: 163–204.
17. Mastrofski, *Policing for People*.
18. Tom Tyler, *Why People Obey the Law* (New Haven, CT: Yale University Press, 1990).
19. http://www.usatoday.com/news/nation/2001/07/12/louima.htm
20. Lou Cannon, "LAPD Confidential," *Los Angeles Times*, 8 October 2000, D-1.
21. M. L. Dantzker, *Police Organization and Management* (Woburn, MA: Butterworth-Heinemann, 1999), 256.
22. International Association of Chiefs of Police National Law Enforcement Policy Center, *Corruption Prevention* (Alexandria, VA: International Association of Chiefs of Police National Law Enforcement Policy Center, 1996).
23. Max T. Raterman, "Progressive Discipline as a Police Management Tool," *Police Department Disciplinary Bulletin* 8, no. 9 (2000): 1–4.
24. Edward A. Thibault, Lawrence M. Lynch, and R. Bruce McBride, *Proactive Police Management* (Upper Saddle River, NJ: Prentice Hall, 1998), 232.
25. Merrick J. Bobb, "New Models for Public Oversight of Law Enforcement," *Subject to Debate, Police Executive Research Forum* 13, no. 11: 1–4.
26. Peter Finn, "Two Meditation Systems Help Manage Citizen Complaints," *The Police Chief* 67, no. 8: 67–80.
27. Teresa Guerrero-Daley, *Independent Police Auditor 2000 Year-End Report* (San Jose, CA: City of San Jose, 2001), 2.
28. Robert M. Shusta, Deena R. Levine, Philip R. Harris, and Herbert Z. Wong, *Multicultural Law Enforcement: Strategies for Peacekeeping in a Diverse Society* (Englewood Cliffs, NJ: Prentice Hall, 1995), 357.
29. Radelet and Carter, *The Police and the Community*, 40–43.
30. Ibid.
31. Michael Hooper, "Civil Disorder and Policing," in *Handbook of Criminal Justice Administration*, (New York: Marcel Dekker, 2001).
32. Thomas Barker and David L. Carter, *Police Deviance* (Cincinnati, OH: Anderson, 1991).
33. Radelet and Carter, *The Police and the Community*.
34. Police Executive Research Forum, "Strengthening Relations between Police and Minority Communities," *Subject to Debate* 14, no. 6 (2000): 1–4.
35. Robert Trojanowicz and Bonnie Bucqueroux, *Community Policing: How to Get Started* (Cincinnati, OH: Anderson, 1998), 9.
36. Police Executive Research Forum, *Subject to Debate*, 1–4.
37. Radelet and Carter, *The Police and the Community*, 226.

Questions for Review

1. What are the three components of police-community relations?
2. What is a citizen review board? What is its main function?
3. Is cultural awareness necessary? Why or why not?
4. What does the acronym SARA stand for?
5. Define and contrast authoritarianism and tempered authoritarianism.
6. What is leapfrogging?
7. Define the concept of team policing and its goals.
8. What is proactive policing?
9. What are the two goals of preventive patrol?
10. Explain the role of solvability factors in a preliminary investigation.
11. What is the role of an internal affairs division?
12. Define the broken windows theory.
13. What is the Big Six?
14. Define informant and outline at least three skills necessary to manage informants.
15. Define mediation and explain its role in police affairs.

Chapter 14
The Role of Research and Planning in Policing

Chapter 15
New Science, Technology, and Paradigms

The Role of Research and Planning in Policing

CHAPTER OBJECTIVES

AFTER COMPLETING THIS CHAPTER, YOU WILL BE ABLE TO:

1. Understand the relationship between research and planning, as well as the importance of both for solving problems.

2. Explain the evolution of policing research from earlier times to the present.

3. Learn the stages for conducting objective and effective research.

4. Apply research to real-life police work.

5. Distinguish strategic planning from contingency planning.

6. Gain familiarity with the key components of strategic and contingency plans.

◄ Plainclothes detective and police officer study crime hotspot map in Dubuque, Iowa.

14.1 Research and Planning

Police work is becoming increasingly complex. Although it cannot be described as a science, scientific methods are being applied to police problems now more than ever before. Literally volumes of new police research are published annually. It is becoming increasingly apparent that new approaches are needed if the police are to respond effectively to emerging problems and citizen expectations. Research and planning have become fundamental instruments for improving decision-making at all organizational levels. Effective use of resources cannot be accomplished without getting facts, analyzing data, considering alternatives, and developing informed plans and procedures.

Although the topics of research and planning are discussed separately in this chapter, it is important to recognize that they have a **symbiotic relationship**, which is a mutually beneficial relationship between two concepts that are dissimilar in form. Research is the foundation of progressive planning, and quality planning cannot occur without the information developed through quality research.[1] For example, research that shows the effectiveness of a gang prevention program will encourage them to plan to use it and allocate resources to it. On the other hand, research that shows its inability to prevent gangs will usually make the program less popular. Furthermore, newer research is constantly replacing outdated research and prompting police management to revise their planning and resource allocation.

symbiotic relationship
Implies a mutually beneficial relationship between two concepts which are dissimilar in form.

The Value of Research

Research and planning are vital elements in police operations. Policing is a highly dynamic enterprise, and as it evolves in its ability to fight crime, research and planning become more valuable. Well-armed juveniles offenders and cybercriminals have emerged as threats that were not experienced in previous eras, and terrorism has taken on new proportions in the United States. To effectively combat these threats, police must do their homework and research the best methods for countering them.

The value of research is sometimes questioned, especially by police administrators who deal with field issues every day and view researchers as working in an ivory tower that has little connection to the real world. One concern is that researchers may not understand police work well enough to fully understand the topics they are studying, but this can be resolved by ensuring that researchers are either active police personnel or have recent field experience. Another concern is whether research is completely objective, or if it reflects the biases of those performing or funding the research.

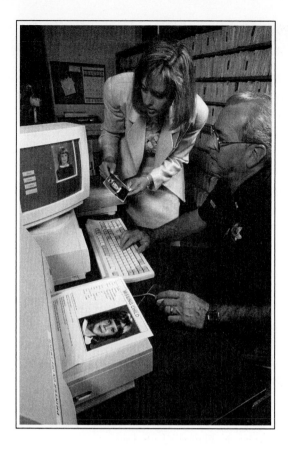

◀ **Basic Research Tools** Being savvy about computers and software tools has become an indispensable skill for contemporary policing.
What type of training is most important to keep officers abreast of new technology and research methods?

After all, if a research idea is unpopular to those who are funding research projects, how will it receive the funding needed to complete a long-term study? Fortunately for police administrators, today there is enough research performed by different government organizations, private research foundations, nonprofit organizations, and legal institutes to provide a wide array of research on police topics. Administrators can compare research to find answers.

The benefits of research and planning directly affect field officers. Moreover, field officers comprise the most important link in the research-planning continuum: information gathering. Without the information obtained through officers' performance of field work, there would be no information base upon which research can be conducted. Crime and arrest reports are the primary source of information for the crime database.

14.1 Self Check

1. Can you describe the relationship between research and planning?
2. What type of issues can affect the value of research?

POLICING *Online*
Check your answers at
www.policing.glencoe.com

14.2 Research in Policing

research Careful study of a subject.

Research is the careful study of a subject. Any subject can be researched, from the typical activities of the burglar casing a house, an officer trying to arrest the perpetrator, to a homeowner attempting to prevent future break-ins. Research can provide insights into community problems and how police agencies operate. It can help create and implement potentially useful programs and show which programs are successful and which ones are not. In short, research is a tool for police officers and citizens who want to make informed decisions.[2]

There are three principal reasons why law enforcement needs good research in a way it has not needed it before:

1. **Unprecedented focus on outcomes** which can be demonstrated by studies that show that police action can affect crime rates. American society has become increasingly concerned about seeing results from its government organizations, including the police. This bottom-line orientation in modern policing is unprecedented and is not expected to diminish. Public budgets and resources are finite, so taxpayers need to see clear benefits from the government agencies that they support. Also, American are increasingly questioning whether society's professionals (such as teachers, lawyers, doctors, and politicians) know what they are doing.

2. **Professionalization of policing** and the need for a body of knowledge on which ethical police actions are most effective. Although other professions are able to objectively grant and revoke professional status—for example, teachers and doctors are given professional status after passing board requirements—policing has no comparable body of standards. As you learned in Chapter 9, there is no uniform, nationwide ethics police with the power to punish transgressors. It must be performed on a case-by-case basis by police management or civilian inquiry boards, which means that punishments are inconsistent and therefore less effective.

3. **Shift to data-driven problem solving** in which research can provide crime mapping and other computerized aids to police. Today, there is no published comprehensive knowledge base on which law enforcement strategies work and which do not. The only way to establish a real body of knowledge is through systematic and prolonged research. Just as a nationwide code of ethical standards will help to professionalize policing, so will a comprehensive guide such as this.

Within the United States, there has been a pronounced shift to community policing, which encompasses problem-solving policing. If these policing processes are to part of all routine police work, then police agencies will need to develop research skills. They will need to analyze, interpret, and act upon research data.[3] The problem is that for the most part, law enforcement personnel have not been effectively trained to do this. Some agencies, such as the NYPD with its renowned CompStat process, have enthusiastically embraced the data-driven paradigm and reaped marked reductions in crime rates over the past decade.[4]

The Evolution of Policing Research

The first systematic study of policing was conducted by the American Bar Foundation (ABF) during 1956–1957. The ABF survey was the first to identify the extensive use of discretion by police officers. It also revealed that police work involved public service as much as it did crime-fighting.[5] A full-fledged movement for police research evolved from policing crises during the turbulent 1960s, in which the police were plunged into the center of national social and political problems. Unlike police changes during earlier parts of the reform era, this unprecedented era of scientific research paved the way for the extraordinary reductions in crime that are still working today. The forces affecting policing during this period included Supreme Court decisions on:

- Police procedures
- The civil rights movement, which challenged discriminatory police practices such as those directed toward civil rights protestors
- Urban riots
- Demonstrations against the war in Vietnam
- Rises in the crime rate

Amid all this, the police found themselves constantly criticized, either for improperly handling crowd control or for conducting illegal detentions, searches, or seizures. This stimulated a burst of inquiry into policing strategies.

Prompted by the high level of public concern about the police and the crime rate in the 1960s, the President's Commission on Law Enforcement and Administration of Justice convened to examine American crime and law enforcement. In essence, the commission members sought to reduce crime while preserving freedom. Their strategy centered on the application of **scientific management** which is fact-based and well-researched decision making.[6] Most importantly, the commission sponsored pioneering research on the tasks performed by police.

Report on Police

In 1973 the National Advisory Commission on Criminal Justice Standards and Goals published its *Report on Police*, a formulation of goals and standards for crime reduction and prevention at local and state levels. The National Advisory Commission's report was unique in that all its standards were researched and documented by working police officers. The task force of officers was required to base all standards on established programs with proven records of success.

SOURCE: National Advisory Commission on Criminal Justice Standards and Goals, *Police*, U.S. Government Printing Office, Washington, D.C., 1973.

scientific management
Fact-based and well-researched decision making.

Other new research and government agencies helped provide new information about police effectiveness. The 1968 Omnibus Crime Control and Safe Streets Act created the National Institute of Justice (NIJ) and the Law Enforcement Assistance Administration (LEAA), which were discussed in previous chapters, funded research that developed and innovated the law enforcement response to crime problems. These agencies spent massive sums of money on policing research, technological innovation, and higher education of police personnel.[7]

Since 1970 the Police Foundation has sponsored some of the most important research on policing, such as research on the effectiveness of preventive patrol and the cause and prevention of civil disorder.[8] Another important research sponsor is the Police Executive Research Forum (PERF),[9] which has conducted impressive contemporary research on such vital topics as use of force and community policing problem-solving mechanisms.[10] In 1972, the American Bar Association published a study that discussed the American police officer's dual role as peacekeeper and crime fighter.[11]

Rapid Police Response You learned about the Kansas City Preventive Patrol Experiment in Chapter 1. Another study of the Kansas City Police Department assessed the value of rapid response by police.[12] Contrary to popular belief, the study concluded that in most cases rapid response did not help solve crimes. Instead it revealed that many serious crimes were not deterred by rapid response. The crime sample that was analyzed revealed that almost two-thirds of crimes were not reported quickly enough for rapid response to be effective.

Although a prompt police response can increase the chance of making an on-scene arrest,[13] the elapsed time taken by a citizen to report a crime largely determines the effect that police response time will have on the outcome. The study revealed a need for formal call-screening procedures to differentiate between emergency and nonemergency calls,[14] and it led to further research that also demonstrated the value of response strategies that ensured that the most urgent calls received the highest priority and the most expeditious dispatch.

MYTH	FACT
Police need to arrive quickly at the scene of a crime in order to have a good chance of solving it.	A Kansas City Police Department study revealed that many serious crimes were not deterred by rapid response.

◀ **Police Management**
The vision, mission, and values of a police department are defined from the top down. *Why do you think there is such a focus on top brass in police departments?*

Community-Oriented Policing The San Diego Police Department conducted several significant research studies during the 1970s. These included:

- An evaluation of one-officer versus two-officer patrol cars
- An assessment of the relationship between field interrogations of suspicious persons and criminal deterrence
- A community-oriented policing (COP) project, which was the first empirical study of community policing

The COP project required patrol officers to become knowledgeable about their beats through "beat-profiling" activities, in which officers studied the topographics, demographics, and call histories of their beats. Officers were also expected to develop directed patrol strategies to address the types of crime and citizen concerns revealed by their profiling activities. Oftentimes, this entailed undercover operations or heavy patrolling (also called *saturation patrol*) at crime hotspots. For example, an area known for curbside drug deals could be cleaned up with a strong patrol presence, in which officers drive by frequently but with no set pattern or schedule. A park known for its high crime, drugs, and gang-related activities may need heavy directed patrol until the problems are resolved.

Officers participating in the COP project concluded that random patrolling was not as important as previously thought. They also concluded that developing stronger ties with members of the community was more important than once believed. In addition, the project demonstrated that interaction with the community could improve the attitudes of officers toward their jobs and toward the communities they served, and could encourage the officers to develop creative solutions to complex problems.[16]

Many of the findings from this study have a direct bearing on contemporary community policing efforts. First, by getting to know members of the community, the officers were able to obtain valuable information about criminal activity and perpetrators. They were also able to obtain realistic assessments of the needs of the community members and their expectations of police services. The study also exposed the need to reevaluate the issue of shift rotation. Officers must be assigned to permanent shifts and beats if they are to participate in community activities. Finally, the COP project demonstrated the critical role that shift lieutenants and sergeants play in program planning and implementation.

Problem-Oriented Policing (POP) As you recall, problem-oriented policing (POP) encourages police to begin thinking differently about how to solve crime and social problems in a community.[17] One 1984 study of POP found it to be an effective approach to addressing many community problems. The study also gathered important data about POP design and implementation.[18] A couple years later, additional independent research confirmed the value of police methodically identifying the hot spots in a community and crafting specific strategies to reduce the number of calls.[19]

Foot Patrols You learned about the Newark Foot Patrol Experiment and the Flint Foot Patrol Experiment in Chapter 11. Both of these hands-on studies showed that foot patrol units could develop more positive attitudes toward community members[20] and could promote positive attitudes toward police.[21] In Flint, Michigan, residents said foot patrols made them feel safer, and they "felt especially safe when the foot patrol officer was well known and highly visible."[22] In addition, it is worth noting that in both cities the use of foot patrols increased officer satisfaction with police work.[23]

Reducing Fears of Crime Fear reduction studies provided factual data on the effectiveness of key community policing tactics. These included the following approaches for reducing fear among residents:

- Community organizing
- Door-to-door contacts
- Neighborhood mini-stations
- Intensified enforcement coupled with community involvement
- Improving community conditions
- Enhancing the image of the police[24]

Driving this study was the notion that if fear could be reduced, community residents would be more inclined to take an active role in preserving safety and tranquility within their neighborhoods. This will encourage the level of involvement necessary for community policing to succeed.

Domestic Violence The 1981 Minneapolis Domestic Violence Experiment examined the deterrent effect of arrest. In selected precincts, incidents of domestic violence were randomly assigned to one of three types of police response: arrest, mediation, or separation. Each officer carried a color-coded pad of report forms and handled each case according to a series of steps. Repeat violence over the next six months was measured through follow-up interviews with victims and police department records of calls to the same address. The findings indicated that arrest prevented further domestic violence more effectively than separation or mediation.[25] The Minneapolis experiment received much national attention and had a significant effect on public policy. In fact, in terms of short-term impact, it may have been one of the most influential research projects in the history of the police.

Investigations Although much early policing research dealt with patrol issues, the Rand Corporation examined the role of detectives' follow-up investigations. This 1975 study concluded that the bulk of the cases solved by detectives hinged on information obtained by patrol officers during the preliminary investigation. This dramatically challenged traditional thinking about the roles of detectives and patrol officers in the handling of investigative functions. The implication was that patrol officers should become more actively involved in criminal investigations. The implementation of appropriate training would allow patrol officers to perform effective preliminary investigating that could help in obtaining timely case closures, therby reducing the tremendous case loads of detectives and allowing them to devote more time to complex investigations.[26]

Stages of Research

Research involves five stages:

1. Defining the problem
2. Designing the research
3. Collecting the data
4. Analyzing the data
5. Reporting the findings

Defining the Problem This is the most important stage of research. The problem determines whether research is necessary, or even possible. It influences the research design, data collection, and data analysis. How the researcher defines the problem greatly determines how useful the study's findings are. (See Figure 14.1 for an example of how research and data can help define a crime problem.)

Figure 14.1

Tempe, Arizona Crime Hot Spots Map

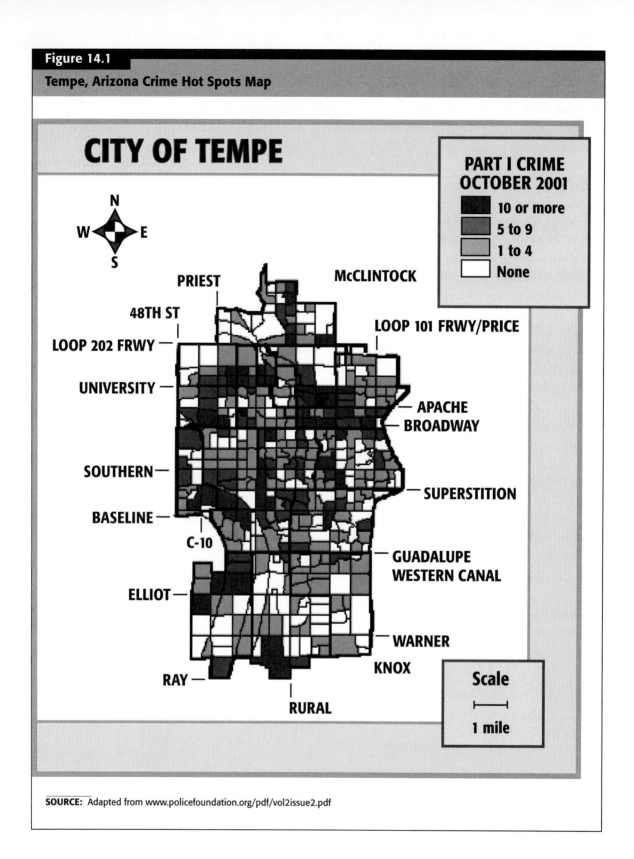

CITY OF TEMPE

PART I CRIME OCTOBER 2001

- 10 or more
- 5 to 9
- 1 to 4
- None

N
W E
S

PRIEST

McCLINTOCK

48TH ST

LOOP 101 FRWY/PRICE

LOOP 202 FRWY

UNIVERSITY

APACHE
BROADWAY

SOUTHERN

SUPERSTITION

BASELINE

C-10

GUADALUPE
WESTERN CANAL

ELLIOT

WARNER

KNOX

RAY

Scale

⊢—⊣

1 mile

RURAL

SOURCE: Adapted from www.policefoundation.org/pdf/vol2issue2.pdf

A clear statement of the problem is necessary before the researcher begins. The statement should be simple and address all the issues involved. The statement sets limits on what the research will address. For example, presume there is much concern about a high number of robberies—specifically, convenience store robberies. Further refining the problem might be useful:

- Are all convenience stores being robbed?
- Are the robberies occurring at the same time of night?
- Are the robberies only a symptom of a larger problem?
- Is community concern a bigger issue than the number of robberies?

Answers to any of these questions may help define the problem, but researchers must be careful to define it accurately. This is a key reason why researchers should have some kind of policing experience: If they misjudge a situation based on incomplete knowledge of what needs to be studied, their information will be useless to police management and officers in the field.

Another part of defining the problem involves studying previous research. Examining previous research can help ensure that new research takes into account the full range of available information on the subject so that such work is drawn upon, but not duplicated needlessly. In many instances, this information is available on the Internet, which has enabled even small agencies to access an extraordinary amount of research findings.

Computer On Patrol

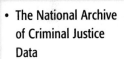

Research on the Internet

The following sites are premier criminal justice research sites. You can access all of these sites through **www.policing.glencoe.com**. Although some of the material may be very long, and perhaps hard to understand, try to read at least the introductions (sometimes called "Abstracts") to learn about the research projects that people are undertaking.

- United States Department of Justice (DOJ)
- Office of Juvenile Justice and Delinquency Prevention (OJJDP)
- The National Archive of Criminal Justice Data
- The National Criminal Justice Reference Service (NCJRS)
- PAVNET (The Partnerships Against Violence Network)
- The Bureau of Justice Statistics (BJS)

Think About It Which site provided the most useful information, and why?

Designing the Research The research design contains the logic of the study. Using the model, the research design organizes the study so that the researcher can obtain answers to questions. The **research design** is a blueprint that is based on accepted research practices and guides the collection of data, the analysis of data, and the interpretation of findings.

Comparing two or more groups of subjects is central to research design. At least one group is subject to a different approach than was used before, such as by providing more community policing units in one area and less in another to find how many units work best for a community. In contrast to these groups is the control group, which is subject to the same approach as before (such as the same number of community policing units) and provides a stable comparison.

Ideally, these groups should differ in only one way. For example, suppose an officer compares two convenience stores from the same chain, serving the same part of the town and having similar physical design, but one store has two clerks on duty and one store only has one. Ideally, because these stores belong to the same chain, they will be almost identical, except for the number of clerks on duty. If one store has fewer robberies than the other, then one may claim that two clerks deter robbers, as expected. The plan for comparing robbery incidents at these two stores is part of the research design. The problem helps to determine the design. Similar stores must be selected to conduct a valid comparison study. If one were to choose a fast-food restaurant for comparison, then the study would be meaningless.

Another important aspect of the design phase is to not only select very similar subjects for comparison, but also to attempt to recognize any other factors that might be accounting for differences between groups of people or crime locations. For example, there might be outside factors impacting one study site but not impacting any other site. There are all kinds of factors that can impact one locale more than another. Such factors could include imposition of a curfew, closure of a street, and increased foot traffic due to opening of a strip mall.

Collecting the Data The systematic gathering of facts and figures is called **data collection**. A police officer must ask whether the data collected measure what is supposed to be measured. For example, are officers sure that two clerks were on duty at a store, or did the officers survey the store during shift change, when two employees happened to be there at the same time? Are two clerks normally on duty when robberies most often occur? Are reported crime data accurate, or do some robberies go unreported? Data quality is a major research issue. Good results require good data.

The most common sources of data used by police officers are official records, such as dispatch tapes, crime reports, and surveys.(See Figure 14.2 on page 547 for a sample survey form.) In the era of community policing,

research design Blueprint, based on accepted research practices, that guides collection of data, analysis of data, and interpretation of research findings.

data collection Systematic gathering of facts and figures for the end purpose of problem solving.

Figure 14.2

Community Policing Citizen Survey *(excerpt)*

In the neighborhood or area where you live, how concerned are you about the following issues? Please select your level of concern.

1. My personal safety Not at all concerned	1 2 3 4 5 6	Extremely Concerned
2. Theft or Burglaries Not at all concerned	1 2 3 4 5 6	Extremely Concerned
3. Juvenile problems Not at all concerned	1 2 3 4 5 6	Extremely Concerned
4. Gang activity Not at all concerned	1 2 3 4 5 6	Extremely Concerned
5. Buying and selling drugs Not at all concerned	1 2 3 4 5 6	Extremely Concerned
6. Prostitution Not at all concerned	1 2 3 4 5 6	Extremely Concerned
7. Vandalism Not at all concerned	1 2 3 4 5 6	Extremely Concerned
8. Abandoned cars Not at all concerned	1 2 3 4 5 6	Extremely Concerned
9. Loitering Not at all concerned	1 2 3 4 5 6	Extremely Concerned
10. Traffic violations or problems Not at all concerned	1 2 3 4 5 6	Extremely Concerned
11. Noise or disturbances Not at all concerned	1 2 3 4 5 6	Extremely Concerned
12. The safety of others Not at all concerned	1 2 3 4 5 6	Extremely Concerned
13. The overall crime rate Not at all concerned	1 2 3 4 5 6	Extremely Concerned

Your Neighborhood Using the map of Jefferson County below, identify the section you live in and select the number which indicates your neighborhood. **1 2 3**

Please enter below any comments you may have.

Thank you!

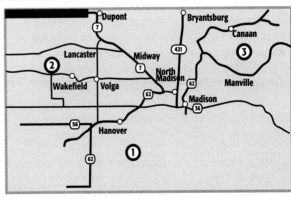

SOURCE: Adapted from Jefferson County, Indiana, Sheriff's Department, "Jefferson County Community Policing: How is it working for you?", accessed online at http://sheriffjeffersoncounty.com/survey.html on December 19, 2001.

survey findings have been commonplace for getting a "pulse" on community concerns. In this regard, it is important to ensure that surveys are conducted in such a manner that all citizens have an equal chance for inclusion in the survey. Observations of the physical environment can also be particularly useful for analyzing community problems. Often, the physical environment is linked to criminal activity or social disorder.

Analyzing the Data Left alone, data tell nothing. Once the researcher collects the data, he or she must convert them into usable information. **Data analysis** is the use of mathematics to convert data to usable information. Analysis may be simple or complex, depending on the research design and types of data collected. However, it is not the complexity of analysis methods that matters. It is the logic behind the analysis. This logic comes from the research design. If a research project is well designed, the results that flow from it will have substantial value, regardless of whether or not sophisticated mathematics are employed. On the other hand, if a research endeavor was poorly constructed, all the findings that flow from it will be flawed, regardless of the power of mathematics employed for data analysis. (See Figure 14.3 on page 549 for a sample analysis and report.)

data analysis Use of simple mathematics to convert data to usable information.

Police Procedure

Who's Calling?

A Philadelphia police sergeant investigated possible causes for an unusually high number of noise complaints—505 calls over a six-month period—made about a neighborhood bar. Officers believed that the loud music at the bar was the problem, and they were repeatedly dispatched to the bar to ask the owner to turn the music down. Still, the complaints continued. The bar owner insisted that he had lowered the music and that it was unreasonable for the police to ask him to lower it more. Hearing this, the sergeant decided to analyze the calls-for-service data to determine who was making the calls and where the complaining parties were located. He discovered that an elderly woman who lived next to the bar had made every single call, mainly out of loneliness. The sergeant had acoustic measures taken in the bar and in the woman's home and found that the sounds from the bar could not be detected in her home. The sergeant brought the bar owner and the woman together so they could directly discuss the noise problem. After that, the calls stopped immediately. The sergeant's study of the problem revealed an unlikely solution: Had he not been so open-minded, his officers might still be dispatched to the bar today, wasting valuable police resources without addressing the real issue.

Critical Thinking If the caller were falsely reporting the bar owner with the malicious intent of getting him arrested, how might the results of this case be different?

SOURCE: John E. Eck and Nancy G. La Vigne, *Using Research*, Police Executive Research Forum, Washington, D.C., 1994, pp. 14–15.

Figure 14.3

The Nature and Extent of Crime

As these maps illustrate, index crime rates in 1998 varied from state to state.

Murder

Robbery

Rape

Aggravated Assault

◆ States that are largely rural, such as Maine, Montana, North Dakota, South Dakota, and Wyoming, tend to have relatively low crime rates, and person crimes are particularly low in these areas.

◆ States that are high in some types of crime are low in other types of crime. New York, for example, has high robbery rates, but low burglary and larceny rates.

◆ Overall, few regional trends are apparent, with the exception of murder rates, which seem to be lighter in the Southeast than in the rest of the country.

Map Key

Note: The colors of the states represent ranges forcrime rates, from low to high, as shown in the map key. Crime rate ranges were established by subtracting the lowest rate from the highest, and dividing the resulting range into four equal increments. The rate ranges, per 100,000 population, for each crime category are:

Murder...1.1–12.8
Rape...18–69
Robbery...10–299
Assault...45–732
Burglary...325–1,394
Larceny..1,498–4,012
Motor Vehicle Theft...........................103–865

Crime Rate Level

Low —————————————→ High

SOURCE: Adapted from www.jrsa.org. Crime and Justice Atlas, 2000

ETHICS ISSUES

Interpreting Data

What are the ethical issues of how data is interpreted? One issue is that researchers strive to be consistent in analyzing data, but are often presented with inconsistent information. For example, each jurisdiction has slightly different wording for each statute. Because of this, those who are arrested for an offense in one jurisdiction may not have been breaking the law in another.

When presenting data, all such variables should be explained so that people using this data do not misunderstand its meaning. Even thought this will make the data seem more complex, it will also help to prevent misunderstandings among those who use such information to plan and create policies.

What other ethical issues could arise in the way that data is interpreted?

Reporting the Findings The findings put results into usable form. They explain the results and form the basis for policy recommendations Additionally, findings frequently point the way for further research.

In fact, discovering unanswered questions is as important as answering them because the unanswered questions help identify existing policies that are based on untested assumptions and may need testing.

In the presentation of research findings, the best approach is through simplicity. Data, whether presented in tables, graphs, or charts, should be formatted as neatly as possible, with no extraneous graphics.

This is because serious readers want to be able to access its information as quickly and easily as possible without distractions. On the other hand, charts and photos that help illustrate the research findings are always helpful.

Applying Research to Police Work

Police officers engage in research activities every day. An officer responding to a burglary call performs the following research:

- Collects data such as evidence and testimony
- Develops hypotheses about when the crime occurred, entry methods, and likely suspects
- Analyzes data such as alibis and suspect descriptions
- Tests hypotheses, or educated guesses, by performing interviews and interrogations
- Arrives at findings by identifying and sometimes arresting an offender

For example, an officer's data collection and analysis methods are drawn from training and agency procedures. Incident reports and supplemental reports are the officer's data collection forms. The criteria for legitimate findings are the officer's rules of evidence and due process.

Police conduct research either to confirm beliefs about the underlying causes of a community problem or to reveal causes of crime that may not be readily apparent.

Most large police departments today have a separate research and planning unit whose role is to compile and analyze research data in order to develop specific strategic or contingency planning.

14.2 Self Check

1. What are the five stages of research?
2. How can research be applied to police work?

POLICING *Online*

Check your answers at
www.policing.glencoe.com

Planning in Policing

A disciple of August Vollmer and one of the best-known police administrators, O. W. Wilson promoted careful police planning and firmly
believed that planning in law enforcement amounted to a blueprint for immediate, practical use. **Planning** is a process of developing a method to achieve
a defined goal. Wilson was very specific about the fact that police planning
should be operationally oriented, which means that it should be geared toward
affecting the real world of objects rather than simply the world of ideas.[30]

planning Process of developing a method, that takes
place in advance of action,
to achieve a defined end
state.

The Planning Before Action

The most important aspect of planning is that it takes place *before* action.
This may appear so obvious as to be trivial, yet the need to act is often so
compelling that people act before they have collected sufficient information
and formed a reasonable plan. When a course of action and its consquences
seem clear, planning may be unnecessary and inefficient. When consequences are not clear, however, or when there may be better or undiscovered
alternative courses of action, the value of planning increases greatly because
it allows police administrators to objectively explore other options.[31]

Planning is really about making decisions. Like research, it is largely
driven by the problems that police face. Just as research is performed to learn
as much as possible about a problem condition, planning is the use of
research and decision-making to solve problems. Police officers use research
to devise plans throughout the course of their daily activities, just as they
compile extensive crime databases through their report-taking activities. If
a department's crime mapping data shows an increase in burglaries among
stores of a particular shopping district, officers can make an effort to provide crime prevention tips to store owners and perform directed patrol at
night time. Detectives can study similar crimes in case they share a common
M.O., which would denote that the same person committed them.

The Value of Planning An example of the value of planning before taking
action is the 1993 conflict at Waco, Texas, between David Koresh's Branch
Davidian religious sect and federal law enforcement agents. The ATF had
suspected Koresh and his Branch Davidian disciples of amassing a large
arsenal of illegal weapons and explosives. In a poorly planned raid on the
sect's Waco compound, the ATF sustained multiple fatalities and injuries.
After a lengthy siege, the compound and its inhabitants were incinerated in
a blaze of questionable origin. The siege of the Branch Davidian compound
has been the subject of countless studies on the quality of decision-making
and planning by federal authorities, who sometimes acted in conflict with

local law enforcement. The federal report on the Waco incident cited major deficiencies in planning, intelligence-gathering, and coordination.[32]

More recently the response of the federal government to the terrorist attacks of September 11, 2001, is another example of a measured and detailed response. For example, federal agencies immediately planned to strengthen the safety of commercial. Although many favored arming pilots with weapons and the idea was given careful consideration, this concept was rejected because of training and liability issues, as well as the possibility that hijackers could turn the weapon against the pilot. Instead, air marshal corps was expanded, National Guard troops were deployed at airports, and targets such as cockpit doors were hardened and strengthened.[33]

Strategic Planning

Within policing, two types of planning are predominant within the operational environment: strategic planning and contingency planning. **Strategic planning** is a department-wide planning endeavor that leads to long-term organizational changes that meet the emerging needs of a community. Strategic plans are agency-wide and routinely cover a span of at least five years. Their planning framework is extensive and solicits input from all reaches of the police agency and the extended community. The presumption in embarking on strategic plan development is attainment of a better fit between the problems and needs of the community and the police department's capability of response.[34]

CopTalk

Planning among Patrol Units

Every day, officers often engage in planning activities before beginning their work shifts in the field. At roll call they share information on crime hotspots and wanted persons, then incorporate that data into their plan for patrolling their beats. Before leaving the station to enter the field, new partners often discuss which one of them will take the lead in approaching a vehicle pulled over or which one will initiate dialogue with suspects that they encounter.

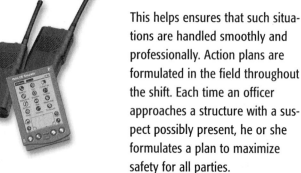

This helps ensures that such situations are handled smoothly and professionally. Action plans are formulated in the field throughout the shift. Each time an officer approaches a structure with a suspect possibly present, he or she formulates a plan to maximize safety for all parties.

What Do You Think? What other issues should patrol partners discuss before entering the field?

◀ **Emergency Plans** New York police prepare to face off mock demonstrators at a mobilization exercise. Effective emergency plans can mean life or death to citizens.
Do you think the public is aware of this specific police role?

Patrol officers and others such as detectives and traffic officers contribute to the formulation of strategic plans, and their field enforcement activities should be the extension of major plan goals. Commonly, strategic plans have goals centered on the reduction of specified types of crimes like residential burglaries, traffic accidents, or drug offenses.

There are standard elements that constitute strategic plans, regardless of the type of agency. You have already learned how these elements contribute to the police role, and now you will learn how this role is planned by police management.

- Vision
- Mission statement
- Values
- Goals
- Objectives
- Strategies
- Resources
- Method of assessment

These items constitute the steps in the planning process as well as the content of the strategic plan document. The relationship among the elements may be understood using the analogy of a staircase. The first step at the base of the staircase is the vision, the foundation upon which the strategic plan rests. Each additional step is applied upon the one preceding it.

Vision The vision is the first step in strategic planning and is the foundation upon which the other components stand. **Vision** is a mental image of a possible and desirable future for the law enforcement agency and its community. Police management create vision statements in order to guide a department's standards and inspire commitment among officers.

vision A mental image of a possible and desirable future for a law enforcement agency and its community.

Mission Statement A statement of purpose that a police department uses to show its responsibilities to its employees and the public **mission statement**. It distinguishes the organization from other governmental agencies and even from another police department. A mission statement reflects the agency values.

mission statement Statement of purpose that expresses a police department's responsibilities and distinguishes the organization from other governmental agencies or even from another police department.

Values Enduring beliefs about what is right and desirable and underlie an agency's mission, goals, and objectives is a common definition of **values**. Typical values are trust, honesty, integrity, service, responsiveness, and community partnership. In constructing a mission statement, police management must gain a measure of consensus among employees as to what the organization aims to accomplish. If not, any plans to develop unified values will fail. Additionally, it is vital to obtain input from the community. This can be accomplished through a community advisory committee that reflects different community populations. Thus the statement should convey a shared vision of the future, as well as shared formal beliefs and formal goals.

values Beliefs that guide an organization and the behavior of its employees.

Goals and Objectives Goals and objectives are part of the mission statement. A **goal** is a measurable long-term end to be attained. Universal law enforcement goals include the following:

goal Measurable long-term end state to be attained.

- Reduction of crime
- Reduction of fear of crime
- Reduction of social and physical disorder
- Strengthening of community involvement

An **objective** is a short-term milestone to be accomplished on the way to achieving a goal. Objectives are easily measurable and are limited by time constraints. Often these terms are used interchangeably, but objectives are actually stepping stones toward a goal. For example, the goal of graduating from a police academy requires passage of numerous performance objectives such as learning an adequate amount of self-defense and criminal law. As another example, a police agency may establish a goal of reducing burglaries in a particular neighborhood. To accomplish that goal, they may establish the objective of starting a Neighborhood Watch Program with at least 40 percent household participation.

objective Short-term milestone to be accomplished enroute to goal achievement.

Just as it is important for police administrators to include employees when planning an agency's vision and mission statements, it is equally

CAREER FOCUS

Police Planner

Job Description

There are two components in my job: policies and procedures, and special projects. The most recent large special project was the installation of in-patrol car video systems. We investigated the various products on the market, traveled to other agencies, and tried out the cameras in arrest vans first since most complaints we get are from citizens who were transported in these vans.

One of our main concerns is always reducing litigation, and we tried to impact that by having the cameras installed to capture evidence.

We review all policies and procedures and make sure they comply not only with federal and state regulation but also with local laws. This means that there are many bases to cover to ensure the department is covered legally. Attorneys always review our findings and recommendations.

Michael Wilson, Kansas City PD

The completion of a major project, such as the in-car cameras, is very satisfying because it has benefits for both the community and the police. It will show whether an officer is right or wrong, and as such it is part of a system of checks and balances.

I was also the 2001 President of the International Association of Law Enforcement Planners, the main organization in the field with 2,000 members.

Employment History

I have been with the department for 28 years. My father was a police officer, and I went through the academy right after high school. I worked as a patrolman, as a detective, undercover as a narc investigator; I also provided security for the mayor, and I finally joined the planning and research unit in 1992.

Follow-Up How do you think planning and research relate to community policing?

important to include them when planning and setting goals and objectives. Field officers often have currently information on field conditions that are valuable to top management, so their input is crucial if police management is going to plan goals that solve the field officers' work-related problems. When planning goals and objectives, police management should set them high enough so that employees will have to strive to meet them, but not so high that they will become discouraged and give up trying to meet them.

strategy Specific action taken toward achieving an objective (and goal).

Strategies A specific action taken toward achieving objectives and goals is termed a **strategy**. Strategic planning requires the consideration of alternative courses of action in order to choose those that will best attain specific objectives and their respective goals. For example, the objective of reducing the incidence of new cases of vandalism by 20 percent could be achieved by strategies such as installing high-intensity lighting or enacting and enforcing anti-loitering ordinances.

It is essential that any strategies employed actually contribute to the achievement of specified objectives and goals, and are not merely "bells and whistles" that appear impressive but lead to nothing concrete. For example, if a police department wants to accomplish an objective of reducing gang violence on and near a school campus, they might employ a strategy that involves establishing a van service that shuttles neighborhood students to school without forcing them to walk through gang-infested streets. See Figure 14.4 below for an example of gang suppression strategies.

Figure 14.4

Planning Gang Suppression Strategies

- Clearly defining common key terms such as *gang*, *gang member*, and *gang-related* so that data comparisons across agencies will be meaningful.
- Using information and intelligence both from inside and outside the agency to clarify the nature and extent of the gang problem.
- Using information and intelligence to target priorities (that is, specific gangs, neighborhoods, and individuals) and then develop enforcement strategies accordingly.
- Inventorying all possible resources inside and outside the department that may be used to address the gang problem.
- Keeping the effort focused by developing specific goals, objectives, and priorities.
- Ensuring that adequate management tools are in place, including a time/task plan, written policies and procedures, and an evaluation plan.

SOURCE: Urban Street Gang Enforcement ww.ncjrs.org. http://www.ncjrs.org/pdffiles/161845.pdf

Figure 14.5

Resources for Gang Suppression Plan

Law Enforcement Resources

- ◆ Internal divisions and units currently responsible for gang intelligence gathering, investigations, database management, and enforcement
- ◆ Support provided by other divisions and specialized units for current gang suppression efforts, including patrol and community police officers; drug enforcement; career criminal and organized crime; tactical (for example, special weapons and tactics (SWAT)); juvenile investigators and school resource officers; and crime analysis, research and planning, and records
- ◆ Support from other criminal justice agencies, including Federal agencies such as the Internal Revenue Service (IRS), U.S. Customs Service, U.S. attorneys' offices, the Bureau of Alcohol, Tobacco and Firearms (ATF), the Federal Bureau of Investigation (FBI), the Drug Enforcement Administration (DEA), and the Immigration and Naturalization Service (INS); State police and prosecutors; corrections; probation and parole and courts; housing authority police and security personnel; and campus police
- ◆ Support from law enforcement agencies in other jurisdictions
- ◆ Current police/prosecutor agreements and systems regarding gang cases
- ◆ Agreements and working relationships with other organizations involved in gang issues (for example, schools, prevention programs, and victim assistance agencies)
- ◆ Training resources
- ◆ Technical assistance resources (for example, regional and national criminal justice associations and organizations and colleges and universities)
- ◆ Equipment needed and available

Resources to support police intervention in targeted neighborhoods may include:

- ◆ Resident organizations
- ◆ Business groups
- ◆ Churches and church organizations
- ◆ Community-based organizations such as gang prevention or intervention programs
- ◆ Public housing tenant associations

SOURCE: Adapted from Urban Street Gang Enforcment. www.ncjrs.org. http://www.ncjrs.org/pdffiles/161845.pdf

Resources The materials and personnel required to execute strategies are **Resources**. All police agencies are acutely aware that resources are limited, and that dedicating them to a specific problem involves budgetary constraints. It is always essential to develop a sound justification for the use of resources. In a police department, as in almost any enterprise, there always will be fierce competition for available resources. An ideal path to take to maximize the chances of winning the resources battle is to demonstrate the cost savings that will eventually result through the strategies to be financed. Therefore, it is well worth the effort to employ strategies that have been well-researched and shown to be successful in other venues. (See Figure 14.5 above for an example of resources lineup.)

resources Materials and personnel required to execute strategies.

Figure 14.6

Five-Paragraph Tactical Plan Format

Situation This paragraph establishes the "who," "what," "where," "when," and "why" of a special event situation. A clearly expressed situation paragraph is critical to the development of the remainder of the plan. It should provide background to the event, including any aggravating factors.

For example: The City of Anytown will host the 30th Annual Motorcycle Rodeo at the Anytown fairgrounds on Friday, May 13. The daylong event will begin at 8:30 A.M. and conclude at 5:00 P.M. Closing ceremonies will consist of an awards ceremony at 6:00 P.M., followed immediately by a fellowship dinner. In the past these functions have been relatively incident-free. However, this year the event is open to international competitors, a number of whom are from countries known to house perpetrators of terrorist incidents within the United States. In addition, a decision was made by the city council to permit the consumption of alcoholic beverages.

Mission The mission is determined by the incident commander after receiving a situation briefing. The statement should clearly define the goal(s) of the police department in as concise a manner as possible. If there is more than one mission involved, the multiple missions must be prioritized.

For example: The overall department mission is to ensure the safety of all persons attending the event. A secondary mission is to expedite the flow of traffic along Interstate 100 and Route 15. A third mission is to facilitate creation of an environment hospitable to the staging of this event. The proceeds that accrue to city coffers from the hosting of this one-day activity are equivalent to one month's revenue under normal circumstances. Therefore, the Motorcycle Rodeo is a potentially valuable recurrent source of revenue for the city.

Concept of Operation The concept of operation has a two-fold purpose. It projects the sequence of policing operations in chronological order and also predesignates tactical concepts and tools to be employed. This can be the most complicated plan section to develop because it requires a mental walk-through of the progression of policing actions prior to their actual occurrence. The key to getting this passage done in the most useful manner is to spend time at the actual concerned venue so the procession of policing activities can be visualized within the environment within which they will occur. When preparing this section, separate the "chronology" text from the "tactical concepts" text.

For example:

> May 12, 0600 hrs.: Sanitize (conduct a bomb sweep) the motorcycle garage
> May 12, 0800 hrs.: Sanitize the exhibition grounds
> May 12, 0900 hrs.: Activate the command post
> May 13, 0600 hrs.: Emplace traffic control devices at control points
> May 13, 0700 hrs.: Set up perimeter security

Tactical Concepts:

Arrest Policy: Officers shall self-limit enforcement activities to those relating to interference with the conduct of the motorcycle rodeo and those that endanger personal safety. Booking approval shall be obtained from the officer-in-charge of the field command post. The portable booking center will be used to detain arrestees prior to their pick up by the sheriff's department.

Use of Force: The standard use of force continuum will be in effect. Officers are reminded of the importance of using the "swarm" technique whenever possible for subduing belligerent suspects.

Figure 14.6

Five-Paragraph Tactical Plan Format *(continued)*

Execution This paragraph is used to make specific assignments to all units involved. Each element's membership must be identified, and each element must be assigned a specific mission. Use of a matrix can significantly simplify and clarify these assignments. A matrix is used in addition to written instructions and provides a quick reference to assignments that have been made and also serves as a check to ensure that there have been no "holes" or duplication of effort in the execution phase. Completing a matrix is fairly simple, with significant activities related to the operation being listed in chronological order across the top boxes and the involved units listed in the boxes along the left side of the matrix.

For example: There will be a total of four elements (or units) deployed to police during this special event. Primary activities are sanitization, command post maintenance, traffic control, and perimeter security. A mobile field force will be deployed to perform roving security tasks and will be available for deployment for other assignments as circumstances require. Individual assignments to elements are listed below, as is a complete description of duties to be performed pursuant to each primary activity. An "Assignments/Activities Matrix" (below) depicts at a glance the primary activities and unit assignments.

Assignments/Activities Matrix				
	Sanitization	**CP**	**Traffic Control**	**Perimeter Security**
Unit 1	May 12, 0600 hrs	May 12, 0900 hrs	May 13, 0600 hrs	
Unit 2		May 12, 1400 hrs		May 13, 0700 hrs
Unit 3		May 12, 2200 hrs		May 13, 1500 hrs
Unit 4		May 13, 0600 hrs		

Administrative Instructions This paragraph addresses any administrative announcements that are necessary to make the operation work. Typical ingredients in this section include: reporting instructions, uniform requirements, and feeding protocols, i.e., how and when meals will be handled.

For example: All personnel will wear class "A" uniforms. Rain gear and helmets (with protective face masks) shall be immediately accessible if needed. Frequency 7 will be the primary radio frequency, and frequency 2 will be the tactical frequency (to be used in "simplex" mode at all times). Feeding times and locations will be at the discretion of squad leaders.

assessment The process of determining the extent to which goals and objectives have been achieved.

Assessment In the course of progressing to achieve objectives and goals, there must be a means for affirming progress. **Assessment**, which is also referred to as evaluation, is the process of studying strategies to determine whether or not they are helping to achieve objectives and goals. The basic measures used for assessment must be directly related to the original objectives and goals. To return to the example of the school gang prevention strategy, the crime rates for the school and its environs would be typical measures. Other common measures include official reports of crimes, surveys, and numbers of persons contacted.

Assessment ensures that baseline data are gathered so that there is a basis for comparison. **Baseline data** assess the situation before police attempt to implement strategies to show what problems existed before strategies were attempted. Typical baseline data are counts of the numbers of crimes or levels of fear just prior to implementation of a strategy. The gathering of baseline data is a standard practice that precedes the implementation of community policing programs. The assessment process needs data determine how much progress has been made toward achieving goals.

baseline data Values of measures prior to implementation of strategies, which provide a means for before/after comparisons.

Example of a Strategic Plan Oftentimes, it is easier to grasp strategic plan concepts by review of an actual plan. has been constructed as an aid for visualizing strategic plan components. The development of a strategic plan is really nothing more than designation of a goal responsive to a problem. Objectives are created in furtherance of accomplishing the designated goal, strategies are the action steps for attaining objectives, and resources for fueling strategies must be specified and cost-justified. Finally, there must be identification of a means for assessing how well strategies and objectives are progressing toward goal accomplishment.

At this point all one needs to do is to specify another objective in furtherance of the goal of reducing the incidence of Part I crimes. In turn, additional strategies, resources, and an assessment method will need to be identified. The process is not difficult; it is merely one that requires careful consideration of the most efficient methods to be applied to combat a problem situation. This is best done in a group problem-solving format in order to capitalize on all levels of expertise in discussing a variety of objectives and strategies.

Emergencies or Disasters?

Perhaps emergency plans should really be called disaster plans because this is more descriptive of the type incident these plans are intended to handle. These incidents are:

- Natural, such as a flood or tornado
- Technological, such as an air crash or toxic cloud
- Human-caused, such as a riot or explosion

contingency planning Preparations made for specific events and occurrences that are not part of the daily activities of police department personnel.

Contingency Planning

There are two categories of contingency plans: tactical plans and emergency plans. See Figure 14.6 on page 558 for a templatized version of a tactical plan. **Contingency planning** is the preparations made for specific events and occurrences that are not part of daily police activities. This short-term planning demands some specific detail in terms of procedures, but because of changing conditions in the field, it often demands more flexibility than other types of planning do. It is an important component of field operations routines, and many large municipal agencies assign officers to contingency planning on a full-time basis in order to enhance the agency's response capability to such matters. Parades and special events such as special holiday shopping days at the local mall or major sporting events, are typical subjects of contingency planning. Less frequently, catastrophic incidents become the subject of contingency planning.

Tactical Plans Tactical plans are tailored around major activities such as rock concerts, athletic events, parades, and dignitary visits. Such plans are formulated based on what is expected to take place. The plans can cover recurrent events as well as first-time events. In the majority of cases, tactical planning uses the resources normally assigned to the agency and does not require consideration of use of other agencies' resources, other than on a minimal scale, e.g., borrowing barricades from a public works department. In most instances, a standard format, such as that outlined in Figure 14.6 on page 558, can be used to fashion a tactical plan, regardless of the specifics of the event.

Emergency Plans Emergency plans are developed to contend with large-scale unusual occurrences that have an impact that exceeds jurisdictional boundaries and that require reconfiguration of the police department in order to control the incident. Reconfiguration means transitioning to 12-hour shifts and a mobilizing off-duty personnel to bolster the control force. Also, emergency plans are normally conceived with the knowledge that a number of duties will be shared with outside responders. Accordingly, such plans include built-in provisions for accommodation of other agencies.

Example of a Tactical Plan While there are several acceptable formats for developing contingency plans, the five-paragraph format shown in Figure 14.6 on page 558 is used by many agencies. It is not difficult to produce and it provides a thorough plan with which to secure a special event. Thus it provides for the creation of a contingency plan that covers all appropriate issues in a succinct and readily understandable manner.

14.3 Self Check

1. What is the most important aspect of planning?
2. What two types of planning are predominant in policing operations?

POLICING *Online*

Check your answers at
www.policing.glencoe.com

The Role of Research and Planning in Policing

Summary By Learning Objectives

1. Understand the relationship between research and planning, as well as the importance of both for problem solving.

Research and planning share a symbiotic relationship because they are both fundamental instruments for improving decision making at all organizational levels. Both are also vital for problem-solving, which has become especially important in the era of community policing, with its emphasis on responsiveness to community-expressed problems. Through learning and applying the best methods for gathering high quality information from the field and by practicing proven planning methods, patrol officers can maximize their effectiveness as problem solvers.

2. Explain the evolution of policing research from earlier times to the present.

The interest in policing research was fueled by the policing crisis of the turbulent 1960s, in which police found themselves embattled in skirmishes that were fueled by social and political problems. During this period the civil rights movement gained momentum and the Vietnam War caused extraordinary controversy and turmoil among Americans. As a consequence of the heightened attention given policing issues, the federal government channeled huge sums of money into research and technology to improve policing methods. The 1968 Omnibus Crime Control and Safe Streets Act subsidized a number of research projects that in some cases turned upside down conventional policing strategies. One Kansas City study disclosed that rapid response to citizen calls often had little effect on the crime-solving rate. Rather, response time became important only if calls to dispatch centers were made at the time of crime commission or shortly thereafter. Additionally, federally funded research enabled much to be learned about matters such as domestic violence, community policing, foot patrols, and detective work.

3. Learn the stages for conducting objective and effective research.

Research is a five-stage process:

1. The process begins with problem identification.
2. After the problem has been identified, a research design must be developed. The research design is a blueprint for collecting and analyzing information relevant to the problem.
3. The third and fourth stages entail actual data collection and analysis. The most common sources of data are police crime and arrest reports and citizen surveys.

4. The analysis of data via simple mathematics provides result-oriented findings such as whether there are decreases or increases in specific crimes, or favorable or unfavorable views toward a community policing program component.

5. The last stage in the research process is the reporting of findings. Formal reports of findings form the basis for policy recommendations.

4. Apply research to real-life police work.

Police officers apply research activities to their police work daily. For example, an officer responding to a burglary call performs the following research:

- Collects data such as evidence and testimony
- Develops hypotheses about when the crime occurred, entry methods, and likely suspects
- Analyzes data such as alibis and suspect descriptions
- Tests hypotheses, or educated guesses, by performing interviews and interrogations
- Arrives at findings by identifying and sometimes arresting an offender

5. Distinguish strategic planning from contingency planning.

Strategic planning is long-term planning, while contingency planning is normally responsive to events occurring in the short term. Strategic planning is departmentwide in its scope and formation. The strategic plan may span five years and addresses major department issues such as crime reduction, traffic safety, and personnel complaint incidence. All department employees are expected to contribute to its development, since all will be beneficiaries. Contingency planning is usually narrow in scope since it is most often focused on matters that involve patrol officers exclusively. It is the customary planning done to prevent disruption at special events such as concerts, parades, or major sporting events.

6. Gain familiarity with the key components of strategic and contingency plans.

Strategic plans are long-range plans that set a course for handling matters that are of primary importance to an agency. Their key components are vision, a mission statement, goals, objectives, strategies, resources, and assessment procedures. Contingency planning most often takes the form of tactical planning. Tactical plans are tailored for the control of major special events such as concerts, sporting events, or parades. Standard areas of coverage include the following: situation, mission, concept of operation, execution, and administrative instructions. The mission statement is critical because it provides the foundation and focus for all policing activities that are planned. Special operational issues are discussed in this section as well. Topics such as arrest policy, use of force policy, and rules of engagement are covered here. The "execution" section is a detailing of specific assignments. Specific missions, eg., crowd control, perimeter security, or traffic control, are assigned. The administrative instructions paragraph addresses incidental matters such as mechanics for reporting overtime, uniform requirements, or feeding protocols.

Key Terms

symbiotic relationship (p. 536)
research (p. 538)
scientific management (p. 539)
research design (p. 546)
data collection (p. 546)
data analysis (p. 548)
planning (p. 551)
strategic planning (p. 552)
vision (p. 554)

mission statement (p. 554)
values (p. 554)
goal (p. 554)
objectives (p. 554)
strategy (p. 556)
resources (p. 557)
assessment (p. 560)
baseline data (p. 560)
contingency planning (p. 560)

Questions for Review

1. Why is problem solving so important to community policing?

2. What are primary sources of information gathered by police officers?

3. What social issues prompted the interest in policing research?

4. What legislation of the 1960s was instrumental in funding policing research?

5. Identify and discuss three significant research projects of the 1970s.

6. Identify the five stages of research.

7. Which type of planning is generally responsive to events occurring in the short term?

8. Which type of planning is generally department-wide in its scope and formation?

9. Identify the primary components of strategic plans.

10. Identify the primary components of tactical plans.

Experiential Activities

11. The Value of Knowledge

Think about how to develop practical and fact-based solutions for the type of law enforcement agency you would like to work for. Find out its current crime-solving problems. Choose one problem and answers these questions:

    a. What problem did you choose and why?

    b. What are your solutions?

    c. How is the value of research and planning impacting the "bottom line" in field operations?

12*. Develop a Strategic Plan for Citywide Traffic Safety

You are the police chief of a city of 65,000 people with a downtown shopping area that attracts tourists from nearby cities. The City Manager has asked you to reduce traffic injuries and deaths by 25 percent over the next two years. Your review of the accident statistical data reveals two interesting time slots when accidents occur: between the hours of 7:00 A.M. to 9:00 A.M. and between 3:00 P.M. to 6:00 P.M., from

NOTE: Exercises 12, 13, 14 can be assigned separately or together. They each use the scenario in Exercise 12.

Experiential Activities continued

Monday through Friday. These accidents involve a number of young drivers, and over 80 percent occur within a two-mile radius of local high schools. Another group of accidents occurs on from Thursday through Sunday at nighttime from 11:00 P.M. through 2:30 A.M. A high percentage of these involve drivers of all ages who have been drinking alcohol.

    a. Draw the framework for a strategic plan by deciding the plan's vision, mission, goal, objectives, strategy, resources, and assessment.

13. Target Public Education

You want to offer targeted public education to the high schools and to local bars and nightclubs. Neither group wants to hear about the possible dangers of their behaviors: Students may tune you out as "just another lecture," and bar owners may play along but not make any attempt to instill safety measures to keep drunks off the road. You need strategies that will catch their attention and make them respond.

    a. What can you do to make the high school students understand the importance of safe driving?

    b. What can you do to compel bar and nightclub owners to stop serving drunk patrons allowing drunks on the road?

    c. How can you assess the effects of your public education effort?

14. The Resource Question

You decide to increase the number of patrol cars that will be available from 11:00 P.M. to 2:30 A.M. from Thursday through Friday. Normally, the swing shift ends at midnight and the graveyard shift begins at the same time.

    a. How will you schedule the patrol resources for this time period?

    b. Will you schedule them differently on Thursday and Sunday than you will on Friday and Saturday?

    c. How would you organize a system of peer review for your plans?

Web Patrol

15. Evaluating Information Resources

Access the National Institute of Justice Web site and their online newsletter through the link at **www.policing.glencoe.com** Read an article.

    Does the subject pertain directly to policing? identify its primary value. If there is an indirect benefit, identify that benefit.

16. National Institute of Justice

Go to **www.policing.glencoe.com** for a link to the National Institute of Justice.

    Which issues current research activities of the NIJ relate to policing?

17. Planning Issues

Go to **www.policing.glencoe.com** to access the International Association of Law Enforcement Planners' site.

    What are some of the planning issues that would impact police most?

Critical Thinking Exercises

18. Getting Your Community Involved

Contemporary police officers cannot merely address community policing with "lip service" that pretends to show concern, but does not offer real solutions. Beat officers are the primary links with the community, and they can provide some of the best solutions for dealing with crime.

In this spirit, and assuming that you are in charge of an area that has five Neighborhood Watches, answer the following questions:

   a. How might you instruct your five Neighborhood Watch Block Captains to lead their respective blocks in a strategic planning session?

   b. Could you provide enough guidance so that they could develop two strategies for combatting a growing neighborhood burglary problem?

19. Motivating Your Peers

You are in the final phase of a six-month police academy program. You, as well as all your classmates, have been given the assignment of researching state-of-the-art methods for field problem-solving.

The "carrot" that has been dangled in front of you for splendid task accomplishment is a promise of assignment to the precinct of your choice.

   a. Identify a couple web sites that might be a good place to start. Why did you choose them?

   b. Now, in a one-page report, apply these ideas to a city of 200,000 with a relatively large gang and violent crime problem.

20. Managing Large Events

This exercise can be done alone, in pairs, or in small groups. Using the five-paragraph tactical plan format that you learned about in this chapter, develop an operational plan for an upcoming rock concert in your city.

Feel free to enhance your plan with charts and matrixes that will make it more easily understood to others. Strive to fashion a plan that clearly communicates the primary operational objectives in the most succinct manner.

   a. When your plan is completed, exchange your plan with another classmate (or pair or group, dependin on how the assignment is completed) and critique each other's plans. Focus on the ease with which the plans are understood and the coverage of main operational issues.

   b. After the critique has been completed, each group should consider the changes suggested and incorporate the changes that appeal to you.

Endnotes

1. National Advisory Commission on Criminal Justice Standards and Goals, *Report on Police*, U.S. Government Printing Office, Washington, D.C., 1973, p. 123.
2. John E. Eck and Nancy G. La Vigne, *Using Research*, Police Executive Research Forum, Washington, D.C., 1994, pp. 2–3.
3. Ibid., pp. 20–25.
4. Donald J. Newman, "Sociologists and the Administration of Criminal Justice," in Arthur B. Shostak, ed., *Sociologists at Work* (Homewood, Illinois: Dorsey Press, 1966), pp. 177–187.
5. Mark Moore, "Looking Backward to Look Forward: The 1967 Crime Commission Report in Retrospect," *National Institute of Justice Journal*, No. 234, December, 1997, pp. 24–30.
6. John K. Hudzik and Gary W. Cordner, *Planning in Criminal Justice Organizations and Systems*, Macmillan Publishing Co., New York, 1983, pp. 90–91.
7. Frank E. Hagan, *Research Methods in Criminal Justice and Criminology*, Allyn and Bacon, Needham Heights, MA, 1997, p. 385.
8. Thomas J. Deakin, "The Police Foundation: A Special Report," *FBI Law Enforcement Bulletin*, No. 55, November, 1986, pp. 1–10.
9. William A. Geller and Michael S. Scott, *Deadly Force: What We Know*, Police Executive Research Forum, Washington, D.C., 1992.
10. Bureau of Justice Assistance, *Understanding Community Policing: A Framework for Action*, U.S. Government Printing Office, Washington, D.C., 1994, p. 7.
11. American Bar Association, *Standards Relating to the Urban Police Function*, American Bar Association, New York, 1972.
12. George L. Kelling, Antony Pate, Duane Dieckman, and Charles E. Brown, *The Kansas City Preventive Patrol Experiment: A Technical Report*, Police Foundation, Washington, D.C., 1974, pp. iii, 533–5.
13. National advisory Commission on Criminal Justice Standards and Goals, *Police*, U.S. Government Printing Office, Washington, D.C., 1973.
14. Kansas City Police Department, *Response Time Analysis: Part I Crimes*, U.S. Government Printing Office, Washington, D.C., 1980, p. iii.
15. John E. Eck and William Spelman, "A Problem-Oriented Approach to Police Service Delivery," *Police and Policing: Contemporary Issues*, ed. Dennis Jay Kenney, Praeger, New York 1989, p. 101.
16. John E. Boydston and Michael E. Sherry, *San Diego Community Profile: Final Report*, Police Foundation, Washington, D.C., 1973, p. 83.
17. Herman Goldstein, "Improving Policing: A Problem-Oriented Approach," *Crime and Delinquency* No. 25, 1979, pp. 241–3.
18. John E. Eck and William Spelman, *Problem Solving: Problem-Oriented Policing in Newport News*, Police Executive Research Forum, Washington, D.C., 1987, pp. 81, 99.
19. Lawrence W. Sherman, Patrick R. Gartin, and Michael E. Breurger, "Hot Spots of Predatory Crime: Routine Activities and the Criminology of Place," *Criminology*, No. 27, 1989, p.39.
20. George L. Kelling, *The Newark Foot Patrol Experiment*, Police Foundation, Washington, D.C., 1981, pp. 94–96.
21. Robert C. Trojanowicz, "An Evaluation of a Neighborhood Foot Patrol Program," *Journal of Police Science and Administration*, No. 11, 1983, pp. 410–419.
22. Robert C. Trojanowicz, *An Evaluation of the Neighborhood Foot Patrol Program in Flint, Michigan*, Michigan State University, East Lansing, MI, 1982, p. 86. See also Robert C. Trojanowicz, "An Evaluation of a Neighborhood Foot Patrol Program," *Journal of Police Science and Administration*, No. 11, 1983.
23. George L. Kelling, *Police and Communities: The Quiet Revolution*, Perspectives on Policing, Washington, D.C., National Institute of Justice and John F. Kennedy School of Government, Harvard University, 1988, p. 5.
24. Antony M. Pate, Mary Ann Wycoff, Wesley G. Skogan, and Lawrence W. Sherman, *Reducing Fear of Crime in Houston and Newark: A Summary Report*, Police Foundation, Washington, D.C., 1986, p. 3.
25. Lawrence W. Sherman and Richard A. Berk, *The Minneapolis Domestic Violence Experiment*, The Police Foundation, Washington, D.C., 1984. Lawrence W. Sherman and Richard A. Berk, "The Specific Deterrent Effects of Arrest for Domestic Assault," *American Sociological Review*, No. 49, April, 1984, pp. 261–272.
26. Joan Petersilia, *The Influence of Criminal Justice Research*, Rand Corporation, Santa Monica, CA, 1987, p.15.
27. Eck and Spelman, op. cit.
28. Eck and La Vigne, op. cit., pp.14–15.
29. Daniel Glaser, *Strategic Criminal Justice Planning*, Center for Studies of Crime and Delinquency, National Institute of Mental Health, Washington, D.C., 1975, p. 3.
30. Edward A. Thibault, Lawrence M. Lynch, and R. Bruce McBride, *Proactive Police Management*, Prentice-Hall, Upper Saddle River, NJ, 1998, p. 348.
31. John K. Hudzik and Gary W. Cordner, *Planning in Criminal Justice Organizations and Systems,* Macmillan Publishing Company, New York, 1983, p. 10.
32. Richard Abshire, "Waco Revisited: A Look Back for an Answer," *Law Enforcement Technology*, Vol. 24, No. 4, April 1997, p. 29.
33. Elliott B. Smith, "U.S. Retaliation Not Imminent, NATO Told," *USA Today*, September 27, 2001, p. A-1.
34. Mark H. Moore and Darrel W. Stephens, *Beyond Command and Control: The Strategic Management of Police Departments*, Police Executive Research Forum, Washington, D.C., 1991, p. 28.

New Science, Technology, and Paradigms

CHAPTER OBJECTIVES

AFTER COMPLETING THIS CHAPTER, YOU WILL BE ABLE TO:

1. Identify the anticipated paradigm shifts in the future of policing.

2. Explain new science and technology applications in policing.

3. Understand the current capabilities of forensic scientists.

4. Comprehend the various types of biometric measures and how they are used.

5. See how computers contribute to the effective use of new science and technology.

6. State why nonlethal weapons are an important factor in the future of policing.

7. Understand the benefits and drawbacks of using new science and technologies.

8. Explain how paradigm pioneers help to integrate new science and technology into policing.

◀ Police officers watch surveillance camera monitors in a command center at Washington, D.C. police headquarters in February 2002.

Looking to the Future

Who would have imagined in 1900 that technologies such as DNA, electronic house arrest, Kevlar protective vests, microcomputers, and psychological profiling would become commonplace in criminal justice? In the late 1800s and early 1900s, criminal justice professionals were witnessing the integration of new science and technologies that, for their time, were equally groundbreaking. (See Figure 15.1 on pages 572–573 to learn more about the innovations of that period.)

The integration of science and technology at the turn of the century was just as difficult to accomplish as the integration of community policing and DNA technology is today. Even commonplace policing tools such as the automobile, telephone, and airplane were criticized by people who insisted that they were not realistic. They argued that motorized vehicles were not safe to drive or useful in catching criminals, that human voices traveling through the air or telephone wires were impossible, and that flying in an airplane was absurd.

Law enforcement officials did adopt these new technologies—they had little choice—and some continued to look for new ways to improve their crime-fighting abilities. Theodore Roosevelt, who served as the police commissioner for New York City between 1895 and 1897, introduced call boxes for the public to report crimes quickly to the police. (This was before most people had telephones in their homes.) Police reformer August Vollmer created a professional model of policing that encouraged the use of new technologies, such as motorized vehicles and radio communications. Vollmer and Roosevelt, as well as other policing innovators, recognized the importance of technology in better serving the needs of the community.

The Need for New Science and Technology

As we move into the twenty-first century, reliance on technology has increased for all law enforcement agencies. Emphasizing this point, U.S. Attorney General John Ashcroft stated,

> The wave of technological advancement that has changed the lives of almost every individual, business, and institution in the nation has also changed the world of criminal justice—from how we fight crime to how we manage law enforcement resources to the types of crimes we face. New technologies can help law enforcement agencies prevent crime, apprehend criminals, manage offender populations, and protect the public from the threat of terrorism.[1]

◄ **Computer Crime** Cybercop James McLaughlin, a veteran of the police force in Keene, New Hampshire, tracks down Internet sexual predators. Crime in cyberspace is a new beat for police, but large departments now all have a computer crime unit. *What do you think the biggest challenge is in policing the Internet?*

A driving force for police reliance on new technology is the fact that the face of crime is dynamic and changing. As researchers have noted, "Crime of the future is going to look much different than it does today. With changes in technology, we will see the advent of new definitions, and the criminal justice system will be asked to respond to these new crimes."[2]

What this means is that most of these crimes will be economically and technologically driven. They will include the use of computers to commit the following:

- Major disruptions of businesses
- Intellectual property theft
- Malicious introduction of false information
- Tampering of medical records
- Confounding and jamming air traffic control activity[3]

To make matters even more difficult, criminals will also adapt new procedures to commit old forms of crime. For example, terrorists and organized criminals can now purchase and use their own satellite communications to commit crimes and avoid detection by law enforcement.[4]

The Future of Crime Fighting

How can law enforcement meet the challenge of dealing with sophisticated crime? Several forms of new technology have been suggested. A few of them are the following:

Figure 15.1

Police Technology Time Line from 1850 to 1996

Year	
1850s	The first multi-shot pistol, introduced by Samuel Colt, goes into mass production. The weapon is adopted by the Texas Rangers and, thereafter, by police agencies nationwide.
1854-59	San Francisco is the site of one of the earliest uses of systematic photography for criminal identification.
1876	Washington, D.C., installs its first telephone in a police station.
1877	The use of the telegraph by police and fire departments begins in Albany, New York in 1877.
1880	Chicago installs telephones in call boxes.
1888	Chicago is the first U.S. city to adopt the Bertillon system of identification. Alphonse Bertillon, a French criminologist, applies techniques of human body measurement used in anthropological classification to the identification of criminals.
1897	Detroit implements bicycle patrols.
1901	Scotland Yard adopts the Henry system of fingerprint classification.
1910	Akron (OH) Police Department uses a Model T Ford as the first police car.
1910	Fingerprints are ruled admissible in American courts. Albert Gross develops a system of authenticating questioned documents. Edmund Locard establishes the first police crime laboratory in Lyon, France.
1911	A criminal is captured in Pittsburgh after his photo was transmitted by facsimile (using telephotography) from New York City.
1913	Fitchburg (MA) Police Department creates the first motorcycle patrol.
1921	John Larson, a medical student working with a member of the Berkeley (CA) Police Department, invents the first polygraph.
1923	The Los Angeles Police Department establishes the first police crime laboratory in the United States. The use of the teletype is inaugurated by the Pennsylvania State Police.
1926	Berkeley creates the first police radio system.
1928	Detroit police begin using the one-way radio.
1929	Five airplanes are purchased by the New York City Police Department.
1934	Boston Police begin using the two-way radio.
1930s	American police begin the widespread use of the automobile. The prototype of the present-day polygraph is developed.
1932	The FBI inaugurates its crime laboratory
1948	Radar is introduced to traffic law enforcement.
1948	The American Academy of Forensic Sciences (AAFS) meets for the first time.
1955	The New Orleans Police Department installs an electronic data processing machine. The machine is not a computer, but a vacuum-tube operated calculator with a punch-card sorter and collator. It summarizes arrests and warrants.
1958	A former marine invents the side-handle baton, a baton with a handle attached at a 90-degree angle near the gripping end. Its versatility and effectiveness eventually make the side-handle baton standard issue in many U.S. police agencies.

Figure 15.1

Police Technology Time Line from 1850 to 1996 *(continued)*

Year	
1960s	The first computer-assisted dispatching system is installed in the St. Louis police department.
1966	The National Law Enforcement Telecommunications System, a message-switching facility linking all state police computers comes into being.
1967	The FBI inaugurates the National Crime Information Center (NCIC), the first national law enforcement computing center. NCIC is a computerized national filing system on wanted persons and stolen vehicles, weapons, and other items of value.
1968	AT&T announces it will establish a special number (911) for emergency calls to the police, fire and other emergency services.
1960s	Many attempts to develop riot control technologies and use-of-force alternatives to the police service revolver and baton. One of the few technologies to successfully emerge is the TASER which shoots two wire-controlled, tiny darts into its victim or the victim's clothes and delivers a 50,000-volt shock. By 1985, police in every state have used the TASER.
1970s	The large-scale computerization of U.S. police departments begins. Major applications in the 1970s include computer-assisted dispatch (CAD), management information systems, centralized call collection using three-digit phone numbers (911), and centralized integrated dispatching of police, fire, and medical services for large metropolitan areas.
1972	Development of lightweight, flexible, and comfortable protective body armor for the police. The body armor is made from Kevlar, a fabric originally developed to replace steel belting for radial tires.
Mid-1970s	The National Institute of Justice funds the Newton, Massachusetts, Police Department to assess the suitability of six models of night vision devices for law enforcement use.
1975	Rockwell International installs the first fingerprint reader at the FBI. In 1979, the Royal Canadian Mounted Police implements the first actual automatic fingerprint identification system (AFIS).
1980	Police departments begin implementing "enhanced" 911, which allows dispatchers to see on their computer screens the addresses and telephone numbers from which 911 emergency calls originated.
1982	Pepper spray, widely used by the police as a force alternative, is first developed. Pepper spray is Oleoresin Capsicum (OC), which is synthesized from capsaicin, a colorless, crystalline, bitter compound present in hot peppers.
1990s	Departments in New York, Chicago, and elsewhere increasingly use sophisticated computer programs to map and analyze crime patterns.
1996	The National Academy of Sciences announces that there is no longer any reason to question the reliability of DNA evidence.

SOURCES: Adapted from Law Enforcement Assistance Administration, Two Hundred Years of American Justice: An LEAA Bicentennial Study (Washington, D.C.: Government Printing Office, 1976), 78–83. The Evolution and Development of Police Technology. A Technical Report prepared for The National Committee on Criminal Justice Technology National Institute of Justice by SEASKATE, INC.555 13th Street, NW 3rd Floor, West Tower Washington, DC 20004 July 1, 1998

Cold Cases

One reason for unsolved crimes is the fact that technology did not give police investigative capabilities that are available today. With DNA technology almost perfected, agencies have begun reopening cold cases and re-examining the evidence for new clues. For example, in 2001, the West Virginia State Police set up a nine-member Cold Case Unit to reinvestigate old crimes, with priority given to murders and other violent crimes.

SOURCE: Vada Mossavat, "Troopers Hope to Shed New Light on Cold Cases," *Charleston Daily* Mail, 2 August 2001, 1C.

holistic crime proofing
Crime proofing in which isolation, stigma, anonymity, accessibility, and hiding places are designed out of the environment; ultimate goal is to make everyone a part of, and accountable to, the same community.

- The increased use of biosensors, lasers, and thermal neutron analysis equipment, which will greatly assist investigators in searching for 1) missing persons or 2) evidence of dangerous white-collar offenses such as toxic waste dumping
- The increased development and use of nonlethal weapons such as laser guns, rubber bullets, phasers, and chemical sprays, which could deter fleeing or aggressive suspects and also save thousands of lives each year
- The use of detachable bionic eyes and eardrums, which could be worn like hearing aids or eyewear and could aid police in surveillance activities
- An increase in computerized law enforcement

In addition, policing experts predict a large number of paradigm shifts, which are changes in the ways in which a group or organization sees its ideals, or paradigms. Some of these expected shifts will be seen in the following:

- A decline in the number of sworn police officers coupled with an increase in civilian policing positions, especially those that do not involve the use of force, searches, or arrests.
- An increased use of automated surveillance, report writing, and information systems, which will reduce the time required to perform these police functions.
- An increased awareness and use of **holistic crime proofing**, which involves designing towns, cities, and environments to minimize isolation, stigma, anonymity, accessibility, and hiding places. This type of design makes it more difficult and less desirable to commit crime. Its implications can be complicated due to privacy and personal rights issues, but its ultimate goal is to make everyone a part of, and accountable to, the same community.
- Reduced police involvement in victimless crime operations, such as stings created to catch nonviolent drug offenders and gamblers, and a greater concentration on tracking and investigating organized and white-collar criminality, such as drug dealers, those who run illegal gambling enterprises, and corporations that endanger human life through harmful products, waste disposal, or deceptive information.
- An increase in cooperation in exchanging information between law enforcement agencies, both nationally and internationally. Information can cover offenders, offenses, criminal investigations, stolen property, and crime victims. This will involve the development of new computers, new crime control software, and improved satellite communications.[5]

Most of these new paradigms predict that technology will affect the way law enforcement conducts its business when dealing with crime. They are based on technology that either exists today or is currently undergoing research and development and can be expected to change the way law enforcement agencies protect the public.

15.1 Self Check **?**

1. Why does law enforcement need new technology more than ever?
2. What is holistic crime proofing?

Check your answers at
www.policing.glencoe.com

15.2 New Science and Technology

Law enforcement agencies are becoming better equipped to deal with increasingly sophisticated criminal activities. Emerging are new weapons, identification technologies, and (perhaps most important) new ways of collecting and analyzing data and evidence. For example, blood samples are taken from all federal inmates and some state inmates, then added to a DNA offender database. New information-processing technologies such as this database will perhaps do the most to reshape the way law enforcement solves crimes.

The challenge is to keep pace with these new technologies, but what exactly are they? Many people have a vague understanding of better-known advances such as DNA testing but still have questions about what exactly they are and if they really work. The future of law enforcement depends on new science and technology to keep pace with new crimes and offenders, collect information and evidence about them, and help apprehend them. There are too many new concepts to discuss in this chapter, but some of the more significant ones will be examined here.

Forensic Science

Forensic science is the enforcement of criminal and civil laws by scientifically gathering evidence to be used in court proceedings. Generally, most people group the term *forensics* to define the sciences that are used to investigate crime. There are two major branches of forensics: criminalistics and forensic medicine. **Criminalistics** focuses on the recording, scientific examination, and interpretation of the minute details to be found in physical evidence, such as hair and clothing fibers. **Forensic medicine** is the use of medicine to determine the cause or time of death, or for other legal purposes.

forensic science The enforcement of criminal and civil laws by scientifically gathering evidence to be used in court proceedings; its two major branches are criminalistics and forensic medicine.

criminalistics Forensic science that focuses on the recording, scientific examination, and interpretation of the minute details to be found in physical evidence, such as hair and clothing fibers.

forensic medicine The use of medicine to determine the cause or time of death or for other legal purposes.

Biological Evidence Perhaps the most important and intriguing advances have been made with evidence that comes from the human body. Because researchers have nearly perfected the technology to determine a genetic fingerprint through DNA testing, any type of intact biological evidence such as blood, hair, or semen can be used to determine innocence or guilt or to identify corpses.

Arguably, DNA (deoxyribonucleic acid) is the most prominent tool used by forensic laboratories. Its use in crime laboratories became possible between 1985 and 1995, when a technique known as polymerase chain reaction (PCR) was perfected. PCR is a technique for amplifying a tiny amount of DNA into almost any desired amount, which makes it easier to analyze and compare with bigger samples.

The use of DNA as evidence has gained credibility within the scientific community, and today's DNA tests have a guaranteed accuracy of 95 percent. This accuracy level is growing as the ability to analyze DNA becomes even more precise.[6]

Combined DNA Index System (CODIS) A national database and searching mechanism for DNA profiles that is maintained by the FBI.

Combined DNA Index System (CODIS) A national database and searching mechanism for DNA profiles has been developed and is maintained by the FBI. The **Combined DNA Index System (CODIS)** is a national DNA index system that allows federal, state, and municipal crime laboratories to exchange and compare DNA profiles. CODIS began in 1990 as a pilot project and became fully operational in October 1998. As of December 2000, there were 441,181 offender profiles and 21,625 forensic profiles in CODIS.[7]

Investigative leads are developed from biological evidence at the crime scene, such as blood, semen, flesh, fingernails, or hair. CODIS can be used as an investigative tool by using the two indexes associated with CODIS. The first index is the forensic index, which contains DNA profiles from crime scene evidence. The second index is the convicted offender index, which contains DNA profiles of individuals convicted of felony sex offenses and other violent crimes. The two can be compared by any crime lab to see if evidence from unsolved crimes can be matched with any information on known offenders.

CODIS also permits local laboratories to store their crime scene DNA evidence for possible matches that may be made later by another laboratory for different crimes. This technique of examining DNA for cold, or unsolved, cases is particularly useful: As of December 2000, CODIS has provided investigative leads in more than 1,500 cases. By the year 2005, CODIS is expected to be able to have more than one million convicted felon profiles in its database. Also, the means to expedite CODIS searches will be manifested in miniaturized mobile DNA laboratories that can analyze evidence at the crime scene.[8]

Mitochondrial DNA (mtDNA) DNA analysis has been used mainly by examining the DNA that is derived from the somatic cells, which are the cells that form the body's tissues, organs, and other parts. The use of **mitochondrial DNA (mtDNA)** is becoming increasingly important as well. These tiny organelles are found in every cell, but they are not associated with the genes in the cell's nucleus. They work separately to produce energy for the body.

Because mitochondrial DNA is transmitted to children by the female egg and not the male sperm, earlier research of mtDNA studied only people related through the female line. However, today's technology is allowing scientists to analyze mtDNA from sperm. As this technology is perfected, it should provide enormous help to cases in which semen is the only evidence available.

Missing Person mtDNA Database Another important aspect of mtDNA is the fact that it is less prone to become unusable over time like regular DNA. The FBI realized this potential and opened the Missing Person mtDNA Database in February 2001. This database helps law enforcement agencies in identifying the remains of an unknown person against the information in the database. It has two components:

1. A database of DNA profiles from the relatives of known missing individuals
2. A database of DNA profiles from the remains of individuals who cannot be identified by fingerprint, dental, medical, or anthropological examinations[9]

mitochondrial DNA (mtDNA) Tiny organelles that are found in every cell and are not associated with the DNA in the cell's nucleus but work separately to produce energy for the body; used in new DNA research.

The DNA from the first part of the database can be compared with DNA from the second part of the database to make a positive identification. As this database continues to grow, fewer and fewer human remains will be classified as unknown.

Facial Reconstruction Traditional techniques of identifying unknown victims rely on the process of **facial reconstruction**, a procedure of making a clay reconstruction of a person's head to help investigators determine how he or she may have looked before death. This procedure is imprecise and often fails to account for obesity, ethnic affiliation, aging, and other variables. Two other problems are that the process of creating clay models is very time-consuming, which can slow down investigations, and the results may vary between different practitioners.

A more efficient computerized facial reconstruction program is currently under development at Sheffield University, England. The system takes a three-dimensional digital image of the skull using a laser scanner, then compares that image to MRI images of living human beings to examine tissue depths. Once the digital images are stored, they are reconstructed and then placed on the Internet. So far, preliminary findings are promising.

Computer Forensics The investigation of any electronic device that is used to commit a crime involves **computer forensics**. This new branch of forensics has a distinct methodology to ensure that proper documentation and investigative techniques are followed so that this evidence can be used in court. This growing field of investigations is due to an increasing reliance on computers by businesses and consumers.

Computer forensics specializes in the identification, preservation, extraction, and documentation of electronic data.[10] It addresses cyber-terrorists, who are criminals who threaten computer systems with malicious viruses and have been responsible for creating the Melissa Virus and the Code Red Worm, both of which disrupted computer systems all over the world and cost millions of dollars in repair costs.[11]

Computer forensic specialists also deal with other crimes that are surfacing on the Internet such as child pornography, denial of service attacks, auction fraud, e-mail threats, cyberstalking, and even prostitution. Their work is not only limited to computers but also to crimes using other electronic devices such as digital cameras, pagers, access control devices, printers, and scanners.[12]

Other New Technologies One system under development, **Identification-Based Information System (IBIS)**, allows officers to obtain evidence such as

facial reconstruction A technique used with the skull of an unidentified individual to help investigators determine how an unidentified person may have looked when alive.

computer forensics The investigation of any electronic device that is used to commit a crime.

Identification-Based Information System (IBIS) A handheld device that allows officers to gather information on suspects, take mug shots, take fingerprints, and call for help.

mug shots and fingerprints at the scene of the crime. In addition, the officer can transmit all of this information to a central database. IBIS ensures that a usable fingerprint is taken and alerts the user if the fingerprint is not adequate. The fingerprint information is transmitted to an Automated Fingerprint Identification System (AFIS) database, which scans for matches with known suspects. Eventually, the time needed to conduct a search with these tools will be no longer than 5 to 10 minutes.[13] Such technology is close to completion and should be available to police officers within the next decade.

Another tool comes from the FBI's crime laboratory. To recover serial numbers that have been destroyed, such as those on stolen weapons, the FBI is currently developing active thermography for serial number restoration. This system will replace the current means of recovering serial numbers, which uses a difficult chemical procedure. The thermography system uses pulsing lights that heat up the metal surface to an exact temperature, and then a heat-sensitive camera photographs the metal as it cools. This process is then repeated in a specific pattern. Image analysis tools are then used to reconstruct the serial number as it was once displayed on the metal.

A third new form of technology is Raman spectrometry, which has been designed for identifying chemical compounds in field investigations. Although it has had limited success so far in the laboratory and is still under development, it has great potential as an investigative tool. It is based on the fact that unique patterns of emissions, known as spectra, are produced by different chemical compounds. The Oak Ridge National Laboratory is developing a self-contained Raman spectrometer for use in investigations in which hazardous materials are suspected. It may also be used for the identification of fibers and may perhaps replace the current method of infrared spectroscopy.

Fighting Computer Crime To address threats against Internet security, the U.S. government created the National Infrastructure Protection Center (NIPC), a special unit of the FBI, in 1998 to thwart computer-related attacks. It was designed to act as an early warning service for network managers and to investigate hackers. With the amount of money lost due to computer-related theft estimated to be billions of dollars, the NIPC has a huge challenge before it.[14]

In summary, the field of forensics will continue to expand in the twenty-first century. It will have to meet the ever-growing needs of the law enforcement community, especially as new types of crimes are generated with new forms of technology. The investigative capabilities of many law enforcement agencies will become much more efficient as the field of forensics takes advantage of new scientific discoveries.

FYI

Carnivore and Magic Lantern

As part of its Cyber-Knight project, the FBI has developed Internet spying technologies that can be used to eavesdrop on suspected criminals' computer communications. Carnivore was designed by the FBI to track the electronic correspondence of suspects. Privacy experts have raised concerns that the program, which is installed at Internet service providers, is capable of also collecting the e-mail of people who are not under investigation. The newest technology, code-named Magic Lantern, plants a Trojan horse keystroke logger on a target's personal computer by sending a computer virus over the Internet. This software is capable of capturing encryption keys and allows agents to read data that has been scrambled by the suspect, something the Carnivore technology could not accomplish.

Biometrics as an Identification Tool

Biometric technology is changing the way people's identities are verified by helping law enforcement positively identify people by their physical characteristics. When used correctly, it can provide a high level of accuracy.

A **biometric** is a measurable, unique physical characteristic or personal trait that can be physiological and behavioral. A physiological characteristic is a stable physical feature of an individual that does not change without an injury, such as fingerprints and retinal eye patterns. A behavioral characteristic reflects a person's psychological makeup, such as handwriting and typing patterns. Overall, physiological characteristics are considered to be the most reliable because they lack variability. Systems that are based on behavioral characteristics must account for changes in the person's behavior, whether deliberate or not.[15]

A **biometric system** works by comparing a known set of individual characteristics, which must be stored in what is known as the reference template, with the person's actual characteristics. For example, an investigator could compare the fingerprints taken from an unsolved case and compare them with the fingerprints in an offender database. If it becomes necessary to verify the person, such as when a suspect is arrested, released, and arrested again, a new reading is made of the individual's characteristics and a comparison is made with the previously stored pattern. The comparison must match to be successful.

Biometrics in Fingerprinting Law enforcement's main use of biometric technology is in fingerprinting. What is changing most rapidly is the efficiency of these investigative methods. Fingerprinting has always provided airtight evidence when prints remain clear and intact, but for years finding a match on fingerprints was a slow and time-consuming process that could take months.

Today, fingerprint searches are usually done with automated identification systems. The state of Minnesota was the first to introduce such a system. It connects law enforcement systems throughout the state and permits the rapid identification of criminals by matching previously stored digitized fingerprints.[16]

NCIC 2000 The FBI has standardized the transmission of digital fingerprints so that they can be shared by other law enforcement agencies. As a result of this standardization, the FBI developed the NCIC 2000 system to expedite identification of suspected criminals. With this system, which is named after the FBI's National Crime Information Center, a portable fingerprint reader can be taken to a scene and a digital fingerprint can be recorded and transmitted to the FBI to determine if the suspect is on the national list of wanted persons. These portable readers can be used in a patrol car or a short distance

biometric A measurable, unique physical characteristic or personal trait that is used to identify or verify the identity of a person.

biometric system A system that compares a known set of individual characteristics, which must be stored in what is known as the reference template, with the person's actual characteristics.

from the patrol car. The NCIC 2000 also allows users to view mug shots of suspects to help in confirming the identity of the wanted person.[17]

Integrated Automated Fingerprint Identification System (IAFIS) Associated with the FBI's NCIC 2000 is the **Integrated Automated Fingerprint Identification System (IAFIS)**. The IAFIS is a national database of criminals' fingerprints that contains approximately 40 million criminals' 10-print fingerprint records. It is used to maintain a criminal history record for each arrested individual and is useful for law enforcement agencies in searching unidentified latent fingerprints from crime scenes to identify possible suspects.

Integrated Automated Fingerprint Identification System (IAFIS) A national database of criminals' fingerprints used to maintain a criminal history record for each arrested individual.

Other Biometric Systems The use of biometrics is not limited only to fingerprinting. It can also be used to prevent crime by restricting access to valuables. For example, it can be used to identify people when they try to cash a check or use an ATM. Some biometric systems have already been very successful:

- Hand geometry software uses a three-dimensional scan and nine-digit code that accounts for finger length and palm shapes. It has been used on U.S. nuclear reactor doors with a reported success rate of 99.9 percent.
- Another biometric system is a fingerprint device in keyboards that is designed for computer security. The device matches a scan of an index finger against a stored representation of that same finger. The device accounts for wounds and aging.[18]
- Face recognition software is being used in several American and British cities, where it is used to scan people at kiosks where they are cashing checks. One London neighborhood attributes a 40 percent reduction in crime due to the use of a surveillance camera network that uses facial recognition software to scan for criminals. Facial recognition software is also used by the Department of Motor Vehicles in West Virginia to prevent people from getting a driver's license under a different name.[19]
- Retinal scanning systems scan the retina of the human eye and are currently being used in high-security institutions, such as nuclear plants. They are, however, not completely reliable because the retina in the human eye is subject to change over time. They are also intrusive and potentially harmful because they shine a light into an individual's eye to illuminate the retina. They are expected to be replaced by iris scanning systems (below).
- Iris scanning systems scan the irises of a person's eyes, which are as unique as fingerprints. They are currently being developed with an expectancy of high accuracy and low error rates because, unlike the retina, the iris remains stable throughout a person's life.

For example, an iris-scanning tool developed by EyeTicket underwent field testing in 2001 at Heathrow Airport in London. International passengers had their irises scanned at the airport, and then their images were digitized and stored in a database. The next time those passengers stood in line at the passport control area of the airport terminal, they had their irises scanned and waited a few seconds until the system matched the image that was previously stored. A similar system is in use to limit access controls to secure areas for airline employees in Charlotte, North Carolina.[20] As the demand for improved airline security increases, this technology may become commonplace in the near future.

Overall, the development of biometric technology is advancing very rapidly. Fingerprinting, a mainstay of law enforcement investigations, will be far more useful with this new technology. The faster identification of individuals, at computer workstations and at confinement facilities, will improve law enforcement efficiency. Biometric technology will greatly enhance the crime prevention and investigative capabilities of law enforcement and will expedite the identification of suspects for crimes.

Imaging as an Identification Tool

imaging The enhancement of optical capabilities for law enforcement personnel, as well as the recording and documenting of crimes as they occur.

Imaging is the enhancement of optical capabilities for law enforcement personnel, as well as the recording and documenting of crimes as they occur.

The future of police imaging capabilities will depend greatly on technology that was developed by the military. Its use in law enforcement can be expected to branch into three main areas:

- **Accountability** Certain types of imaging are being used today to record police officers as they conduct traffic stops. This video monitoring can be used to ensure that the officer is showing appropriate behavior, and it also records the actions of the suspect who is being detained.
- **Recording and documenting crimes** Systems are in place that can record traffic violations at intersections and speeding cars. Systems can also scan crowds for law violators, including those who are on wanted lists.
- **Illumination** This would occur particularly in the areas of night vision and thermal imaging, which will be covered later in this section.

mobile video systems Systems in patrol cars that can film all officer-citizen interactions; key goals are accountability and documentation.

Mobile Video Systems Perhaps the most common police use of imaging is with **mobile video systems** in patrol cars. These video systems merge two important concepts for law enforcement: accountability and documentation. They also provide excellent training resources for law enforcement officials.

Mobile video systems were originally designed to record roadside field sobriety tests as well as vehicle searches. Many of the early models used everyday video cameras, which were placed on makeshift plywood mounts that were installed in the dashboards of patrol cars. Today's mobile video system consists of a recording device, a controller, a mounting or enclosure for the equipment, and a wireless audio system that is placed on the officer's belt. Most systems are activated manually by the officer, through the light bar when it is turned on, or by a body microphone.[21]

Uses of Mobile Video Systems The video system gathers audio and video evidence simultaneously and is enhanced by techniques that officers are being taught today. Officers can talk into a microphone as soon as the video is activated to explain what is happening. For example:

- If an officer notices a swerving vehicle, he or she can talk into the microphone while the film is running and recite the various speeds that the vehicle is traveling.
- During a traffic stop, the officer can record various observations, such as whether the suspect smells like alcohol.
- The officer can also use the system to record evidence such as alcohol or drugs found in a car.

Since the invention of mobile video systems, many departments have adopted them. Departments that have had lawsuits filed against them for

◄ **New Video Tools** Equipment such as the Mobile Video System helps police gather better evidence.
How can it also protect police officers?

improper police behavior during traffic stops find that the video systems can prove either their innocence or guilt, depending on the circumstances. In either event, mobile video systems are a cost-effective way to handle many citizen complaints before they go to trial. If an officer is innocent, video documentation could be the best testimony he or she could take to court.

The video also allows the jury to see the suspect's behavior at the time of arrest. As someone pointed out, "When you're a slobbering drunk at three in the morning, you look quite different than when you show up in the courtroom with your lawyer three weeks later in a business suit, looking like an angel."[22]

Apart from these uses, mobile video systems also provide excellent training tools because they provide immediate feedback about how an officer performed at an incident. They can also show whether an officer may have gotten too close to suspects, as well as other bad habits. Police officer training academies can also use the videos as training aides.

Wireless Video Systems Researchers are currently designing video systems that allow officers to wear micro-cameras that record everything the officer sees as he or she leaves the patrol car. For example, if an officer stops the car and enters a convenience store, the system will record exactly what the officer sees and hears. The device will transmit the audio and video back to the patrol car where it is captured and recorded. Eventually, such evidence will be archived on computers that could be transmitted to a courtroom. Judges would then be able to access the archival system to show any evidence that the jury needs to see.

Identifying and Documenting Crimes Law enforcement will also use recording devices designed to assist them in the identification and documentation of crimes. Cameras are becoming a popular way to assist law enforcement agencies in traffic enforcement. Many police departments prefer them because they decrease the number of personnel needed for traffic enforcement as well as liability claims.[23] As more vehicles travel the roads, it will become harder for law enforcement to handle traffic offenders, and the use of camera systems will greatly help them.

One of the more popular ways to use cameras has been to place them at intersections to enforce traffic light laws. Another approach is to use them to enforce speed limits. For example, the South Dakota Department of Transportation employs a system designed to improve safety in work zones. It uses only a radar gun and a video camera. When a motorist speeds past, the radar gun triggers the camera to tape the car. Tickets are issued to individuals based on individual photographic prints made from the video.

Identifying Criminals in Crowds Camera technology is also being used to catch criminals in crowds. One system, FaceIt, helps law enforcement agencies catch individuals wanted for crimes. The system works by continually running a camera, with the software constantly comparing any faces to those stored in a database.

FaceIt computes at a rate of 60 million records per minute. The software works as long as both eyes are visible and can compensate for lighting conditions, skin color, eyeglasses, facial expressions, facial hair, and aging.[24] It is being developed for the following applications in assisting law enforcement:

- Searching crowded areas to watch for people known to incite violence
- Automatically searching for and identifying human faces in any scene
- Searching a database of images for pictures matching a composite drawing
- Identifying possible suspects from images captured by surveillance cameras during a robbery
- Assembling an electronic photographic lineup of similar-looking suspects
- Sending and receiving image files of the same size, color, and clarity for sharing with other agencies
- Comparing Internet images of exploited children to faces maintained in a database of missing children to identify some of the suspects

FaceIt was first used in January 2001 at Superbowl XXXV in Tampa, Florida. FaceIt cameras found 19 people with outstanding warrants. Although all of the warrants were for minor offenses, the operation was a success because it accurately identified so many suspects.[25] Today, the system in Tampa uses 36 cameras in the town's popular nightlife district.

Law enforcement agencies also use imaging technology to assist the human eye of the beat patrol officer. Many devices assist police officers in seeing the environment in which they work. Some of these devices, such as night vision and thermal imaging, were originally military devices that law enforcement agencies adopted for several uses, even routine patrols. Night vision devices, for example, were originally designed for snipers and infantry during the Vietnam conflict.

Today, law enforcement agencies are using night vision devices such as the PVS-14, a third-generation night vision device that can be mounted to a head mount or hand carried. The devices are useful for surveillance and searching buildings, as well as stealth and gathering intelligence. The PVS-14 is normally used in starlight, but even in conditions that do not have any lighting, it can still provide vision by using an infrared illuminator.

Thermal Imaging Thermal imaging uses heat that is radiating from every person and object to create an infrared image. Its capabilities are frequently misunderstood because of Hollywood dramatizations that portray it as being able to see through walls. In the U.S. Supreme Court case of *Kyllo v United States*, agents used a thermal imaging system to scan the outside of a suspected drug dealer's home. They found heat signatures that would indicate that the suspect was using high-intensity lamps to grow marijuana. The suspect claimed that the agents' use of thermal imaging was an illegal search. The Court decided that thermal imaging constituted a search and was, therefore, unconstitutional.[26] Thermal imaging can be useful in other applications, however. One example is attempting to locate individuals who are hiding or missing, such as in an overgrown field or wooded area.

Radar Flashlight Another form of imaging is the radar flashlight, which uses radar to detect the presence of another person based on the individual's respiration. It uses electromagnetic energy to see through brick, wood, plasterboard, glass, and concrete walls up to eight inches thick and at distances of up to 10 feet.[27]

Crime Mapping

The amount of information and data obtained by law enforcement agencies is enormous. Not only do police departments answer public calls for service, but they also gather their own information through investigations and many other sources, such as other law enforcement agencies. How law enforcement agencies deal with these data determines how effective and efficient they will be in clearing crimes. If the information they receive is not sorted or stored accurately, it can become lost or forgotten and thus unusable.

MYTH	FACT
Police departments are on their own when it comes to buying and developing new forms of technology. That is why so few have new equipment or methods.	Federal agencies help municipal police departments with grants, training, and literature on how to implement new technology. For example, the Bowling Green (OH) police department received an $11,000 grant from the Office of National Drug Policy's Counter-Drug Technology Assessment Center for thermal imaging cameras.

One approach to this is the graphical representation of crime. This actually began before computers were used, when investigators would use colored or labeled thumbtacks on a wall map to show where crimes had taken place. Although this representation was useful as a means to determine where crimes were committed, it did not give any information about when they occurred or by whom.

Today, computerized systems address the location, time, and demographics of any criminal event that is reported to the police (see Figure 15.2 on page 588). One of the most powerful tools used by law enforcement agencies today is **crime mapping**, which is the use of maps that show location and time in relation to crimes that have been committed. It permits officers to analyze crime in certain locations, analyze the times at which crimes occurred, and study demographic patterns. It can also be broken down according to different types of crimes.

crime mapping The use of maps that show location, time, and demographics in relation to crimes that have been committed.

Geographic Information Systems (GIS) Crime mapping has been greatly helped by **Geographic Information Systems (GIS)** technology, which offers a computerized mapping system that produces layered, detailed descriptions of conditions and analyzes the relationships between variables such as location and time. GIS technology has revolutionized the way maps are viewed today. It has been used not just in law enforcement but also in surveying, navigation, geology, space exploration, tourism, and urban planning.

GIS permits an integration of many different data sets at once. This means that several new variables can be examined when a crime analysis session is taking place. For example, urban planning maps and health, illness, or injury demographics could be used to examine possible crime trends and causes. GIS can also conduct statistical analysis that can help police executives in assessing their crime-fighting abilities (See Figure 15.3 on page 590).

Geographic Information System (GIS) A computerized mapping system that produces layered, detailed descriptions of conditions and analyzes the relationships between variables such as location and time; the backbone of crime mapping.

GIS allows departments to examine the most complex trends through such techniques as pattern analysis, which takes into account the time, location, and demographic information simultaneously. Another new analysis technique is environmental profiling, which assumes that criminals work within the comfort zone of familiar environments. This technique narrows a list of suspects based on facts in the case, such as the suspect's place of employment or residence and the location of the crime.

The use of GIS systems is expected to increase in police departments as its technology becomes more powerful and cost-effective. A survey of police departments conducted in 1997 and 1998 found that only 13 percent of 2,004 responding departments used computer crime mapping. Approximately 33 percent of the departments with 100 or more police officers were conducting crime mapping with computers, but only 3 percent of the smaller departments were doing so.

Figure 15.2

Using GIS to Track Offenders

These maps show how GIS crime mapping tracked the many offenses of Shaky, a homeless man living in Charlotte-Mecklenburg, North Carolina. These maps can separate offenses by type, category (violent versus property or felony versus misdemeanor), and other factors such as time and date.

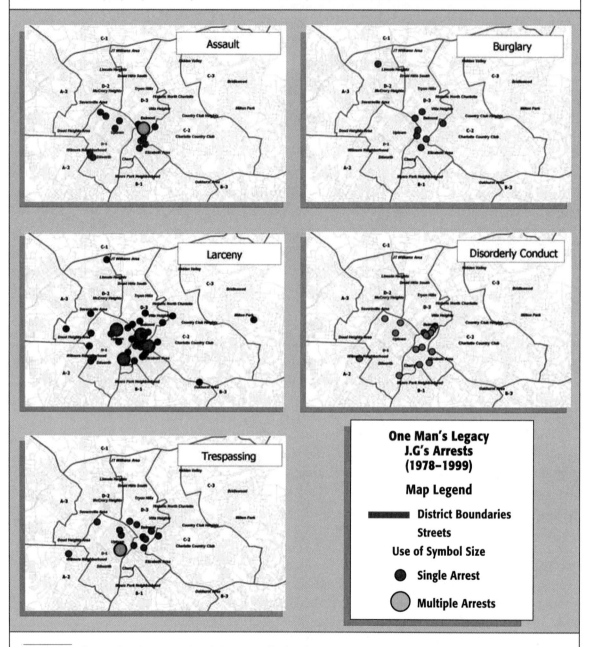

**One Man's Legacy
J.G's Arrests
(1978–1999)**

Map Legend

▬▬▬ **District Boundaries**

Streets

Use of Symbol Size

● **Single Arrest**

◯ **Multiple Arrests**

SOURCE: Carolinas Institute for Community Policing, "One Offender's Legacy," retrieved from the World Wide Web: http://www.cicp.org/legacy.htm.

The growing use of computer crime mapping has led to the creation of the Crime Mapping Research Center (CMRC), which develops, researches, promotes, evaluates, and spreads crime mapping analysis. The CMRC conducts training on the latest software developments and is developing a national geocoded archive for all law enforcement agencies to access.

CompStat GIS capability has been enhanced by **CompStat**, which is an integrative process that was first developed by the New York Police Department in 1994. CompStat, which stands for "computerized statistics," is a process by which the information from crime maps is integrated with an exchange of information between a department's leaders.[28] It increases the flow of information between a law enforcement agency's executives and the commanders of its operational units. The CompStat process contains several crime reduction elements:

CompStat A process in which information from crime maps is integrated with an exchange of information between a police department's leaders.

- Accurate and timely intelligence
- Identification and monitoring of shifting crime trends
- Effective tactics that must be comprehensive, flexible, and adaptable to these shifting crime trends
- Rapid deployment of personnel and resources
- Relentless follow-up and assessment

CompStat is often conducted as a weekly meeting. When a CompStat meeting is conducted, crime maps are used not only for crime analysis but also for accountability of the district commanders and for evaluation of their policing efforts.

The future of computer crime mapping holds great promise, especially in the area of crime analysis and problem solving. The affordability of GIS system platforms for even the smallest of law enforcement agencies makes the technology available to all departments. Some GIS software is free, although other forms can be expensive. It is anticipated that GIS will provide many analytical tools for departments and may even be integrated with intelligence analysis software similar to that used by the CIA and the Secret Service.

Using the New Technology

Crime mapping and CompStat are only two examples of the many ways in which police use computers today. Police agencies use computers in patrol cars, to investigate crimes, and to share information. They also face the challenge of trying to update older computer systems on a limited budget.

Figure 15.3

GIS Crime Mapping and Problem Solving

For police problem solving, GIS mapping can be broken down into four stages: scanning (watching for problematic situations), analysis (determining what the problem is), response (implementing a response to the problem), and assessment (determining if the response was successful). Below is a crime overview (the scanning stage) for Cambridge, MA, from March 2002 to April 2002.

Cambridge Police Department: Current Crime Overview

Housebreaks

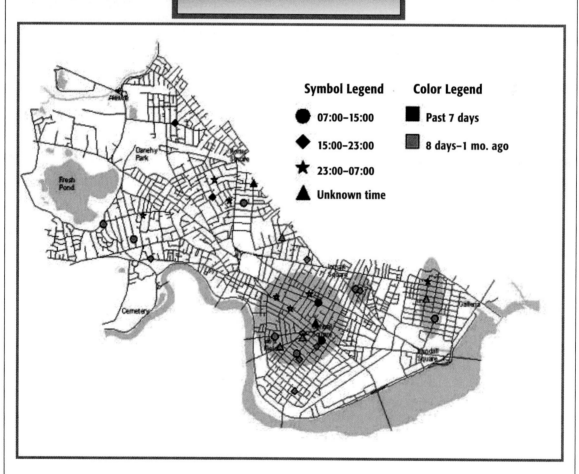

There were 32 housebreaks reported throughout the City in the past 30 days, an increase of 7 percent from last year at this time, which was 30. Of the eight housebreaks that have occurred within the past week, three had suspect descriptions.

SOURCE: Cambridge Police Department at http://www.ci.cambridge.ma.us/~CPD/crime/housebreak_new.html

This section will discuss:

- Interoperability among agencies
- The need for updated computers
- How police can adopt ideas from the military

Interoperability As law enforcement agencies learn more about crime trends through crime mapping, they also confirm the fact that many criminals do not limit themselves to a single jurisdiction. A criminal may terrorize two or more adjacent areas because they offer the same types of criminal opportunities, or he or she may commit crimes across a county, state, or region. Law enforcement agencies cannot act alone in apprehending these criminals but must share information and resources.

The ability to transfer information between different agencies and across jurisdictional lines is known as **interoperability**. With developing

interoperability The ability to share information among different agencies in different jurisdictions.

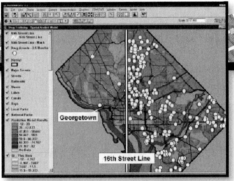

Computer On Patrol

Information Technology

Information technology can be categorized into four fundamental types. These types can apply to law enforcement or to any other agency within the criminal justice system.

1. *Administrative Systems:* These systems allow agencies to perform routine record-keeping tasks such as crime reporting, budgeting, data collection, and other reporting requirements.
2. *Data Retrieval Systems:* These systems provide individual law enforcement officers with public safety information that can help in solving a crime. Examples of these systems include the National Crime Information Center (NCIC) and wanted persons' files from any agency.
3. *Analytical Systems:* These systems provide police management with summaries that help improve a police commander's awareness of policing or public safety problems or issues. They can also enhance their ability to manage tactical operations in the field. Examples of these systems include crime analysis reports and crime mapping.
4. *Process Control Systems:* These systems directly perform operational tasks such as computer-assisted dispatch, which allows law enforcement personnel to perform other tasks.

Think About It Why is it important that law enforcement agencies have user-friendly information technology systems?

SOURCE: James McCarty, *The Impact of New Technology and Organizational Stress on Public Safety Decision Making,* Criminology Studies, vol. 5 (Lewiston, NY: Edwin Mellen, 1999), 27–28.

technology and a more mobile society, law enforcement agencies must be prepared to operate and cooperate between jurisdictions. Interoperability is necessary to ensure that offenders are apprehended in a timely fashion and have to face all possible evidence that can be brought against them.

Obstacles to Interoperability   Sometimes law enforcement agencies cannot communicate with each other and share information due to territoriality or mistrust (which is sometimes justified) that another agency will take all the credit for a shared investigation. When these obstacles arise, interjurisdic-tional investigations will be slowed down at best. At worst, cases can remain unsolved due to a lack of cooperation.

Along with the human obstacles, another major obstacle to interoper-ability is the lack of compatible computer equipment. The National Institute of Justice (NIJ) is currently funding three efforts to promote interoperability:

- The Advanced Generation of Interoperability for Law Enforcement (AGILE) was developed to bring together several interoperability programs under one umbrella. AGILE seeks both short-term and long-term solutions geared at standardizing wireless communications and information technology applications among law enforcement agencies.
- The Software Radio Interoperation Device (SRID) program will create reprogrammable patches between different police radios operating at different frequencies or between radios operating on AM and FM frequencies.
- The State and Local Communications Interoperability Analysis Program was established to conduct a survey between state and local law enforcement agencies to examine the extent of the inter-operability issue. It is hoped that its findings will help policymakers and planners correct the interoperability issue.[29]

The Need for Updated Computers   If law enforcement agencies are to be efficient and interoperable, they need efficient computer systems that han-dle and share data effectively. Without such systems, police cannot success-fully implement community policing or problem-oriented policing.[30]

Today, many police departments are swaying from the large mainframe computer systems that were popular in the 1970s and 1980s to the modern alternative of personal computers. PCs are powerful enough to support the decision-making needs of a policing organization. They are usually placed in a local Intranet or management information system (MIS) so that they can communicate and share files with each other. PCs seem best at sup-porting agencies that are trying to shift their paradigms by seeking a decen-tralized approach.

The problem associated with switching from the old, laborious mainframe computers to the more efficient PCs is that it is an expensive process. This is especially true of smaller departments that do not have the taxpayer support to modernize their systems. In answer to this, many departments are developing partnerships with nearby departments and pooling their resources to develop a centralized computer-aided dispatch system (CAD), as well as other data-sharing tools.

One example of this is the South Central Minnesota Public Safety System (SCMPS), where law enforcement agencies in a 4,000-square-mile area southwest of Minneapolis have found a way to solve the problem by sharing their information system needs. SCMPS unites five dispatch centers, four jails, and 150 workstations to provide greater efficiency for dispatchers, increased accountability, and better crime statistics and crime analysis than was previously used by the individual agencies.[31]

For larger departments that need a supercomputer, current technology allows for them to be built with minimal cost. Agencies can even use existing, outdated computers so that they do not have to purchase all-new equipment. For example, the Oak Ridge National Laboratory in Oak Ridge, Tennessee, needed a supercomputer to draw a national map of ecoregions. A task this large required something more powerful than a single PC. The solution was to collect all the outdated PCs, then link them into a much more powerful computing cluster. This cluster was powerful enough to map the ecoregions and make environmental predictions based on current global warming trends.

Ideas from the Military Because the military uses much of the same technology as law enforcement, it will provide many ideas for new technology and ways of implementing it. The military's approach to technological resources is based on the concept of **C3I**: command, control, communications, and intelligence. Command and control refer to resource allocation and mission planning, and intelligence refers to collecting information about the enemy and environment, such as carefully cataloging maps, pictures, and all sources of data. The communications aspect is what ties everything together. It includes all forms of communication, such as radio communications and computer links.

The military uses the C3I paradigm to permit commanders to execute plans, monitor progress, and make corrections and changes as a mission unfolds. Law enforcement can easily adopt the concept of C3I, which will make the integration of military technology easy. This will include the use of many wireless systems for information sharing, as well as powerful networks that will enable agencies to quickly share and access an information database with other law enforcement agencies, such as one's state agency or the FBI.[32]

C3I An acronym that stands for "command, control, communications, and intelligence," a key military concept for the adoption of technology.

Another new technology appropriated from military use is the "Digital MP System." Originally designed for military police, this system uses miniature cameras, view screens, a computer, electronic gloves, and other devices to help police do their jobs. It allows video, audio, and silent communications with headquarters and partners. For example, by making hand signals with the electronic glove, an officer can communicate a message such as, "Suspect ahead," to a partner. The cameras can provide video feeds to headquarters. There is even a program that can translate English into one of nine languages, or vice versa, with only a five-second lag.

Vehicle and Weapon Technology

Some of the most visible aspects of police work relate to pursuing fleeing suspects and the use of force with deadly weapons. Researchers are working to invent new tools that would reduce these risks.

Immobilizing Vehicles What if science and technology could devise a means to slow down or even stop fleeing offenders in vehicles? A number of technologies have evolved that promise a safer and more effective way of doing this. New technologies that could improve officer and citizen safety, along with their benefits and drawbacks, are shown in Figure 15.4 on page 595. The National Institute of Justice (NIJ) is currently supporting two other initiatives aimed at stopping fleeing vehicles:

electromagnetic vehicle stopping Technology that allows officers to neutralize the electronic systems of moving vehicles, resulting in the vehicles coasting to a stop.

1. **Electromagnetic vehicle stopping** allows officers to neutralize the electronic systems of moving vehicles so they coast to a stop. The NIJ and U.S. Army Research Laboratory are currently involved in evaluating this new technology for law enforcement.
2. The Pursuit Management Task Force (PMTF) defines police practice and the role of technology in high-speed fleeing vehicle pursuits. The PMTF is composed of senior law enforcement officials from a variety of local, state, regional, and federal agencies.

Nonlethal Weapons Weapons are a major instrument for law enforcement in the United States. New police recruits undergo numerous hours in pistol marksmanship, and police departments maintain these skills by continual education programs and annual weapons qualifications.

The future of weapons in policing may eventually shift from the traditional lethal kinds employed today to more nonlethal options. The military began to develop nonlethal weapons for recent peacekeeping missions, such as the U.N. missions to Somalia and Bosnia. This technology will be

Figure 15.4

Safe Ways to Stop a Car?

The following innovations can help officers slow down or stop fleeing vehicles. Each has its benefits and drawbacks, but all represent progress toward eliminating dangerous high-speed car chases.

Technology	Benefits	Drawbacks
Radio Communicator A low-powered police transmitter that overrides other radio broadcasts.	Enables police to communicate with the driver of the fleeing vehicle; relatively inexpensive.	Cannot force the suspect to stop.
Enhanced Police Sirens Directs a louder siren toward the suspect.	Ensures that suspect and other motorists can hear the siren at high speeds and increasing distance.	Cannot force the suspect to stop; too much noise may cause fear and distraction in other motorists.
Vehicle Barriers Barriers that are adapted to stop vehicles.	Flexible technology allows for fixed or movable barriers, depending on needs of police.	May result in vehicle crashes if suspect cannot stop in time.
Caltrops Iron ball with four projecting spikes, used to disable vehicle tires.	Technology can allow for controlled air leak in tires; may be deployed in stringed formation from frangible canister.	May cause blow-outs and vehicle crashes; may cause unnecessary car damage; may misfire.
Deployable Nets Nets that can cause drag or reduce performance to stop fleeing vehicles.	Can be deployed from police vehicle or aircraft, or from a fixed location that will attach the vehicle to a permanent barrier.	Can cause confusion or vision problems for fleeing driver, which could cause accidents that harm innocent bystanders.
Tire Shredders	Excellent for use at border checkpoints to prevent high-speed pursuits before they start; device will shred, not puncture, tires.	Less likely to cause blowouts than devices that puncture tires but still may cause unnecessary auto damage.

SOURCE: The National Committee on Criminal Justice Technology, *The Evolution and Development of Police Technology: A Technical Report*, National Institute of Justice, retrieved September 15, 2001, from the World Wide Web: http://www.nlectc.org.

smart gun technology A security system for a firearm that will only allow a specific user to fire it.

adaptable to law enforcement agencies. Other nonlethal weapons are also in development for law enforcement:

- A laser dazzler that is used to disorient and distract a subject by using random flashing green laser lights
- An anti-personnel beam weapon that shoots a laser that will immobilize a suspect
- A number of other projects that are examining ways to disable subjects using physiological responses such as nausea, dizziness, and disorientation
- A disabling net and launching system that will ensnare attacking or fleeing subjects
- A ring airfoil projectile, which is a doughnut-shaped rubber projectile that is used to deter a single individual at a standoff range by producing a sting when it strikes
- A sticky shocker is also under assessment, which is a low-impact, wireless projectile that is fired from a compressed gas or powder launcher. The projectile sticks to the subject with a glue-like substance or with clothing barbs, then delivers a small but disabling electrical shock.[33]

Smart Gun Technology Another technology that holds great promise for law enforcement is **smart gun technology**, which is a security system for a firearm that will only allow a specific user to fire the weapon. Researchers are currently examining how the user should be identified. Some are examining the application of biometric measures, such as the grip and fingerprints of a specific user, and others are testing a radio-controlled device.

The development of smart gun technology resulted from a study that found that between 1979 and 1992, 16 percent of officers killed in the line of duty were killed by an adversary using a service weapon. In other words, they were killed in the line of duty when their own weapon or that of another officer was turned against them. This new technology may have another application as well. Citizens who own guns may be able to apply this technology to their privately owned weapons to ensure that children and other nonowners cannot fire them.

Benefits of Nonlethal Weapons There are four obvious benefits to employing nonlethal weapons:

1. The disabling capability of most nonlethal weapons allows officers to detain an individual who otherwise may have caused harm to the public or the officer.

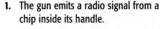

CopTalk

Smart-Gun Features for Public Safety Officers

Law enforcement officers who helped develop the specifications for a "smart" service weapon say the firearm should:

- Operate reliably in all environments.
- Have all the capabilities of a current firearm.
- Be able to be fired by other police officers.
- Be easy to operate and maintain.
- Verify and approve the user in the time it takes to draw and aim.
- Only work when the transponder is behind the gun.

1. The gun emits a radio signal from a chip inside its handle.
2. As the weapon is drawn from the holster, a watch-like device worn by the person holding the gun receives this signal and returns a coded radio signal.
3. The weapon is enabled when it receives the return signal. All this happens in the time it takes for the officer to draw the gun.

- Include an indicator that tells the user if the system is enabled.
- Fire even if the electronics fail.

What Do You Think? Should departments be required to provide this technology for all police firearms?

SOURCE: NCJRS, Making Guns Safer for Law Enforcement Officers and Consumers at http://www.ncjrs.org/pdffiles1/jr000244d.pdf

---

2. The nonlethal weapons will result in less need for medical attention, which will result in less taxpayer costs.
3. Deployment of nonlethal weapons will require less internal investigative time than if a lethal weapon was deployed.
4. If an officer mistakenly identifies a threat and reacts with a nonlethal weapon, the outcome is less serious than if he or she had used lethal force.

Ultimately, law enforcement will be affected by the development of both smart gun technology and nonlethal weapons. Certainly, both will have benefits for the police and the public because they will make law enforcement situations less deadly for both.

15.2 Self Check

1. What is CompStat?
2. Define interoperability.

POLICING *Online*

Check your answers at
www.policing.glencoe.com

15.3 New Science and Technology

New science and technology are approached with great enthusiasm by some but with caution by others. One problem is the fact that new science and technology seem to always be appearing on the horizon and are often sold without thought of their implications. In law enforcement, new science and technology face skepticism because of the costs involved. As new technology is manifested and new possible crimes evolve from them, law enforcement is expected to maintain the ability to stay ahead of the criminal element, but this is often expensive.

Despite these drawbacks, the use of new technology and science does enhance the abilities of law enforcement agencies. This section will examine the general benefits and drawbacks of new science and technology in greater depth.

Benefits of Innovation

There are obvious benefits to using new science and technology. Five of the most important benefits are:

1. New technology offers police better efficiency and accuracy in the collection and documentation of evidence. With the use of mobile video, officers will be able to record an incident from the moment they are dispatched. This will allow juries to see the crime scenes and the suspects as they appeared at the time of the crime. For example, during the O. J. Simpson trial, the amount of time the court spent examining evidentiary issues resulted in countless delays, misinterpretation of evidence, and exorbitant court costs that could have been prevented if the investigation had been videotaped.

2. The use of biometric technology will assist officers in correct identification of wanted persons.

3. Technology such as GIS will assist the public and law enforcement agencies in establishing accountability. GIS will assist in holding the police accountable to the public and will assist in holding district commanders accountable for the actions in their districts.

4. New information management technology will permit a more decentralized decision-making process. Data will be given in a more timely manner and will be more likely to assist in an accurate decision-making process. This capability is essential for departments that are employing a community policing paradigm, which requires decentralized authority and must provide officers with the resources to make sound, accurate decisions.[34]

CAREER FOCUS

Crime Analyst

Job Description

I collect data, collate and analyze it. The analysis is the hardest part and the least frequently done because of lack of time, tools, and training, but it is crucial. If you have 30 burglaries and they might be related, you have to do some analysis. In the old days, detectives would recognize a criminal's signature, his or her MO, and analyze data in their heads, informally. With computers, we now can run hundreds or thousands of reports and have officers assigned to specific crimes.

Susan C. Wernicke, Overland Park, KS PD

Crime analysts have to understand law enforcement, how crooks work, how the criminal justice system works, and that the data is only as accurate as the people who report it and enter it. For example, sex crimes are typically hard to analyze because they are often under-reported or over-reported (fraudulent reports are made). Analysts must be proficient with computers and databases, and understand statistics. You must always try to find everything you can so your analyses are accurate, timely, and useful.

What I enjoy the most is that I am in law enforcement and I am an investigator—with a computer, not a gun—and I help make the city better and safer.

Employment History

I have been a crime analyst for about ten years and been with the department for five years. I started as a dispatcher, then I worked with police records and property records, and I took a position as an assistant crime analyst when it came open.

Education

I graduated with a B.A. in human services and criminal justice. I am now going back to school for a Master's degree in criminal justice with a minor in statistics.

Follow-Up Why do you think understanding statistics is so important in this position?

5. Interoperability between different agencies will increase. In the past, different agencies have not been able to communicate with one another because their communication modes were incompatible. New technology will eliminate this problem and will allow for greater efficiency between different agencies and jurisdictions. This should translate into a higher number of arrests for suspects who attempt to flee to different jurisdictions.

Social Costs of Innovation

Along with the benefits of new science and technology, there are some costs to consider. Probably the main concern the public has with the constant development of new science and technology is the possibility that law enforcement may become too intrusive on their privacy. This level of surveillance is contrary to the American values of privacy and individual rights.

For instance, some people are concerned that DNA databases may also store the DNA of innocent people, which could be taken from any blood sample or donation. The FaceIt technology is also intrusive because it continually monitors faces in a crowd. The concern that people may have is whether these different types of technology will be used to store information about the average citizen who has not committed crimes. This is not mere paranoia: Many Americans are now aware that J. Edgar Hoover, who

▶ **Looking for Criminals** The IBIS portable id device manufactured by Visionics, Corp., captures and transmits photos and fingerprints to databases for identification. The use of new and more invasive technology, while efficient, can also provoke a social backlash.
Why do you think the issue of privacy is so much at the forefront of debates on new surveillance techniques?

Police Procedure

Predicting Crime Trends

Noted criminologists John Klofas and Stan Stojkovic make these predictions about policing in the near future:

Criminal justice will incorporate evolving technologies to arrest, prosecute, adjudicate, and supervise criminal populations. In this way, the traditional roles of criminal justice workers will also change dramatically in the future. Increased specialization of work assignments will be likely, and the work itself will become more complex.

Critical Thinking How will this affect police procedures over the next ten years?

SOURCE: John Klofas and Stan Stojkovic, *Crime and Justice in the Year 2010* (Belmont, CA: Wadsworth, 1994).

---

was director of the FBI from 1924 to 1972, kept lengthy files on hundreds of law-abiding Americans whose political beliefs differed from his.

Another problem with using new technology is that it is often costly. Many departments are unable to update their equipment because of budgetary constraints, which creates a technological lag for them, especially if they are smaller and receive less funding.

New technology also requires new training, and mistakes may be made early in the use of new technology. This means that these early uses could result in misuse, which will lower the public's confidence. Misuse can also generate more challenges in the courts regarding the infringement of constitutional rights. It may also be hard for police to convince courts that their use of new technology is ethical. This has been especially true for departments that use thermal imaging, which many courts believe to be intrusive. In fact, the Supreme Court has already ruled that using thermal imaging constitutes an unconstitutional search when used to check a house for heat levels.

When faced with these issues, the main question is still whether the technology will result in greater efficiency and effectiveness. After all, the use of new science and technology has always been a slow process that faces mistakes and misapplications. The early use of patrol vehicles is one famous example. As technology is used and better understood, efficiency and effectiveness often increase. Indeed, few scholars and police leaders doubt that new science and technology will change American policing. It will affect its roles and goals as well as its training and education.

15.3 Self Check

1. What are the benefits of innovation?
2. What are the social costs of innovation?

POLICING *Online*

Check your answers at
www.policing.glencoe.com

15.4 Science and Technology

Any integration of science and technology by law enforcement requires vision, which can be defined as the ability to perceive something through foresight or deepened understanding. Since positive vision is essential to the survival of organizations, police agencies need to develop it to succeed in the future. It must also be accompanied by careful action. As futurist Joel Barker said, "Vision without action is only a dream, action without vision only passes the time, but vision with action can change the world."[35]

The Need for Vision

As America moves into the next millennium, police must be poised to address new crime problems that will test their resources, talents, and commitment. To move successfully into the future by integrating new science and technology, police organizations must demonstrate four key concepts:

1. Innovation is necessary to have a competitive edge over the criminal.
2. Excellence ensures that an organization, through continuous improvement and goal setting, is delivering the highest quality service possible.
3. Anticipation is determining your clients' needs and then developing services or products to meet those needs. In law enforcement, this means projecting future crime trends, then developing and implementing new methods to effectively fight crime and increase public safety.
4. Vision, which is discussed above and in the next section.

What is a Successful Vision? Successful visions share a number of common characteristics:

- They are leader initiated.
- They are shared and supported by all.
- They are comprehensive and detailed, which means that they address the what, when, how, and why of a problem.
- They are genuinely positive and inspiring. This means that they reach for a challenging but realistic goal, require a full range of skills, have a worthy reward that is worth the effort, and recognize that it is better to err on the side of greatness.

For example, August Vollmer's vision was to integrate science and technology into law enforcement and reshape the police officer into more of a social worker. His contributions were instrumental in encouraging new thinking about how law enforcement approached crime fighting. Today, police leadership across America is experimenting with a new vision: the use of science and technology to modernize policing and place it at a strong advantage against today's criminals.

Police Leaders as Paradigm Pioneers

The purpose of vision in law enforcement is to anticipate new paradigms in fighting crime and guiding police agencies through paradigm shifts. A police chief's vision is not enough; he or she must become a paradigm pioneer. **Paradigm pioneers** are leaders who take new ideas and concepts developing at the fringe of a profession and bring them into professional use. This means that he or she must lead the rest of the agency in implementing a paradigm shift. For example, if a traditional police department wants to switch to community policing, the move from centralized to decentralized authority will represent a paradigm shift.

paradigm pioneers
Innovative leaders who take new ideas and concepts and bring them into professional use.

To return to the example of August Vollmer, he was both a paradigm shifter and paradigm pioneer. Vollmer tried several new innovations:

- He made Berkeley the first American city to put all of its officers on bicycles and later in automobiles.
- He pioneered radio communications in patrol cars and the use of the polygraph.
- He was the first in the nation to create a crime investigation laboratory and police academy. His academy curriculum included courses in criminalistics that were taught by scientists.

Paradigm pioneers, such as Vollmer, are skilled in whole-brain thinking, problem solving, interpersonal communications and critical thinking, which were discussed in Chapter 7. In addition, they are risk takers. All of Vollmer's innovations were questioned by other police leaders, and certain innovations (such as requiring a college education for officers) are still ignored by some.

In the past 100 years, law enforcement has seen the application of science and technology. With this came new challenges, demands, and frustrations. If American policing is to meet the challenges of the next century, police must become visionaries and paradigm pioneers to effectively integrate and apply science and technology in law enforcement.

15.4 Self Check

1. What are the characteristics of a successful vision?
2. How can a police supervisor or chief play the role of a paradigm pioneer?

POLICING *Online*
Check your answers at
www.policing.glencoe.com

Chapter 15

New Science, Technology, and Paradigms

Summary By Learning Objectives

1. Identify the anticipated paradigm shifts in the future of policing.

Much new science and technology in policing were created in response to a new breed of creative, technologically advanced criminal. Futurists and criminal justice scholars project many changes in policing in the future, including the increased use of nonlethal weapons, bionic eyes and ears, computers, and information technology.

2. Explain new science and technology applications in policing.

In policing, some new concepts are in the design stages and others are in use.

- Biometrics offers a technology to use physical characteristics such as fingerprints for identification, authentication, and access control.
- New information technologies offer increased capability for interoperability.
- Crime mapping allows police to collect, analyze, and map criminal statistics.
- Advances in forensic science, such as mtDNA analysis and facial reconstruction, provide new means to more effectively identify the dead and the living.
- Computer forensics offers the capability to investigate cyber-crimes.

3. Understand the current capabilities of forensic scientists.

Forensic scientists currently use:
- DNA testing
- CODIS, a national DNA index system
- Mitochondrial DNA in the Missing Person mtDNA Database
- Traditional or three-dimensional facial reconstruction
- Computer forensics
- Identification-Based Information System (IBIS)
- Active thermography
- Raman spectrometry

4. Comprehend the various types of biometric measures and how they are used.

Law enforcement's main use of biometric technology is in fingerprinting, which today is usually done with automated identification systems. The Integrated Automated Fingerprint Identification System (IAFIS) is a national database of about 40 million criminals' fingerprints. Other systems are:
- Hand geometry software
- A fingerprint device in keyboards
- Face recognition software
- Retinal scanning systems
- Iris scanning systems

5. **See how computers contribute to the effective use of new science and technology.**

   - Current DNA testing and automated fingerprint identification relies on computer systems to run quickly and accurately.
   - Crime mapping is a computerized mapping system based on GIS software. the use of GIS systems is expected to increase as its technology becomes more cost-effective. The Crime Mapping research center (CMRC) is developing a geocoded archive for police use.
   - CompStat is the integration of computer statistics and personal interaction among department leaders to assess the quality of their policing work.
   - Police agencies use computers in patrol cars to investigate crimes and to share information. The mobile video systems that are now often used in patrol cars provide improved accountability and documentation as well as excellent training resources.

6. **State why nonlethal weapons are an important factor in the future of policing.**

   There are four primary benefits to nonlethal weapons:

   1. The disabling capability of most nonlethal weapons allows officers to detain an individual who otherwise may have caused harm to the public or the officer.
   2. Nonlethal weapons result in less need for medical attention.
   3. Deployment of nonlethal weapons requires less internal investigative time than the use of lethal weapons does.
   4. If an officer mistakenly identifies a threat and reacts with a nonlethal weapon, the outcome is less serious than if he or she had used lethal force.

7. **Understand the benefits and drawbacks of using new science and technologies.**

   Evidence presented in court will have greater validity. New information technologies will give police accurate information to make timely decisions. It will also help decentralize decision making, which is necessary for community policing. Interoperability will improve greatly. One drawback is that police departments struggle to remain current. More court cases will likely challenge the constitutionality of using some of these new technologies. The cost of new technologies will limit their implementation in small departments.

8. **Explain how paradigm pioneers help to integrate new science and technology into policing.**

   Paradigm pioneers are leaders who take new ideas and concepts and bring them into professional use. They are risk takers who are intuitive in their thinking and typically use whole-brain thinking, problem solving, interpersonal communication, and critical thinking.

Key Terms

holistic crime proofing (p. 574)
forensic science (p. 575)
criminalistics (p. 575)
forensic medicine (p. 575)
Combined DNA Index System (CODIS) (p. 576)
mitochondrial DNA (mtDNA) (p. 577)
facial reconstruction (p. 578)
computer forensics (p. 578)
Identification-Based Information System (IBIS) (p. 578)
biometric (p. 580)
biometric system (p. 580)

Integrated Automated Fingerprint Identification System (IAFIS) (p. 581)
imaging (p. 582)
mobile video systems (p. 582)
crime mapping (p. 587)
Geographic Information System (GIS) (p. 587)
CompStat (p. 589)
interoperability (p. 591)
C3I (p. 593)
electromagnetic vehicle stopping (p. 594)
smart gun technology (p. 596)
paradigm pioneers (p. 603)

Questions for Review

1. Why is it imperative that law enforcement integrate science and technology into its crime-fighting role?

2. What are biometrics and how would you apply them in policing?

3. What is crime mapping?

4. What is mtDNA? Facial reconstruction? Computer forensics? How would you use these technologies in policing?

5. What are some of the new imaging technologies?

6. What is electromagnetic technology and how would you use it in policing?

7. Why is developing nonlethal weapons essential to the future of policing?

8. What are the benefits and costs of integrating new science and technology into law enforcement?

9. Why is vision critical in the integration of science and technology into policing?

10. What is a paradigm pioneer, and why is August Vollmer considered a good example of one?

Experiential Activities

11. **How Do Officers Feel About Technology?**
Contact a local police officer and ask him or her what new science and technology the department has begun to use in the past ten years.
    a. What responses did you receive?

    b. Do you think the responses would have been different coming from an officer at a department of a different size?

    c. If you detect resistance, what may be some of the reasons for this resistance?

Experiential Activities continued

12. Nonlethal Weapons
Research the current use of nonlethal weapons in several police departments.
- **a.** What is the greatest benefit to using more nonlethal weapons in policing?
- **b.** What is the greatest drawback to using more nonlethal weapons?
- **c.** What shortcomings need to be overcome before nonlethal weapons become standard policing equipment?

13. Technology and Police
Interview two or three people who are not involved in police work and ask for their opinions about the current state of American policing and its use of technology.
- **a.** What were their opinions?
- **b.** What technological advances did they want to see?
- **c.** What concerns did they have about criminals and technology?

14. Technology and Criminal Justice
Interview two or three other students and ask them which of the technologies they learned about in this chapter are the most important. Next, ask them which of the technologies seemed to be unrealistic, unconstitutional, or possibly dangerous. Be sure to find out why they feel this way.
- **a.** Which technology seemed most important to them?
- **b.** Which technologies seemed to have the greatest drawbacks?
- **c.** Which technology seems the most beneficial and the most detrimental to you?

Web Patrol

15. Facial Reconstruction
Learn more about three-dimensional facial reconstruction by reading "Modeling Age, Obesity, and Ethnicity in a Computerized 3-D Facial Reconstruction." Through the link at **www.policing.glencoe.com**.
How can a facial reconstruction artist work with these variables to ensure a realistic reconstruction?

16. What Is the Latest Technology?
Go to the Justice Technology Information Network through the link at **www.policing.glencoe.com** and access the Law Enforcement & Corrections Technology News Summary.
What kind of impact will any of these new items have on policing?

17. Cybercrime
Go to the U.S. Department of Justice's Web site that is devoted to the fight against cybercrime. You can access this site at **www.policing.glencoe.com**. Read the Attorney General's speech.
Of all the challenges outlined in the speech which one seems the most difficult to you? Why?

Critical Thinking Exercises

18. Imaging Technology

You have been asked to serve on a police task force to evaluate the legal implications of using imaging technology.

The most important device for you to investigate is a new radar scanner that looks through walls. It can detect people or objects moving behind up to three feet of concrete. It works so quietly and has such a long range that no one on the other side of the wall would be able to tell that the device was being used.

a. What constitutional problems may this new technology raise?

b. What can the police department do to ensure that the rights of innocent citizens and suspects are not violated?

19. Police, Terrorism, and Technology

Study the circumstances and events surrounding the terrorist attack on the World Trade Center in New York City on September 11, 2001.

Next explore new technologies in policing and in security. You can look in technology or policing magazines or search on the Internet.

Based on the new science and technology discussed in this chapter and those that you researched, identify technologies that might have prevented the terrorist attack.

a. Which technologies did you choose, and why?

b. What is your rationale for using a particular science or technology?

20. An Insider's View on Technology

Read a current issue of a law enforcement magazine, either in print or online. Some good examples are *Law Enforcement Technology, Police,* and *Police Chief.* Pay close attention to articles dealing with the future of policing and new technology.

Identify how science and technology are discussed in these publications to fight crime or improve officer safety.

a. How do you think the issues you learned about will affect the future of policing?

b. How would you like to see them affect the future of policing?

Endnotes

1. Office of Justice Programs and Office of Community Oriented Policing Services, *A Resource Guide to Law Enforcement, Corrections, and Forensic Technologies* (Washington, D.C.: U.S. Department of Justice, 2001), iii.
2. John Klofas and Stan Stojkovic, *Crime and Justice in the Year 2010* (Belmont, CA: Wadsworth, *YEAR*), 286.
3. Richter Moore, Jr., "Wiseguys: Smarter Criminals and Smarter Crime in the 21st Century," *The Futurist*, September 1994, 33.
4. Gary Feinberg, "United States: Developed Nation-State," in *Crime and Control*, edited by Gregg Barak (Westport, CT: Greenwood, 2000), 248–49.
5. Georgette Bennett, *Crime Warps: The Future of Crime in America* (Garden City, NY: Anchor, 1987); Feinberg, "United States," 249.
6. The National Commission on the Future of DNA Evidence, *The Future of Forensic DNA Testing: Predictions of the Research and Development Working Group* (Washington, D.C.: National Institute of Justice, 2000), 17.
7. Lallie D. Leighton, Yvette E. Trozzi, and Colleen Wade, eds., *FBI Laboratory 2000* (Washington, D.C.: FBI, 2000), 1.
8. The National Commission on the Future of DNA Evidence, *The Future of Forensic DNA Testing*, 3.
9. Leighton et al., *FBI Laboratory*, 2.
10. James R. Borck, "Leave the Cybersleuthing to the Experts," *Infoworld*, April 2001, 54–57.
11. Hollis Stambaugh, David S. Beaupre, David J. Icove, Richard Baker, Wayne Cassady, and Wayne P. Williams, *Electronic Crime Needs Assessment for State and Local Law Enforcement* (Washington, D.C.: National Institute of Justice, 2001), iv.
12. The Technical Working Group for Electronic Crime Scene Investigation, *Electronic Crime Scene Investigation: A Guide for First Responders* (Washington, D.C.: National Institute of Justice, 2001), 9–22, 37–46.
13. Rebbecca Kannable, "A Grip on Identification Information," *Law Enforcement Technology*, June 2000, 122–25.
14. Charles Piller, "Anti-Hacker Center Fights for Respect" *Los Angeles Times*, 5 March 2000, A1.
15. D. R. Weiss, *Smart Gun Technology Project: Final Report* (Washington, D.C.: National Institute of Justice, 1996), 90–91.
16. Stephen Coleman, *Biometrics in Law Enforcement and Crime Prevention: A Report to the Minnesota Legislature* (St. Paul, MN: Center for Applied Research and Analysis, School of Law Enforcement, Criminal Justice and Public Safety, Metropolitan State University, 1999).
17. Scott Tillett, "FBI Turns On New Crime-Fighting System," CNN.com, 19 July 1999, retrieved September 7, 2001, from the World Wide Web: http://www.cnn.com/TECH/computing/9907/19/system.idg/.
18. Paul Lagerman, "Biometric Evolution and Proliferation," retrieved September 6, 2001, from the World Wide Web: http://faculty.ed.umuc.edu/~meinkej/inss690/lagerman/lagerman.htm.
19. William M. Bulkeley, "Your Face or Mine? Ask a Computer," *Wall Street Journal*, 12 July 1999, retrieved September 6, 2001, from the World Wide Web: http://www.infowar.com/class_1/99/class1_120899b_j.shtml.
20. Catherine Greenman, "Airports Trying Out Iris Identification," *Baltimore Sun*, 6 August 2001, 1C.
21. Ronnie L. Paynter, "Patrol Car Video" *Law Enforcement Technology*, June 1999, 34–35.
22. Ronnie L. Paynter, "Big Brother's Not Watching," *Law Enforcement Technology*, June 1999, 54.
23. Carl Fors, "Take a Picture: Study Finds Photo Enforcement Systems Reduce Traffic Violations," *Law Enforcement Technology*, September 1999, 18.
24. Greg Gerber, "FaceIt: You're Busted," *Law Enforcement Technology*, June 2000, 142.
25. "In US First, Tampa Cameras Study Crowds for Criminals," *Miami Herald*, 2 July 2001, 5B, retrieved August 15, 2001, from the World Wide Web: http://www.nlectc.org/inthenews/newssummary/weeklynews.html.
26. *Kyllo v. United States*, case #99-8508 (2001).
27. Design News, "Radar Device Peeks Through Walls," *Design News*, 6 August 2001, 14, retrieved August 20, 2001, from the World Wide Web: http://www.nlectc.org/inthenews/newssummary/weeklynews.html
28. Thomas Rich, "Mapping the Path to Problem Solving," *National Institute of Justice Journal*, October 1999, 3–4.
29. Keith Harries, *Mapping Crime: Principle and Practice* (Washington, D.C.: U.S. Department of Justice, 1999), 92.
30. Office of Justice Programs and Office of Community Oriented Policing Services, A *Resource Guide to Law Enforcement, Corrections, and Forensic Technologies* (Washington, D.C.: U.S. Department of Justice, 2001), 38–39.
31. Lorraine Green Mazerolle and Robert C. Haas, "The Problem-Solver: The Development of Information Technology to Support Problem-Oriented Policing," in *Criminal Justice Technology in the 21st Century*, edited by Laura J. Moriarty and David L. Carter (Springfield, IL: Charles C Thomas, 1998), 100.
32. Jerry Huettl, "Public Safety Partnership Debuts CAD, Records, and Jail System Serving 24 Agencies" *Police Chief*, January 2001, 31–36.
33. The Rome Technology Laboratory Team, "The New Horizon: Transferring Defense Technology to Law Enforcement," retrieved August 20, 2001, from the World Wide Web: http://www.aci.net/kalliste/deftech.htm.
34. Office of Justice Programs and Office of Community Oriented Policing Services, *A Resource Guide to Law Enforcement, Corrections, and Forensic Technologies* (Washington, D.C.: U.S. Department of Justice, 2001), 12.
35. Joel Barker, *The Power of Paradigms: The Business of Discovering the Future* (Burnsville, MN: Chart House International, 1992).

Questions for Review

1. Explain the concept of symbolic relationship and how it applies to research and planning in policing.
2. Why does the field of policing need good research?
3. What is scientific management?
4. What is saturation patrol?
5. What are the five stages of research?
6. What is data collection?
7. Explain the concept of planning.
8. What is strategic planning?
9. What are the steps in the planning process?
10. Name two different types of planning.
11. Explain the concept of holistic crime proofing and how it is related to scientific developments.
12. What is criminalistics?
13. What is biometrics and how is it used in policing?
14. What is CompStat?
15. Explain the concept of interoperability.

Glossary

A

accident investigation Collection and assessment of facts surrounding vehicular collisions. (12)

accommodators People whose learning style involves perceiving information concretely and processing it actively. (7)

administrative law The branch of law that provides the rules and regulations established by governments to control the actions of industry, business, and individuals. (10)

Age Discrimination Act of 1967 A federal law that prohibits employment discrimination against persons older than 40. (6)

Americans with Disabilities Act (ADA) A federal law that makes it illegal to discriminate against qualified individuals with disabilities. (6)

arrest A seizure of a suspect by an officer; requires probable cause. (10)

aspirational code of conduct Implies a type of code of ethics that motivates adherence to the highest standards of policing. (9)

assessment The process of determining the extent to which goals and objectives have been achieved. (14)

assessment center An alternative or supplement to the written exam that provides a series of exercises or simulations. (6)

assimilators People whose learning style involves perceiving information abstractly and processing it reflectively. (7)

assumption A statement accepted or supposed as true without any proof or demonstration; an unstated premise or belief. (7)

attending Giving your attention to another person with a strong focus on non-verbal communication. (7)

attitudes Behavior that a person chooses to align himself or herself with that the person feels will help him or her attain important goals. (13)

authoritarianism A personality trait that favors obedience over freedom, which is often found in police officers. (13)

authoritarianism The conspicuous exercise of legal powers. (8)

Automated Fingerprint Identification System (AFIS) A computer-based fingerprint technology that uses a mathematically created image of a fingerprint that identifies up to 250 characteristics for each print. (12)

Autonomic Nervous System (ANS) A system that supplies impulses to the heart, muscles, and glands. (8)

B

background investigation An extensive investigation of police applicants that examines several prior behaviors, including past drug use, crime record, driving record, and job performance. (6)

bailiff An officer, found in each English town, who was responsible for checking on all residents and visitors to that town. (2)

baseline data Values of measures prior to implementation of strategies, which provide a means for before/after comparisons. (14)

Glossary

beat profiling Study of beat topographics, demographics, and call histories to develop tailored patrol strategies to address the types of crimes and citizen concerns pertinent to the beat. (11)

Big Six Principal groups that must work together to ensure the success of community policing efforts: police, general community, businesses, civic officials, media, and public and non-profit agencies. Also called stakeholders. (3, 11)

Bill of Rights Ten amendments to the Constitution that protect American citizens from government abuses. (10)

biometric A measurable unique physical characteristic or personal trait that is used to identify or verify the identity of a person. (15)

biometric system A system that compares a known set of individual characteristics, which must be stored in what is known as the reference template, with the person's actual characteristics. (15)

blending An officer assuming the role and dress of an ordinary citizen in order to remain undetected in an area of high crime potential. (12)

Bow Street Runners A plainclothes detective force whose responsibility was to move quickly to crime scenes and begin investigations; the first modern detective unit. (2)

broken windows theory A theory that finds that when citizens allow their communities to deteriorate—such as by allowing broken windows, trash, and abandoned cars to accumulate—they send a silent message to criminals that no one cares about their neighborhood. (3, 11)

burst stress Stress that is caused by important single events (such as a shootout) rather than continual low-grade stressors (such as department politics). (8)

buy and bust An operation in which an undercover officer purchases a quantity of drugs in order to arrest the seller; also called a sting. (12)

C

C3I An acronym that stands for "command, control, communications, and intelligence," a key military concept for the adoption of technology. (15)

California Psychological Inventory (CPI) A psychological test that provides an indication of how the applicant compares to the general population on several job-related personality factors. (6)

casual deputies A sworn police reserve of private citizens who served on posses, guarded jails, and filled in for regular police. (3)

centralized state agency A "one-stop" state policing model in which officers have statewide jurisdiction in all typical policing matters, such as criminal investigations. (5)

chain of command A police department's order of authority, which begins at the top of the pyramid with the chief or sheriff and flows downward to the next level or echelon. (5)

citizen review board A method for processing citizen complaints that consists of citizens who subpoena officers and witnesses, find facts, and recommend or determine discipline. (13)

civil law The branch of law that provides a means of controlling the noncriminal relationships between individuals, businesses, or organizations. (10)

Glossary

civil liability In policing, liability for civil action that is taken by private citizens against police misdeeds. (10)

Civil Rights Act of 1964, Title VII A federal law that prohibits employment discrimination on the basis of race, color, religion, sex, age, or national origin by employers who employ 15 or more persons and are engaged in an industry affecting commerce; applies to all police departments. (6)

code of conduct A code of conduct specific to the behavior of individual officers. (9)

Code of Hammurabi A collection of laws and edicts that provided guidance for a variety of issues, from civil matters to criminal acts; based on the concept of *lex talionis*. (2)

cognitive training Training focuses on developing critical thinking, problem-solving, and decision-making skills, all of which are necessary for successful community policing. (6)

Combined DNA Index System (CODIS) A national database and searching mechanism for DNA profiles that is maintained by the FBI. (15)

community policing An organizational philosophy based on a set of values emphasizing problem-solving partnerships between community members and their police in which both work together to identify, prioritize, and solve crime problems to attain improved quality of life in the community. (1, 3, 11)

community policing era An era of policing (1980- present) that focuses on police-community collaborations to identify and solve problems that affect the quality of life in a community. (3)

community relations The relationship that a department and its individual staff have with the public; it may be either positive or negative. (13)

CompStat A process in which information from crime maps is integrated with an exchange of information between a police department's leaders. (15)

computer forensics The investigation of any electronic device that is used to commit a crime. (15)

conceptual programming model A model for planning, design, and delivery of police services that focuses on needs assessments, design, implementation, and evaluation; and stresses quality and accountability. (1)

conflict model A system model in which subsystems are believed to work best when they are in conflict, because they strive for the best possible outcome for themselves. (1)

consensus model A system model in which subsystems work together in agreement to reach a similar goal, promote harmony, and maximize efficiency; in criminal justice, the shared goal is justice. (1)

conservatism Supportive of the status quo, particularly regarding society's laws and customs. (8)

constable An early English officer who supervised the weapons and equipment of the hundred, which was ten tithings. (2)

contingency planning Preparations made for specific events and occurrences that are not part of the daily activities of police department personnel. (14)

Glossary

continuum of force An escalation or de-escalation of force in response to a suspect's actions. (4)

convergers People whose learning style involves perceiving information abstractly but processing it actively. (7)

coroner A person assigned to each shire who maintained death records, investigated sudden and unnatural deaths, handled forfeitures to the king, and performed other duties. (2)

corruption Acting on opportunities created by virtue of one's authority, for personal gain, at the expense of the public one is authorized to serve. (9)

county law enforcement Countywide law enforcement services that are most often performed by a sheriff's department. (5)

crime A voluntary and intentional act that a person commits, or allows to occur by neglecting a lawful; prohibited by law and punishable in the name of the state. (1)

crime clearance The status assigned to a case when the concerned detective has solved the crime and has taken all possible, appropriate action against at least one suspect. (12)

crime mapping The use of maps that show location, time, and demographics in relation to crimes that have been committed.

criminal investigation The capacity to sift through complex bodies of evidence in order to verify or establish the facts of a case. (4)

criminal justice system The government's use of police, courts, and corrections to prevent, control, and reduce crime and delinquency. (1)

criminal law The branch of law that defines crimes and punishment; also called penal law. (10)

criminal procedure The regulatory guidance for officers' actions in matters involving the criminal law, including the rules governing matters such as search and seizure and field detentions and arrests. (9)

criminalistics Forensic science that focuses on the recording, scientific examination, and interpretation of the minute details to be found in the physical evidence, such as hair and clothing fibers. (15)

Critical Incident Stress Debriefing Team (CISDT) A unit that provides emergency counseling services to officers experiencing PTSD. (8)

critical thinking The analysis of ideas in the process of solving a problem or formulating a belief. (7)

cultural awareness A level of understanding that enables one to comprehend characteristics of culture in general and apply them to specific cultures. (13)

cultural awareness program A program for improving police-community relations that consists of active support by the agency head, self-assessment by the police agency, community assessment, and development of a training plan. (13)

curtilage The area and out-buildings surrounding a house that are considered private property. (10)

custodial interrogation When an officer interrogates a person who is under arrest or whose freedom to leave is restricted in some significant manner. (10)

cynicism Distrust of human nature and motives. (8)

Glossary

D

data analysis Use of simple mathematics to convert data to usable information. (14)

data collection Systematic gathering of facts and figures for the end purpose of problem solving. (14)

decentralized state agency A state policing model in which state law enforcement duties are performed by different divisions, such as a highway patrol. (5)

decoy An undercover operation in which an officer dresses as and assumes the role of a potential victim and then waits to be the subject of a crime. (12)

deep cover Submersion in a false identity for an extended time period, sometimes months. (12)

delinquency The criminal behavior, but committed by juveniles instead of adults. (1)

denial A means of avoiding a problem by pretending that it does not exist; common among alcoholics and substance abusers. (8)

differential response A dispatch method in which responses to citizens' calls for service are matched to the importance of each call, and a police unit is either assigned or not assigned accordingly. (11)

directed patrol A patrol strategy that provides dedicated patrol units to special problems as time allows during the course of a shift. (11)

directed patrol Patrol that targets a certain crime hot spot, a certain type of crime (such as drug loitering on street corners), or a certain type of criminal. (3)

discretion The autonomy or freedom an officer has in choosing an appropriate course of action. A police officer has discretion whenever the effective limits of the officer's power leave him or her free to make a choice among possible courses of action or inaction. (9)

distress Any type of negative or unpleasant stress. (8)

divergers People whose learning style involves perceiving information concretely and processing it reflectively. (7)

DNA testing Technology that identifies offenders and corpses by testing biological evidence to find its DNA sequence. (12)

door openers A process one uses to initiate communications. (7)

draconian code A very harsh ancient Greek code that made many crimes, even property crimes, into capital offenses; also allowed debtors to be sold into slavery. (2)

due process A system of procedural laws that safeguards citizens' constitutional rights. (1)

E

early warning mental health program An in-house police mental health program in which sergeants are taught to detect early symptoms in officers. (8)

egocentrism A way of thinking that chooses to see the world from a very narrow and self-serving perspective, which can lead to manipulation and self-serving behavior. (7)

electromagnetic vehicle stopping Technology that allows officers to neutralize the electronic systems of moving vehicles, resulting in the vehicles coasting to a stop. (15)

Glossary

electronic eavesdropping Surveillance over computers and other electronic devices. (10)

empowerment is the act of creating an opportunity for expressions of power and ownership, such as over a community. (11)

ethics Study and analysis of what constitutes good or bad conduct, addressing specific moral choices an individual makes in relating to others. (9)

eustress Stress that results from positive events. (8)

exclusionary rule A rule of evidence that does not allow any court to use evidence that is obtained in violation of a defendant's constitutional rights. (10)

F

facial reconstruction A technique used with the skull of an unidentified individual to help investigators determine how an unidentified person may have looked when alive. (15)

federal law enforcement Law enforcement agencies that are responsible for enforcing federal criminal law statutes. (5)

field supervisor A police supervisor, usually a sergeant, primarily charged with overseeing the quality of service delivery and supervising demanding tactical situations. (4)

Field Training Officer (FTO) An experienced officer who becomes a mentor to a new officer by teaching him or her to apply academy training to situations on the street. (6)

following skills Listening skills that focus on staying out of the speaker's way so that the listener can discover how the speaker views his or her situation. (7)

follow-up investigation Continuation of the preliminary investigation conducted by patrol officers in an attempt to reconstruct the circumstances of an illegal act. (12)

forensic medicine The use of medicine to determine the cause or time of death or for other legal purposes. (15)

forensic science The enforcement of criminal and civil laws by scientifically gathering evidence to be used in court proceedings; its two major branches are criminalistics and forensic medicine. (15)

formal disciplinary system A system by which complaints are processed and resolved; a necessity for reinforcing public trust and organizational policies. (13)

G

Geographic Information System (GIS) A computerized mapping system that produces layered, detailed descriptions of conditions and analyzes the relationships between variables such as location and time; the backbone of crime mapping. (15)

goal Measurable long-term end state to be attained. (14)

good faith exception An exception to the exclusionary rule that holds that evidence is admissible when obtained from a seemingly acceptable warrant that is later determined to be invalid for reasons that police did not foresee. (10)

gratuity Something given freely to a police officer, which may or may not be in return for a favor or for an expectation of a future favor. (9)

Glossary

H

hierarchy An organization that is characterized by several levels of command, with authority increasing as the levels reach the top of the pyramid. (5)

high-stress training A widely criticized training method that places officers in a very stressful training environment similar to that of military boot camp. (6)

holistic crime proofing Crime proofing in which isolation, stigma, anonymity, accessibility, and hiding places are designed out of the environment; ultimate goal is to make everyone a part of, and accountable to, the same community. (15)

holistic policing Provision of a full array of community treatment regimens to attack crime conditions. (4)

I

Identification-Based Information System (IBIS) A handheld device that allows officers to gather information on suspects, take mug shots, take fingerprints, and call for help. (15)

imaging The enhancement of optical capabilities for law enforcement personnel, as well as the recording and documenting of crimes as they occur. (15)

individual rights advocates Those who focus on protecting the constitutional rights of those who come in contact with, or are processed through, the criminal justice system. (1)

inference An intellectual act by which one concludes that something is so in light of something else's being so, or seeming to be so. (7)

informant A person who informs against another suspected of violating some penal statute. (12)

in-service training Training that the officer receives once on the job, such as field training and professional development. (6)

Integrated Automated Fingerprint Identification System (IAFIS) A national database of criminals' fingerprints used to maintain a criminal history record for each arrested individual. (15)

integrity Integrated collection and application of virtues that bring about the goals of an organization. It is the applied outcome of the combination of the concepts of professionalism, discretion and ethics. (9)

internal affairs division A section of a police agency that handles citizen complaints or initiates investigations of officers who are committing crimes or misusing their authority. (13)

interoperability The ability to share information among different agencies in different jurisdictions. (15)

isolationism The effect of exclusion from mainstream society from being a police officer. (8)

J

jurisdiction The geographic area or crime issue over which the authority of a law enforcement organization extends. (5)

justice The ideal of fairness, applied in an objective and consistent manner; the goal of the criminal justice system. (1)

justice of the peace An official with law enforcement and judicial powers who had the authority to pursue, arrest, sentence, and imprison offenders. (2)

Glossary

K

Kerner Commission A 1967 commission that found that a deep hostility between police and ghetto communities had been a significant factor in causing inner-city riots. (3)

kin police An early policing system in which family, tribe, or clan members assumed responsibility for dispensing justice. (2)

L

Law Enforcement Assistance Administration (LEAA) A government agency that provided states and local governments with funds and guidance for crime prevention and reduction; in operation from 1969 to 1982. (3)

law of agency The belief that the police, who are the public's agent for providing law enforcement, possess only the authority that is granted to them by society. (1)

Law of the Twelve Tablets The first set of written law in ancient Rome; grouped civil and criminal law, legal procedures, and some social regulations. (2)

leapfrogging A technique used to rotate various surveillance team members into a close contact position with an individual being watched. (12)

legalistic style A style of policing that uses uniform enforcement of codified law with a minimal exercise of discretion. (4)

Leges Henrici A legal code that divided England into 30 judicial districts and made serious crimes into breaches of the peace against the king. (2)

legislative mandate A legal requirement that is enacted by government lawmakers, such as three strikes laws that require three-time felony offenders to receive life sentences. (4)

lex talionis An ancient philosophy of justice, which means equal retaliation or "an eye for an eye." (2)

lifelong learning Continuous learning, either formal or self-directed, that is directed toward personal enrichment and professional development. (7)

light cover An undercover assignment of very short duration, such as stings or decoy work. (12)

line functions Policing functions that encompass policing units directly involved in the provisions of field services. (5)

lineup Having several persons appear before a victim or witness for the purpose of identification. (10)

lynch law A type of vigilante justice in which any alleged criminal could be caught by a mob and executed on the spot. (3)

M

Magna Carta An English document that extended a number of rights to commoners and nobles, many of which are predecessors of rights found in the U.S. Constitution. (2)

Managing Criminal Investigation (MCI) An array of scientifically tested suggestions for improving the investigative process such as case screening. (12)

master thinker People who are at the highest level of critical thinking because they are conscious of the workings of their minds. (7)

Glossary

mere suspicion The gut feeling that officers have when they suspect that something is wrong but have no proof; cannot be used to justify legal action. (10)

minimal encouragers Phrases such as "Tell me more" or "Go on" to keep the speaker active in the communication process. (7)

minimum standards Employment standards such as age, height, weight, education, absence of criminal record, and residency, which are established by the state and the individual police organization. (6)

Minnesota Multiphasic Personality Inventory (MMPI-2) A psychological self-test that is used to diagnose mental disorders and select appropriate treatment. (6)

Miranda warning A rule that police must advise a suspect of his or her constitutional right to remain silent and request the assistance of counsel; a result of *Miranda v. Arizona* (1966). (10)

mission statement A statement that clearly and concisely describes what actions a department will take to achieve its vision and values. (1)

mission statement Statement of purpose that expresses a police department's responsibilities and distinguishes the organization from other governmental agencies or even from another police department. (14)

mitochondrial DNA (mtDNA) Tiny organelles that are found in every cell and are not associated with the DNA in the cell's nucleus but work separately to produce energy for the body; used in new DNA research. (15)

mobile video systems Systems in patrol cars that can film all officer-citizen interactions; The key goals are accountability and documentation. (15)

modus operandi A unique identifying action or characteristic of a crime that can identify a particular criminal's involvement in that crime. (4)

monitors Public representatives who are given unprecedented access to law enforcement files, records, and personnel to review agency performance. (13)

multiple-role phenomenon A variable that influences an officer's role enactment; consists of role conflict, role ambiguity, role strain, or any combination of these. (4)

municipal police City-based policing agencies; also known as local police. (5)

Myers-Briggs Type Indicator (MBTI) A widely used psychological test that can be administered to individuals age 14 and older. (6)

N

nonsystem A non functioning system in which components fail to recognize their relationships, depend upon each other, and work together in a way that promotes its goal. (1)

norms Principles of conduct that guide acceptable behavior. (4)

O

objective Short-term milestone to be accomplished enroute to goal achievement. (14)

omnipresence A characteristic of successful preventive patrol that creates the impression that the police are always present. (11)

Glossary

organizational stressor Any factor within an organization that can contribute to a police officer's stress. (8)

P

paradigm pioneers Innovative leaders who take new ideas and concepts and bring them into professional use. (15)

paralanguage Auditory and visual cues such as specific words, voice tone, voice speed, frequency and length of pauses, and the use of words like "aah" and "mmm." (7)

paraphrasing Restating the essence of the speaker's content in the listener's own words. (7)

parasympathetic system The part of the autonomic nervous system that slows down the heart and lungs and stimulates the digestive organs during periods of relaxation. (8)

patrol The walk or drive through an area to ensure public order. (11)

Peace Officer Standards and Training (POST) Statewide programs for individual police officers, which ensures that they meet minimum standards of competency and ethical behavior. (5)

Peel's principles of policing A set of nine concepts created by Robert Peel as the foundation of the London Metropolitan Police; still in use today. (2)

perimeter A tactical positioning of police officers to contain someone attempting to escape from the scene of a crime. (4)

perpetual loan The belief that the authority of the police is loaned to them by the community. (1)

photo lineup Having a victim or witness view several photographs of possible suspects for the purpose of identification. (10)

plain view doctrine A doctrine that allows officers who observe evidence in plain view to seize it without a warrant or probable cause. (10)

planning Process of developing a method, that takes place in advance of action, to achieve a defined end state. (14)

police operations The preventative, investigative, and crime-fighting work that police do; determined mainly by citizen requests. (5)

police role Customary police functions such as investigations, arrest, and social services; what officers perceived as the uses of their authority; and their problem-solving methods. (4)

police stress unit A non-profit organization that is not affiliated with any law enforcement agency but provides specialized and confidential help for officers and their families. (8)

police subculture The meanings, values, and behavior patterns that are unique to those in policing. (8)

police-community relations A relationship based on public relations, community service, and community participation. (13)

political era An era of policing (1840-1920) that was characterized by political involvement in the administration and operation of police. (3)

polygraph examination A standard lie detector test that is used in policing to screen applicants. (6)

Glossary

posse comitatus A power of the shire reeve that allowed him to call able-bodied men of the shire together when he needed assistance. (2)

Post-Traumatic Stress Disorder (PTSD) A psychological condition that sometimes occurs after an individual has been exposed to a traumatic experience. (8)

praetor A Roman Judge who changed the law and created new laws as necessary. (2)

praetorian guard A Roman police force that existed mainly to protect the life of the emperor and his property, specifically his palace. (2)

precedent Past judicial decisions are followed in making future decisions; base on *stare decisis* which means, "let the decision stand." (10)

prejudice A type of attitude that is formed regarding objects, persons, groups, or values on the basis of limited information, association or experience. (13)

preliminary investigation Encompasses the evidence-gathering activities that take place at the scene of a crime immediately after the crime has been reported to or discovered by the police. (12)

preservice training Training in which recruits learn a wide variety of subjects ranging from defensive tactics to working with special populations. Also called academy training. (6)

President's Commission on Law Enforcement A 1967 commission that examined how effective the criminal justice system was in controlling crime. (3)

preventive patrol A type of patrol that deters crime through a visible police presence while enabling police to detect potential criminal incidents. (11)

proactive policing Policing that acts on the belief that the best way to control crime is to prevent it from occurring in the first place. (13)

probable cause A level of suspicion, based on evidence, that can lead a reasonable person to believe that a suspect has committed or will commit a specific crime; required for an arrest or to obtain a legal arrest warrant or search warrant. (10)

problem solving The act of recognizing and solving a problem; an essential part of effective policing. (7)

problem-based learning Recruit training that fosters the skills necessary for effective community policing, such as critical thinking, team building, interpersonal communication, and leadership. (6)

Problem-Oriented Policing (POP) A problem-solving process that helps officers identify and solve persistent problems on their beats; central to this process is SARA. (3, 7, 11)

professionalism Preparation for work in accordance with standards that include advanced education, demonstrated familiarity with the field's core body of knowledge, accountability through peer review, and a code of ethics. (9)

progressive discipline A type of officer discipline that calls for increasing the severity of punishments as an officer's transgressions become more frequent. (13)

progressives A political movement that advocated efficiency in governmental operations and the involvement of government in improving the lives of the poor and disadvantaged. (3)

Glossary

GLOSSARY

provost marshall Military official in charge of one of England's 12 military districts under the rule of Oliver Cromwell; acted as both police chief and judge. (2)

proxemics The study of personal space and how it is used. (7)

psychological profiling A method of suspect identification that seeks to identify an individual's mental, emotional, and personality characteristics as manifested in things done or left behind at a crime scene. (12)

public order advocates Those who believe that when criminals threaten public safety, the interests of society take priority over the criminals' individual rights. (1)

public relations A police department's efforts to communicate with the public about the work it does. (13)

Public Safety Partnership and Community Policing Act of 1994 An act that emphasized community policing as a crime-fighting strategy and made more funding available for community policing activities. (3)

Q

quiet revolution The growth of community policing. (1)

R

rapport A friendly relationship that results from establishing open communication by acting in a courteous and restrained manner at all times. (13)

rattle watch A night watch system in which each watchman had a rattle to signal to citizens, to other night watchmen and call for help. (3)

reasonable suspicion The amount of knowledge necessary to make an ordinary and cautious person believe that criminal activity is occurring; necessary for a stop and frisk. (10)

recruitment The use of strategies and benefits to entice people to work as police officers. (6)

reflective listening A listening skill that involves listening to the speaker and repeating the feeling and content in the message back to demonstrate understanding and acceptance. (7)

reform era An era of policing (1920-1980) that was characterized by the removal of politics and corruption from police. (3)

research Careful study of a subject. (14)

research design Blueprint, based on accepted research practices, that guides collection of data, analysis of data, and interpretation of research findings. (14)

resources Materials and personnel required to execute strategies. (14)

reverse sting An undercover officer poses as a seller of drugs for the purpose of arresting a predisposed purchaser of drugs. (12)

role acquisition The process of learning one's role, learning one's role set, and knowing how to select a role from one's inventory that is appropriate to the situation at hand. (4)

role ambiguity Any uncertainty about one's role; goes along with the police role. (4)

role conflict Conflict that arises when an officer encounters two sets of expectations that are inconsistent with each other. (4)

role enactment The social conduct exhibited by a police officer, shaped by four factors: role expectations, role acquisition, organizational goals, and multiple-role phenomenon. (4)

Glossary

role expectations The rights, privileges, duties, and obligations of any occupant of a social position, as perceived by those occupying other positions in the social structure. (4)

role set A group of people who perform different roles together. (4)

role strain In which an officer's role is limited by what he or she is authorized to do. (4)

roll call A police check-in procedure in which officers receive their duty assignments and briefings on a variety of subjects. (4)

rule of law Society's guideline for what is acceptable and unacceptable human behavior; sometimes referred to as legality. (1)

S

SARA An acronym that stands for the analytical and problem-solving process of Scan, Analysis, Respond, and Assess. (7)

scientific management Fact-based and well-researched decision making. (14)

search Occurs when police search a person, object (such as a vehicle or package), or location (such as a business or residence) to find evidence of criminal activity; generally requires a search warrant. (10)

search warrant A document that is prepared by an officer, sworn to be true and accurate by the officer, and then issued by a judicial official in order to support the probable cause required for a search. (10)

seizure Occurs when police take physical evidence or property to help build a case. (10)

selection pool All of the candidates from which a small number of officers are selected. (6)

selection process The process of testing and interviewing policing candidates to see if they qualify for police work. (6)

selective enforcement Concentrating enforcement action on those motorists who are violating the laws that contribute most often to injurious accidents. (12)

service style A style of policing that emphasizes enhancement of the quality of life, and informal sanctions are employed in conformance with broad community norms. (4)

shire reeve A traveling official that was the head of the shire and had both law enforcement and judicial responsibilities. (2)

showup Having one suspect appear before a victim or witness for the purpose of identification. (10)

siege mentality A police mind-set that groups people into two categories: us (police) and them (everybody who is not a police officer). (8)

slave patrols Citizens police patrols that were created in the South to prevent slave insurrections and control crime. (3)

smart gun technology A security system for a firearm that will only allow a specific user to fire it. (15)

social control All social arrangements that either motivate or compel people to conform to society's rules; a way of maximizing the predictability of social behavior. (4)

solvability factor Reliable indicators of the potential for solving cases. (12)

span of control The number of people or units supervised by one manager. (5)

Glossary

specialization An organizational approach that occurs when an organization's structure is divided into units that are given specific tasks to perform. (5)

split-force patrol Assigning most of a patrol force to respond to calls for service while assigning a smaller special problems unit to give attention to preventive patrol or special crime problems. (11)

staff functions Policing functions that encompass activities provided in support of field operations. (5)

station supervisor A police supervisor who ensures that activities stay on track within the precinct station; also known as the watch commander. (4)

Statute of Winchester A law that attempted to develop a police system of watches and wards, or guard forces, across England. (2)

stereotyping A form of perceptual shorthand in which a person categorizes someone or something before fully understanding it. (13)

stop and frisk An action in which police stop, briefly detain, and frisk individuals in the course of a field interrogation; requires reasonable suspicion. (10)

strategic planning Department-wide planning endeavor designed to effect long-term organizational changes that are responsive to the emerging needs of the community and law enforcement agency. (14)

strategy Specific action taken toward achieving an objective (and goal). (14)

stress Any even that requires a person to adjust in some manner; the body's nonspecific response to any demand placed on it. (8)

stress inoculation Developing a lifestyle that makes one resistant to the effects of stress. (8)

stress management Reducing or eliminating unhealthy stress in order to lead a balanced lifestyle. (8)

stressor Any event that elicits a response from the Autonomic Nervous System (ANS). (8)

Strong Interest Inventory (SIT) A psychological test that measures an individual's interest in a broad range of occupations. (6)

suicide by cop A severe single-event stressor that occurs when citizens act in ways that endanger life, forcing police to respond with deadly force.

suicide by criminal An indirect form of police suicide, in which officers place themselves in unsafe situations or ignore standard safety precautions out of indifference for their own lives. (8)

surveillance Observation of a person, place, or thing in such a manner that the observer is undetected. (12)

sworn officers Officers who are trained and empowered to perform full police duties, such as making arrests and carrying firearms. (5)

symbiotic relationship Implies a mutually beneficial relationship between two concepts which are dissimilar in form. (14)

symbolic assailant Someone whose gestures, language, or attire signify to police a capability of being dangerous. (8)

sympathetic system The part of the ANS that accelerates the function of the heart and lungs and slows down the digestive organs during periods of excitement. (8)

Glossary

T

task-oriented training Training that focuses on developing repetitive skills and conditioned responses in recruits, such as by training them in defensive tactics, firearms, and writing traffic citations. (6)

team policing A policing strategy that was built on the idea of assigning a group of officers to a geographic area on a permanent basis; used mainly in the 1960s and 1970s. (3)

team policing Combining officers who perform different duties such as patrol, investigative, and traffic into teams assigned to specific geographic regions, with primary responsibility for all policing within a team's geographic region. (11)

technical surveillance The use of electronic and visual enhancement devices to overhear or view suspects in the conduct of their affairs. (12)

tempered authoritarianism Authoritarianism that is used only when needed, such as in situations requiring the use of force. (13)

territorial imperative When a person defines and defends a geographical territory in which he or she lives and moves. (3)

thief takers Bounty hunters, often corrupt, who were given monetary rewards for apprehending and turning in criminals. (2)

tithing The heart of the English mutual pledge system, in which groups of ten families were held responsible for each other's behavior. (2)

Title 42 of the United States Code Section 1983 An act passed by Congress in 1871 to ensure that the civil rights of men and women of all races were protected. (10)

tort The wrong charged against defendants in civil cases. (10)

traffic control Three types of traffic safety functions: enforcement, accident investigation, and parking and intersection control; the first two are performed by the police. (4)

traffic direction and control Entails actions taken to ensure the expeditious and safe movement of traffic, as well as the enforcement of laws regulating parking. (12)

traffic law enforcement The total police effort directed toward obtaining compliance with traffic movement regulations after programs of education and engineering have failed to reach this goal. (12)

U

U.S. Supreme Court The court of last resort for all cases that it hears, which means that all cases decided by the Supreme Court cannot be appealed again; the final interpreter of all constitution matters. (10)

undercover investigation An investigation in which an investigator assumes, for organizationally approved purposes, a different identity to obtain information or achieve another investigative purpose. (12)

Uniform Crime Report (UCR) A uniform system of classifying and reporting crimes; developed by August Vollmer and the IACP and today administered by the FBI. (3)

Glossary

unity of command A part of sound organizational design, in which every individual in an organization has only one immediate superior or supervisor. (5)

urban cohort A Roman police force that dealt with problems of street crimes and mob violence by patrolling the streets and maintaining public order. (2)

V

values Beliefs that guide an organization and the behavior of its employees. (14)

values statement A statement that declares an organization's values and beliefs in clear terms. (1)

vice comites A traveling judge who was the forerunner to today's federal circuit judge. (2)

vice investigation Investigation that focuses on crimes against the morals of a community. (12)

vigilante groups Informal self-protection societies created in the American West; also called vigilance committees or regulators. (3)

vigiles A special Roman corps of 7,000 men who served as both as fireman and night police. (2)

vision A mental image of a possible and desirable future for a law enforcement agency and its community. (14)

vision statement A statement that illustrates the ideal beliefs and actions of an organization. (1)

vizier A high-ranking ancient Egyptian official who was the only person other than the pharaoh who could act on all civil matters. (2)

W

watchman style A police style that centers on order maintenance; criminal violations are evaluated in terms of their immediate consequences rather than what the law says about them. (4)

Watson-Glaser Critical Thinking Appraisal (WGCTA) A psychological test that assesses an individual's critical thinking skills by testing five areas: inference, recognition of assumptions, deduction, interpretation, and evaluation of arguments. (6)

Wickersham Commission A special commission created in 1929 to study the increasing crime problem and the quality of the police response. (3)

wiretapping Secretly listening to telephone conversations for investigative purposes. (10)

writ of certiorari A written request to the Supreme Court asking it to review a particular case. (10)

Z

zone of stability The amount of stress that a person can effectively manage. (8)

Appendix A
Report-Writing Guidelines

What law enforcement tool does a police officer use most often? Handcuffs, a gun, a two-way radio, a baton, a bulletproof vest? Although these are the pieces of equipment we usually associate with police work, another object is an essential part of every officer's job: a pencil (or, more likely, a ballpoint pen) to take notes. Report writing is one of the most important yet unappreciated parts of a criminal justice professional's job. Taking field notes and preparing reports can make up to three fourths of a day's workload.

Written documents play a key role at every stage of the criminal justice process. A criminal investigation often begins when a police officer is called to a crime scene by a victim or a bystander. The officer's written account of what he or she saw, said, and was told—the police report—can play a key role in the successful investigation and prosecution of a crime. An accurate, thorough, and clearly written report can also help exonerate an innocent person and explain the actions taken by the police. An inaccurate, incomplete, or carelessly written report can lead to wrongful conviction, allow a guilty person to go free, and raise questions about the actions of the officers involved. With so much at stake, strong writing skills and an understanding of the report-writing process are of utmost importance. This appendix provides an overview of these skills and of the steps involved in producing a high-quality report.

The Three Phases of the Interview

A good police report begins with a good interview, which is usually a three-part process. The emphasis in the first stage is on careful listening; in the second stage, you will ask questions and take notes to get the facts you will need for the report. The third stage is your opportunity to verify the facts. Let's look in more detail at the tasks involved in each of these steps.

Phase 1: Listening

When you respond to a call, your first tasks are to determine whether the victim needs medical treatment and whether the suspect is still in the area. The interview itself then begins with your allowing the victim to tell his or her story without interruptions. A crucial aspect at this stage of the process is showing empathy and establishing a good rapport with the victim. During this phase of the interview, you do not take notes. Rather, by listening attentively and respectfully, you build a positive relationship with the victim and encourage his or her cooperation in the fact-finding process.

Appendix A
Report-Writing Guidelines

Phase 2: Gathering and Recording Information

At this stage of the interview, the victim retells his or her story, guided by your questions. You take careful notes and ask specific questions to elicit complete information. Like a newspaper reporter, your goal is to find out as much as you can about the "who, what, when, where, why, and how" of the incident.

Phase 3: Verifying and Clarifying the Facts

After completing your questioning, you read your notes back to the victim. This step gives the interviewee a chance to recall additional information, and it allows you to confirm that you have accurately recorded the conversation. This also gives you a chance to review the victim's statements and identify any inconsistencies or omissions, and clarify or expand your notes if necessary.

Key Questions in the Interview

What information should you look for in the interview? As you explore the incident, be sure that you are covering each of the five "Ws and H" questions. For example, these questions may involve:

- *Who?* Answers to "who" questions may refer to suspects, victims, witnesses, informants, other police officers, medical personnel, and any other persons on the scene.
- *What?* What happened? What was taken? What was damaged? What injuries have occurred? What crime has been committed?
- *When?* When did the crime occur? When was it reported? When did officers arrive on the scene? When was the suspect last seen?
- *Where?* Where was the victim when the crime was committed? Where was the suspect? Where was the victim prior to the crime? If the suspect is not on the scene, what areas should be searched?
- *Why?* What was the victim doing at the crime scene? What motives does the victim think the suspect may have had? If there was a delay in reporting the crime, why did the victim wait to call the police?
- *How?* What methods were used by the suspect in committing the crime? Did the victim resist? If so, how?

Appendix A
Report-Writing Guidelines

Establishing the Elements of a Crime

Remember that you are providing information to be used by criminal justice professionals as they seek to investigate and prosecute crimes. Your report can help establish that the elements of a crime have occurred.

For example, suppose you are called to the scene of an apparent burglary. According to statutory law, burglary generally requires three elements:

1. An entry,
2. of a dwelling or building,
3. with the intent to commit a crime inside.

As you conduct your interview, ask yourself what evidence might establish this crime. Are there signs of a forced entry, such as broken glass? If not, how might the entry have been made? How many entrances to the building are there? Did the suspect have a key to the building? Some jurisdictions also require that for an entry to be a burglary, the act must be committed at night, so "when" questions will be important.

If you are responding to a domestic violence call or if you are on the scene when fighting breaks out, you may be a witness to the crime of battery (a completed assault). To establish this crime, prosecutors must show that

1. A person intentionally touched another person,
2. with the intent to injure or with criminal negligence (or, in some jurisdictions, with the intent to commit another unlawful act), and
3. harm was done to the victim (bodily injury or offensive touching).

Your report of the events you witness or investigate can play a key role in determining whether the crime of battery took place. Notice that intention plays a key role in answering that question. What can you find out about why the suspect acted as he or she did? Are there reasons to think that any party involved was acting in self-defense? Your alertness in identifying the events and exploring the motives of those involved can be invaluable—but in order to be an effective contributor to the process, you must document your observations in your report.

Field Notes

Field notes are abbreviated notations written by an officer at a crime scene. Well-organized and neat field notes are the basis for a well-organized and clear report. Organize your field notes according to the topics you will need to cover in your departmental report, and record

Appendix A
Report-Writing Guidelines

information in a format with which you are comfortable. It is most important that the field notes document factual and relevant information about the crime scene. Field notes should contain the information that will aid the officer in answering the questions *who, what, when, where, why*, and *how*. Remember that your field notes can be subpoenaed and can be used to defend the credibility of a crime or arrest report. During a trial, field notes can be an indicator of an officer's thoroughness and efficiency.

Structuring Your Report

Chronological Order Think of your report as telling a story to someone about an event that has already happened. In taking notes and writing your report, describe the events in the order which they occurred, and list statements made in the order in which they were received. Organizing your notes in chronological order will give you a framework to use for the narrative portion of your report. Because you are writing about an event that has already happened, use the past tense.

Active Versus Passive Voice Your description of what happened will usually be clearer if you write in active rather than in the passive voice. In a sentence written in the active voice, the subject of the sentence performs the action. With the passive voice, the subject in acted upon.

For example:
Active: Jones broke the window. (4 words)
Passive: The window was broken by John. (6 words)

Active: Officer Murphy found broken glass on the floor below the window. (11 words)
Passive: Broken glass on the floor below the window was found by Officer Murphy. (13 words)

Note that writing in the active voice usually reduces the number of words needed to describe an event. By using the active voice when possible, you can make your report more concise and readable.

Avoiding Jargon The first step in writing any document is to consider the audience. Remember that you are writing a report that may be read not only by other police officers but also by prosecutors, defense attorneys, judges, jurors, and others. Avoid jargon and slang that may be easily understood by police but may not be familiar to others.

First Person Write your report in the first person. Saying, "The author of this report saw the subject drive past" or, "This officer then proceeded to the scene" sounds pretentious and may confuse the reader. Simply stating, "I saw the subject drive past" or, "I then went to the scene" communicates the information more simply and effectively.

Appendix A
Report-Writing Guidelines

Sentence Length Pay attention to the length of your sentences. Very long sentences often spin out of the writer's control and confuse the reader. For example, this long sentence gives so many details that the main point—that the witness saw two men knock down another—gets lost:

> I interviewed one of the witnesses, Agnes Smith, who said that at 10:49 A.M. she saw two men in Lazy Z Barbecue parking lot, one dressed in a blue baseball jacket with "Red Rockets" written in yellow across the back and the other in tan shorts and a white shirt, knock an older man in jogging clothes to the ground.

In this sentence, the report writer first identifies the central event and then provides descriptive details:

> I interviewed one of the witnesses, Agnes Smith, who said that at 10:49 A.M. she saw two men in the Lazy Z Barbecue parking lot knock an older man to the ground. One of the attackers was dressed in a blue baseball jacket with "Red Rockets" written in yellow across the back. The other wore tan shorts and a white shirt. The older man was dressed in jogging clothes.

Short, choppy sentences can also interfere with your goal of giving a complete explanation. For example, these three sentences don't identify the causal relationship between road conditions and hazardous driving:

> The roads near Payette were glazed with a thin layer of ice. Then they were covered by a dusting of snow. It was dangerous to drive.

Instead, show the connection:

> Because the roads near Payette were glazed with a think layer of ice and then dusted with snow, driving in that area was dangerous.

Making Your Report Credible

Remember that your report may be used in court to help establish what happened at the scene. Rather than vague generalizations that are open to various interpretations, be specific and include information that will help the reader imagine the scene. For example, phrases such as "combative posture," "furtive movement," and "suspicious glance" appear to be unsubstantiated opinion. Focus on the details that would justify the use of such adjectives. Rather than "the suspect took a combative posture," you might say:

Appendix A
Report-Writing Guidelines

The suspect assumed a stance like one used in martial arts or boxing, with his fists clenched and raised to shoulder level. I could also see that his face was red and that the veins on the sides of his neck stood out. He spoke very loudly and glared at me as he shouted. He seemed to be very angry at me.

When you provide such details, you provide supporting evidence for the conclusions you draw. The focus of your report is to provide an accurate description of the incidents you investigated, rather than to record unsubstantiated opinions. For example, stating only that, "the victim seemed disoriented" presents an opinion with no evidence. In contrast, consider this statement:

The victim could not give his full name, had no explanation as to why he had parked behind the warehouse, and could not provide details of the attack that had caused profuse facial bleeding. He seemed disoriented and was confused about where to go when the paramedic asked him to step toward the ambulance.

This description enables the reader to visualize the scene and provides a basis for the conclusion that the victim seemed disoriented.

Your report should be free of personal bias and prejudice. A report is essentially a sworn document, so it is vital that it be truthful and based on fact.

The Final Report: A Job Well Done

After you've written your report, take time to be sure that it is as good as you can make it.

- Always proofread your report. If possible, ask a coworker to review your work before you submit it to a supervisor.
- Use a dictionary to be sure that your spelling is correct and that you are stating what you mean to say. A thesaurus is useful when you are looking for synonyms or trying to find the best term to capture what you want to describe.
- Study model reports and develop guidelines to follow as you develop your narrative.

If you feel that you need to brush up your writing skills, consider a college-level English course or a course on police report writing. The Web site of the Police Training Network offers resources including two handbooks and videos (See the link provided at **www.glencoe.policing.com**).

A complete, accurate, clearly written report reflects your commitment to the job and your attention to detail. In many cases, what you write may be the primary basis your supervisor has for evaluating your job performance. Make sure that you develop the skills needed for report writing—remember that it's a crucial part of a police officer's job.

Appendix B
Essential Spanish for the Law Enforcement Officer

Days of the Week

Sunday	domingo
Monday	lunes
Tuesday	martes
Wednesday	miércoles
Thursday	jueves
Friday	viernes
Saturday	sábado

Months of the Year

January	enero
February	febrero
March	marzo
April	abril
May	mayo
June	junio
July	julio
August	agosto
September	septiembre
October	octubre
November	noviembre
December	diciembre

Greetings and Farewells

1. Good morning, Miss.
   Buenos días, Señorita.

2. Good afternoon.
   Buenas tardes.

3. Good evening, sir (good night)
   Buenas noches, Señor.

Appendix B
Essential Spanish for the Law Enforcement Officer

Greetings and Farewells continued

4. How are you?
   ¿Cómo está usted?

5. Very well, thank you.
   Muy bien, gracias.

6. Hello!
   ¡Hola!

7. Goodbye
   Adiós

8. So long
   Hasta luego

Low Risk Frisk

1. Stop!   Police!
   ¡Pare!   ¡Policía!

2. Put your hands up!   Spread your fingers!
   ¡Manos arriba!   ¡Separe sus dedos!

3. Slowly turn around!   Stop!
   ¡Voltéese despacio!   ¡Pare!

4. Put your hands behind you back/head, palms together!
   ¡Ponga sus manos atrás de su espalda/cabeza, con sus palmas juntas!

5. Spread your feet!
   ¡Separe sus pies!

6. Cross your fingers!   Relax your fingers!
   ¡Cruce sus dedos!   ¡Afloje sus dedos !

7. Don't move!
   ¡No se mueva!

Appendix B
Essential Spanish for the Law Enforcement Officer

High Risk Frisk

1. Stop!   Police!
   ¡Pare!   ¡Policía!

2. Put your hands up! (higher)   Spread your fingers!
   ¡Manos arriba! (más)   ¡Separe sus dedos

3. Slowly with your hands up, come down to your knees!
   ¡Con sus manos arriba, bajese a sus rodillas, despacio!

4. Slowly, with your hands in front of you, come down to your stomach!
   ¡Con sus manos en frente de usted, acuestese boca abajo, despacio!

5. Bury your forehead!
   ¡Ponga su frente en el suelo!

6. Put your arms out to your side, palms up!
   ¡Ponga sus brazos a sus lados, con las palmas boca arriba!

7. Spread your legs!
   ¡Abra sus piernas!

8. Bury your heels!
   ¡Ponga sus talons en el suelo!

9. Put your right/left hand on the small of your back, palm up!
   ¡Ponga su mano derecha/izquierda en el medio de su espalda, con la palma boca arriba!

10. Put your right/left hand on top of your right/left hand with the palm up!
   ¡Ponga su mano derecha/izquierda arriba de su mano derecha/izquierda con la palma boca arriba!

11. Turn your head to the left!
   ¡Voltee su cabeza, a la izquierda!

12. Don't move!
   ¡No se mueva!

ESSENTIAL SPANISH

Appendix B
Essential Spanish for the Law Enforcement Officer

Removal of High Risk Suspects From the Vehicle

Put your hands outside the windows.
Ponga sus manos afuera de la ventana.

Driver, slowly with your left hand turn off the engine and drop the keys outside.
Chófer, con su mano izquierda apague el motor y suelte las llaves afuera despacio.

Driver, with you right hand, open the door from outside.
Chófer, con su mano derecha abra despacio la puerta por afuera.

Driver, slowly with your hands up, get out of the car.
Chófer, con sus manos arriba bajese del carro despacio.

Turn around, stop.
Volteese, pare.

Walk backwards. Stop.
Camine para atras. Pare.

Walk to the right or left.
Camine a la derecha o izquierda.

With your hands up, slowly come down to your knees.
Con sus manos arriba, bajese a sus rodillas despacio.

Passenger, slowly with your hands up, get out of the car through the driver side.
Pasajero, con sus manos arriba bajese del carro del lado del chófer despacio.

Commands

Drop the weapon!	¡Suelte el arma!
Drop the gun!	¡Suelte la pistola!
Drop the knife!	¡Suelte la navaja!
Drop it!	¡Suéltela/(o)!
Hands behind your head	Manos atrás de su cabeza
Hurry up	Apúrese
Speak slower	Hable más despacio

Appendix B
Essential Spanish for the Law Enforcement Officer

Commands continued

Repeat please	Repita, por favor
Listen to me	Escúcheme
Do it!	¡Hágalo!
Come with me	Venga conmigo
Stay there	Quédese allá
Sit down	Siéntase
Stand up or stop	Párese
Quickly	Rápido
Let's go	Vamos
Don't talk	No hable
Follow me	Sígame
Come here	Venga aquí
Go over there	Vaya allá
Go away	Váyase
Stay outside	Quédese afuera
Tell me quickly	Dígame rápido
Tell me the truth	Dígame la verdad
Give me your license	Deme su licencia
Sign your name here	Firme su nombre aquí
Where are the keys?	¿Donde estan las llaves?
Fire	Fuego
Get out of the house/apt.	Salgase de la casa/apartamento

The Predominant Colors

Black	Negro (negra)
Blue	Azul
Brown	Café (complexión moreno)
Hazel/Lt. Brown (eyes/hair)	Castaño
Green	Verde
Grey	Gris

Appendix B
Essential Spanish for the Law Enforcement Officer

The Predominant Colors continued

Orange	Naranja (anaranjado, anaranjada)
Pink	Rosa
Red	Rojo (roja), colorado (colorada)
White	Blanco (blanca)
Yellow	Amarillo (amarilla)
Light Color/Clear	Claro (clara)
Dark Color/Obscure	Obscuro (obscura)

Medical Aid Terms

1. Are you injured?
   ¿Está Herido?

2. Does your chest hurt? (The) stomach? (The) head?
   ¿Le duele el pecho?   ¿(el) estómago ? ¿(la) cabeza ?

3. Where does it hurt? Show me!
   ¿Dónde le duele? ¡Muéstreme!

4. You're injured, pleased don't move.
   Está herido, no se mueva, por favor!

5. Are you ill?
   ¿Está enfermo?

6. Are you diabetic?
   ¿Es usted diabetico?

7. Are you an epileptic?
   ¿Es usted epileptico?

8. Do you have heart trouble?
   ¿Sufre del corazón?

9. How do you feel?
   ¿Cómo se siente?

Appendix B
Essential Spanish for the
Law Enforcement Officer

Medical Aid Terms continued

10. Are you taking medication?
   ¿Está usted tomando alguna medicina?

11. Where is your medicine?
   ¿Dónde esta su medicina?

12. You need medical help.
   Usted necesita ayuda médica.

13. Do you want a doctor?
   ¿Quiere usted un médico?

14. Do you want an ambulance?
   ¿Quiere usted una ambulancia?

15. You should see a doctor.
   Usted debe ver a un médico.

16. Do you want to go to the hospital?
   ¿Quiere usted ir al hospital?

17. You have to go to the hospital.
   Usted tiene que ir al hospital.

Anatomy

1. (The) Arm   (El) Brazo
2. (The) Back   (La) Espalda
3. (The) Body   (El) Cuerpo
4. (The) Blood   (La) Sangre
5. (The) Chest   (El) Pecho
6. (The) Ear   (El) Oido/La Oreja
7. (The) Eyes   (Los) Ojos
8. (The) Face   (La) Cara
9. (The) Fingers   (Los) Dedos
10. (The) Foot   (El) Pie

Appendix B
Essential Spanish for the Law Enforcement Officer

Anatomy continued

11.	(The) Forehead	(La) Frente	
12.	(The) Hand	(La) Mano	
13.	(The) Head	(La) Cabeza	
14.	(The) Knee	(La) Rodilla	
15.	(The) Leg	(La) Pierna	
16.	(The) Mouth	(La) Boca	
17.	(The) Nose	(La) Nariz	
18.	(The) Stomach	(El) Estomago	
19.	(The) Throat	(La) Garganta	
20.	(The) Waist	(La) Cintura	

High Risk Kneeling Frisk

Stop!
¡Pare!

Put your hands up! /Spread your fingers.
¡Manos arriba ! /Mas abra sus dedos.

Slowly turn around. Stop.
Voltéese despacio. Pare.

Put your hands behind your head.
Ponga sus manos atras de su cabeza.

Cross your fingers.
Cruce sus dedos.

Cross your feet/legs.
Cruce sus pies/piernas.

Don't move.
No se mueva.

Don't talk.
No hable.

Appendix B
Essential Spanish for the Law Enforcement Officer

Field Interview/Citation/Personal Data

1. Your license, please.
   Su licencia, por favor.

2. Do you have identification?
   ¿Tiene identificación?

3. What is your name?
   ¿Cómo se llama usted?

4. What is your last name?
   ¿Cuál es su apellido?

5. What is your first name?
   ¿Cuál es su primer nombre?

6. What is your father's name?
   ¿Como se llama su papa?

7. What is your address?
   ¿Cuál es su domicilio? (Dirección)

8. How tall are you?
   ¿Cuánto mide usted?

9. How much do you weigh?
   ¿Cuánto pesa usted?

10. What is your date of birth? How old are you?
    ¿Cuál es su fecha de nacimiento? Cuantos años tiene?

11. What is your phone number with area code? (Home) (Work)
    ¿Cuál es su número de telefono con área? (De casa) (De trabajo)

12. Where do you work?
    ¿Dónde trabaja usted?

13. What is your address at work?
    ¿Cuál es la direccion de su trabajo ?

14. What is your Social Security Number?
    ¿Cuál es su número de seguro social?

15. Do you have a nickname? (another name?)
    ¿Tiene usted sobrenombre? (¿otro nombre?)

Appendix B
Essential Spanish for the Law Enforcement Officer

Field Interview/Citation/Personal Data continued

16. Do you belong to a gang? Which one?
    ¿Pertenece usted a una pandilla/ganga? ¿Cuál?

17. What is your mother's name ?
    ¿Cómo se llama su mamá ?

18. Which school do you go to? Where is the school located?
    ¿A cuál escuela vas? ¿Dónde está la escuela?

19. Where were you born ?
    ¿Dónde nació usted?

Desk Guide Command Sentence

Is it an emergency?	¿Es una emergencia?
Do you need help?	¿Necesita ayuda?
Was there a wreck?	¿Hubo un choque?
Was someone run over?	¿Hubo un atropellado?
Son/Daughter ran away?	¿Su hijo/hija huyó de la casa
Do you need the police?	¿Necesita la policía?
Do you need the fire department?	¿Necesita a los bomberos?
Was there a burglary?	¿Hubo robo de casa?
Did they rob you?	¿Le robaron a usted?
Did they steal your car?	¿Le robaron su carro?
What is the license plate number to you car?	¿Cuáles son los números de sus placas?
Was there a drive-by shooting	¿Hubo una balacera desde un carro?
Are there any weapons?	¿Hay armas/Tienen armas?
Where do you live?	¿Dónde vive usted?
Where did it occur?	¿Dónde ocurrió?
Do you speak English?	¿Habla inglés?
Please calm down	Cálmese, por favor
Goodbye	Adiós
Car insurance	Seguro de carro

Index

Index

Index

Index

Index

INDEX

Index

Index

INDEX

Index

Index

Index

Photo Credits